This Train Is Bound for Glory

This Train Is Bound for Glory

The Story of America's Chapel Cars

To Beverly and Allen,
Beverly, you were the light that led us through the writing of this book. We shall never forget your loving support and guidance.
Wilma Rugh Taylor
Norman Thomas Taylor

Wilma Rugh Taylor and Norman Thomas Taylor

Judson Press • Valley Forge

Many of the images used in this publication are from the photographic archives of The American Baptist Historical Society.

Bible quotations marked KJV are from *The Holy Bible*, King James Version.

Bible quotations marked NASB are from the *New American Standard Bible*, ©1960, 1962, 1963, 1968, 1971, 1972, 1973, 1975, 1977 by the Lockman Foundation. Used by permission.

Bible quotations marked NRSV are from the New Revised Standard Version of the Bible, copyright ©1989 by the Division of Christian Education of the National Council of the Churches of Christ in the United States of America. Used by permission. All rights reserved.

Library of Congress Cataloging-in-Publication Data
Taylor, Wilma Rugh.
  This train is bound for glory : the story of America's chapel cars / Wilma Rugh Taylor and Norman Thomas Taylor.
    p. cm.
Includes bibliographical references and index.
ISBN 0-8170-1284-2 (alk. paper)
1. Railroads—United States—Passenger-cars. 2. Chapels—United States. I. Taylor, Norman Thomas. II. Title.
TF455.T39 1999
277.3'081—dc21   98-53388

Printed in the U.S.A.
06 05 04 03 02 01 00 99
10 9 8 7 6 5 4 3 2 1

To all the chapel car workers and chaplains,

and to the denominational leaders, railroad officials, railroad workers, chapel car builders,

and men and women of good faith

who helped bring the message of God's love and faithfulness

to hundreds of little towns along America's railways

during the heyday of rail travel.

"This Train Is Bound for Glory"

This train is bound for glory, this train (my Lord).
This train is bound for glory, this train;
This train is bound for glory, and if you ride you must be holy,
This train, my Lord, this train.

Chorus of song by same name, origin unknown.

First recorded in 1920 by Wood's Blind Jubilee Singers and made popular by American folk singer Woody Guthrie.

CONTENTS

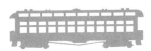

In October of 1997, at the start of the fall semester reading week when classes did not meet, I met Wilma and Norman Taylor for the first time in my office in Berkeley, California. In the meaningful events of one's life, as well as the course of human events, timing—both planned and unplanned—is crucial. Our meeting that day was accidental, unplanned, because normally I would have been teaching, and our paths might not have crossed. We had no appointment, and we did not know one another. The Taylors had stopped by the seminary on a hunch, following a tip from someone who might know, that maybe the school's archives would contain something about Baptist railroad chapel cars that had come through northern California many years ago. I had stopped by my office for a few minutes to check my mail. For me, and for them, our chance meeting turned out to be memorable.

Such memorable meetings had accumulated for the Taylors during the previous two years. In the fall of 1995 they had embarked on an adventure that began in West Virginia, retracing the route of chapel car *Herald of Hope* nearly a century earlier. This adventure would take them more than seventeen thousand miles in thirty-two states throughout the nation, with many planned and unplanned meetings and discoveries along the way. Their fall 1997 swing through northern California came during a five-week trip in the western United States that followed an ambitious schedule, though it was flexible enough to allow time for unplanned discoveries.

The Taylors remember our meeting in my office because it led to their surprise discovery of a gold mine of information about Baptist chapel cars in the seminary's archives and special collections. Their planned brief visit lasted the week as they mined these unexpected resources. (No one else has read as much during a seminary's reading week than they did that week.) I recall the meeting not only because the Taylors were engaging persons who became my friends but also because I marveled at their disciplined passion in pursuing their research and at their accumulated wealth of information about the subject. I long had known about the American Baptist chapel cars, but I had no idea of the breadth and scope of the larger story or of the rich resources documenting the history. We had so much to talk about! Their research adventures would continue another year, resulting in their remarkable book *This Train Is Bound for Glory: The Story of America's Chapel Cars*, a book that will give readers like me much to ponder and talk about in the years ahead.

Two stories unfold in this book, one explicit and the other implicit in the text. The primary story traces the adventures of thirteen railroad chapel cars and their Episcopal, Baptist, and Roman Catholic colporter missionaries throughout the western United States during the half-century of the 1890s through the 1930s. Railroad history and church history intertwine creatively in this saga of national westward expansion and settlement. Personalities and events come alive in the descriptions of developing towns and cities within diverse regional landscapes wherever chapel cars visited. Two such events are the great storm of Galveston, Texas, in 1900 and San Francisco's 1915 Panama-Pacific International Exhibition. We learn much about the ethnic, cultural, and religious diversity that permeates this story. We learn about the inside workings of church mission enterprises and American railroading, their developing strategies and technologies, the interactions of their respective human motives and aspirations, their successes and failures.

This history, told here in its full parameters and in detail for the first time, is the book's explicit story. The other story implicit in the text, one that surfaces here and there and gives added life to the historical narrative, follows the Taylors' travels along the routes of the thirteen chapel cars over their several decades of accumulated service. The Taylors followed the tracks, visited the towns, the related churches, the surviving witnesses, and their descendants; they read old newspapers, archival records, letters and journals, and local histories as well as church and railroad histories. Indeed, they came so close to reliving the history itself that their narration of the stories brings railroad chapel car history alive to its readers.

Dr. Eldon G. Ernst
Professor of American Church History
American Baptist Seminary of the West

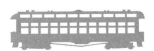

This book has been a long time in coming. It has many authors, for many have said in word and deed that the story of the chapel cars of America must not be forgotten. Our helpers include the staffs of state, historical, and denominational archives across America and many local churches and individuals. Especially we want to thank all those people who shared their first-person stories with us as we traveled more than seventeen thousand miles following the paths of the chapel cars.

In miraculous ways, the primary sources of this story were made available to us—the original journals and letters of the workers who traveled on the cars. Some of those records had been thought lost but were merely out of sight, waiting to be found and shared.

Although we have worked diligently in writing this book and searched through exhaustive records and talked to numerous sources, the story will never be finished or without error. We are aware that some of our information may be inaccurate due to incomplete, faulty, and missing reports. We are also aware that for every town we found mentioned in reports, there were at least a handful not mentioned. We apologize to churches or towns that were visited by a chapel car but are not in our logs or if dates and places are conflicting.

We have tried to tell the story as well as we could, but we know it would have taken us another lifetime to check all our facts. We thought it was important to share the inspiration of this story as we have been privileged to know it and been blessed by it.

We give special credit to Beverly Carlson, retired administrator/archivist, American Baptist Historical Society, who has given us support from the beginning of the project. Without Beverly's zeal and enthusiasm, the book probably would not be.

To Brother Michael J. Grace, S.J., University Archivist, Cudahy Library, Loyola University, Chicago, who provided us with such hospitality and who served as consultant for our chapters on Roman Catholic chapel cars; and Roscoe Keeney Jr., who helped us learn the story of the chapel cars in West Virginia on our first chapel car journey and who became a friend and cheerleader; and Father Herman Page, Episcopal priest from Topeka, Kansas, and Lois Prusok, editor, Episcopal Diocese of Northern Michigan. We could not have written about the Northern Michigan cars without their help.

To Arlene Spencer, who because of her love for journalism and church history consented to help in the editing of this book; and Harriet Dowdy, chapel car supporter and friend, who read the Baptist chapters to provide insight from her years of leading visitors through chapel car *Grace*.

How honored we were when Dr. Eldon G. Ernst, professor of church history at the American Baptist Seminary of the West and a respected church historian, agreed to write the foreword; and when Monsignor Kenneth Velo, president of the Catholic Church Extension Society; Rev. Thomas Ray, Bishop, Episcopal Diocese of Northern Michigan; Rev. Andrew H. Fairchild, Bishop, Episcopal Diocese of North Dakota, Fargo; Dr. H. Roger Grant, chair of the history department of Clemson University and rail author; and Dr. Daniel Weiss, general secretary of American Baptist Churches, U.S.A. offered their support.

To presidents Paul LaDue and Ken Giacolleto and the staff of the American Baptist Assembly at Green Lake, who permitted us to work on chapel car *Grace* and graciously housed and supported us on our visits.

To Dr. Richard Francaviglia, of the Center for Greater Southwest Studies, at the University of Texas/Arlington, who invited us to share our story at the seminar on "Railroads and the West" in September 1996. The reception of our program there and the ensuing support of many in the rail community gave us the motivation to try and make this a scholarly work worthy of a role in American rail history.

Others who deserve special mention are Dean Frank Clark, Gethsemane Cathedral, Fargo, North Dakota; Bradley A. Collins, editor of *Extension* magazine; Dave Carmichael, archivist, YMCA of United States; Bud Carroll, Baptist chapel car supporter and friend; Robert Parmelee of the Sonoma Valley Historical Society, who helped us find chapel car *Good Will*; Mr. and Mrs. John Diani, owners of chapel car *Good Will*; Jasper Sanfillipo, owner of the second Episcopal Northern Michigan chapel car; Dr. Roger Fredrickson, chapel car champion and mentor; Rev. Alvin Elliot, Michigan historian; Rev. Eldon L. Elmore, who has long had an interest in the chapel cars; Rev. Janet Ewing, Church of the Master, Denver, who provided hospitality; Mary and Selmer Hagen, who have done much to restore chapel car *Emmanuel*; Pete Kelly, writer, *Extension* magazine; Marion Kobow, American Baptist Assembly, Green Lake, Wisconsin; Michael Korson, editor of *The Montana Catholic*, Diocese of Helena, Montana; Betty Layton, archivist, American Baptist Historical Society; Mac Kennickell, whose fascination about the chapel cars inspired us.

Also John and Bertha (Barney) McTaggart, whose connection with the Barney family enhanced our research; Dr. Dana Martin, administrator/archivist, Colgate Rochester Divinity School, Samuel Colgate Baptist Historical Collection; Jim Neubauer, Mid-Continent Museum member, who was as excited about *St. Anthony* as we were; Kristina

Southwell, archivist, Episcopal Church USA, Austin, Texas; Marge Spragg, archivist, Diocese of Great Falls–Billings, Great Falls, Montana; Catherine Tilzey, assistant editor, *The Montana Catholic*, Diocese of Helena, Montana; Gregory P. Ames, curator, John W. Barringer III Railroad Library and the staff of the St. Louis Mercantile Library at the University of Missouri–St. Louis, St. Louis, Missouri; and Roberto A. Sarmiento, Head, Transportation Library, and Mary McCreadie, Assistant Head, of the Northwestern University Library, Evanston, Illinois.

We appreciated the hospitality of these ABC regional offices: ABC of the West, ABC of the Northwest, ABC of the Pacific Northwest, ABC of the Pacific Southwest, ABC of the Rocky Mountains, ABC of Nebraska, ABC of Ohio, ABC of Oregon, ABC of Great Rivers, ABC of Mid-America, ABC of the Central Region, West Virginia Baptist Convention, ABC of Wisconsin; ABC of the Dakotas, and ABC of Michigan.

We searched the Baptist Collections at Baylor University, Waco, Texas; Oklahoma Baptist Convention, Oklahoma City, Oklahoma; Franklin College, Franklin, Indiana; American Baptist Seminary of the West, Berkeley, California; William Jewell College, Liberty, Missouri; Kalamazoo College, Kalamazoo, Michigan; and the Townsend Collection at Mary Hardin-Baylor University, Belton, Texas.

Other names that constantly popped up when researching the Baptist chapel cars were Jacquie McKeon, Harold Mitchell, Gary Wagner, Larry Janssen, Clayton F. Smith, L. Phillip Samuelson, and Arlo Reichter. Each in his or her own way tried to preserve the memory and presence of the chapel cars, and we are indebted to them.

In a personal note, we thank the long line of railroaders who over forty years added to Norman's appreciation for life on the railroad. When he was seventeen years old, he walked into the Beech Grove shops of the New York Central Railroad. When he walked out in October 1995, he walked into the world of railroad church cars, restoring chapel car *Grace*, and researching for this book. His close friend and fellow worker Harlan Finley always supported his interest and encouraged him. Norman has a railroader's heart touched by God's grace.

For Wilma, forty years as a high school and college teacher and journalist led her in retirement to write and publish two stories of God's unfailing love—first her novel, *The Valley of the Blue Heron*, and then this book. Steeped in Baptist history and theology from her childhood by her mother and grandfather, as a young women she was sent by the American Baptist Convention to many of the same states and churches visited by the Baptist chapel cars.

Our appreciation goes to Jean B. Kim, Executive Director, Educational Ministries, American Baptist Churches, U.S.A., and publisher Kristy Arnesen Pullen, who saw the promise in the book. To our editors and the production staff at Judson Press, we owe many thanks: Randy Frame, Victoria McGoey, Mary Nicol, Linda Triemstra, Rebecca Irwin Diehl, and Christina Edginton. Their patience and dedication to the story made all the difference to us.

A special tribute goes to our children and grandchildren. For more than three years, they watched us leave our home and their homes to trace the routes of the chapel cars. To our daughter Norma Faye, who spent many hours helping her dad on chapel car *Grace*; to son Timothy Mark and daughter-in-law Catherine Barker Taylor; to daughter Catheen Marie and son-in-law Steven Scott Hardwick; to daughter Bethany Ann and son-in-law Ronald Lloyd Warren; and to our grandchildren, Chelsea, Natalie, Jonathan, and little Grace, who was born just as this book went to press. They soon learned about "Grandpa's Train Car."

To Norman's mother, Ida Taylor, and Barbara and Charles, and Martha and David, and all our nieces and nephews, whose sincere interest in our projects gave us heart to continue.

Wilma's brother, Weldon Rugh, faithful servant, went to be with the Lord in November 1996, in the midst of our travels. Right before his passing, he read our first article about the chapel cars and conveyed to us his pride in the project. We are grateful to our sister-in-law Doris Rugh, who faithfully read each chapter and whose comments made the book more readable, and to Wilma's sister, Dorothy Fulmer, who has always encouraged Wilma in her creative work.

Our research trips were not without sacrifices—personal, physical, and financial—the most important the time spent away from our loved ones, friends, and home church. Without some sacrifices, we would not have been able to count ourselves a part of the chapel car family, who left their homes and friends and traveled many miles to serve Christ and his gospel.

Wilma Rugh Taylor
and Norman Thomas Taylor
September 1998

CHAPTER 1

Western Railroads: "Hell on Wheels" or Heaven

Rawlins, Wyoming, 1995 — A plain brick church stands on a corner in a quiet neighborhood in this working-class city, a railroad town. The church has a simple white cross on its front door, no ornate stained-glass windows, no towering spires, except for the peaks of the surrounding Sierra Madres that straddle both sides of the Continental Divide. But inside the heart of the First Baptist Church of Rawlins, literally, is a wooden symbol of a unique era of rail and church history.

This church was built around a rail chapel car, one of thirteen that followed the railroads west in the late 1800s and early 1900s. Those churches on rails carried men and women of God who were willing to suffer hardships to bring faith and stability to the multiplying rail towns where faith and civilized life struggled to survive.

To understand why and how those cars came to be and what they accomplished, we must look back to a Rawlins of another time — a wilder, more violent time.

Rawlins, Wyoming, 1867 — The flap of the muddy canvas tent swung open. Through its smoky hole flew the drunken form of a young man, little more than twenty years of age — a Union Pacific railhand, blood spurting from his nostrils, face battered by someone's fist. A farm boy, perhaps from Indiana or Ohio, raised on his pa's corn-fed bacon and his ma's biscuits an' gravy and worn family Bible. As a Union recruit at sixteen, he might have fought valiantly at Antietam, Gettysburg, the Wilderness, and Spotsylvania. Surviving the

Civil War that made him a man, he, like so many others, thought workin' on the railroad would bring him fame and fortune. Instead, it had brought him to the vices of this hell-on-wheels town — eating blood-splattered dust and tasting the bile of shame and liquor that burned through his esophagus.

What brought young men like this one to Rawlins was the construction of the first transcontinental railroad. In 1862 the controllers of the Central Pacific and the Union Pacific railroads began their own race to achieve fame and fortune. Congress and President Abraham Lincoln had finally agreed to grant them right of way over federal lands and to cede sixty-four hundred acres of public lands and a considerable subsidy for each track mile toward the completion of a transcontinental route.

The Central Pacific was to begin in Sacramento, California, and head east; the Union Pacific was to begin in Nebraska Territory and head west. The railroad that laid the most miles of track would reap the greatest wealth. Speed was the name of the game, and the stakes were high. Men were needed for the race. Thousands of men.

So they came to work on the railroad. Not just young veterans and farmhands came to these newly platted towns along the rails, but also former slaves, failed eastern businessmen, and immigrants who had fled to the promised land by the shiploads. Payday brought them by the droves to the tent saloons, poker games, and brothels of railheads like Truckee,

Fig. 1.1 Railroad workers gather in front of a Union Pacific pay train at Blue Creek, Utah, during the construction of the transcontinental railroad. These men, from the very young to the most seasoned, were mainly Irish and Western European immigrants and ex–Civil War soldiers seeking their fortunes on the railroad. (A. J. Russell photo, Union Pacific Railroad Museum Collection, 11-83)

Dutch Flat, Winnemucca, Julesburg, North Platte, Cheyenne, and Rawlins.

Towns Become "Hell on Wheels"

To rack up the most miles and profit expediently, the Central Pacific and Union Pacific established end-of-track points to provide food, lodging, and supplies for the companies' growing stables of workers. Along with these basics, other "necessities" were allowed if not promoted by the railroads: gambling, women, and alcohol. These needs, real and desired, stacked on rail cars, moved from place to place and soon gained the name "Hell on Wheels."

Fig. 1.2 Colfax, California, an early rail town, was not so quiet when night brought rowdy rail workers to Saloon Row across from the depot. (California State Railroad Museum)

Many of those early boom towns vanished as the rails reached beyond them — towns like Gold Run on the California side of Donner Pass, where now there is almost nothing. No saloon rows, no raucous crowds, no gold coins clanking, no gunshots echoing — just a few houses, a convenience store, the old Union church built by miners, and the silence of the nearby cemetery. Other towns, among them Julesburg, Cheyenne, North Platte, and Rawlins, remained and are stable communities with generally law-abiding citizens.

Julesburg does not want to remember its hell-on-wheels reputation but chooses instead to accent its Pony Express and Oregon/California Trail heritage. However, historian Dallas Williams values that part of the town's history and preserved it in *Hell Hole on the Platte*. The rails reached Julesburg June 25, 1867, and the sporting houses were open for business the next day. Williams characterizes the scene: "Arriving with the Union Pacific were various pimps, gamblers, pickpockets, bunko artists, thieves, shills, and other assorted nasty types. And women; not the marrying kind but rather several hundred prostitutes. This mobile Hell on Wheels was controlled by Eastern syndicates who had staked the madams, saloon proprietors, and gambling hall operators and employed gunmen, thieves, and whores on a commission basis."[1]

Major Henry C. Parry, an army surgeon with the Union Pacific Railway Commission, stationed at Fort Sedgwick near Julesburg, described the arrival of that first train to Julesburg. "You can readily think how rejoiced we all were, when we heard the shrill whistle of the engine and saw in the dim distance, its dark form coming puffing toward us. Every cloud of its white smoke, seemed to bring with it peace and civilization over the plains of the far West." It was not long before the good doctor was dealing with other effects of that "cloud of white smoke,"[2] not quite peace and civilization. For the girls of Hell on Wheels brought another problem: venereal disease. It was estimated that more than half of the women were infected.[3] In turn, 25 to 50 percent of the Union Pacific's crews[4] were infected, as well as many of the soldiers stationed at nearby Fort Sedgwick.

Williams reported that booming new Julesburg, the third town by that name, did not last long. The settlement, which contained twelve hundred wood-framed canvas buildings or prefabs, of which at least nine hundred were dedicated to some sort of vice, lasted long enough to brand the thousands of men and women who passed through. Williams added, "When end-of-track had moved on to Cheyenne a few months later, Julesburg was little more than a ghost town with a very large garbage dump."[5]

Something other than the towns themselves remained in those settlements mainly west of the Mississippi. Remaining were the lawless attitudes and life-strangling addictions adopted in those early towns, attitudes that created loss of life and limb on the railroads and stifled the establishment of law and order and religion for years to come. It was not just the Central Pacific and Union Pacific routes that supported hell towns. They were everywhere along the steel ribbons west.

The railroad companies advanced America's so-called Manifest Destiny, jump-started its post–Civil War economy, and provided mobility and undreamed-of opportunities for many. But in their greedy rush to crisscross the nation, they had fostered a moral wasteland.

Who could have foreseen that such a great technological accomplishment would leave in its wake such an ungodly wilderness? The eastern public, for the most part, had welcomed and marveled at the speed and improved comfort of rail travel. Railroads had proven that they were better than turnpikes, canals, and steamboats for passenger and shipping purposes. The opening of the West via rail, with all its possibilities for progress, would be a boon to many, with the exception of those American Indian tribes who called those vast territories home.

Congressman Charles W. Cathcart of Indiana, speaking on the floor of the House of Representatives on February 6, 1846, voiced the view of most Americans: "The Iron Horse [the steam car] with the wings of the wind, his nostrils distended with flame, salamander-like vomiting fire and smoke, trembling with power, but submissive to the steel curb imposed upon him by the hand of man, flies from one end of the continent to the other in less time than our ancestry required to visit a neighboring city."[6] The majority of citizens saw the railroad as "the wings of the wind," which would take them where they desired to go.

Could it be that Nathaniel Hawthorne, from his vantage point in Salem, Massachusetts, in the 1840s, was the only one who had a forewarning of the social changes that a transcontinental railroad might bring the American West?

Hawthorne's Tale Proves Prophetic

Hawthorne's allegorical tale "The Celestial Railroad," patterned after John Bunyan's *Pilgrim's Progress*, provides some insight into his fears. Hawthorne describes a group of pilgrims who board a train that they hoped would take them to the Celestial City of Heaven. Hawthorne's train, unlike Congressman Cathcart's vision, is not the holy "wings of the wind" of Psalm 18 or the cherubim wings and the wheels of the prophet Ezekiel's vision.

On board Hawthorne's train is a gentleman, Mr. Smooth-it-away, a townsman of the City of Destruction, a director of the railroad corporation and one of its largest stockholders. As the train pulls into the station, the narrator describes that on top of the train "sat a personage, almost enveloped in smoke and flame, which . . . appeared to gush from his own mouth and stomach, as well as from the engine's brazen abdomen." Just outside the city, the train passes over a bridge

Fig. 1.3 The celebration of the driving of the golden spike at Promontory Point, Utah, May 10, 1869, symbolized the completion of the first transcontinental route that joined the Central Pacific and Union Pacific railroads. Along the construction route were many railroad towns, left behind in a spiritual wasteland. (A. J. Russell photo, Union Pacific Railroad Museum Collection, 1–23)

of elegant construction, and "on both sides lay an extensive quagmire, which could not have been more disagreeable, either to sight or smell, had all the kennels of the earth emptied their pollution there."

"This," remarked Mr. Smooth-it-away, "is the famous Slough of Despond, a disgrace to all the neighborhood; and the greater that it might so easily be converted into firm ground."[7]

In *All Aboard! The Railroad in American Life*, George H. Douglas interprets Hawthorne's moral. He notes that the narrator of the story, while on his journey to the Celestial City, makes sly observations on how poorly the railroad is built, how its bridges shake, and how the cars rattle. But he is even more perturbed about how the railroad has transformed the landscape, ruining settled institutions and traditional ways of life. People who board the train are hurried, agitated; they seem to want to drop their values by the wayside.

"The narrator understood," Douglas comments, "how the railroad could be advertised as providing a smooth ride to heaven, but in fact it was the work of the devil himself."[8]

Little Godliness between Planned Prayers

By a combination of motives and methods, the race for rails finally began from the west January 8, 1863, in Sacramento, California. Crowds on the levee on Front Street near "K," dampened by steady drizzle and sprinkled with the top hats of state and local dignitaries, were warmed by the music of the brass bands and the sight of bright flags hanging from the speakers' platform and nearby buildings. Well-to-do women, wrapped against the chill, looked on from behind wooden balustrades of hotel balconies. They no doubt gossiped a bit about the roly-poly wholesale grocer turned governor, Leland Sanford, who was the newly elected president of the Central Pacific Railroad, and former dry-goods merchant Charlie Crocker, now superintendent of the Central Pacific, who bustled about below preparing to start the ceremonies.

After many delays, Sanford finally broke ground around noon. To add sanctity to the ceremony, a prominent preacher called for divine blessing on the venture, and, according to accounts, it was a very, very long blessing.

Now the race was on. With the fidelity of gangs of Chinese coolies on the Central Pacific and the doggedness of Irish, British, and European immigrants and ex–Civil War soldiers on the Union Pacific, tracks were laid across the mountains, plains, and rivers, even through the winter storms of 1866–1867. Central Pacific vice president, Collis Huntington, wrote to Crocker July 1, 1868, "So work on as though Heaven were before you and Hell behind you." By October a note was even stronger. "By God, Charley, you must work as man never worked before. Our salvation is you."[9]

In early 1869, the Central Pacific finally made summit and dragged its construction cars over the Donner Pass to

Fig. 1.4 Although religion was noticeably absent in the towns along the right of way, the sound of hymns could be heard on board many trains. Services were held to appease religious leaders who objected to trains running on Sunday. (Library of Congress)

Truckee. The crews then sped across the Nevada desert toward the tracks of the Union Pacific, the object of devious destruction tactics by Northern Cheyenne and Sioux war parties that did not appreciate being crowded out of their hunting grounds. After many months of grading, blasting, and laying track in the midst of heat, blizzards, and Indian attacks, the Central Pacific and the Union Pacific first bridged the continent May 10, 1869, at Promontory Point, Utah *(see fig. 1.3)*. Before the turn of the century, more railroads would complete transcontinental routes with government aid, among them the Northern Pacific, the Denver & Rio Grande, the Southern Pacific, the Santa Fe, and the Great Northern.

At Promontory Point, the Union Pacific and the Central Pacific engines finally met. In spite of the fact that both Sanford and Thomas Durant, president of the Union Pacific, missed striking the ceremonial spike, the deed was declared done with much fanfare. The Reverend John Todd of Boston, official correspondent for two eastern religious magazines, prayed. His prayer, which couldn't be heard above the drunken revelry, was short and contained these words: "that Peace may flow unto them as a gentle stream, and that this mighty enterprise may be unto us as the Atlantic of Thy strength and the Pacific of Thy love."[10]

Someone remembered that John Sharp, the Latter-day Saint "railroad bishop," was there as Brigham Young's representative, and he was asked to pray too. At 12:40 P.M. the telegraph operator impatiently tapped, "WE HAVE GOT DONE PRAYING. THE SPIKE IS ABOUT TO BE PRESENTED."[11] Engraved along the side of that golden spike, which was quickly removed for posterity, were these words: "May God continue the unity of our Country as this Railroad unites the two great Oceans of the world."[12]

The extraordinary enterprise that had started with a prayer ended with a prayer, but there was little godliness between. Instead, especially on the Union Pacific portion, were the hell-on-wheels towns scattered along the routes — flimsy tents and dirt hovels populated by saloon keepers, gamblers, and desperadoes of every kind, plus the soiled doves who flocked wherever the men settled. Like Hawthorne's Slough of Despond, towns like North Platte, Julesburg, Cheyenne, and Rawlins, where young railhands from Indiana, New York, South Carolina, Michigan, and Missouri found and lost themselves, were the beginning of morality run amok along rail right of ways.

The Paradox of the Rush for Rails

Richard O'Connor in *Iron Wheels and Broken Men* presents the paradox. "In less than two generations Americans conquered the West, or possibly savaged it beyond redemption." That ravaging began, O'Connor goes on to say, the day they drove the golden spike to symbolize the linking of the first railroad to the Pacific coast. "The corporate balance sheets of the railroads would not wait upon humane process or orderly planning, or even history," O'Connor emphasizes. "In their desire to create an active market for their various enterprises, the railroads promoted a hasty and heedless settlement of the lands along their rights-of-way, simultaneously profiting by the sale of lands given them by an overly generous government."[13] The railroad heralded by many as the grand "Agent of Civilization" apparently had lost sight of any divine design and instead had cut a deal with Hawthorne's devil.

Ironically, if religion was absent in the towns along the right of way, the sound of hymns could be heard on board the trains *(fig. 1.4)*. To appease religious leaders who were opposed to running trains on the Sabbath, a profitable day for the rail industry, it was customary on Sundays to hold religious services en route. Although it was a Vermont law of 1850 that required conductors to read Sunday Scriptures from Bibles,[14] frequently presented to railroads by the American Bible Society, the practice was generally observed on most lines.

On a train rolling through western Wyoming in 1872, John Lester read the Episcopal service, the Reverend Mr. Murray delivered a sermon entitled "To Die Is Gain," and a choir sang. Lester wrote in a letter, "Here in the very midst of the Rocky Mountain wilderness our thanksgivings were offered up; and our music floated out upon the air, and resounded through the deep caverns, and among the towering hills."[15]

Fig. 1.5 American Baptist colporters came west in the mid-1800s and baptized hundreds, but to establish a church in the rail towns was difficult because there were seldom places large enough to accommodate a congregation. (American Baptist Historical Society, Valley Forge)

However, deboarding brought not the sound of hymns and Scriptures but sounds of a different kind. A group of passengers from New England, traveling on one of the first trains to the West in 1869, was delayed by bad tracks near Wasatch, Utah, and had to spend the night there. "What a place to stop in! No buildings — nothing but tents or shanties, and all of them 'whiskey hells' of the lowest kinds. We worked our way through the most villainous-looking crowd that man ever yet set eyes on, to an old sleeping car on a discontinued sidetrack, which proved to be densely populated with 'creeping things.'"

Wasatch was filled with several hundred discharged railroad workers who had been paid off after the malicious capture of the private car of Dr. Durant, an official of the Union Pacific. Drunk and disorderly, they "made the night hideous, of howling, cursing, swearing and pistol shots."[16]

Hawthorne and his "Celestial Railroad" may not have represented the views of most of his fellow Americans in the 1850s, yet there must have been everywhere some of the same doubt about the too-rapid expansion of rails west. Douglas concludes, "The railroad led away from arcadian America, from the virginal continent, to a new and shadowy nation. It would transform the American people; it would subvert their values. It would make a promise of leading to a city of wonders, to new and gleaming life-styles, but would it really lead to our salvation as a people?"[17]

Religion an Afterthought of Railroads

Religion, especially salvation, seemed to be an afterthought of the railroad companies in those early years, unless it was in the form of a token prayer at the start or completion of a construction project. After all, the job of the railroad companies was to build railroads and create profit, not churches. What did churches have to do with wise enterprise? What did morality, moderation, and public order have to do with good business practices? Wasn't it enough that the railroads provided the broad economic base to place America at the forefront of the world economy?

After the rashness of the early construction period, many railroad companies would come to realize that completion of churches in a settlement lifted the spirits of the people and improved the climate of the towns. In her book on the early churches of Washington State, Esther Pearson concludes that the church was a place for not only worship but also fellowship; a link between the primitive environment of the present and the more civilized life most people left behind. The church provided a proper setting for religious services and a place for the joyous church rituals of baptism, confirmation, and marriage as well as the services for the dead, for in the frontier community, as Pearson points out, death came early to many.[18]

Even after the hell-on-wheels lifestyles had moderated, churches were among the last structures to be built in many railroad towns. Faith in the form of organized religion — the stabilizing center of morality, moderation, and public order in the more judicious establishment of towns in the East — had a much lower priority in the western rail towns. John Hoyt Williams, in *A Great and Shining Road*, wrote that in 1864 Omaha was home to 127 saloons, 25 so-called temples of vice, and 10 full-fledged gambling establishments, but only 20 places of worship. Five years later, the number of saloons had shrunk to 38, plus 5 liquor wholesalers, but so had the number of churches: 6 for a population of twenty thousand.[19]

Towns Churchless, but Not Godless

Eldon Ernst, professor of American church history at the American Baptist Seminary of the West at Berkeley, cautions in *Religion and Society in the American West* that although the image of a godless frontier is an exaggeration, research verifies that, with the exception of Utah, the Far West still has the highest percentage of unchurched persons in America.[20] He concludes that religious institutions did not have a strong impact on the Pacific Northwest, and the large majority of westerners never affiliated with churches.[21]

In some cases, western migrants left religion behind amid what seventeenth-century church historian Robert Baird called the "engrossing cares and manifold temptations" of the frontier. In other cases, they evolved new, less austere creeds,[22] frequently of a more secular kind. For example, towns were likely to have lodge halls — the Masons, Red Men, Woodmen, Eagles, Moose, and Elks — than churches. Many prominent men belonged to the Masons, except Catholics, who were forbidden to join, and some evangelicals, including Baptists, who objected to the secret rites. Freemasonry demonstrated the appeal of secret and magical beliefs to middle- and upper-class men, sometimes more so than the rituals of Christian congregations. Between 1790 and 1840 perhaps as many as a hundred thousand men joined Masonic lodges.[23]

Those early rail communities may have been churchless, but they were not godless, especially when women began to travel west to join their husbands, fathers, and brothers. The woman would become the force behind the organization of many of the western rail town churches. Small bands of believers, mainly women and children, frequently met in homes, opera houses, depots, and schoolhouses. When they outgrew their space, they seldom had the money or support to erect a building, even though the ladies' aid societies were known to keep many a church open and active through their cake sales and mission projects.

The indifference toward established religion did not help those faithful flocks. Although the Union Pacific Railroad offered free lots to congregations along the line, as did most of the other railroads, lack of funds delayed the construction of buildings.[24]

Saloonkeepers, frequently the wealthiest, most influential people in town, knew that religion was bad for their business, although they sometimes permitted their premises to be used for services. They especially feared the temperance societies, supported largely by the Methodists and Baptists, and generally did everything they could to prevent a church from formally organizing and building. In Holbrook, Arizona, on the Santa Fe line, the Bucket of Blood Saloon kept churches out of town until 1913. When a church was finally built, the Bucket of Blood had to shut down.[25]

Men and women of faith had been in the West long before the building of the railroad, starting with the Catholic padres and the Spanish missions of the Southwest and followed by a brave, if somewhat naïve, parade of mainstream Protestant preachers and missionaries.

On December 1, 1817, Baptist missionary John Mason Peck and his family arrived at the foot of Elm Street in St. Louis aboard a keelboat. He found a town that was no longer merely a French trading post but a town awaking to its importance as the gateway to the West. The village was receiving restless, property-hungry people too rapidly to house them properly. Save Bellissame's French tavern for farmers, there was not a hotel or boarding house in the place. A barrel of flour cost 12 dollars and coffee from 62 to 75 cents per pound.

Neither the excessive prices for food nor the extreme inconvenience of living accommodations awakened Peck's concern as much as did the state of religion and morals in St. Louis and the neighboring settlements. Among the village sights he saw were "nightly orgies and scenes of drunkenness and profane revelry, and among the frantic rites observed were the mock celebration of the Lord's supper and burning of the Bible."[26] The boast was often made to Peck that the Sabbath would never cross the Mississippi, but it did.

Starting in the 1860s with the construction of the transcontinental roads, the clergy rushed to the base towns and settlements along the rail lines (see fig. 1.5). Those early voices were like John the Baptist "crying in the wilderness," but their message was gratefully received by the few who had the rare opportunity to hear them. It was not unknown for a homesteader to exclaim: "Here's a Methodist preacher before I get my wagon unloaded!"[27]

Need Was Great, Missionaries Few

There were not enough preachers to meet the need. Pleading for help, John F. Spalding, Episcopal missionary bishop of Colorado and Wyoming, wrote:

> The country is full of young men, on ranches, in mining camps, in railroad shops, in smelting works and manufacturers and stores and offices, to whom the minister of the Church can go . . . to the large extent young men, who can be warned against the dangers around them, led back while going astray, helped up, redeemed, saved to Christianity and to good society, and good citizenship. Nothing, but the Church of Christ, embodying and holding forth the blessed Gospel by loving, sympathizing pastors and people, can help them.[28]

By 1889 there were only five Catholic priests besides the bishop in Wyoming. Bishop Maurice W. Burke of Cheyenne found conditions so intolerable that he went to Rome to get the Diocese of Cheyenne attached to a neighboring diocese, but he was turned down. He wrote to eastern Catholics for help: "With no prospects for the future, no increase in the Catholic population, with absolutely no support for a bishop,

with a large debt on the little church at Cheyenne, and without any possibility of doing anything whatever in the interests of religion, I find the situation insupportable."[29]

The farther west the traveling preachers and padres rode, the less evidence they found of Christianity, not just in the rail base towns but also in the scattered frontier settlements a day's ride from the depots. The common saying was, "There is no law west of Kansas City, and west of Fort Scott, no God."

One story says that a Presbyterian missionary arrived at a lonely cabin in a clearing and, hoping to find some fellow member of his denomination, asked the woman of the cabin: "Are there any Presbyterians in this country?" The woman, assuming that the man, like her husband, must be a hunter of animals, replied: "Wal, I just couldn't say for sure about that. These woods is full of most every kind of varmet, but I ain't paid much attention to 'em. You might take a look around there on the back side of the cabin where my husband keeps his varmet hides, and see if he's got any Presbyterian hides nailed up. If there's any Presbyterians in this country, he's bound to have caught one by now."[30]

Men and women of faith came, willing to suffer hardships to bring faith and stability to the multiplying rail communities like Rawlins, where faith and civilized life struggled to survive. Hawthorne's Slough of Despond surrounded them. The distances were great, the rail boom was quick, and the rowdy rail towns were vile. Facilities for organizing congregations were far too limited, and the support for building churches was sadly lacking.

But God was not ticketless as the rails stretched from coast to coast. From 1890, through two world wars, and beyond, because of the prayers and actions of God-inspired men and women, thirteen chapel cars — three Episcopal, three Catholic, and seven Baptist — were hauled across many of the same tracks that first carried those hell-on-wheels towns. During the early years of their service, those churches on rails were pulled at the expense of and with the permission and invitation of railroad companies that had learned from hard experience that a railroad, or a great nation, cannot be built on speeding iron wheels alone. When faith prepared the roadbed, then wheels did fly across the rails "with the wings of the wind."

Their destination: heaven.

Notes

[1] Dallas Williams, *Fort Sedgwick: Colorado Territory, Hell Hole on the Platte* (Julesburg, Colo.: Fort Sedgwick Historical Society, 1996), 49.

[2] "The History of Sedgwick County, Colorado," The Sedgwick County Historical Society, C-12, Julesburg Public Library, Julesburg, Colo., 1982.

[3] Williams, 50.

[4] Robert West Howard, *The Great Iron Trail: The Story of the First Transcontinental Railroad* (New York: G. P. Putnam's Sons, 1962), 249.

[5] Williams, 46.

[6] *Congressional Globe*, February 6, 1846, 323; quoted in Dee Brown, *Hear That Lonesome Whistle Blow* (New York: Holt, Rinehart and Winston, 1977), 26.

[7] Nathaniel Hawthorne, "The Celestial Railroad," in *The Complete Works of Nathaniel Hawthorne*, Riverside ed. (Cambridge, Mass.: Houghton Mifflin & Co., 1854), 212–13.

[8] George H. Douglas, *All Aboard! The Railroad in American Life* (New York: Marlowe & Company, 1995), 92.

[9] California Railroad Museum exhibit display card, California Railroad Museum, Sacramento, Calif.

[10] Howard, 326.

[11] Ibid., 328.

[12] *The Railroaders*, The Old West series (New York: Time-Life Books, 1973), 116.

[13] Richard O'Connor, *Iron Wheels and Broken Men: The Railroad Barons and the Plunder of the West* (New York: G. P. Putnam's Sons, 1973), 7.

[14] Loose sheet with information about American Bible Society, Box-Colportage and Chapel Cars information acquired and/or produced in 1980 and 1990s, articles, lists, hymns, correspondence, etc., American Baptist Historical Society, Valley Forge (henceforth ABHS, VF).

[15] John Erastus Lester, *The Atlantic to the Pacific*, 16; as published in Brown, 158.

[16] William L. Humason, *From the Atlantic Surf to the Golden Gate*, 19–20; as published in Brown, 161.

[17] Douglas, 92.

[18] Esther Pearson, *Early Churches of Washington State* (Seattle, Wash.: University of Washington Press, 1980), 6.

[19] John Hoyt Williams, *A Great and Shining Road: The Epic Story of the Transcontinental Railroad* (New York: Time Books, 1988), 126.

[20] Carl Guarneri and David Alvarez, "Introduction," in *Religion and Society in the American West*, ed. Carl Guarneri (New York: University Press of America, 1987), xi.

[21] Eldon G. Ernst, "American Religious History from a Pacific Coast Perspective," in *Religion and Society in the American West*, ed. Carl Guarneri (New York: University Press of America, 1987), 9.

[22] Carl Guarneri, ed., *Religion and Society in the American West* (New York: University Press of America, 1987), x.

[23] Jon Butler, *Awash in a Sea of Faith* (Cambridge, Mass.: Harvard University Press, 1990), 235–36.

[24] T. A. Larson, *History of Wyoming* (Lincoln: University of Nebraska Press, 1965), 221.

[25] "History of Holbrook, Arizona," Holbrook Public Library, Holbrook, Ariz.

[26] Coe Hayne, *Vanguard of the Caravans* (Philadelphia: Judson Press, 1931), 53–55.

[27] Lawrence F. Small, *Religion in Montana*, 2 vols. (Billings, Mont.: Rocky Mountain College, 1992), 1:133.

[28] John F. Spalding, *The Spirit of Missions*, March 1886, 97.

[29] Larson, 223–24.

[30] Ross Phares, *Bible in Pocket, Gun in Hand: The Story of Frontier Religion* (Lincoln: University of Nebraska Press, 1964), 2–4.

CHAPTER 2

The Church-on-Rails Concept: Nothing New under the Sun

I f the railroads had abetted in the creation of a spiritual wasteland along the newly laid tracks west, then the railroads needed to be part of the solution. One of the first to come to that conclusion and to visualize a possible solution to the spiritual deprivation along the rail lines was Boston W. Smith *(fig. 2.2)*. Known to almost everyone as Uncle Boston, he had responsibility for Baptist Sunday school work in Minnesota.

In a Minnesota town along a new rail line in the 1880s, Smith met a woman who appealed to him, "Uncle Boston, won't you help me start a Sunday school?" He immediately gathered a library of Christian books and Sunday school papers from the American Baptist Publication Society and took them to her. She then asked her skeptical husband for use of his buckboard, and she scoured the prairies for ten miles around, stopping at every claim shanty to ask, "Would you like to come to Sunday school?"

About twenty excited children promised to come. Many others wanted to, but their parents forbade them or other problems stood in their way. The thought then occurred to her, Where should the school be held? They had no place in the town larger than her claim shanty of two crowded, dirt-floored rooms, so here she decided to hold it.

Soon the school was so large that on nice days they met out of doors. Parents sent their children to get free reading material, as they had no papers and few precious books, and the books and papers that the publication society gave the pupils

drew people from all parts of the country.[1] As the weather became frigid, there was nowhere to hold the school, and so it had to be abandoned until spring. Smith knew the same scenario was being repeated all over his vast missionary territory.

A few years later at St. James, Minnesota, G. H. Herrick, a Sunday school superintendent in that district, also found himself without a place to conduct Sunday school. He made a request of the railroad company that a passenger coach be sidetracked in town; the company responded favorably, and for an entire winter a Sunday school was conducted in that passenger car. In that car, Smith wrote, "a Sunday school was organized which grew into a flourishing Baptist church." More importantly, Uncle Boston said, "I at once dreamed that the day would come when a missionary car would be built for the purpose of carrying the gospel to new communities."[2]

Earlier Chapels on Wheels

Smith was not the first to conceive of a church on wheels. Perhaps one of the first churches on wheels was the "little ark," a wooden box on wheels, set on the road of Kilbaha Beach at the mouth of the Shannon River in Ireland *(fig. 2.3)*. A priest said Mass there for people who walked miles to attend. Built by the priest in 1852, the box was only 6 feet long, 5 feet wide, and 7 feet high. It was raised on four wheels so that even those kneeling at the outskirts of the crowd could follow the Mass.[3]

Fig. 2.1 The chapel cars of the Russian Orthodox Church, which were constructed to carry the sacraments and services of the church to the thousands who lived and worked along the route of the Trans-Caspian and Trans-Siberian railroads, were the inspiration for the American chapel cars. (Courtesy of Stephen G. Marks)

Fig. 2.2 Minnesota Baptist Sunday school missionary Boston W. Smith, called "Uncle Boston" by hundreds of children across the nation, was one of the first to dream of a rail chapel car. (American Baptist Historical Society, Valley Forge)

Another chapel on wheels was the coach Pope Pius IX, the longest reigning pontiff in the history of the church, reportedly used while traveling through the Papal States during his reign in the 1860s.[4] An innovative man, he set up a commission to introduce railways into the Papal States in 1846.[5] The coach was fitted for administering the sacraments and receiving guests, as well as for the comfort of the pope.

The earliest church on rails probably was the train of three (some say five) Russian Orthodox church cars that moved in the late 1880s with construction gangs first along the Trans-Caspian Railroad, which links the Caspian Sea to Tashkent,[6] and then along the Trans-Siberian Railroad (see fig. 2.1). Like the settlers of the American plains and prairies, the people who lived in eastern Siberia existed in an environment that could be described as bleak, and their situation was parallel in many ways to the plight of those living along American western routes.

Steven G. Marks, in *Road to Power*, records the account of railroad engineer L. N. Liubimov:

The conditions of life wear especially hard on people of the "educated class" arriving here from European Russia, who yearn for their distant homeland. The oppressive feeling of solitude and dissatisfied spiritual needs, in conjunction with an unfamiliar climate, ruins the nervous system and engenders an irresistible desire to escape from the region once and for all. Add to that the almost daily murders, committed for the most part by fugitive hard-labor convicts, . . . and the frequent funeral processions; one can easily imagine that life for the Vladivostok resident is not sweet. For this reason, [as] nowhere else, it seems, do they seek to drown their sorrows in spirits in such measure as in this dreary city. Here they drink to the utmost from morning until late at night and end up either suicides or insane . . . and to make up for it all, there is an abundance of drinking houses, taverns, and houses of pleasure.[7]

Like Nathaniel Hawthorne and some others in America, there were those in Russia who had forebodings about what a transcontinental rail route would do to their way of life. They feared the settlers and exiles, people of easy money, shady characters, and swindlers who would come in on the trains. "They and the mass of their kind will crop up from both ends of the empire, grabbing all trade and industry into their hands. The railroad will give birth to a period of speculation of the most roguish type ever to have a place in society. In contemporary Siberian society there is much confusion and disorder, but essentially it is vigorous."[8]

These alarmed Russian regionalists must have received reports about what was happening along the American transcontinental lines. They felt that the healthy traits of Siberian life would be destroyed by the industrial fever of railroad promoters and other speculators.

As was the case with the American transcontinental railways, the Siberian railway, which became the longest continuous rail line in the world, was to fulfill Russia's version of Manifest Destiny — to develop the resources of Siberia and to constitute a new commercial route for rapid travel and exchange of products from East and West.[9]

Some Russian churchmen saw the Siberian spiritual wasteland and determined to do something about it. *The Spirit of Missions*, a brief from the *London Church Review* reported, "A traveling church will be put upon the Trans-Caspian railway shortly to provide occasional services for the Russian officials of the line and the settlers scattered about. Externally the church resembles an ordinary railway carriage except for a cross over the roof and a little belfry at the entrance. Inside, however, it is beautifully fitted up for the service of the Orthodox Church, with a carved wooden altar and accommodation for seventy worshipers. The Priest and his assistants travel in a tiny coupe attached to the church-carriage" (see fig. 2.1).[10]

Nicholas Faith, in his study of the railway and religion, points out that the faith of many people in England, Scotland, and Wales put them at odds with the railways, especially with the practice of running trains on Sunday. After a disastrous Sunday accident in 1842 in Versailles, France, and another Sunday tragedy in the Clayton tunnel just outside Brighton,

England, twenty years later, "plenty of people rushed about proclaiming the accidents as a judgment of God." According to Michael Robbins in *The Railway Age*, it was the need for mail trains to run on Sunday that broke the resistance of the Sabbatarians in both Scotland and Wales.

Similar battles were fought in the United States. In Galesburg, Illinois, the railroad was the blunt instrument that broke the power of the Sabbatarians. The first Sunday train was boarded by the impressive figure of President Blanchard of Knox College, who was told to "go to hell" when he ordered the engineer to take the engine back to the roundhouse.[11] That seemed to be the end of the Galesburg crusade.

Harris's Chapel Car

At the same time Boston Smith was dreaming of a Baptist gospel train car that would hold services on Sundays as well as on other days of the week, the following item appeared in *The National Car-Builder*:

Edwin A. Harris, of Fitchburg, for twelve years a railroad conductor, connected with the Railroad Men's Christian Associations, has for about nine months traveled among railroad men holding religious meetings. Mr. Harris proposes to build and equip a mission car to be called "Bethlehem," and has already procured from the Jackson & Sharp Co., of Wilmington, Del., a plan of the proposed car, estimated cost of which is from $10,000 to $13,000. The proposition is made to churches and individuals to subscribe to a fund of $18,000, . . . for the construction and equipment of a mission car to be used in evangelistic work among railway men.

The car is to be constructed after models suggested by railroad men, and is arranged that it furnishes a room for meetings and is also supplied with cooking and sleeping apartments for those engaged in the work. It is to be built to run over any ordinary gauge railroad. It is designed as a convenient headquarters for mission work among railway men, for the distribution of Bibles and reading matter, and is to be manned by workers of practical railway experience . . . a car commissioned in this service, stopping in the railway centers . . . may be an efficient auxiliary to the agencies already established.

Subscriptions may be sent, or plans and circulars giving further particulars will be furnished, on applications to E. A. Harris, Fitchburg, Mass.[12]

Whether such a car ever was constructed is unknown, and whether Smith ever saw that news item is also unknown, but Harris had the basic plan, from need, to design, to effect.

The First American Chapel Car

It would be Episcopal Bishop William David Walker of North Dakota who first took the concept, produced a chapel car, and put it into service. On a trip to Russia in the late 1890s, Bishop Walker saw the Russian Orthodox chapel cars

Fig. 2.3 One of the earliest forms of a chapel on wheels was the "little ark," a wooden box on wheels, built in Ireland. Its purpose was to provide a place where the local priest could say Mass for the faithful who would walk miles to attend services. This drawing illustrates a congregation in May 1852. (*Extension*, November 1911)

on the Siberian Railway. Although Bishop Walker never mentioned it, he had also no doubt read in *The Spirit of Missions*, his denominational publication, about a chapel car suggested by the Reverend Edward Abbott.

Like Harris, Abbott had a scheme whereby a missionary bishop might make the most of his itinerary in an extended jurisdiction where towns were springing up along railways but where facilities for holding services were poor.

> . . . as there are directors' cars, paymasters' cars, and construction cars, so there might be a Bishop's car in which he and his wife (he must be childless) might live and move from place to place. The car should be fitted up so that it may be readily converted into a chapel and the people in the village gathered in for worship and counsel. The idea is novel, but not revolutionary, and in a country of magnificent distances and quick development, the conditions are such as to require modern methods. There might be stranger things than for a Bishop to occupy a moving palace, a home and chapel on wheels.[13]

That article, if Bishop Walker saw it, plus his view of the Russian Orthodox chapel cars, would have caused some wheels to whirl in the bishop's head. In April 1890, while Smith was still gathering support for a Baptist chapel car, Bishop Walker had contracted for such a car to be built by the Pullman Palace Car Company in Pullman, Illinois, and took possession of it in early November 1890. Called the *Church of the Advent*, the Cathedral Car of North Dakota, Walker's car was the first American chapel car put in service. The Baptist car, contracted in August at the Barney & Smith Car Company shops in Dayton, Ohio, would not be completed until the spring of 1891.

In 1904, after his Cathedral Car had been out of service and sold and he had left North Dakota, Walker visited the Baptist chapel car *Messenger of Peace* at the St. Louis World's Fair. He told missionary Joe Jacobs about his experience.

> I was on a tour around the world and while crossing Siberia I noted on Sunday morning that an extra coach was attached to our train and upon reaching the next town the train was held there while the people attended Mass. Curious to know how this service was conducted, I entered the car and stood with others while a Greek Catholic Priest said Mass. This over, the train moved on to the next town where a similar service was held, and so through the day.
>
> Living as I did then in North Dakota, I thought how convenient an arrangement like this would be for me to conduct confirmation services and organize churches on that frontier. Upon my return to America I made known my plans to some wealthy friends and it was not long before my dream was realized, and I began work in the great Northwest with the first chapel car that was ever built in America. When I left that Diocese for Buffalo I left to my successor the car, but he made little use of it. Your Boston Smith and Wayland Hoyt gathered their ideas from me, just as I had done from the Greek Catholics and I am really delighted to see that you Baptists have greatly profited by an Episcopalian idea.[14]

Some Baptists were not gracious about the fact that Bishop Walker had beaten them to the draw. The editor of *The Pacific Baptist*, the Reverend Charles Wooddy, published what might be considered an uncharitable account of the *Church of the Advent*, although there was some truth to it.

> . . . the Episcopalians had a cathedral car running in Minnesota and North Dakota six months before Evangel entered upon the scene. Did the Baptists borrow the idea from the Episcopals or did the Episcopals divine or anticipate it? There are some who believe that Bishop Walker caught the idea from descriptions of a Sunday school gathered in a freight car by Uncle Boston and given by him in many places and reported in many papers, east and west, sacred and secular.
>
> At any rate, while the idea was brewing in Baptist brains, Bishop Walker hurried his plan into execution and out came a gaudy car, with flanging steps, proud cupola and painted pictures of saints and sinners. The hit [success] of

that car was not very satisfactory. Before going in its first tunnel, the steps had to be knocked off and before passing under the first bridge, the spire had to be taken down, and after running awhile in Dakota, the car was stowed away in Fargo for months.[15]

As Bishop Walker was sharing his experiences with Jacobs in the chapel of *Messenger of Peace*, the Baptist paper *The Word and the Way* provided more details of the Russian Orthodox cars, which were still in service. "The cost per car is 30,000 rubles or about $18,000. The interior of each coach is modestly furnished. Light is furnished by means of tallow candles and a wood stove furnished heat. At one end of the car is the kitchen and at the other end the sleeping apartments. A priest and two assistants occupy the church on wheels. On top of the car are bells that are used to call the worshipers to service. There is nothing new under the sun."[16]

Although perhaps there is nothing new under the sun, the chapel cars revolutionized the missionary operations of at least three denominations and, by their novel appearance and approach, drew thousands of Americans into a unique religious experience and a better way of life.

Notes

[1] Boston W. Smith Papers (henceforth referred to as BSP), ABHS, VF.

[2] "Church and Parsonage on Railway Wheels," BSP 1831–1908, Group 2, Box 3 P, ABHS, VF.

[3] Julia R. Doyle, "The Evolution of the 'Church on Wheels,'" *Extension*, November 1911, 15, Catholic Church Extension Society Archives, Chicago.

[4] Francis P. Leipzig, *Extension in Oregon* (St. Benedict, Ore.: The Benedictine Press, 1956), 33.

[5] Eamon Duffy, *Saints and Sinners: A History of the Popes* (New Haven, Conn.: Yale University Press, 1997), 222.

[6] John F. Stover, "Trans-Caspian Railroad," Bibliography: Stephenson, Graham, Russia from 1812 to 1945 (Grolier Electronic Publishing, 1996).

[7] Steven G. Marks, *Road to Power: The Trans-Siberian Railroad and the Colonization of Asian Russia, 1850–1917* (Ithaca, N.Y.: Cornell University Press, 1991), 13–14.

[8] Ibid., 87–88.

[9] Ibid.

[10] *The Spirit of Missions*, September 1890.

[11] Nicholas Faith, *The World the Railways Made* (New York: Carroll & Graf, 1990), 269–70.

[12] The article from the *Boston Herald* appeared in *The National Car-Builder*, October 1883.

[13] *The Spirit of Missions*, February 1889, 49.

[14] *Missions*, September 1912, 657.

[15] *The Pacific Baptist*, December 24, 1891, 7, American Baptist Seminary of the West, Berkeley, Calif.

[16] *The Word and the Way*, April 14, 1904.

CHAPTER 3

The First American Chapel Car: Cathedral Car of North Dakota

In 1883, a fifty-year-old native of New York City, a Columbia University graduate with doctorates from Oxford and Trinity, came to North Dakota — a journey of extremes. He had advanced to the priesthood in Calvary Church, New York, where he displayed ability as a man of affairs, wise judgment, and conservative churchmanship, which added to his powers as a preacher and sermonizer. His sympathies for all classes led the House of Bishops to nominate him for the missionary episcopate of North Dakota. He was consecrated in Calvary Church, New York, December 20, 1883.[1]

Even as a young priest he was known for his innovative and courageous approaches to missionary work. He would need all those traits in his new home. A year after William David Walker (*see fig. 3.2*) came to North Dakota and before "it had been toned down much by civilization," *The Illustrated American* reported that he proved his compassion for the common men and their condition in that frontier.

In front of a saloon he saw seventy or eighty men forming a ring around two others, who were engaged in a desperate fight. The clothes of the combatants were torn and bloodstained, and one was nearly blinded. Bishop Walker broke into the ring, and going up to one of the struggling men, who was kicking the other in the face, attempted to drag him away. Unaided, he [Bishop Walker] could accomplish nothing, and was himself in danger of injury. He appealed to the crowd.

"Will no one of you help to separate these men?" he asked.

The crowd jeered. "Let them have it out," one man cried.

Then the bishop lifted himself up to his full height and cried, with eyes blazing with indignation: "Is it possible that the manhood of all of you is gone? Are you only wolves? Shame on you!"[2]

This was not a prudent way to address an excited crowd in Dakota in those days. The crowd stood dazed and amazed for a moment. Then four or five men rushed forward and helped the bishop. His hands and clothes were stained with blood and dirt in the struggle, but he had the demeanor of a conqueror. Standing between the two combatants, who were glaring at each other and eager to renew the fight, he directed two or three of the crowd to take each man home and see that they did not begin the struggle again. The crowd meekly obeyed.

The challenge of mission work in North Dakota seemed fitted for the bishop, but this was generally not the case. A

Fig. 3.1 The stained-glass miniature rose window in the cupola-style transept of the Cathedral Car may have been copied from a similar design on the exterior of the Russian Orthodox cars. Here the Cathedral Car is parked at the Chicago Pullman shops in November 1890, ready for delivery to Bishop Walker. (Smithsonian Institution Photograph)

Fig. 3.2 Bishop William David Walker built the first American chapel car, the *Church of the Advent*, the Cathedral Car of North Dakota, in 1890. (Courtesy of the Episcopal Diocese of North Dakota. © Copyright DFMS: Archives of the Episcopal Church U.S.A. Used by permission.)

vision for missions was not at the top of the agenda for many in the Episcopal clergy. James Thayer Addison, in his history of the Episcopal Church in the United States, describes the situation when Walker became bishop of North Dakota.

Development was rapid in the West, and by 1890 five of the eight territories of Dakota, Montana, Wyoming, Idaho, Washington, Utah, New Mexico, and Indian Territory had become states, and their population had risen to 1.5 million whites, drawn largely from the Middle West.

"The census of 1890 officially recorded the passing of the frontier. Thenceforth there was to be no fringe of settlement in the United States, for the whole country belonged in the 'settled area,' although in some parts the settlement was still thin . . . [but] much of the West remained a frontier region for the Church long after it had ceased to be a frontier for population."[3]

Support for mission work in these territories was weak, "painful evidences of wide indifference and of inadequate support," and if money was hard to raise, so were men. According to the bishops, writing in 1895, "It is the fault of much of our training for the ministry that it fails to produce the kind and number of clergy demanded by the Church for its missionary work at home and abroad. . . . To call for such men, and to call in vain, is the bitterest experience that can befall the Church."[4]

At that time, the Episcopal Diocese of North Dakota had eighteen churches and about thirty-five missions, services being conducted in hotel parlors, stores, schoolhouses, halls, skating rinks, and theaters. Across the state Bishop Walker found stretched four great rail lines — the Northern Pacific, the Great Northern, the Milwaukee and St. Paul, the Minneapolis and Pacific, with feeders thrown out in all directions. "A large number of hamlets dot the country at short intervals. Many farms are grouped around each station of the principal and branch railways." The bishop could count as many as sixty or seventy of these very small places on the railroads. "In frequent instances such settlements contain no school houses or churches,"[5] and often he could find no room large enough to hold twenty people.

After seeing the Russian Orthodox cars, the missionary bishop pondered a situation in his wild diocese for which creeds were not responsible — a lack of church buildings. Walker felt that the innovative approach of rail cars was what he needed to reach the outposts of his diocese. In 1889 Walker approached friends in the East for money to build a railway chapel *(fig. 3.1)*. A member of the Mission Board of the Protestant Episcopal Church, Cornelius Vanderbilt II, whose grandfather made the family fortunes on steamship and railway lines in ways that many thought scandalous, made the first contribution.[6]

Pullman and His Palace Car Company

On April 28, 1890, Bishop Walker contracted with the Pullman Palace Car Company, in an agreement signed by George M. Pullman, to build a 60-foot-long, 9-foot, 8-inch-wide, oak finish car. According to the Newberry Library's Pullman Collection, $4,224.16 was paid November 14, 1890, for Lot 1746.[7]

The shop where this first American chapel car was built was a busy place at the close of 1890. When Pullman signed the contract to build the Cathedral Car of North Dakota, his company had 2,135 vehicles running over 120,686 of the approximately 160,000 miles of railroad track in the United States. Prospects looked even better for the 1890s because of demands for the upcoming Chicago World's Fair; in addition, more Americans appeared to be traveling as the nineteenth century entered its final decade.[8]

Pullman, just months short of sixty years old when the Cathedral Car took form in his shop complex, had been reared to be honest, frugal, thrifty, and industrious. An example of these traits was the model company town of Pullman, built in 1880–1881 to improve worker efficiency in order to increase the output and profits of Pullman's Palace Car Company.

The town had parks, a school, a marketplace, shops, a library, a church, a bank, and recreational facilities. The brick housing had running water and a sewage disposal system, and the company maintained attractive parks, streets, and lawns as part of the rent — which was high enough for Pullman to make a 6 percent profit from the town.[9] In 1905, Jacob D. Moskowitz, following Pullman's example, built a model company town for the main chapel car builder, the Barney & Smith Car Company in Dayton, Ohio, called the Kossuth Colony (see chap. 14).

Returning from a trip east, Bishop Walker stopped at the Pullman shops in Chicago in November 1890. According to the agreement, the car was to have been completed in August, but for some reason it was not ready until late October. *The Spirit of Missions* reported that the bishop left Chicago for Fargo on November 13 in possession of the car. The car excited a great deal of interest in Chicago, and many persons visited it. It was the intent of the bishop to reach every village and hamlet along the railroads in his jurisdiction, living and holding services in the car.[10]

Bishop Walker and His Cathedral Car

On the return journey to North Dakota, about one thousand people inspected the car at Minneapolis.[11] Among those viewing the car were several members of the Baptist church, who asked questions regarding it and its proposed work. On the second day, three of them returned, two of them most likely Boston W. Smith and the Reverend Wayland Hoyt, pastor of the First Baptist Church of Minneapolis. They asked more questions and then stated that they looked on it as solving a difficult question: what to do spiritually with the small towns on the railroads during the transition period.

"We have therefore, Bishop," said one of the gentlemen, "concluded to have one built for the Baptist church."

The bishop replied, "I haven't a patent on it, and so of course you can."

Walker related later that about three days thereafter the Twin Cities papers announced that an order already had been given for such a car, and in about six months it was running in these northwestern states.

Harper's Weekly described the Cathedral Car of North Dakota:

This car is sixty feet long, and arranged with what has been known to the manufacturers as a "state-room" at one end. In the centre of the exterior on either side is an elevation with sunken panels to give in some degree the cathedral appearance. This transept plan was arranged by Mr. C. [Charles] C. Haight, of New York, well-known architect for Trinity Church Association, Columbia College, and the Episcopal Theological Seminary, in addition to a general course of important work in this city and its environs.

The finish is in oak, and the car is equipped with double windows on account of the cold country in which it will be used. A Baker heater is selected for warming this moving house of worship. Toward the rear of the car is the chancel with its altar, lectern, and font. A cabinet organ provides the music. The seating space is filled with portable chairs to the number of about eighty. The room partitioned off in the rear is ten feet long by about nine feet four inches wide.

Its twofold use as vestry and bedroom is best signified in the bishop's words: "In it I can put on my robes. It will also be a dormitory for me when the people of the hamlet will not have room to shelter me. It will be simple in decoration and in its equipment."[12]

When Bishop Walker boasted, "This is, of course, the first church of the kind that has been built in the world, in all the ages of its history,"[13] he must have had a memory lapse, for he failed to mention the Russian cars that had inspired his chapel car. He emphasized the simplicity of the car. "It would be incongruous for a missionary bishop to go about in a luxurious and pompous way. The object is in a simple way to preach Christ's Gospel and administer the sacraments to many who have few or no opportunities to avail themselves of these spiritual comforts."[14]

The Illustrated American described the furnishing, which reflected involvement of Episcopalians across the nation. For example, the altar was given by a Summit, New Jersey, church; the lectern by a Philadelphia clergyman as a memorial for his father; Mrs. Colt, of Hartford, Connecticut, widow of the manufacturer of small arms, gave the silken altar cloth; the altar linen was provided by the wife of the bishop of Fredericton, New Brunswick. The church school of St. Catharine's at Davenport, Iowa, contributed the bishop's chair; and the Sunday school of St. James's Church in Brooklyn sent the books for the altar. The font was the gift of the Missionary Society of Calvary Church, New York; and

the Bible a memorial of the late General George W. Cass, long-time senior warden of Christ Church. Chicago friends of Bishop Walker supplied the communion service; the kneeling cushions came from the family of the bishop of Iowa; and the organ was presented by the Young Ladies' Missionary Association of the Church of the Heavenly Rest, New York.

In the same issue of *The Illustrated American*, Bishop Walker described why he wanted the chapel car. He felt that to erect churches in towns, until their stability was assured, would be a waste of capital. In the neighborhood of each town large numbers of farmers had taken claims. To meet these people's spiritual wants, a church on wheels would be effective. His plan was to send a placard announcing his coming, to be posted in the railroad station ten days before he arrived. The car would then be drawn to the place by a freight train and switched to a sidetrack. After the service was over, the car would be attached to another train when it appeared and dragged to the next place at which services were to be held. Thus the work would go on from day to day.[15]

The Cathedral Car's ministry was seventy thousand square miles within the jurisdiction of the Northern Pacific and the St. Paul, Minneapolis, and Manitoba railroads. Of his mission field, Walker wrote, "I do not believe it to be a western exaggeration to say that a larger torrent of able-bodied people has swept into this section than ever entered any section of land since time began."[16]

Walker wrote:

I reach through the occasional ministrations of the "cathedral car" thousands of people whom I could not otherwise touch. I am now on another tour in it. Everywhere it is filled or crowded. The only exception was at a little place last night. The hamlet, however, consisted of only four dwelling houses, two wheat elevators, and a railroad station. Yet there were from thirty to forty persons present at our worship. The same service in a cheerless school-house, if there had been one, would probably not have called out one quarter the

Fig. 3.3 The ceiling designs and wood paneling of the Cathedral Car were typical of the workmanship of Pullman craftsmen. (Smithsonian Institution Photograph)

number of people, and this is the story everywhere. The compactness, the dignity, the simple beauty of the car wins the people. Its hearty service, too, reaches their hearts.[17]

Bishop Walker found the population of North Dakota — including large numbers of Englishmen of good family, Canadians, and industrious, orderly Scandinavians — even in the smallest households, remarkable in several respects, especially in education, intelligence, and cultivation.

In such homes refinement is shown in the books carefully treasured, in the tasteful if inexpensive decorations of the rooms, and in the speech of the occupants. The proportion of college-graduates who are farming in North Dakota is surprisingly large. In one settlement, consisting of twenty houses, a visitor was assured that there were twelve college-graduates among the inhabitants. Many of these remarkable inhabitants were led to settle in North Dakota through Northern Pacific bonds held by them or by relations. When payment of interest on these bonds was stopped, after the panic of 1873, while the bonds themselves were quoted at very low figures in the market, they could still be used at face value for the purpose of buying lands included in the Northern Pacific grant.[18]

The Episcopal chapel car was well received. People were moved by its compactness, dignity, and simple churchly beauty, and the bishop's spartan way of living probably accounted for much of his success with pioneer men. He cooked his own meals, made his own bed, swept the floor, distributed leaflets, made the fires, and kept the car in order; he usually had to play the organ as well.[19]

Bishop Walker acknowledged that many people were prompted to come to visit the church car by curiosity alone. One farmer told him, "I've been to a good many circuses, and I've seen all the grandest exhibitions that have come west; but this is the biggest show yet."[20]

By July 1891, accounts of the Cathedral Car had appeared in China, Japan, India, New Zealand, Canada, Australia, Scotland, Great Britain, Germany, Norway, Syria, Italy, and the West Indies. In a somewhat mangled report, the Reverend Mr. Dooman, in a letter from Nara, Japan, wrote: "A couple of days ago, I saw in a Japanese secular paper the following item: 'Mr. Dakota has built a railroad car in the city of New York to use it as a church in which he will travel all over the United States.'"[21]

Church Ambulant Recognized As Success

An 1891 *Illustrated American* reported that the *Church of the Advent*, Cathedral Car of North Dakota, was already bearing fruit, even though the car had not been in operation long enough for great results to be achieved:

Upon his next tour of visitation he [Bishop Walker] expects to make a number of confirmations and two or three missions have already been established in consequence of his work. Another striking result is that several agnostics, professed infidels, and other persons, who made a practice of never going to church, have attended services conducted in the car, not once, but again and again. Perhaps it is the novelty; but there seems to be something particularly attractive in the atmosphere of the car which draws in those for whom ordinary churches have no attraction.[22]

Wherever the car traveled, large crowds gathered to see it. Robert Wilkins and Wynona Wilkins, in *God Giveth the Increase*, tell of the reception of the car. Frequently as many as ninety persons crowded into the car, and often three people had to share two chairs. In some villages, attendance was equal to twice the population. In the first three months, Bishop Walker visited thirteen places, and in only three of these the car was not filled to capacity.

When the bishop was at a dinner at Christ Church College, Oxford, in 1894, "one of the Oxford MP's said 'Bishop, you don't belong to the Church militant or the

Church triumphant.' I asked, 'what do I belong to then?' His reply was: 'To the Church ambulant.'"[23]

It seemed to many other bishops that Walker's commitment was more to a church ambulant than to a church permanent. Although Walker sometimes was called a builder of churches, he had refused to build a cathedral in Fargo, suitable to its position as the see city of the diocese. The *Church of the Advent* chapel car was the bishop's church — his cathedral, the seat of his see.[24]

Because of the name of the Cathedral Car, the *Church of the Advent*, several people asked whether the bishop was a Seventh-Day Adventist. They were burning to ask his view regarding the millennium and the date when the world would end. The bishop pleaded ignorance on the subject.

On another day, the car was anchored at a village. Service was announced for that evening. The place upon the sidetrack where the car had been switched was somewhat inconvenient. The bishop asked the agent to have it removed to a more suitable location. He promised to request the conductor of the next freight train to change it.

In about an hour a freight train arrived. The bishop observed that the conductor had great difficulty in managing it. He was excited, and the brakemen were in the same condition and were running about with a great deal of vim. Suddenly the conductor jumped from the caboose and came to the bishop. He said, "Elder, I want to ask you a question. Don't you think a conductor of a freight train has more right to swear than a preacher?"

The bishop replied emphatically, "No, but why do you ask such a question?"

"Well," said he, "I have the dumbest brakemen that ever you saw on that train. They are so stupid that I am afraid they will break it in two. I feel like ripping out oaths at them and I can't help it. I guess you'd swear too if you had them to deal with."

"Well," said the bishop, "I don't think I would give vent to my wrath in oaths. Now, what good does it do you? What do you accomplish by it? Does it add any force to your order or

any ability to your men to do their work?"

"No," was the reply, "but I feel so mad that I can't help it."

"Now let me ask you a question or two," said the bishop. "Do you swear when you are in the presence of preachers?"

"Of course not. I would not insult them by swearing before them."

"Do you swear in the presence of ladies?"

He said no again. "That would be very impolite."

"Well," said the bishop, "if you can restrain yourself in the presence of parsons and ladies you can just as well in the presence of those under you. They are men and they are entitled to polite usage as well as anybody else. Besides, the Bible tells you and me that it is a sin to use profane language. Remember there is such a thing as insulting God Almighty."

At this point the train began to move away. The conductor took hold of the bishop's hand, said goodbye, and leaped upon the caboose. Two days later the Cathedral Car was stationed at another point. In the course of the day, the same conductor appeared with his train and assured the bishop that he had had no occasion to use profane language since their conversation.[25]

Traveling in sleighs or walking over the prairies, the bishop's missionaries were often in danger, especially when they were overtaken by the blizzards that could develop without warning. The thermometer frequently fell to 35 or 40 degrees below zero. One winter when the mercury reached 52 degrees below zero, Bishop Walker froze both cheeks and one ear. Even indoors the risk was great. One priest's nose was frozen on a night when the temperature in an unheated room fell to 25 degrees below zero.

The severity of the winters affected both the missionary efforts of the clergy and the zeal of the laity. Unless they were warmly clad, people ran a great risk in attending services during the winter, and they were thus inclined to attend the nearest place of worship, regardless of denomination. It was therefore important that Episcopal churches must be centrally located if members were not to be lost.[26]

When the railroads crossed the North Dakota prairie, they established water stops every thirty miles or so and shop stops every hundred miles or so. Some of those stops became towns, and major rail shop towns along the Northern Pacific line were Fargo, Jamestown, Bismarck, and Dickinson. A surprising effect of Walker's chapel car ministry was with railroad workers.

As a rule, railroad men were not churchgoers. They were away from home so much that they were not reached by the ordinary church methods, and often they were obliged to work on Sundays. The Cathedral Car could not have had greater success among them if it had been designed especially for them. It was only natural that they should feel at home in it and that they should regard their railroad uniforms and working clothes as the proper thing to wear in a car, although such attire would be out of place in an ordinary church.[27]

Walker reported that the men joined in the services, took part in the responses, and sang with a spirit rarely manifested in ordinary churches. "This is in part due to the fact that the members of the congregation have to sit so close together in the car. They feel none of the awe or embarrassment about raising their voices that is inspired by a large hall not well filled. But the enthusiasm has also a more solid foundation and is born in a large degree of the fact that the religious needs of the people are supplied."[28]

As is true with any innovation, there were those who criticized Bishop Walker's Cathedral Car, even though *Harper's Weekly* stressed a positive approach.

The only possible criticism to which this journeying cathedral may be subject is indicated in this fine simplicity. The hope must prevail; nevertheless, that no detriment to the triumphant course of the institution is foreshadowed in its extremely simple form — in similitude with the plan of the new French court drawn up by M. de Remusat at Bonaparte's request, of which, the emperor said, "There is not sufficient display in it, all that would not throw dust in people's eyes." No one can doubt that a wise bishop knows as clearly and comprehensively for what he had built as did ever a political

sovereign. Although not without dignity and elegance, this novel type of cathedral will depend for popularity on its usefulness rather than on its stateliness.[29]

The bishop and his chapel car were a familiar sight from the rolling woodlands of the Red River Valley to the Montana border as Walker officiated at church services, conducted marriages and funerals, and tended his scattered sheep. Bishop Walker with the Cathedral Car visited Drayton, a town of seven hundred inhabitants, in 1895. It touched his heart to hear a farmhand singing beautifully at one of the meetings and to learn that this man used to sing in the choir of Lincoln Cathedral, England. "Your car," said the man, "seems like a bit of home to me."[30]

Walker Leaves His Cathedral on Rails

In the spring of 1897 Bishop Walker was called to serve in western New York State, again a journey of extremes, and Bishop James Dow Morrison, bishop of Duluth, was asked to take charge of the jurisdiction of North Dakota. Presiding bishop for the occasion was G. Mott Williams, who one year before had been elected to the newly created position of bishop of Northern Michigan. Bishop Williams had something in common with the departing Bishop Walker. He too operated a chapel car, the second such car to be used in the Upper Peninsula of Michigan.

Bishop Morrison, upon assuming his responsibilities at the annual meeting of September 1897, was overwhelmed at his temporary charge.

I doubt if you can find anywhere, in a missionary jurisdiction, mission churches that will compare with those beautiful little houses of worship with their walls of prairie boulders, which we find so frequently in this state. If some of our stations have languished we must remember that they have only suffered the fate which had overtaken everything during those trying years of scarcity and financial depression that told so heavily on North Dakota. But now that God's kind Providence is permitting us once more to see the smiling face of prosperity, it is our duty to open every church door and make every altar and chancel beautiful with the sight and sound of praise and prayer and to remember gratefully the splendid work of good Bishop Walker, whose energy and devotion have given us these churches to occupy and if please God to fill with worshipers.[31]

The acting bishop, although he praised Bishop Walker's missionary energy and devotion, was also dismayed that there was not a better church building in Fargo. Somewhat critical of Bishop Walker's decision to build the *Church of the Advent* chapel car cathedral instead of a traditional edifice, he commented about his tour of the territory:

The last place that I visited was this church in Fargo, and while I was delighted with the spacious church lot, and its excellent location, I was surprised not to find a better church building. I am sure that the churchmen here have only been reserving their energies that they might erect here a stately and beautiful church, which would be in keeping with the principal town of the state and the residence of the bishop . . . and I confidently anticipate that at no distant day the churchmen at Fargo will arise and build.[32]

In his tour of the diocese, on the North Dakota line of the Northern Pacific Railroad, Morrison discovered that Dickinson had a nice church but no services; Mandan and Bismarck had churches but no pastors. Jamestown had both a church and an active pastor, but he was too busy with his own parish to fill the needs of Carrington, which had neither a church nor a pastor. He found the same situations along the Langdon branch and the Mayville line of the Great Northern.[33]

Bishop Morrison also had a bone to pick with the railroads, in this case the Northern Pacific, and the subject of his ire was public access to the steel and wrought-iron railroad bridge that had been built over the Missouri in 1882, ten months before the northern route of the transcontinental railway was finished. Up to that time, the only way to get across the Missouri at that point was by steamboat or ferry, or in the winter by crossing the ice.[34]

On Sunday, June 19, 1898, he held service in the church at Bismarck and preached, and afterward Morrison visited some of the people who were ill. He had intended to hold evening service at Mandan but was unable to cross the river, because all permits to cross the bridge had been revoked that morning. An effort of his host, General Hughes, to obtain a concession in his favor was fruitless.

Angered, the bishop pronounced, "The Northern Pacific Railway has received many favors in North Dakota, and its existence is only justified at all, on the theory that it serves the people of the state. Some of its officials seem to have forgotten this. There is no reason why the railway bridge over the Missouri should not be made a public highway where the foot passenger could safely cross at all times. The cost would be a trifle, and the accommodation to the public would be appreciated by many in the wretched condition of the train service."[35]

In the forty years of its use, the Bismarck/Mandan bridge would be crisscrossed by several chapel cars, but the Cathedral Car was the first, followed closely by *Evangel*, the first Baptist car, on its maiden trip.

Only once, according to Bishop Walker, probably in 1891 on *Evangel*'s maiden voyage, had the Baptist car and the Cathedral Car been together in the same town. It was at a junction, where the end of one touched the end of the other. "It was like a clasping of hands," Walker said. In neither was service held on that night. There was therefore no conflict of theology in the churches on wheels. The following morning they parted, one being hauled west and the other northwest. Walker added, "Since that time the Baptist church, finding the work of the chapel cars effective, have built three more, and they are accomplishing much on several railroads west, south and east."[36]

Cathedral Car Parked, Sold

In 1899 Bishop Samuel C. Edsall became head of the North Dakota diocese. The new bishop, busy getting diocese matters back in order after thirty months without a resident bishop, had other interests than chapel cars. After his arrival, he found the much-publicized *Church of the Advent* in need of repairs in its shed in Fargo on the Northern Pacific track and more than one hundred dollars in arrears in its rent. Edsall felt that while the car had attracted much attention, it was too cumbersome and expensive to be practical. Moreover, Bishop Edsall explained, it ran only at the convenience of the railroads, and as railroad business increased, they were less and less disposed to move the car free of charge (although Bishop Walker and the five Baptist cars in operation at this time were not having any difficulty with obtaining free passage).

The bishop, unable to negotiate for its handling by the railroads and seemingly unwilling to see its value as a missionary tool, sent the Cathedral Car — no longer the Bishop's Church — to Carrington to be used as a chapel. A lay reader held Sunday services in the car until winter, when extreme cold made it impossible to continue.[37]

Bishop Edsall did have a concern for missions, and he was disheartened at the lack of financial support he was receiving from the board of missions. He had observed certain problems in planting the church on the frontier. "A missionary was often successful when he first appeared in a new town, but interest in his services soon fell off as 'civilization' came in the form of fraternal lodges, hotels, and women's clubs."

He felt the problem was that because the people were so scattered and too few to support a minister, they must have outside help. And that help was not coming.[38] In his vision, that outside help was not in the form of a chapel car. At the annual convocation in 1900, Edsall reported:

On the day of my Consecration [Wednesday, January 25, 1899, at St. Peter's in Chicago], Bishop Walker turned over to me $8,205 and subsequently $500 additional which he had accumulated and held in trust for the church in North Dakota. He has also deeded to me a block of ground in Fargo and quarter section of land in Foster county and given me a bill of sale of the cathedral car. These properties were turned over to me without any terms of restriction as to their use; although some of the money had been received at a time when it was hoped that a Church school for girls might be built at Fargo, and a smaller portion had been tentatively promised to Gethsemane Church Fargo, toward the erection of their new Church.[39]

At a meeting held November 30, 1901, the bishop reported that eleven years after it was put into service, the Cathedral Car had been sold for one thousand dollars and the mortgage on the bishop's residence had been reduced by that amount. The bishop had a beautiful new residence, "a dignified structure in the colonial style, spacious, comfortable and home-

Fig. 3.4 This interior view shows that, unlike the chapel cars to follow, the Cathedral Car had wooden chairs instead of pews. At the front of the car can be seen an ornate stand adorned by a massive eagle. An organ stands against the window wall of the car. (Courtesy of the Episcopal Diocese of North Dakota)

Fig. 3.5 Inside Gethsemane Church, Fargo, is a stained-glass window depicting the origin of the church. Among the panels is a scene including the *Church of the Advent,* the Cathedral Car of North Dakota. (Norman T. Taylor)

like." The house was equipped with modern plumbing; five brick fireplaces ensured "physical comfort, even in our coldest weather." At the rear of the lot, a barn was built of lumber taken from the dismantled shed of the Cathedral Car.[40]

On the North Dakota prairie the need was still great, and a chapel car could have been a blessing to one young priest. On Ascension Day in 1900 he went thither and, after investigation, decided to start a mission, but he had no place to meet. Thirty-four children and adults were baptized in the mission within a few months and twenty confirmed,[41] and there was still no church for them to meet in.

As late as 1906, Protestant Episcopal Reverend E. W. Burleson of Minnesota said, "We are so short of clergy, only twenty in an area of almost 71,000 square miles with a population of some 600,000, it is impossible to seize these openings as should be done, . . . there are by the thousands 'sheep having no shepherd' . . . and scores of children who never saw a missionary and countless others who see one only at long intervals."[42]

Cathedral Car Lives On

Even though Bishop Walker's cathedral on rails had been sold, that was not the end of the *Church of the Advent.* McHenry, North Dakota, a typical Dakota town, was started in 1899 when the Northern Pacific Railway extended a

branch line. "It is now, and likely to be for some time, the terminus of the branch, and so is a place of considerable importance, being the headquarters and distributing point for a large tract of surrounding county."[43]

The new town had a population of three hundred within a year, including two communicants of the Episcopal church, but not a church building of any denomination. The Reverend D. H. Clarkson of Jamestown visited the village, and he and Bishop Mann organized St. Michael's Mission. Outfitted with furniture from the dismantled Cathedral Car, a building was completed and the first service was held in 1903. But in 1913 the building had to be sold, since it seemed impossible to interest the largely foreign-born population in the Episcopal church.

Still, parts of the Cathedral Car continued in use. During the summer of 1919, St. Mary's Church was built in Guelph, and among its furnishings were the font and lectern from the Cathedral Car. When St. Mary's Church in Guelph was combined with nearby St. Mark's Episcopal in Oakes, the font and lectern were incorporated into the worship of the new St. Mary's and St. Mark's Episcopal Church of Oakes.

Rising high above surrounding suburban housing on the outskirts of present-day Fargo, the see city of the Diocese of North Dakota, is a striking church. Praised for its pure prairie architecture, its soaring towers emulate the clean lines of the grain elevators that still dot the landscape. It is the cathedral church of the Episcopal Diocese of North Dakota — Gethsemane Cathedral. It is a fitting cathedral, one that Bishop Edsall would have approved.

Inside, two treasured brass chandeliers from the *Church of the Advent,* the Cathedral Car of North Dakota, converted to electric lights, are mounted on a wall in a church lounge, and in a display case is a glass globe from a lighting fixture used in the car. At the west end of the Great Hall, light from the striking "The Great Commission" stained-glass window dances across tables where members enjoy a coffee hour.

This window is the history heart of Gethsemane's congregation. Recorded there in the vivid art-glass blues and reds and shades of gold are scenes depicting the founding of the church. A Northern Pacific Railroad surveyor's tent at Northern Pacific Avenue and Broadway in 1872 is pictured at the lower left. At the lower right is another scene — the *Church of the Advent*, the Cathedral Car of North Dakota (fig. 3.5).

That chapel car too was a fitting cathedral, one of which Bishop William David Walker, a man with true missionary vision, was proud — a cathedral to take to the people who could not come to it.

In the words of Hymn 223 in the *Book of Common Prayer*,

> Onward we go, for still we hear them singing,
> "Come, weary souls, for Jesus bids you come;"
> And through the dark, its echoes sweetly ringing,
> The music of the gospel leads us home.[44]

Notes

[1] William Stevens Perry, *The Bishops of the American Church Past and Present* (New York: Christian Literature Co., 1897), 281.

[2] "Cathedral on Wheels," *The Illustrated American*, March 21, 1891, 222.

[3] James Thayer Addison, *The Episcopal Church in the United States: 1789–1931* (New York: Charles Scribner's Sons, 1951), 230.

[4] Ibid.

[5] *Harper's Weekly*, January 31, 1891, 90.

[6] *The Spirit of Missions*, May 1891, 169; Robert Wilkins and Wynona Wilkins, *God Giveth the Increase: The History of the Episcopal Church in North Dakota* (Fargo: North Dakota Institute for Regional Studies, Fargo, 1959), 49

[7] Newberry Library, Chicago, Pullman Collection: Pullman 07/00/02, Completion and Delivery of Cars, vol. 3, 93.

[8] Liston Edgington Leyendecker, *Palace Car Prince: A Biography of George Mortimer Pullman* (Niwot: University Press of Colorado, 1992), 198.

[9] Susan McKee, "Princes of business rode like kings inside Pullman's Palace train cars," *The Indianapolis Star*, November 20, 1994, K4.

[10] *The Spirit of Missions*, December 1890, 470.

[11] Wilkins and Wilkins, 49.

[12] *Harper's Weekly*, January 31, 1891, 90.

[13] *The Illustrated American*, March 21, 1891, 222.

[14] *Harpers Weekly*, January 31, 1891, 90.

[15] *The Illustrated American*, 223.

[16] *The Spirit of Missions*, December 1890, 470.

[17] *The Spirit of Missions*, October 1892, 378.

[18] *The Illustrated American*, 224.

[19] *The Spirit of Missions*, December 1890, 470.

[20] Ibid.

[21] *The Spirit of Missions*, April 1891, 153.

[22] *The Illustrated American*, 224.

[23] Wilkins and Wilkins, 50.

[24] *The Record*, May 1895–June 1898, 4, roll 3202, State Historical Society of North Dakota.

[25] Ibid., August 1895, 5.

[26] Ibid.

[27] Ibid.

[28] *The Illustrated American*, 224.

[29] *Harper's Weekly*, January 31, 1891, 90.

[30] Personal papers of the Reverend H. "Mac" Kennickell, Asheville, North Carolina.

[31] *The Spirit of Missions*, May 1897, 7.

[32] *Journal of Proceedings*, North Dakota Convocation, 1897, 9.

[33] Ibid. 8–9.

[34] Edward C. Murphy, "The Northern Pacific Railway Bridge at Bismarck," *North Dakota History, Journal of the Northern Plains*, spring 1995, 10.

[35] Journal of Proceedings, North Dakota Convocation, 1898, 16.

[36] The Record, August 1895, 5, roll 3202, State Historical Society of North Dakota.

[37] Wilkins and Wilkins, 91.

[38] Ibid., 67.

[39] Missionary District of North Dakota, 1902, Appendix C, report of secretary and treasurer of the standing committee, 29.

[40] Wilkins and Wilkins, 66, 75.

[41] The Reverend Edward Welles Burleson's account in *The Spirit of Missions*, March 1906, 171.

[42] Ibid.

[43] Wilkins and Wilkins, 127.

[44] *Book of Common Prayer, General Hymns*, 223, "Hark, Hark, My Soul" (London: Collins' Clear-Type Press), 60.

CHAPTER 4

The Hoyt Brothers, J. D. Rockefeller, and the Chapel Car Syndicate

Early in 1890, as the Cathedral Car was being constructed in the shops at Pullman, Illinois, Dr. Wayland Hoyt, pastor of the First Baptist Church of Minneapolis, went on an extended journey through Wisconsin and Minnesota with his brother Colgate Hoyt, a railroad executive. This was not the first time that the two had journeyed together. In the summer of 1878 they had a memorable adventure traveling as a part of the Nelson Miles/Colgate Hoyt expedition to Yellowstone Park and the Yellowstone Valley (*see fig. 4.1*).

Colgate Hoyt, then a member of the business elite of Cleveland, Ohio, was married to a niece of General W. T. Sherman. Her sister was the wife of Colonel Nelson A. Miles, probably the army's most successful Indian fighter.

By the summer of 1878, relative peace had come to the Yellowstone Valley, and Miles believed that the country was safe enough for civilian excursion parties. He invited Colgate Hoyt to join him, and Colgate gathered a group of friends, including his brother Wayland, and headed west for a two-month excursion. Later Colgate wrote an account of this frontier expedition.[1]

The journey of the brothers twelve years later was of a different nature. Their father, the Honorable James M. Hoyt,

was an influential Cleveland lawyer and an active Baptist layman, and he had reared his sons in the Euclid Avenue Baptist Church of Cleveland, the same church that played an important role in the childhood of John D. Rockefeller. Wayland Hoyt (*fig. 4.2*), a graduate of Brown University and Rochester Divinity School, was serving his first year as pastor of the First Baptist Church after pastoring several prominent churches in Cincinnati and Philadelphia.

As the brothers traveled in Colgate's private car on the Duluth/St. Paul branch, Wayland was much disturbed by what he saw from his window — a sight he knew could be repeated a thousand times in these vast regions. A brilliant preacher, he later shared what he saw with the delegates of the sixty-sixth anniversary of the American Baptist Publication Society who met at Chicago on May 28, 1890.

The other day I was riding in a railroad car. The train stopped at a station. I looked out of the car window, and I saw — well, I saw nothing unusual. You could parallel what I saw a thousand times in the vast regions of this new Northwest. I saw a hamlet of perhaps thirty or forty houses, log Houses, — it chanced to be a lumber region, — but well built and comfortable. There were

Fig. 4.1 In July 1878, Baptist businessman Colgate Hoyt (eighth from the left), at the invitation of Colonel Nelson A. Miles, traveled with a party that included the Reverend Wayland Hoyt (far left) to Yellowstone Park during a lull in Indian hostilities. The Hoyt brothers would take another trip together, a trip that would result in the building of the first of seven American Baptist Publication Society chapel cars. (Montana Historical Society, Helena)

Fig. 4.2 The Reverend Wayland Hoyt, a pastor distressed by his view of churchless towns along the route of the Wisconsin Central Railroad in the late 1880s, convinced his brother Colgate Hoyt, a railroad executive, to engage his wealthy friends and build the first Baptist chapel car. (Photo c. 1875 by George Kendall Warren of Boston, courtesy of James S. Brust, M.D.)

several stores; people walking about; men at their various handicrafts; men hanging about the station; little children playing in the streets.

Of course I saw it — the saloon, and it was not difficult to imagine the serpent slime of blight and wretchedness it would draw through that humble settlement. I did not notice the name of the town. It would be no cause for wonder if it already called itself a city and was staring into the future with the most unblinking and audacious eyes of enterprise; certain it would be a metropolis with a swiftness of growth which Jonah's gourd could not begin to match.

But looking out of that car window did I see a church? That sight did not greet me. Then there came upon me what the absence of a church must mean there — desecrated sabbaths, the hard humdrum of life, simply material with never a push toward higher things, the sad plight of the little children, on the spiritual side, I saw playing in the streets, and I could almost look into some one of those houses, and discern some poor pioneering saint, deprived of all religious privilege, struggling to keep the spiritual life throbbing amid such bitter, irreligious winter.

"Well, the train started, and I found myself asking myself the question," Hoyt said. "What does that town need for its moral regeneration and uplifting and how can its needs be met?"[2]

This concern moved Wayland Hoyt to further action. He turned to his brother Colgate and said, "You railroad men ought to be doing more for this new country than you are doing."[3]

Colgate Hoyt's Syndicate of Friends

Colgate Hoyt had moved from Cleveland to New York City in 1881 to be a partner in the banking house of James B. Colgate and Company. The elder Colgates and Hoyts had been longtime friends, and Colgate Hoyt's name symbolized

that bond. Now a vice president of the Northern Pacific Railroad, Colgate Hoyt's resume also listed vice president of the Duluth & Manitoba Railroad, trustee of the Wisconsin Central Railroad, and chief officer of the Chicago and Northern Pacific Railway. He had just been elected vice president of the Oregon and Transcontinental Company, and soon he would be vice president of the new Missouri, Kansas & Texas Railroad.[4]

When Colgate spoke on behalf of railroad executives, he spoke with authority. He replied, "We think we are doing considerable: we provide the way for them [people in the towns along the route] to ship in and ship out, to get in and to get out. What more can we do?"

Dr. Hoyt called his brother's attention to the fact that in all these new towns there were from one to five saloons, and in scores of them no places of worship. "Why not build a missionary car of some kind to give these lonely and destitute communities an opportunity of hearing the gospel of Jesus Christ?"[5]

The matter was dropped then, Hoyt related, "but shortly afterward, when in New York, in my brother's office, I saw a pigeon hole in his desk labeled 'Chapel Car Syndicate.' Then I knew that something had come of it. Something always does come of syndicates."[6]

A few weeks later, Wayland Hoyt summoned Minnesota Sunday school missionary Boston Smith to see him at his church office. Wayland told Smith, "I have a letter from my brother; he is thinking favorably concerning the building of that missionary car. He has organized a chapel car syndicate in Wall Street. Now I want you to sketch what you think would be a good plan in which the missionary can both live and hold services."

Smith would later recall, "I hurried to an architect's office [Harry W. Jones of Minneapolis][7] and in two hours I had the drawings of what I thought would be a good car in which to hold services. This was at once forwarded to the Chapel Car Syndicate consisting of John D. Rockefeller, Charles L. Colby, John R. Trevor, James B. Colgate, E. J. Barney,

William Hills, and a few other level-headed business men."[8]

These "level-headed business men" were all Baptists with Wall Street connections who had personal stakes in making profit and insuring stability in rail communities. Three of them — Rockefeller, Colgate Hoyt, and Charles Colby — were members of the Fifth Avenue Baptist Church.

The syndicate was a family affair for the Hoyts, Colgates, Colbys, and Trevors, bound by years of Baptist associations, marriages, and friendships. Colgate's father, William Colgate, like his father before him, was a soap maker, the founder of what is now Colgate-Palmolive-Peet Company. The elder Colgate was the prime benefactor of two major institutions, the American Bible Society and Colgate University, and James B. Colgate continued those family traditions.

In 1852 James formed with J. B. Trevor a partnership known as James B. Colgate and Company, dealers in stocks, securities, and precious metals. James B. Colgate's substantial loans to the United States government strengthened the credit of the country,[9] and for several years he served as president of the New York Gold Exchange.[10] Colgate's first wife was a Hoyt, and his second wife was a Colby, the daughter of the twenty-second governor of New Hampshire.[11]

As for Charles L. Colby, his father was Gardner Colby, who had given large amounts to Baptist missions and Waterville College (Maine), which was later named Colby College in his honor. After he retired as a successful merchant, Gardner Colby became the president of the Wisconsin Central Railroad,[12] exhibiting considerable executive ability and courage by undertaking the construction of 340 miles of railroad through primeval forests and unsettled territory. He developed extensive railroads throughout the northwestern part of the United States and was connected in prominent official capacities with one after another of the great companies operating in that region.[13]

Another Baptist tie was Charles L. Colby's brother, Dr. Henry Francis Colby, who served from 1868 to 1903 as pastor of the First Baptist Church of Dayton, Ohio, building that church to national prominence.[14]

Contributing to the chapel car project was one of the last charitable gestures of J. B. Trevor, a former business partner of James B. Colgate. Trevor and James Colgate were fiscal agents of the U.S. government during the attempt of railroad financiers Jay Gould and James Fisk to corner the gold market in 1869.[15]

On Monday night, December 22, 1890, a few weeks after his gift of $500 was made to the syndicate, Trevor died unexpectedly at his winter residence in New York. A former president of the American Baptist Home Mission Society, he was known for his generous gifts to the Divinity School at Rochester, New York (now Colgate-Rochester/Bexley Hall/Crozer Theological Seminary), and his interest in and support of Baptist missions.[16]

William Hills's connection to the rest of the syndicate is less clear. He did not seem to be a part of the inner circle of friends. Hills was not only a donor to the first Baptist chapel car but also would pay for the costs of chapel car 3, *Glad Tidings*, in honor of his wife. He also guaranteed the addition of chapel car 4, *Good Will*. A member of the Mt. Morris Baptist Church in New York, he was the founder of the Hills Brothers Company.

The chapel car was not the only project of this select group of wealthy Baptist laymen. At least four of them — Colgate Hoyt, James Colgate, Charles Colby, and John D. Rockefeller — had combined their treasuries and talents in several other endeavors of much greater investment risk than the chapel car. At the same time these men were giving toward the building of the first Baptist car, *Evangel*, several of them were also deeply involved in the development and the resulting downfall of the city of Everett, Washington (see chap. 5).

In November 1890, according to Bishop William David Walker, three Baptists (most likely, Boston Smith and the two Hoyts) came to see the *Church of the Advent*, the first American chapel car, when it was on exhibit in Minneapolis.[17] They questioned Bishop Walker about the operation of the Episcopal chapel car. At the time of the Baptists' visit to Bishop Walker's chapel car, the first Baptist car, which Barney

Fig. 4.3 John D. Rockefeller, seen here in 1884, was a donor to the first Baptist chapel car. The influence of several friends caused him to turn away from the support of the chapel car project. (Courtesy of the Rockefeller Archive Center, Tarrytown, New York)

& Smith inked on their blueprint nameplates as "The Northern Pacific Gospel Car," was already in construction in the Dayton shops.

At the 1891 publication society meeting in Cincinnati, the board reported "the very generous and noble gift of a chapel car for this Society."

Whereas, Messrs Colgate Hoyt, John D. Rockefeller, James B. Colgate, John B. Trevor, Charles L. Colby, William Hills, and E. J. Barney have generously ordered and paid for the construction and complete equipment of a chapel car, for the use and purposes of the American Baptist Publication Society in its colporteur Sunday school and Bible work: therefore, Resolved, That this Board of managers hereby accepts for the work of this society, the said chapel car as the generous gift of the brethren above named, and that this society does hereby agree to use the said car only for the purposes for which it was constructed and donated, to keep said car in proper repair, and to provide for this car a missionary or colporteur and necessary assistance, to carry on the work of this society as designed and practicable, and all this free from any expense whatsoever to the donors of the said chapel car.[18]

On the motion of L. E. Kline of Missouri, a vote of thanks with cheers was unanimously given to the donors, although some in the audience probably flinched at the mention of John D. Rockefeller (*see fig. 4.3*).

The Standard Oil Company practices of Rockefeller led many Americans, including Baptists who benefited greatly from his gifts, to question his motives and methods. In 1879 Rockefeller was indicted by a Pennsylvania grand jury for criminal conspiracy to violate the laws of trade, especially those that forbade a common carrier to discriminate against some shippers in favor of others.

That case never came to trial, but Rockefeller continued to be tried in the court of public opinion. In the decade to come, he would give millions to charity, and for each gift, the charge

of "tainted money" would be flung. Seldom was "tainted money" taunted by Baptists. Rockefeller was hailed by most as "a leader and a giver who God has provided," as a "God-fearing man of colossal fortune" whom "God had ready" and "society raised up."[19]

Although many questioned the principles of Rockefeller, that he was a devout Baptist there was no question. As a boy, inspired by his mother's devotion, he joined the Cleveland Erie Street Baptist Church, which became Euclid Avenue Baptist Church, and seldom missed services. In his adult years, he served as Sunday school superintendent at both the Cleveland church and the Fifth Avenue Baptist Church in New York.

In June 1890, Colgate Hoyt asked Rockefeller to be a part of the chapel car investment. Hoyt had long been an adviser and associate to Rockefeller, a fellow trustee of the New York Fifth Avenue Baptist Church. In response to his friend's request, Rockefeller gave one thousand dollars for the building of the first Baptist chapel car.

According to a memo headed "Standard Oil Company's Private Telegraph Line," dated NY 6/26, 1890, to Mr. JDR, supposedly from Colgate Hoyt, "The gospel car subscription syndicate is closed and I have subscribed for you one thousand dollars on time. The amount is made up as follows — Colgate Hoyt 500, Charles Colby 500, John Trevor 500, James Colgate 500, Rockefeller 1000, Total $3000."[20]

Rockefeller Drops Support of Chapel Cars

A reading of later letters suggests that the giving was hardly enthusiastic. To be fair, it was not Rockefeller's choice that his name be used so liberally by the American Baptist Publication Society in connection with the chapel cars. Many times he was advertised as being the leader of the project. In actuality the Hoyts, especially Wayland Hoyt, were the heart of the chapel car project. To Rockefeller, the thousand dollars he gave toward the building of *Evangel* was probably just a gesture of support for this current project of Colgate Hoyt.

When Rockefeller was asked in 1892 to contribute toward

the building of a second chapel car by chapel car missionary E. G. Wheeler, he refused. Timing might have had something to do with the refusal. On March 2, 1892, the Supreme Court of Ohio decided that the Standard Oil Trust agreement was void, not only because the Standard Oil Company of Ohio was a party to the agreement but also because the agreement itself was in restraint of trade and amounted to the creation of an unlawful monopoly.[21]

On June 15, 1892, Rockefeller responded to Wheeler's request, "Your letter of the 9th is received: but I have so many other undertakings on hand, I cannot make any contributions for the proposed second Chapel Car."[22]

Even if the times and circumstances had been more auspicious, it is doubtful that Rockefeller would have given more money to the chapel cars. One of his close friends was American Baptist Home Mission Society and Baptist Education Society official Henry L. Morehouse, for whom Morehouse College would be named.

Morehouse had convinced Rockefeller that while the chapel car work is "doubtless doing good it is far more expensive in proportion to the results than the work of a practically similar nature done by the Home Mission Society; furthermore, that the Home Mission Society is amply able and thoroughly equipped to do all of this work; moreover it was the first in the field, and to have two societies competing for the work is unwise, expensive and confusing to the public. We agree in advising that you should not respond to this appeal."[23]

In spite of pleas from Boston Smith and other chapel car missionaries, Rockefeller's mind was closed to the subject.

E. J. Barney and His Car Company

The last member of the syndicate, E. J. Barney, did not seem to be in the category of the elite friends, although he no doubt knew Charles L. Colby and Colgate Hoyt well. Barney was a trustee of the First Baptist Church of Dayton, Ohio, pastored by Dr. Francis Colby; and Barney was connected to the railroad industry as a builder and as a trustee of the Wisconsin Central Railroad. He was head of the Barney &

Smith Manufacturing Company, which was founded in 1849 by his father, Eliam. It became Dayton's most important company in the years following the Civil War.

A prospectus issued to potential buyers as the company went public in 1892 stated that the Barney & Smith Car Company *(fig. 4.5)*, as it was now to be called, was the second largest of its kind in the United States. Its equipment was

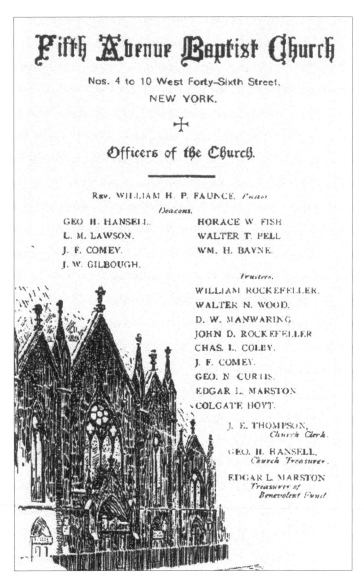

Fig. 4.4 Three of the syndicate members, including John D. Rockefeller, were trustees of the Fifth Avenue Baptist Church in New York City. (American Baptist Historical Society, Valley Forge)

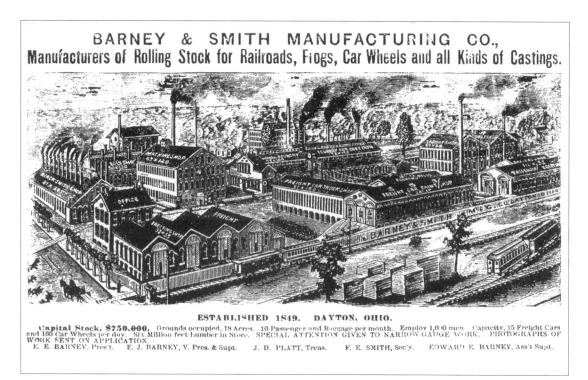

BARNEY & SMITH MANUFACTURING CO.,
Manufacturers of Rolling Stock for Railroads, Frogs, Car Wheels and all Kinds of Castings.

ESTABLISHED 1849. DAYTON, OHIO.

Capital Stock, $750,000. Grounds occupied, 18 Acres. 10 Passenger and Baggage per month. Employ 1,000 men. Capacity, 15 Freight Cars and 100 Car Wheels per day. Six Million feet Lumber in Store. SPECIAL ATTENTION GIVEN TO NARROW-GAUGE WORK. PHOTOGRAPHS OF WORK SENT ON APPLICATION.

E. E. BARNEY, Pres't.   E. J. BARNEY, V. Pres. & Supt.   J. D. PLATT, Treas.   F. E. SMITH, Sec'y.   EDWARD E. BARNEY, Ass't Supt.

Fig. 4.5 The Barney & Smith Car Company, a competitor of the Pullman Palace Car Company, was known for its craftsmanship and use of fine woods. E. J. Barney, an active Baptist layman, would contract to build the first Baptist chapel car at cost. Six other Baptist cars and two of the Catholic Extension Society cars would be built by Barney & Smith. (American Baptist Historical Society, Valley Forge)

recognized as of the highest grade by its customers, among whom were included nearly all of the principal railroad companies in the country.[24]

Many of the workers employed by Barney were immigrants, brought from the Black Forest region of Germany for their skill in wood carving and fine cabinet making.[25] More than 80 percent owned their own homes, averaging a wage of $1.70 for a twelve-hour day, 310 days a year. Barney & Smith was probably ahead of other car builders in respect to its outlook toward its employees. They would survive the 1893 depression better than did Pullman employees, who lived in company houses and had to pay rent to Pullman although they were laid off.[26]

Much of the concern for the welfare of the employees as well as the quality of the work was due to the Barney family's religious beliefs, which had passed down from father to sons.

Uncle Boston's First View of *Evangel*

In the summer of 1890, Boston Smith was asked to share his concept for the design of the first Baptist car with the syndicate, and the Barney & Smith Car Company agreed to build it at cost for around four thousand dollars.[27]

Smith described his first visit to the car with its catalpa-wood exterior and oak interior, at the sprawling, 130-acre Barney & Smith shop along the banks of the Mad River.

The following spring I was summoned to Dayton, Ohio. I was instructed to call at the shops of the Barney and Smith Car Company. Mr. Eugene Barney, the president, received me most kindly, and at once invited me to accompany him to the yards of the great plant. There, upon one of the tracks, stood an elegant car, resembling a Pullman sleeper. On the side of the car I read at the top, "Chapel Car," and just below the windows the number "1," and the name, "Evangel." As I stood looking at the "Evangel" after the inspection, I could but think how a dream of mine a dozen years before had been realized. . . . [28]

As Smith, overwhelmed with the beauty of the car he had dreamed of and hoped for so many years, left the shops after viewing *Evangel*, he could only say, "Surely God's hand is in this."

In a letter to Colgate Hoyt, the grateful missionary wrote:

Dear Sir & Bro:

After more than two months of work in "The CHAPEL CAR," I feel constrained to write and tell you that my expectations have been more than realized. The Car meets a want that has long been felt. Already I see enough work in sight to keep the Car in constant use for the next twelve months and invitations from the smaller railroad towns are pouring in.

Mr. Mellen has indeed made my work on the Northern Pacific of the most pleasant character. His letter [just] about gives me the Northern Pacific System. It could not be arranged more pleasantly.

I have made the trip from Chicago to Livingston, Montana. The Car has been crowded and scores of souls have been saved. On my last trip no less than fifty I think decided for Christ and confessed Him with their mouths. I sincerely trust the donors of "THE CHAPEL CAR" may never regret their investment. Yours very sincerely, BOSTON W. SMITH[29]

Notes

[1] James S. Brust and Lee H. Whittlesey, "'Roughing It Up the Yellowstone to Wonderland': The Nelson Miles/Colgate Hoyt Party in Yellowstone National Park, September 1878," *Montana, the Magazine of Western History*, spring 1996, 56.

[2] Anniversary Report of the American Baptist Publication Society, Chicago, 1890, 69.

[3] Lemuel Call Barnes, *Pioneers of Light: The First Century of The American Baptist Publication Society*, 1821–1921 (Philadelphia: American Baptist Publication Society, 1924), 104.

[4] Publication No. 104, Annual Report for 1921–1922 (Cleveland, Ohio: The Western Reserve Historical Society, 1922), 20.

[5] Boston W. Smith, *The Story of Our Chapel Car Work* (Philadelphia: American Baptitst Publication Society, n.d.), 3–4.

[6] Ibid., 4.

[7] BSP, ABHS, VF.

[8] Ibid.

[9] *The National Cyclopaedia of American Biography*, vol. 24, 329.

[10] *Robert Colgate: The Immigrant: A Genealogy of the New York Colgates*, comp. Truman Abbe and Hubert Abbe Howson (New Haven, Conn.: The Tuttle, Morehouse & Taylor Company, 1941), 92, Samuel Colgate Baptist Historical Library, Colgate-Rochester Divinity School, Rochester, New York.

[11] Ibid., 94.

[12] *The Colby Family: Something of Its History in Europe and America* (Waterville, Maine: Colby College, 1931), 17, Samuel Colgate Baptist Historical Library, Colgate-Rochester Divinity School, Rochester, New York.

[13] *The National Cyclopaedia of American Biography*, vol. 8, 404.

[14] Proceedings of the Ninetieth Annual Meeting of the Ohio Baptist Convention, October 1915, 65, Samuel Colgate Baptist Historical Library, Colgate-Rochester Divinity School, Rochester, New York.

[15] *The National Cyclopaedia of American Biography*, vol. 32, 360.

[16] *The Home Mission Monthly*, February 1891, 30, Samuel Colgate Historical Library, Colgate-Rochester Divinity School, Rochester, New York.

[17] "Cathedral on Wheels," *The Illustrated American*, March 21, 1891, 222.

[18] Anniversary Report of the American Baptist Publication Society, Cincinnati, Ohio, 1891, 65.

[19] William H. Allen, *Rockefeller: Giant, Dwarf, Symbol* (New York: Institute for Public Service, 1930), 353.

[20] Early chapel car correspondence, Rockefeller 7 Others, Box 22, Samuelson Collection, Colporter files, ABHS.

[21] Flynn, 301.

[22] Correspondence between John D. Rockefeller and the Reverend E. G. Wheeler, dated June 15, 1892, Early chapel car correspondence, Rockefeller & Others, Box 22, Samuelson Collection, Colporter files, ABHSA.

[23] Correspondence between John D. Rockefeller and John D. Rockefeller Jr., dated September 11, 1900, letterhead address 26 Broadway, New York, Early chapel car correspondence, Rockefeller & Others, Box 22, Samuelson Collection, Colporter files, ABHS.

[24] Scott D. Trostel, *The Barney & Smith Car Company: Car Builders* (Fletcher, Ohio: Cam-Tech Publishing, 1993), 87.

[25] Ibid., 29.

[26] Ibid., 49.

[27] BSP, scrapbook, "Kind Words," "The Gospel on Wheels," Minneapolis newspaper, Box 76 P, 1831–1908, ABHS. (Figures in different reports vary from $4000 to $8000, but our best sources say that Barney & Smith built the car at cost for $4000, giving perhaps a 50 percent discount.)

[28] Smith, *The Story of Our Chapel Cars*, 5.

[29] BSP, ABHS, VF. The letter is dated August 10, 1891.

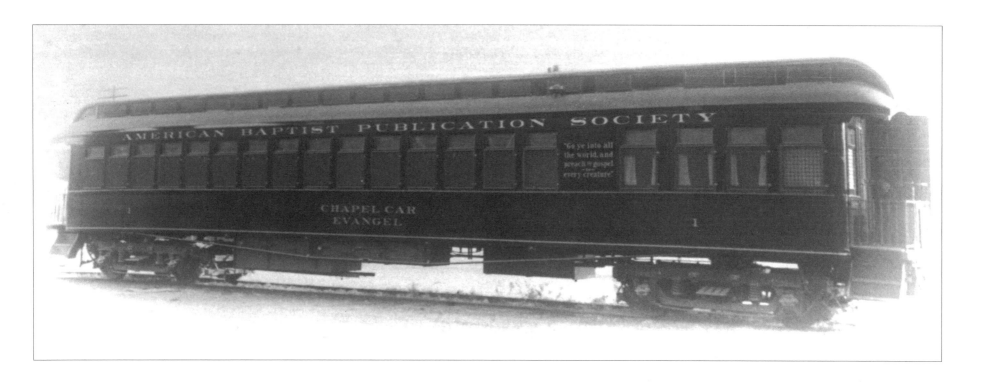

CHAPTER 5

Baptist Car 1: Uncle Boston's Dream, Bright *Evangel*

It must have been quite a scene the morning of May 23, 1891, as the delegates of the American Baptist Publication Society marched in a body one thousand strong to the imposing Grand Central Depot in Cincinnati for the dedication of *Evangel (see fig. 5.1).* After everyone in the concourse sang hymns and stood with bowed heads for prayer, Wayland Hoyt, who had turned Boston Smith's dream of a Baptist chapel car into a reality, delivered the address. Dr. Hoyt stepped to the platform and began by asking, "Why should not the Lord Jesus Christ have the best things? Why should his missionaries upon earth go to conventions in a stagecoach, when they own a magnificent palace car?"[1]

At this point, the blowing of steam and ringing of bells of a locomotive that had backed into the station interrupted the speaker. The bells and pops of locomotives and the low whissss of the air brakes seemed singularly appropriate. The doctor proved himself equal to the occasion, however, by shouting, "It's hard work to talk against a locomotive but Divine Providence may so strengthen my voice that I can."[2] The noise immediately ceased, providentially, many thought. Hoyt told the crowd what he saw from the train windows on the trip through Minnesota with his brother, railroad official Colgate Hoyt, in 1889 — towns with many saloons but no churches — and how he urged his brother and other railroad officials to do something about it.

Hoyt boasted that *Evangel* had been made so strong it could be butted against any freight train without damage, which was not the case. He announced the written assurance of railroad magnates all over the West and Northwest that *Evangel* "shall be carried by their great system of lines absolutely free, everywhere." This was greeted with tremendous applause. In closing, Dr. Hoyt told the delegates, "Its initial trip is to be from Chicago to the Pacific coast, making indefinite stops at three points in each state, through which the route lies, one to be a railroad division terminus, another where there is a small Baptist church, and the third at some village without a Baptist church."[3]

One observer wrote that "Uncle" Boston Smith next made the speech of his life in telling how he proposed to use this church on wheels. "Dr. Chase prayed; God heard him, but the audience didn't; and then we sang that beautiful and appropriate hymn of Brother Geistweit's ["Roll On, Bright Evangel"], in which brakemen and firemen and a fat old engineer lustily joined. It was a scene never to be forgotten. My blood tingles as I write about it. God bless Uncle Boston and chapel car *Evangel.* God bless the people to whom he goes, especially that vast army of public servants whom we call 'Railroad men.'"[4]

Miss Mary G. Burdette of the Woman's Baptist Home Mission Society would later recall another scene at the dedication. When she and a Mrs. Kennedy reached the chapel car, one of the officials stood on the rear platform.

Fig. 5.1 The first Baptist chapel car, *Evangel*, at its dedication at Grand Central Depot in Cincinnati. Paid for with donations from a syndicate of wealthy Baptist businessmen, the car was built by the Barney & Smith Car Company of Dayton, Ohio. (American Baptist Assembly, Green Lake, Wisconsin)

Fig. 5.2 Boston W. Smith on the platform of *Evangel* greeted guests who visited the car while it was on exhibit in Minneapolis, Minnesota, in the summer of 1892. (American Baptist Historical Society, Valley Forge)

"To him we said, 'Will you help us on the car?'

"'Yes,' he said, 'this time, but it is your last chance. Women will never travel on the chapel car.'

"'Oh, Doctor,' we replied, 'you cannot run the chapel car without the women.'"[5]

Miss Burdette was right. The wives of the missionaries played an irreplaceable role in the work of the chapel cars. For the men who worked along the tracks, the sight of a missionary wife singing a hymn, playing the organ, or telling a Bible story would be a sweet reminder of home and times past. The wives' influence on the women and children of the settlements would prove to be a promise of better times to come.

Smith was proud of *Evangel*, which measured 10 feet by 60 feet.[6] "In one end were the living apartments . . . a writing desk and book shelves to the top of the car, a large wardrobe and locker. In one section an upper and lower berth. A little kitchen was completely equipped with an Adams and

Westlake stove. There was a copper-lined sink connected with a tank overhead, a sideboard, and china closet. As Smith exclaimed, 'Everything complete as it could be.'"[7]

The chapel portion of the car was equally compact. A small coat closet was just inside and to the right of the boarding door, and a deacon's bench, which also served as an extra bed, was at the altar end. Colonel J. J. Estey of Vermont had given one of his pump organs, and Mrs. Lucy Littlefield of New York donated a magnificent brass lectern. At the back of each pew were hymnal racks, and under each pew were storage boxes for Bibles and tracts. Hanging from the center of the domed ceiling were brass chandeliers, and above the windows were smaller panes of stained glass. As Smith said, "To the last detail, it was a church on wheels."[8]

The New York *Daily Advocate* reported Smith's concept of the seating arrangement:

> The aisle does not run down the center of the car, but is a little to one side, and there are two seats to one side and three on the other. This puzzled me for a time, but I finally thought that the builders were economizing space, and had concluded it was much better to divide five seats with three on one side and two on the other than it was to have two and a half seats on each side.[9]

A Baker heater stood in a small closet inside the rear entrance to the car. This hot-air system, intended to be the major source of heat, proved to be inadequate and the topic of much grief in years to come.

Beginning the Journey

Following the dedication, the car arrived in St. Paul on May 30. Area Baptist women furnished *Evangel* with linens, silverware and dishes, aisle matting, and fine Smyrna rugs in the office and on the platform. The young people's societies committed to placing wire screens over the windows, which Smith said was necessary in mosquito country. This required the car to go back to the Northern Pacific shops for about ten days.[10]

Not surprisingly, the matter of a baptistry for the car was brought up. Baptism by immersion was a cardinal tenet of Baptist doctrine, one that most set it apart from other Protestant denominations. The Reverend W. H. Geistweit suggested a rubber baptistry that could be put up in a box frame and put away when not in use.[11] Dr. William C. Bitting, pastor of Mt. Morris Baptist Church in New York, also thought it would be a good idea to provide the car with a baptistry. He suggested a good portable one — a rubber one that could be brought out when the occasion demanded — could be had cheaply.[12] No practical solution seemed to be found, so *Evangel* and most of the Baptist cars had no baptistry.[13]

That lack did not stop the missionaries from baptizing — in every pond, creek, river, and ocean along the way, as well as being creative with makeshift arrangements from rain barrels to holes in the ground to horse troughs. In one western town, the section boss of the railroad dug a trough and brought down an irrigating stream for the missionaries' use.[14] At times handcars were used to transport baptismal candidates to the nearest body of water, and stories were told of icy rails that overturned carloads of candidates who suffered frostbite en route to be baptized.[15]

After a visit by Boston Smith with William S. Mellen, the general manager of the Northern Pacific system at Minneapolis, Smith was provided with a letter to superintendents and conductors that issued free movement along railroad lines. "You will pass Mr. Boston W. Smith and one attendant, with chapel car *Evangel* over our lines. You will arrange to take the car on any train he desires; you will sidetrack it wherever he wishes. Make it as pleasant for Mr. Smith as you can. Signed: Wm. S. Mellen, General Manager."[16]

Evangel's free and unlimited passage was a generous gift. In the late 1890s the rate for hauling cars was around 54 cents per mile. Without free passage, *Evangel*'s initial trip could have cost $1,080.[17] Free passage continued to be granted to the chapel cars during the early years of their existence and greatly reduced the cost of their operation. Without the free,

and later reduced, transportation fees, the chapel car program could not have succeeded.

Not having yet secured an assistant for the car, Smith, a father of five, took his twelve-year-old daughter along as organist. On the Wisconsin Central line between Chicago and Minneapolis, after supper one evening, Boston invited passengers and trainmen to a service in *Evangel*. One of the Pullman porters presided at the Estey organ. Familiar pieces in the *Select Gems* hymnal, with which the car was furnished, were sung. A second porter whispered that he "was a Baptist too," and cordially grasped Smith's hand as he said, "Well I am mighty glad the Baptists have got such a car on the road; we railroaders can go to meeting once in awhile now."[18]

The first question asked by Northern Pacific officials before *Evangel* started on its maiden journey west was "Is your car equipped with paper wheels having steel tires?"

"It was a conundrum I could not answer," Smith reported, "being new in the railroad business."

He hastily sent a telegram to the Barney & Smith Car Company and learned that the car had ordinary cast-iron wheels. The Northern Pacific Railroad had adopted a rule requiring that all special cars be equipped with paper wheels (laminated) to guard against accident.

"What was to be done? It did puzzle me for a little while," Smith said. Out of deference to the "illustrious donors" of the car, one of whom was a former vice president of the publication society, and another the richest man in America, the company consented to carry the *Evangel* as far west as Livingston, Montana, until October 15. Then the wheels had to be changed *(see fig. 5.4)*.[19]

What Would *Evangel* Find Along the Way?

When all the mechanical problems were solved, what would *Evangel* find besides churchless towns? According to an 1882 promotional booklet distributed by the Northern Pacific Railroad *(see fig. 5.3)*, the route from Minneapolis to the coast was a paradise.

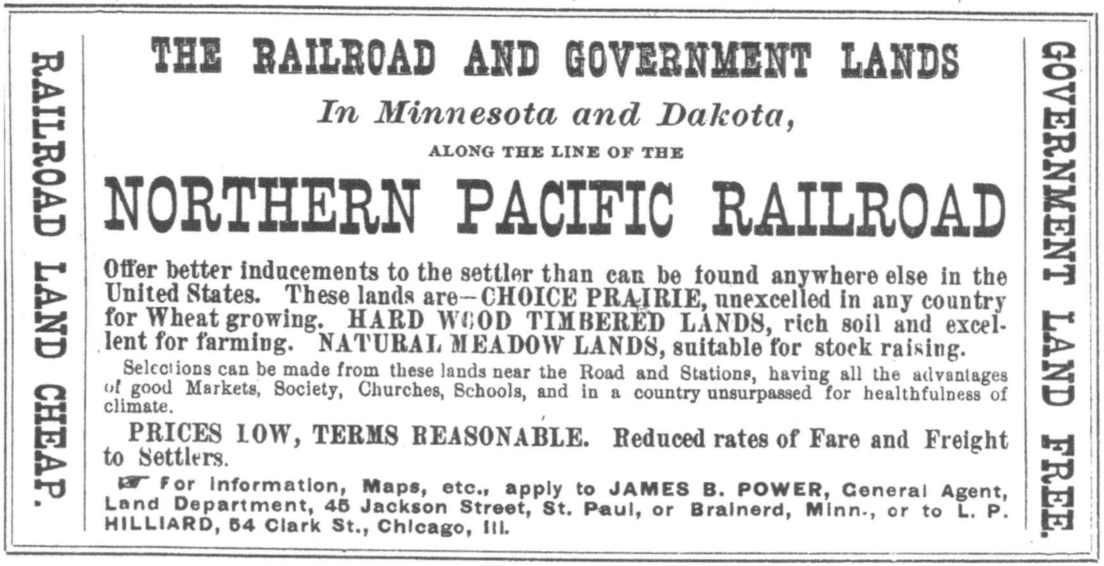

THE RAILROAD AND GOVERNMENT LANDS

In Minnesota and Dakota,

ALONG THE LINE OF THE

NORTHERN PACIFIC RAILROAD

Offer better inducements to the settler than can be found anywhere else in the United States. These lands are—CHOICE PRAIRIE, unexcelled in any country for Wheat growing. HARD WOOD TIMBERED LANDS, rich soil and excellent for farming. NATURAL MEADOW LANDS, suitable for stock raising.

Selections can be made from these lands near the Road and Stations, having all the advantages of good Markets, Society, Churches, Schools, and in a country unsurpassed for healthfulness of climate.

PRICES LOW, TERMS REASONABLE. Reduced rates of Fare and Freight to Settlers.

☞ For Information, Maps, etc., apply to JAMES B. POWER, General Agent, Land Department, 45 Jackson Street, St. Paul, or Brainerd, Minn., or to L. P. HILLIARD, 54 Clark St., Chicago, Ill.

Fig. 5.3 Posters and brochures advertising the opportunities along the routes of the Northern Pacific Railroad tempted many immigrants and easterners to come west. Seldom was life as easy as the advertisements promised. (American Baptist Historical Society, Valley Forge)

Large quantities of pine lumber are manufactured at various points on the line and furnished to settlers at reasonable price. These lumbering interests give employment to thousands of men, especially during the winter. Many of the settlers on the prairies find occupation for themselves and their teams, at the season of the year when they are not employed on their farms, in logging, and in getting out wood and ties for the railroad company in these timbered regions. . . . Vast areas of rich land still lie vacant and subject to free homestead entry. Natural pastures of the best grasses furnish unlimited grazing for flocks and herds. Inexhaustible coal fields are ready for the pick and shovel. . . .

Aside from its great capacity for agriculture and grazing, this country possessed extensive deposits of gold, silver, coal, iron, and other minerals. Timber, adapted to all the uses of life, and especially valuable for ship building, exists in immense quantities. Fish, of finest quality and in enormous quantity fill Puget Sound. . . .

Too much cannot be written to describe the unbounded natural resources which lie ready for development and which will amply remunerate all who go on

to either Washington or Oregon, and, with industrious application, endeavor to convert them into actual wealth. The Northern Pacific Railroad has millions of acres of land west of the Missouri River, offered chiefly at from $2.60 to 44 cents per acre.[20]

People believed what the attractive booklets and posters said, and they came by the thousands. The home mission society reported that from 1882 to 1891 more than five million people passed through Ellis Island.[21] Many sought their fortunes along the routes of the Northern Pacific Railroad, but what they found for the most part was not what the promotional material described.

Evangel had a publicity campaign that seemed to work well on that first trip and that served as a prototype for the following chapel cars. Publicity was patterned after that of traveling circuses and theater cars that visited many of the same rail towns. In several cases, the chapel cars, circus cars, and theater cars vied for crowds.

The chapel car was attached to the rear of a westbound passenger train. As the train tarried for orders, each person at the station was handed a circular that advertised the coming of the car, inside of which was placed a bit of Christian literature. Along the route, the chapel car workers threw Sunday school papers to the excited boys and girls who came to watch the train go by. In this way the gospel was carried into thousands of homes along a thousand miles of the Northern Pacific line through Minnesota, North Dakota, and Montana.

Flyers were also posted on every store and saloon in town, as well as around the rail depot. Thousands of circulars were printed containing a picture of the chapel car, the names of those who made it possible, and a brief outline of what the missionaries hoped to accomplish. The final words on that original circular were these: Would the car be of service in your town or neighborhood? If so, please write to *Evangel*, Minneapolis, Minnesota.

Within a month Smith received enough invitations to book the car for two years. Smith reported that the car averaged two meetings every day and from five to seven services each Sunday and stayed at each stop for one to three days. For every place it stopped there were a dozen more where it could not stop.

The Maiden Voyage

Brainerd, Minnesota, was the first stop on the maiden voyage west. The car arrived Saturday and remained until Monday. On Sunday six meetings were held, every one crowded to overflowing. Most people who attended had not been inside a church for many years. Across the state line in North Dakota was Fargo, the great wheat-buying center of the Dakota Territory. *Evangel* stopped for three successful meetings with the Fargo church, organized in 1881 — the first Baptist church established in North Dakota.[22] The territory had entered the Union in 1889, just two years before.

Many of the settlers in this area worked on bonanza farms built by the Northern Pacific Railroad, operating as many as a hundred thousand acres in the valleys of the James and Red rivers. "You are in a sea of wheat," one visitor to a bonanza farm wrote, "the railroad train rolls through an ocean of grain."[23] Hundreds of horses and dozens of mammoth steam-powered machines, seeders, harvesters, and threshers were required to operate these massive operations. The few faithful at Fargo urged that the car return for work in several towns where they felt Baptist churches should be organized.

At Jamestown, in the valley between the waters of the Cheyenne and the Missouri, where the earth not too many years hence had shaken with the tread of millions of buffalo, two crowded meetings were held. Many people came to the two services held next at Bismarck, the new state capital, and then *Evangel* crossed the Missouri River to Mandan on the new railroad bridge. This boom town was stirred by the visit of the chapel car, and businessmen of the town, mostly nonchurchgoers, Smith reported, saw the stabilizing value of the car's presence and hoped the car would come back.

At Miles City, Montana, *Evangel* visited the first completed Baptist house of worship between Fargo and Washington Territory, built in 1882.[24]

Even though there was not yet a Baptist church in Billings, crowds welcomed the car. Although the census of 1890 officially marked the closing of the frontier, there was no lack of excitement in town. Smith related: "We conducted several meetings in the car to which came a number of Montana cowboys. A murder, a lynching, and the killing of two Indians were among the happenings of the town about the time of our arrival at this place where the gospel is surely needed. The meetings attracted many of these poor sinners who never had attended a religious service, and the songs were especially pleasing to those who came into meetings. Two Indians were killed here the morning we left."[25]

Livingston, Montana, where the car had to turn around because of the Northern Pacific ruling on paper tires, had good results, especially at the meetings with the men at the large Northern Pacific shops. Even those who had little interest in religion could not resist a look inside this beautiful railroad car built to be a church on rails. Among the curious were those railroaders who had not entered a church or heard a preacher since their boyhood back East or in the old country. Even if they had the interest, they were embarrassed to attend one of the churches in town, but they seemed at home in a railroad car.

On the return trip, Uncle Boston held services in other towns, among them Lisbon, North Dakota, where the car remained three days to encourage a church organized in the office of a Judge Rhymer in 1882,[26] and Steele, where there was no meeting house and the residents heartily appreciated the coming of a church on wheels. Every meeting along the route was packed.

Smith distributed much literature and gave away several Bibles. One German boy ran home to tell his mother that she could get a Bible in their language at the church car. He ran back, bareheaded through the cold wind, barely able to gasp his request for a Bible. On receiving the Bible, he clasped it to his breast and sped away to his waiting mother. Smith related, "It was a most touching sight."[27]

The car returned to Minneapolis early in September, when

it was taken to the shops to have the paper-wheel project completed. Smith did not think it seemed right to ask the donors to assume further expense. Originally Pullman said it would cost about five hundred dollars to change from cast-iron to paper wheels but then made a generous offer to equip the *Evangel* with steel-tired paper wheels for four hundred dollars.

"It occurred to me that it would be a nice thing to get eight Baptist Sunday-schools, East and West, to 'take a wheel' apiece. That would be fifty dollars a wheel. Could I find the schools?"[28]

From wealthy Sunday schools in New York State to rural Sunday schools in Minnesota, Uncle Boston got the money for wheels from his "nieces and nephews" — children he had reached through his Sunday school publications, children who had no idea what paper wheels were. Then, proud as a father with a child wearing new shoes, he started west again with *Evangel* and the prescribed paper wheels.

Uncle Boston published a letter to his nieces and nephews about the trip. He recorded that in the evening services all passengers were invited from the immigrant and tourist cars to the Pullman travelers. "All classes came, the tired mother who left her baby with a kind woman in the tourist sleeper, the man on his way to look after his mining interests, the commercial traveler, the gambler, train attendants, conductor, brakeman, and a few Christians."

The paper wheels added much to the pleasure and safety of riding on the *Evangel*, according to Smith. "They made so little noise that while in motion the voice of the speaker can be heard to the farthest seat in the Chapel."

Not only was he pleased with the paper wheels, but Smith's ride over the mountains was also an inspiration. "The grand scenery was looked upon during a perfect day, when the sky was that beautiful blue that makes a faultless background for the snow covered mountains. As the Chapel Car was at the rear of the train, our outlook was simply magnificent."[29]

Wheelers Take Charge in Oregon

In early December 1891, *Evangel* and Smith arrived in Portland to meet the Reverend and Mrs. E. G. Wheeler, the first appointed chapel car missionaries. Smith turned *Evangel* over to the Wheelers on December 6, and the local paper recorded the event. Imagine Wheeler's excitement when he viewed that brightly varnished, Tuscan Red car on a siding in the Northern Pacific yards at Front and Glisan Street. The words brushed in gold — at the top "Chapel Car" and below the windows "Evangel" — gleamed in the sun. It was a railroad car fit for a prince — the Prince of Peace.

Wheeler extolled the rail evangelism venture at that year's spring gathering of the publication society. "If nothing is better than God, nothing is too good for God. Why should we crawl like snails when we might better take the rails?"[30]

The exhilarated missionary, who as a colporter had experienced the hardships of witnessing in the outposts of the Northwest on foot and by horse and buggy, could not praise the railroad officials enough for their cooperation. He announced that everywhere the car had gone the word from the highest officer down to the lowest had been, "It will give us pleasure to do anything we can for the chapel car."[31] He thanked the Northern Pacific, Southern Pacific, Union Pacific, Oregon Pacific, and Great Northern lines, Wells

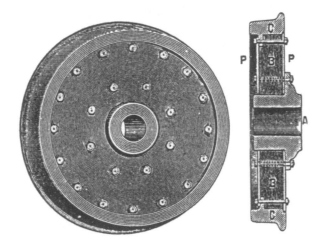

Fig. 5.4 After *Evangel*'s initial trip to Livingston, Montana, the Northern Pacific railroad would not permit the car to travel until it had new Allen paper wheels installed. The wheels were paid for by Uncle Boston Smith's "little nieces and nephews" in Sunday schools across the country. (Authors' Collection)

Fargo Express, and the postal telegraph companies for valuable favors to the car.

Among the railway fraternity we have our strongest friends. Many railway men are praising God tonight for what the chapel car has done for them. Section men, conductors, brakemen, telegraph men, shop hands and others have been touched by the power of God's love.[32]

On December 9, *Evangel* started its mission. It went south on the Oregon Pacific section of the Southern Pacific, first stopping at Oregon City, the oldest incorporated town west of the Rockies. Crowds from the large Baptist church in town, as well as other citizens, came to see the gospel car sided near the depot.

At Woodburn, where there was no Baptist church, they held services; and at Salem they organized the first Sunday school started in the car, calling it the Evangel Baptist Sunday School at Yew Park. After the chapel car made a short stop at Albany, the Wheelers traveled to Harrisburg, where two hundred ecstatic children greeted Mrs. Wheeler at the depot. They organized a church at Harrisburg on December 22 during a terrible storm.

People showed numerous kindnesses to the Wheelers all along the line. Portland Baptists had stocked the car with provisions. Oregon City urged "a little more," as did Salem and Albany. At Harrisburg, they assured Brother Wheeler that he need not buy anything there.[33]

As the chapel car approached Cottage Grove, Oregon, the Wheelers noticed that the depot sported two names. Inscribed in large letters at the top was "Cottage Grove," and "Lemati," meaning "peaceful valley," appeared lower in smaller letters. They would discover that a community split had occurred around 1887 — over town sites, roads, and the location of the post office — between those who lived east of the bridge and those who lived west of the bridge.

When *Evangel* pulled into the dual-identity town, a mining boom had resulted in the town swelling from eight hundred people to more than three thousand. Building also boomed:

hotels, opera house, drugstore, butcher shops, and saloons, many saloons. The Bohemia Saloon, the Helena Saloon, and many others sprang up on both sides of the bridge. Miners and town rowdies whooped it up in the saloons in one town, and then they dashed across the bridge to evade the town marshal. According to town history, the tinhorn gamblers, the get-rich schemers, and the ladies of the night followed close on the heels of the miners.[34] The Wheelers' visit encouraged the nineteen Baptists in town, who had organized a church but did not yet have a building.

As was true at Harrisburg, Merlin, and Corvallis, children were especially attracted to the chapel car. At one stopping place the Wheelers were met by a delegation of schoolboys, who reported to the other students the car's arrival. At four o'clock, looking down the street, *Evangel*'s missionaries beheld more than one hundred children marching to the car, with a teacher heading each division. Mrs. Wheeler remembered that in another town the car rolled into the station and the children greeted them with cheers. The crowd was so great, the Wheelers held two services to accommodate the immediate throng. The Wheelers varied methods of conducting the children's meetings according to the ages, using blackboards, charts, objects, and Bible stories.

Although children's work took much of the Wheelers' time, they were always amazed at the variety of adults who came to the car. "Gamblers, saloon men, and wicked women have been saved by the power of God. The Bibles, books, tracts and papers have been of great service and greatly appreciated. One man came twenty miles to meet the 'Baptist Publishing Car' for a supply, and a whiskey drummer brought a nice Bible to take home."[35]

As Goes the Railroad, So Go the Towns

As the chapel car traveled to the tip of one of the islands that string out toward Canadian waters north of Puget Sound, the Wheelers found the fishing port of Anacortes. They came in on the Seattle and Northern Railroad and gathered a small but dedicated congregation. Wheeler reported that it was not easy to raise money and support the churches in this Skagit River area. The area had experienced its boom years in 1889–1890, when town leaders hoped that the main line of the Northern Pacific would come through the town.

Excitement ran high then and many businesses opened, with real estate offices the most numerous, closely followed by saloons. The Skagit County Historical Society recorded that some churches began in the midst of the boom, finding what housing they could. Their spiritual impact made them, like the San Juan islands the citizens overlooked, "tiny islands in a sea of materialism," and their influence, as the Wheelers discovered, was minimal.[36]

When the Northern Pacific main line did not come, the tide turned against the churches in town. In the summer of 1890, Anacortes Presbyterians bought the canvas top from a beer hall in order to have a roof over their heads, and with just a frame front, the church opened for services.[37]

After the Wheelers left, the Baptist group disbanded, except for four hardy women who ten years later organized a ladies aid. Mmes. Trafton, Bushey, Amsbury, and Marshall cooked and quilted to raise money for a church. They advertised in local papers that they would take in plain sewing and would pay the editor by sewing for him. With their growing profits, they erected a one-room building and held services November 21, 1907.[38] The building those women worked so hard to build was the origin of the First Baptist Church of Anacortes, a beautiful structure overlooking Juan de Fuca Strait. Seeds sown by the Wheelers' witness finally had their harvest.

East on the mainland from Anacortes, at the junction of three railroads, Woolley had been platted in June 1890. Like Cottage Grove, the town had a rival in nearby Sedro. Because of its position on the railroad, Woolley soon outgrew its non-rail neighbor. About two thousand men were employed in and around town by the Bennett coal mines, six miles northeast of town. *Evangel* came into town to hold services for the miners and their families, and in February 1892, a church was organized.

Rockefeller, Friends, and the Everett Story

While *Evangel* was at Woolley, investors, including Wisconsin speculator Henry Hewitt and New York Baptists Charles L. Colby and Colgate Hoyt, hoped that Jim Hill would bring his Great Northern line over the Cascades, down the valley of the Skykomish, and to the sea. There they hoped a great city called Everett would rise on the peninsula above Port Gardner Bay.[39]

Colby and Hoyt, both former directors of the Northern Pacific Railroad and members of the syndicate that had given funds to build *Evangel*, had invested a goodly sum of their fortunes in forming the Everett Land Company. Their fame and fortune would be assured if they could persuade their friend and fellow Baptist John D. Rockefeller to apply his wisdom and wealth, mainly his wealth, to boosting the future of Everett.

According to Norman H. Clark, who wrote *Mill Town*, the story of Everett, the town was not much to boost in the spring of 1892.

They had perhaps eight hundred houses on the fringes of what they called their city, but hundreds of men and women were sleeping in tents and even cruder shelters. A few slept in coffins which others had carried to the peninsula on the rumor that at Everett one could sell anything. During every hour of daylight men labored to erect a huge shipyard and, beside it, a factory for the manufacture of steel barges. Others worked far into the night on the construction of a nail factory, a smelter, and a paper mill. Still others pounded spikes to steady the rail line they had hastily laid to connect their city with Tacoma and Seattle. Five hundred men were clearing land in an area defined as the city.

Yet, these people had no church, no graveyard, no jail. And no one could buy or rent any of the cleared land, for the men who with providential wisdom had laid out the city were withholding its substance for an indefinite and highly speculative reason.[40]

A few weeks later the Everett *Herald* reported that Wall Street millionaires, including Colby and Hoyt, had already invested $1,501,000 in manufacturing plants, and a contract had been let to grade ten miles of streets.[41]

Evangel came into Everett on the Northern Pacific line after organizing a church at Snohomish. The car made history as the first church to hold services on the bay side of Everett on April 11, before the saloons were in operation. "We were in 'on the ground floor' as the real estate men would say," Wheeler glowingly reported. That first night Wheeler baptized a young man from Philadelphia in the bay near the car. Wheeler rejoiced, "It is a beautiful sight! It was the first baptism, as far as we know, in that country."[42]

The Everett *Times* reported that "Easter services were very appropriately observed in chapel car 'Evangel' last Sunday morning. Wheeler and his wife conducted four other meetings during the day, but the men's meeting at 4 o'clock was one of the most impressive of all, and several accepted Christ. At 3 o'clock a church was organized in the car."[43]

The town managers gave five lots on the corner of Wall and Rockefeller streets overlooking the sound on the west and the river on the east. A magnificent building was promised, reported to come from Charles Colby and to be turned over to the church free as soon as the church could pay its pastor a salary of fifteen hundred dollars a year. Starting with twenty members, the church called the Reverend D. J. Pierce as pastor, to be paid as the agreement required.

It was rumored that John D. Rockefeller, "more than usually concerned about the moral environment in which he had invested,"[44] had sent the Baptist chapel car to be a good influence on the town. This was not the case, for Rockefeller no longer had any interest in the chapel cars. It was more likely that Hoyt or Colby was the motivator behind the chapel car's arrival.

When the panic of 1893 struck, the assets of most Americans and American cities faded, and the infant city of Everett was no exception. Clark writes that Rockefeller sent

Frederick Gates — Baptist pastor turned Rockefeller financier — to discredit and remove Colby and Colgate Hoyt and to clear out Rockefeller's interests in Everett, leaving the town on the edge of the beautiful bay floundering.

Eventually Jim Hill and the Great Northern Railroad and Frederick Weyerhauser gave the struggling town the financial foundation to survive. As for the men who had forged such close ties through their fellowship as Baptists of wealth and position, their lives would never be the same. Colby would soon die of a heart attack, and Colgate Hoyt would seemingly seek a lower public and denominational profile. The atmosphere of the trustees' meetings of the Fifth Avenue Baptist Church, of which all three men were members, was no doubt less cordial. The ties that bind are not always blessed, contrary to the words of the old hymn.

Nevertheless, the First Baptist Church of Everett, started by *Evangel* before the town was a town, would survive its dark days and continue its witness *(see fig. 5.5).*

The only church that stands now at the corner of Wall and Rockefeller streets is a grand old Presbyterian church. It is in the place once held by the First Baptist Church of Evearett, started by Evangel. *Down the street, at the corner of Colby and Pacific, is the present First Baptist Church of Everett. A huge banner over the front entrance of the sprawling, low, masonry building reads, "Welcome, Navy."*

Inside crowds of young families, senior citizens, and navy personnel in civilian dress find seats for the first worship service of the morning. It is a contemporary one, rich with children's voices, praise choruses accompanied by keyboard chords and words flashed on television screens. Babies are dedicated, prayers are heard, and a senior pastor earnestly talks about the importance of finding quiet time alone with God. The invitation is given.

Visitors leaving the service are asked to sign a guest register propped on an ornate brass stand in the foyer. Many in that large congregation may not be aware of its place in history. It is the lectern from Evangel *that once held the Bible from which*

the Word of God was preached to thousands of people along the tracks west. We touch the stand and admire its brightness.

Perhaps the lesson we have learned in Everett is that in spite of the rise and fall of men and their fortunes, God's Word still stands in the city on the hill by Puget Sound.

Evangel was proving to be a great success, and crowds everywhere flocked to see it. During the 1892 annual meeting of the publication society in Philadelphia in late May, a newspaper said, "It is expected that large crowds will be attracted to the Pennsylvania railroad yard during *Evangel*'s stay, and to guard against the crush, it has been decided to admit no one without card of admission, which may be obtained at 1420 Chestnut Street. Next week the car will start on a second trip through Minnesota."[45]

Another Philadelphia newspaper reported, "A train from Pittsburgh yesterday dropped a queer looking car at Powelton Avenue station, which was run down to the big shed beneath which the Pullman cars are kept. It was wine-colored, like an ordinary Pennsylvania parlor car, and in gilt letters at the top was painted the words 'Chapel Car,' while on the sides was the name 'Evangel.' It was the famous Baptist chapel car 'Evangel,' which for a year past, under the guidance of Boston W. Smith, the famous evangelist, has carried religion unto small railroad towns where the word of God in public worship is seldom heard."[46]

It did not take long before grumblings were heard from an opposition movement led by officials of the American Baptist Home Mission Society. Since 1832 the home mission society had sent dedicated missionaries through the country. Now it seemed to be having difficulty in dealing with competition for funds and attention, especially competition in the form of the unique and glamorous rail churches. Home mission society leaders contended that the rail chapel cars were trendy, impractical, and too expensive for mission work.

"Uncle Boston's Toy" Attacked

At the dedication in 1891, some representatives of the home mission society ridiculed *Evangel*, saying that it was an innovation and would soon have had its day. "Why, sir," one of these men was heard to say, "Uncle Boston has a new toy, but he will not know what to do with it in a little while."[47]

As curious crowds waited in line to go through the car at the Pennsylvania rail yard, Mrs. Wheeler described the first year on *Evangel* at the yearly meeting. Then her husband pleaded with the delegates.

Can we afford to drop the chapel car work when just upon the threshold of greater success? Shall we not increase the service with another car for the Pacific coast which today offers a most promising field for just such unique missionary endeavor? Hundreds of places inviting the car in California, Oregon, Washington, Idaho, and Nevada, are as much in need as the forty places visited. Just before leaving I received information that the Southern Pacific Railroad would gladly furnish transportation for this car into California.[48]

Fig. 5.5 The town of Everett, Washington, was founded by a group of eastern investors, some of whom also sponsored *Evangel*. The chapel car started the first church in the town, and this painting in the First Baptist Church of Everett commemorates that heritage. (Norman T. Taylor)

Wheeler announced gifts from donors for a second car, and then Dr. C. C. Bitting, missionary secretary for the publication society, called for offerings toward construction of a second car. In response, $3,071 was collected, almost half of the amount that would pay for the car.

After the meeting, the Wheelers and *Evangel* returned to the West Coast and Hanford, in the San Joaquin Valley of California. By 1890 Hanford was one of the most flourishing towns south of Stockton. Passing through fields and vineyards, *Evangel* came to a town rebuilding and reorganizing after two devastating fires in 1887 and 1891.

Wheeler had many things on his mind as he came to Hanford. He knew that there were those who wanted the chapel car work stopped. But before leaving town, in spite of his discouragement, he established another church.

Wheelers Leave, *Evangel* Goes East

The Wheelers, without *Evangel*, went east to promote a second chapel car, and *Evangel* went east, too — to Minnesota, with the young and less experienced Reverend J. Malcolm Sawers as the missionary. On October 9, in the chilly waters of the Mississippi River, Sawers baptized new converts of the First Baptist Church of Little Falls, which had organized August 18. On November 13, Sawers immersed more people in even chillier waters.[49] That once discussed baptistry for the car would have been most appreciated.

Many immigrants who had settled in the lands west of the Mississippi were attracted to the chapel car. In 1893 a Mr. Johnson, commissioned by the publication society to minister to Danes and Norwegians in their own tongue, joined Sawers. They distributed Bibles, New Testaments, and tracts written in six languages — French, German, Swedish, Norwegian, Danish, and English.

The haste to build rail settlements was evident to the chapel car workers by the number of sorry hamlets they passed on their journey, as was the resulting scarcity of churches. In one Wisconsin village in 1894, there had been no preaching before *Evangel* came. It had four saloons but not an avowed Christian. In this place two girls died in the autumn, and the six little girls who repeated the Lord's Prayer at the grave provided the only religious service to be had.[50] At Greenwood, Wisconsin, *Evangel* barely escaped a forest fire that swept through the town, and at Barker, a town of 150 with no religious services, crowds filled the car.[51]

At Wheeler, Wisconsin, with only eight houses and a saloon, many people came to the chapel car and were saved. They pleaded for Sawers not to leave. Sawers, a single man, had good help on the car from Wisconsin state missionary Edmunds and pastors Sprague and Pattingill.[52] In the spring of 1894 Sawers reported, "We have just closed a seventeen day successful campaign in one of the very worst communities in the northwest. We were sidetracked on the very spot where a man was murdered three weeks ago."[53]

The Thomases' Years in the South

After two years of working in Minnesota and Wisconsin, the publication society accepted an offer in July 1894 for *Evangel* to work in Arkansas, with the Reverend and Mrs. John S. Thomas as missionaries. *Evangel* would leave the cold North to witness in the warm South, but the situation in the South for Baptists had not always been warm. A division had occurred between the Baptists of the North and the South in 1845, mainly over questions of slavery and resulting missionary operations, and the Southern Baptist Convention was organized at Augusta, Georgia, on May 8 of that year.[54] However, the next few years would find the publication society still contributing toward the mission needs of several of the southern states, including Arkansas.

Arkansas began to reconstruct its economy, and efforts were made to attract settlers after the difficult years following the Civil War. Italians were the most numerous of the immigrants, joined by Hungarians, Slovenians, and Germans, and the towns along the tracks were growing in number. J. M. Loughborough, commissioner of the Iron Mountain and Southern Railroad, and T. B. Mills, a Little Rock real estate man, promoted life in Arkansas nationwide with their paper,

"The New Arkansas Traveler."[55] Rail lines, like the Pittsburgh and Gulf in the east and the Choctaw in the west, crawled across the red hills and pine forests, carrying settlers who founded towns.

Evangel did not reach Arkansas until October, and with good cause. In May 1894, Pullman workers in Chicago went on strike to protest cuts in wages and excessive rents for housing owned by Pullman. June found Eugene Debs, the fiery president of the American Railroad Union, calling all rail workers to strike in solidarity, and most United States railroads were affected by the action. Debs's A.R.U. members and other railroad workers vowed they would not move any train that carried a Pullman car. A hundred thousand railroad men walked off their jobs, and trains stopped moving, including *Evangel*. The strike did not end until August.

Since Mrs. Thomas had to be away from the chapel car to tend their family of five, Thomas, who had pastored in Tennessee and Arkansas, was joined at times by Arkansas pastors Rev. J. G. Doyle and Bro. W. P. Kline. Thomas wrote, "We are working among the whites and Negroes with great success and entirely without friction. The Negroes are nearly all Baptists here, and are getting on well in their work."[56]

Not all was so successful. "We made some disgusting failures . . . so far as human observations could grasp results," Thomas and Doyle reported.[57] In spite of "some disgusting failures," Arkansas Baptists were pleased with the work of *Evangel*.

Ill Health, Hard Times Hit Thomas

Chapel car life took its toll on Thomas's health. During August 1895 he had been working in northeastern Arkansas among the swamps, where he was taken with fever, though not before he had resuscitated two nearly dead churches and organized a church at Earle on the "Cotton Belt Route."[58]

In December Thomas, ill again, reported from his home in Searcy, Arkansas:

When the St. Louis, Iron Mountain and Southern

Railroad was being constructed, capitalists regarded it as a good investment because it was the great trunk line out of St. Louis to all points in the West and South. Many saw pecuniary interest in it simply as a business transaction. But God saw more, and in the fullness of time put men at the head ready to advance his cause on a grand scale.

Look on your map and see the great Missouri Pacific system stretching to the South and West, and then think of Col. W. B. Doddridge, general manager at the head of affairs, speaking the word that sends our Chapel Cars in every direction carrying the word of life. The Iron Mountain Pacific railroad has the men and money to do things on a large scale. An order was sent to all inspectors to furnish "Evangel" supplies without charge. When we keep up with the program God makes for us to work by, the cause goes well. Shall we not push on?[59]

Hard times came to Arkansas in the form of smallpox. In the winter and spring of 1896, the quarantine regulations were so rigid that armed men stood at railroad stations and on the roads leading into towns. On no account was anyone allowed to enter. Business was paralyzed, and travel was almost suspended. Yet in the midst of this scourge, the chapel car pushed on.

It became necessary during the quarantine to move the car in order to hold a meeting in the town of Palestine. Doyle reported, "What could we do? No one was allowed to enter the town and the trains were not even allowed to stop. Imagine our joy when, the day before the meetings were to commence, we received a telegram stating that the town council had held a meeting and that the quarantine, so far as it related to Chapel car 'Evangel,' was raised. We were pulled into the town the next day, held the meeting, the Lord blessed the work."[60]

In 1897 the publication society announced, "This year the *Evangel* has continued in Arkansas, winning the good will of the people." Not everyone who came to the car had good will. In one out-of-the-way point, Bradford, several wild-eyed chaps made a disturbance. The missionary remonstrated with them, but to no avail. Finally, he seized the heavy stick used to open the ventilators at the top of the car and told them if they did not quiet down, he would use it on their heads.[61]

When it was reported that *Evangel* was to leave Arkansas, Thomas was overwhelmed with letters saying, "Stay, stay! Do not leave Arkansas; we need you here."

For *Evangel*, the next stop before the turn of the century was Louisiana, a strong Catholic area. In 1897 Boston Smith described Louisiana as a difficult field and said workers found opposition from priests. "Nevertheless, the car is filled night after night, many of whom, disgusted with Catholicism, are receiving the truth. The brethren of the churches in Louisiana have given the car hearty support and commendation."[62]

At Donaldsonville, the missionaries started a chapel. At Woodworth, a mill town, they had good meetings. The last week they were there, both the saw and planing mills ran two hours overtime at night, greatly impeding attendance at the meetings, but they completed the meeting house that had stood so long unfinished.

Evangel held one of its most profitable meetings at Olla, a sawmill town along the Natchez Trace, near the Castor Springs resort area. After good meetings, Thomas baptized several people in the Castor River in the presence of about a hundred onlookers. One of the leading merchants of Olla, an educated man, commented that it was the first baptismal service he had ever seen. Thomas raised money for a church, ordered literature, and launched a Sunday school.[63]

Thomas reported that a little wreck at Forest Hill in 1899 had put the car in bad shape for handling. Because Christmas was near, he thought it best to run in where he could get the repairs ordered by Smith. Thomas wrote: "The car is in great favor with the men on the Missouri Pacific system and Texas and Pacific, and they extend every courtesy. They run their engines along side the car to give us coal and water when occasion requires. I have conceived the idea of putting a Bible on every engine. The engineer, fireman and head brakeman

have many opportunities to read, especially on the switch engines."[64]

The Southern Baptist partnership turned sour in 1900 with opposition from some leaders who resented the presence of the American Baptist Publication Society workers and materials. In addition to this predicament, Thomas was beset with physical and family concerns. In spite of many conciliatory letters from Dr. Robert Seymour, the secretary of the publication society, the car was withdrawn from the South.

Indian Territory Beckons

Evangel was transferred to Indian Territory in 1901 — territory that proved friendlier than the South had been. The land of the Five Tribes had not yet joined with the Oklahoma Territory to become a state. About sixty-five years earlier, Baptist missionary Isaac McCoy had arrived in Indian Territory by keel boat and established the first Baptist church on the north side of the Arkansas River. Soon more Baptist and Methodist missionaries came to compete with the Congregationalists and Presbyterians, who had long held the Indian field.

On rails of steel instead of in wooden keel boats, the workers of *Evangel* traveled on The Choctaw Route, a new line running west from Little Rock, Arkansas, to Oklahoma. From the oldest town in Indian Territory, Fort Gibson, W. S. Wiley wrote in May 1902, "*Evangel*, Rev. J. S. Thomas in charge, has been holding meetings here for five days, and the congregations exceeding the accommodations of the car; the Presbyterians have offered the use of their church. There is no Baptist church in Fort Gibson, but a number of Baptist families have been found and a church will soon be organized. Indian Territory hails the coming of *Evangel* and its efficient manager with delight."[65]

Six Baptist chapel cars were now on the road: *Evangel*, *Emmanuel*, *Glad Tidings*, *Good Will*, *Messenger of Peace*, and *Herald of Hope*. All the missionaries had a warm fellowship at the Second Chapel Car Conference held in Kansas City September 27 to October 5, 1902; the first had been held in

1898. Thomas, who had nearly died of overwork and malaria a few months earlier, was recovered enough from his illness to lead several sessions, including "Selecting Towns for Work" and "Heating and Lighting Chapel Cars." It would have been enlightening to hear the dialogue in the latter, as this seemed to be the main mechanical problem all the missionaries faced. Complaints about the heating and lighting were increasing in monthly reports, with the Baker heater being the main culprit.[66]

W. G. Brimson, an official of the publication society and general manager of the Omaha, Kansas, Quincy (O.K.) Route entertained the chapel car missionaries on his luxurious private car *Marialys*, which proved to be a memorable event. Brimson, with his many railroad connections — president and general manager of the Chicago and Eastern Illinois, Calumet and Blue Island, Chicago and South Eastern, Chicago & Kenosha, Joliet and Blue Island, and Milwaukee Bay View & Chicago railroads[67] — proved to be a valuable friend to the chapel car movement.

Large crowds gathered at the 1903 State Baptist Convention in Oklahoma City, including the crew of *Evangel*, which was parked on the Frisco track in South Town. Boston Smith spoke to the assembly, including delegates from the Indian Nations dressed in "every shade and variety of citizen's clothes to many-colored blankets and moccasins."

The climax of the meeting was reached as "Left Hand," chief of the Arapahoes, was testifying to the power of Christ to save a wild Indian — a scalp-taking savage. Visiting Lake District Home Mission secretary, T. K. Tyson of Michigan, rushed to the platform, threw his arms around Chief Left Hand, and amidst tears of joy declared that forty years almost to the day, he was a United States soldier in battle at Sand Creek, Colorado, when their troops were in mortal combat with the Arapahoes led by Chief Left Hand. They recognized each other, all the more remarkable from the fact they had not met from that day to this. The vast audience

was soon in tears of joy singing "Praise God from Whom All Blessings Flow."[68]

Across the state line from Fort Smith was Spiro, the general end of the Choctaw Trail of Tears. Le Flore County passed to the Choctaw Nation by the treaty of Dancing Rabbit Creek in Mississippi in 1830, by which the Choctaws agreed to give up land in Mississippi for lands in Indian Territory. Removal of the Choctaws began in 1831, and with it began the Trail of Tears. Choctaws knew well that they did not want to come west; however, if they stayed in Mississippi, their government would be abolished and they would be under the white man's law.

Many died in flooded swamps in which they traveled waist-deep in water, when snow and sleet of the worst blizzard in decades caught them in the Mississippi and Arkansas swamps. They froze to death; they died of exposure, malaria, cholera, and smallpox. Twenty-five hundred perished on the journey and soon after arrival in Le Flore County near Spiro.[69]

Sixty years after the Trail of Tears began for the Choctaws, a small group chartered the First Baptist Church of Spiro in a store building near the Kansas City Southern Railroad depot. Around 1905, *Evangel* came into town and was placed on a KCS siding, and the Thomases helped to get the church building started.[70]

One hundred years later, in the fall of 1996, Pastor "Big John" Flanagan of the First Baptist Church of Spiro was gracious to his visitors from Indiana, even though he had a number of things to do. No, he had never heard of a church on rails called Evangel *or that it had anything to do with the history of the church, although it sounded interesting. But if anyone knew about it, it would be church member Geneva Overstreet, the pastor said with a wide grin. "She's really something. She's ninety-three, but her memory's better than mine."*

And he was right. He placed the call, and after ascertaining that Geneva was "feelin' good today," he asked, "I've got some visitors here who say the church was started by a railroad church car. Know anything about that?" The big smile flashed again across the preacher's face. "You do? Well hang on just a minute. I want you to tell these folks just what you told me."

The voice over the speaker phone was a bit unsteady but clear. "I can remember folks sayin' the church was started by a boxcar. It was parked down by the tracks, and the people met in it. The missionaries on the car helped build the first church."

We told Mrs. Overstreet how much we appreciated her good memory and explained that the chapel car was not a boxcar but a beautiful church car, with stained glass, pews, organ, and living quarters.

"I'd love to have seen it," she said. "I guess the Lord keeps me around for some reasons. I do remember hearing about that old boxcar."

As we left the pastor's office, we saw a concrete edge about 40 by 80 feet outlined in the front yard of the present church — the foundation of the original church, laid almost a century ago.

Among the members of the present First Baptist Church of Spiro are still those of Choctaw blood.

District missionary J. H. Franklin reported in the fall of 1905, "One must visit the territories every few weeks if he would keep up with the development of the country. A little more than a year ago I made a trip over a new railroad into Indian Territory and found there was hardly a station on it of any considerable size. Now there are towns on this road with 2,000 or 2,500 people each."[71]

Adamson, Indian Territory, with about seven hundred people, was so new that one-third of the people lived in tents and the others in rough board houses. The missionaries began without anything, but at the end of eight days, they organized a church with fourteen members. In one week, it grew to thirty-one souls. The Thomases left with the lumber on the ground for a new meeting house. There was no other house of worship in town.[72]

On January 21, 1907, Thomas wrote that they were leaving Indian Territory.

We go from here to Denison, Texas, to work in the interest of the railroad men in the shops. We are to hold meetings at 12 o'clock midnight, and at noon. That work is in cooperation with the Railroad Y.M.C.A. There are two thousand men there at work. Great cities are standing where a few board "shanties" stood seven years ago. It takes work to evangelize those places.[73]

In November 1907, *Evangel* crossed the Oklahoma state line and began work in Kansas with white settlers at Parsons. The first missionary in Kansas was a Catholic priest, Juan de Padilla, who accompanied Coronado and then returned to live among the Wichitas in 1542. He died a martyr's death at the hands of those he loved and befriended because they were jealous that he planned to preach the gospel to their foes. Much later, in 1824, Isaac McCoy came to Kansas to witness to the Indians, and other missionary societies established missions. Five denominations pioneered in the work with the Five Tribes — Catholic, Presbyterian, Methodist, Friends, and Baptist.[74]

September 1901 was a sad month for the chapel car movement and the Indians of Oklahoma and Kansas. The death of Boston Smith was reported on September 10. The warm, funny, dynamic Uncle Boston, who was called "Na-chum" Boston by the Cheyennes, "Ad-dah" Boston by the Comanches, and "Ne-hush" Boston by the Wichitas,[75] was gone, lost also to thousands of his beloved nieces and nephews nationwide. On September 27, the death of Wayland Hoyt, who was responsible for the realization of the chapel car concept, was announced.

The Killians, Kansas, and Railroad Men

Thomas, who had persevered for more than seventeen difficult years on *Evangel*, resigned in 1910, and the Reverend John C. Killian and his wife, of Trenton, New Jersey, came to *Evangel*. Before leaving the chapel car, Thomas asked the women of Kansas to help put the chapel car in "splendid order" for the new missionaries. "It would probably cost $100

Fig. 5.6 The Reverend and Mrs. John Killian spent many months on *Evangel*, especially in Oklahoma, Indian Territory, Kansas, and Nebraska. Killian went on to have responsibility for the chapel car work for the American Baptist Publication Society. (American Baptist Assembly, Green Lake, Wisconsin)

to furnish carpets, bedding, linens, dishes, cooking utensils, and other needed equipment."[76]

The women of Kansas responded in good faith. In addition, John Killian soon received news that caused Mrs. Killian to rejoice. The First Baptist Church of Kansas City, Missouri, had adopted the car, and in a few weeks a box was received: silverware from Talbert Jewelry of Kingman; quilts from the ladies' aids of Kingman, Cedar Valley, and Arkansas City; pillowcases and towels from the Priscilla Club of Tauy Church and the women of Cawker City; a comforter from Phillipsburg, all of which brightened the car and made life more comfortable, and 47 dollars in cash, broken into gifts of 1 dollar, 3 dollars, and 5 dollars.[77]

One of the first churches the Killians visited was First Baptist of Wichita. While they were there, they took advantage of dealing with the temperamental lighting on *Evangel*, and in doing so they met W. C. Coleman.[78] Coleman, inventor of a special gasoline lamp, visited *Evangel*, saw the need, and offered to install one of his outfits without charge. Along with two men from the Coleman plant, Coleman personally completed the installation of the new lighting system. Killian reported that now the car was brilliantly lighted. A devout layman, Coleman would become president of the Northern Baptist Convention in the 1920s. His lamps would light all of the Baptist cars as well as the later Catholic cars.

The Killians came to love the noonday meetings with the railroad men, and soon they met the midnight shift too. "We average about 30 men who bring their dinner. They eat, then sing several pieces. Mrs. K. sings, then I speak. About 12:30 one night a caller came and said, 'Please sir, we men who work at night have no chance to go [to the services], what could be done for us?' And I said, 'We will be delighted to have the same kind of service for you at midnight,' so we have been holding services from 12:05 to 12:50."[79]

It was not beneath Killian to make a little business deal on the side for the benefit of the work. Thomas Edison eventually gave one of his phonographs to all but the last of the chapel cars and personally presented his gift to *Evangel*. Killian related, "When the phonograph was given to us by Mr. Edison, I thought its main work would be at children's meetings, but it is in the men's. We have only about seventy-five records, so when I land in a place, I go to one of the dealers and tell him about the meetings and suggest that if he will keep me supplied with the records I want to use, I will tell the men the titles of the records I am using. They are eager to help."[80]

Killian felt strongly about the railroad men. "One of the most beautiful sights is to see the men, coming to the car just as they are and as they listen and are convicted of sin to see the tears plow through the faces dirty with honest toil."[81]

Throughout the work of the chapel cars, there was a spirit of cooperation with other denominations. That did not mean that occasional clashes did not occur, but when a chapel car came into town, other churches usually participated in the services. Such was the case in 1911 at Lyons, Kansas, where the car became so crowded that neither it nor the local Baptist church could accommodate everyone. They moved to the Methodist church for Sunday night. The Presbyterians joined in, and the congregation grew to seven hundred.[82] The work at Lyons also touched the communities of Frederick and Hoisington. The Pittsburg visit occurred only two years after the founding of the town, which at that time had a population of about a thousand but no religious services.[83]

Car Hopscotches Kansas, Oklahoma

Kansas railroad laws interfered with the success *Evangel* was having in the state. At the state convention in October 1911, it was explained that the car would have to travel between Oklahoma and Kansas because Kansas law forbade free transportation between two points in the state.[84] In 1912 *Evangel* hopped to Oklahoma. At Haskell, Killian led the congregation in erecting a building on a site they already owned. "We can only imagine the furious pace at which the construction took place — services were held just a few weeks after the stakes were driven."[85]

When *Evangel* reached Watonga, Oklahoma, in February or March 1912, the Baptist church was apparently ready to cease. During a terrible snowstorm, the Killians held revival services and baptized many. At Ames, the work was equally successful. "We could use six cars in this state alone," Killian would say. "It was heart-rending to hear, 'Don't leave us until we have a pastor; else we will go down.'"[86]

Hopscotching back to Kansas, *Evangel* was crowded in Dodge City, where the first building of the First Baptist Church had been completed in 1879. The pastor then was Domine Collins, a "very democratic person, who mingled with gamblers and gunmen, and was beloved by the entire town." The church needed money to pay off the building debt and decided that the women should have a box supper. A local businessman made a deal with Bat Masterson to corral his gang to buy boxes as a favor to Pastor Collins. Masterson arrived that night followed by gamblers, gunmen, and cowboys who bought the boxes at a good price and stayed for the hymn sing. Collins was fortunate Masterson favored him, for legend has it that Masterson had run many a preacher out of Dodge.[87]

News in the spring of 1913 was that a new railroad was being planned from Dodge City's depot on Wyatt Earp Boulevard southwest, creating towns along its line. Two of those towns that the Santa Fe Railroad (known during construction as the Dodge City and Cimarron Valley) created were Elkhart and Rolla.

Morton County history relates that when the first train came through Rolla on March 15, 1913, an excited crowd gathered at the station. The people used a just-sided "passenger car" for a chapel and gave thanks for the coming of the railroad.[88] That so-called passenger car was *Evangel*.

The deed from the Santa Fe Land Improvement Company for the townsite of Elkhart was filed April 28, 1913, at 2 P.M. On April 29 the first lots were sold and tents put up, and Elkhart was established.

Ten days later, one hundred business lots plus several residential lots had been sold. Cash Wilson's pool hall was one of the first buildings in town, along with Roberts Grocery, Ora Carey's livery business, Mrs. Farmer's Hotel and Restaurant, and the Star Lumber Company. Charlie Burkett opened the first barber shop in a tent and had the distinction of installing the first street light. He strung a wire from Roberts Grocery to his barber shop, hanging a gasoline lamp in the middle. It had to be filled and pumped but burned the entire night.[89]

The farmers of Elkhart were worried about an invasion of grasshoppers eighteen miles long and five miles wide, reported to be moving northeast from northeastern New Mexico. They read in the *Richfield News* about a bait that would prevent the destruction of crops by grasshoppers, a bait prepared by mixing dry bran with Paris green and then made into a mash in which had been stirred cheap syrup and the finely chopped pulp and juice of an orange or a lemon.[90]

Townspeople who gathered every day to gossip about grasshoppers and recipes and to watch the trains come into town received an extra thrill on June 16 or 17. On the rear end of the daily train was *Evangel*, with the Killians on the observation deck waving to children along the tracks. On June 18, the Killians and state missionary A. W. Idhe met with residents and formed the First Baptist Church of Elkhart. Dr. W. V. Tucker, co-owner of the Welch and Tucker Groceries and Feed Store, was a charter member and gave the land on which the first frame building was erected at a cost of one thousand dollars.[91]

In late June 1913, after helping start the Elkhart church,

Evangel pulled into the Rolla station again to help build a Baptist church. Killian reported for the *Kansas Baptist* newspaper in July, "Two things are true here: they all want a church and are eager for it. The people are poor in this world's goods. They are worthy, and money put in here will bring good returns to the kingdom. These dark and windy nights they drive five or more miles to the car."[92]

Later in the summer, the train watchers on the Dodge City, Elkhart, and Rolla line would see another unusual rail car pull into the station, this one run by the Chicago, Rock Island & Pacific Railway. It was a silo demonstration train, sent to show the farmers how better to manage their crops.[93] Demonstration trains were frequently sided in towns spreading the gospel of good farming at the same time as the chapel cars were spreading the gospel of good news.

Evangel was taken to the shops in Muskogee for an overhaul in the summer of 1913. The Killians went east for a much-needed vacation, including a promotional tour for chapel car work. "On coming back we found the car 'a thing of beauty,' shining outside and inside. The lettering on the side is new and a great improvement; for now you read at the top, American Baptist Publication Society, and the words 'Chapel Car Evangel' are also on each side. While the car stands on the siding, hundreds from passing trains and townspeople read our name and verses of Scripture. While this car is the oldest, it can now more fully represent our denomination and do us credit. Railroad men talk about its beauty and give it careful consideration."[94]

Transportation Turnovers Create Concern

In 1914 the chapel car secretary reported that the problem of transportation had become increasingly serious. Railroad companies that in former years had been glad to transport the cars free of charge were no longer able to do so because of new legislation. Chapel automobiles were replacing worn-out wagons in California, and three boats were added to the mission fleet in western Oregon and northern California. In Utah, camp wagons were in use. Nevertheless, the chapel cars were still in great demand.

While the society was trying to determine which mode was the most efficient and economical for their work, the *Evangel* and five other cars continued to serve well. At the annual meeting of 1915 in Los Angeles, the seventh and last car, *Grace*, was dedicated, and money was being set aside for another rail chapel car and funds to support the work.

After leading a series of meetings at Englewood, outside of Denver, the Killians went east to Limon, where they organized a church on August 12. They held successful services at Deer Trail and Bijon, stopped at Cokedale in September, and at Hastings, a coal camp with about nine hundred people in the southern district.[95]

By January 1916, *Evangel* was with the Bethany church in Denver. Many railroad men lived in the area, and it seemed an ideal place for the car and its workers. Working in Colorado among a group of mining camps of about fifteen thousand people, the Killians found "the well educated and the illiterate; the faithful Christian and the hardened sinner; the hungry soul waiting for the right word, the callous and indifferent."[96]

After six years on *Evangel*, the Killians left chapel car work for administrative duties with the publication society. Honeymooners Arthur V. Allen and his wife replaced the Killians in the spring of 1916.

Along with adjusting to married life (as well as life on a chapel car, which didn't provide much privacy), Allen and his bride, the daughter of a former missionary to China, soon discovered that the coal fields of Colorado had a great need for pastors. Allen knew a lot about pastors: his father and three brothers were pastors.

Evangel was moved to west Nebraska in 1917, with the Allens still on board. Along the Burlington line, they stopped at Merna, where they hoped to join the church with Cliff. At Columbus, where the church had been closed for seven years and the property was in decay, a fellowship supper was given. In a month the church was reorganized and renovated.

After one year of service, the Allens resigned in August

1917 to assume a pastorate, taking with them one of the few babies born on a chapel car.[97] In a letter written later, Allen said, "It was fascinating work and we would have continued except that the car with its limited water supply was not an ideal place to raise babies."[98]

Killian was called to come back to *Evangel* until a new missionary could be found and to finish the work at Ord. The Killians were relieved of their duties in September 1917, when the Reverend and Mrs. W. M. Kennedy came to the car for a short time. Kennedy was a Nebraska state missionary. Superior, Wisconsin, was the first stop, where, in spite of depressing newspaper headlines about war, the church was revived.

World War I Brings Hardships

The United States declared war on November 17, 1917. The Northern Baptist Convention's "Emergency War Measures" stated, "The world war in which America is now called to play a part creates a national crisis and lays heavy responsibilities upon the people. It is a time for personal initiative, for universal cooperation, for willingness on the part of each to do his share. The deciding human factors in the war are the condition of the men at the front, the resources of the nation, an adequate food supply, a spirit of unity, and a sacrificial loyalty to democracy."[99] Churches were encouraged to cultivate close relationships with army and navy chaplains; to the YMCA, which was ministering to men in the camps; and to the American Bible Society, which made Scriptures available for every soldier and sailor.

The government took over operation of the railways in December 1917 and did not relinquish control until March 1, 1920. The Reverend V. E. Clarke and his wife came to Nebraska in 1918 to work on *Evangel* during this difficult time. Vernie Clarke was a man of many talents but little formal schooling. Coming from a poor family of English, Dutch, and Welsh origin, he was converted at the age of seven as a result of reading the New Testament by himself for two years. Obviously bright, he tried to work and put himself through school to become a minister, but his health failed.

Left only with the resources of the Los Angeles Public Library, Clarke spent many hours educating himself. In his leisure, he learned to play the harp.

Clarke came to the Reverend George L. White, the missionary secretary for the western district, and asked for a chance to serve as a missionary. As a test he was sent to Chloride, California, to build a church and establish work. After four months, he had shown his ability to preach and organize the affairs of a congregation. As a result Clarke was placed on *Evangel* for a term of service.[100]

One of Clarke's first stops was Lodi. A letter from Francis G. Gschwind of Callaway, Nebraska, explains: "Lodi was a very small rural community about seven miles southeast of the present town of Callaway and consisted only of a railroad station, grain elevator, livestock loading pens, store, post office, church, school, and a home or two. It was located on the Union Pacific's Kearney Branch, which then ran from Kearney to Stapleton, Nebraska, since cut back to Arnold, Nebraska. No trace of Lodi exists today. It has long since disappeared, like many of the other towns along the lines of the railroads."[101]

Complications of transportation and trackage privileges were trying during 1918. Samuel Neil reported to chapel car workers, "These problems will continue while the war lasts, and we must face the possibility of having to withdraw the cars altogether for a time. We hope, however, to avoid this."[102]

On January 19, 1919, a new government regulation was enforced. That regulation forbade free transportation for all private cars, including those used for religious purposes. Even though the lines were restored to private operation in 1920, free passage continued to be a major problem. Neil reported that owing to the railroad conditions created by the war, it had been difficult to arrange for the movement of cars, but it was hoped that now this handicap would be speedily removed. If war was not enough, "the aggressive work of both [rail and motor] cars and [boat] cruisers has been hindered by the influenza epidemic," Neil told delegates to the publication society's annual meeting.[103]

At Ord, the flu caught up the ministry of the Clarkes, and they had to move to other towns. At Dannebrog, a girl named Norma, who had been adopted by a Christian couple when she was ten days old, came to the chapel car for the after-school sessions. At the age of eighty-four, Norma Cargill wrote to tell what a positive influence those times, and the lessons and Scriptures learned, were on her life.[104]

After extensive repairs to the increasingly vintage *Evangel* in 1920, Clarke left the chapel car, and new missionaries, the Reverend and Mrs. B. H. Ward, came for a very short stay from their pastorate of the Riverside and Silver Creek churches, to work at Wellfleet and Stella, Nebraska.

In October the Omaha Baptist Union believed the time had come for a Baptist church to serve the northern part of the city. They held the first service in the chapel car on October 31, 1920, and then formed the Parkside Baptist Church.[105]

At Loup City, one of the last stopping places in Nebraska, *Evangel* served as a temporary church because the church had burned to the ground.[106]

The Reverend and Mrs. Frank Blanchard were now in residence, having been transferred from *Glad Tidings* in August 1921. First stop for the Blanchards on *Evangel* was at Rockville, Nebraska, a village of fewer than five hundred souls, where it seemed they were not wanted, although there was no Protestant church in town. The citizens had been kept in ignorance of their arrival, and some citizens had broadcasted the word that no ministers or churches were wanted. The Blanchards soon discovered that not a pastor, minister, missionary, or evangelist had succeeded in organizing any religious work in the community, although many had attempted to do so.

Blanchard visited every family in the town but failed to find a Baptist. He found some Lutherans and finally discovered a young Baptist three miles out in the country. This was their nucleus, and at the end of eight weeks they had organized a church with fourteen members, including some of the most prominent residents of the village.[107]

The effects of the war were devastating to the publication society and the chapel car program. The publication society, as well as most businesses, struggled to survive. At the 1922 meeting at Indianapolis, Indiana, secretary Sam Neil spoke. The genial Scot was usually able to find the positive side of problems, but even he was somber. "The riot of after-war reaction has not yet spent itself. The condition of the people socially, morally, religiously is such as to alarm all who study it." Neil warned that the situation for the society was serious.[108]

Wyoming and the End of *Evangel*'s Line

While the publication society struggled to make ends meet, *Evangel* found work in Wyoming. In September 1922, church lots were secured in Casper and a pastor was located. The Blanchards erected a chapel at Evansville, three and a half miles from Casper, where the Texas Oil Company was building a refinery.[109]

At Lucerne, along the Wind River in the Owl Creek range of the Rockies, they helped to build a church. Before they could get used to *Evangel*, the Blanchards were transferred again on April 1, 1924, this time to car 2, *Emmanuel*.

The quick turnover of chapel car workers was a result of the aging of the chapel car family, both equipment and workers, and resulting health problems, many related to the unique stresses of chapel car life. White was constantly trying to arrange transportation over railroads that were not interested in hauling the old wooden cars without steel underframes. He spent days arranging repairs at rail shops that were too busy with their own work to be bothered.

Attention at the publication society headquarters was being turned from the troublesome chapel cars with their increasing maintenance problems toward the auto chapel cars, which cost less, were easier to maintain, and could travel more easily on the improving roadways. Two new auto chapel cars, each costing less than ten thousand dollars, featuring living areas for missionaries and carrying tents, were assigned to California. Auto chapel car 1, the Crawford Memorial, was assigned to the Mexican colonies around Los Angeles. Auto chapel car 2, the Ernest Leigh Tustin Memorial, considered to be state of the art in furnishing and equipment, was assigned to northern California.[110]

In November 1924 *Evangel* came to Rawlins, Wyoming, its last station of service, brought in on the Union Pacific Railroad. Located near the freight depot, the car was used for one year as a meeting place by the people who endeavored to establish a church in Rawlins. The *Rawlins Reporter* of June 16, 1925, said:

Early last fall [1924] Rev. John D. Smith, General Colporter, came to Rawlins in the interest of the Baptist denomination and found a number of Baptists who had not united with any of the Rawlins churches. In November the Chapel Car, Evangel, was sent here by Rev. Joe P. Jacobs, Superintendent of Missions for the Baptist churches of Wyoming, with a view to conducting revival services, but the wife of Rev. Herbert Richmond, Missionary of the Chapel car, was not able to remain on the car and Mr. Richmond resigned before any meetings were held.

On April first Rev. Smith returned and expected to conduct a series of meetings when a coal oil stove being filled with gasoline exploded and severely burned him and set fire to the car. Dr. Jacobs was present when the accident occurred and conducted services that night, and took Rev. Smith to his home in Douglas [Wyoming].

Later Rev. Carl Fischer was sent here and finding a number of children not in Sunday school, organized in the Chapel car a Baptist Sunday school. On Sunday, May 24th, he was joined by Rev. Carl C. Harwood, Missionary from Jackson's Hole, and began revival services. Dr. Jacobs came from Casper last Saturday and on Sunday [June 7, 1925] organized the First Baptist Church.

At the meeting in the car on Sunday night, Dr. Jacobs, on behalf of the Wyoming Baptist Convention, formally tendered to this newly organized church the use of the Chapel Car for one year as a permanent meeting place for the church, or until such time as the church can provide a more commodious building. This car is now the property of the Wyoming Baptist Convention, having been presented to the convention by the American Baptist Publication Society.[111]

In hopes that a church could be built in that historic rail town, in September 1929 the publication society sent the Reverend A. C. Blinzinger, who had a national reputation as the "chapel car church builder," to Rawlins with chapel car *Grace*. The cornerstone was laid April 6, 1930, a gift from Mr. Gray, president of the Union Pacific Railroad and a Baptist layman from Omaha. The church was dedicated October 5, 1930, but Blinzinger remained until the building was completed.

Evangel Becomes Heart of Church

To some, the inclusion of *Evangel* into the structure of the new church might have seemed a practical measure. When the first part of the building was constructed, the chapel car was turned 90 degrees and incorporated into the rear of the church sanctuary. Years later *Evangel* became part of the educational plant, its long row of windows facing the mountains to the west. When a new educational wing was added, *Evangel* found itself holding forth at the center of the entire church, exactly where it was meant to be.

Visitors to the Rawlins church can look through *Evangel*'s original windows. Windows that once reflected sod homes and saloon rows in the Dakotas, Minnesota, and Montana; bustling depots in raw coastal towns in Washington, Oregon, and California; the framework of new churches in the golden wheat fields of Kansas and Nebraska; baptisms in the great rivers of Oklahoma, Arkansas, and Louisiana; and mountain views in Colorado and Wyoming. The same windows had been washed by railroad men in shops across the West, who had stopped their work to pray, sing a hymn, or shake the missionary's hand.

They can even go through one of *Evangel*'s end doors that had been carefully preserved and worked into the structure. The same door that thousands entered to find the Good News.

For that was the purpose of this first Baptist *car* — *evangelos*, to bring good news. *Evangel* is still bringing good news as the heart and soul of the First Baptist Church of Rawlins, Wyoming.

It was as Boston Smith said when he first saw *Evangel* at the Barney & Smith shops in the spring of 1891: "Surely God's hand is in this."

> Roll on, thou Bright Evangel,
> Go like the flying wind
> Till all shall know of Jesus
> The savior of mankind.[112]

Notes

[1] "Church and Parsonage on Wheels," BSP, ABHS, Philadelphia, 21–22.

[2] Ibid.

[3] Ibid.

[4] Ibid.

[5] Anniversary Report of the American Baptist Publication Society, Philadelphia, 1898, 21–22.

[6] "The Gospel on Wheels," BSP, ABHS, VF.

[7] BSP, scrapbook, "Merry Christmas," ABHS, VF.

[8] Ibid.

[9] Ibid.

[10] "Report of Chapel Car Service," BSP, ABHS, VF.

[11] W. H. Geistweit, "The Chapel Car," *The National Baptist*, in BSP, scrapbook, "Kind Words."

[12] BSP, New York *Daily Advocate* clipping, in scrapbook, "Kind Words," ABHS, VF.

Fig. 5.7 At the physical and spiritual heart of the First Baptist Church of Rawlins, Wyoming, is *Evangel*, which was built into the structure of the church. (Norman T. Taylor)

13 At least one Baptist chapel car, *Good Will*, had a baptistry installed, but upon examination of the car when it was discovered in 1998 in Boyes Springs, California, no marks could be found that indicated where the baptistry had been installed. The thought is that the baptistry was one like the ones suggested for *Evangel*, a rubber folding arrangement that collapsed in the area under the platform.

14 BSP, colporter records, newspaper clippings.

15 Samuel Neil address, Samuel Neil files, Colporter Department Box, ABHS, VF.

16 Boston W. Smith, *The Story of Our Chapel Car Work* (Philadelphia: American Baptist Publication Society, n.d.), 6.

17 Ibid.

18 "A Chapel Car Incident," BSP, ABHS, VF.

19 "The Story of the Wheels," scrapbook, "Merry Christmas," BSP.

20 A Northern Pacific Railroad promotional brochure dated July 1, 1882, found in BSP.

21 *The Home Mission Monthly*, June, 1892, 179.

22 JoAnne and Don Shoemaker, *North Dakota Baptist State Convention, 1884–1984: The First Centennial* (Barre, Vt.: Northlight Studio Press, Inc., 1984), 5.

23 Dee Brown, *The American West* (New York: Simon & Schuster, 1994), 155.

24 Flora K. Willett, "Baptist History in Montana," in *Religion in Montana*, 2 vols., ed. Lawrence F. Small (Billings, Mont.: Rocky Mountain College, 1992), 1:208.

25 "Report of Chapel Car Services," scrapbook, "Merry Christmas," BSP.

26 Shoemaker and Shoemaker, 42.

27 "The Chapel Car *Evangel*," scrapbook, "Merry Christmas," ABHS, VF.

28 "The Story of the Wheels," BSP, scrapbook, "Merry Christmas," ABHS, VF.

29 BSP, personal letters in scrapbook, "Merry Christmas," article from Baptist Young People's Union, ABHS, VF.

30 Sixty-Eighth Anniversary of the American Baptist Publication Society, 1892, 38.

31 Ibid.

32 Ibid.

33 C. H. Matoon, *Baptist Annals of Oregon* (McMinnville, Ore.: Pacific Baptist Press, 1913), vol. 2, 281, Oregon Baptist State Convention, American Baptist Conference of Oregon.

34 The Writers Discussion Group, Cottage Grove, *Golden Was the Past: 1850–1970* (Cottage Grove, Ore.: Sentinal Print Shop, 1970), 20–24, Cottage Grove Library.

35 Sixty-eighth Anniversary of the ABPS, 38.

36 Margaret Willis, ed., *Chechacos All, The Pioneering of Skagit*, Skagit County Historical Society series no. 3 (Mount Vernon, Wash.: Skagit County Historical Society, 1973), 158.

37 Ibid., 188.

38 Ginger Houston, "First Baptist Church: And it all started in a railroad car," *Fidalgo*, Wednesday, October 27, 1993.

39 Norman H. Clark, *Mill Town: A Social History of Everett, Washington, from Its Earliest Beginnings on the Shore of Puget Sound to the Tragic and Infamous Event Known as the Everett Massacre* (Seattle: University of Washington Press, 1972), 6.

40 Ibid.

41 *The Pacific Baptist*, July 28, 1892, 2.

42 Ibid.

43 The Everett *Times*, "Baptist Church Organized," Wednesday, April 20, 1892, Everett Public Library, Everett, Wash.

44 Clark, 8.

45 BSP, personal papers, scrapbook, "Kind Words," ABHS, VF.

46 Ibid.

47 BSP, personal papers, "Mark Twain's Scrapbook," ABHS, VF.

48 Annual Report of the American Baptist Publication Society, Philadelphia, 1892, 39.

49 Letter to Jacquie McKeon from Roy B. Larson, clerk, First Baptist Church, Little Falls, Minnesota, September 29, 1974, American Baptist Assembly files, Green Lake, Wis.

50 BPS, personal papers, scrapbook, "Kind Words," ABHS, VF.

51 *The Wisconsin Baptist*, January 1901, 4, American Baptist Conference of Wisconsin files, 5.

52 Minutes of the Wisconsin Baptist Anniversaries, October 1894, 55, American Baptist Conference of Wisconsin, 52.

53 BSP, *Home Chimes*, April 1895, ABHS, VF.

54 Southern Baptist Convention Report for 1895, 78, Ouachita Baptist University Archives.

55 *Arkansas and Its People*, ed. David Y. Thomas (New York: The American Historical Society, 1930), vol. 1.

56 Anniversary Report of the American Baptist Publication Society, Saratoga, N.Y., 1895, 47.

57 Arkansas Baptist Convention, 1895, 22, Ouachita Baptist University Archives.

58 *The Colporter*, August 1895, 18.

59 *The Colporter*, February 1896, 6.

60 J. C. Doyle, "Two Years on a Chapel Car," Chapel Car series, 1898, American Baptist Publication Society, Philadelphia.

61 Ibid.

62 Smith, *The Story of Our Chapel Car Work*, 17.

63 Anniversary Report of the American Baptist Publication Society, Rochester, N.Y., 1898, 108– 9.

64 *The Colporter*, December 1899, 8.

65 *Evangel* report sheet, American Baptist Assembly files, Green Lake, Wis.

66 BSP, Howard Parry Collection.

67 *The Biographical Directory of the Railway Officials of America* (Chicago: The Railway Age and Northwestern Railroader, 1896), 54.

68 Rev. F. B. Palmer, "New Acts of the Apostles," BSP, ABHS, VF. (Folder labeled "Articles").

69 Henry L. Peck, *The Proud Heritage of Le Flore County*, 4th ed. (self-published, 1996), 12.

70 "Town History of Spiro," Spiro Public Library, Spiro, Okla.

71 *The Word and Way*, September 21, 1905, 8.

72 *The Word and Way*, May 9, 1907, 11, Archives of William Jewell University, Liberty, Mo.

73 A letter from J. S. Thomas, dated January 21, 1907, to I. T. McAlester, Included in "Fresh from the Firing Line," a brochure published by Boston W. Smith, BSP, ABHS, VF.

74 W. A. Seward Sharp, *The History of Kansas Baptists* (Kansas Historical Society, 1939), 3–5. *The Kansas Baptist*, September 1901, 5.

75 "An Indian Meeting in the Jesus Car," BSP, ABHS, VF.

76 *The Kansas Baptist*, July 1910, 3.

77 *The Kansas Baptist*, September 1910, 5.

78 *Missions*, February 1911, 140.

79 *Missions*, October 1911, 703.

80 Ibid.

81 *The Kansas Baptist*, March 1911, 7.

82 Hoadley, "Chapel Car Ministry in the Southern States," *American Baptist Quarterly*, March 1991, 28.

83 Ibid.

84 Fifty-first Annual Meeting of the Kansas Baptist Convention, October 9–12, 1911, 15.

85 Hoadley, 29.

86 Oklahoma Baptist Convention Report, 1912, 8.

87 *The High Plains Journal*, April 2, 1949, 2.

88 *History of Morton County*, Morton County Historical Society, 108, Morton County Library.

89 Ibid., 120.

90 Richfield, Kansas, newspaper, May 1, 1913, 1.

91 *History of Morton County*, 743, Morton County Library.

92 *The Kansas Baptist*, July 1913, 6.

93 Richfield, Kansas, newspaper, May 1, 1913, 1.

94 *Missions*, May 1914, 353.

95 Ibid.

96 1914 Anniversary Report of the American Baptist Publication Society, Boston, Mass., 1914, 653.

97 See chapter 9 on chapel car *Good Will*.

98 Joseph H. Heartberg, "Chapel Car Evangelism Recalled," *ABC Magazine*, February 1974.

99 Northern Baptist Convention Report, 1917, Bulletin No. 24, War Measures, 300–307.

100 *Nebraska Baptist Bulletin*, September 1918, 92–93.

101 Letter from Francis G. Gschwind, E. G. Publications, Callaway, Neb., October 30, 1980. American Baptist Assembly, Green Lake, Wisc.

102 Anniversary Report of the American Baptist Publication Society, Denver, Colo., 1919, 40.

103 Ibid.

104 Letter from Norma Cargill, December 24, 1997, from Grand Island, Neb.

105 Letter from Parkside Baptist Church, Omaha, American Baptist Assembly files, Green Lake, Wis.

106 *Missions*, January 1919, 3.

107 F. I. Blanchard, "The Seed Is the Word of God," tract, American Baptist Publication Society/American Baptist Historical Society, ABHS, VF.

108 Anniversary Report of the American Baptist Publication Society, Indianapolis, Ind., 1922, report of Samuel G. Neil, 53.

109 *Missions*, January 1919, 3.

110 Annual Report of the Board of Managers, American Baptist Publications Society, Atlantic City, N.J., 1923, 34–35, ABHS, VF.

111 History of the First Baptist Church of Rawlins, Wyo. Courtesy of Rawlins First Baptist Church.

112 Hymn written for chapel car *Evangel* by the Reverend W. H. Geistweit.

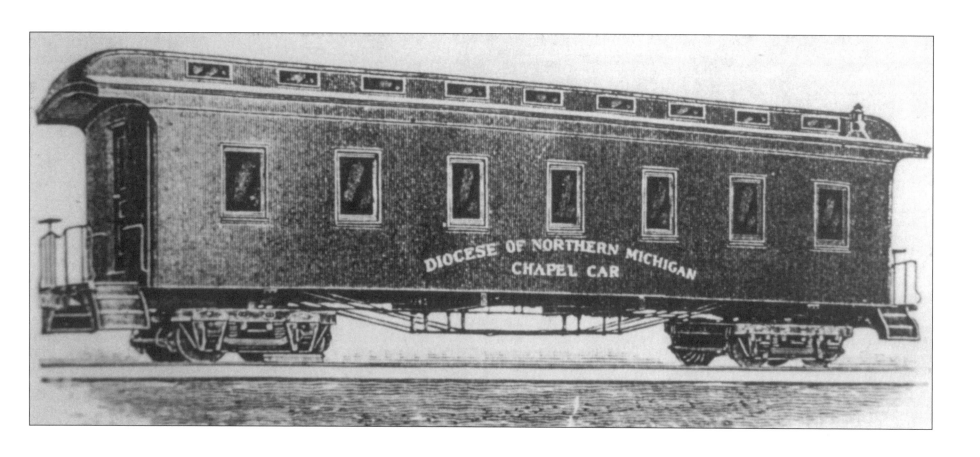

CHAPTER 6

Bishop Mott's Episcopal Cars of Northern Michigan

"*The town of Ontonagon completely wiped out by fire on August 25th 1896.*"

This was the entry in the Ontonagon Fire Department log on that date. The alarm sounded at 1:10 P.M. and, according to fire department reports, the town, except for some outlying areas, had burned by 5:00 P.M.

On the day that disaster struck, a southwest wind had sprung up, igniting a smoldering swamp. No one was overly concerned in the late hours of the morning of August 25, a Tuesday, though the smoke reaching the town had become bothersome and visibility on River Street was limited. Everyone broke for the noon hour at the Diamond Match Company (DMC) mills, but upon returning to work at 1:00, the men at the west side mill were alarmed to see that the swamp fires had advanced on the mill buildings.

The wind was picking up in velocity, and the smoke was quite thick. Evacuation of the dozen or so houses on the west side of the river was begun; minutes later, one of the mill buildings took fire. From this point on, there was little hope. DMC had stockpiled forty million board feet of dried and seasoned lumber in piles up to four stories high near the mill buildings. For weeks the situation had been an invitation for disaster, and now it had come.[1]

Along with the town went the Episcopal church, the second Protestant church in town, built in 1854 of materials transported from Detroit on a chartered schooner. That church, the oldest continuously still active in the diocese, played an important role in the Michigan chapel car history. For it was at Ontonagon that a third Episcopal chapel car — the second chapel car of the Diocese of the Upper Peninsula of Michigan — came to serve as the religious center for that community while the people set about rebuilding their town and their lives.

Michigan's Upper Peninsula

The Episcopal church in Michigan's Upper Peninsula had put two rail chapel cars in service between 1891 and 1893 in that beautiful and wild north country that nobody seemed to want. Originally Michigan was forced to trade the much more accessible and civilized Toledo strip for the area.

Before 1854, many thought that the Upper Peninsula, considered to be "a land of perpetual ice and snow,"[2] would never be populated by more than a few adventurous souls. Yet, within less than a decade after Michigan was admitted to the Union, Douglas Houghton's report revealed that rich deposits of copper were there. Shortly afterward, a surveying party led by William A. Burt discovered iron near Negaunee. During the years that followed, copper and iron mining attracted thousands of people to the Upper Peninsula, and towns and cities sprang up.[3]

Lois Prusok, editor of *The Church in Hiawathaland*, relates that the Episcopal church had ties in the Upper

Fig. 6.1 This sketch of the second chapel car of the Episcopal Diocese of Northern Michigan was used in a promotional brochure. The car perhaps was purchased from the North Western Railroad, where it may have been used as a business car, chair car, or caboose. (Courtesy Central and Upper Peninsula and University Archives, Northern Michigan University)

Peninsula as early as 1761, when the British troops stationed in the area "undoubtedly brought their Anglican tradition and the book of Common Prayer with them to their remote outposts."[4]

The Keweenaw Peninsula was first settled around Copper Harbor, at the very tip, but the discovery in August 1845 of the rich Cliff Lode twenty miles south on the Eagle River sparked a rush to that area. The town of Clifton grew up around the mine. Eagle River, with a new dock, roads, a stamp mill, warehouses, and homes, was evidence that Copper Harbor was booming. In 1845, the discovery of the Minnesota Mine near Ontonagon swelled that town to a city of six thousand people.[5]

Because the rapids of the St. Mary's River prevented ships from traveling from Lake Huron to Lake Superior, the first canal at Sault Ste. Marie was built in 1855. The effect on the Upper Peninsula was like that of a dam bursting. Timber and minerals flooded out, and immigrants and development flooded in. Marquette quickly became the leading port for shipping iron ore, and in 1856 the town had 1,664 residents. The parish of St. Paul's Church was founded with "barely a handful of communicants."[6]

Ten years later, the Civil War brought another boom to the iron range, and the cities of Ishpeming and Negaunee grew up around the mines there. Commercial fishing expanded, and the great lumber boom in the eastern Upper Peninsula began. The 1880s saw the beginnings of the towns of Bessemer and Ironwood around the new Gogebic iron range. By the late 1880s and early 1890s they were rough-and-tumble mining towns. But there were some signs of religious impact in Ironwood, where "hot controversy raged over proposals to reopen the 'variety theatres' which moralists had closed," and the Methodist Temperance Society held weekly meetings in the church. "But these were voices crying in the wilderness."[7]

Williams and His Zeal for Missions

In 1884 a young Episcopal priest named Gershom Mott Williams (*fig. 6.2*) visited his uncle on Mackinac Island. His father, once commander of the fort on the island, had been transferred to upstate New York just weeks before Williams was born in 1857. According to Prusok, Mott was a man of many accomplishments: linguist, author, hymnologist, lawyer, and authority on relations with the Swedish church.

He also had a passion for missionary work. When Williams returned to the Upper Peninsula in 1891, he was named archdeacon as well as rector of St. Paul's in Marquette, and in 1896 he would be elected bishop of the Diocese of Marquette, later renamed the Diocese of Northern Michigan.[8]

The young churchman's diocese was a territory with an "immense foreign population, non-English speaking. A vast majority were French, German, Czech, Italian, Polish and 'other Romanists,'" as Williams would say. The language problem plus cultural polarities created problems.

"One difficulty of church work in a mining town is the social rift between the educated and scientific officers, and the miners. Another is the fact that half the miners are always on 'night shift' and can get to church with difficulty. Then there is the polyglot trouble that so few of our clergy know how to handle. It is a shame that we Americans never learn the hospitality of using another man's speech."[9]

Williams had a burning concern for the unchurched in his isolated land. He explained that the community was long shut in as soon as lake navigation ceased and was left to itself, often without a clergyman, for six to seven months. Sunday was generally disregarded. Liquor interests were all-powerful. "Physical pleasure ruled as an ideal. Some of the effects of this early society remain. . . . I wonder whether the world knows how frightfully dear living is here, where we import everything? This makes it exceptionally hard for the clergy, and torments me to know how to get more rectories built."[10]

At the opposite end of the Upper Peninsula, the *Newberry News*, established in 1886, was describing in its columns "lively times in the village." In many other Upper Peninsula lumber towns, this was apt to be especially so in the spring, when the ice-hauling roads melted, logging camps were abandoned, and workmen came to town to "blow their stakes."

In 1888 Newberry had three churches, but it also had eight saloons. The latter increased with greater activity in the woods and peaked in number — according to whose testimony one takes — at eleven or sixteen. It appears that saloon license fees for a long while paid most if not all the costs of running the village government.[11]

Many lumber and mining towns did not have an Episcopal church. Williams worried about these areas, many of which were served, if at all, by itinerant missionaries. By 1893 Episcopal strength in the area resulted in the region being organized as a missionary district of the Diocese of Michigan. Seven parishes and twenty-seven missions were reported in the journal of the district's primary convocation held that year at Ishpeming.

First Car of Northern Michigan

Innovative ways were needed to bring the gospel to those who lived off the beaten track. One of those methods was the use of the Upper Peninsula Episcopal rail chapel cars, perhaps inspired by Bishop William D. Walker's *Church of the Advent*. In Michigan, the cars were not built new. The first chapel car was probably a loaned railroad car, most likely from the Chicago & North Western Railroad, which was outfitted as a chapel.[12]

According to Father Herman Page, a retired Episcopal priest whose father and grandfather once served as bishops in Northern Michigan, the first Michigan car may have been in use as early as 1891 and was probably an oversized caboose. Archdeacon G. Mott Williams said of that first car, "It was an old affair, borrowed at that, and inconvenient." It was used to hold regular worship in communities along the east-west lines of the Duluth, South Shore & Atlantic. At times it ventured into the copper country and to locations along the Chicago & North Western.[13]

The list of places the car served in 1893 included lumber and mining camps, vanished villages that grew up around railroad crossings, and towns that continue to exist. Echoing from the past are names like Whitefish, Iroquois, Donaldson,

Shunk, Seney, Trout Creek, Trout Lake, L'Anse, Pequaming, Kitchi, Ewen, Bessemer, Rockland, Flint Steel, Baraga, Chassell, Portage Entry, Sagola, Republic, Michigamme, Spur, Norway, Hermansville, Stephenson, Ingalls, Thomaston, Whitney, and Dollarville. Some places were preaching stations, others established missions where churches were later built.[14]

By late 1893 it appears the first Upper Michigan chapel car had been retired. Williams told the delegates to the 1894 convention at St. Paul's Church in Marquette, "I want also to report on the chapel car. It was operated long enough to prove serviceable, but was an old affair, borrowed at that, and inconvenient. I am having a new one built, it will be rigidly plain, but very strong, and I hope, convenient. It can be used to much greater advantage here, I think, than in any other part of the church. It will serve admirable [sic] in places where the rapid fate of a church would be to go up in a forest fire."[15]

The Second Chapel Car Put in Service

The new car must have been in the planning in 1893, because the following news item appeared in *The Standard*, a Minnesota Baptist paper: "I read with much interest the other day, a brief article in a daily paper about a new enterprise in Northern Michigan, the building of a chapel car for missionary work among the people of that part of the country, under the lead of a prelate by the name of Archdeacon Williams; a Catholic enterprise, as I took it, from the reading of the article."[16]

Then the author, Marcus Duncan, attacked the Catholic church and priests in general, saying the Catholics had no right to claim their car was a new enterprise, because the Baptist chapel car *Evangel* deserved that credit. The truth was that this car was not a Catholic car but the second Upper Peninsula Episcopal car, and the first Upper Peninsula chapel car could have been on the rails before *Evangel* was.

Unlike the *Church of the Advent*, the seven American Baptist Publications Society chapel cars, and the three Catholic Church Extension Society cars, the two chapel cars of the

Fig. 6.2 Bishop G. Mott Williams had two chapel cars in service in Northern Michigan because of his concern for the unchurched (Courtesy of the Archives of the Episcopal Church USA., Austin, Texas)

Upper Peninsula of Michigan seemed to have no wealthy angels to help build new and elaborate equipment. Bishop Williams mentions somewhat bitterly, "Millions of money have gone East from these copper mines to Massachusetts and New York capitalists, but only one Boston churchman and only one New York churchman have ever given so much as a thousand dollars for church work in our diocese."[17]

In available sources about the Michigan Episcopal cars, there is no mention of the *Church of the Advent*, which had been highly publicized both at home, in Episcopal publications, and abroad. The North Dakota car and the Michigan cars were in operation at the same time, as were the Baptist cars. It is a matter of record that the two bishops were well acquainted and bound together by many Episcopal ties.

This second Upper Peninsula car, although it was earlier reported as being used on the Union Pacific, may have been a North Western car.[18] It was a wooden truss-rod, monitor-roof, open-platform car, 9 feet, 7 inches wide and 45 feet long over the car body. Its four-wheel passenger trucks were of an old style that included wooden parts.

Page explains that cars of similar size and general configuration were made by various builders, including Jackson & Sharp and Barney & Smith. Some were built as business cars; others were converted for business or company use from chair cars or cabooses (*see fig. 6.1*). Railroad uses of this type of car included division superintendents' cars, inspection, wire service, or pay car.

In *Santa Fe Business Cars*, a drawing of a Santa Fe superintendent's car, #40 (previously #210), a wooden car built in 1870, and car #404 are very similar to the second Episcopal car. Car #404 had been first used as a division superintendent's car and later a farm demonstration car, which would have required space uses similar to those of a chapel car.[19]

For church purposes there were three separate compartments: chapel, sleeping quarters, and a place to prepare and eat meals. The usual business car bedroom(s), observation room, and dining room could have been removed, leaving the small kitchen and the attendant's room for the person traveling in the car. Then the rest of the car could be fitted with an altar and other church furnishings. It probably would have seated thirty or thirty-five people. Wood stoves at either end heated the car, which had seven windows on each side and a door on each end opening to the platforms. Hidden in a closet was a primitive toilet.[20]

Bishop's Car Travels Many Lines

The second Episcopal church on wheels would be known as "The Bishop's Chapel Car," although unlike the North Dakota chapel car, it was not the bishop's cathedral. The election of Bishop Williams in 1896, the proceedings confidential and conducted behind closed doors, was the main order of the primary convention of the Diocese of Northern Michigan, as it was so designated in 1895. After prayer, an informal vote was taken of all candidates offered by the delegates. After two ballots had been taken, it was announced that Williams was elected first bishop of the Diocese of Marquette.[21]

Another historic motion was passed at this convention, reflecting the changing tide in womens' rights that reached to the outermost points of the Michigan peninsula.

Whereas, believing the interests of the parishes of the Diocese of Marquette will be subserved by giving the women of those parishes the same right as to voting as the men in parish meetings, Resolved, that we seek cooperation with the other diocese of the state to petition the Legislature of the State of Michigan to enact a law or to amend the present law so as to permit the various parishes of this diocese to extend to the women thereof equal privileges with the men in the matter of voting in the parish meetings.[22]

Bishop Travels Across Upper Peninsula

In the year of his election, Bishop Williams visited many towns along the scenic shores of Lake Superior. He listed in an abstract of parochial and personal reports: "Chapel Car. Services at Thomaston, Ballentine, Marchwood, Three

Lakes, Humboldt, Champion, Crystal Lake, Kenton, Ewen, Munising, Eagle Mills, Wetmore. Occasional services at Detour, Flint Steel, Quinnesec, Spalding, Ford River, Seney, Deer Park, Osceola, Eagle River, Bruce's Crossing."[23]

In the heyday of the railroads, seventy-seven different lines operated across the Upper Peninsula. The chapel car was given free use of their tracks, traversing the peninsula east to west and north to south. Williams himself was a frequent traveler on the rails, baptizing and confirming new members to the faith in the towns along the way. All were depots along the Duluth, South Shore and Atlantic Railroad. Many were logging settlements at the time, and the railroad was helpful in arranging for the car's use.[24]

In Bishop Williams's charge to the clergy of the diocese in 1896, he reminded them, "We belong to a church which we are taught to believe is the historical and natural Church of the English-speaking people" and urged them to the task of winning back those "who, once belonging to us, have for political or other reasons drifted into various separations from the Historic Church." He thanked God that "this is, as far as Church and State go, a free country."

Then he urged his clergy to be careful in the established services of the church, including the use of unleavened bread, his preference, even though ordinary bread had Episcopal approval. He also made a point that emphasized why the rail chapel car was such a benefit. "Our Church should be presented everywhere, when possible, as a church with an altar. This is why school house services are so unsatisfactory."

The bishop, distressed over clerical conditions in his parish, also discussed ministerial character:

Our clergy must impress the world as industrious and studious. Further, they must remember that the religious world, as represented by Methodism and its influences, is suspicious of the discipline of the church, and apt to consider that it is relaxed so as to represent a lower moral platform, because our people are not specifically forbidden certain forms of amusement or

gratification. Many of our co-workers in this field are avowed Prohibitionists, and have a lurking tendency toward the Manicheeism which sees positive evil in things, instead of our relations to them. Drinking is a sin to them, where drunkenness is to us. Or gluttony is the sin known to the books, while many religious people do not accuse themselves severely for eating too much, but do for drinking a glass of wine. We must be as temperate in speech as in action.[25]

Bishop Williams's prediction that the chapel car might be used where a town's church would go up in a forest fire came true. The Church of the Ascension in Ontonagon, a strong congregation with eighty-six members, an active church organization, and a church and rectory in good repair, was insured, with indebtedness chiefly for a new stained glass window, which cost $307.[26] The second car was then placed there to serve as a church (fig. 6.3). The bishop explained the situation:

The burning of the Ontonagon church, August 25 last, with the whole town, almost destroyed the parish as well as the church building and rectory. Fortunately, considerable insurance was carried, though not nearly the value of the property, and we received some $3000 to replace $7000 of burned property. The fine bell was uninjured, and the stone foundation of the church.

An appeal to the general church brought me over $600 by which means, and sending the chapel car, the Rev. Mr. Mulligan was enabled to live three months at Ontonagon after the fire, living and preaching in the car, and to relieve a great deal of distress. I have still a small invested balance on which I draw from time to time for materials to assist the Woman's Guild in relief work there.

Mr. Mulligan and his duty to his family moved him to accept work in Nebraska in December and in February the Reverend Edward Warren, a former

Fig. 6.3 This old print, which is included in the centennial history of the Church of the Ascension in Ontonagon, Michigan, shows the Reverend W. A. Mulligan, the pastor, on the car while it was serving in Ontonagon, with his Friendly Girls Society class, plus some little boys. (Courtesy of the Ontonagon Historical Society)

rector, came back to take charge and expressed his willingness to continue for a while, and has been transferred to the diocese. Mr. Mulligan built a small chapel from insurance money before he went away, seating seventy-five people. The Sunday School is maintained, and two guilds. Just before the fire, new windows of cathedral glass had been put in the church, which in completeness of equipment rivaled any in Diocese.[27]

The Ontonagon couple who wanted to be married in an Episcopal church were among the many who were thankful for the presence of the chapel car in town, and the first wedding in the chapel car took place in 1897. The car remained on the #1 siding there until a new building could be completed in 1898.[28]

The person who would erect that new church on the foundation of the old church was the Reverend William Poyseor, a Welsh Congregationalist turned Episcopalian. Poyseor would become a respected leader in the Episcopal church of

Northern Michigan. Like Bishop Williams, he was concerned for those living in outposts away from the parish church, but unlike Williams and his chapel car, which was sided in Poyseor's town, Poyseor's mode of transportation to reach new missions was a dog sled.[29]

In the bishop's report in 1897, Williams tells that he made a thorough visitation of the diocese, although he does not mention the chapel car.

> Every mission and parish has been visited save Bessemer, Crystal Falls and Manistique. . . . My willingness to go whenever sent for has been largely because I was anxious to see what the result would be. In some respects the results were unsatisfactory, the expenses of visitation were not nearly met by the principal parishes, and in some cases it was evident that no attempt had been made to impress upon the people that they had a special duty to the Episcopate. I have traveled 300 miles, involving sleeping car travel as well, and received a collection of $2.41.[30]

Whether he did any of this traveling by chapel car is unknown.

The prevailing problem in Williams's diocese, as with other denominations across the country, was how to keep ministers. It did no good to start congregations if a pastor could not be kept on the field. Why did clergymen leave their parishes? The beleaguered bishop felt he knew why.

> Recently I received letters in which the signatures might have been interchanged without any particular difficulty. From one end of the diocese to the other at odd times, I get this story, "the church is $200, $300, or more, behind in my salary. At the end of the year a report is rendered showing that the salary is $1,000, or less, that the amount raised for the year is from $1,500 to $2,000, that the vestry had done thus and so with their money, and has given a total of $9.43 to the Board of Missions, and that the Easter Offering 'squared' them up with the

rector, who has paid his debts, and begins with the fiscal year another grocery bill. On Advent Sunday, he has to preach on the text 'Owe no man anything but to love one another.'" That is why clergymen leave parishes.[31]

Baptist car manager Boston Smith, who had four cars on the road, was keeping track of the Michigan Episcopal cars and stuck this news item on a page in one of his many scrapbooks about chapel car work. The date and source had been trimmed away, but the other articles on that page were dated May 21, 1898. "The Episcopalian chapel car, which has for some time stood idly in the railroad yards, will probably soon enter upon a new sphere of usefulness. Arrangements are being made to have it moved to Stephenson (an unorganized mission), in Memominee county where it will be used permanently for church purposes. The car is nicely fitted up for such use and will comfortably seat fifty people, though there is room for a large congregation."[32]

Clouds of war (the Spanish-American War) caused concern for the people of the Upper Peninsula in 1898, and Bishop Williams spoke to the matter.

> I notice that the Bishops generally are having something to say about the war. I would chiefly bid you to prayer on the subject. I believe it is a just war. But I am not sure that all of our people have as high motives as they should. If you can hear of great bloodshed unmoved, you are not yet in a proper frame of mind. Would God that people were as anxious to obey our laws, to live for our country as to die for her. God save the United States, new problems open before her. May her legislators have wisdom and virtue to face them. and the best sort of victories ever be ours.[33]

Little is known of the car's use after 1898. In *Marquette*, Bishop Williams reports on the condition of his diocese and says when naming church buildings and chapels, "Besides, we have our chapel car, which does duty now as a mission chapel, though it may soon begin its travels again."[34]

The chapel car was listed in the 1900 inventory of churches and facilities, and its service was also mentioned in a 1901 bishop's report as being in Chippewa County. In the journal of the fifth annual convention it was reported: Munising, Alger County. The Chapel Car. Rev. A. H. Brook, officiating to Oct. 1st. Baptisms, 2; services, 20; families, 8,[35] and it was listed again in the inventory of facilities.[36]

In Bishop Williams's address to the annual convention of the diocese he said, "In Chippewa County, the parish at the Sault is very prosperous and daily gaining . . . the Chapel Car is being used in a railroad suburb."[37] The car was still listed in the facilities' inventory.

Chapel Car Use, Interest Fades

At the beginning of the twentieth century, problems in the diocese included controversy over a recent ordination to the priesthood in New York State and ritual troubles in England over the meaning of the Ornaments Rubric and other matters of ritual, such as the use of altar lights, tabernacles, and colored vestments, as well as leavened or unleavened bread and watered-down communion wine. The lighting of tapers, how the Epistle and Gospel should be read, the use of incense, the use of the sign of the cross, and reserving the blessed sacrament for communion of the sick were also issues in American Episcopal circles. Many laymen in Bishop Williams's parish were troubled by what they called "the encroachment of the Romanizing party in the Church."

> I would point out, first, that it is in the nature of things that the attitude of a liturgical scholar should be somewhat different toward the prayer book than that of the layman, and second that there can be no permanent encroachment as long as we have a common prayer book. The prayer book is 350 years old, and it is still the prayer book. The principles which dictated the first compilation are still valid, and taking our present American standard, it met with very few changes after use of 100 years. It will not be changed again.[38]

It seems that the car did not begin its travels again, as the bishop had hoped. The bishop had a busy year in 1902, as the list of his journal entries shows:

Wednesday, Sept. 4, St. Paul's Cathedral, Marquette. Celebrated Holy Communion at Sixth Annual Convention of the Diocese of Marquette. Presided all day. Made annual address and also addressed missionary meeting in the evening.

Thursday, Sept. 19, Day of President McKinley's funeral. Gave three addresses, the first before the Marquette high school, the second at the Cathedral, and the third in the opera house at Newberry.

Thursday, Oct. 3, San Francisco, Grace Church. Took my seat in the House of Bishops: in attendance at General Convention until Oct. 17th.

Saturday, Oct. 19, San Mateo, attended cornerstone exercises of new Divinity school.

Sunday, Nov. 3, Denver, attended the Cathedral.

Sunday, Nov. 24, Preached and celebrated Holy Communion at St. James, Grosse Isle.

Thursday, Nov. 28, Thanksgiving Day, preached at the Cathedral.

Monday, Dec. 2, Preached in school house at Maple Ridge.

Nowhere in the records for that year was the chapel car mentioned. It was not in the inventory of services and facilities for that year or the next. In 1904, without his chapel car, Bishop Williams was still searching for ways to provide for "reverent and churchly services in places where we have no church buildings."

Schoolhouses, according to tradition and the spirit of the Ordinance of 1787, ought to be open to us, but the trustees often lock us out just as we seem to be going good. But even schoolrooms are often very inconvenient. While we are often tendered the use of other religious buildings, we cannot reciprocate and are obliged to conform our service to inconvenient arrangements. Besides this, our people are slow to build when they are sure of such hospitality, and I, myself in preaching in such places do not like to say the precise thing I think most necessary to the community.

Could we have, almost everywhere, a small, accessible room, we could turn it into an oratory, providing simple furniture, and have reverent celebrations of the Holy Communion. We could use such rooms whenever we pass by, which might be many times a year. If annexed to private houses, they could be easily cared for and bless their guardians with many opportunities for devotion.[39]

Bishop Williams had not given up on his desire to reach the outposts of his diocese. "Country work and railway work could, doubtless, be done by ministers in charge at Newberry, St. Ignace and the Sault, as well as many other points, but horse hire and railroad fare are serious considerations where there is but a bare living salary and butter selling at 28 and 32 cents, with crate eggs strictly not fresh, at 2 and one-half cents each and embalmed milk at the usual moderate price. One can't very well go out to a school-house or farm-house service once a month, baptize a baby, and pass the hat. If one did, the hat might come back — with 23 cents, if there were a good congregation and the sermon suited them."[40]

After the chapel car was sold, a boat was used to serve congregations in the eastern islands. In 1907 Williams had a small portable chapel built by the Mershon-Morley Company, a chapel "which will accommodate about fifty worshipers and furnish the rallying point for the erection of a permanent church." It was put together with bolts and wing nuts and could be set up easily in a lumbering camp and transported by horse and wagon and probably from time to time by train to its new location. Like the rail chapel car, it was eventually retired to another use.

In 1907 Williams announced in his convention address that mission work was now being accomplished "with some modern auxiliaries. The automobile is being tried out in the Delta County field. Initial expense was not much more than that of a good horse and driving equipment."[41]

From Work Car to Museum Piece

Sometime in 1902 or 1903, the chapel car was apparently sold by the diocese to the Munising Railroad. Father Page records that in 1905, now no longer the bishop's chapel car but a lowly work car on the railroad, the second Episcopal car of the Upper Peninsula was used on the East Branch on bridge and building maintenance service. An authorization for expenditure (AFE) dated August 1905 authorized adding side doors and air brakes. Later it went to the Lake Superior & Ishpeming (Munising Railway), where it was numbered XB111, used as a boarding car, and painted boxcar red. Pictures of the 45-foot-long and 9-foot-7-inch-wide car taken in the Marquette yard in 1961 show no side doors, the center window closed over on each side, knuckle couplers, and air brakes.

On a visit to the car in 1996, Father Page made several observations. "Wooden cross-wise braces in the clerestory, every six feet or so were quite unusual and were a style of reinforcing when first introduced in 1860–70s. The trucks appeared to be quite old, many wooden parts, and the wheels all had the wording, 'Pullman Palace Car Co' cast in the sides. One journal box cover had the initials of 'PPC' cast in; the other seven were blank. The last servicing by the LS&I was 'MQT 6-19-65 LS&I' stenciled on the air tank."[42]

After its retirement from the Lake Superior & Ishpeming (LS & I) in 1980, the car was bought by Clint Jones, along with some LS & I cabooses, and stored in the Duluth, South Shore & Atlantic's (DSS & A) West Yard in Marquette. In 1982 it was bought by potter Marilyn Mutch, who after considerable difficulty, had it moved to her studio located in the old freight house in Negaunee, close to the former passenger line of the DSS & A. Interior walls were removed, and the car was adapted as a gift shop.

Fig. 6.4 The second chapel car of the Diocese of Northern Michigan after it was sold to the Lake Superior and Ishpeming (Munising Railway), where it was numbered XB111 and used as a boarding car. (Courtesy of Father Herman Page)

Behind the stacks of wooden ducks and crafts and candles, a visitor could still see the metal plate outline of two opposite upper berths where Bishop Williams and other priests slept as they visited outposts where no other form of the Episcopal church could go.

The second Episcopal chapel car was purchased in 1998 by Jasper B. Sanfilippo of Elk Grove, Illinois. Sanfilippo is restoring the car and renovating it as a first-class private passenger day coach. It will become a part of the Victorian Palace Museum, which is known for its collections of beautifully, restored antique music machines as well as other antiques. The car will be used on a private rail line to carry guests visiting the estate for charitable and social events.

Lengthening the car by four feet, Sanfilippo plans to add wheel-cut, etched, and beveled glass. The woodwork will be mahogany in the high Victorian style, as will be the furnishings. All of the exterior siding will be replaced and made to look like the original, using clear poplar so as to make a high-quality painted surface. Sanfilippo anticipated the car's completion to be early 1999. "We are adhering very precisely to all exterior details. A plaque commemorating the car's history as the Episcopal Chapel Car of the Diocese of Northern Michigan will be on display on the car."

Fig. 6.5 The second Northern Michigan chapel car was used as a gift shop in Negaunee. The interior of the chapel car reflects its original use. The deep shelf on the left is where the upper berth was located. Another berth was at the opposite end of the car. The shelf under the clerestory windows was used for storage of the bishop's personal items. (Norman T. Taylor)

In his bishop's journal of the third annual convention of the Diocese of Marquette (Saturday, June 5, 1897), Bishop Williams wrote: "I was presented with a beautiful pectoral cross by the cathedral congregation."

In October 1996, Bishop Thomas K. Ray kindly shared the beauty of that same cross with the authors of this book. It has been passed down to bishops in the Episcopal Diocese of Northern Michigan — just as has the spirit of its owner, Bishop G. Mott Williams, the supporter of the two chapel cars of Northern Michigan.

> Jesus, lover of my soul,
> Let me to thy bosom fly,
> While the nearer waters roll,
> While the tempest still is high,
> Hide me, O my Saviour, hide,
> Till the storm of life is past;
> Safe into the haven guide,
> Oh, receive my soul at last.[43]

Notes

[1] "Fireman's Record Book," *The History of the Ontonagon Fire Department*, by Bruce H. Johanson, Web page, visit.ontonagon.com.

[2] Willis F. Dunbar, "The Northland and Its Railroads," *All Aboard: A History of Railroading in Michigan* (Grand Rapids: Eerdmans, 1969), 155.

[3] Ibid.

[4] Lois Prusok, ed., *The Church in Hiawathaland*, October 1995, 1 (centennial edition, Episcopal Diocese of Northern Michigan).

[5] Ibid.

[6] Ibid.

[7] Ibid.

[8] Ibid., D.

[9] "Church Extension in the Diocese of Marquette," *Marquette*, June 1900, n.p.; a publication of the Domestic and Foreign Missionary Society of the Protestant Episcopal Church in the United States of America at the Church Missions House, 281 Fourth Ave., N.Y.

[10] Ibid.

[11] Files of the Episcopal Diocese of Northern Michigan, Marquette.

[12] Ibid.

[13] Letter from Father Herman Page, Topeka, Kansas, to Norman and Wilma Taylor, March 28, 1996.

[14] Lois Prusok, "The Episcopal Diocese of Northern Michigan," *Marquette Monthly*, January 1996, 28.

[15] Journal of the Second Annual Convocation of the Missionary District of Northern Michigan, 14. The convocation was held in St. Paul's Church, Marquette, Wednesday, June 20, 1894.

[16] *The Standard*, printed in 1893, BSP, ABHS, VF.

[17] "Church Extension in the Diocese of Marquette," *Marquette*, June 1900.

[18] Letter from Father Herman Page, July 1, 1998, to Norman and Wilma Taylor.

[19] Ibid.

[20] Ibid.

[21] Report of the Primary Convention of the Diocese of Marquette, 1895–1896, 10.

[22] Report of the Primary Convention, 21.

[23] Third Annual Convocation Report of the Missionary District of Northern Michigan and Primary Convention, and the First Annual Convention of the Diocese of Marquette, 1895–1896, 33.

[24] Prusok, "The Episcopal Diocese of Northern Michigan," *Marquette Monthly*, January 1996, 28.

[25] Third Annual Convocation Report, 45–46.

[26] Robert Wilkins and Wynona Wilkins, *God Giveth the Increase: The History of the Episcopal Church in North Dakota* (Fargo: North Dakota Institute for Regional Studies, 1959), 33.

[27] Journal of the Second Annual Convention of the Diocese of Marquette, 1897, 8.

[28] Letter from Father Page, March 28, 1996.

[29] Prusok, *The Church in Hiawathaland*, F.

[30] Journal of the Second Annual Convention, 8–9.

[31] Journal of the Third Annual Convention of the Diocese of Marquette, 1898, 14.

[32] BSP, ABHS, VF, scrapbook.

[33] Journal of the Third Annual Convention, 20.

[34] "Church Extension in the Diocese of Northern Michigan," *Marquette*, June 1900.

[35] Journal of the Fifth Annual Convention of the Diocese of Marquette, 1900, 39.

[36] Ibid., 40.

[37] Journal of the Sixth Annual Convention of the Diocese of Marquette, 1901, 21. The convention was held at St. Paul's Church in Marquette.

[38] Journal of the Fourth Annual Convention of the Diocese of Marquette, 1899, 16–18.

[39] Journal of the Ninth Annual Convention of the Diocese of Marquette, 1904, 34, bishop's address.

[40] Journal of the Eleventh Annual Convention of the Diocese of Marquette, 1906, 12.

[41] Prusok, "The Episcopal Diocese of Northern Michigan," *Marquette Monthly*, January 1996, 28.

[42] Letter from Father Page, July 1, 1998.

[43] Hymn by Charles Wesley. "Jesus, Love of My Soul." Reprinted in *The Baptist Hymnal* (Valley Forge, Pa.: Judson Press, 1991), 499.

Baptist Car 2:
All Hail, *Emmanuel*

It was a miracle that chapel car *Emmanuel*, dedicated in Denver May 24, 1893, was completed. Times had changed since 1891. Because of the financial panic of 1893, Barney & Smith Car Works, like most of the nation's businesses, found itself in deep trouble.

Both E. J. Barney, a devoted Baptist layman, and Frederick Smith had reached middle age and had become very wealthy. Both wished to ease out of the responsibilities of the plant, having declining interest in the business inherited from their fathers. In May 1892, they sold the company to some Cincinnati investors for $4,500,000 but bought enough stock to control and retain their positions on the board of directors.[1] By April 1893, their fortunes had changed.

Between May and October of 1893 more than eight thousand businesses failed, and 156 railroads fell into the hands of receivers.[2] The Barney & Smith Car Company went public, hoping to broaden its base for survival. However, in 1893 the railroad trade journals reported that the company had orders for only 250 freight cars and 4 passenger cars, 7 percent of its normal production.[3] *Emmanuel* was one of those 4 passenger cars, and the company was thankful for the business.

The company built *Emmanuel* for approximately seventy-five hundred dollars, not at cost as they had done for *Evangel*; they could scarcely afford such charity. The contract price did not include the interior hardware and accessories, which the Dayton Manufacturing Company, an offspring of Barney & Smith, provided for a 25 percent discount.

Other items were donated: air-brake equipment from Westinghouse Air Brake Company, couplers from the Buhoup-Miller Company, a heater from William Baker, springs from Aaron French, one half of the wheels from Julius G. French, wheels from Paige, a sweeper from Bissell, a gong from Buckeye Bell Company, a range from Chicago Range Company, blankets from Oregon Woolen Mills, mats from Revere Rubber Company of Boston, and silverplate from the Meriden Britannia Company. The women of the First Baptist churches of San Francisco and Oakland furnished the car.

Barney & Smith called men back to work in order to complete this second Baptist car. Longer by ten feet than *Evangel*, reportedly with an exterior of catalpa wood, *Emmanuel* was divided into two sections, the chapel, with a seating capacity of 150, 94 in pews, 10 in study seats, 35 or more on camp stools; and the living quarters. Mr. Barney favored catalpa wood and planted large areas of the trees in Dayton for production purposes. *The Railroad Gazette* praised the use of catalpa wood, mentioning its strength and power in resisting decay, even in the most exposed situations, and its lightness and toughness. These qualities were in addition to having a beautiful grain and color, susceptible to an excellent finish as an ornamental wood.[4] Throughout the interior of the car were graceful touches of catalpa inlay.

In the chapel area, oak plywood pews with slightly curved seats and paneled backs were arranged to

Fig. 7.1 This interior view of chapel car *Emmanuel* shows the beauty of its construction. To the left of the minister, the Reverend B. B. Jacques, is the memorial door made in honor of the Reverend E. G. Wheeler, who was killed in a train accident on his way home to Minnesota while the chapel car was in the shop at Sacramento. (American Baptist Historical Society, Valley Forge)

accommodate three persons to the right of a narrow aisle and two to the left. About ninety persons could comfortably sit in the eighteen rows, but sometimes as many as 150 children crowded into the car for Sunday school. Racks for hymnals were attached to the back of pews. . . . Bibles, tracts, and evangelistic material were stored in boxes under the pews. The car also carried magazines, newspapers, and books that the workers loaned upon request when the car was sidetracked.

Ornate brass light fixtures hung from the ceiling the length of the car with an exquisitely fashioned brass chandelier in the middle. An acetylene gas plant lighted the lamps. Small panes of white glass, staggered in triplicate, stretched the length of the car on both sides just below the concave oak ceiling. Twelve vertical shaded windows on both sides of the car were topped with racks for clothing and supplies. The inside walls began a curved ascent with two highly varnished sections of oak plywood stretching between three rows of racks and the small horizontal skylights.

A horizontal strip of framed glass stretched above the oak-paneled wall tzg quarters bearing the words, "God is Love." The lectern was made of solid brass, its desk portion supported with outstretched wings of an eagle perched atop a globe. The base stood on four claws above which a square section bore the date of the car's dedication and the name donor Mrs. Mary E. Baker, New York City. A brass bell attached to the rear of the car was used to summon worshipers.[5]

The Empire Bronze Corporation of Franklin Park, Illinois, appraised the lectern in 1978 for three thousand dollars, noting that the eagle on the base would have had to be cast via the lost-wax process, a process that is most expensive and difficult to have executed in America. To the left of the lectern on a six-inch platform was an Estey reed organ, donated by Colonel J. J. Estey, president of Estey & Company of Brattleboro, Vermont, and a member of the First Baptist Church of Brattleboro. Estey, a brigadier general of the Vermont militia who had served as a state senator in 1882, had already given an organ to *Evangel* and would give organs to the next four cars.[6]

Wheelers Start on Pacific Coast

In 1893 immigrants by the thousands were pouring into Ellis Island, sometimes called the Island of Tears — tears of those who were sent back to their home country for one reason or another. Those who were privileged to stay headed west, wherever the rails would take them, to small towns and settlements. The two Baptist chapel cars were in much demand by state conventions, and the Wheelers were eager to start.

From May 1893 to November 1894, the Wheelers traveled to the coastal district of the Southern Pacific Railroad and then, in the winter months, down the San Joaquin Valley. The Reverend Wheeler reported, "The officers of the company have shown their appreciation by placing their waiting rooms at our disposal to conduct regular services among these railroad men."[7]

At Lindsay, a church was founded, and at Hanford, where they had first stopped in chapel car *Evangel* a year earlier, they held revival services.[8] In the summer of 1894, they found themselves on a ten-day mission in Melrose, California, where there was no church. Wheeler baptized seventeen in a huge baptistry built alongside the chapel car.[9]

At one terminal town, again they found no religious organization, but "saloons, gambling, Sunday horse racing, and the like held full sway." A three-week meeting resulted in the organization of a church, Sunday school, Baptist Young People's Union, and temperance society. The railroad company gave a lot, and the congregation was able to move out of a dance hall where they had been meeting.[10]

Boston Smith, the chapel car manager, was traveling across the country to raise money for more chapel cars when he and Mrs. Smith took a vacation to celebrate their anniversary. Their favorite spot was Northfield, Massachusetts, the assembly grounds run by evangelist Dwight L. Moody. While traveling there in the fall of 1894, the Smiths were on a train crossing Canada. "As we rode over that great railroad known as the Canadian Pacific, I noticed how many little towns we passed where there were no church buildings. In all of these places there were many boys and girls. Surely we ought to have a Chapel Car on this great line of railroad which runs through Canada clear to the Pacific. The Canadian brethren to whom I mentioned it, felt that it ought to be given attention at once."[11]

While Smith tried to promote a Canadian chapel car, the Wheelers headed for the Southwest, where Texas Baptists pleaded for them to come. In El Paso with *Emmanuel* in the spring of 1895, they established a mission on Main Street for the Chinese, a night school under the direction of the First Baptist Church, and an American Sunday school. They worked extensively among the railroad workers, although the Reverend Groat, the district missionary who had joined the Wheelers on *Emmanuel* for some of their Southwest trip, mentioned that Mr. Wheeler was not in the best of health.

Harry Hills, a local businessman turned evangelist, served as an assistant to the Wheelers. Wheeler had worked as a railroad telegraph operator earlier in his career. He said of Hills, "He proved very efficient in work and soul saving, especially with the railroad boys, for he himself had been a brakeman on the road and so knew their needs."[12]

The El Paso *Daily Herald* reported, "Mr. Wheeler is a forcible and interesting speaker, and his wife is a lovely and entertaining woman. The public are taking very kindly to them both and the car may be expected to be crowded at all of the services."[13]

In February 1895, at Roswell in New Mexico Territory, a small band of Baptists had started a two-room church under the leadership of missionary O. P. Miles. Miles was looking for ways to encourage the growth of the fledgling fellowship and heard through Smith that the chapel car was in El Paso. On April Fool's day, *Emmanuel* rolled into the Roswell depot on the new Pecos Valley Railroad in the midst of a terrible sandstorm.[14]

Methodists in town were stirring up a sandstorm of their own — revival-style — when *Emmanuel* arrived. It is likely that Miles needed the spark of the chapel car to offset the excitement created by evangelist Abe Mulkey. Mulkey was "turning Roswell upside down, as it were, and giving it a cleaning out, . . . with strong men with tears streaming down their faces."[15] Some of the 125 people saved in the meetings came to the Baptist church, but the Methodists were reaping the most rewards.

Wheeler was not about to take a backseat to anyone when it came to soul-saving. Twenty-three people come forward after the first meeting in *Emmanuel*, and sometime the next day Wheeler baptized a number in the river that flowed from the artesian springs that helped make the area famous. Since the chapel car could not hold all the crowd, meetings were moved to the New Mexico Military Institute. With his knack for public relations and perhaps a sense of one-upmanship over Mulkey, Wheeler took pictures of the baptism and had them displayed in the lobby of the prominent El Capitan Hotel.[16]

A week later, after considerable success in spite of the competition, the Wheelers and *Emmanuel* left for Eddy, now known as Carlsbad.[17] The two-year-old Eddy Baptist Church had strict rules of discipline. Deacons would withdraw the hand of fellowship from members who danced or drank, and attendance at all meetings was a must. If a member was absent without reason, a committee was sent to counsel with the absentee.[18]

The membership at Eddy was about to be tested. They would be expected to attend the meetings of the chapel car, and under normal circumstances there would have been no conflict. But who reached Eddy before *Emmanuel* did? Abe Mulkey, drawing huge crowds and turning Eddy "upside down, as it were, and giving it a cleaning out." He had left Roswell with a love offering of $250, which he said would be used for charity. The Wheelers must have felt it was not worth another revival battle, for they left Eddy after only a few meetings,[19] traveling down to Pecos, Texas, and then working their way west to Arizona's southern frontier.

Arizona Towns Wide Open for Ministry

Arizona border mining towns like Nogales, Naco, and Bisbee were an exotic challenge for the Wheelers in the late spring of 1895 — a different kind of lifestyle from their Midwestern backgrounds and Pacific Northwest experience. The Wheelers may have seen many outlandish and uncivilized places in their missionary travels, but Bisbee may have been the most noxious.

"In the 1890s Bisbee could accurately be described as a filthy, smelly, and smoke-filled camp," Carlos A. Schwantes writes in his study of the town. "Yet even if sulfur fumes filled the air of the enclosed valley, they were not universally regarded as evil. Some people believed that sulfur smoke was beneficial in protecting the community from the ravages of typhoid fever, and even if that assertion was suspect, few could argue that smelter stacks belching smoke were signs of prosperity."[20] Phelps Dodge Mining Corporation acquired the Atlanta Claim at Bisbee in 1881 and combined it with the rich Copper Queen in 1895.

Emmanuel came into Bisbee on the Arizona and Southeastern Railroad, completed in 1889 and connected with the Santa Fe Railroad at Fairbanks. During those early years of *Emmanuel*'s visit, Bisbee had fifty saloons, fifteen of which were located in Brewery Gulch, just across the sewer-filled road from the depot where the car was sided and held services. The area was "long the haunt of a floating population of tramp miners, gamblers, con artists, and prostitutes who congregated in its saloons."[21]

In 1895 the town was still wide open, although the devout and would-be devout among the mixture of Cornish, Welsh, Italian, Slavic, Mexican, and other immigrants[22] met at the old wooden schoolhouse or at the new adobe schoolhouse. The Union Church Association of Episcopalians, Methodists, Baptists, and Catholics comprised the spiritual presence in town and used those facilities.[23]

Along what would become Route 66, the chapel car made brief stops. At Holbrook, near the Petrified Forest, where there were no churches, the Wheelers met with a few faithful who had been gathering in homes for Sunday school. Well into the twentieth century Holbrook boasted that it was the only county seat in the United States that did not have a church. Some faithful met in homes and in the schoolhouse, but according to local legend, the cowboys and the Bucket of Blood Saloon controlled the town, and they did not want churches.[24]

The Bucket of Blood Saloon, known as the most popular meeting place in northeastern Arizona, ruled this section with an iron hand. The cowboys were frequently asked for a donation for the new church, but practically all of them refused. Judge Sapp, who headed the committee to organize a church, said that the influence behind this was considered to be the Bucket of Blood. The judge often laughed over an incident that occurred in 1913. One prominent citizen of Holbrook was a cowboy with plenty of money. Judge Sapp asked him for a donation.

"What's the money for?" he asked.

Judge Sapp told him it was for a church building so families could be induced to live in Holbrook.

"Who wants to bring women and children here anyway? This is a man's country," the cowboy said.

The judge explained that he brought his wife with him and expected to make his home here. He was told, "Take your wife back to Oklahoma" if he wanted her to go to church.[25]

At Holbrook no church would be established until 1913.[26] The Bucket of Blood had good reason to fear, for after the Methodists built the first church in town, the old saloon closed its doors.

At Flagstaff the Wheelers thrilled to views of the majestic, still snow-laden San Francisco Peaks and found a dozen Baptists, but only the Methodists and Presbyterians had churches. Incorporated a year earlier, the Atlantic and Pacific Railroad had set up Flagstaff in 1880 as a base site. Delay in construction of the Canyon Diablo Bridge keep the railroad crews at Flagstaff, where they spent their money on diversions such as gambling, drinking, and prostitution. Along with the railroad, the Arizona Lumber & Timber Company, the largest in the West, helped Flagstaff become a permanent town.

The town was still wild, dangerous, and crime-ridden when the Wheelers were sided near the depot for a series of meetings. Gambling was wide open, and not all the games were honest. Prostitution flourished in the saloons that were located across the street from the depot where *Emmanuel* held services. The "soiled doves" were a constant affront to the decent women of the town, and in addition to such vice, the saloons were the site of frequent fights, often punctuated with gunfire.[27]

At Williams, the end of a division of the Atlantic and Pacific road, "the car, which was sided just a few yards across from saloon row, was packed with sinners." At Hackberry, where there was no church or Sunday school, Indian children, "many of whom spoke good English," filled the pews. At Winslow the Wheelers probably used the Union Hall, where "anyone who wanted to preach" could preach. Although records are sketchy, it appears that *Emmanuel* was at Winslow before Sunday morning, April 8, when the roundhouse and shops of the Atlantic & Pacific Railroad burned to the ground along with eight of their finest engines.[28]

Wheeler Killed in Train Wreck

After returning to California in 1895 and stopping at Aromas and other California towns, the Wheelers placed the chapel car in the Sacramento shops for repairs. There they held services with the employees until the superintendent insisted they vacate the car so that it could be painted. In leaving *Emmanuel*, Wheeler said, "Good-bye, dear old chapel car, but not for long."

Two days later, on August 8, as they were on an Atlantic and Pacific train bound for home in Winona, Minnesota, Wheeler was killed in a washout near Grants Station, New Mexico. Washouts occur often in desert country, as the normally rare rains can come in heavy doses in winter and in late summer. Under the shadow of volcanic Mt. Taylor, Wheeler was thrown from the car when it went off the track. Mrs. Wheeler miraculously was not seriously injured.[29]

The young widow related the tragic moment to the delegates of the 1896 publication society convention: "a sudden shriek of the whistle, a sudden putting on of the brakes, a crash, and all was over, and my dear one had gone." Many in the audience wept as she quoted a poem.

> At last when our journeys up and down shall be done,
> And life's train shall in triumph to the terminus come;
> We shall sing as we're nearing heaven's portals so
>   bright,
> Praise the Lord! Hallelujah! All the signals are right![30]

After Wheeler's death, a memorial was placed in chapel car *Emmanuel* — a new upper half of the door that led into the living quarters bore his image in stained glass (*see fig. 7.1*). The lower half was paneled in the form of a Latin cross, commonly referred to as a Christian door.[31]

Hills, who had helped the Wheelers in El Paso, took temporary charge of the car until March 10, 1896. Hills explained why he left an office job to help out on the chapel car. "I felt I must go on the car. . . . I prayed over the matter, asking the Lord that if He had work for me on the car to open the way for me to go, and if not to show me what were his plans for me. I attended nearly every service while the car was in the city [El Paso], and the more I attended the more I felt called on that there was work for me on the car. I gave up my position and went on the car and from that time till we left the car at Sacramento on the fourth of last August, were the happiest days of my life."[32]

Harry Hills Carries On Work

Badly shaken by the death of his mentor and friend, Hills determined to keep the car in service until someone else could be appointed. At one point, the car had reached Montague, a junction town of the Southern Pacific and Yreka road and the supply point for the Shasta and Little Shasta valleys. Hills probably stopped at Mount Shasta City, Weed, and Hornbrook, also on the line, although records of his short tenure on the car are missing.

The Southern Pacific Railroad took the challenge in 1883 of constructing the steep grades over the Shasta Siskiyou Mountains between Portland and San Francisco that other railroads, like the California & Oregon, had shunned. The grades were so steep along that line that one station was aptly dubbed Pusher. Pusher, later changed to Dunsmuir, grew into an important rail center with a roundhouse and repair facility. Hills would have made a priority of having chapel car shop meetings in Dunsmuir.

An account in the *Siskiyou Pioneer* newspaper told of the superhuman exertion it took to grade the almost perpendicular bluffs *Emmanuel* would have traveled over, with Chinese as the major graders, outnumbering white workers twenty to one. Among the many dangers of completing the Southern Pacific line were Moduc Indians who called that territory home. They believed the Great Spirit lived at Mt. Shasta's summit in the bubbling hot springs.[33]

While holding successful meetings at Montague, Hills left the car and went up to Yreka to pick up express mail. Yreka was not on the Southern Pacific main line, and the Yreka Railroad had commenced operation several years earlier to connect Yreka with the main line at Montague. Even though there were already several churches in Yreka, started when gold was discovered in the spring of 1851,[34] Hills was invited to bring *Emmanuel* to town. Up the steep grade of Butcher Hill, for Yreka was at 2,630 elevation; past the Catholic, Chinese, and pioneer cemeteries, the hanging tree, over the slow-moving Shasta River, all the way into town, with majestic Mt. Shasta always in view. He did not have to pay a cent, compliments of the accommodating president of the Yreka Railroad.

While in the post office a man said, "Why don't you come here to Yreka with your wonderful car?"

Hills answered simply, "Because the conductor wants ten dollars to haul it over, and we have never paid that to any line of road for any cars."

Then the man said, "I am president, general manager, and passenger agent, traffic manager, and owner of this line; what do you want?"

Mr. Hills, much astonished, said, "Why sir, you are very kind; I would only like to have the car hauled here to your beautiful city."

"It shall be done," was the answer.

The next day the little engine coupled on to the car and started up a steep grade with many curves. After a time the car nearly stopped. Mr. Hills got out the pinch bar, and he and the conductor went behind and pushed and the car went to the top of the hill. Then the engine stopped for breath, the engineer blew the whistle and rang the bell, and so started for the town. The missionary caught the inspiration, raised the flag on the chapel car, and rang the church bell and brought all at the depot to welcome the car.[35]

Jacques Revisits Hell Towns

The Reverend and Mrs. B. B. Jacques from Massachusetts took over the work March 10, 1896, with Hills staying with them for a while, first witnessing to the railroad men in Los Angeles at the River Street Station. Towns visited in California by the Jacques and *Emmanuel* in 1896 read like a roll call of earlier whiskey hells, including Dutch Flat, Gold Run, Alta, and Truckee.

The Central Pacific Railroad reached Dutch Flat, then a gold-mine boom town in 1866, but the Methodists were already there, having built their church in 1861. When the chapel car arrived at the depot in Dutch Flat thirty years later, the Jacques would have noticed a large number of Chinese in town. The Chinese population in Dutch Flat at one time numbered two thousand. Many of the Chinese came during the building of the railroad and stayed on to maintain shops, become laborers, or try their hand at mining. The Masonic Hall (*fig. 7.2*), organized in 1856, was the center of town life, aside from the saloons and bootleg joints.[36] Churches would not come until later.

After services at nearby Gold Run, perched on the side of the Sierra Nevadas, the car went down grade to Truckee. Men had come to find their fortunes in gold at Truckee at midcentury. It was not until Theodore D. Judah decided to bring the Central Pacific Railroad over the Sierra Nevada via the Donner Pass, making the towns of Dutch Flat and Truckee important supply bases, that the town developed. When the Jacques came to hold services at Truckee, the town was more known for the account of the Donner Party, whose trek from Illinois to California in 1846 left most dead along the way. In ironic contrast, another center of local news was a fantasy icicle and ice palace created to be the center of winter carnivals.[37]

The Jacques spent sixteen days at Truckee, visiting homes and saloons, distributing gospel tracts, and having meetings. They saw that Truckee still had a hell-on-wheels side. "Although sin of every kind abounds, and the majority of the people seem so fully given to Satan, yet we found some of the most kind hearted I ever met. We had great children's meetings, and Protestant and Catholic alike flocked to the car." Owing to the large number who wished to be present at the farewell service, they accepted the pressing invitation of the Methodist pastor and held their meeting in his church. This proved to be a wise action, as the car could not have accommodated the people, about two hundred being present. The text was Matthew 7:21: "Not every one who says to me, 'Lord, Lord,' shall enter the kingdom of heaven, but he who does the will of my Father who is in heaven."[38]

Then *Emmanuel* crossed the Donner Pass to a little town just across the Nevada state line.

At present we are at Verdi, about ten miles from Reno, which is a beautiful little spot, nestled in among the mountains with a population of 300. As we looked over the place, we found three saloons, shops of nearly every kind, a nice school house, but no church, and on inquiry learned that there was no religious service in the place at all, except as a Catholic priest came in a few times a year. . . . The Catholic element is quite strong but we hope to organize a Sunday school and also establish a preaching station to be supplied at least once a month by the Baptist Church at Reno.[39]

The Jacques were distressed to see "boys and girls running wild on Sunday," and they quickly organized a Sunday school the last week of September 1896.

From Verdi the car went on to Reno, where the only Baptist church in Nevada was located, and the missionaries had services twice a day for two weeks. Pastor of the Reno church was W. C. Driver, who would later become a chapel car missionary.

Reno was already known for its wide-open gambling. Just a few months earlier a thirty-three-year-old San Francisco mechanic created the first slot machine, a small black machine he named the Liberty Bell. It paid off in nickels.[40] The Liberty Bell would be followed by many other versions of its kind.

Fig. 7.2 In most towns visited by the chapel cars, lodges, such as the Masonic Lodge, were built before churches were. This was the case in Dutch Flat, California, where the Masonic Lodge was organized May 8, 1896, several years before the first church in town. The Reverend and Mrs. Jacques brought the chapel car to Dutch Flat in the fall of 1896. (Norman T. Taylor)

The Reverend N. L. Freeman, pastor of the Reno church, praised the work of the chapel car. "To say that I am won over on the side of chapel car work does not express my feelings nor my convictions. The work, the car, the workers must be met, seen, felt, to fully realize the method of thus spreading the gospel to be of God. If I ever had any doubts of the advisability of such methods, they are forever banished."[41]

Reno had hoped to be the maintenance base for the Central Pacific Railroad but was disappointed when Wadsworth, "a dinky town 15 miles down the line," received that honor. Wadsworth's roundhouse was busy from its founding, and it remained one of the most important maintenance centers in Nevada for the next forty years. One of the jokes of the day

was that Reno was scheduled to be folded up and shipped by flatcar to Wadsworth. That joke eventually came true in 1904, but it was Wadsworth, not Reno, that was packaged up and shipped away to another new town, Sparks.[42]

Jacques baptized many in the waters of the Truckee River at Wadsworth, and November 7, 1896, the second Baptist church in Nevada was organized.

When the Southern Pacific Railroad (Central Pacific) shops were moved from Wadsworth to Sparks, the Baptist chapel was also moved, with the rest of the town, and reorganized under the name of Emmanuel Baptist Church of Sparks. It was the first church in Sparks, and Governor John Sparks, for whom the town was named, gave a beautiful glass window to

Fig. 7.3 In 1896 a group of townspeople in Towles, California, gather by the chapel car, where a banner announces the meetings. (American Baptist Historical Society, Valley Forge)

the church. That window still exists in the new building.[43]

At Lovelock, meetings were held in "a town largely given over to the saloon element,"[44] and at Winnemucca, Jacques spoke to six hundred people on the river banks during a baptismal service.[45] Nevada journalist Jim Hulse wrote that when Nevada was young, it had little time for God.

Unlike Utah, which was carved from the desert wilderness by the devout Mormons, and California, which in the beginning was the dominion of God-fearing Spanish missionaries, Nevada was spawned by rowdy, irreverent men who owed their allegiance to mammon. . . . A hundred Nevada ghost towns have, among their forgotten streets and shadows, the ashes of burned churches or the ruin of temporary meeting houses. The forces which helped to kill so many tiny religious movements in their infancy had something to do with the creation of the present Nevada. The hard life and commercially unattractive land which discouraged the early churchmen, plus the get-rich-quick spirit of the railroaders and miners, helped to build the present society which gives haven to gamblers.[46]

It had been difficult for Baptists to organize, build, and survive in Nevada, and the coming of chapel car *Emmanuel* was a boost. The Jacques visited the Nevada towns again in the spring of 1897, and then went to Towles, California. Among the crags and peaks of the Sierras, the Jacques built a church on land given by the Towles brothers, who owned a large lumber business.[47] They then traveled to Clipper Gap, where the candidates "who went down into the pure running water as it flowed through the orchard preached a greater sermon to the people assembled than words could ever do."[48]

At Sacramento, day by day the car was filled with men from the Southern Pacific shops. In October Mrs. Jacques became ill enough to be hospitalized in San Francisco but was well enough to continue on to Willows, Cottonwood, and north, where on Thanksgiving Day they held services for everyone in Redding.

Mrs. Jacques in Failing Health

Across the state line in Oregon, they stopped at Cottage Grove, where the Wheelers had organized a church that had failed. Then they went down the line to Creswell, Eugene, Irving, Riddles, Shedds, Corvallis, Fort Stevens, with the army; Eugene, Astoria, Knappa on the Columbia River, Wells Station, and many others.

Emmanuel reached Ashland on December 3, 1897. At Talent the Jacques found a unique mixture of beliefs. Jacques explained, "Nearly everything is represented, from Baptist down to Unitarians, infidels and socialists, yet God gave victory." Their next stop was Medford, where it was ice-breaking time, so those who wanted to be baptized had to wait until warmer weather and warmer water. At Tolo, the Jacques found themselves out in the woods, with only a half dozen houses in sight, but they managed to start a Sunday school.

In February of 1898, *Emmanuel* came into Grants Pass, along the rocky Rogue River where gold had been discovered in 1851. Jacques hoped to encourage the Baptists there who had seen one building burn to the ground.[49] As it would happen, their new building would also burn down in 1902.[50] Mrs. Jacques's health broke down at Grants Pass, as it had on previous occasions. A physician was called in, and he told her that if she wanted to live, she must leave the work. "No one can tell the struggle it was for her to step out and say 'good-bye' to the dear car for a time at least, but weakness compelled her to do it, and thus I was left alone," her disheartened husband wrote.

Jacques was joined in the work by Wilfred Dimock at Merlin, who would be on the car for eight and one-half months. At Dillard, where they stayed two weeks, interest did not abate. One night, Jacques related, as the meeting was going on, a carload of lumber was run in on the track and removed to ground donated by the general manager, ready for a church to be built.

In one Oregon town, a Methodist minister came to the meetings in the car and said, "This is the best thing I ever saw. I am going to petition the Methodist conference to build me a chapel car."[51] No record has been found that the Methodists ever built such a car.

Back in California in December 1899, Mrs. Jacques joined her husband for a brief time, and the Jacques established a church at Camarillo. "We have never seen souls so stirred," a member wrote. The *Oxnard Courier* reported:

> The car "Emmanuel" is a pillar of cloud by day and a pillar of fire by night, to lead lost souls wandering in Egyptian darkness to the feet of the Lord. On week days the daytime services are confined to young folks, but as the shades of night fall, the twinkling lights from many windows and the musical intonations from the chapel bell of the car proclaim the welcome to partake of the joy of the Redeemer extended to rich and poor alike, in full measure, without money and without price. The chapel car has not been large enough to accommodate the crowd; so long as the interest in the services lasts and people gather to worship in the car, it will remain with us. . . .[52]

On their way back to Los Angeles, Jacques reported: "Last Saturday, we held a train service. Among those who came in were four railroad officials from the Union Pacific and the Chicago and Northwestern roads. They were just delighted with the work and expressed much sympathy for it. I do not think that *Emmanuel* was ever in better favor with the railroads than now."[53]

Along with organizing the Baptist church in Pasadena and reaching several other California towns, Jacques and Thomas Moffatt, who had come to help in Mrs. Jacques's absence, attended the Arizona Baptist Convention in Tempe in April 1901. On the return trip, they visited Guadalupe, Mexico, one of the few times a chapel car crossed a United States border.

Worried about his wife, whose health had not improved, Jacques left chapel car service in the fall of 1903 for the pastorate of the Baptist church in Santa Clara, California, one of their earlier chapel car stops. This permitted them to have a more normal family life with their two daughters, who had been left in the care of relatives much of the time, and for Mrs. Jacques to regain her health. Their service on chapel car *Emmanuel* was without blemish or complaint.

Hermistons Bring New Approach

A new, quite aggressive approach to rail evangelism came to *Emmanuel* with the appointment of the Reverend E. R. Hermiston and his wife to the car. The Hermistons, and at times their daughter Marjorie, were on the car from October 1903 to July 1915. Hermiston frequently referred to and took great pride in his years as a baseball player with the International League, founded in 1877 as one of the first minor leagues. It was acknowledged that several of its teams were as good as or better than some in the National League.[54]

> I can understand some things in my own life. I left the Mills Academy in my sophomore year to join the baseball boys. I traveled two years with the International League, and those the canker-worm has eaten. Mother never ceased to pray for me, and the night I returned home she put her arms around my neck and said: "My boy, I gave you to God when you were an infant child and I know some day that you are going to be converted and preach the gospel." At that time I wept over my sins and I believed I was ordained for the chapel-car work." Hermiston remembered this verse, "I thought little of it then, Though memory touched my heart, For her whose love sought from above, For me the better part."[55]

Like his contemporary and hero, evangelist Billy Sunday, who played for Chicago and Pittsburgh from 1883 to 1890, Hermiston was not well educated. However, he had a knack for evangelistic preaching and a zest for reaching the unsaved, especially railroad men. "I spoke to one thousand men in the railroad shops last summer, and they [shop managers] gave one half hour of their time without docking the men. I feel that I am pastor to four million railroad men."[56]

Hermiston began his work on *Emmanuel* in Oregon in March 1903. Reports of the Oregon Baptist State Convention missionary in 1901 indicated that the moral condition in many parts of the state were sad indeed. ". . . the wickedness and destitution appalling. Saloons, gambling dens, houses of ill-fame, and other abominations have taken root in this fertile soil, and are bringing forth a dire harvest of corruption and death. In some of these towns there is no religious work of any kind."[57]

Hermiston's first stop was in Tallman, Oregon; then he went to Halsey and Portland before making a run to Nevada to revisit and revive the churches started by Jacques. From Red Bluff, California, in 1905, he had the audacity to write to John D. Rockefeller and ask for help with transportation problems with *Emmanuel*. That was his first mistake. Hermiston's superiors at the publication society were dismayed that he had done so. His second mistake was to misspell Rockefeller's name in the inside address. Although the letter was typed, it had many errors, and Hermiston had made crossouts (in the following text they are indicated by brackets).

John D. Rockafellow
Cleveland, Ohio
Red. Bluff. Cal. 2.15.05.
Dear Sir: —

I m sure [you] will be delighted to here about the work of Chapel Car Emmanual. Our trip north has been a continual revival and over one hundred have been baptised into this association as a result of the car work and this is one of the most needy [fields] in the State. At this place a great work is in progress and [H]arry [M]ainard the chapion Puglist has been converted, and closed his saloon He had one of the finest in the place and he is working to save others, Four other saloon men have been in our meetings. Untold good is being done among the railroad men 30 have been baptised here and two are railroad men.

I write to say that a [p]haroh that knows not Joseph had come into power on the Southern Pacific. R. R. And we have to pay half fare for the transportation of the car. And I thought you might have influence in the matter to get us free transportation; I have great confidence that you will do all you can in this matter and it will confer a lasting blessing on these [places] that need the work so much.

Yours after the lost. ER Hermiston[58]

There is no evidence that Rockefeller responded to the letter.

The San Francisco Examiner gave the following account of the conversion of the fighter Harry Maynard that Hermiston referred to in the Rockefeller letter.

Harry Maynard, the once famous San Francisco prize fighter had found religion and he has closed his saloon at Red Bluff, and it would take a burglar to break in through the barred doors. The Maynard–Satan (Devil) bout took place in Red Bluff. The pair had met before many times and Satan had always won so easily that it looked like a lay down. This time Harry pulled himself together and went after his old enemy at the tap of the gong. The fight lasted for days and all of the time Harry was ducking and countering and sidestepping and occasionally going down for the count but always coming back until Satan got so weary of his job that he jumped out of the ring and the referee gave the decision to Harry.[59]

After two years of Christian witness, many times speaking on *Emmanuel*, Maynard died. Just before he died, he called to his friends and asked them to pray and sing. "The end is near," he said. "I have one request. Tell Brother Hermiston that I am so glad that he brought the old chapel car 'Emmanuel' to Red Bluff."[60]

Fig. 7.4 Frequently the chapel car workers would speak to large crowds at the shops where the cars were being serviced. This meeting in the locomotive shop at Sacramento shows the Reverend and Mrs. Hermiston and their daughter, Marjorie, leading a service. Note the trumpet player near the platform. (American Baptist Historical Society, Valley Forge)

Hermiston Leaves Mark in Oregon

Hermiston tells of the naming of the Oregon town whose name he shared. "When I arrived at Hermiston, Oregon [March 18, 1907], they were quarreling about the name of the town and as I was the only neutral person in town — I was on the railroad — they accepted my name, and we built a monument of chapel-car work, the Hermiston Baptist Church. The entire cost was five thousand dollars." Other versions verify that Hermiston had nothing to do with the town's name, that it was chosen from a novel, *Weir of Hermiston*, by Robert Louis Stevenson.[61] But this was Hermiston's version.

The tragic death of a local saloon girl put both the chapel car Hermiston and the town of Hermiston in the local news. One evening after the service an attractive brunette named Carolyn Ross asked to talk with Hermiston. The talk lasted until midnight. She said that she was a saloon girl from Kansas City and could sing and dance and mix with the customers. Her life was shattered, however, when one night a cowboy made an advance toward her. Unable to fight him off, she pulled his gun from his holster and shot him. "From that time on I've just been traveling from one place to another," she explained.

Hermiston found Carolyn a place to stay, and to show her gratitude, she sang at chapel car services for a time. But after living the life of a saloon girl since she was eighteen, she found the village of Hermiston too quiet for her. Within a month she left. After thanking Hermiston for his help, she walked out of *Emmanuel*. Despondent over her inability to make a respectable life for herself, she went to her room and wrote a note to Hermiston, explaining that she was sorry for all the bad things she had done. A postscript read: "A bad person doesn't deserve good people." As she left town, she was killed in a buggy accident. Hermiston preached her funeral sermon, which drew crowds of people.[62]

Idaho Towns, Churches Growing

To the east, Idaho was growing rapidly with the new rail lines crossing the state. The Hermistons took *Emmanuel* on the Idaho Southern Railroad to Jerome. "Only a few months ago it was all sagebrush," Hermiston wrote, "and now the roar of commerce and the click of the telegraph and the whistle of the locomotive have driven out the coyote and jack rabbit and made way for the Chapel Car in the winning of the west."[63]

Hermiston, who would become known for his colorful stories, some true and some truth-stretched, told of the cowboy in Idaho who complained about finding *Emmanuel* in an unexpected spot on a deserted siding. "I am going to leave this country, as I think it is ruined, for you cannot go half a mile without running into a church or a barbed-wire fence."[64]

Across southern Idaho, *Emmanuel* traveled on the Minidoka & Southwestern branch of the Oregon Short Line, visiting towns with churches and more that were without, at least without a Baptist church. At Caldwell, when Hermiston stopped, there had been one church — a Baptist church — and people of all denominations gathered in it. With the growth of the town, other denominations started their own churches, taking many of the members from the Baptist church. Mrs. A. E. Gipson commented on the situation at the sixty-sixth anniversary of the church. "They [the Christians] organized their own church in 1892 and when they left us, taking with them at least half of the Sunday School scholars, it was a time of deep discouragement to the weakened Baptist church."[65]

The Baptist church in Pocatello was established some years after the Utah and Northern Railroad came across the state line in 1877 and through the town. The Congregationalists had built the first church in town, with the first religious service held February 24, 1888.

One Presbyterian missionary from New York came to the southern Idaho valley at Hailey and was politely asked to leave. "Some of the boys in town appointed a Committee to wait upon him and request him to leave. . . . They stated their conviction that if a church were started here, it would seriously retard the growth of the town, if not kill it altogether. But Pratt said that he would gladly oblige the boys but he had been sent here by his church to perform what he considered a sacred duty . . . and would remain until he had performed that duty. They offered him a purse of $500 if he would leave," but he refused.[66]

Despite the efforts of the Reverend Dwight Spencer of the Home Mission Society to start churches in southern Idaho, the Baptists did not establish a strong base until the late 1880s. In Pocatello in 1909, working in harmony with the Railroad Y, Hermiston held meetings in the largest hall in the city. Being a fan of Billy Sunday, it is likely he would have

Fig. 7.5 At Medford, Oregon, these children, some holding leaflets given them by the missionaries, gather around the chapel car. (American Baptist Historical Society, Valley Forge)

traveled to Spokane, Washington, to hear Sunday preach on Christmas Day in 1908.

More than ten thousand people crowded into the tent at Spokane with hundreds more trying to get in the door. "Billy told colorful stories as he denounced millionaires, college graduates and money-hungry churches. Working up a loud and passionate closing, Billy thundered, 'When I die, have the butcher take my hide and tan it, make it into drumheads and let men go up and down the land beating the drums against the Devil.'"[67]

Hermiston, taking his lead from Billy Sunday, must have thundered and pounded his Bible at Pocatello, as he reported, "There was a large number of converts and one-fifth of them were railroad men. The entire city was moved, the gambling dens were closed, the saloons were put out of business, and the young men filled the churches."[68]

Railroad Men and Wicked Towns

At the Hillyard shops outside Spokane, Mrs. Hermiston spoke to six hundred men who, according to reports, were much moved by her message. The chapel cars would spend much time at the Great Northern Railroad Hillyard shops during their tenure in the Northwest. Named after the president of the Great Northern, James Jerome "Jim" Hill, the shops, built in 1892, were among the largest in the nation, drawing men from all over to work on the railroad.[69]

During the summer of 1911, *Emmanuel* was busy in Washington State. But when the summer's heat turned the chapel car into an oven, the Hermistons headed for the mountains and held meetings at Kittitas, Ellenburg, and Cle Elum. When *Emmanuel* came into Cle Elum in 1911, two railroads shared the town: the Great Northern and the Chicago Milwaukee and St. Paul. The CM & St. Paul came through town in 1908 and constructed a depot, roundhouse and ice house that employed many men, along with coal and lumber businesses. The town's population was diverse. Italians, Croats, Poles, and Slovaks heard of Cle Elum and the coal mines and railroads, and they came by the hundreds.[70]

The first religious services in town were held in places like Tillman Hall, the Reed Hotel dining room, a log cabin, and the Cle Elum school, but by 1899 the Baptists had the distinction of being one of the first organized churches in the city.[71] By 1904 the Presbyterians, Methodists, Catholics, and Free Methodists had also established churches. A history of the town records that it was not uncommon for people from other denominations to attend different churches, throw peanuts at the ministers, and boo them. That behavior seemed better suited for the amateur-night shows at the opera house, which was featuring the music of the Chudley-Kennedy five-piece union orchestra[72] when Hermiston was in town. Hermiston, however, saw more wickedness than a five-piece dance band.

At Cle Elum we had the meetings in the mining town and the car was side-tracked right in the slums, and it

Fig. 7.6 Railroad workers, from the young boy in the back row to the very old gentleman in the front, gather with several officials after attending a service in *Emmanuel*. The worker in the center is holding a Bible given to him by the missionaries. (American Baptist Historical Society, Valley Forge)

was certainly a wicked place. I do not believe that we were ever in a place where things were so wide open. In some respects it was worse than in the gold fields of Nevada. Any hour of the night we would wake up and hear them singing their Bacchanalian songs and sometimes fighting.

They told us when we arrived it was no use to try to hold services as the people did not go to church. But, the chapel car was a little different. They came and filled the car night after night. The lumber jacks gave my little girl money to sing for them. On Sunday nights the saloon men and publicans and sinners crowded the car and some women from the red-light district came in.[73]

Hermiston's Behavior Dismays Bosses

Hermiston had the knack of going wherever he wanted to go, whenever he wanted to go there, and this caused problems with his superiors and the state missionaries with whom he was supposed to be cooperating. In October 1911, George White, his boss in the western district, lost him again. Hermiston had left Washongal, Washington, without notice, and the people at Washongal were angry. They had wanted the chapel car to remain there to help in defusing attempts of the Campbellites in town to divide their church. White, exasperated, wrote to his boss, "I find it impossible to keep track of him [Hermiston] . . . running about, regardless of others. No one knows where he is except the station agent, and he told me several places the car had visited along the line."[74]

Ignoring the controversy surrounding his erratic behavior, Hermiston, at Camus now, wrote to White boasting about his success at Goldendale, where he was not to have gone. Great crowds came to the depot when *Emmanuel* was getting ready to depart; they sang and wept and shouted and cheered. How much of that description was exaggerated, it would be hard to tell, although Hermiston's personality and preaching style did seem to have dramatic effects on people.

As White had requested, and for once on time, Hermiston sent an inventory of the car, explaining "the oil stove is a

goner and the silver cornet was stolen a year ago." The items listed, in his own spelling, were an Edison Phonograph with records, $25.00, Copying machine, $15.00, Ten dollars worth of Silverware, Five dollars worth of dishes, Twenty dollars worth of Bedding, Ice cream freezer and Coal scoop shovel, Hand saw, Ax, Sledgehammer, ice forks, carpet beater; 3 Folding chairs One rocking chair & One Study chair, covering for vestibule, Organ, Pulpit, Organ chair, Flag pole, 2 box lamp chiminies, Paper punching machine, and some oil cans.[75]

This chapel car list was an interesting contrast to that of fellow publication society colporter H. P. Anderson and his wagon working in Moab, Utah, during the same time period: wagon, $155, Two horses $335, Set of harness $50, Horse blankets and bed blanket $18, Whip, feed bags, curry comb and brush $4.50, Lantern, oil can and stove $3.40, and Trunks and grips $25.[76]

Even though Hermiston was told by White not to go to Vancouver, Washington, Hermiston wrote that he was going there anyway. His cheery approach had developed a sharp edge. "Gypsy Smith [another evangelist in the mold of Billy Sunday] is there. It is a good railroad center and we have a right to go."[77]

Not too many things seemed to unnerve Hermiston, but the rumor of another chapel car on the road gave him quite a scare while he was at Brawley, California. On January 20, 1912, he hurriedly scribbled another note, which was obviously not edited by Mrs. Hermiston, to White. "I learn that the Nazerene Church has put a Chapel Car on the Road and that they are headed for this Valley and I wish you would find out and see if we cannot work together and not cover the same Territory at the same time. There headquarters is in Los Angeles, Calif. We are well. Another man made a decision last night and seemed to be converted. I am going to leave here Monday, as I want to get to Holtville before the other Car as we can build a Church there."[78]

On February 2, a bit relieved, he wrote White again, "I am glad to learn through Watson that the Nazerine People have no Chapel Car and dont intend to put one on it was false report."

Hermiston Not Happy in Arizona

In October 1912, chapel car *Emmanuel* returned to Arizona, where it had last been with the Wheelers in 1895. The years from 1900 to 1917 were difficult times for Arizona Baptists because of the move toward modernism on the part of some in the Northern Baptist leadership and growing Landmark conservatism. Publication society leaders thought that the irrepressible yet irresistible Hermiston might be able to bring some spark to the struggling churches. At the convention in 1912, the Arizona board, in the midst of considerable dissent, voted to remain with the Northern Baptist Convention.

Hermiston, with the humor that helped him survive many chapel car hardships when other less jovial men weakened, wrote another unedited note to White from Yuma. "We are now at Yuma and things are down to the bottom and it looks like a wicked town and it makes me think of what the little girl said when her people came to Ariz. she said 'good Bye God' we are going to Ariz. I hope it will not be that bad. It is very hot here and yet they say it is fine now. If this is fine I dont know what it is when it is hot. Gen Sherden [Sheridan], said if he had a Ranch in Yuma and one in Hades he would rent the one in Yuma and live on the other."[79]

In spite of his poke at Yuma, the meeting there was a "great revival," and Brother McCourtney, the state missionary, said "it was the best meeting he had seen in the state."[80] Hermiston said he had been misinformed about Yuma. "While Yuma has been described as a wicked and godless place of 4,000 people, yet a change has come with the entrance of so many new people. To explain this, it should be said that the Government has spent over eight millions of dollars here and the railroad two million more, and most of it had passed through the saloons. But there is a new era of prosperity on in this country, and I think without doubt it will be one of the big towns of the state."

There were a large number of United States soldiers in Yuma, as it was a border town, and because of the Mexican trouble, they had to be on guard. Some of the soldiers attended the services in the car and "were caught in the gospel net," as Hermiston reported, and the pastor baptized eight of the young men.[81]

On November 1, 1912, the chapel car arrived in Safford, a strong Mormon town. The *Graham Guardian* reported the arrival of *Emmanuel* and the Hermistons, who were given a nice reception by church members.[82] The chapel car did not receive quite as nice a reception from the station master. There was no siding for the chapel car and no passing track. This was the first time this had happened to Hermiston.

> We were afraid we would have to leave. Then the railroad people did the magnanimous thing and built us a spur free of cost. Say what you will about the railroad corporations, they have certainly treated the chapel cars kindly. Then there was a good deal of excitement about politics which engrossed the men. Added to that a circus came to town and the Mormons had a big dance to put the finishing touches on the week's celebration. But we preached the simple gospel and it proved to be the power of God unto salvation to the Mormon as well as to the Gentile.[83]

In spite of the opposition of the Mormons, crowds filled the car every evening, according to the newspaper. "All Christian people are taking a part in the work. . . . Expect large service Sunday. There will be a meeting for the men in the Safford Theater on Main Street Sunday at 3 p.m."[84] Before leaving, Hermiston reported that he started a movement to have all the evangelical churches work with the Baptist people and make one strong Gentile church.

Sick from the effects of Arizona water and tired from the journey, Hermiston wrote from Globe on November 25 that they had a great closing climax at Safford and a fine baptismal service. Twenty-five or more people made decisions, and they doubled the membership.[85]

Globe, sandwiched between the Apache and Pinal mountains, called itself the Capital City of the County with the Copper Bottom, although originally men came to mine silver, not copper, in its red mountains. In the early 1900s Globe was a Wild West metropolis of twenty thousand, boasting fifty dance halls and saloons that never closed. In one week, the operator of a North Broad Street soft-drink stand witnessed three murders. Miners, from their new union hall, gaped while spreeing cowboys herded a wild-eyed steer through the plate-glass window of a luxury gambling house,[86] but in spite of the wildness, there were those in Globe who wanted more of a religious influence in town — they wanted a Baptist church.

The Globe *Silver Belt* reported Sunday, December 1, 1912, that Hermiston preached in the morning and at the evening service. Mrs. Hermiston "will deliver one of her best addresses to parents on 'Mother, Home and Heaven.' Mr. Hermiston will sing the beautiful solo, 'Tell Mother I Will Be There.'" The following Sunday, the Hermistons followed a similar routine in services, and then the *Silver Belt* announced on December 11 that the couple were leaving Globe for other points in Arizona.

The *Silver Belt* reported January 23, 1913, that the chapel car was now in Miami, where a church was under construction on land donated by Inspiration Copper Mining Company. Much progress had been made in the development of the Inspiration Company: construction of a mill and power plant, water supplies secured, one hundred employee houses built, a lodging house and a boarding house provided, and doctors and a company hospital in town.[87] A Presbyterian church had been started in 1911 in Miami, and the Baptists, who had been meeting in the schoolhouse, would boast the second church in town.

All the meetings were held in the car, and the car and Mrs. Hermiston, who preached one evening on "Shall We Know Each Other in Heaven?" were admired by a local journalist.

Mrs. Hermiston has contributed much toward the success of the meetings. She is a forceful and eloquent

speaker and has been instrumental in the work of conversion. The car in which the services are conducted is arranged conveniently and is comfortable in every respect. The combination chapel and missionary car is novel in its self and an object of attraction.[88]

Just as *Emmanuel* was getting ready to leave the Globe/Miami area, the Presbyterians took up the revival spirit where the Baptists left off with another full week of evangelistic services.[89] In this rich, open-pit copper-mining country, the devil was getting his due.

Troubles with Rail Laws, Revolutionaries

The immediate concern, beside the heat, as Hermiston wrote from Naco on the border on May 12, 1913, was that the Southern Pacific might not carry the car back to

Fig. 7.7 The open-pit copper-mining towns of Douglas, Bisbee, Miami, Globe, and Morenci welcomed the coming of *Emmanuel* and the Hermistons to town, and churches were organized and strengthened by these visits. This is a view of the mines near Morenci, which are still active. (Greenlee County Historical Society, Clifton, Arizona)

California. To get back on the line, they would have to put on several new appliances and add a steel platform with vestibule ends and steam connections. Hermiston had applied to the shops at El Paso and hoped to hear that they would take the car. To White he wrote, "I will be glad to hear from you and if you will not be down to say what to do as it would be a bad blow to be thrown off the S.P."[90]

Still on the border at Naco May 15, where he was having good meetings, Hermiston sent his report for the year. "For the ten years my books show 63000 miles traveled, 4750 meetings held, 4490 sermons preached, 70000 tracts distributed, 3305 professed converts, 1852 baptisms, 23 churches organized, reorganized, and built. I have covered eight states in ten years. The churches built cost from five hundred to ten thousand. I have assisted in raisin thirty thousand dollers at twelve different dedications aside from the special car work. We have seen the desire of our heart in the salvation of the west."[91]

The prayers offered in the churches of Douglas and Agua Prieta across the border on Easter morning of 1911 had special significance. The residents of Douglas were alarmed over the coming battle for Agua Prieta, and they had good reason to be. Border battles continued about the time Hermiston brought *Emmanuel* into town.

When the Hermistons arrived at the copper mining town of Douglas in June 1913, the Baptists were worshiping in a fine church on Church Square, once listed in *Ripley's Believe It or Not* as being the only place in the world where four churches were located on the same block.[92] The congregation was no longer meeting in the ragged tent where the church began in 1902 and where a baptistry had been dug in the ground inside the tent and a curtain hung up around it.[93]

The chapel car stayed only ten days. It was not safe in Douglas for man or chapel car, and it would not be for a number of years to come. The Mexican revolutionary Pancho Villa sent out a proclamation in October 1915. "I wish you would request every man, woman, and child in Douglas to remain off the streets and in their homes in the event of fighting across the border. Tell them to get behind adobe walls and not trust wooden ones. The penetration of a high power rifle ball is too great for any reliance to be placed on wood."[94]

There was another reason *Emmanuel* hurried out of town. Hermiston did not feel well. He and "the missus" had taken a room at the elegant Hotel Gadsden to cool off and rest a bit. His note to White May 23, on the stationery of the hotel where Pancho Villa would soon ride up the marble stairs on his horse, scrawled, "I am not well and dont feel a bit good it is the heat or water that has upset me. We are now at Douglas a few days but will not stay as they had a 5 weeks union meeting and also Bisbee has union meeting on now so we will go on to Clifton."[95]

Hermiston never wanted to go to Clifton. From Globe in the fall of 1912, he had told White that he could not take the car into Clifton because the curves were too short. From Naco on May 14 he again wrote that the track to Clifton was dangerous and the curves were very short, and one railroad man had told him it would be dangerous. However, the car went to Clifton after all and made it around the curves in fine order, and Hermiston reported a good meeting. "Although it is so hot it is like an oven in between these rocks in a deep canyon."[96]

Discouraged with chapel car work, Hermiston was thinking of taking a job in the East but could not decide to leave the West. He thought "it might be best for the good of the car work to let some one else take it." He had found someone in Clifton to do some minor repair work on the car (varnish, running gear overhauled). He begged White to let them return to California near the beach, where it was cooler, and "a little let down from the strenuous speed limit of the last season."[97]

Something else was bothering Hermiston. He had been doing some land speculating in northern California, around Gerber, and some of those deals had gone bad. He had asked for a loan from the Home Mission Society for $1,200 to help purchase the lot. Now he was in a financial bind and no doubt embarrassed. He was afraid others would find out his situation. He did not know that his superior already knew. Other matters besides clean water and ocean breezes were on his mind. However, regardless of Hermiston's personal problems, the meeting at Clifton was a great success.

By the end of June, having navigated the precarious curves at Clifton, the chapel car and the Hermistons had made their way back to California. Hot, dangerous, difficult Arizona, where dozens were reported saved, was left behind.

At the large First Baptist Church of San Bernardino, a railroad town with nearly two thousand men employed in the shops and on the road, Hermiston was having a great revival. He was where he wanted to be, doing what he wanted to be doing. He was holding meetings nearly every day in the big Santa Fe shops as well as at the church. The men at the shop meetings donated ten thousand dollars to the new YMCA,[98] another of Hermiston's favorite projects.

The Pacific Baptist reported that the worst thing Hermiston had to contend with as he moved on to San Luis Obispo was "the miserable dance in the lodge and high school." At Paso Robles, ten were immersed in the Salinas River, and interest in the meeting was so intense that it broke up a tightrope exhibition show that was scheduled to take place in the city park. There were hundreds of people on the river bank. Hermiston sang, and Pastor Colyar waded into the river and preached and explained the Baptist beliefs. That night the 50 x 76-foot tent was crowded and many stood outside to hear the forceful and eloquent message of Mrs. Hermiston.[99]

Blanchards Move Car to Montana

In the spring of 1915, the first steel Baptist chapel car, named *Grace*, was being built at the Barney & Smith shops. The donors of *Grace* designated its first field of service to be California, and they requested to have the Hermistons transferred to the new car. Hermiston's popularity and powerful preaching, plus the large numbers of decisions and baptisms, seemed to outweigh his peculiarities and penchant for trouble with superiors. Also, Mrs. Hermiston was a plus to their ministry. At one of their last stops before transferring to *Grace*, at Santa Ana, seventy-three persons went forward in confession and thirty-three were baptized.[100]

Mrs. Hermiston had heard that *Grace* had a real bedroom with "a real brass bed," not just two small single berths. She would be the envy of all the other chapel car women. She could hardly wait.

After extensive repairs and installation of a new Baker heater, plus keeping a stove the Hermistons had been using, *Emmanuel* arrived in Montana in the fall of 1915. Much to everyone's dismay, it spent its first five months on a rail siding because it lacked workers to run it. The missionaries, the Reverend and Mrs. F. I. Blanchard, did not arrive from Pontiac, Michigan, until February 6, 1916. Although the car was in good mechanical shape, it was dirty inside and out.[101] By the following week, after some brisk housecleaning by Mrs. Blanchard, the car moved to begin revivals with the church in Anaconda. After four weeks in Anaconda, the car visited Missoula, Victor, Darby, Hamilton, and Belt over the next six months.[102]

The *Daily Missoulian* reported on March 23, 1916, "Chapel Car *Emmanuel* arrived in Missoula yesterday morning and was set out on the sidetrack at the Northern Pacific station for a three weeks' stay," and continued coverage until on April 11 it announced that the meetings would close on the coming Saturday. "There has been an increased interest in the services during the past few days. Sunday evening a large number were converted."

The Blanchards had success at Lewistown, and at Roundup in 1917, a church of twenty-one members was organized on New Year's Day with a praise service and an old-fashioned picnic with basketsful of the finest food. Blanchard reported, "Six months ago we did not know there were five Baptists in town."[103] Stops at Laurel, Livingston, and Manhattan resulted in conversions and additions to the churches. At Belgrade, which proved to be a disappointment as to interest, Blanchard became ill. The car was moved to Bozeman until services could begin again.

In 1917 war clouds on the Mexican border had given way to the storm of World War I. White inquired of a YMCA executive in California as to where and how the chapel cars might help with the war effort. He was especially interested in camps at Presidio, Vallejo, Goat Island, Fort McDowell, Camp Fremont, and Monterey. Chapel cars had already made contacts at Camp Kearney and Camp Lewis.[104]

In 1918 the Blanchards returned to Roundup, helping with the completion of the new church before being transferred to chapel car *Evangel*. The Reverend and Mrs. A. C. Blinzinger came to *Emmanuel* in the spring of 1919 and managed the work as it moved from Montana to Colorado. They secured lots, organized churches, and erected buildings, including churches at Fort Lupton, Simla, and Limon. Former brick-layer Blinzinger was known as a skilled church builder, although perhaps a little rough around the edges when it came to preaching and pastoring.

The spread of influenza in the fall of 1919, while *Emmanuel* was at Boone, Colorado, created distinct losses — religious, financial, and social — to churches all over the Northwest. As the Montana Baptist Convention Annual reported, "Its only apparent good came in creating conditions in which our ministers and workers left the usual formal routine of service and became veritable ministers of mercy in calling, prayer, care of the sick, burial of the dead and in relieving the material and spiritual needs of their several communities."[105]

The shuffle began again. The Blinzingers were transferred to *Grace* April 1, 1924, and Blanchards transferred from *Evangel* back to *Emmanuel*. For them, it was like coming home.

The Craig, Colorado, newspaper reported on June 1, 1924, "A chapel car belonging to the American Baptist Publication Society was parked just north of the freight depot opposite the Moffat station, and with it are Rev. and Mrs. F. I. Blanchard."[106] *Emmanuel* left Craig for Greybull, Wyoming, where a great revival was held, and traveled to the mining town of Gebo, Wyoming, where the only church in town was organized. Soon the Blanchards were back on the Moffat Road to start a church in Steamboat Springs, Colorado.[107] Then they went on to the mining camps at Clark and Bear River.

Blanchards Visit Beet Towns

Things were not going well for Frank Blanchard in 1926, although he was pleased to be back on *Emmanuel*. He was not pleased that the Colorado state secretary had refused to arrange his schedule in detail for him, just the opposite from the independent, free-wheeling Hermiston, but had turned the responsibility over to someone else.

Blanchard, who required order and structure in his life, complained, "this has not been very satisfactory; he [the Colorado state secretary] just says go to Ovid where there is a big sugar factory going up, organize a church and erect a church building, and then go to Sedgwick and Julesburg and if possible build a church and tie them up with Ovid." Blanchard, who had confessed to having nervous problems before, seemed overwhelmed and showed signs of depression.

The three towns that Blanchard was so reluctant to visit are in the northeast corner of Colorado. Ovid and Sedgwick are names that most Americans would not recognize, but many Americans, particularly rail historians, cannot forget the name of Julesburg. For Julesburg was one of the hell-on-wheels towns on the Union Pacific route of the transcontinental railroad, and before that, it had been at the crossroads of several pioneer trails along the Platte River. Records indicate that Blanchard did visit Julesburg, then a law-abiding town, but did not organize a church there, hoping to link a Julesburg fellowship to the Ovid church.

At Sedgwick the Blanchards held meetings in cooperation with the Union Church and Sunday school, also hoping to link with the Ovid ministry. Also a sugar-beet town, Sedgwick was named after Fort Sedgwick, which was located along the nearby Platte River, an important outpost to protect settlers and railroad workers during the mid-1800s.

On August 6, 1925, announcement was made that Colorado's nineteenth sugar factory would be located in Ovid, and headlines in the local papers shouted the news. First a tent city sprang up, and then two-room shacks were roughly constructed for housing the workers, and a boarding house and dormitory were leased to accommodate the workers, as well as the Sugar Cafe.[108] By October 1926, Ovid had three lumber yards, two theaters, a bakery, two cafes, two hardware stores, a beauty shop, two pool halls with barbers, two grocery stores, a furniture store, a pickle factory, a florist, a cheese factory, a men's clothing store, two garages, and two churches. One of those two was the new Baptist church, whose members met in the basement of their church in construction.[109] That church was started by the Blanchards in chapel car *Emmanuel*.

> *The hustle and bustle of 1926 Ovid is gone. We stand outside the huge brick shell of the Great Western Sugar Company and look for reflections in its shattered glass eyes. Where are those people now, the ones who flocked to the tiny town? The congregation of the Methodist church, the first church in town? The twenty faithful charter members who formed the First Baptist Church in chapel car* Emmanuel? *The little children who learned their lines for the Christmas program under the tutoring of Mrs. Blanchard? The seventy-five who increased the flock? The seventeen who came to know Christ through Blanchard's Spirit-led words during the revivals? Those who were baptized in the Platte?*
>
> *The autumn wind, the only sound in the town, warns the nearby trees of the winter to come. First to come to these lands were the immigrants on trains full of household goods, livestock, and farm equipment. Then came the strangers from faraway lands, to work in this wreck of broken brick that still looms tall. Together they built businesses and schools, had dances and went to picture shows, carried their Bibles to Sunday school and married and christened and buried at church.*
>
> *There are still a few people in Ovid, although we saw none along the main street lined with buildings no longer used. There are still farmers growing sugar beets. Across the river from town is a flagpole marking the spot of old Fort Sedgwick. There is nothing there now but the river, and the trees, and the wind.*
>
> *In the emptiness of the streets and in the sound of the wind, the words of the Gospel of Matthew come to mind. Could Blanchard have shared them with his congregation? Could they*

have known this is how it would end? Did they find comfort in hearing them? "Heaven and earth will pass away, but my words will not pass away" (Matthew 24:35, NRSV).

In June 1928, Blanchard reported that the church at Padroni, Colorado, wanted to erect an edifice costing three thousand dollars. "That would not be much for a good size community but with a farming town of about 100 people and the surrounding farming community composed largely of Mexicans, Italians, and Russians, and the Americans dry land farmers hardly able to exist, $3,000 is considerable. Nobody from the Home Mission Society or State Baptist office will help." He guessed morosely that he would have to figure things out on his own.[110]

In 1929 the chapel car was back on the Moffat Road at Phippsburg, where things were not getting better for the Blanchards, despite the fact that Blanchard had been given a raise of $200, bringing his yearly salary up from $1,800 to $2,000. *Emmanuel* had been touched up and repairs made for $607 by the Denver & Rio Grande Western Railroad.

Fire Damages Car, Distresses Blanchard

Then trouble struck. *Emmanuel* was hit by lightning and caught fire. A distressed Frank Blanchard reported to White:

It caught on fire the afternoon of August 3 while we were away on a two weeks' vacation . . . it was one of the most terrific electrical storms ever known in this section of the state. The fire could be seen playing here and there throughout town and then came a great crash but it was fully ten minutes before the people knew where the lightning struck and then they saw smoke coming out of the church end of the chapel car, but no one knows how it came into the car, nothing to show.

The outside of the car is scarcely touched, but oh, the inside. All of ceiling in the church part is black and the sheets of ceiling are hanging down in strips and even the ceiling in the house part is practically gone. All of the deck windows, especially of church, are gone, the woodwork around them destroyed. The electric wires, though in conduits, are melted together. Men from the car shops rushed in by breaking in the glass in the doors and used chemicals and carried our clothing to safety. I am thinking the hollow wire gasoline plant is destroyed.[111]

The Denver and Rio Grande Western shops at Denver made the fire repairs for $1,359.34 plus $460.48 for additional work. Most costs were covered by insurance, and *Emmanuel* was back on the road. After building churches at Agate, Bijou, and Bennett, Blanchard was told by the Colorado secretary that he did not want any more churches built because of the financial depression. So they left the chapel car on a spur at Bennett in October 1932 for a year to save expenses and went to Denver to aid the Mt. Hermon Church.

The strain of chapel car life became too much for Frank Blanchard, and in December 1934, after working at Deer Trail, Littleton, and Peyton, he wrote, "Now I am down and out in health. Hope to be back again in Christian work at least part of the time, but I believe Mrs. Blanchard and I have a right to rejoice in the record of the past."[112]

Blanchard, suffering a serious mental breakdown in 1936, was pensioned at the rate of $357.20 per year, and in June 1937 passed away. Mrs. Blanchard described his funeral: flowers sent by many of the churches where they had served and pallbearers from Craig, Agate, Bennett, and Gebo churches. She had 19 dollars a month from the ministers and missionary board to live on, along with help from family. At her age it would be difficult to find work.

Parrys Offer Stability to Aging Car

As the oldest boy of five parentless children, the Reverend Howard Parry grew up in Girard College in Philadelphia, a school for "poor, white, male orphans."[113] He pulled himself up by the proverbial bootstraps by hard work and determination, becoming one of the best qualified men in the chapel car ministry. Work at New York Biblical Seminary and

Wooster Academy, degrees from Denison University and Crozer Seminary, and academic distinction in Philosophy and Psychology, were testimonies to Parry's determination and integrity. After several years as a successful Ohio pastor, Parry and his wife, Mary Ellen, were appointed to *Emmanuel* on May 1, 1935. Having lost infant twins, the Parrys were childless, which made their situation for chapel car work more tenable.[114]

The Howard Parry years are recorded by meticulous accounts in his journals, which were given to the Samuel Colgate Historical Collection at Colgate-Rochester Divinity School in Rochester, New York. As the Parrys left their home on their way to join *Emmanuel* in Colorado, on Tuesday, January 29, Howard recorded that Mary was not feeling well. They left Chicago at 10:30 A.M. on the train, and Howard spent the day getting to know the train crew. The conductor had left the Pennsylvania Railroad five years ago, and they had several common acquaintances from that connection. The Pullman porter was a member of the Pullman Company basso quartet and the Copley Methodist Episcopal Church in Chicago.

Weather, Headaches Plague Parry

From their first destination in Peyton, Colorado, elevation 6,800 feet, in the spring of 1935, the Parrys experienced a wide range of weather. On February 15 the entry includes "Dust storm, wind high, car rocking, snow, and heavy winds." On February 24, "Blizzard, power off, Temp. 9 degrees, wind gale force, car rocking with the wind, hard to keep warm, no power, cooked dinner on oil heater." By March 15, "dust storm with snow at night," and on March 26, "Terrific dust storm, dropped 25 degrees in hour, cleaned chapel but dust storm undid."

April did not bring much improvement. On April 6, "Dust storm," and April 10, "Bad Dust storm." On April 12, Howard got to get out of the car and have a little sport, "Shot three jack rabbits." On April 17, it was "Dust storm," again, and on April 23 and 24, "Blizzard, the funeral of a four-year-old postponed, drifts high, trains late."

May did bring some spring showers, plus hail on May 8. After performing his calling duties and before his evening meetings, Parry hunted prairie dogs and rattlesnakes. By the end of May, there was still no relief from the weather. On May 30, "rain, hail three and four feet deep, flooding, no power, roads washed away." The last day of the month brought "one of the worst dust storms, no trains, no mail." But June 1, although there still were no trains or mail, brought a special sight to the weather-beaten *Emmanuel* and the Parrys — "a double rainbow."

By July, three words began to appear in Parry's daily journal. "Headache again today." For most of the years of his ministry, Parry suffered severe headaches, much like migraines. But all that was prescribed by local doctors were headache remedies and rest. Frequently Howard Parry would take some time to go hiking, hunting, or fishing — a way to find some peace for the pain in his head.

From Briggsdale to Crowley in the spring of 1937, the Parrys made themselves effective in the chapel car service by remaining cheerful and energetic. According to the Ordway *New Era*, "In the present era, the car is taken to communities where economic disasters due to failures of crops, depression and other extenuating circumstances have made necessary a rebuilding of the spiritual life of the community and the local church organization. Cooperation with all evangelical denominations is the spirit of the workers . . . and all citizens of the Crowley/Ordway area are invited to the services."[115] Despite a snowstorm and the appearance of a smallpox case in Ordway, which caused the Parrys to be vaccinated, the first service brought out twenty people.

The IGA store in Crowley gave free advertisement to the presence of the chapel car at the bottom of an ad that promoted men's work shoes for $1.98, ladies' hose for 15 cents, and three pounds of coffee for 50 cents.[116] Those who may have responded to the ad were a diversified flock. For example, in Mrs. Parry's children's work, she had three Japanese girls, an Armenian child born of that historic group of refugees driven out of their native land during the world war, and several Mexican children.

"The other morning a Japanese lady called at the chapel car and we had a pleasant visit all morning. She read in her own language John 3:16. Both she and her husband are Buddhists. Every two or three weeks a Japanese Buddhist priest comes and holds a meeting to which they are expected to come. But the young Japanese who are in high school do not like their religion, and want to be Christians. We are soon to cooperate in an effort to entertain all Japanese youth in the community that we can get together," Mary Parry reported.[117]

Howard Parry recorded in the summer of 1937 that the weather was merciless: hot sun, temperature close to 100, no rain, crops beyond help. And in November, an infantile paralyses quarantine for over a month made children's services impossible.

Parry, an astute surveyor and student of psychology, saw South Fork as a case study in rural problems. His surveys of the towns he visited were carefully prepared, no doubt a surprise and pleasure to his superiors, who were not used to such efficiency. His report of the towns of Del Norte and South Fork on January 2, 1939, noted:

— pop. 1500; Churches Roman Catholic, Presbyterian, Methodist, Episcopal, Baptist (1914); large Mexican pop. employed in vegetable fields, cattle and sheep; Economic condition fair; Good schools; South Fork report — pop. 100; lumber camp, privately owned by Denver man; large number of Mexicans, some Americans; Workers of Lumber Co. paid in coupon form; Roman Catholic Mexican, no priest, no service; no church, no itinerant ministry; started services Jan. 8, 1939.[118]

It is duplicate of the peonage system of rural America as described in all current social approaches to Christian ministry [Parry refers to Mark Dawber's *Rural America*.] The town, privately owned and operated, once in clutches of the owner, must buy from him only in units he operates. Pay is in coupon form, only good in the

Fig. 7.8 After being retired from active service, *Emmanuel* was eventually moved from a Baptist camp in South Dakota to a salvage company, where it was scrapped for its metals. A craftsman from Prairie Village, Madison, South Dakota, saw the potential for restoration of the car. It was then saved from destruction and restored by a group at Prairie Village. (American Baptist Historical Society, Valley Forge)

village. The Mill is now shut down and will be for the month; the workers become hopelessly in debt, which if they still want to meet must remain until more work comes usually in the spring. Thus folks must either stay or move away and repudiate their debts.[119]

More immediate problems replaced Parry's sociological thoughts on that day. "Before light a severe snowstorm struck here, at least a foot of snow; now the wind is drifting it about. Radio out of commission due to storm and strong wind." For most of 1938, the Parrys worked out of *Emmanuel* at Deer Trail and also established a joint work at nearby Byers. It was hoped that a larger parish work could be established in the area, but that was not to be. Instead, Parry would take the chapel car to South Fork and the related communities of Del Norte and Ordway.

At South Fork a unique work would be accomplished among a transient population. On December 31, 1938,

Emmanuel was spurred at South Fork, high in the Rockies between Creede and Wolfe Creek canyons. As a result of Parry's leadership in South Fork, the Emmanuel Mission Chapel & Hall was organized and built; it was dedicated December 8, 1940. In a report to the secretary of the Colporter-Missionary Division of the Home Mission Society, Parry said there was no church or community hall within fifteen miles of South Fork, and members of the Emmanuel Mission Chapel believed it was going to change the color of the entire community.[120]

Emmanuel Retires Almost to Oblivion

The Parrys were loved and respected in their Colorado ministry, markedly for their obvious care for the people of the communities they served, especially the young people. For all the good they were doing, Howard still recorded those three words frequently: headache again today.

By 1942 the chapel car ministry had changed dramatically. Free passage was a thing of the past, the old wooden cars were not welcome on the rails, and as a result stays were much longer in towns, and the focus of the ministry had changed greatly.

In view of the expanding scope of the auto chapel car work launched in 1923, coupled with increased transportation and maintenance costs and a decline in effectiveness of the chapel cars, the board of managers of the home mission society and the publication society began to evaluate objectively the future of the fifty-year-old chapel car ministry. On April 30, 1942, Mark Rich reported to the home mission and publication societies: "Due to several changes it is increasingly difficult to find challenging fields of service for the chapel cars. For this reason a thorough study has been made of available fields in states west of the Mississippi River. The results indicate that in no state is there a large field for the use of these cars. . . . It is probable that within the next few years one or two of the chapel cars will be retired from itinerant service."[121]

The publication society made the decision to send the chapel car to the South Dakota Baptist Camp at Swan Lake.

Parry preached his last sermon in *Emmanuel* in February 1942. His salary during his tenure in South Fork was $1,660 plus a $400 expense allowance shared by the two societies. The insured value of *Emmanuel* at that time was $4,440.[122]

With Howard Parry on *Emmanuel* every inch of the journey, the chapel car left Del Norte July 23, 1942, en route to Swan Lake, Viborg, South Dakota. It was removed from rail right of way to avoid demurrage charges, and drawn by heavy-duty trucks with cable winch devices the last eight miles to the grounds. Then the workers swung the eighty-foot car, which at one time was the longest passenger-type car in America, into its proper placement upon its own trucks.

It must have been difficult for Parry to leave *Emmanuel*, but the car had earned its rest. At a meeting of the board of the American Baptist Home Mission Society on January 27, 1943, it was voted to sell *Emmanuel*, exclusive of the lectern, which remained the property of the American Baptist Publication Society, to the South Dakota Baptist Convention for the sum of one dollar.

During its thirteen years at Swan Lake, *Emmanuel* "took a horrible beating from the weather — wind and rain storms and blistering heat in the summer and snow storms and bitter cold in the winter."[123] The car had become an eyesore. In 1955 financial constraints made it necessary for South Dakota Baptists to sell Swan Lake camp to the Northern District of the General Conference Mennonite Church with the understanding that the chapel car would be removed.

Sold to two men from Sioux Falls in the salvage business, the car was stripped of metal *(see fig. 7.8)*. Then the Brandt Engineering Company purchased the car and used it for storage.

While it was on Brandt property, John O. Olson, a master carpenter employed by Prairie Village, a pioneer museum near Madison, South Dakota, saw and examined the car. He was "greatly impressed with the quality of workmanship and was amazed that the car had endured harsh weather conditions for some thirty years without even normal maintenance procedures."[124] A group from Prairie Village expressed inter-

Fig. 7.9 Placed on the National Register for Historic Places in 1976, *Emmanuel* is being beautifully restored by a group of workers at Prairie Village, where it is on display with other buildings in this turn-of-the-century village. (Norman T. Taylor)

est in the car, but Dina Brandt Holgate, the owner of Brandt Engineering, declined to negotiate with them at that time.

Before finding its just place of honor at Prairie Village, *Emmanuel* was transferred with permission of Brandt owners to a group of young people at the First Baptist Church of Sioux Falls, under the ministry of Dr. Roger Fredrickson. They had good intentions of preserving the car and having it serve as a community center for VISTA volunteers, but local homeowners objected to the appearance of the car, and it was returned to Brandt Engineering Company. At this turn of events, Dina Brandt Holgate gave permission to transfer the car to Prairie Village.

Restoration Brings *Emmanuel* Honor

Emmanuel qualified for the South Dakota Register of Historic Places and was placed on the national register in 1976 through the dedicated efforts of volunteers and Jacquie McKeon, who wrote *If That Don't Beat the Devil*, an early book about the chapel cars. By the fall of 1982 restoration of the exterior of the chapel car had been completed at a cost of $34,896. William J. Janklow, governor of South Dakota, proclaimed May 22, 1983, Chapel Car *Emmanuel* Day. "I join South Dakotans of all religious persuasions in saluting this enduring landmark of stalwart faith and steadfast works."[125]

A small but dedicated group at Prairie Village continues to bring *Emmanuel* back to its full glory, with shiny new oak pews crafted after the pattern of the originals, new windows, and newly sanded and varnished walls and ceiling *(see fig 7.9)*. At home in its place near a 1900s country church and period rail depot in the charming model town, *Emmanuel* is again being used as a place of worship as well as a memorial to the men and women who guided its path across the great West.

> Salvation's Chariot, roll
> On, till from pole to pole
> Christ reigns alone;
> Till darkness turns to day,
> Till earth shall choose his sway,
> And all its trophies lay
> Before his throne.[126]

Notes

1 *The Barney & Smith Car Company* (n.p., n.d.), Dayton and Montgomery County Public Library, Dayton, Ohio.

2 John A. Krout, *United States Since 1865*, College Outline series, 12th ed. (New York: Barnes & Noble, 1953), 66.

3 Scott Trostel, *The Barney & Smith Car Company* (Fletcher, Ohio: Cam-Tech Publishing, 1993), 88.

4 Ibid., 40.

5 Clayton F. Smith, *American Baptist Quarterly*, March 1991, 70.

6 Ibid.

7 *The Colporter*, February 1894, 1.

8 The History of the First Baptist Church of Hanford, Calif.

9 *The Colporter*, September 1894, 3.

10 Ibid.

11 Ibid., 4.

12 BSP, ABHS, VF.

13 *The Pacific Baptist*, March 21, 1895, 3, American Baptist Seminary of the West, Berkeley, Calif.

14 Ibid.

15 *Roswell (New Mexico) Register*, April 3, 1895.

16 Ibid.

17 *Roswell (New Mexico) Register*, April 10, 1895.

18 Seventy-fifth anniversary book, First Baptist Church, Carlsbad, N.M., 1965, 9.

19 *Eddy*, a semi-weekly, Wednesday, April 10, 1895, n.p.

20 Carlos A. Schwantes, ed., *Bisbee: Urban Outpost on the Frontier* (Tucson: University of Arizona Press), 9.

21 Ibid., 12.

22 Ibid., 35.

23 Annie M. Cox, "History of Bisbee, 1877 to 1937" (thesis for the Department of History of University of Arizona, 1936), 91.

24 Lyle Johnston, ed., *Centennial Memories of Holbrook, Arizona, 1881–1981*, 39–40, Friends of the Holbrook Public Library, Holbrook, Ariz.

25 Ibid.

26 Harold C. Wayte Jr., "A History of Holbrook and the Little Colorado Country, 1540–1962" (unpublished thesis, Department of History, University of Arizona, 1962), 115.

27 Richard K. Mangum and Sherry G. Mangum, *Flagstaff Album: Flagstaff's First 50 Years in Photographs* (Flagstaff: Hexagon Press, 1993), 26.

28 "History of Winslow," Arizona, Navajo County Historical Society, Memorial Library, Winslow, Ariz.

29 *The Colporter*, October 1895, 3.

30 Anniversary Report of the American Baptist Publication Society, 1896, Asbury Park, N.J., 79.

31 Smith, 71.

32 *The Pacific Baptist*, November 14, 1895, 4, American Baptist Seminary of the West, Berkeley, Calif.

33 Nancy Drennon, "Southern Pacific Begins Trek Up Shastas," *Siskiyou County Railroad Gazette*, 10, 1997 editions, Yreka, Calif.

34 "History of Yreka, California," Yreka Chamber of Commerce.

35 Anniversary Report of the American Baptist Publication Society, Asbury Park, N.J., 1896, 82.

36 "Dutch Flat" (Dutch Flat: The Dutch Flat Community Club).

37 Joanne Meschery, *Truckee: An Illustrated History of the Town and Its Surroundings* (Truckee, Calif.: Rocking Stone Press, 1978), 81.

38 *The Pacific Baptist*, October 1, 1896, 11, American Baptist Seminary of the West, Berkeley, Calif.

39 Ibid.

40 Phyllis Zauner and Lou Zauner, *Reno-Sparks, Nevada: A Mini-History* (Reno, Nev.: Zanel Publications, 1978), 50.

41 BSP, scrapbook, "Mark Twain," ABHS, VF.

42 Zauner and Zauner, 17.

43 Anne Kellogg, "Long-time Sparks church has roots that pre-date the Rail City," Daily Sparks Tribune, November 10, 1996.

44 Smith, 74.

45 *The Colporter*, February 1890, n.p.

46 Jim Hulse, "Pioneer Preachers Found Nevada Tough," *Nevada State Journal*, 1954, Washoe County Library, Sparks, Nev.

47 *The Pacific Baptist*, March 18, 1897, 10, American Baptist Seminary of the West, Berkeley, Calif.

48 *The Pacific Baptist*, April 15, 1897, 6, ABSW, BC.

49 Perry T. Booth, *Grants Pass: The Golden Years, 1884–1984* (Grants Pass, Ore.: Grants Pass Centennial Commission, 1984), 109.

50 Edna May Hill, *Josephine County Historical Highlights* (Grants Pass, Ore.: Josephine County Historical Society, 1976), 74.

51 *The Pacific Baptist*, November 16, 1898, 5–10.

52 *Oxnard Courier*, Ventura County, Calif., Saturday, March 3, 1900, 1, Colportage & Chapel Cars, information acquired and/or produced in 1980 & 1900, Box, ABHS, VF.

53 *The Colporter*, May 1900, n.p.

54 Bob Hoie, "Minor Leagues: A Historical Overview," Total Sports Web Site, 1996.

55 Anniversary Report of the American Baptist Publication Society, 1908, Oklahoma City, Okla., 88–89.

56 Ibid.

57 Report of the Board, Oregon Baptist State Convention, October 14–16, 1901, American Baptist Conference of Oregon, Portland, Ore.

58 Letter from E. R. Hermiston to John D. Rockefeller, Red Bluff, Calif., February 15, 1905, Samuelson Collection Box, Early Chapel Car Correspondence, Rockefeller and others, ABHS, VF.

59 "A Prize-Fight on the Chapel Car; Pugilist Harry Maynard, of Red Bluff, California, Wins," a tract by the American Baptist Publication Society.

60 Ibid.

61 Dee Dorran, "Abiding Faith Carries It On," *The Hermiston (Oregon) Herald*, Wednesday, March 31, 1982, 4, material sent to authors from Mrs. Doris E. Herman, 134 Central, Orland, Calif., January 21, 1997.

62 *The Hermiston Herald*, column of Hermiston history, "Saloon Girl's Death Ends Life of Tragedy," Thursday, May 21, 1964, n.p.

63 *Missions*, September 1914, 765–66.

64 Anniversary Report of the American Baptist Publication Society, 1908, Oklahoma City, Okla., 80.

65 Tracy Greer Gipson, "Forty Years with Baptist Pioneers in South Idaho: A History of Baptist Work in the Area from 1864 to 1904" (unpublished thesis submitted in candidacy for the degree of Master of Arts in the Berkeley Baptist Divinity School, Department of Church History, 1945), 97.

66 Ibid., 86.

67 June Summers, *Follow the Light: A 76-Year History, 1910–1986* (Spokane, Wash.: Richard's Printing Company, 1987), 6, Spokane Public Library.

68 *Missions*, April 1910, 278.

69 Summers, 4.

70 *A History of Kittitas County*, Washington (Kittitas, Wash.: Kittiitas County Centennial Committee, 1989), 1:55-58, Kittitas Public Library, Kittitas, Wash.

71 History Report of Cle Elum, Washington (Community Development Study, May 1955), 133.

72 Ibid., 114.

73 Anniversary Report of the American Baptist Publication Society, Philadelphia, 1911, n.p.

74 Letter from George L. White to Robert Seymour, October 30, 1911, ABHS, VF.

75 Letter from E. R. Hermiston to George L. White, October 31, 1911, ABHS, VF.

76 Letter to George L. White from H. P. Anderson, October 1911, ABHS, VF.

77 Letter from E. R. Hermiston to George L. White, November 14, 1911, ABHS, VF.

78 George L. White files, ABHS, VF.

79 Letter from E. R. Hermiston to George L. White, Yuma, Ariz., October 11, 1912, 27.12, Box 27, ABHS, VF.

80 Letter from E. R. Hermiston to George White, October 25, 1912, 27.12, Box 27, ABHS, VF.

81 *Missions*, March 1913, 282–83.

82 *Graham Guardian*, Stafford, Ariz., November 1, 1912.

83 Letter from E. R. Hermiston to George L. White, Stafford, Ariz., November 3, 1912, ABHS, VF.

84 *Graham Guardian*, November 8, 1912.

85 Letter from E. R. Hermiston to George L. White, Globe, Ariz., November 25, 1912, 27.12, Box 27, ABHS, VF.

86 Maggie Wilson, "Globe, Arizona: A Remembrance," *Arizona Highways*, 23, vertical file, Miami Memorial Library, Globe.

87 Wilma Gray Sain, *Miami: A History of the Miami Area*, Ariz., (Gila County Historical Society, Globe, Ariz., and Miami Memorial Library), 12.

88 *The Silver Belt*, "Revival Meetings Are Ending at Miami," Globe, Ariz., January 23, 1913, 1.

89 Ibid.

90 Letter from E. R. Hermiston to George L. White, Naco, Ariz., May 12, 1913, 27.12, Box 27, ABHS, VF.

91 Letter from E. R. Hermiston to George L. White, Naco, Ariz., May 15, 1913, 27.12, Box 27, ABHS, VF.

92 "This Is Your Life," seventy-fifth anniversary of First Baptist Church of Douglas, Ariz., 1977.

93 Ibid.

94 Robert S. Jeffrey, unpublished thesis, University of Arizona, 1951, 87.

95 Letter from E. R. Hermiston to George L. White, from Douglas, Arizona, May 23, 1913. George L. White files, ABHS. VF.

96 Letter from E. R. Hermiston to George L. White, Clifton, Ariz., June 4, 1913, 27.12, Box 27, ABHS, VF.

97 Ibid.

98 *Missions*, August 1912, 641.

99 *The Pacific Baptist*, April 11, 1914, American Baptist Seminary of the West, Berkeley, Calif.

100 *Watchman-Examiner*, May 13, 1915, 587.

101 Letter from George L. White to Joe P. Jacobs, August 17, 1915, George L, White file, ABHS, VF.

102 Lawrence F. Small, ed., *Religion in Montana*, 2 vols. (Billings, Mont.: Rocky Mountain College, 1992), 1:223.

103 *Missions*, 1917, 203.

104 Letter from George L. White to W. H. Towner, Presidio YMCA, San Francisco, February 11, 1918, George L. White files, ABHS, VF.

105 Montana Baptist Convention Annual, October 7–10, 1919, American Baptist Conference of the Northwest, Kent, Wash.

106 P. R. "Bob" Griswold, *Denver and Salt Lake Railroad*, 1913–1926 (Denver: Rocky Mountain Railroad Club, 1996), 183.

107 Ibid., 189.

108 *The History of Sedgwick County*, Colorado (The Fort Sedgwick Historical Society, 1982), C–56, Julesburg Public Library, Julesburg, Colo.

109 Ibid., C–42.

110 Letter from F. I. Blanchard to George L. White, June 15, 1928, George L. White files, ABHS, VF.

111 Letter from F. I. Blanchard to George L. White, August 11, 1930, George L. White files, ABHS, VF.

112 Letter from F. I. Blanchard to George L. White, April 2, 1935, George L. White files, ABHS, VF.

113 "Girard, Stephen," *Encyclopaedia Britannica*, vol. 10 (Chicago: Encyclopaedia Britannica, Inc., 1968), 430.

114 Telephone conversation with Beverly Carlson, ABHS, VF, from information given by a niece of Howard Parry.

115 The *New Era*, Ordway, Colorado, May 26, 1936, Howard Parry files, ABHS, VF.

116 Ibid.

117 Anniversary Report of the American Baptist Publication Society, Philadelphia, 1937, 44.

118 January 24, 1939, report, Killian file, Colporter box, ABHS, VF.

119 Ibid.

120 Smith, 80.

121 Ibid.

122 Ibid., 81.

123 Ibid., 81–82.

124 Ibid.

125 Jacquie McKeon, *If That Don't Beat the Devil* (self-published), 45.

126 Written by Samuel Francis Smith, author of "My Country, 'Tis of Thee," and sung to the tune of "Come Thou Almighty King."

CHAPTER 8

Baptist Car 3: *Glad Tidings* across the Plains and Prairies

Nestled in blankets, the baby swung in a hammock between the two berths as chapel car *Glad Tidings* rolled through the Iowa countryside. Her mother monitored the arc of the swing with her hand, and her father watched apprehensively from above. It did not take long for the Charles Herbert Rusts to discover that a chapel car was no place to raise a baby.

The Reverend and Mrs. Rust were newlyweds at the dedication of chapel car *Glad Tidings*. The young couple, like thousands at Saratoga, New York, had decided to visit the new chapel car at the station of the Delaware and Hudson Railroad on May 25, 1894. There they found the Reverend E. B. Edmunds, a missionary from Wisconsin, in charge.

He was trying to cook some oatmeal for breakfast on a stove that did not seem to have any heating power. As we met him, he said, 'I have been over an hour trying to get a little lunch here.' As we passed out the door, I exclaimed, 'Well, I rather pity the missionaries who are to live on that car.' Little did we think that in four months we would be the missionaries on that very car.[1]

This third Baptist car built by the Barney & Smith Car Company was a gift of William Hills, a member of the chapel car syndicate from the Mt. Morris Baptist Church of New York City and head of the Hills Brothers Company. The car was given upon the condition that matching funds be raised

for the building of the fourth car, *Good Will*, by the close of 1894.

Rain drenched the exposed sections of the Saratoga depot and dampened the enthusiasm of the large crowd gathered for the dedication. In his address, shortened because of the inclement weather, the Reverend W. C. Bitting of New York declared, "Well may the whirling of its wheels, the hum of its hurry, and the whiz of its speed express the strength of sacred impulses to bear the 'Glad Tidings' to others. This work is all the sweeter because these wheels will rest from their revolutions, not in the crowded cities where church spires rise, but in the desert spots where the weary advance guard of our national life is struggling with the slow soil in the tired hope of winning new victories for our loved land."

To the delegates crowded under a canopy of umbrellas, the secretary of the publications society, the Reverend Robert G. Seymour, proclaimed, "It is time for the revival of old methods harnessed to new forces. We are not going back to pedestrianism or ox–carts, the age is of steam and electricity. But we need to rest in the power of the old methods pushed forward by steam and electricity. . . . It is a startling fact, to which careful students of religious statistics will agree, that more than one-third of our sixty-two million of people in the United States are outside of and unreached by the organized churches."[2]

After the dedication, Boston Smith, who had heard about the Rusts, came to the Warren Avenue Baptist Church in

Fig. 8.1 At Wheeler, Wisconsin, the Charles Herbert Rusts spent many weeks organizing a Sunday school that later became the Grace United Methodist Church. (Grace United Methodist Church of Wheeler, Wisconsin)

Boston, where Rust, a graduate of Gordon Bible School, was serving as assistant pastor. After asking the young couple to consider becoming missionaries on *Glad Tidings* and praying with them, Boston left the young couple, giving them three months to make their decision.

The last days of the time were fast going, according to Rust. The matter had to be settled. "Mrs. Rust went to one room and I went to another. On our knees we told the Lord we would go anywhere he would have us go; we only wanted to be sure. One verse, Isaiah 1:19, kept coming before me — 'If ye be willing and obedient, ye shall eat the good of the land.' We came together and expressed our mutual convictions that God wanted us to go and we were willing."

Newlyweds Begin Life on *Glad Tidings*

When the Rusts became the missionaries on *Glad Tidings*, they began to appreciate their new home, which had been on a siding waiting for their arrival.

It is a handsome car and certainly a worthy addition to any train. It is seventy-seven feet long and eleven feet wide. On the top of the side you see the words 'Chapel Car' and in the center of the side the name 'Glad Tidings,' both in gold. There is an eaves-trough on the roof with hose attachment, so that the water tanks can be filled with soft water during the greater part of the year. Under the car you will find boxes to hold thirty-five hundred pounds of coal, storm sash and screens, oil stove and oven, and provisions and books and tracts. A ladder, storm door and four screen doors are hanging under the floor.[3]

Like most people, the Rusts were amazed at the compactness of the living quarters. "As we step from the chapel toward the living rooms we find ourselves in a miniature parsonage, 18 feet long and 10 feet wide. In this space we have a bedroom with two berths, a dining room with table, a study with typewriter, desk and library, a kitchen with range and closet, an ice chest, pantry, wardrobe, toilet room, and heater

to heat the entire car with."[4] The couple would soon discover that the Baker heater would become the source of many perturbed letters to chapel car officials.

Rust would relate, "People in Boston told us that we could never endure the blizzards and cold of the West. They pictured the sufferings that we would certainly have to pass through. And I confess all was very dark to us, because we had never been west of New York, and while I knew Chicago and Minneapolis were excellent cities, yet what we might find west of them frightened us."[5]

After filling the chapel car pantry with supplies, the young couple started their adventure west in the early fall of 1894. Operating along the lines of the Northern Pacific and Wisconsin Central roads, their first stop was Brainerd, Minnesota, where Smith had stopped in 1891. In 1890 the Northern Pacific had initiated building wooden boxcars at the huge shops located there. As a result of ensuing costs, foreclosure proceedings had begun,[6] but the company survived by reorganizing as the Northern Pacific Railway Company. In 1895 it was still the busy focal point of the community. Because of the switching of engines in the busy yards where the chapel car was parked, Mrs. Rust found that sleeping in the car was almost impossible.

At Staples, the Rusts were stationed behind the coal chute, and workers loaded the engines all night. They got little rest. "If this had continued in every town we would have been obliged to get a room outside, but in the small towns we were not bothered as much," Rust related. The success of the meetings at Staples compensated for the inconvenience of the lost rest. "God came with *Glad Tidings* to Staples, and the Holy Spirit accompanied the word with power. The town was stirred to its depths, and sinners were soon on their knees crying before God. A Sunday school was organized with forty-four members the first day and was added to right along — fathers, mothers, and their children studying the word together."[7]

After a shop stop in St. Paul, where storm windows were installed, and visits to several Minnesota and North Dakota settlements, the Rusts found Bismarck, the North Dakota capital, a bustling town. The division of the Dakotas had just occurred in 1889. Settlers flooded into the Dakotas from 1878 to 1886, but few ventured west of the Missouri River until the surrender of Sitting Bull in 1881. Situated on the Missouri, Bismarck was the stopping place for many immigrants. The nationalities most represented were Scandinavians, Germans, and Russians. The 1895 census for the Dakotas showed 19,257 from Norway, 7,746 from Sweden, and 4,369 from Denmark; from Germany, 18,188, and from Russia, 12,398.[8]

The Baptists in Bismarck were happy with the car's visit, "The chapel car *Glad Tidings* in charge of Mr. and Mrs. Rust has visited our city. Mr. Rust preached the gospel and the sweet singing rendered by Mrs. Rust was most attractive. Two more consecrated disciples of our Lord have never visited our city, and this young Sodom has had the greatest shaking up spiritually that I have witnessed in about twelve years. There soon was not room in the car to hold those who were interested."[9]

Rust talked about typical Minnesota and North Dakota towns in 1895.

In most of these little towns an immense amount of business is done, as the merchants have to supply the country for miles around. As a rule we seldom visit a town that has more than five hundred people in it, and in a great many instances only thirty, forty, seventy-five, and one hundred. In these smaller places there are no churches nor Sunday-schools as a rule. . . .

These North Dakota towns have no saloons, but just as soon as you get across the line into Minnesota you see saloons by wholesale. In one of these towns which we visited in September, 1895, with only five hundred population, there were twelve saloons, and these in a line within five blocks. Sometimes there is a steady stream of men traveling across the line from North Dakota to Minnesota to get their drinks. I have seen the train on the Great Northern come into one of these

Minnesota towns from across the North Dakota prairies, with its load of harvesters on their way to the Eastern cities, and I have seen fully thirty men jump from the train, hardly waiting for it to stop, and rush to the saloons to get their whiskey.[10]

On sight, people had a problem with figuring out what the chapel cars were. One time the Rusts were sidetracked at a large division point and some traveling salesmen were standing on the platform at the station. They were gazing intently upon the car, and Rust heard them say: "Glad Tidings, Glad Tidings. . . . That must be the pay car."[11]

Other reactions to the car were less amusing, for many elements did not welcome the presence of a church on rails in

Fig. 8.2 Much of Rust's work across the Dakotas, Minnesota, and Wisconsin was with railroad workers like these meeting in the car in a shop in Minnesota. (American Baptist Historical Society, Valley Forge)

their town. Rust recalled one time when as day was breaking and he had gone outside to fill his coal bucket, he looked up and there in bright red paint, someone had scrawled "Cattle Car" over a thirty-foot area. As the paint was still wet, he was able to remove it with much scrubbing.[12]

Rust often spoke of his work with the railroad men in the shops along the lines in Minnesota, the Dakotas, Nebraska, and Iowa. "I think I can safely say that there is never a meeting without some railroad men in it. I could give you letters from section-men, brakemen, conductors, dispatchers, wire agents, and many others who have been saved and blessed because of the meetings in 'Glad Tidings.'" This phase of the work was appreciated by the general managers and division superintendents all along the line. "I remember writing to an agent in a town where we had once been sidetracked asking him if he could give me the same trackage again; I received a message in a day or two which read like this: 'Dear Mr. Rust; your letter at hand. You may have any track you want but the main line; if that will not do, I will make one that will.'"[13]

Railroad Ministry Vital to Chapel Cars

During the 1880s the railroad network of the United States grew to 93,671 miles, equal to 70 percent of the mileage built in the preceding half century.[14] Along with the growth of the railroad came an increase of workers. In 1895 there were employed in the United States 873,602 railroad employees.[15]

Midday and midnight the chapel car workers held services for these men in yards and shops. Rust handed out cards saying "Come just as you are." Bare-armed, dirty, work-clothed, they came — by the thousands. Rust related that he stood at the door of the chapel car and grasped the hand of each man.

"Look at this man who is reaching up now in some haste. He is the engineer of a stationary engine in the shop. He has been in the car each noon, but cannot stay to the entire service, as he is obliged to run to his engine to blow the whistle at 12:45. He hardly can part with the missionary, and says in parting: 'God alone knows what the chapel car has meant to

me. I have not been in church for years, but you have brought the church to me.'"[16]

Glad Tidings traveled many miles on the Chicago, Burlington, and Quincy route. From 1880 to 1905, the CB & Q colonization plan brought hundreds of people from England, Scotland, Sweden, and Germany to Illinois, Iowa, and Nebraska. Unlike the earlier disregard of some railroad enterprises for religious life, the CB & Q Railroad encouraged whole religious communities to come, bringing their pastors. At Crete, Nebraska, the railroad helped start a Congregationalist college, and since no church was present in the town, the railroad offered the depot as a meeting house with rail commissioner Harris as Sunday school superintendent.

Since there was no depot at Harvard, the CB & Q sidetracked a coach every Sunday for use as a chapel. Colonies of Russo-Mennonites, Bohemians, Yankee Congregationalists, a band of New England temperance advocates, and thousands of Scotch Presbyterians came to Harvard. In Iowa the Burlington fostered colonies of Swedish Lutherans, Methodists, Welsh Episcopalians, French Icarians, and Catholics. From its beginning, the Burlington tried to promote the community as a whole and safeguard its well-being.[17]

Rust believed that the success of the chapel cars on the rail lines depended mainly on the personal character of the railroad official with whom the missionary had to deal. "If that man is a conscientious Christian, or recognizes the moral benefit derived from Christ's teachings being inculcated in the minds of his men, he will be much more favorably impressed with the chapel car than one who has no tolerance for religion. Let me add, however, that there had never been a time previous to the present when railroad companies were so free to recognize the demand and need for moral character among their employees as today. They are enforcing rules regarding drinking and frequenting saloons that would not have been tolerated a few years ago."[18]

Many times rail officials and others were mistaken about the financial situation of the cars, as Rust discovered. "I was in the office of an official of a very large Western system not long ago. During our conversation he said, 'Why you have a great deal of wealth back of your chapel car, haven't you?' I answered, 'No, sir. We depend entirely upon the contributions from churches and individuals.' 'Oh yes,' he said, 'I recognize that, but there is one particular individual, is there not?' He believed that a certain wealthy and prominent Baptist [John D. Rockefeller] was forwarding the money to pay our bills, including transportation."[19]

Without a pass on a rail line, the missionaries would have to pay, even if the car had permission to travel on that line. The annual passes given to the missionaries by a rail line usually read something like "Pass C. H. Rust and assistant." They were good on any train on that line. "We are very careful never to abuse our privileges in any way. The railway companies trust us, and we surely want them to continue to do so. We have had people come to us a number of times and ask if they could not ride with us. One man wanted us to put him under the seats. Our answer is always 'No.'"[20]

It was important to keep the goodwill of the railroad officials. Hauling the chapel cars did not bother the officials as much as how they could allow the car to be on a side track for any length of time without seriously hindering them in their business. Rust explained that the companies charged two dollars for every twenty-four hours after the first forty-eight hours that a loaded boxcar was left on the track, oftentimes ten dollars for a theater or circus car. "Thus you see that the railroads are very considerate to allow us to stay at all. It is only because of their desire to do all they can to help on a good cause."

Since siding the chapel cars could cause problems, Rust found a solution that would work for other chapel car missionaries as well. He conferred with officials and asked them if they could not have their section men build a short spur from the side track and run the car onto it, then swing the side track back into place and leave the chapel car on rails of its own, out of the way of all traffic. "In answer to my request, orders were given to have it done. It costs the company about eight dollars to build the track and take it up again when we leave town. We have offered to pay for it but they have never sent any bill yet, and they have done this for us many times."[21]

Life on Chapel Car Cozy but Cramped

Life on the chapel car was often described as cozy, maybe too cozy. Rust explained that everything seemed to be in the way, and "we were always in each other's way. At the end of the first three months we had numberless bruises, because of our running into sharp corners and things in general. Once when rushing from the parsonage to the chapel I struck my head so hard on the small closet near the door, that I dropped to the floor like a felled ox and almost lost consciousness."[22]

Glad Tidings was on the end of a long freight train one day when Mrs. Rust said, "Put up the table for dinner, please; we are about ready." Rust started to get the table when the train lurched and knocked him against his desk, jamming his hand. That dinner was sent from the kitchen stove, away under the desk in the library. At another time Mrs. Rust was getting breakfast on the oil stove. "I saw a switch engine coming, and was sure it was going to strike hard. I rushed in and in Yankee style yelled, 'Look out, Bertha, it's coming.' She looked out

Fig. 8.3 Rail workers watch as Mrs. Rust hangs her laundry on the rear platform of chapel car *Glad Tidings* on a siding at Wheeler, Wisconsin. What looks like a wringer washing machine is on the platform behind her. (Grace United Methodist Church, Wheeler, Wisconsin)

the window to see what was coming, and just then an engine struck the car, and away went the entire breakfast on the kitchen floor."[23]

Home life on the chapel car was often disturbed. "You never know just what is to happen. If the car is not on a special spur of its own it must be switched nearly every day and night. During one night last summer we were switched five times, and handled quite roughly. I remember that my head was severely banged against the end of my berth. The railroad men always handle the car as quietly as possible, but when it is between freight cars and these cars must be switched, then ours must be handled with the others."[24]

Fig. 8.4, 8.5 The Reverend Charles Rust brought his bride to the chapel car, where the young couple learned to endure the hardships of chapel car life and prospered in their ministry through the Plains states. Mrs. Rust soon learned that life on a chapel car was not practical with infants. She established a home away from the chapel car for the family, although the Rusts were distressed about being apart for long periods of time. (American Baptist Historical Society, Valley Forge)

Frequently the missionary wives handled major portions of the work, especially when the husband was ill or had to be away from the car. In most situations when the wife was on the car, she would be responsible for children's and women's work, singing and playing the organ, some book work, and the general housekeeping of the car. Wives who had small children stayed at home and saw their husbands only when they were in the area, sometimes spending vacations on the car. Rust remembers the agony of hearing his daughter Ruth say on one of his infrequent trips home, "How long are you going to stay, Papa?"[25] In several cases, older children would

be left with family members, seeing their parents only on school breaks. Frequently young adult children would assist their parents on the cars, generally with musical talents.

Chapel car life was especially difficult for the missionary wives. They had practically no privacy, and that was exceedingly hard for Mrs. Rust. They were seldom given the opportunity to be alone. Mrs. Rust had no room or closet she could call her own — no dresser on which to lay pins, ribbons, and numerous other belongings. The only place was her husband's desk, and he needed that for other things. "It was good discipline for us and tested our religion," Rust said. "We prayed for special grace and wisdom every day in our en-deavor to fit into the demands of the place and the work."[26]

Early in December 1896, the Rusts visited a churchless town on the Wisconsin Central Line where there had been no religious services for two and a half years. The townsfolk hailed the car with delight, especially the children, whose spiritual training had been sorely neglected. One boy came and asked Rust to write out the Lord's Prayer for him, but instead Rust took thirty-five Testaments, marked the Lord's Prayer in each, and presented one to each child. "We went through the prayer carefully, word by word. They learned it readily, and in two or three days were able to repeat it from memory."

Wheeler, Wisconsin, on the Wisconsin Central, was sometimes referred to as "Guzzler's Glory" because town life seemed to center on the saloons. The Rusts found no church in 1897, although chapel car *Evangel* had visited there several years earlier. But crowds came to the chapel car. With the thermometer reading from zero to thirty below, people would walk four or five miles and back, and some would drive a dozen miles or more. One woman, a member of the Methodist church in the East, said that for the first twelve years after she was brought West, she only heard one sermon and that was at a funeral.[27]

After several visits, a Sunday school was started, and it grew and grew. The Rusts hoped that this faithful band would develop into a Baptist church.

In early September 1997, we visited the town of Wheeler, eager to find the Baptist church started one hundred years ago. It was a bright Wisconsin sabbath as we drove into Wheeler and looked down the street of this town of about five hundred people. The empty storefronts were still there. Things had not changed much since 1897 and 1898 when Glad Tidings *was last there.*

We saw the spire of a well-kept church with quite a crowd of cars in the parking lot. The Baptist church, we hoped, but the sign said Wheeler Lutheran. Just around the bend on Church Street, we saw another small church. The Baptist church, we hoped. The sign said Wheeler United Methodist. Disappointed, we turned away from the building and began another search for the Baptist church.

After circling the town, and in the absence of a Baptist church, we decided to worship with the Methodists. We were warmly greeted by the members, and when we asked one if there was a Baptist church in town, the response was "No, not since I've lived here, and I've lived here all my life." Before settling into the pew, my husband whispered, "Look at the front of the church." On the wall hung a huge banner emblazoned with the Methodist flame symbol, and beneath it was a silhouette of a chapel car. We looked at each other in astonishment.

After the service, as we queried members about the chapel car influence, we were shown a scrapbook with pictures of Glad Tidings *and members of the church — only it wasn't a church then, it was a Sunday school. That Sunday school started by chapel car* Glad Tidings *and the Rusts developed into an Evangelical, then a United Brethren church, and then into the United Methodist church (see fig. 8.1).*

How happy we were that we had been led to worship with the Methodists in Wheeler on that Sunday morning.

Black smoke spiraling into the sky was a frequent and frightening sight for people throughout the chapel car's range. At Plainfield, Wisconsin, a center of country trade in the Potato Belt, many homesteads had been destroyed, along with churches and whole town blocks, as dry haystacks would burst into flames fanned by the wind. The Rusts came in 1898 to help revitalize the church.

The always present danger to the towns was not fire but the influence of the saloons. In one Wisconsin town, Rust had been giving a talk on "Danger Signals" to a carload of children. The town was "full of wickedness, and there were saloons and beer barrels all around us." He told the children that he wished they could write "danger" (in their minds) over every saloon in the city. They went from that car and taking chalk, wrote "DANGER" on the doors of the saloon, on the sidewalk in front of the saloons, and also upon the beer storage houses (*see fig. 8.7*).[28]

Fig. 8.6 Ruth Rust (left) was born while her parents were on *Glad Tidings* and stayed on the car until her sister Marjorie was born. (American Baptist Historical Society, Valley Forge)

Rust discussed the early problems facing the chapel cars.

There were many questions in the minds of the denomination when the Publication Society accepted the first chapel car. It was considered by some to be the result of the dreaming of an impractical mind; by others it was styled a "white elephant," by others "Uncle Boston's Toy," and even the most enthusiastic questioned its permanent usefulness under the most favorable conditions. It certainly was an experiment.

It was one thing to have a car [rail chapel car]; it was another to get it hauled. If it could not be hauled at a small sum per mile how could it be used? And when we consider the fact that the universal price charged by railroad companies for hauling a car is fifty-four cents a mile, and that those who gave the first car, although being railroad officials, would not guarantee to use their influence toward getting reduced rates for the car, what could the most sanguine expect?[29]

When the Rusts' second daughter was born, the family established a home in the St. Paul area where Mrs. Rust and the children spent most of their time (see fig. 8.6).

Since Mrs. Rust was frequently at home with a growing family, Rust needed help on the car. C. W. Meacham helped during 1897 and 1898, and at Frazee, Minnesota, Rust had another helper on the car, a young bachelor, Arthur Isaac Tipton. Two sisters were baptized during that stay and came frequently to the car for services. Tipton returned in June 1901 to marry one of them, Mabel Adele Weymouth, affectionately called Della. In later years Mr. and Mrs. Tipton served as colporters in Wyoming with their buggy and their span of black horses, Dick and Dock. The fairy-tale beginning did not have a beautiful ending, as Mrs. Tipton was paralyzed in childbirth during their term of service in Wyoming.[30]

The *Nebegamon Enterprise* reported that "The Chapel Car 'Glad Tidings' was sidetracked at this place Saturday evening last, and has remained during the week."[31] W. F. Fitch, general manager of the Duluth, South Shore & Atlantic, received a letter of appreciation for the car during May.

Dear Sir:

The people of Lake Nebagamon in meeting assembled last evening, voted to have me extend to you their hearty thanks, for the benefit and pleasure derived from the chapel Car "Glad Tidings", under the able management of Missionary C. H. Rust, and brought over your lines to this place, and hope that they will again be allowed the pleasure of another visit from the car in the near future.

In behalf of the people of Lake Negagamon,
C. G. Towne, Agent[32]

From Lake Nebegamon, the *Nebegamon Enterprise* reported May 13 that the car was taken to West Superior, where Rust won many friends. Between 1890 and 1900 the population of Superior, Wisconsin, increased so rapidly that by the turn of the century Superior was the second largest city in the state. McDougall whaleback ships, designed to withstand the sharp, choppy waves of the Great Lakes, were launched by the dozen from Superior shipyards, and people flocked to the area.[33]

The absence of libraries and bookstores in those rail communities like Superior, plus the dearth of religious information, made the distribution of literature a vital part of chapel car work, and the chapel car libraries provided hours of education and enjoyment for the many who came into the car and read.

No books were sold under the terms of free transportation, but tracts and books by the thousands were given away. The car had a library of about sixty volumes of selected Christian reading, and at the first meeting in a small town people were told that the books were for them to enjoy. Rust was often kept busy loaning books. The young people were eager to borrow them, sometimes reading three or four in a week. Rust said, "We seldom lose a book, as they are notified when the car will leave. I have seen them coming just before the train was to haul us out, walking along the track reading their books, anxious to finish before the chapel left."[34]

In the early 1900s *Glad Tidings* revisited Minnesota towns like Frazee before going to Golconda, where a woman told them that she had not been to a church in twenty-seven years. Her son had died at age twenty without ever hearing a gospel sermon or knowing what a Sunday school was.[35] The new congregation at Detroit, Minnesota, presented Mrs. Rust with money for a gold watch in appreciation for her singing.

At Jordan, a town of about twelve hundred people on the Minneapolis and St. Louis Railroad where nine-tenths of the town were Catholic, there was no English preaching. The car was full each night with people standing at the door and on the platform.[36] Rust participated in an unusual funeral while he was in Jordan in the summer of 1900, as he related:

Seven saloons open wide day and night, business stores open on Sunday, Sunday ball games, etc., claiming the attention of nearly everyone and a general disregard of anything godly, but when the chapel car rolled into town it was filled at all services. A man who had been a drunkard for years had died of "delirium tremens." He was a lone personage and had no relative near. The saloon-keeper who had sold him a great deal of the liquor which was his ruin, decided to be kind and purchased a shroud, and others chipped in to buy the casket and hire the hearse.

The saloon-keeper came to me and asked if I would assist in giving the man a decent burial by speaking and praying at the grave. Only a short service was needed. It seems that the deceased had been quite a musician, written music, and at one time had charge of his own band, which was a good one. It was his dying request that the band play at the grave.

The funeral was on Sunday afternoon. The band came and the procession formed. The saloon-keeper with the chapel-car missionary in the first carriage, just behind the band, then the hearse with six pall bearers, six poor, ruined, liquor-soaked friends of the deceased, and then a string of carriages. The streets were lined

with people, and we went to the graveyard, and in a few minutes more than four hundred people had gathered at the grave in the paupers' lot. I endeavored to speak loving words to the people concerning the things of God.

It was evidently well received. God had used the message. There were many evidences of it. The saloons which had been wide open all night and Sunday were closed at the appointed hour. Less drinking and gambling, and a church was organized and a preacher called to the field.[37]

On a return visit at Brainerd, the car was sidetracked at the shops for noon meetings with the men. At Bemidji, the second week in September 1900, the Rusts revitalized the small

Fig. 8.7 At this Wisconsin town, the children who came to the car were told to think "danger" when they saw liquor or saloons, but instead of only thinking it, they took chalk and wrote "DANGER" on the drinking establishments of the town. (American Baptist Historical Society, Valley Forge)

congregation they had organized on an earlier trip. In Iowa, at Corwith, crowds filled the car as they did later at Valley Junction, Woolstock, Greenville, Landon, and Montgomery.

At Holmes, organized when the Chicago and Rock Island Railroad pushed westward in 1881, the grandparents of radio personality Paul Harvey ran the hotel. The car was put on a spur in September, and meetings were at full capacity for two months while a church was organized. The town, consisting of two elevators, four stores, the hotel, a blacksmith shop, and eight houses, up to that time had no church for English-speaking people.

The new Baptist church soon became the center of community life. Ice cream socials were held on the lawn by the Ladies "Glad Tidings" Circle, and the young people gathered on the depot's wooden platform for party games like "Miller Boy" and "Old Dan Tucker." Sometimes the young Baptists might be tempted to have their fortunes told by the gypsies who would come to town in covered wagons, along with the novelty of visiting the medicine tent shows.[38]

At Woolstock, down the line, served by the Chicago & North Western Railroad, the townspeople were mainly French from Alsace-Lorraine. The name of the town came from the large sheep herds that operated along the Boone River.[39]

Rust came to Spirit Lake, Iowa, in December 1901 and had excellent results with a struggling church in the town. Some of the members could no doubt remember by first-person account the Spirit Lake massacre of 1857 that made the town infamous. All others knew the story well. At least forty settlers were killed in that Indian attack, grisly proof that life was not safe in Iowa's isolated settlements. During these happier and safer times, an addition was made to the Spirit Lake church, and the building was rededicated.

Wisconsin Towns Welcome Rusts

Two strangers had appeared on the streets of Almond in January 1900, interviewing businessmen and farmers. Several days later it was announced that they were officials from the Chicago & North Western Railroad. They were planning to build a line from Fond du Lac to Marshfield and then through Wild Rose, Almond, and Bancroft. The C & NW came to Almond in September 1901, and a picnic, complete with brass bands, was held in town to celebrate the event.[40] Farmers who had stopped growing wheat because of crop failure and were now growing potatoes were especially happy. The railroad would make it possible for them to ship their crops rather than have them freeze, as happened with other long-distance hauling options.[41]

Glad Tidings first came into Plainfield and Bancroft, siding on the earlier Soo Line track at Bancroft in August 1902. The Rusts organized a church and the Glad Tidings Ladies Circle before heading down the track to Almond, where the church was organized November 19, 1903, with twenty-two members. The English Methodists in town were dismayed, for many of the Baptists had attended their church before the chapel car came into town.[42]

Mrs. Joseph Walter wrote in the church history of her days on the chapel car. "The time *Glad Tidings* came to Almond on the CNW. Rev. Rust and his wife held meetings, and here is where yours truly began her remembrance of the good times we children had when we would rush home from school and go to the chapel car for learning Bible verses and the books of the Old and New Testament. I received my first very own Bible, which I had for years, for memorizing the books of the Old Testament. What good times we all had at these children's meetings."[43]

The church built from the work of *Glad Tidings* at Almond, along with the other churches in town, were miraculously saved several years later when a fire almost destroyed the town over a period of eighteen months. Dr. L. E. Olson, a Baptist minister who was a teenager in town at the time, described the events. One building after the other was reduced to ashes, he related. The hardware store, the billiard hall, the Ford garage, then the hotel and restaurant; several weeks later, the meat market, the newspaper, the millinery shop and the shoe repair shop.

If this was not discouraging enough for the townsfolk, they watched in horror as the Woodmen's Lodge Hall burst into flames. There was something of the ludicrous that night, Olson recalled. "The Woodmen were concerned about their traps and initiation equipment. The building was certainly going down, but the Woodmen insisted on saving their trappings. A rescue team was organized and into the secret walls they went. In their hurry they failed fully to cover the head of the old proverbial goat. The goat was spared the ravaging destruction of fire, but his secret presence in the hall became a matter of public knowledge. Thus one of the secrets that all good Woodmen are under obligations forever to conceal became public knowledge."[44]

In a discussion of the dearth of churches in Northern Wisconsin at the 1904 Wisconsin State Convention, the suggestion was made, "Why not run the chapel car up the new Soo line that is being built from Dresser Junction to Superior? That road is being built through a section where the Swede Baptists have been at work for years and you can organize a Baptist church in every town along that line." The response was "Why organize new churches to die for lack of support, when churches already organized are dying for lack of support?"

Yet the delegates agreed that it was a shame that in Wisconsin, in villages where girls don't have the opportunity to hear a gospel sermon until fourteen years of age, and where mothers with tears in their eyes plead for gospel preaching to help save their sons from awful ravages at the saloon, workers were instructed not to build churches.[45]

At the town of Grand Rapids, Wisconsin, which would later be called Wisconsin Rapids, the *Wood County Reporter* recounted that *Glad Tidings* was spurred out at the Wisconsin Central Depot. Crowds were turned away Sunday morning, and Rust hoped to have a larger place for the Sunday evening meeting. He was inviting everyone to come and find out more about Baptist beliefs. The Rusts helped organize a church on June 15, before the chapel car left town late that month.[46]

Another major attraction was coming into town June 20. The World's Strongest Man was going to give demonstrations in John Daly's drugstore, performing such amazing feats as breaking a logging chain in two. In spite of that attraction, the ladies of the town were busy with a Women's Circle that had been organized on the chapel car. On Thursday, June 23, they were going to discuss "Is it right to expect the young people to give up amusements when they become Christians?"

The people of Scotts Bluff, Nebraska, welcomed *Glad Tidings* in 1904 and founded a church after several weeks of evangelistic meetings.[47] In the fall of 1904, *Glad Tidings* spent three months visiting South Dakota towns, including Clear Lake, Watertown, and Elkton. The Home Mission Society recorded in 1864–1865, "In Dakota a Baptist church and Sunday school have been organized at Yankton, the capital of the territory." This was the pioneer religious organization among evangelical denominations in South Dakota.

Fig. 8.8 At Louisville, Nebraska, in 1906, Sunday school members pose in front of *Glad Tidings* at the Missouri Pacific Railroad depot. (Courtesy of Jim Reisdorff, South Platte Press, David City, Nebraska)

Rust Joins Family, Whites Come

Rust continually agonized over his absence from his family, and in 1905 he decided to leave chapel car work. *The Baptist Examiner* of September 28, 1905, reported that Rust had been appointed the new district secretary of the publication society in New York State, and a few years later he took a pastorate where he could spend more time with his family. His book *A Church on Wheels*, published by the American Baptist Publication Society in 1905, made a major contribution to the chapel car ministry.

In 1906 the Reverend George L. White, a Nebraska pastor and a graduate of the University of Chicago and its Divinity School, was on *Glad Tidings*. After visiting Randolph and Wellfleet, on a cold January 19, White baptized five hardy souls in the Elkhorn River at Stanton, where they had to chop through twenty inches of ice. "Most of the people in the town are German Lutherans. We are now bound for the northwestern part of the state on the Chicago and Northwestern Railway. There is a stretch of road three hundred miles in length this side of Chadron, Nebraska, where there is not one Baptist church, and many towns have no church of any denomination."[48]

At Louisville, Nebraska, in 1906, the Whites had an active two-year-old on the car. That did not seem to hamper his father's successful meetings there and in other northeast Nebraska towns, although Mrs. White no doubt had her hands full.

When *Glad Tidings* came into Auburn in the fall of 1906, the town was in an uproar. For months it had been rumored that the Missouri Pacific might choose the town for a division point. When the old Missouri Pacific hotel in Auburn burned August 3, 1906, its proprietor held off on replacing the building until he was assured the crewmen would not be leaving town.[49] The presence of the chapel car provided citizens with a different topic of conversation.

A reporter for *The Republican* paper of Plainview, Nebraska, tried to explain the transportation situation of the chapel cars as he covered the visit of *Glad Tidings* there.

The railroads charge each of these cars that run over their roads at the rate of eighteen first class passengers, or fifty-four cents a mile for every mile traveled. The minimum charge is fifteen dollars between stations. The fare between Plainview and Creighton [where the car also stopped] was thirty cents for each passenger before the new law passed. It is now twenty. For the eighteen the fare will be $3.60. Perhaps the railroad will reduce the cost of the transfer to ten dollars to agree with the new order of things. If not it will cost $15 to get the car to Creighton. The railroads charged nothing for leaving the car on the sidetrack. The theatrical troupe cars that travel in this way get cut rate of 36 cents a mile or one third cheaper than the chapel car, but they are not allowed to remain on the sidetrack only a limited time. The cost of operating one of these cars for a year is $3000.[50]

White reported 178 professed conversions at Plainview, with eighty people joining the Baptist church and the rest aligning with the Methodists, Congregational, and Friends churches in town.[51]

The Whites, like the Rusts, concluded that a chapel car was not a good place for a small child. White was appointed general missionary, working out of Salt Lake City. L. A. Drumwright took charge of the car in September 1907.

Drumwright worked in Nebraska, stopping at Albion, Valparaiso, David City, Polk, Central City, Grand Island, Cotesfield, and Maxwell. *Glad Tidings* went to the shops for repairs in August, and in September, after a year on board, Drumwright became ill and left chapel car work. The Reverend E. A. Spear and his wife became the new missionaries in charge.

White, now a general missionary, had many things to worry about in addition to the changes on *Glad Tidings*. The question was not just who was on the car but how the car was going to get from place to place. He reported in 1908, "Some of the railroads which for many years have carried cars without cost are now demanding remuneration. We are grateful for their present and past generosity, but we must call the attention of our people to the need of increased contributions because of these increased expenditures."[52]

While he was on *Glad Tidings* at Laurel, Montana, in 1910, Spear was inspired by the sight of a bridge — a different kind of bridge. He reported they were on a railway siding where the one mail train a day did not stop except upon flag; one store, a post office, and a section house with two Greeks. The chapel car missionaries increased the population more than one-fifth. Around were desolate, barren hills with their red soil indicating the presence of gypsum; a gorgeous sunset; a mighty river frozen nearly two feet deep forming a natural bridge.

> Over this river from the valleys and bench lands came the people — men, women and children, some of them old-timers, others recently from the more densely populated sections of the country; some impelled by curiosity, others with a thirst for the words of truth, all respectful and friendly, glad to have something to relieve the monotony of a long, cold winter in a section where they have no Bible school and preaching but once a month. The first day a terrible wind was blowing from the north, and the audience consisted of three men and three boys; the rest of the time they came, some afoot, others on horseback, and still others in rigs loaded to the axle with a happy, carefree company. Five nights and an all-day meeting on Sunday, and the car was compelled to move on to the next engagement.[53]

White, who was overseeing Spear's travels, knew the need for the gospel in the Utah/Wyoming district. He recalled his first experience as a missionary secretary for the area. White's first stop in Wyoming was at Gillette, where he came in on a train. Gillette was a godless place. Every form of sin seemed to be practiced openly. The largest building and the center of interest in the town was a combined saloon, dance hall, gambling house, and brothel.

I secured a room for the night between two saloons where the noise was so great that it was impossible to sleep. About two o'clock in the morning the uproar ceased for a little while, a beautiful tenor voice in one of the saloons below sang 'The Holy City!' In the moment of silence in the night, someone remembered his earlier Christian training. It was as if an anguished heart was searching for Christ and the better way of life.[54]

Missionaries See Promise in Big Horn

The real pioneer preacher in the Big Horn Basin of Wyoming was the Reverend Louis Thompson. Thompson traveled the basin in the late 1880s without the benefits of a chapel car, holding services in tents, log buildings, dining rooms, or wherever he could get people together. He told of starting from Thermopolis for Tensleep during one heavy snow. Upon reaching the D Ranch, he found it impossible to go further. He started back to Thermopolis with the stage driver. The two of them shoveled snow all the way from the ranch to Thermopolis, some fifty miles, in order to get through. Exhausted, they lay down many times in the narrow tracks to rest, only to get up and go on with the shoveling. It took hours of this grueling labor before they reached their destination.

Like Thompson, Catholic Father Endres, a Belgian, traveled over the basin in all kinds of weather to minister, on horseback, with team or sled, as the occasion demanded. He was loved alike by Protestant and Catholic.[55] The chapel cars made life easier for the Spears than were the journeys of their forerunners.

In 1900 the Mormon church had begun advertising the Big Horn Basin. Mormons came by the thousands, moving along the Old Mormon Trail to join other Mormons who had come earlier to the area to help in the building of the irrigation canals under the Carey Act project. The Mormons were also responsible for the growing of sugar beets and bringing into the Basin the sugar factories.[56] The Church of the Latter-day Saints is still a strong religious and economic force in the area.

The Baptists would also see great promise in the Basin. In the *Colorado Baptist Bulletin*, the Hanover Company, whose president was Baptist layman D. T. Pulliam of Loveland, Colorado, advertised 35,000 acres of the finest land to be found along the Big Horn River, with a perpetual water right on every acre sold. They encouraged Baptists to come and enjoy the bounty of the land. Although several rail lines were projected, only one railroad entered the valley then — the Cody branch of the Burlington.

Fig. 8.9 Children cluster before *Glad Tidings* at Greybull, Wyoming, in 1912, in the Great Basin area, where toughs from a nearby town gave pastor Arthur Sangston trouble. (American Baptist Historical Society, Valley Forge)

To reach the Big horn river… you leave the road at Garland, and stage the rest. This long ride will, however, soon be a thing of the past. In a very few months the Burlington will have extended a branch line from Fannie on the Cody branch to Thermopolis in the southwestern part of the Basin. This line will be rushed as fast as possible in order to handle the rush into the Shoshone Indian Reservation at its opening in June, 1906…. With the coming of a railroad no section of the country can compare in rapid development to that

portion of the Big Horn Basin that extends along the river. Here the homeseeker wants to go and go quickly, if he is looking for cheap land.[57]

Glad Tidings was brought to the Big Horn Basin of Wyoming to work at several towns in 1910, including Manderson, Basin, Powell, Greybull, Lovell, and Thermopolis, known for its hot springs. At Powell, originally called Colter, the headquarters of the government's great Shoshone irrigation project was located. In every direction stretched fertile fields, young orchards, and the beginnings of many homesteads.

People, mostly young, had come from all points east to take advantage of the opportunity for land. After choosing a site, the homesteader would file, agreeing to pay the government $45 per acre for his land, this to be divided into yearly payments of $4.50 per acre, with ten years to pay.[58] William Howard Taft had been inaugurated when Powell's numbers were counted at near three hundred homesteading families, and growing.

One homestead wife recorded that her father filed a claim in August 1909. After filing, he held a farm sale at his place in Nebraska, loaded his belongings on an immigrant car, and left for Powell, with her mother and the rest of the family following. "The Powell flat looked like 'no man's land.' No trees, no roads, just sage brush and cactus. The small owls, prairie dogs, horny toads and rattle snakes all lived in the same holes. We killed 22 rattle snakes around our house the first summer."[59]

The Shoshone dam project was completed January 18, 1910, and the dry land began to become green. It was July when the chapel car came to town, and Spears offered the car as a resting place for the town during the Fourth of July festivities. Sunday, July 11, was a special day. No matter in what direction the eye turned that day, majestic mountains, the loftiest peaks crowned with perpetual snow, range upon range, met the vision. In the car, flowers crowned the Estey organ, and Spear preached a grand sermon, followed by a basket dinner. In the afternoon the Powell Valley Baptist Church was organized. The crowning event was the baptism. A crowd of more than 150 of all faiths or no faith followed the chapel car to the Shoshone River to observe the baptism.

The baptistery was the wild, beautiful Shoshone River, probably the first time its waters were ever used for this impressive, symbolic rite. In its hurling course from its mountain source to the thirsty, waiting plains below, it found time to linger in a sheltered spot, spreading into a quiet pool, overhung by great trees. The overlapping trees formed a green background to the scene; curtains were stretched for dressing rooms, and the assembled company numbered not less than one hundred and fifty. Seven candidates awaited the ordinance, and as the evangelist led them into the rippling waters and laid them beneath the waves, the hearts of parents and friends were thrilled with solemn joy. "Shall we gather at the river?" was sung from full hearts.[60]

By the summer of 1910, White was promoted to general missionary of the Pacific district with offices at the YMCA building in Portland, Oregon. Times continued to be unsettling for Baptists. The feud between the publication and home mission societies in regard to the chapel cars had not abated. The Southern Baptist board had gained exclusive rights in New Mexico and was attempting to do the same in several other states. White began to feel that life on one of his chapel cars in the Big Horn Basin would be a breeze compared to trying to micromanage the chapel cars, fight denominational battles, and attempt to build bridges of understanding between men and societies.[61]

A number of Baptists settled near Burlington soon after the Mormons started the town. The church they founded had the distinction of being the oldest church in continuous service in the Big Horn Basin.[62]

When the Chicago, Burlington & Quincy Railroad let it be known that the railroad would come to Basin if the railroad would be given a large area of land south of the original townsite, there was excitement in the community. This would have meant real growth for the town. But the owners of that land refused to give the section to the CB & Q, and so Greybull got the division point.[63]

In addition to that setback, a spectacular murder trial had cast a shadow over Basin's reputation, and the town had difficulty shaking its reputation as a wild place to live. Former Basin City Baptist pastor Floyd Ellison recalled an incident that happened just after *Glad Tidings* and the Spears had left town. He said that one day a man and his wife stopped by the parsonage. This man said to Ellison, "We came by to see the church and the town which my father said was too wild to have his children raised there." This man's father was a minister who had come to Basin on a Saturday sometime between 1910 and 1912. His trunk was taken to the Markham Hotel, where he put up for the night. That night there was a fracas in the saloon involving two cowboys from Hyattville. One of

Fig. 8.10 The Reverend H. R. Morton, Arizona Baptist secretary; Dr. Samuel G. Neil, Bible secretary of the publication society; Mrs. and the Reverend A. B. Howell, *Glad Tidings* missionaries; Dr. George L. White, joint secretary; and the Reverend Pablo J. Villanueva, colporter among the Mexicans of Arizona, met to discuss the Mexican work. (American Baptist Historical Society, Valley Forge)

them pulled his gun out and began to shoot. Ellison's uncle happened to be coming in the door and was accidentally shot in the knee. The visiting minister heard about the fracas. Next morning he preached the sermon at the eleven o'clock service, went back to the hotel and got his trunk loaded on the train, and left the rough town, never to return.[64]

In Cheyenne in September 1910, the Spears held services. At Lovell in November, a successful revival was held with more than one hundred people attending, at least eighty of these Mormons who remained at the after meeting as "earnest seekers."[65]

Sangstons Welcomed with Eggs

At Lucerne, Wyoming, the first station on the Burlington line out of Thermopolis, the terminal of the railroad in the Big Horn, *Glad Tidings* dropped anchor on the side track in January 1911 for the purpose of holding a meeting and gathering up all the Baptist forces. The Reverend and Mrs. Arthur Sangston were now on the chapel car. The newly organized town of Lucerne seemed to be an ideal location for a church. A shipping center for ranchers and stockmen, the town had a two-story general store that served as a post office, a lumber yard, a blacksmith shop, a freight and passenger depot, a wool house, corrals, and stock-yards. A boarding house was soon to be built, and later a two-room brick school house and a sugar-beet dump were added.[66]

"Pastor-at-large Wilbur Howell had done some heroic work on this field prior to our coming and when the train cut loose from us, our lights were lit and we were ready for business. We had an audience of 12 people the first night and by Sunday, four days later, the car had 75 people in it, and four ready for baptism. These we took to Thermopolis and baptized in the hot springs pool [also called the Star Plunge]," Sangston reported.[67]

During a meeting at Greybull, the saloon element at Worland, five miles north, incited three young men to attend the meetings and if possible break them up by loud talking, whispering, and other tomfoolery. They made some headway for a night or two, but on being warned of trouble ceased these annoyances only to begin on another tack, putting in the collection box comic postals with vulgar and ugly sentences on them. When they were again reproved, they met at the boxcar station after the congregation was dismissed and egged the car *(see fig. 8.9)*.

The next morning the Sangstons found the outside of the car streaked in fourteen places; the culprits had fled, leaving several good eggs in a linen handkerchief on the ground. These Mrs. Sangston scrambled for breakfast, as eggs were forty cents a dozen. As a final statement, she washed the handkerchief and sent it to Worland. When the Worland thugs came again to service to see the effect of their work, Sangston reported, "God put them under conviction for sin, which was better than jailing them."[68]

At Scotts Bluff, Nebraska, in July 1912, Sangston was up against tough competition, this time not town thugs. He had a hard act to follow, for Dwight L. Moody had recently held a revival in town.[69] Folks crowded the chapel car, and the missionary's sermons, inspired by Moody, "did not spare the prevalent sins of the community" and caused much excitement.

Moody might not have done Sangston a favor as a model for his sermons. Sangston was attacked on the street with a whip, and the papers wrote up the matter sensationally. According to reports, the attempted persecution only increased the power of the meetings.[70]

The death of Robert G. Seymour, general secretary for colporter work, created more restlessness among the chapel car missionaries. He was a man the chapel car missionaries had respected and depended upon to keep the chapel car ships afloat. In October Sangston wrote to White that he was distressed by the void Seymour had left and the changing tides of Baptist politics. He suggested that he might leave chapel car work. Sangston, whose wife and son were not on the car with him at the time, requested that White look for a job for him on the Pacific coast,[71] but the discouraged missionary still faithfully continued his ministerial duties on the car.

In November 1912, Sangston, having successful meetings in Vona, Colorado, wrote to White saying that he was still dismayed by matters in the chapel car management. He was considering buying property in Roseburg, Oregon, and moving his family there to seek other possibilities. Could White advise him?[72]

White responded, "I have consulted with some who understand that district [Oregon] and who tell me that it is very unwise to invest any money in land in Oregon, by dealing with land agents . . . you might expect to lose every dollar you put into it." White's advice was that Sangston go to Oregon and inquire among the ranchers. In that way he could buy land for one-third the amount that land agents would charge.[73]

Glad Tidings spent four months in the San Luis Valley at Del Norte, Monte Vista, Alamosa, La Veta, and Walsenburg. Denver and Rio Grande Railroad officials and employees along the line were most obliging and often attended the meetings.[74] Although the Sangstons had success with their meetings, things did not work out as they wished. They really wanted to take *Glad Tidings* to the Pacific area and make a new life there under the leadership of White, but the decision was made to keep *Glad Tidings* in Colorado — without the Sangstons.

Much discouraged and feeling rejected and betrayed, Sangston wrote White in June 1913, "I wrote to Rev. Joe Jacobs and got a reply stating what disposition had been made of us. It will be useless to press the matter further for he would not tell the real reason, nor do I ask it of you. We will within the next 2 months get off the car and go to Russell, Iowa, and make that our headquarters and do public evangelistic work."[75]

All of the chapel car missionaries seemed disheartened by the constantly changing tides of the troublesome situation between the home mission and publication societies. They were tired of changing the lettering on the sides of their cars, of preparing multiple reports, of conflicting assignments, of trying to please two masters, of trying to keep aging cars in

good repair — tired of keeping railroad costs down and free-will offerings up.

Henry L. Morehouse of the home mission society could not get the thorn of the chapel cars out of his side, and now the soreness had grown to include the gospel wagons and boats, all of which were attracting much attention for the publication society.

His friend and associate, Charles A. Wooddy was still receiving reports from the survey about the chapel cars he had sent out earlier. North Dakota's Baptist secretary felt he could do without chapel cars and use field missionaries if he had to, although the Northern Pacific, Great Northern, and Soo railroads built new roads during the past year, and the Milwaukee Road was reported to contemplate construction of a line through the eastern portion of the state to Winnipeg. The South Dakota secretary also felt field missionaries could do the work in the thirty-seven towns along rail lines that were presently struggling without a church.

But Kansas officials were excited about the chapel cars. "The car attracts attention and offers an opportunity for special meetings for men or children."[76] Montana's state secretary felt the chapel cars were the best way to witness to all the new towns along the recently constructed lines of the Chicago, Milwaukee & Puget Sound Railway and the Soo Line.

Fig. 8.11 *Glad Tidings* ended its long service in Arizona. Before going to Flagstaff, where it would be dismantled after serving as a temporary church, the car made several stops in Arizona, including Douglas. All the chapel cars had bicycles, like the one in the picture, so that the missionaries could make calls around town. (American Baptist Historical Society, Valley Forge)

The Wyoming secretary agreed. "We can use a chapel car indefinitely, and as we can use no other agency. The Burlington Sound to Coast Line is being completed and trains are already running on it. It crosses the State from North West to South East. There are large towns along the lines of the Union Pacific where we should like to send a chapel car."[77]

Davis Stays at Douglas, Wyoming

If Morehouse and Wooddy were not excited about the chapel cars, a newspaper reporter in Fort Morgan, Colorado, was. Impressed by *Glad Tidings* when it pulled into town and was sided on the Burlington tracks at the south end of Main Street in April 1914, he gave glowing reports of the attractiveness of the unique car and of the Reverend and Mrs. J. S. Davis, now on board. "Rev. J. S. Davis is accompanied by his wife in this form of missionary work. He is an interesting speaker and his hearers are impressed that his life is in the cause he represents. He has been in charge of a chapel car a number of years and has met with many remarkable experiences. He has been in the railroad shops, in the barren territories of the frontier and in the most cultured communities as well."[78]

The people who lived in Deer Trail in 1914 would long remember the winter *Glad Tidings* came to town.

Deer Trail, Colorado, September 1997: An old gentleman sits on a wooden bench outside a lone cafe on a strip of storefronts that could have been built when in 1875 the Kansas Pacific Railroad granted the town plat of Deer Trail. He stares ahead, and the presence of strangers does not detract from his concentration.

He is looking at the ribbon of railroad track. It is likely that if he has lived in this town long, he worked for the railroad — the Kansas Pacific or the Union Pacific or the Denver and Rio Grande, whichever one claimed ownership at the time. Almost every man in town did.

The town behind him is quiet. On a side dirt street not far from where the old man sits is a tidy Baptist church. The sign

announces worship services. The church is alive and well. When it was built life was livelier, the town crowded, businesses flourishing.

In February of 1914, a great revival had been held in town, and the Holy Spirit's presence had been felt. On Sunday the largest congregation ever gathered in Deer Trail had come to Glad Tidings, and many souls, including whole families, had come to the Kingdom. The effects of the chapel car's visit could be seen all over town.[79]

Now the streets are quiet in Deer Trail. No excitement in town. Just an old man looking at the rails and remembering.

From Deer Trail, the car traveled north to Kersey and Gilcrest before settling in at Douglas. When Father Patrick came to Brophy in 1887, he recalled, "I found no Catholics there and the town looked like Goldsmith's Deserted Village."[80] Father Brophy would also have found few Baptists. St. James Catholic Church would be built in 1898. It would not be until the summer of 1915, after the CB & Q Railroad was built through Douglas, that *Glad Tidings* came into town and was placed on a prominent siding.

The local paper noted the car's presence and reported an unusual occurrence. Chapel car missionaries held baptisms anywhere they could, even in grease pits. At Douglas, in what was still homesteading country, twelve candidates were dipped into what hopefully was a clean pit in an abandoned garage. Some might classify that not a baptism as much as an oil anointing. It had not been an easy task to establish a church in this town due to opposition by other churches in town — including an impressive new St. James Catholic Church — and the general indifference of local Baptists.

It was here missionary J. S. Davis also ran afoul of the home mission society. Bruce Kinney, a beloved area home missionary, wrote to Morehouse with his concern about the chapel car work at Douglas. "They will want all the credit of beginning the work, organizing the church, building the building and at the same time are asking us to put in at once an investment of two or three times as much as they have spent all told to say nothing of the cost to us to support a pastor for an indefinite number of years. . . . It is simply incongruous."[81]

Kinney's objection had validity, for there were times when the home mission society was left with a church debt incurred by chapel car–built churches. Davis started a building campaign in 1919 for the Douglas church. Because of World War I and difficulty in raising the money for the edifice, the church was not finished until August 1923, and then only with the help of the state convention and the home mission society and sacrificial giving on the part of members.[82]

No doubt the building of the new steel chapel car *Grace* in the spring of 1915, a gift from the Conaway and Birch families of Los Angeles, triggered some of the increased anxiety attacks of the home mission society. *Grace*'s exposure at the San Francisco Exposition in 1915 only enhanced the image of the chapel cars, and the home missions society saw its coffers suffering.

It was at Douglas that *Glad Tidings* would spend much of the World War I years. Those were both the best of times and the worst of times for the people of Wyoming. The *Laramie Republican* in September 1917 reported, "Never in the history of Wyoming has the entire people been more prosperous than now," and those statements were backed up by the report of the state commissioner of labor and statistics.

Victory bonds were oversubscribed. Significant anti-Americanism seemed to have been absent in Wyoming, although extra guards were stationed at the Standard and Midwest refineries, the Pathfinder Dam, and railroad bridges. A Basin man was forced to kiss the flag because he had criticized President Wilson, and a Union Pacific employee of Russian ancestry in Cheyenne was stripped and painted yellow because he refused to buy a Victory bond. Basin, Thermopolis, Lander, and Douglas had vigilance committees, and at Greybull and a few other places, German books were burned.[83]

There was heavy traffic on Wyoming railroads, particularly on the Union Pacific. The lessons learned in the Civil War

that railway cars must be used only for the movement of troops and supplies, not for storage, had been forgotten. Cars were loaded and sent on their way with no place to unload them. As a result of this practice, congestion approaching paralysis hit the nation's railway system in 1917.[84]

In December the Union Pacific's general manager, in an attempt to increase the efficiency of some of his workers, persuaded the governor to appeal to mayors to close saloons at nine in the evening. Ten days later, on December 28, the federal government took over the nation's railroads with assurances of fair compensation to the owners.[85]

On January 4, 1917, the *Douglas Budget* reported, "Rev. J. S. Davis will take the Baptist chapel car to Dwyer this week for a series of meetings at that place. Delay in going has been caused by a shortage of coal for the car, which uses anthracite only and the supply of that kind of coal in Wyoming is limited. The car will be back the 1st of March and during its absence services will be held in Unity Temple."

After being sided at Douglas for over two years as a result of wartime restrictions, *Glad Tidings* was in need of an overhaul. There had been some consideration of moving the car to southern California, but the railroads there would not handle a car without steel underframes.[86] In February 1917, a discouraged Davis resigned from chapel car work.[87]

As World War I was going on and government restrictions were in place, the decision was made to keep *Glad Tidings* in Wyoming, and William Kennedy of Millville, New Jersey, was assigned to the car. In the game of chapel car musical chairs, the Kennedys were transferred to *Evangel* in October, and Mr. and Mrs. W. J. Bell, from Pipestone, Minnesota, were the novices on board.

Glad Tidings Serves Through War

One of Bell's early experiences in 1917 was at Chugwater, Wyoming, a small but progressive village in view of the magnificent Laramie Peak. By 1910, settlers were arriving daily by train, some five hundred. Drought, hail, and grasshoppers played havoc with the homesteaders' dreams, and more than half of the settlers were soon gone. The town was first platted in 1914, but enough remained to ensure the future of the town.

People who had been meeting in the Chugwater school came to the meetings in July 1917 and wanted to start a church. They needed a more permanent meeting place, but the doors all seemed closed. The missionaries, however, solved the problem. A poolroom owner had a fine white stucco bungalow, thirty-two feet square, in the process of erection, but the work was at a standstill for lack of funds. This condition, plus the fact all the young men were leaving the town because of the military draft, caused the poolroom owner to decide the poolroom business was not a necessity. He sold the property to the newly organized church, and the structure was completed in 1919.[88]

The diversity of religious materials available on the chapel cars had increased. At the board meeting in September 1917 the publication society reported that the entire New Testament had been completed in Hungarian, the Gospel of Luke had been printed in English and Hungarian in parallel columns, and the Gospel of John had been finished in Bohemian. The four Gospels in Polish were about to be printed, and the New Testament in Polish had been set up as far as Titus. The Gospel of Matthew was also in type and was being broken into pages. They were also printing a Polish hymnal with selected Scripture readings.

What a joy it must have been for the chapel car missionaries to be able to put into the hands of a person from Hungary or Poland the Gospel or a hymnal in their own tongue.

The war had made great changes in the way the railroads conducted business, and the publication society and the other societies were pressed for money. White was informed in April 1919 that *Glad Tidings* was going to be transferred from Wyoming to North Kansas City, Missouri, with a limited range of service. The Blanchards of *Emmanuel* would be in charge.

The Blanchards began their Missouri mission at North Kansas City, a growing factory city, but with less than a thousand population, where they rebuilt a collapsed membership from ten souls to an active membership of fifty. In the old Jesse James region of Missouri, at Little Blue, nearly everyone they met and those who came into the car had, at one time or another, been church members somewhere else. "The interest was good, and after about ten days I took an expression, asking all Christians to rise, when, to my surprise, only six stood. I wondered at this, for most of those remaining seated in the crowded church had admitted church relations in personal conversation. The next night told the story, as wanderers began to return and sinners confessed their need of a Savior."[89]

Missouri provided some time for the chapel car to be put in better shape. Much of the missionaries' work involved car maintenance and repair. The cars were to be varnished and have general renovation at least every two years, but other emergencies would find them in local or main shops too frequently.

In June 1920, permission was granted by the American Baptist Publication Society for repair work on *Glad Tidings* at the Union Pacific Shops near Kansas City at Armstrong.

Voted: To authorize repairs on chapel car "Glad Tidings" at an estimated cost of $416.00 This is the estimate of the Union Pacific Railway Company.
    Note: the repairs on "Glad Tidings" will include:
Painting of car, scraping off all loose paint
Painting of wheels and trucks
Gold leaf lettering
Painting of top of car. It was last painted in September, 1916
Several leaks in the roof must be soldered
2 copper screens to be placed in screen windows
2 window glasses to be laced in frames
1 screen door in bad condition
Doors repaired a little
A new smoke stack on top of car
New boxes underneath the car which contain the

Baker-Heater pipe
The cleaning of air box underneath the car, etc.[90]

Twenty-seven years old but looking shiny and new, *Glad Tidings* was reborn and ready for a new adventure. Early in 1921 there was an earnest effort to reach more of the Mexican populations in California and Arizona. The Reverend and Mrs. Howell, formerly missionaries in Mexico, Cuba, and Puerto Rico, were assigned to take *Glad Tidings* to Arizona. On April 14, 1921, Samuel G. Neil, publication society secretary, informed White that the car would be transferred from Missouri to the Howells in Arizona.

Getting the car to Arizona became a complex problem. Several options were considered after discovering that new tariff rates for chapel cars had been established August 1, 1921, which placed them in the same class as Red Cross cars. The rate was eighteen dollars for a minimum charge, and ten full fares for hauling the car a considerable distance. They charged no demurrage, and six persons could ride on the car at rates suggested.

White agreed with Neil that it would be best for the Howells to go on the car at Armstrong. In that case they would save their own car fare from Kansas City to Douglas, Arizona, and that would mean a saving to the society.[91] After traveling from Armstrong on the Union Pacific and switching at Kansas City to the Rock Island, *Glad Tidings*, with the Howells aboard, was on its way to Douglas, Arizona.

At Douglas, the *Daily Dispatch* announced that *Glad Tidings* was at the El Paso and Southwestern depot, and Howell "has been holding meetings along the route from Kansas City and has a large fund of humorous incidents to relate."[92]

Although privately there were problems with Howell and the Mexican mission, the publicity surrounding the unique project was glowing. Howell praised his new mission work. He and Mrs. Howell had never seen a chapel car before. They had spent twenty-eight years of service in the Latin American fields of the Home Mission Society, but a chapel car had never been part of their equipment.

Howells Begin Mexican Mission

When he found the car in the Union Pacific yards at Armstrong, Kansas, Howell said, "I liked the name, painted in large gold letters on the dark background. 'Glad Tidings' would mean so much when translated into Spanish. 'Buenas Nuevas' were to be taken to these people who had been forced, by ten years of civil strife to leave their native land and seek refuge in our country. This, then, would be the general theme of the message."

The Howells tried to explain how they felt about being on the chapel car. As they sat on the platform of the chapel, they tried to visualize the thousands who had occupied its pews during the years of its ministry and the hundreds who had here confessed Christ for the first time. Now an unfamiliar language was to be heard from the pulpit, and the organ was to carry the gospel music in Spanish hymns.

They were amazed at the efficiency of *Glad Tidings*. Howell marveled, "At the back of the rostrum, a door opened into the living quarters. Here the genius of the car builder succeeded in producing a magic house. The one room could be changed at night into a bedroom, and by day into a dining-room, sitting-room and study. From this two doors led, one to a kitchenette. In the little kitchen nothing was lacking and everything was within reach. The other door led down a hall, with lockers for clothes and provisions. At the end of the hall was the door to the rear platform and to the right, into the washroom. Inventive skill had made these thirty feet of car space into a comfortable, modern parsonage." When they finished looking the car over, they felt as if "we were going somewhere."

It was decided that their work was to begin in the mining town of Bisbee. From the start the car was filled with eager listeners. The Mexicans came first because this was something new. It was an unheard-of arrangement: "Una capilla en un carro-pulman" (a chapel in a Pullman car). Then the message gripped them. At the end of two weeks twenty-five confessed Christ as their Savior. Within two weeks after the close of the meetings, half that number had joined the local Mexican church.

From Bisbee *Glad Tidings* went to Naco, right to the border of Mexico. The car was located within two hundred feet of the boundary line. For six weeks the car was where they could reach the people from both sides of the line. Here they had the help of Mexican Publication Society colporter, the Reverend Pablo J. Villanueva *(see fig. 8.10)*. Twice during the stay at Naco Villanueva exhausted his supply of Bibles and Testaments, besides disposing of all that were in the car. "I never anywhere saw a people so anxious to read God's Word. Nearly every night there were conversions in the car. At the end of the meetings thirty-five had accepted Jesus. There was no local Mexican church in Naco, so we had to leave these converts to shift for themselves. I have since heard of six who moved to Empalme, Mexico, and immediately joined the local Baptist church."

The next stay was Nogales, the twin city of the border. Here they were in the midst of a Mexican population of more than fifteen hundred people. Nogales, Arizona, and Nogales, Mexico, were really one city. "One crosses the street passing through the wide gate, guarded by the custom officers, and is in Mexico. We had a splendid location for the car, on one of the main streets of the American city, directly in front of the court house. During our six weeks' stay in Nogales, fifty-one made public confession of Jesus. We took two pictures of our Sunday school attendance on the two last Sundays we were in Nogales. These pictures are graphic testimonies of the increasing interest in the work."[93]

Not all was harmonious in the Howell arrangement. White felt that Howell did not have the heart for chapel car work, that he did not want to visit homes and greet the local Mexican people in the streets. He did not want to stay in Arizona during the summer months, although White had given him permission to get a room outside the car and use the car only for meetings. Other chapel car missionaries had endured such conditions and had done the work; so should Howell.

White and Neil were not pleased with Howell's attitude and insisted that he stay in Arizona for the full year pledged.

White concluded, "He has had good results so far as professed conversions are concerned, and we appreciate him. He is capable of accomplishing a great deal of good, but evidently has not conceived the genius of chapel-car work."[94]

Staying longer than he desired, Howell was relieved to leave chapel car work in June. *Glad Tidings* was in Glendale near Phoenix, and he was instructed to leave the car on its siding and turn the keys over to the state superintendent until his successor could be found.

Glad Tidings Begins Final Trip

Howell's successor was the Reverend W. C. Driver, an old hand at chapel car work, who had served with his wife in Oregon for many years. Driver knew that after weeks in Arizona's sandpaper wind, *Glad Tidings* needed new paint. Because there was no major car shop near that could handle the work, the Detroit Auto Paint Shop in Phoenix did the work in December 1922 for $295.08.

The job description included "two coats of Pratt & Lambert's Pullman Green Vitralite enamel on one side of the car which is far too much weather-worn to receive varnish. The other side it is possible to bring out fairly well with two coats of Pratt & Lambert's Spar Varnish, the best grade procurable here. For the roof, we will use a coat of the best grade of Gilsonite or asphaltum base paint which will protect, waterproof, and give a good lustre. On the side upon which we use the enamel, it will be necessary to go over the sign-work again and to keep down the cost, we have figured the use of gold Bronze instead of the usual Gold Leaf. The result obtained in this manner is so near the same that only a trained eye can tell the difference, but it makes quite a little difference in the price."[95]

In its new coat of paint, after having services in Phoenix and Mesa, *Glad Tidings* worked at Chandler in the spring of 1923. On April 5, the Chandler newspaper ran the story, "A regular Missionary Baptist Church is to be organized in Chandler next Friday evening April 6. The evangelistic services at the Chapel Car during the past month have resulted in thirty conversions, nineteen baptisms and a number of reclamations. On Sunday, April 8th, at 10:00 o'clock, a Sunday School will be organized in the Chapel car. It is believed that the church membership will reach 50 or more and the enrollment of the Sunday School will be not less than sixty."

Flagstaff Becomes Last Stop

At the Arizona Baptist Convention in May 1923, several items of major concern were on the agenda. "According to the reports the two greatest problems confronting the churches are indifference, and the amusement craze. Other problems, all of which are more or less general, are how to secure and keep a pastor, how to reach the unsaved, lack of spirituality, uninformed members regarding Baptist beliefs, building, removals, unlisted Baptists, shift work, securing Baptist teachers in public schools, and indebtedness of the people."[96]

A year later, the state convention report noted, "the church at Flagstaff, after several years of quiet existence, had come to life again as an organization, and for the time being will join with the Methodists and Presbyterian churches in the city in support of a pastor. It would become a Federated Church." Almost as an afterthought, the same agenda item announced that the Glad Tidings Baptist Church of Chandler, after a brief existence, voted to disband. This was the church that *Glad Tidings* and the Drivers had worked so hard to organize not too many months before.

In February 1926, *Glad Tidings* arrived in Flagstaff and was pulled through town, past the new Santa Fe depot and past marvelous views of the San Francisco Peaks, and put on a siding at the lumber mill. The Drivers dropped the car off and traveled on to California.

Services began in the car under the care of Arizona Baptist missionary W. A. Vanderhoof and continued in that location until the end of the year.[97] The *Coconino Sun* reported that Vanderhoof was ill and that George White of Los Angeles, who was formerly chapel car missionary for *Glad Tidings* (now in charge of chapel car work in the West) would be preaching the following Sunday evening, and that good crowds were coming to the car.[98]

In the same issue was a picture of a railroad car that looked amazingly like *Glad Tidings*. It was a school car, equipped and operated by the Canadian National Railway for the Ontario government in order to bring educational facilities to the children of Canada. When a car just as attractive and novel was sitting on a visible siding in his own town, it is interesting that the newspaper editor would choose to ignore it and promote as news a car hundreds of miles away in another country.

There were those in town who were not happy to see *Glad Tidings*, especially perhaps those in the Federated Church. The Baptists had been trying for a number of years to start a church in town and until now had not been successful. Whether or not the picture of the Canadian car was a slam, an intentional slight, or an innocent slip will never be known, but it was an intriguing coincidence. A week later this lead appeared in the paper: "In spite of bad location, the audiences have been growing at the chapel car. Sunday's services were well attended and enthusiastic."

Almost a year since its arrival in Flagstaff, the car was moved from that "bad location" at the sawmill to a siding on South Beaver Street and the Santa Fe track crossing. It was parked next to a stone warehouse not more than a hundred yards from the Santa Fe depot. A huge snowstorm prevented the car from getting ready for a move less than two blocks down South Beaver Street — to a spot where it would be used until a church could be erected. In the midst of that storm the Reverend W. F. Starring, president of the Arizona Baptist Convention, arrived from the Winslow Baptist Church, where he preached at the morning and evening service to a small but brave crowd.

On February 25, the paper announced that the car had been placed on timbers ready to be moved, and meetings were held in the car despite the inconveniences. The week of March 4, *Glad Tidings* became a "street car," due to downright irritating circumstances.

The moving of the chapel car after many delays and dis-appointments is progressing satisfactory. The car stood in the street Monday and Tuesday without moving any because Mr. Washington's help deserted him. It was discovered later that one of the men had skipped leaving several unpaid bills about town. The people of the town have been patient during the delays and inconvenience caused by the moving of the car and the Baptist folks appreciate the kindnesses shown them.

The kindness of the Santa Fe Railroad people and Paul Morton of the Central Commercial Company in giving the Baptist people space and permission to unload the car on their property is quite note-worthy and is appreciated.

Flagstaff's "street car" has caused considerable comment, but it will shortly cease to be a "street car" having made only one trip down the street.

As the car nears its destination interest in it grows and the services grow. The audiences were good Sunday even though the car was out in the street and it was raining.

F. E. Hart who has been helping to move the Baptist Chapel car failed to show up for work Monday morning. And it was finally ascertained that he had departed for parts unknown.[99]

Glad Tidings *had reached its new location on South Beaver; it was not yet on its foundation the following week, minus trucks and wheels — still beautiful and useful as a house of God but robbed of its "go." It had become the Glad Tidings Baptist Church and would serve that purpose until sometime in 1931 or 1932, when it was dismantled and its congregation moved to a building once owned by the Seventh-Day Adventists.*

Harold Harper, who attended church as a young boy in Glad Tidings, *remembers the chapel car well as it was his job to clean and prepare it for worship. He remembers rubbing down the golden oak pews and dusting the Estey organ and the ornate*

pulpit in the chapel. He remembers the Reverend Dixon, who taught him the Scriptures that have sustained him all his eighty-three years. He remembers watching Dixon take that chapel car apart with his own hands, ending up with a ton of brass screws in the process. He will never forget the warmth and fun and fellowship of the Christians in that chapel car.

Harper thought he would never see Glad Tidings *again. As he watched slides of* Glad Tidings *and other chapel cars in his home in Flagstaff in the spring of 1997, he wiped his eyes and murmured to his wife of sixty-four years, who never got to see the church on rails he talked so much about, "Now isn't that something, isn't that something. I never thought I'd see it again. Isn't that something."*

Glad Tidings, so the angels sang,
Until the heav'ns with gladness rang;
Glad Tidings late my soul replied,
For me my Lord was crucified.[100]

Notes

[1] C. H. Rust, *A Church on Wheels* (Philadelphia: American Baptist Publication Society, 1905), 3.

[2] *The Colporter*, July 1894, 3.

[3] Rust, 8–9.

[4] Ibid.

[5] Ibid., 6.

[6] Carl Zapffe, "75" *Brainerd, Minnesota*, 75, a publication of the Brainerd Civic Association, Brainerd, Minn., Public Library.

[7] Boston W. Smith, *The Story of Our Chapel Car Work* (Philadelphia: American Baptist Publication Society, n.d.).

[8] T. M. Shanafelt, *The Baptist History of South Dakota* (Sioux Falls, S.D.: South Dakota Baptist Convention, n.d.), 65.

[9] BSP, scrapbook, "Merry Christmas," ABHS, VF.

[10] *Missions*, April 1910, 278.

[11] Anniversary Report of the American Baptist Publication Society, Pittsburgh, Pa., 1897, 22.

[12] Rust, 9.

[13] Anniversary Report, 1897, 23.

[14] R. C. Overton, *The First Ninety Years: An Historical Sketch of the Burlington Railroad* (Chicago, 1940), 13.

15 Seventy-first Anniversary of the ABPS, 1895, an address by Donald D. MacLaurin, American Baptist Publication Society, Philadelphia, 49.

16 Anniversary Report of the American Baptist Publication Society, 1901, Springfield, Mass., 48.

17 Overton, 24.

18 Rust, 15.

19 Ibid., 17.

20 Ibid., 18.

21 Ibid., 19.

22 Ibid., 23.

23 Ibid., 27.

24 Ibid., 26.

25 Ibid.

26 Ibid., 23–24.

27 C. W. Meacham, "Three Weeks on a Chapel Car," brochure, ABHS, VF.

28 Rust, 57.

29 Ibid., 13.

30 Letter from Margaret Hargrave to Mrs. Dorothy A. Martin, Board of Education and Publication, Valley Forge, Pa., dated July 21, 1971, ABHS, VF.

31 The *Nebegamon Enterprise*, April 29, 1899, courtesy of Father Herman Page and of Andrew Roth, of the Duluth, South Shore & Atlantic Railroad Historical Society.

32 Ibid.

33 *Encyclopedia of Wisconsin: A Volume of Encyclopedia of the United States* (New York: Somerset Publishers, 1990), 346.

34 Rust, 73–74.

35 *The Colporter*, February 1900, 8.

36 *The Colporter*, May 1900, 8.

37 *The Colporter*, August 1900, 7.

38 "Holmes," in *The History of Belmont County*, Iowa (Iowa Historical Society, 1976), Bicentennial Commission, 214.

39 "Town of Woolstock," from the files of the Iowa Historical Society, 250.

40 Ralph Tess, Our Heritage: *Almond and Vicinity* (Almond, Wis.: Almond Historical Society, 1986), 64.

41 Ibid., 62.

42 Ibid., 42.

43 "Almond Baptist Church History," Almond Historical Society, Almond, Wis.

44 L. E. Olson, *Beyond the County Line* (Ft. Wayne, Ind.: self-published) Almond Public Library, Almond, Wis.

45 Proceedings of Wisconsin Baptist Anniversaries, October 3–6, 1904, American Baptist Conference of Wisconsin, 35.

46 *Wood County Reporter*, Grand Rapids, Wood County, Wis., Thursday, May 21, 1903, front page, Wisconsin Rapids Memorial Library, Wisconsin Rapids, Wis.

47 "Baptist Church Celebrates 90 Years," *Star-Herald* (Scottsbluff, Neb.), August 20, 1994, 1B, n.p.

48 BSP, chapel car pamphlets and tracts, ABHS, VF.

49 Michael M. Bartels, *Missouri Pacific: River and Prairie Rails* (David City, Neb.: South Platte Press, 1997), 94.

50 Plainview Paper. (newspaper clipping).

51 Letter from George L. White to Guy C. Lamson, January 29, 1915, George L. White file, ABHS, VF.

52 Anniversary Report of the American Baptist Publication Society, Oklahoma City, Okla., 1908, 37.

53 *Missions*, April 1910, 278.

54 Frank Schweissing, *The History of Wyoming Baptists* (Wyoming Baptist Convention, 1952), 26.

55 Tacetta B. Walker, *Big Horn Basin: Stories of Early Days in Wyoming* (Casper, Wyo.: Prairie Publishing Co., 1936), 61–62.

56 Ibid., 133.

57 *Colorado Baptist Bulletin*, March 1905, 3, Archives of the American Baptist Conference of the Rocky Mountains, Lakewood, Colo.

58 Virginia Turner, "More Reminiscing of Pioneer Days in History of Sagebrush Flat, Now Fertile Powell Valley," *The Powell (Wyoming) Tribune*, Friday, October 27, 1950, 3.

59 *Pioneer Memories* (Powell, Wyo.: Powell Business and Professional Women and the Powell American Association of University Women, 1975), Powell Public Library.

60 Sophie Bronson, "A Day with Glad Tidings," *Missions*, January 1911, 23–25.

61 Letters between Joe Jacobs, secretary for the western division, and George L. White, missionary for the western division, July 9 and July 17, 1912, George White files, ABHS, VF.

62 David J. Wasden, From Beaver to Oil (Cheyenne: Pioneer Printing, 1978), 253.

63 Lylas Skovgard, *Basin City: The First County Seat in the Big Horn Basin* (Basin, Wyo.: Timbertrails Press, 1988), 34–35.

64 Ibid., 124.

65 Schweissing, 62.

66 Unpublished history of the Thermopolis and Lucerne Baptist Churches, comp. Hazel Bender Cochran, 1964.

67 *Missions*, September 1915, 704, Franklin College Library, Franklin, Ind.

68 Ibid.

[69] Letter to George L. White from Arthur Sangston, Scotts Bluff, Neb., July 29, 1912, George L. White files, ABHS, VF.

[70] *Missions*, December 1912, 945.

[71] Letter to George L. White from Arthur Sangston, Alliance, Neb., October 1912, George L. White files, ABHS, VF.

[72] Letter to George L. White from Arthur Sangston, Vona, Colo., November 25, 1912, George L. White files, ABHS, VF.

[73] Letter to Arthur Sangston from George L. White, Portland, Ore., December 3, 1912, George L. White files, ABHS, VF.

[74] *Colorado Baptist Bulletin*, April 1913, Archives of the American Baptist Conference of the Rocky Mountains, Lakewood, Colo.

[75] Letter to George L. White from Arthur Sangston, Alamosa, Colo., June 6, 1913, George L. White files, ABHS, VF.

[76] Letters to Bruce Kinney from Montana, Wyoming, North Dakota, South Dakota, Kansas Baptist Headquarters, 1915, Bruce Kinney files, ABHS, VF.

[77] Report of C. A. Woody survey results, George L. White files, ABHS, VF.

[78] Newspaper clipping from Fort Morgan, Colo., April 10, 1914, ABHS, VF.

[79] *Colorado Baptist Bulletin*, May 1914, Archives of American Baptist Conference of the Rocky Mountains, Lakewood, Colorado.

[80] "A History of St. James Catholic Church," Douglas, Wyo.., Mass of Dedication, April 28, 1981.

[81] Letter to H. L. Morehouse from Bruce Kinney, August 9, 1915, Bruce Kinney files, ABHS, VF.

[82] Schweissing, 76.

[83] T. A. Larson, *The History of Wyoming* (Lincoln: University of Nebraska Press, 1965), 400.

[84] *Encyclopaedia Britannica*, "Railway," 1968, vol. 18, 1108.

[85] Larson, 397.

[86] Letter to Guy C. Lamson from George L. White, December 21, 1916, George L. White files, ABHS, VF.

[87] Letter to George L. White from Guy C. Lamson, January 4, 1917, George L. White files, ABHS, VF.

[88] Anniversary Report of the American Baptist Publication Society, Atlantic City, N.J., 1918, 32.

[89] F. I. Blanchard, "The Seed Is the Word of God," tract, American Baptist Publication Society/American Baptist Historical Society, ABHS, VF.

[90] Bill from Union Pacific Railroad, George L. White files, ABHS, VF.

[91] Letter to Samuel Neil from George L. White, George L. White files, ABHS, VF.

[92] *Daily Dispatch*, September 16, 1921, n.p., Douglas Public Library, Douglas, Ariz.

[93] *Missions*, September 1922, 470.

[94] Letter from George L. White to Samuel G. Neil, April 15, 1922, American Baptist Assembly files, Green Lake, Wis.

[95] Letter from Detroit Auto Paint Shop, 613 South Central Avenue, Phoenix, Ariz., to American Baptist Publication Society office, Phoenix, Ariz., November 27, 1922, miscellaneous correspondence, ABHS, VF.

[96] Arizona Baptist Convention Report, May 1923, American Baptist Conference of the Southwest, Phoenix office.

[97] Churches Column, *The Coconino Sun*, Flagstaff, Friday, February 12, 1926.

[98] Ibid., Friday, February 12, 1926.

[99] "Glad Tidings Baptist Church," *Coconino Sun*, Flagstaff, March 4, 1927.

[100] This hymn, assigned to chapel car *Glad Tidings*, was written by Indian missionary Isaac McCoy after an Indian-settler battle fought in Indiana, sometime between 1817 and 1846. The hymn was sung to the tune of GRATITUDE L.M. or "Lord, Speak to Me That I May Speak."

CHAPTER 9

Baptist Car 4: *Good Will* from the Southwest to the Northwest

Texas in the 1890s was divided into three frontiers of magnificent distances, great destitution, and splendid possibilities: east Texas, south Texas, and west Texas, including the contiguous territory of New Mexico. The Texas Baptist Convention reported in 1894, "Hard as the times are, these vast regions are being settled. There is nowhere else for the people to go, and he who has an ear to hear can already hear the tramp of the oncoming millions. Our missionaries should not wait to ride on the cowcatcher of the first engine of the new railroad, but should already be on the ground ready to welcome the engineer and his passengers, preaching the gospel to them, and baptizing them as fast as they believe."[1]

Constructed to ride not on the cowcatcher but coupled behind the engine, chapel car *Good Will* came to Texas after its dedication at Saratoga Springs, New York, June 1, 1895, with the Reverend Edwin Stanton Stucker and his wife on board. Stucker, an Ottawa University and University of Chicago Divinity School graduate, came to the chapel car ministry from a pastorate at Aurora, Illinois.

The father of the chapel car movement, Wayland Hoyt, told those gathered at the seventy-first anniversary meeting of the publication society:

. . . it is the peculiar function of the colporter to go, to keep going; to persist in going, and to go into places where nobody else would be apt to go, and the chapel car with its whirring wheels, with its prayer meetings often speeding on transcontinental trains at the rate of forty miles a hour, and its swift visits here, then yonder to this destitute place and that, and with its ability of harnessed steam to search out any hamlet on prairie or nook or mountain side to which nineteenth century railroads can push themselves — why, your chapel car is simply the most compact and alert specimen of a gospel-going.[2]

This fourth Baptist car, built with seventy-five hundred dollars in subscriptions to fulfill the agreement with William Hills when he made the gift for *Glad Tidings* the year before, began its work in Texas in cooperation with the Southern Baptists. Besides native Texans — mainly ranchers, cowboys, merchants, and professionals — there were thousands of Bohemians, Swedes, and as many as three hundred thousand[3] Germans who had migrated to the state, plus a large Norwegian settlement in the Texas Basque country and a growing population of African Americans. Around San Antonio, San Marcos, along the Rio Grande, at El Paso,

Fig. 9.1 When *Good Will* first visited Texas, the state was a wild and diverse land of opportunities and extremes. In the land west of the Pecos River, Judge Roy Bean was the law of the land. (Western History Collections, University of Oklahoma Libraries)

along the Mexican border, and into New Mexico Territory, there were many needy Mexican settlements.[4] Texas Baptists were eager for *Good Will* to minister to these snowballing colonies, many without churches.

With new railroads spreading all across Texas, witnessing to railroaders was another major focus for the chapel car ministry, and it was at a railroad center that Stucker first stopped — Denison, the shops of the Missouri, Kansas, and Texas Railroad (MK & T).

> The car was placed between the round house and machine shops and services were held at noon, p.m. and midnight, for ten days. The meetings at midnight were especially fruitful. The men seemed to realize that we were there with *"Good Will,"* when we left our home uptown (the combination of heat, noise, and smoke prevented our staying in the car here) and came over a mile through mud and rain, which were not lacking for a single twenty-four hours while we were there. . . . The midnight audience averaged forty men, who would hurriedly eat their lunches and come "just as they were" and give us at least fifty minutes, and usually a full hour. A more attentive audience could not easily be found. The result was over fifty public professions among men many of whom had not been in a religious service from five to fifteen years, according to their own testimony.[5]

After stopping at Dallas to ask the superintendent of the MK & T to park a coach at the Denison shops for the use of Christian laymen, the Stuckers went on to Fort Worth and made their way into the extreme northwestern part of the state, the fabled Llano Estacado or Staked Plains. For two months *Good Will* held two to three services daily in the frontier towns above the Canadian River where the gospel had never been preached.

When *Good Will* arrived in 1895 at Texline, a Fort Worth and Denver Railroad junction town in the desolate stretches of Llano Estacado, the tent city was changing into a permanent town. A town hall, which was being used for school

sessions, had been built along with a hotel and a number of businesses.[6] In spite of the town's expansion, however, there was no church. From the first night of *Good Will*'s arrival, the car was filled, with practically all of the one hundred town residents in attendance.[7] For two weeks, meetings were held twice each day and four times on Sundays in the chapel car, and a little church was formed.

Along the Texas and Pacific line at Big Sandy, the car was filled every afternoon with bright, responsive boys and girls, and the car was filled in the evening with their mothers and fathers. At the Texas and Pacific shops at Marshall, the car was the center of a circle of eight large shops employing five to six hundred men. Stucker reported, "During the seven months since the dedication of *Good Will*, it has traveled five thousand miles and witnessed the preaching of over three hundred gospel sermons. It has not found a single railroad over which it may not freely journey on its mission of love."[8]

Stucker left the chapel car in November 1895 to become a Texas district secretary.

Freedom Fighter Diaz Operates Clinic

Blackballed from practicing medicine in Cuba as a result of preaching Baptist doctrine, Dr. Alberto J. Diaz came to the attention of the Southern Baptist board. The Committee on Cuban Missions described Diaz as an earnest, godly man whose zeal, enthusiasm, and unfaltering faith, even through bitter persecution, were mighty factors in carrying on the work.[9] During that time of persecution, he was even rejected by his own mother, whose opposition finally melted away when she saw the impact of her son's ministry. She came to Diaz and asked, "Alberto, are you not willing for me to join your church?" When Diaz baptized her, in his joy he forgot the formula words and simply said, "Here, Lord Jesus, this is my mother."[10]

Boston Smith had met Diaz at the American Baptist Publication Society national gathering in Milwaukee in May 1895, where the *Glad Tidings* was on display. "How would you like to take charge of Chapel Car *Good Will* and go to Mexico to preach the gospel in that republic?" Boston proposed to Diaz. "You should have seen the sparkle in his black eyes when I asked the question," Smith said.[11]

So it happened that in November 1895, Diaz was the missionary on board. It was hoped that he would be able to carry the chapel car work into Mexico, but after a few weeks of service among the Spanish-speaking people of Texas, the call for aid to Cuba came, which Diaz could not resist, and he resigned his chapel car assignment and joined the army that was on its way to Cuba.

Smith visited Diaz on the chapel car in San Antonio in 1896, before Diaz left for Cuba, and was surprised by what he found.

Sidetracked in the most densely populated section of that quaint city, among the Spanish speaking people, I found *Good Will*. As I entered the beautiful study, I found the bookcase, instead of containing a well-selected library, filled with surgical instruments of all kinds. Opposite the bookcase was an operating table. "Why, Doctor, what does this mean?" I asked. He told me in his broken but intensely interesting way, how from nine to eleven o'clock each morning he treated, free of charge, all the sick and afflicted who came to the car. This, he said, gave him entrance into the homes and hearts of the people. After lunch each day, he visited from house to house, reading the word of God, distributing Spanish tracts and praying with the people.[12]

After Diaz left, the Stuckers returned to San Antonio on the chapel car in February to conduct a series of meetings near area railroad depots. The first meeting of the series was held near the international depot, and then at Smithville, where the night services overflowed into the opera house.[13]

Meanwhile, Baptists in the border town of Del Rio had called for support in organizing a church, and in May 1896 *Good Will* pulled into Del Rio and parked in the local railroad yard. Catholic priests had held the first religious services in the area around 1808, and a priest of the Episcopal church

and a chaplain in the United States Army stationed at nearby Fort Clark held Protestant services in the 1850s. The Methodists did not organize until 1878, and from 1887 through 1890, the few Baptists who were in Del Rio held only occasional meetings.

Local historians suggest that the threat of Indians and the work that had to be done to civilize this raw country didn't allow much time for worship other than what settlers could do in the fields or at home. Then the Reverend Frank Marrs, a pioneer Del Rioan, joined the car fresh from his studies at Southern Baptist Seminary in Louisville, Kentucky, and soon afterward he organized the First Baptist Church of Del Rio.[14]

By the 1890s, Del Rio had grown to 1,980 people, and the Southern Pacific Railroad was the town's biggest employer with collective salaries amounting to nearly twelve-thousand dollars monthly.[15] When construction on the Southern Pacific stretched across the federal territories in the late 1870s and early 1880s and reached Texas, the inveterately thirsty crews, like the crews of the other western railroads, demanded that saloons move along with the building of town tracts.

Following the railroad from San Antonio to Del Rio were many saloons, including Mr. Ware's Hell's Acre[16] and the legendary Judge Roy Bean's saloon. These taverns, mainly tents, still flourished during the time *Good Will* was in Del Rio (*see fig. 9.1*).

At some point the notorious Roy Bean discovered that a tent saloon was a comparatively lucrative enterprise, so he acquired such a business, which he moved from place to place as the track-builders moved along. Somewhere between El Paso and the Pecos River, he became renowned enough to attract the notice of the Texas Rangers, who observed that he could handle himself well and triumph over all sorts of troublesome characters who frequented such resorts as he kept. Troublemakers behaved well under his supervision.

Whether he solicited a job as justice of the peace or not, he seems to have been called into that service by

Texas Rangers, who found it a hindrance to have no judge before whom to arraign prisoners who had been arrested for thievery and other crimes. On the long stretch of railroad where there were virtually no towns, the temporary town at the "end of the track" had to serve from time to time as a place of arraignment, and the housing for such an arraignment might conveniently be a saloon.

Roy Bean stood tall, cuffed men about in his saloon if they were unruly and altogether had made a name for himself as a man to be respected (later famous for his affection for the actress Lillian "Jersey Lil" Langtry). Appointed justice of the peace, he grew fond of the title Judge and soon posted a shingle giving his name and title, and making the claim that he was "The Law West of the Pecos."[17]

From the lawlessness of the Pecos, *Good Will* went to the more citified Dallas, where it played Cupid in cahoots with genial Uncle Boston Smith. The chapel car became the honeymoon location for the Reverend E. G. Townsend and Hollie Harper Townsend, who met at the First Baptist Church of Dallas in 1896. He was pastor of a small church, and she was engaged in city Bible work among women and children. The young people were both excited about chapel car work as a result of hearing an address by Uncle Boston at the First Baptist Church of Dallas, where the eminent George Truett was pastor. Uncle Boston, never bashful, encouraged them to wed and come to work on the chapel car.

Newlywed Townsends Delight in Work

As newlyweds the Townsends climbed aboard *Good Will* in 1897 when Stucker returned to his work as district missionary. Townsend would say of Smith's urgings, "The result was, after much consultation and prayer, I undertook the following March, what few men are willing to do, the management of two brides at once!"[18]

Townsend reported to the seventy-fourth session of the publication society about the work in Tenaha, a shipping point on the Houston, East and West Texas Railroad that had been founded only two years before *Good Will*'s arrival. By 1897 the town had grown to 680 residents and had become a center for area farmers and lumbermen.[19]

The work in Texas, as elsewhere, is along these lines: among railroad men and their families, at division points and in large shops; with weak, half-organized churches; and in railroad towns where there are no churches. In many portions of west, south, and eastern Texas there are weak, struggling churches. To these churches, poor, untrained, and often pastorless for a year, the visit of the chapel car is the event of a lifetime.

Such a place was Tenaha, sixteen miles from the eastern border of Texas, in the heart of the piney wood. We stopped for only a day or so, waiting for mail, before going west to a cooler clime. We began to preach four times a day. The people began to come for miles and miles around. They came to see that church on wheels — that wonder car, and a woman [Mrs. Townsend] who was "a heap better talker than the man." . . .

Twice we were forced to move, seeking a larger building. On the third Saturday I say there were a thousand people present. We worked two weeks longer, baptizing in all forty-six and receiving into the church sixty-five, and some twenty joined neighboring country churches.[20]

Things did not go so well at another stop late that summer. "We found a church but it was doing absolutely nothing. Some large brick works and coal mines near the town brought a gang of drinking, gambling men. We longed to stay for weeks here, but after one week I was forced to leave, worn out with the heat and malaria fever. . . ."

Children were a delight to the Townsends, especially to Hollie. "I wish you could look in sometimes on the car filled with a squirming mass of young humanity, . . . their heroic attempts to sing the new songs; their blank dismay when called upon for Scripture verses; and their pathetic apology, 'We ain't never been to no sunday school to learn one,' or 'we ain't got no Bible at our house;' their delight when we give them the story papers and Scripture cards; the eagerness with which they listen to the Scripture lesson and the bright, amusing stories. When we get the children, it is not a hard task to get their parents."

At one town they were sidetracked in the middle of the plaza. "Every afternoon I would hold services for men only," Townsend said, "and except the little band of workers, I had a different crowd every day, men from the farms and ranches, fifty and one hundred miles away, who would be gone tomorrow."[21]

At Abilene in October 1897, Townsend set up a tent seating two thousand by the chapel car. All denominations in town participated in the meetings, sponsored by the First Baptist Church. It was Townsend's hope that God would lead and this would be the greatest meeting ever held in western Texas.

In reporting to Smith, Townsend wrote about the meeting and testified about his wife's stellar Christian qualities, "About 80 conversions to date. Many backsliders reclaimed and the town is being stirred religiously from center to circumference. My faith is that 200 souls will be saved. Sister Townsend holds women's meetings at 3:30 and a children's meeting at 5 p.m., both largely attended. She is modest, wise, consecrated and is a great soul winner and organizer, and is a power for good."[22]

Mrs. Townsend Dies after Childbirth

Townsend did not mention the fact that his wife was also pregnant and not in good health. Little over a year after their marriage and their coming to *Good Will*, Hollie Townsend died after giving birth to a baby boy, one of only three babies born in chapel car service. The memory of Hollie Harper Townsend's goodness would long outlast her short, devoted life.

One of the last things Hollie Townsend did was to write a tract for the publication society describing life on the chapel car. She writes of her kitchen on the car.

On one side of this hall is a little room, a doll house you would think, but it is my kitchen! Just standing room, fitted up with refrigerator, cupboard, sink for washing dishes, and a good range: the missionaries cook and eat same as other folks. We have a large pantry across the hall, and next to it another closet for clothes. . . .

My porches are rather small, but a yard as big as — Texas! In this yard is always to be found the choicest flowers, for the children bring them to me every day, until I often have every vase full and in desperation bring in the dish pan to hold the love offerings. . . . When we pull in at a little country station, we attract more attention than a circus. All the boys and girls and big folks too, come crowding around the car to see what it means, such a fine car — it cost seventy-five hundred dollars — and it does shine![23]

In December, after his wife's death, Townsend visited Del Rio, where Stucker had started a church, and then he went west to Comstock and established a new congregation. Maybe keeping his mind on the work his wife loved so much would abate his grief. Pastor Marrs came from the Del Rio Baptist Church to help organize the church at Comstock, located in that desolate area of the Devil's River. The Galveston, Harrisburg and San Antonio Railroad Company built a railroad westward through Val Verde County in the late 1880s, and along this railroad in thirty-mile intervals town sites were laid out, including the town of Comstock. The thirty-mile distance between towns was convenient in that it represented one day's travel by horse and buggy.

We are now on the southwestern border not only of Texas but also of the United States. Across the Rio Grande River in Mexico, the Santa Rosa Mountains lift their heads far above the clouds. This is the frontier of two republics. . . . Leaving Del Rio Christmas week, we climbed upward till we reached the table-land that is the great cattle country of Texas. We found a resting place at a little station, Comstock. There are not a dozen houses in sight yet from the ranches for twelve and twenty miles the people came and filled the car.

A gray-haired woman, the mother of twelve children, who had lived all of her life on a ranch, became interested in the meetings. She said: "I have never heard anything about the gospel, because I have never had any chance to go to preaching. But this you preach about is just what I have been longing for these many years."

Fig. 9.2 Some of the members of the church started at Comstock, Texas, worked on the Pecos High Bridge, once considered the eighth wonder of the world, completed in 1892. (Prints and Photographs Collection, CH 03235, Center for American History, University of Texas at Austin)

There is a Baptist church here now [with] fifteen members. The clerk of it, a young man, was sixteen years old before he ever heard a sermon. His mother, now an earnest Christian woman, spent eighteen years on a ranch without ever attending a religious service. The reign of his Satanic Majesty has been so universal here in the past that they named one of their principal rivers after him, Devil's River.[24]

In spring 1997 Dollie M. Carter, longtime member of the Comstock Baptist church organized by E. G. Townsend, welcomed us into her cozy living room, lined with pictures of smiling children and grandchildren. On one wall she pointed out an oval-framed, sepia-toned photograph of her husband, now

deceased. Like many who lived in Comstock in the first forty years of the twentieth century, Mr. Carter worked for the Southern Pacific Railroad at the Pecos High Bridge (see fig. 9.2).

Mrs. Carter could think of no better way to help us understand the story of life in the Comstock area than to give us a book written by Jack Skiles, former school superintendent, rancher, and manager of the Judge Roy Bean Visitor Center. From Skiles's book, we learned many interesting facts about this land of the Pecos, including the story of the High Bridge.

Because the previous rail route to cross the Pecos River was dangerous and difficult to maintain, construction started on the high bridge by the Southern Pacific Railroad in March 1891, leaving the original roadbed about three miles east of Comstock, proceeding northwest to the Pecos, and rejoining the old roadbed at Shumla on the west side of the river. The bridge was 321 feet high and 2,180 feet long. At one time considered to be the eighth wonder of the world, the high bridge was open to railroad traffic in March 1892.

Many passengers were afraid to ride across such a tall, spindly structure. At least one time passengers had to walk across the bridge because the wind was blowing so hard that the trainmen feared the light wooden coaches might blow off the bridge. In 1910 the bridge was reinforced and shortened 665 feet, with rock fill placed at both ends. Valuable to the U.S. transportation system, it was guarded by the military for many years, including during the Mexican Revolution and two world wars, and finally was replaced by a stronger concrete-and-steel structure in 1944.[25]

As a pumper, Dollie's husband had to descend 196 wooden stairs down into the canyon to reach the pump house, which provided water for the employees and the railroad. It was a physically demanding job, hard on Mr. Carter's health. Mrs. Carter raised the family in some interesting homes, including in cramped employee quarters of two rooms near the bridge.

Before the Carters came, when Good Will was at Comstock, some wives in the community would remember having to find caves in the bluffs for shelter or willow limbs and river canes to construct crude homes. Tents were expensive, and few people had much money for things other than livestock. The most abundant construction material was railroad cross ties, which were used to build houses and barns, for fence posts, and to keep wood stoves burning.[26]

Life was hard, food was scarce — bread, potatoes, rice, coffee, chili, flour, beans, lard, sugar, some pork and lots of goat meat were the staples, plus canned corn or tomatoes once in a while.

Dollie remembers hard times and good times. She is grateful for family and friends, to a husband whose railroad job provided her with some security, and for her church, a church started by a young, grieving widower, E. G. Townsend, the father of a motherless babe. Freight trains still roll down the main line no more than a hundred yards from Dollie's living-room window, the same line that brought chapel car Good Will *to Comstock almost a hundred years ago.*

After visiting the border towns of Comstock and Del Rio, on the Galveston, Harrisburg and San Antonio Railway, Townsend stopped at the railroad shops of Somerville and Herne.

Each night the car was crowded. The car stood right at the round-house, and there would be as many men on the outside as on the inside. When the windows are all up, they can hear equally as well outside. One night, outside, there stood an engineer, cursing and abusing Christian people. He was reproved by one of the Christian yard men. The man attracted a good deal of attention by his violence. Two nights after this he was shot and killed. It made a very profound impression on everyone. It is just this class of men that our work is among. Many times we are able to lead them to Christ.

This is a typical chapel car town. Not more than twelve months old. More than a hundred houses have gone up in the last four months. There is not an organization of a church house in the place. There are plenty of saloons, and far into the night I can hear the shouts

of their drunken carousals. Interest is growing every night. Last night and night before there were a number that promised to trust the Savior. It is my hope to organize a church here soon and build a house. I have the promise of a lot. May all the dear friends of the chapel car work pray for this place.[27]

Townsend left chapel car work in early 1900 to pastor the First Baptist Church of Waco. During her illness his late wife had suggested to her husband that he marry her best friend, Elli Moore. This Townsend did in September 1899.[28] Elli came from a prominent family; her grandfather led the Texas forces at the Battle of Gonzales during the War for Independence. Later both Townsend and Elli Moore Townsend would become leaders of Mary Hardin-Baylor University.[29]

The Reverend G. B. Rogers, a well-known Texas pastor in his senior years, replaced Townsend on *Good Will*. His first tour took him to Fort Worth and Houston among railroad men, and then to Cleveland, forty-three miles from Houston, a town of only about three hundred inhabitants and no church. The meetings were a success with more than thirty-six confessions, and a church was organized with building plans underway. The next stop was Livingston, where results were not quite so encouraging, but Rogers reported that Thomas Moffatt of St. Louis had come to assist and sing for him.[30]

Rogers had to learn the rules of operating a chapel car, and in April 1900, he received a strong warning from publications secretary Robert G. Seymour about not allowing unauthorized persons to ride on the chapel car in transient. "If the Railroad will carry the car you can do as you please of course about using it for prayer meeting purposes, etc. on the way but it is manifestly unjust to the railroads to carry passengers unless they have a regular railroad ticket for which they have paid full price. We have to be exceeding cautious about such matters. The railroads are very kind to us in carrying the cars and it would be wrong for us to presume upon their kindness by accommodating those who would otherwise have to pay regular fares."

There were more rules to abide by, and in May Seymour again cautioned Rogers to not take the car to conventions and for exhibit unless given express permission. ". . . the railroad companies make a fuss if we go simply to exhibit; so we have to be very cautious when applications come to you to take the car to associations and things like that, that we do not seem to be exhibitors."

The Great Storm of Galveston

On September 8 and 9, 1900, Galveston, Texas, was struck with what was to be known as The Great Storm of Galveston *(fig. 9.3)*. *Good Will* was in the shops at Galveston at the time of the storm, but two years earlier, Townsend and his wife had worked with the Third Baptist Church in Galveston and had gotten to know Pastor Elder G. W. Lane and his family well. Pastor Lane, with his entire family, was swept away in the flood,[31] which claimed six thousand to eight thousand lives and was the worst natural disaster in United States history.

J. W. Maxwell, general superintendent of the Missouri, Kansas and Texas Railway, saw no fewer than three hundred bodies floating in the water, and many more were being buried on the mainland shore.

This proves what many have contended from the first, that the casualties from the beginning have been understated. Under the debris of wrecked houses all over the city there is every reason to believe there are hundreds of bodies, and these must be disposed of as early as possible. In the rafts of the bay there are yet many bodies which must be looked after.

It will never be possible to get the names of all who are lost, but every day makes the list more definite. It will never be possible to get an accurate estimate of victims. The estimate of 3000 is the most conservative, but those who place the estimate at an earlier 5000 are not considered unreasonable by many people. It is safe to say that more that 3000 bodies have been seen so far and the gulf and bay and the debris of the city will unquestionably bring many more to view.

If Mr. Lewis of Dallas has not overestimated the number he observed in Buffalo Bayou, that stream may largely swell the total. How many have been buried beneath the shifting sand of the beach will probably remain a secret forever.[32]

According to a Baptist state convention report, the meeting houses of the First and Second Churches in Galveston were destroyed and also the church at Alta Loma. The Third Church was practically destroyed, although it was still standing. A number of other meeting houses on the coast, near inland, were destroyed or greatly damaged. "Many of the brethren or sisters were swept into eternity, and many others have left that part of the country. Those remaining are left in destitute circumstances."

Good Will suffered damage from the storm, although there are differing accounts as to how much and what kind of damage. At the time of the storm, Brother Vallie C. Hart was

Fig. 9.3 The worst natural disaster to hit the United States was the great storm of Galveston, in which more than five thousand lives were lost amid mass destruction. *Good Will* was in the Santa Fe shops during the storm, and although chapel car assistant Vallie Hart lost his home and all his belongings, including those of the car, the car itself was not seriously damaged. (Courtesy of the Rosenberg Library, Galveston, Texas)

assisting Rogers on the chapel car, and in a letter to *The Colporter*, he explained how his home was wrecked but the chapel car was providentially protected.

I have found the painter who has the contract for painting the car. He lost four cottages and all he had, but saved every member of his family. He is suffering from wounds in his right foot, which are not serious. He will be ready to resume work on the car in a few days. He has already done a good deal of work in the way of burning off the old paint, taking out the windows in the chapel preparatory to cleaning and painting, and was making good headway when the storm came on Saturday, September 8. I think we are exceedingly fortunate in having this man's life spared to us, because he is fully competent to do the work that the car needs, and he will do it well, judging from what the officials of the Galveston Railroad have to say about him, and the character of work he turns out for their roads.

I have visited the car sheds of the Santa Fe shops, where the car is, and the management has placed the car in the best possible position. The fearful storm demonstrated this. To the east of the chapel car on the track is placed a great engine, which protected the car from the drift in that direction, and the drift from the bay side was caught and held by large posts supporting the shed, and while the debris is piled up all around and inside the shed, not one plank was hurled against the car. While one portion of the sheds was torn away and wrecked, that portion over the Chapel Car *Good Will* was not harmed.

Upon my arrival at the sheds I found an old German citizen looking after the interests of the Santa Fe property, and inquired of him about the safety of his family. He told me, between his sobs of grief, how he had struggled all night with wind and waves trying to save his family, and that he had saved them, but lost his home and its contents. When I went inside of the car and played on the organ and sang songs of praise to the Lord for our deliverance, he came to the window and listened.

I found that the books under the platform had not been injured, and I gave this old gentleman a German Bible as a present from Chapel car *Good Will*. He was so grateful for it! He said this Bible was the first and only thing he had to begin life over with except the clothes on the backs of his loved ones, and he and all his family would appreciate the gift.

The blankets, pillows, and mattresses, and chapel car silver were all taken to my home for safekeeping when the car was turned over to the contractor. Brother Rogers, as well as the contractor, advised this, and all was wrecked with my home. Since the storm I have found the blankets, pillows, and mattresses, but they are so damaged by wind and water that I do not think it advisable to try and use them in the car. Later on, when the debris is cleared, I hope to get the silverware.[33]

Because of the need for funds to repair the chapel car and a disagreement between Hart and Rogers, Boston Smith came to Texas in November 1900 to speak at several churches about the work of the chapel cars *(fig. 9.4)*. Stops included Dublin, Denison, Dallas, Brownwood, Belton, Lancaster, Denton, Giansville, Greenville, Whitewright, Plano, and Waco. With donations from Texas churches, the car's repair bill was paid and the contents replaced, peace was restored more or less between Rogers and Hart, and *Good Will* continued its mission.[34]

After the new year, publications secretary Seymour received the news that Rogers was not in good health. The chapel car was also having physical problems and needed more repairs, and the funds for repair were in scarce supply. At the Texas Baptist General Convention in November 1902, funds were granted to help with the repair expenses of the car.

At the same convention, a small visitor brought bittersweet memories. The Sunbeam Band of the Columbus Street

Church in Waco performed for the delegates, and a member of that group was the son of *Good Will* missionaries E. G. Townsend and Hollie Harper Townsend. A convention spokesman said, "As a fitting close to this sweet service, Harper Townsend, the precious little Sunbeam left by his sainted mother, Hollie Harper Townsend, was presented to the body."[35]

To-Night!
AT THE
First Baptist Church

Mr. Boston W. Smith, familiarly known as "Uncle Boston," of Minneapolis, Minn., general manager of the Chapel Car System of the United States, owned and operated by the American Baptist Publication Society of Philadelphia, Pa., will deliver an illustrated address to-night at the First Baptist Church concerning the early history of the American Baptist Publication society and the origin and the work of the chapel cars. This lecture is highly interesting and edifying, and is interspersed with beautiful views thrown on the screen by a powerful stereopticon with calcium lights, operated by Prof.

Good Will reached urban areas like Fort Worth and Dallas, burgs like Alamogorda, and growing eastern Texas towns like Carthage. The Texas, Sabine Valley and Northwestern Railway was extended to Carthage in 1888.[36] Now fourteen years later, crowds overflowed the chapel car and met in the opera house, where a church was organized. Hart was no longer with *Good Will*, due to personal problems with Rogers, and singer Hugh L. Heitt was assisting with the work.

Former *Good Will* missionary Diaz's name frequently popped up in Texas Baptist news. Once revered for his devotion and zeal in bringing the gospel to his own people in Cuba and his bravery in returning to Cuba to fight for his country's independence, Diaz had come into disfavor. He had been arrested in Cuba several times because of his overzealous actions and had been disenfranchised by the Southern Baptist Convention and rejected by the American Baptist Publication Society. His pleas to be heard and accepted again were unrelenting.[37]

Because of ill health and the wearing pace of chapel car life, the aging Rogers resigned in the fall of 1905. On the chapel car to begin its journey from Texas to Missouri to Colorado in 1906 were the Reverend and Mrs. T. S. Fretz. "Our car was in Pattonsburg, Missouri, for a time when we first started out. The church was badly divided, and while we had our twenty professed conversions, very few were willing to come into the church. We began a thorough organization of the Sunday school and among other things organized a Baraca Class for young men. In three months' time this class had grown from six to thirty-five. The Sunday school had more than doubled its membership and was the stronghold of the church."

One of the first long stops in Colorado was at Ordway, where the Fretzes spent six months with the car. "We were there in the busy spring season and contended with storms and poor location for the car, but left behind a church of twenty members, with three good lots for building, and twelve hundred dollars in good subscriptions for the house of worship." Upon hearing that some young men in the community were trying to get support to construct a building on the pretense it would be used for a reading room and gymnasium, but in actuality to be used for gambling, the church decided to build a room in their new church for a gymnasium, reading room, and other community events.[38]

The Fretzes visited a number of towns where churches had been organized but there were no houses to worship in. "These good people whose loyalty had been thoroughly tested in their efforts against hindering obstacles, are almost overjoyed to see a thoroughly equipped Baptist church come rolling in, with evangelist aboard, and this all their own."

We have to do with people from everywhere. In almost every western community you will find persons from almost every eastern state, as well as a liberal constituency of foreigners. Yet each community will have a local coloring of its own. In one community we found a colony from Kentucky; in another a colony from North Carolina; in another a great many Missourians, and wherever we find a sugar factory we find quite a number of Germans and Russians. We had a German woman in our audience last night who sang German words to our English tunes. I did not learn whether the book from which she sang was a copy of our book in German or not, but she sang our tunes and probably used the German words.

This cosmopolitan element among our people sometimes becomes our greatest trial when we get together the strict anti-alien immersionists of the south with the free open communionists of Canada, and every shade and complexion of denominational belief between these extremes, there is frequently some trouble to get the forces amalgamated, but when once they are interested, the possibilities of good work are encouraging.[39]

L. T. Barkman Causes Stir Over Lodges

The Fretzes did not stay on the car long, and in the summer of 1911, the Reverend and Mrs. L. T. Barkman were at New Plymouth, Idaho. The car could not hold all the people, so a tent was erected, which was also packed. From New Plymouth, the car moved to Boise. In October they stopped at Elko, Nevada. In Barkman's journal on *Good Will* in 1912, he wrote, "The next morning we started for Elko, Nevada, crossing the Great Salt Lake, then entering the Nevada desert, where we saw nothing but sagebrush for 228 miles, with the exception of a few little railroad towns, and not a church in all that distance."[40]

As *Good Will* progressed across Idaho, Nevada, and into Utah, Barkman began to have problems. Some people did not like his attitude and approach. On November 28, 1911, after working at Springville and other Utah towns, Seymour wrote to George L. White in defense of Barkman. "Brother Barkman is harsh, but some of the criticism is not worth mentioning, because you cannot turn a man down because his facial expression does not suit a few women; but, as you and I both know from hearing him that some of this criticism is true, and I think you better take the matter up with Mr. Barkman immediately."[41]

Three days later another letter from White pinned the problem down. "One of the most injurious attacks which he [Barkman] makes is against the lodges. He says they are Hell holes, that those who belong to them are the spawn of the devil and on the road to Hell. The Odd Fellows at Murray [Utah] talked of having him arrested but finally decided to let him alone unless he should repeat the attacks in Salt Lake City. I am told that he did not abuse them in Salt Lake City, and so nothing came of it. My fear is that such attacks will reach high up railroad officials through the Masons and that we will lose transportation of his car and others on the Harriman system."[42]

Sparks and Mason, Nevada, were two scheduled stops on Barkman's itinerary in 1912, but he was told by White in December 1911 that it would not be wise to go to Sparks, just outside of Reno, because the railroad company would not allow people in the yard on account of a strike. But the real reason was Barkman's railing against the lodges.[43]

In almost every town established along the rail lines, fraternal lodges like the Masons, the Moose, Odd Fellows, Order of the Red Men, Eagles, and the Woodmen of the World and their women's auxiliaries were organized in town long before churches were. It seemed to Barkman that many lodge members felt that their lodges were a substitute for churches.

Biblically, the teaching against secret societies was also an important issue for more than just Barkman. One Baptist association in New York drew up the following proclamation: "In our opinion, the honour of God, and the peace and purity of the church require that the church should purge itself from this relic of the dark ages, and withdraw from those who still adhere."[44] Baptists were not the only ones to lash out at the

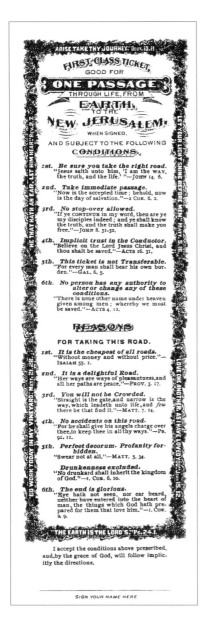

Fig. 9.5 Tickets like this, good for one First Class Service Through Life to the New Jerusalem, were given to visitors to the chapel car. Note the pledge card line at the bottom. (American Baptist Historical Society, Valley Forge)

lodges. Other denominations were also divided about whether to permit their members to belong to secret societies, and the Catholics had strict rules forbidding membership.

Instead of going to Sparks, the Barkmans traveled north-east to Winnemucca, a town nestled at the foot of mountains containing rich ore, where he reported, "car sidetracked on desert with nothing in sight but sage brush and mountains in the distance; a station was found and the car brought closer to it so people could find it. A little Indian girl came into the car and was given a Testament. Then her mother and sister came and were converted and baptized. The Indians said, 'We want to be taught like the white people.' So they came."[45]

At Winnemucca, a new feature had been installed in *Good Will* — a baptistry, placed under the platform area, and Barkman reported, "In regard to the baptistry, it is in and looks fine, no one would know it is in by the looks of it, and we have baptized in it."[46] They had good meetings at Winnemucca, despite Barkman telling White, "This is the hardest field we ever worked. I baptized three Indians and the car is packed to the door, organized a Sunday school and expect to organize a church."[47]

From Winnemucca the Barkmans went to Imlay and then in March 1912 to Mason, Nevada. G. M. Fraser, superintendent of the Nevada Copper Belt railroad, was one of the leaders in the Mason [Utah] fellowship and always was eager to provide passes on his line. Meetings at first started well, but within a few days trouble began brewing again for Barkman. The chapel car left town and stopped at Wabuska, where the Barkmans encouraged the young church before traveling on to Tremonton, Utah.

In the chapel car with the Barkmans was their son Floyd, an ordained minister, who frequently preached and participated in the services. Another talent Floyd had was the ability to soften his father's hard edges and serve as a go-between in church disputes, but Floyd was unsuccessful in getting his father to change enough to continue to serve effectively on the chapel car.

Seymour, the esteemed general secretary of the publication society and director of chapel car work, died unexpectedly September 20, 1912. Besides being one of the leaders of the publication society, he had served with distinction as an officer in the Civil War, heading one of the first all-black units. One of the last letters Seymour received was from White, bemoaning all the problems they were having as a result of Barkman's manners and attitudes. Something had to be done about him.[48]

Even without Seymour's steady presence and wise counsel, the problem seemed to resolve itself. Mrs. Barkman's health became the deciding factor, and the Barkmans, after having good meetings at Spencer and Debois, Idaho, on the Oregon Short Line Railroad, left *Good Will* January 1, 1913.

The Reverend Frank H. Farley was assigned to *Good Will* as interim for three months until the Reverend and Mrs. J. Franklin Day could take charge of the car. Farley started his work on the car at Downey, Idaho, January 6; went to American Falls; arrived at Twin Falls February 9; and closed out the month at Buhl. At Twin Falls, Farley, needing a baptistry, urged the church to build one. No one had bothered to tell him that under the platform of *Good Will*, hidden, where as Barkman reported, "no one could tell it was there," was a baptistry.

Arriving at Filer, Idaho, on March 30, the Farleys received a cold shoulder from the Methodists. They were planning to build a church and needed the goodly number of Baptists presently in their congregation, and they vigorously campaigned against the building of a Baptist church. The Methodists won, no church was built, and *Good Will* left town. Filer was the last stop for the Farleys. The chapel car was left at Pocatello in the spring of 1913 for Day to take charge.

Good Will was in bad physical shape. The Barkmans had left it almost unfit for the Farleys to live in, and since the Farleys were going to be in the car for only a few months, they cleaned it as well as they could and, for the first few weeks, lived in rented rooms and ate in local restaurants. Day, who had been a colporter in Washington State, saw that the repairs and appearance could wait no longer. They had waited too long.

The Oregon Short Line Railroad (OSL) suggested that the painting, both exterior and interior, could be done by painters at Pocatello, and they would do the light repairs to the trucks and body of the car at their shops in Portland. But the OSL was so backed up with work that they could not take the car. As there was no sheltered building available where *Good Will* could be painted in Pocatello, the car was reconditioned at the Denver and Rio Grande shops in Salt Lake.

Days Short on Linens, Long on Woes

Mrs. Day also found the linens in sad condition, with not a dish towel in the car. It was hoped some church would donate new sheets and towels. The Days' son, Owen, was on the car with them while he was on vacation from college and added much to the music ministry, but he also added a body to be bedded and fed.

Pleased with the renovation and repair work done on *Good Will*, Day wrote in his usual style, omitting some punctuation and frequently ignoring other traditions of spelling and syntax, "She is looking fine the fellows did a splendid job, wish you could see the car. The D and RG filled all my bunkers with coal and all my oil cans with oil they were very nice to me. I moved the car over to the OSL Depot Friday and put her in shape and Sunday afternoon we had a great service."

From Salt Lake the Days went to Milner, Idaho, and then to Oakley. They wanted to take the car to Idaho Falls, but when they told the pastor there they needed some meals and a free-will offering, the pastor said they couldn't meet those conditions.[49] Somewhere along the way, Day crossed the path of the Reverend Thomas Gale on *Messenger of Peace*, which was built several years after *Good Will*. He made some observations. "I went over the car carefully, it is a fine car, he has his much better arranged than *Good Will*, then his lighting plant has it all over this one, his is just fine. Gale said that he wouldn't have coal oil lamps. He said throw them out and put in a gasoline plant. We will have to do something at once

these lamps just leak. We laughed at Farley for having buckets under the lamps, but I am doing the same thing. Have to in order to save the carpets and the pews. The men put on new bulbs at the bottom but they leak up at the stem where you turn the wick up, and I cant find any way to stop them."[50]

After stopping at Twin Falls and Hollister, Day arrived at Bellevue on October 7. He was not in a good mood. Mrs. Day was not on the car with him. He had not received his paycheck from the publication society, and "these Idaho people wouldnt do a thing for you unless you would just come out and ask them. I have given them all the hints that it would seem necessary but not a soul has offered to give me a meal since I came here. Well, what is the use to kick just grin and bear it. I havent been well for the last week my stomache is all out of fix some way . . . and something had to be done about the lighting on the car."[51]

At Bellevue, Day was joined by Lee Crownover, who had been hired to assist him in the absence of Mrs. Day. Day was overjoyed with one of Crownover's talents: "He is a fine COOK, and that counts with me quite a little after a month of batching, we have everything in hygenic and eugenic order here thank you."[52]

White wrote Day about the lighting problem on the car and could not remember the name of the man who did the lighting on the other cars. But he provided the name of a Los Angeles company, the Beacon Light Company, that Day might want to contact. The name of the company was the Hydro-Carbon Company, later the Coleman Lamp Company. W. C. Coleman, a prominent Baptist layman from Wichita, Kansas, and active in the Northern Baptist Convention, personally had installed the lights on *Evangel* and then handled the same work on several of the other cars. Coleman's was the name White couldn't remember.

The estimate for installing a lighting system on the car totaled $337.33, a price that included a discount of more than 50 percent.[53]

From Hailey, Idaho, on November 12, Day begged White for bedding. "We must have two three quarter cotton blankets and two full size cotton blankets. Then we should have a pair of pillows, the old ones we have are so old that they are all matted and so hard that there is no comfort in sleeping on them . . . you know we are in a cold country hills all covered with snow ice thick enough and strong enough this morning to hold a person up."

Day planned to take the car to Shoshone to have the Coleman lighting system installed, but in Picabo, a town with a store and just a few houses, where a crowd of fifty came to the car, Day noted instead that he was looking forward to going home for Christmas. He missed his wife and family. "I tell you I am getting real homesick."

Crownover was anxious to leave the car too, because he was not enjoying the work. Day's critical ways might have had something to do with his young helper's unhappiness. Day liked the young man and hated the thought of losing such a good cook, but he admitted that Crownover was not very effective at the meetings and didn't like to do the necessary house-to-house visiting.[54]

The new year, 1914, began well for Day and the chapel car. "Got a man to help me and we have put the new lighting plant in today and it is a dandy, I am just delighted with it. The car is just as light as day it makes it seem like a different place." A watch night service was held at Shoshone with a great crowd, and at Gooding, Idaho, Day waded in knee-deep snow and dreamed about leaving Idaho and heading west to Oregon. By January 20, still in Gooding, Day had another problem besides snow — his bowels. "I do not know the cause unless it is the water or the altitude or both, I never had anything like it before and am becoming a little disturbed about it since it is hanging on so long."[55]

Day was not the only one with a problem. The Reverend Guy C. Lamson, who took the place of Seymour as general secretary of the missionary department, wrote to White that Day's expenses were the highest of all the chapel car missionaries, especially his coal and fuel bills, and his offerings were very small. Idaho might be cold, but it couldn't be that cold, Lamson complained. "It is costing very much more for oil

and fuel for that Chapel Car than it costs me to heat a twelve room house and pay the gas and electric light bills in Germantown. Now, I don't believe that. One thing is sure; we cannot continue Day on the car as things are going."[56]

White and Lamson were beginning to realize that in Idaho Day was not given a chance to have successful missions where his expenses could have been met. He was sent mainly to small churches that could give little if any offerings and to communities where, for a number of reasons, charity was in scarce supply. White was suspicious that "certain parties would like to show that the chapel car work is a failure." So it was decided that Day, who had lost twenty pounds and was not well, would take *Good Will* to Oregon on the Oregon, Washington Railroad and Navigation Lines[57] and see if conditions there would be more hospitable.

At Glenns Ferry, a railroad center where meetings were going well, Day had been to see the doctor and was feeling better. The problems, according to the doctor, were the alkaline water and the high altitude.[58] He thought that when Day got to Oregon, he would feel better.

In Oregon, Day, who seemed to have had some relief from his bowel problems, had a new challenge with the "noisy crowd" that came to the car. "I found out last night that a lot of them claim a second blessing. Dont know how we will come out with sane evangelistic methods. It is not uncommon where you find these Holiness people, that it is very difficult to do a good quiet strong work for the Lord."

Day had also been told by local pastors of a circular letter sent out by Charles Wooddy of the home mission society with questions like "Has your church ever had the help of a chapel car? Did you consider it a success or a failure?" He was concerned about the implications of such a survey,[59] knowing that the home mission society was looking to find ways to fault the chapel car program.

From Ontario, Oregon, near the Idaho border, Day wanted to go to Huntington, where he could get cheaper coal. He knew he was being criticized by Lamson because of his high coal and fuel bills, but he didn't know what he could do about it. He had to pay freight from Pocatello for the hard coal, as the Baker heaters on the chapel cars could not burn soft coal (*see fig. 9.6*). It seemed that Lamson in the East could not understand the difference of coal prices in the West. "I have to pay them 25% advance on the entire bill. That looks like a grab game to me," Day wrote White, who was more understanding, having been a chapel car missionary himself.

At Haines, Oregon, in April, Day was again having trouble with the alkaline water and the high altitude and was thinking about leaving *Good Will*. By the time they reached North Powder, Oregon, he had made a decision. "I am just in receipt of a letter informing me that I had been called pastor of a good church down in the Willamette Valley," at Carlton.

He could not endure another year in the alkali country. He and Mrs. Day were sick about the thought of leaving the publication society, but they planned to leave the car in June to see their son graduate from college. Then they would return to see to some car repairs — external varnishing and external painting — and report to the new charge the first of July.[60] After bringing to a close his last stop at Elgin, Oregon, and seeing his son graduate from college, Day took the car to Pendleton. He hoped to get it into the shops at Portland for work and have it ready for the new missionaries.

The Drivers Take the Wheel

The new missionaries were the Reverend and Mrs. W. C. Driver, who were offered a salary of twelve hundred dollars a year and the usual allowance for expense, provided they could start immediately. White explained that usual expenses meant that the society provided fuel for heating and cooking, necessary repairs on the car, light, postage, stationery, occasional car fare when they had to travel in the interest of the chapel car work, and hotel bills on such trips.

The society did not pay for living upon the car. The missionaries had to provide that themselves, just as they would in a parsonage. "We find from experience, however, that the living expenses on a chapel car are much less than in a parsonage. In going from place to place, the people are often very

kind about providing the missionary with supplies for the table and in some places nearly everything needed along that line is given."[61]

Certainly Day would fault that last statement from his bare-cupboard experiences in Idaho, but maybe the Drivers would fare better. The Drivers could not start immediately. In fact, they could not start until November 1. Driver, formerly from Chehalis, Washington, was an evangelist and had already committed to several revivals in Vermont.

The Portland shops of the Oregon and Washington Railroad informed Day that because *Good Will* was old, it needed a number of items to comply with state law: brake handholds, and the entrance railing as well as platform did not meet the legal requirement for safety of those entering and leaving the car. If the car would be varnished now, it should be good for several more years. Their estimate for

Fig. 9.6 The Baker heater was a bane to all the chapel car missionaries, and in parts of the West it was almost impossible to find the hard coal needed for its operation. (*Railroad Car Builder's Pictorial Dictionary*)

such repairs was $191.09,[62] which was approved by Lamson, so the car would be ready for the Drivers when they came.

The Drivers had no children, and this fact fitted a new policy concerning chapel car workers. White explained, "It is almost impossible to care for children on the car and we have about concluded that we will employ, hereafter, only men and their wives, who can devote their whole time to the work. I think that was one reason Bro. Day felt that he must make a change, because he was compelled to be away from his family so much."[63] Also, Mrs. Driver was an ordained minister, which was unusual for a woman at that time, and her skills as a musician and personal worker would help tremendously on the car.

On the Drivers' first visit to *Good Will*, something important was missing, although they looked everywhere for it — a toilet. What they found for use in the car was not what they had hoped, probably just a railroad hopper-type toilet. The matter of an acceptable toilet, a common complaint of chapel car workers, would come up again.

After leaving the shops with *Good Will* in good repair again, the Drivers spent most of the first month of service at the Calvary and Tabernacle churches in the Portland area and near a churchless section around the Portland Railway Light and Power Company and the Southern Pacific yards. A pleased Driver reported, "If our six chapel cars were coupled together they would make one of the finest trains ever seen on an American railroad, and if the men and women, boys and girls, who have been converted and gathered into the Sunday schools and churches through their ministry during the last 23 years were gathered together in one city, it would make a new Jerusalem of nearly 40,000 souls."[64]

After leaving Portland in December 1914, one of the Drivers' first stops was Adams, Oregon. Already Driver had discovered the expense of feeding hard coal into the Baker heater. Lamson in Philadelphia had not taken the advice to remove the Baker heater. The meetings at Adams went well. On the first day of the new year, *Good Will* was at Freewater, where a letter of appreciation was written by the church officers to the Oregon Washington Railroad and Navigation Company for bringing the car and permitting it to be sided in its yard during the time there.

Both the Drivers came down with the "grippe" at Athen, and the meeting suffered in consequence.[65] They had revived enough to have good services in April at The Dalles and at Prineville, Redmond, and Gresham, where the railroad men took fine care of them and the car. White informed them that the First Baptist Church of Long Beach, California, was thinking about sponsoring the car, and that would mean replacing linens and household supplies and some other needs. That was good news.

Driver was amazed at the crowds that were coming to the car at Pleasant Home, in spite of it being harvest time, but at Hood River they were only modestly successful. The Drivers had not heard from the Long Beach church since sending them a list of needs of the car. Maybe the list scared them?

Good Will was in need of repair and painting work again, and Driver was having a man from the Southern Pacific shops look the car over. By September the car was in Portland having the chapel floor painted, other minor repairs, and the exterior varnished for the cost of ninety dollars. To go along with the newly bright *Good Will*, at Eugene a box came in the mail from a women's club at Tremont Temple in Boston with silverware, and a check for fifty dollars from the B.Y.P.U. of the Long Beach church, to purchase dishes and linens.[66]

A foot of snow was on the ground at Maple Lane, and both Drivers had been sick again, no doubt due to the cold chapel car. "The weather has moderated some so we can at least keep the car warm — a thing that was impossible during the coldest, windiest weather."[67]

Someone other than Driver informed White that *Good Will* had been in a wreck, and so he anxiously inquired about it. Driver quieted his fears. "Your letter of Jan. 19th reached us this morning. The facts concerning our wreck like those of Mark Twain's death many years before he died, 'were very much exaggerated.' I don't know who volunteered the information but it was entirely without authority and foundation. We went around a little curve at Milwaukee on the Portland

Electric Line that made the car and trucks squeak a little and broke a hook off a chain which the R.R. men volunteered to repair without charge."[68]

White needed some good news. The conflict between the home mission society and the publication society had heated up to the point that White and Lamson had almost reached a breaking point.[69] Not only had there been a serious breach between the two societies, but also there had been a breach in the roof of *Good Will*. Driver needed to have the leak fixed before they could take the car to damp Coos Bay for the summer.

Driver wrote in June that at Wellsdale on the Southern Pacific line, 40 percent of the population within two and one-half miles of the station attended every night for a month during this busy season of the year, and 85 or 90 percent of the people within a radius of three or four miles attended the baptismal service at the Willamette River on June 11. Seventeen were baptized there — ten men and seven women, including three generations of women from one family. "I believe the community is transformed for a generation."[70]

Many times the reports sent from the chapel cars were written by the missionary wife. Such was the case with Mrs. Driver. Seldom did the wife correspond directly with chapel car administrators under her own name, but Mrs. Driver would do that several times. She was not a bashful woman; after all, she had a college education and was an ordained minister in her own right.

From Lafayette Mrs. Driver wrote in June 1916, "You may remember that I wrote to you about the possible remodeling of our very crowded and inconvenient washroom." She asked very nicely, "It could be made very much more convenient, I think and the missionary wife at least a little happier, at slight expense. It would require a new water tank and wash basin, one of the folding kind would be least in the way, in case it was necessary to escape to said washrooms for dressing when unexpected callers were arriving."

She was not done asking favors. "The lack of a first class postcard camera has caused us much grief. . . . Wish some good friend could be found who would be interested in such a gift to our work."[71] In spite of her diplomacy, Mrs. Driver did not receive any of her requests or even a response.

Show houses and the movies also made the agenda of the Oregon Baptist Convention in the fall of 1916. "The Moving Picture has come to stay and is linked with every other social problem. Whether it proves a menace or a blessing lies, largely, with Christian people. The right kind of censorship will help mightily. Here is a fertile field for social service work."[72] The most objectionable film of that year might have been William S. Hart's *Hell's Hinges*, but the impact of D. W. Griffith's *Birth of a Nation*, premiering in 1915, could still be felt everywhere, with its blatantly white-supremacist theme that glorified the Ku Klux Klan.[73]

News of the war was the major concern in 1917, and the raising of funds for the distribution of Bibles for soldiers kept the publication society and missionaries busy. A letter from C. C. Bateman, chaplain of the Fourteenth U.S. Cavalry at Camp Del Rio, Texas, pertained to a Corporal Grady, a newly baptized member of the First Baptist Church of Del Rio, which had been started by *Good Will*. In speaking to other members of his regiment, Grady said, "Do not take the Bibles or Testaments as mere books which you can have for the asking, but read them comrades, read them!"

The chaplain requested more Bibles for his soldiers. "Now if you are able to favor us with another shipment of Bibles in any number under one thousand copies, they can be used here or at the outpost stations along the Rio Grande within the Del Rio Military District. We need more at once."[74]

The war brought one good change to the nation's capital. *Missions* reported that on November 1, 1917, Washington was declared a saloonless city. Congress put it in the prohibition list. The saloonkeepers tried to have the law declared unconstitutional, but the law was enforced. Although many people hoarded liquor, the saloons were closed. On the same page of *Missions*, the plea was made for Baptists to conserve food, to substitute cornmeal or rye for wheat flour, which had to be sent to their allies. "The bread ticket will come soon enough, unless our people will respond to Mr. Hoover's warnings and appeals. The situation is going to be steadily more acute, even if the war stops sooner than now seems probable."

Washroom Repairs on Want List

Although the war was the main concern, from Creswell, Oregon, in March 1918, the matter of the toilet was brought up again. *Good Will* needed large-scale repair work, and Driver reminded White that Mrs. Driver really wanted a better washroom — and a better toilet. "We haven't one." The list of repairs was long: the floors needed inspecting and repairing, the roof was leaking again in a spot or two, the steps and platforms were getting old. The whole interior needed going over with some repairs and thorough painting and varnishing. Driver thought all this could cost three or four hundred dollars, and it should be done soon.[75] He was planning to go down the Columbia River area in the summer and needed the repairs done for that trip.

From Springfield Driver sent some advice concerning the Oregon area thirty miles long from Reedsport to North Bend. "They have 700 people, 7 school districts with 8 teachers and no gospel minister of any denomination." A missionary needed to be appointed for that area.

White, who was aware of the many needs of Oregon, had been trying to keep his chapel car and colporter missionaries happy while dealing with the tense situation with the home mission society. He needed some play. On April 21, 1917, he wrote to John F. Powers of the Pacific Coast Baseball League on his stationery, "I understand that you frequently issue annual passes for attendance upon games of the Pacific League. If you can send me a pass for the coming season. The favor will be greatly appreciated."[76] A rousing ball game could go a long way in reducing stress.

A few days later White wrote to the Drivers about getting an estimate on car repairs and perhaps a new toilet. "It is possible that a toilet closet may be built on one side off the platform at the living end of the car. It is not satisfactory in any other place. We would not want anything built there, however, which is not finished as well as the rest of the car. The new car 'Grace' has a splendid arrangement. You might write to Bro. E. R. Hermiston, who is now at Colton, California, and get suggestions concerning that matter."

But the estimate could reach nine hundred dollars, and Lamson did not understand the importance of some of the repairs, especially the item, "Alterations on small dressing room with basin and gravity water." Driver tried to explain again, writing from Clatskanie, stressing the need for an adequate toilet.

The steam pipes for train connections are necessary unless we are to be handled on the freights and that means jamming up the car, breaking lamp fixtures and paying extra fares for Mrs. Driver. The toilet is necessary. We have grown awfully tired of the old unsanitary railroad and other toilets. The ceiling of the car was ruined last winter a year by the leaking and needs the repairs suggested very much. In fact there is not a single item that can be left out and still have a first class job and a good equipment. I consulted the OWR&N Co. [Oregon Washington Railroad and Navigation] and also the North Bank Co. Their labor shortage is so great and their work so heavy that they would not even consider it. It is the S. P or nothing.[77]

At Astoria in July 1917, while the Drivers were waiting for a reply about car repairs, *Good Will* was in a "hair raising" place. "It is certainly the devil's headquarters and yet they say it is improving," Driver reported. "Two years ago it was the worse saloon, gambling, and prostitute camp on the Coast — Public dance halls with women dancing nude every day. It is a little better now and is being reformed and rebuilt on cleaner lines. There are 17,000 people and only three of the popular English speaking churches, Baptist, Methodist, Presbyterian. There are some Scandinavian foreign speaking churches and three thousand of the people are fisherman."[78]

Approval was given for the repairs to be made on *Good Will*, but before going to the Southern Pacific shops at

Portland with the car, the Drivers stopped at Fort Stevens for two weeks to have services for the soldiers. At Fort Stevens Driver received news that the Southern Pacific shops would not be able to handle the car.

I then went to Portland and visited all the main railroad offices and the various companies. They all said the same thing. Shortage of men and war work of their own is more than they can handle. It was suggested by one SP man that the car be sent to Sacramento but the men higher up turned it down saying their Sacramento shops were 1000 men short because of the war. I then went to Twohey Bros. Portland, large car builders, repairers and contractors. They are the largest concern of their kind in the Northwest, doing such work aside from railroad companies. They told me they would do their best for us on the basis of the estimates given by the Southern Pacific. In as much as this seems the only thing we can do, I am writing to ask for approval to take the car to Twohey Bros. the first of Sept.[79]

War, Influenza, Fire Enforce Restrictions

The Baptist cars experienced many problems because of war restrictions on movement and levies, and some areas and railroads were more lenient than others. Driver reported from Portland in January 1919 about his conversation with the manager of the Catholic car *St. Peter*.

I talked with Mr. Hennessey yesterday who is manager of the Catholic Car in Oregon. He tells me the new rates will put their cars out of business. I suggested to him what I suggested to you the other day in a letter, namely that the Catholics and ourselves make common cause in a strong appeal to the Director General for a new hearing. Surely when the Federal officials know that we are entirely free from commercial interests and income, they will see they have made a mistake. They have evidently lumped us off with show, exhibition and rich men's promotion enterprises.[80]

Despite Driver's common complaint, along with George Hennessey of the Catholic car, the Baptist cars in California and Oregon were generally enjoying free transportation continuously without restrictions. But they had no assurance as to how long this luxury would last. In other parts of the country, Baptist cars had been brought to a standstill.

It was not the war but Spanish influenza that brought *Good Will* to a halt in Portland in October 1918. In the down time, Driver continued his project of raising money for New Testaments for the soldiers, which were distributed by Baptist chaplains, camp pastors, and Baptist Red Cross nurses. Finally, after many weeks and many deaths, the influenza quarantine was lifted, and the car, although it needed revarnishing again, moved along the Oregon rails more freely.

But the rail conditions were not good at Beaver Hill, a coal mining town. "We are having no end of trouble on this coal and logging road, with bad track, having to be moved once and twice a day, and standing on bad curves and siding tracks all the time. We don't want to get top sided for the next 30 or 40 years."[81]

In January 1919 all the chapel cars, including *Good Will*, were put under strict restrictions as a new order had been issued by W. G. McAdoo, director general of railroads of the United States Railroad Administration. Only minimum movement of the cars would be permitted and then at a charge of fifty dollars and trackage at three dollars a day. White told Driver, "it may mean the tying up of our Chapel Car work for a considerable time until readjustments can be made."[82] He advised Driver to find a private spur somewhere and stay there until other orders were given, so the car was parked in a back shop area of the Southern Pacific yards at Portland. Driver worked at churches in the Portland area, including the Baptist Russian Mission.

War, influenza, and fire were on the list of trials of *Good Will*. On April 15, 1919, White sent a telegram to Samuel G. Neil, now general secretary of the publication society, explaining that "Chapel Car *Good Will* has been damaged by fire caused by live electric wires. Damage amounts to several

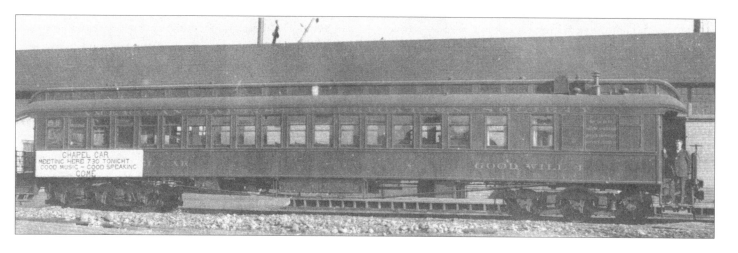

Fig. 9.7 With the completion of the Southern Pacific railroad line to Marshfield in 1916, it was possible to bring *Good Will* to Marshfield, Coquille, Myrtle Point, Powers, and many other Oregon towns. (First Baptist Church of Coos Bay, Oregon)

hundred dollars. Please advise Rev. W. C. Driver by telegram concerning insurance."[83]

Driver wrote explaining more about the fire. "We were being moved out from our old standing place by an electric train, when a lost trolley struck the roof. The current was conducted by our gasoline lamp wire and grounded just inside the door where the car caught fire. Damage estimated at $200 . . . badly burned and scorched in the living apartment and some damage to the lighting system." First he told the bad news, then the good news. The Southern Pacific would continue to grant *Good Will* free passage and movement. Driver was pleased by this decision and felt the action showed the railroad appreciated the work the chapel car was doing in the towns along the line.[84]

Because the Southern Pacific Railroad was so busy with its own work in the Portland shops, *Good Will* was not ready for service again until the end of November. By December the car was back on the road, this time to Independence, and the Drivers were pleased about another prospective raise. The check this time would come from the home mission society, not the publication society.[85] A more compatible relationship had evolved between the societies, and now they were married in handling mission work and sharing responsibilities. One inconvenience for the chapel car missionaries was that they must turn in multiple reports to both societies, and lack

of communication sometimes caused mixups of people, cars, and schedules.

Driver was not feeling well. His heart was acting up, and Mrs. Driver took action. From Portland the first week in September 1920, she notified White that since her husband was not well, she had arranged for an estimate for repairs on the car.

At Veneta in early December, Driver was back in service, still not well, but angry, very angry. He had been informed that Mrs. Driver would no longer be entitled to co-missionary status, "although of course she is still going to be at about 400 services a year and presiding at the organ to play and sing more than three hundred times a year, besides doing a whole budget of other important and indispensable things in connection with the car service. It seems that she no longer has a right to accident or life insurance and it is doubtful whether she has a legitimate right to ask for half fare railroad permit, with which to do our necessary traveling. I may say to you frankly and without complaint, that I dont feel very good about it."[86]

Blanche Driver Assumes Car Duties

Driver's health continued to worsen, and in April 1921, Mrs. Driver wrote White asking for assistance and support. Driver notified White May 29 that he must give up the car work for a few months,[87] and the Drivers felt this would be a good time to put *Good Will* into the shops for repairs. Mrs. Driver wanted specific repairs, and this time her list was different and her approach more direct.

> Our bed is very uncomfortable. We have used it seven years and it was used before that — springs are in bad shape — and it is too short for a 6-1 man, then too, it has to be made and unmade, bedding, mattress, etc. lugged around. Our carpets are badly worn. I have wondered if the partition between the living room and chapel could be moved into the chapel the depth of the present platform and thus give us one long living room with a comfortable bed and a table that could be extended when we wished to entertain — something like Grace, with possible a full length clothes closet, in farther end of Chapel where a chest of screens is now kept.[88]

She also wanted a new floor and rugs for floors instead of carpets. This seemed a long, expensive list for a woman whose husband was having serious health problems and might not be able to continue in chapel car work. Neil and White felt, in view of the sad financial affairs of the home and publication societies and the more pressing needs of other chapel cars, that this request needed much consideration.

Through the months of 1921 and 1922, Driver's health kept the car from service. He continually told White that he was feeling and getting better, in fear of losing his chapel car assignment. But he had been getting worse. Not only was his heart damaged, but also he was having nervous problems.

Although she was not considered eligible for a missionary pass on the railroad, Blanche Driver had been looking after the chapel car and keeping contact with the shop work and seemingly having success. Mrs. Driver said that one of the foremen on the job threw in some extras because "he knew of our chapel car work in Coos Bay — two extra fruit boxes under seats, painting of floor, washing of ceilings and enameling in kitchenette. The lamps have been put in good order,

also, with a slight expense for new wicking." It was finally acknowledged that Driver would not be able to work on the chapel car again, at least not for quite a while. Mrs. Driver knew it too, and she was willing to prepare the car for the person to follow, although, she said, "I want to tell you it is no easy thing to turn the keys of the dear old car over."[89]

No one received those keys for a number of months, as it was decided to keep *Good Will* in storage to help cut expenses. Then Driver, whose health had suddenly improved beyond all expectations, was assigned to *Glad Tidings* in Arizona, to see if the Arizona climate would be an improvement.

New Workers Include Families

Although it was against the general policy to place a man with small children on the chapel car, in June 1923 John B. Speed was placed on *Good Will* with his wife and five-year-old daughter. Their first stop was Swisshome, Oregon, "just a very small place and nothing very large as it would seem can be done, but I feel we have really administered to a need." They organized a Sunday school and "several made decisions for Christ." Next they went to North Bend. In less than four months, Speed decided that chapel car work was not for him, his family, and his health.[90]

Speed had served faithfully before his brief time on the chapel car as an auto colporter. He became stricken with guilt that he had not been able to make the chapel car assignment work. He wrote from a rest ranch in Tulare, California, October 17, "I thought at first of a transfer but got so run down that I did not feel as if I could make good anywhere and now I am a bit discouraged to think I can not measure up to all my friends expect of me."[91]

After recuperating from his illness, Speed was assigned to the new Henry L. Morehouse Memorial chapel auto work in California, where he served faithfully and well.

Fortunately for the publication society at the time, Speed had good friends. The Reverend and Mrs. J. D. Chappelle, friends of the Speeds, took over the car temporarily and stayed on it for four years. One of their stops in June 1927 was Cottage Grove, Oregon, where a beautiful new church building was completed.[92] It was at Cottage Grove that the Wheelers with *Evangel* stopped on their first mission trip in 1891.

In August the Chappelles organized a church in Mt. Shasta, California, against the backdrop of America's fourth highest peak, in the ring-of-fire volcanoes of the Cascade Range. The name Shasta originated from the French for "chaste," but at one time the mountain was called Jesus and Mary, because of its two peaks.[93] The Mt. Shasta work was to be a regional work, having its members in several of the neighboring towns with Mt. Shasta as a center, where a new meeting house would be erected.[94] Before *Good Will* came to the Mt. Shasta area, there was no church from Redding, California, to Ashland, Oregon, a distance of 160 miles.[95]

In February 1930, the Reverend A. C. McChesney and his wife, parents of four boys ranging from five to ten years, plus a girl, two and one-half years, took over the work of the car and found *Good Will* in very bad condition. It seemed that the Chappelles had not lived on the car and therefore had not kept it in good order. And for the last few years they spent on the car, they had kept few records.[96]

McChesney himself, handy with a brush and wash pail, cleaned the car and headed for Marin County, California, a county "rich in resources, with many splendid cities, and practically no Baptist churches."[97]

Whether the McChesneys had all the children with them on the car is uncertain. It is difficult to think that Mrs. McChesney would not have had the preschool children with her, although it was not unusual for schoolchildren to be left in the care of relatives. The imagination could run wild at the thought of five children between the ages of ten and two-and-one-half living in a chapel car. *Good Will* did not have a separate bedroom. There would have been the two berths, upper and lower, the pull-out couch behind the pulpit, and pews. The wash and toilet facilities were limited to say the least, and the kitchen was a galley. Even occasional visits from all the children would have been a logistical challenge.

In one letter to McChesney, Neil closed by saying, "Our prayers and sympathies are with you in all your work." Maybe Neil too was visualizing five children chasing each other up and down the narrow aisle of *Good Will*, and multiples of pants and shirts and socks draped over the brass railings on the front and rear vestibules. It would be a sight to make the meticulous Neil shudder and offer solicitudes.

It seems that McChesney was not daunted, but he did have a few requests. McChesney wrote Neil, "To start with, we need a new oil stove for cooking purposes . . . the bedding and pads in the car are so dilapidated and frayed out that we will need something in this line. That which will bear laundrying I can have done, but we need at least four new blankets, two mattress pads, some sheets, dishes, etc."[98]

For ten months in 1931, the car worked at Tracy, California, where the McChesneys erected a beautiful church with fifty-three new members, twenty united through baptism.[99] The children could have gone to school at Tracy, as they were there long enough.

According to the records of the First Baptist Church of Paradise, California, which celebrated its centennial in 1999, the chapel car came to town in May 1932. In 1933 *Good Will* helped to a build a new church on the site of the original church, built in 1905, which had been destroyed in a storm. The men of the church did most of the work, and the first services were held on Easter Sunday. It is regrettable that few records are available of the four years the McChesneys were on the chapel car, including their tenure at Paradise. Accounts of their family life on the car would have been priceless.

Dryers Center Work in Santa Rosa

In 1935 *Good Will* was turned over to the Reverend I. Morse Dryer. It was used at Santa Rosa, California, for a number of years in strengthening the church there and witnessing to surrounding areas. Several members of the present First Baptist Church of Santa Rosa recall that the chapel car was located at Julliard Park for a time, adjacent to the grounds of horticulturist Luther Burbank's home and gardens.[100] In that park is still located the "Church of One Tree." Baptists of Santa Rosa built the 56 x 37-foot church in 1875 from the wood of one redwood tree, with an edifice from base to elevation of tower and spire measuring 69 feet.[101]

Nearby Petaluma was also a chapel car stop, and the story of the Petaluma Baptist bell has become legendary. In 1858 Petaluma citizens, without regard to church membership, decided that the town should have a bell for social and religious purposes and that the proper place to install it would be in the Baptist church steeple, then the highest tower in town. So a bell weighing about 1,150 pounds, which once was rung by the Vigilante Committee of San Francisco, was purchased for five hundred dollars and hung.

There was a common understanding that the bell was to be used not only for church services but also for the city on those occasions when such an instrument is usually employed. The bell was said to have the sweetest, mellowest tone of any in the state and could be heard distinctly eight or ten miles distant, and when the wind was favorable, even farther. But its popularity proved its undoing. It was in demand for many things, and confusion arose as to the meaning of its summons. People were unable to tell whether it was indicating the time of day, calling church members to prayer, summoning councilmen to session, or ringing the curfew.

Another discordant factor was injected into the situation. Those were Civil War days, and a large majority of Petalumans were strong Union partisans. When victory crowned the Northern armies, Union sympathizers would ring the bell to notify residents. This displeased citizens whose sympathy lay with the Confederacy, particularly those who had contributed liberally toward the purchase of the bell.

One dark night the Southern sympathizers cut down the bell, loaded it into a dray, and hid it in a warehouse under several bushels of potatoes. Several days later about forty citizens took possession of the bell and restored it to its place in the church steeple, marching through the main street behind a dray carrying the bell over which waved an American flag.

Santa Rosa at this time was in particular disfavor with

Petaluma over abolition doctrine, and many Santa Rosa Baptists were Southern sympathizers. At midnight, a few days after the old bell had been triumphantly returned to the Petaluma Baptist church belfry, slumbering citizens were awakened by a terrific clang. The bell had sounded a single note, the loudest in its history, which ended discordantly. Investigation disclosed that the bell was cracked from the rim some distance up the side, a large dent indicating it had been struck with a sledgehammer or other heavy tool. It was thought that its silvery pealing was to be heard no more. But Union partisans refused to permit the bell to be removed from the church. For years afterward its mournful thudding summoned the Baptist congregation to Sunday services and midweek prayer.[102]

Fig. 9.8 Families flocked to *Good Will* in 1929 when the car visited San Anselmo, California, and started a Sunday school and a church. (American Baptist Historical Society, Valley Forge)

When *Good Will* traveled back and forth between Santa Rosa and Petaluma, the Dryers did not have the pleasure of hearing the thud of the legendary bell. It had been donated to the M. H. DeYoung Museum in Golden Gate Park, San Francisco, a symbol of the Petaluma and Santa Rosa Baptist Civil War.

In 1936 came news for *Good Will* that missionaries on all the older, wooden cars dreaded to hear: "The car had now reached physical condition whereby the railroads refuse to haul it." Publication officials reported, "They have, however, consented to haul it once more, taking it to Santa Cruz . . . in that territory there is work which will take perhaps fifteen or twenty years to accomplish. Therefore, we recommend that the chapel car be moved to Santa Cruz and this become the permanent headquarters and home for our chapel car worker, he going out from this point into surrounding territory."

By all accounts, the car did not go to Santa Cruz. Correspondence indicates that in July 1937 the car was also supposed to be moved instead to Pinecroft Baptist Camp, south of Colfax, to serve as a home for the Dryers and an office and chapel for the camp.[103] The Reverend S. S. Aplin wrote the Reverend John C. Killian on July 4, 1937: "You will be glad to get the news that the Chapel Car is due to be in Colfax on Tuesday or Wednesday of this week and I hope by next Sunday that it will be in 'Its last resting place' as Dryer speaks of, all safe and sound. It will be a big task to get it over the road but we have a reliable firm in Sacramento on the job and I feel confident in their ability to do it."[104]

It appears that *Good Will* did not make it up that steep dirt road, and if it did, it did not stay there. On October 21, 1937, Killian wrote Dryer, who had been ill but was still working and living on the chapel car, "I confess I am somewhat anxious to know when you move that car about the expense, because each month your expense account has been high. Now I don't like to write a letter like this, especially to a man who is sick, and I don't want you to worry about it, but to think it over."[105]

Resting Place in Valley of the Moon

Dryer, still ill, wrote from Ross, California, January 15, 1938, "Next week we go to Santa Rosa and Boys [Boyes] Springs in the 'Valley of the Moon' of Jack London fame to settle the chapel car on its permanent foundation. We think we have found a perfect place — no churches or religious meetings, many children and thousands of San Francisco folk vacationing all summer. We are in the midst of hotels, baths, hot springs and sports."[106]

Dryer wanted the perfect place to put *Good Will* and himself to rest, and he thought he had found it.

A memo in the files of the American Baptist Historical Society says that the chapel car was given to the Northern California Baptist Convention to be used as a home and headquarters for the chapel car worker in 1938. The publication society paid $190 for moving the car, and Northern California paid $114 for rental of the lot. In 1940 *Good Will* was sold by the Northern California Baptist Convention for $275 to F. A. Maley of Boyes Springs. The publication society received its proportionate share of the $275.[107]

The spot where Dryer placed the chapel car in 1938 was where it stayed — behind the Boyes Hot Springs Hotel. For over sixty years the chapel car sat behind that hotel, waiting to be found, to be remembered, to be honored.

There it was! Where Morse Dryer left it. Within about 90 feet of the fancy French doors opening into the luxurious lounge of the exclusive Sonoma Mission Inn & Spa. Now off hotel property, almost completely hidden by fence, trees, and landscaping.

Greeted cordially by the present owner and escorted to the location of the car in the first week of April 1998, we felt shy, almost embarrassed — like two old friends seeing another old friend for the first time after many years. We knew Good Will would not be in great shape, maybe in sad shape. The car was 103 years old, and the present owners did not know that their old railroad car had once been a beautiful Baptist church on wheels. So it could be but a shadow of its former self.

Apprehensively, we looked the direction we were being led, trying to carry on polite conversation with our host, fearing yet longing for the first sight of the car that had been assumed destroyed, lost.

The faded, peeling exterior was what we had expected, but the parsonage-end door was open — dark, with some light streaming in through glassless windows, yet inviting. We stepped up and in, and the men talked of windows and walls. I looked up, and what I saw caused a catch in my throat.

The ceiling! It was painted in beautiful scrolls of turquoise on a golden background, along the sides and across the top, scrolls and scrolls. Faded, cracking, peeling, but lovely still. Never had we dreamed that any of the chapel cars had been so decorated. We had seen only the subdued stenciled rosettes at the corners of the cream ceilings of Grace and St. Paul. These designs were not subtle. They were sumptuous, gracefully rococo, rolling, like the waves of a turquoise sea, caught and frozen in tandem (fig. 9.9).

Why had the missionaries on board never mentioned their embellished ceilings, so un-Baptistlike? Why had Mrs. Townsend, who described her home on wheels so eloquently before her untimely death, not mentioned the presence of such artistry? Or Mrs. Fretz, or Mrs. Barkman, or Mrs. Day? Or Mrs. Driver, who so badly wanted a toilet that worked. Were they too busy with husbands, sons, and chapel car duties to look up? Or had they become accustomed to such beauty?

In 103 years, through years when the car had been used as a church and parsonage on rails, a house of worship, a home for missionaries, a chapel car missions office, a press car for the navy during World War II, a place of storage, a neighborhood playroom, those stenciled scrolls had been preserved.

Good Will was waiting: to be found, to be admired, to be remembered, to be honored. As the apostle Paul wrote in 2 Corinthians 8:19, "for the glory of the Lord himself and to show our goodwill" (NRSV).

For forty years Good Will traveled from Texas to Colorado, Nevada, Idaho, Oregon, and California, leaving behind churches and towns that stood witness to its beauty and its mission.

Fig. 9.9 This view of what was the platform of *Good Will* shows the wooden frame where the art-glass "God Is Love" was displayed. The panels that formed the platform wall, which were characteristic in all the wooden chapel cars, are partially intact. (Norman T. Taylor)

Notes

1 Proceedings of the Southern Baptist Convention, May 11–15, 1894 (Atlanta: Franklin Printing and Publishing Company), 42, Ouachita Baptist University Library, Arkadelphia, Ark.

2 Anniversary Report of the American Baptist Publication Society, Saratoga Springs, 1895, 16.

3 Proceedings of the Baptist General Convention of Texas, October 11–14, 1895 (Waco: Baptist Standard Printing House, 1895), 27, Baylor University Texas Collection, Waco, Tex.

4 Proceedings of the Baptist General Convention of Texas, October 12–16, 1894 (Waco: Baptist Standard Printing House, 1894), 24–25, Baylor University Texas Collection, Waco, Tex.

5 *The Colporter*, October 1895, 6.

6 Kathryn Hefley, *Texline, the Front Door to Texas* (Texline, Tex.: Texline Centennial Committee, 1988), 1–2.

7 Ibid.

8 Boston W. Smith, *The Story of Our Chapel Car Work* (Philadelphia: American Baptist Publication Society, n.d.), 31.

9 Proceedings of the Thirty-Seventh Session, Forty-Seventh Year of the Southern Baptist Convention, May 6–10, 1892 (Atlanta: Franklin Publishing House, 1892), 43.

10 Mary Emily Wright, *The Missionary Work of the Southern Baptist Convention* (Philadelphia: American Baptist Publication Society), 364–68, First Baptist Church of Belton, Tex.

11 BSP, 1831–1908, scrapbook, "Merry Christmas," ABHS, VF.

12 BSP, scrapbook, "Merry Christmas," ABHS, VF.

13 *The Colporter*, March 1896, 4.

14 "Del Rio Baptists: From Six Members to 1,450 in 70 Years," May 24, 1966 newspaper clipping, notes on First Baptist Church history in vertical file, Valle Verde Library, Del Rio, Tex.

15 *Biographical Sketches of Val Verde County's Old Timers* (Quality Printing Co.), 1993, 2, Val Verde Library.

16 Ibid., 250.

17 Ibid., 277.

18 Anniversary Report of the American Baptist Publication Society, Rochester, N.Y., 1898, 59.

19 "Tenaha," *The New Handbook of Texas* (Austin: The Texas State Historical Association, 1996), vol. 6, 252.

20 Seventy-fourth Anniversary Report of the American Baptist Publication Society.

21 Ibid.

22 Colporter records, newspaper clippings, ABHS, VF.

23 Hollie Harper Townsend, Chapel Car Series no. 7, "About Chapel Cars" (Philadelphia: American Baptist Publication Society, n.d.), ABHS, VF.

24 *The Colporter*, March 1900, n.p.

25 Jack Skiles, Judge *Roy Bean Country* (Lubbock, Tex.: Texas Tech University Press, 1996), 87–94.

26 Ibid., 121.

27 *The Colporter*, March 1900, 7.

28 Eleanor James, *Forth from Her Portals: The First 100 Years in Belton*, University of Mary Hardin-Baylor (Belton, Tex.: University of Mary Hardin-Baylor Press), 41.

29 Very little was mentioned in Baylor files of the chapel car ministry of Townsend, a Baylor graduate. At the campus of Mary Hardin-Baylor University, in Belton, Texas, in the Townsend Library, we were able to find almost nothing about Townsend's years on the chapel car and his first marriage. Elli Moore Townsend was an influential graduate of Mary Hardin and a classmate of Hollie Harper Townsend. Through her influence and his abilities, Townsend assumed high positions in the college.

30 *The Colporter*, April 1900.

31 J. M. Carroll, *A History of Texas Baptists* (Dallas: Baptist Standard Publishing Co., 1923), 794.

32 Souvenir of the Galveston Storm, Saturday, September 8th, 1900 (Houston: J. J. Pastorisa Printing Ad Litho. Co.), 16–17.

33 *The Colporter*, November 1900, 6.

34 Anniversary Report of the American Baptist Publication Society, Springfield, Mass., 1901, 109–10.

35 Fifty-fourth annual session of the Baptist General Convention of Texas, November 7–10, 1902, Baptist Collection, Baylor University, Waco, Tex.

36 *The New Handbook of Texas* (Austin, Tex.: The Texas Historical Association, 1996), vol. 1, 1003.

37 *The Word and the Way*, October 22, 1903, 1, Oklahoma Baptist Convention, Archives, The Baptist Building, Oklahoma City, Okla.

38 *The Colorado Baptist Bulletin*, April 1906, 7, American Baptist Conference of the Rocky Mountains, Denver, Colo.

39 BSP, pamphlet on chapel car work, chapel car pamphlets and tracts, ABHS, VF.

40 *Missions*, January 1912, 37.

41 Letter from Robert G. Seymour, Philadelphia, to George L. White, November 29, 1911, George L. White file, ABHS, VF.

42 Letter from George L. White to Robert G. Seymour, December 1, 1911, George L. White file, ABHS, VF.

43 Letter from George L. White to L. T. Barkman, January 13, 1912, George L. White file, ABHS, VF.

44 *Baptist Life and Thought: 1600–1980*, ed. William H. Brackney (Valley Forge: Judson Press, 1983), 212.

45 *Missions*, December 1912, 944.

46 Letter from L. T. Barkman to George L. White, January 8, 1912, George L. White file, ABHS, VF.

47 Letter from L. T. Barkman to George L. White, January 25, 1912, George L. White file, ABHS, VF.

48 Letter from George L. White to Robert G. Seymour, September 5, 1912, George L. White file, ABHS, VF.

49 Letter from J. Franklin Day to George L. White, August 13, 1913, George L. White file, ABHS, VF.

50 Ibid.

51 Letter from J. Franklin Day to George L. White, October 11, 1913, George L. White file, ABHS, VF.

52 Letter from J. Franklin Day to George L. White, October 23, 1913, George L. White file, ABHS, VF.

53 Letter from the Coleman Lamp Company to George L. White, October 28, 1913.

54 Letter from J. Franklin Day to George L. White, December 15, 1913, George L. White file, ABHS, VF.

55 Letter from J. Franklin Day to George L. White, January 20, 1914, George L. White file, ABHS, VF.

56 Letter from Guy C. Lamson to George L. White, February 5, 1914, George L. White file, ABHS, VF.

57 Letter from George L. White to J. Franklin Day, March 5, 1914, George L. White file, ABHS, VF.

58 Letter from J. Franklin Day to George L. White, February 14, 1914, George L. White file, ABHS, VF.

59 Letter from J. Franklin Day to George L. White, March 1, 1914, George L. White file, ABHS, VF.

60 Letter from J. Franklin Day to George L. White, May 16, 1914, George L. White file, ABHS, VF.

61 Letter from George L. White to W. C. Driver, July 24, 1914, George L. White file, ABHS, VF.

62 Letter from J. Franklin Day to George L. White, July 31, 1914, George L. White file, ABHS, VF.

63 Letter from George L. White to J. W. Stockton, September 23, 1914, George L. White file, ABHS, VF.

64 *Missions*, March 1915, 27.

65 Letter from W. C. Driver to George L. White, February 21, 1915, George L. White file, ABHS, VF.

66 Letter from W. C. Driver to George L. White, November 21, 1915, George L. White file, ABHS, VF.

67 Letter from W. C. Driver to George L. White, January 25, 1916, George L. White file, ABHS, VF.

68 Letter from W. C. Driver to George L. White, January 25, 1916, George L. White file, ABHS, VF.

69 Letters between George L. White and Guy Lamson, from February 10 to May 6, 1916, George L. White file, ABHS, VF.

70 Letter from W. C. Driver to George L. White, June 26, 1916, George L. White file, ABHS, VF.

71 Letter from W. C. Driver to George L. White, June 29, 1916, George L. White file, ABHS, VF.

72 Oregon Baptist Convention Report, October 17–20, 1916, Salem, Ore., American Baptist Conference of Oregon, Portland, Ore.

73 "1915: Popular Culture," and "1916: Art & Culture," *Our Times*, Multimedia Encyclopedia of the 20th Century (Vicarious, Inc., 1996).

74 *Missions*, April 1917, 342, Franklin College Library, Franklin, Ind.

75 Letter from W. C. Driver to George L. White, March 18, 1917, George L. White file, ABHS, VF.

76 Letter from George L. White to John F. Powers of the Pacific Coast Baseball League, April 21, 1917, George L. White files, ABHS, VF.

77 Letter from W. C. Driver to George L. White, June 9, 1917, George L. White file, ABHS, VF.

78 Letter from W. C. Driver to George L. White, July 25, 1917, George L. White file, ABHS, VF.

79 Letter from W. C. Driver to George L. White, August 20, 1917, George L. White file, ABHS, VF.

80 George L. White correspondence, letter from W. C. Driver, January 25, 1919, ABHS, VF.

81 Letter from W. C. Driver to George L. White, January 1, 1919, George L. White file, ABHS, VF.

82 Letter from George L. White to W. C. Driver, January 6, 1919, George L. White file, ABHS, VF.

83 Telegram from George L. White to Samuel G. Neil, April 15, 1919, George L. White file, ABHS, VF.

84 Letter from W. C. Driver to George L. White, April 22, 1919, George L. White file, ABHS, VF.

85 Letter from George L. White to W. C. Driver, April 29, 1920, George L. White file, ABHS, VF.

86 Letter from W. C. Driver to George L. White, December 7, 1920, George L. White file, ABHS, VF.

87 Letter from W. C. Driver to George L. White, May 29, 1921, George L. White file, ABHS, VF.

88 Letter from Samuel G. Neil to George L. White, September, 1921, George L. White file, ABHS, VF.

89 Letter from Mrs. W. C. Driver to George L. White, March 5, 1922, George L. White file, ABHS, VF.

90 Letter from John B. Speed to George L. White, October 4, 1923, George L. White file, ABHS, VF.

91 Letter from John B. Speed to George L. White, October 27, 1923, George L. White filed, ABHS, VF.

92 Letter from Samuel G. Neil to potential donors, June 30, 1927, George L. White file, ABHS, VF.

93 A promotional brochure published by Lake Siskiyou Camp Resort, Inc., Mt. Shasta Resort, and Mt. Shasta Ski Park.

94 *The Baptist Banner*, September 15, 1927, 17.

95 *Missions*, September 1927, 623.

96 Letter from A. C. McChesney to Samuel G. Neil, January 1, 1931, Samuel G. Neil file, (February 7, 96, T), ABHS, VF.

97 Letter from A. C. McChesney to Samuel G. Neil, January 20, 1930, Samuel G. Neil file, ABHS, VF.

98 Ibid.

99 Publication society report of churches erected by chapel car in 1930–1931 (February 2, 96, I), ABHS, VF.

100 Recollections of Mrs. Satterfield, member of First Baptist Church of Santa Rosa, Calif.

101 *History of Sonoma County, California: Its People and Its Resources*, ed. Ernest Latimer Finley (Santa Rosa, Calif.: The Press Democrat Publishing Co., 1937), 284, Sonoma County Library, Santa Rosa, Calif.

102 Ibid., 281–82.

103 Letter from John C. Killian to I. Morse Dryer, July 27, 1937, Box: Colporter Records, Workers N-W, Branch Managers, I. Morris Dryer Folder, ABHS, VF.

104 Letter from S. S. Aplin to John C. Killian, July 4, 1937, Box: Colporter Records, Workers N-W, Branch Managers, I. Morse Dryer Folder, ABHS, VF.

105 Letter from John C. Killian to I. Morse Dryer, October 21, 1937, Box: Colporter Records, Workers N-W, Branch Managers, I. Morse Dryer Folder, ABHS, VF.

106 Letter from I. Morse Dryer to John C. Killian, January 15, 1938, Box: Colporter Records, Workers N-W, Branch Managers, I. Morse Dryer Folder, ABHS, VF.

107 Memo in files of ABHS, VF. Folder Dorothy Martin Correspondence, "Grace" article request.

CHAPTER 10

Baptist Car 5: *Messenger of Peace* the 1904 World's Fair, and the Railroad Y

Because Baptist women across the country raised the funds for its construction, *Messenger of Peace* would be called the Ladies' Car. Viewed by thousands at the 1904 World's Fair, it carried a dying Dwight L. Moody on his journey home, traveled across the United States and Canada under the auspices of the Railroad YMCA, and delivered the gospel from the Ozark hills to the Olympic Mountains.

The Reverend Samuel G. Neil, a Scot who came to America as an officer of the Salvation Army, became *Messenger of Peace*'s first missionary with his wife, Millie. Sam Neil preached his first sermon at the age of fifteen in a Scottish schoolhouse, and in 1882 he joined the Salvation Army and became known all over Britain as "the young Scotch prophet" *(see fig. 10.2)*.

After leaving the Salvation Army Training College at Clapton, London, he was conducting a meeting on the Radcliffe Highway and was knocked head over heels by a brothel keeper. The blow on his right ear was so severe that for several minutes his friends and companions thought he was killed. From that day until the time of his death, he was never able to hear a sound in that ear.[1]

At the dedication May 21, 1898, at Rochester, New York's Union Station, the Scottish Neil was not stingy with his praise for the chapel car. "*Messenger of Peace* is the largest, the loveliest, the lightest, and brightest of them all. The ladies do not do things by halves."[2]

The Barney & Smith Car Works was bringing men back to work on a regular basis in 1898 as the nation began to recover from the panic of 1893. On March 23, severe spring rains created flood conditions on the canal system formed by the Great Miami, the Mad, and the Stillwater rivers. The waters of the canal overflowed into the car works, washing away supplies of lumber and filling the lower floors and basement work area with several feet of water.

It was March 26 before the waters receded and the cleanup could begin. Little if any damage was done to rolling stock under construction, and newspaper accounts indicate that the plant was back in full operation within two weeks. *Messenger of Peace* was released from the shops in May.[3]

With Boston Smith on board with the Neils, the car left Rochester on May 24 and stopped at Buffalo, New York; Erie, Pennsylvania; Cleveland and Toledo, Ohio; and St.

Fig. 10.1 The sight of children standing along the railroad tracks waiting for the chapel car to come into their Washington State town greeted *Messenger of Peace* missionaries. (American Baptist Historical Society, Valley Forge)

Fig. 10.2 Samuel G. Neil was the first missionary assigned to *Messenger of Peace*. A Scotsman with a Salvation Army background, Neil would go on to be missionary secretary in charge of chapel car work. (American Baptist Historical Society, Valley Forge)

Louis, Missouri. Large numbers of visitors inspected the car, and, according to Neil, nothing but exclamations of delight were heard. From St. Louis they journeyed to Kansas City, where the Baptists gave them a royal welcome and even the mayor acknowledged their presence.

By June the car had already made its mark in Argentine, Kansas, with lively and productive services. A long list including railroad foremen, clerks, the train master, shop engineer, city attorney, city clerk, mayor, postmaster, editor of the local paper, board of education member, and even local laundry men wrote to *The Evening Herald* praising the "unique, instructive, comforting and inspiring" work. They also thanked the Santa Fe Railway Company for bringing the car to town.[4]

Mrs. Neil would not forget Argentine, Kansas, because it was there she "lost" her fine granite milk can. The milkman came to the car every morning. Mrs. Neil put out her milk can on the rear of the platform with two milk tickets. In the morning when the milkman came, he knocked on the door, thinking the Neils were asleep. Mrs. Neil called out, "The milk can is on the platform, and the tickets are in the can." The milkman replied, "The tickets are here but the milk can is gone." At breakfast her husband asked her what he ought to preach on as an introductory sermon, and she said, "You better preach from the text 'Thou shalt not steal.'"[5]

Several important events happened to this fifth Baptist car during its tenure, in addition to its travels and missionary endeavors through Missouri, Kansas, Montana, Washington, and Oregon. At the World Exposition of 1898 in St. Louis, Missouri, the newly dedicated *Messenger of Peace* was on display for much of the exhibition, and Smith conducted a number of daily evangelistic crusades from the car. One of the outstanding personalities to visit the exhibit was Dwight L. Moody, the noted traveling evangelist of the late nineteenth century, who preached from the platform of the chapel car.

Moody Dying, Souls Saved in Missouri

In November 1899, the sixty-two-year-old Moody was in Kansas City conducting a religious campaign at the Bales Baptist Church.[6] The loss of a grandchild, the pressures of his preaching and evangelism work, and other concerns were weighing heavily on his heart, and he was not well. He was not able to sleep, even to lie down. He was pale, not eating, but he continued to preach. After Thursday night's sermon he was "in a dripping sweat . . . I had never seen him so exhausted," his associate Charley Vining would say. On Friday afternoon, November 17, the denomination made arrangements to have Moody taken home to Northfield, Massachusetts.[7]

Neil, a dynamic preacher in his own right, was asked to continue preaching in Moody's absence, and the dying evangelist was placed aboard *Messenger of Peace* and accompanied to St. Louis by Mrs. Neil, his associates, and his doctor. There he was moved to an eastbound train for his final trip home to Northfield. On Saturday evening the train reached Detroit late owing to engine trouble, and Vining feared the next connection would be missed.

When the engineer who was to take Train No. 4 the next stage heard that Moody, sick, was on the train, he sent a message: "Tell him I was converted under him fifteen years ago and owe everything to him. Tell Mr. Moody one of his friends is at the throttle, and just hold your breath!" They covered the stretch from Detroit through Canada to St. Thomas, including stops, at a mile a minute.[8] After he returned to his home, Moody died December 22.

Around the turn of the century at Carrolton, Missouri, a young boy saw the chapel car on a siding and drawled, "Now what kind of a car do you reckon that is?" After being told that it was a church car, he exclaimed, "Well, I swan! I've seen a cattle car, a hog car, a sleeping car, a smoking car, a baggage car, and a passenger car; but I'll be blessed if I ever saw a car like that. Now, if that don't beat the devil!" Neil replied, "That's exactly what it's supposed to do. Beat the devil!"[9]

At Delta, down the Cotton Belt Line, members of the church the Neils helped build surprised them by placing a dove, the symbol of *Messenger of Peace*, in the new stained-glass window.[10] In addition, the Iron Mountain Railroad and the Cotton Belt Railroad both gave him fifty dollars toward the church building.[11] At Ardeola, where there was a stave factory, the car was not large enough to hold the crowds, and many had to be turned away. One afternoon the Neils held a service for the "colored people of the town. They turned out finely from all round this section of the country and the meeting was a great success. While I was preaching to them on the inside, a congregation of fully one hundred white people stood on the outside and drank in every word."[12]

Missouri Baptists had always loved the revivals and camp meetings that first spread from the East in the early 1800s. They loved the social aspects of getting together with neighbors, and they loved the singin' and preachin.'

J. Gordon Kingsley, in his history of Missouri Baptists, mentions how the rousing songs of the camp meetings sometimes reflected denominational battles. The Methodists, for example, offered this sally in their woodland warfare with the Baptists:

> We've searched the law of heaven,
> Throughout the Sacred code;
> Of Baptism there by dipping
> We've never found a word . . .
> To plunge is inconsistent
> Compared with holy rites;
> An instance of such business
> We've never found as yet.

And the Baptists were not to be outdone:

> Not at the River Jordan
> But in the flowing stream
> Stood John the Baptist preacher
> When he baptized Him.
> John was a Baptist preacher
> When he Baptiz'd the Lamb;
> Then Jesus was a Baptist
> And thus the Baptist[s] came.[13]

Neil left the chapel car for a pastorate in the East in 1902 and would later direct the chapel car work, but there was still some of that revival spirit when the chapel car, now with the Reverend Joe P. Jacobs and his wife, came to Novinger in 1902.

In 1900, the population of Novinger had been only sixty-eight, but in 1902, including the mines for half a mile around, there were between two and three thousand. On March 4 *Messenger of Peace* was sidetracked there and began work. There was neither church house nor schoolhouse in the town and no religious organization except a kind of union Sunday school, with a superintendent who did not even claim to be a Christian. The railroad company built a track just for the chapel car and made a walk from the main street to the car and depot.

To the Jacobses' surprise, at the first night service every seat in the chapel car was taken, mostly by men, with not more than six women present. The second night the car would not hold the people. On the third, they made arrangements to move the meeting to the town hall, a large, unattractive frame building with a seating capacity of about five hundred, used for shows, mass meetings, and every other gathering in town.

It was at Novinger that Jacobs led a young man to Christ, creating quite a stir in the mines and community. Born in England, coming from a troubled family but with a faithful mother, the young man had sworn off religion and sworn onto drink. He had not been in a house of worship for twelve years, and as he said, "If I had not been drinking and full of curiosity to see what this thing was I would not have heard one then. I came in here drunk. Oh, my friend, I believe you are my friend, I have drunk up two good homes and been in bar-room brawls when beer glasses and bottles flew seemingly as thick as hailstones. Your first sermon, drunk as I was, made a deep impression and I have not missed a service since."

For days Jacobs talked, read Scripture, prayed, and pleaded with the young man to accept Christ, but to no avail. One morning the missionary heard him running to the car, shouting, "O Jacobs, O Jacobs! Open the door! Satan is after me! Hurry up, Satan hath desired my soul! Be quick! O my God! I have run all the way from the mines here. I had to come; I could not stay away."

Jacobs opened the door and in rushed Andy in his mining clothes — cap, lamp, and all, just as he had come from his work in the pit. His face was black, his clothes were dirty, and there was a wild look in his eyes. "Oh, they said in the mines that I was crazy, and they shouted, 'catch him, catch him, he is crazy.'" Andy fell upon his knees and confessed his faith in Jesus Christ.[14]

At Brimson, Missouri, on the Omaha, Quincy, and Kansas City (OK) Railroad in March 1903, the car was surrounded by well-kept, prosperous farms. The town was named after William G. Brimson, an officer of the railroad and a prominent Baptist layman, who had hosted the chapel car conferences and befriended the chapel car workers in many ways. There was no church at Brimson, but before the chapel car left, the townspeople had crowded into the largest hall for services and pledged to support a building and a pastor. Local farmers promised to provide the preacher with a cow and a barn filled with hay.[15]

With consternation on June 1, 1903, Jacobs read of the flood that devastated Kansas City and surrounding towns. *Messenger of Peace* had visited many of these towns. Up the Missouri and Kaw valleys the rain descended, and down the rivers the floods came. Both rivers reached a mark above anything on record. Armourdale and Argentine, where the chapel car had spent much shop time, were almost wiped out.

The West Bottoms, in which were the stockyards, railroad yards and shops, factories and machine shops, great packing houses, wholesale houses, and the Union depot, was a scene of wild desolation. Trains were stopped because the depot was flooded to the second story. Business was paralyzed. The city was without water and in darkness. Sixteen steel bridges connecting the two Kansas Cities went down.

The Baptist paper, *The Word and the Way*, in its first issue after the flood, commented about the action of Kansas City officials in closing all the saloons during the emergency. "Not a dry goods store, not a fruit store, not a grocery, not a shoe store, not a bakery, was ordered closed. And why? Because there is nothing in any of these lines of business that in any

way endangers the interests of the community. They are not makers of brawls. They do not demoralize men and incite them to lawlessness and indecency. . . . It will go into history that in the time of its greatest trouble and peril, Kansas City was afraid of its saloons."[16]

In *The Word and Way* of July 23, 1903, Jacobs told Missouri Baptists that *Messenger of Peace* would be leaving "dear old Missouri" and traveling to Colorado. "Since our arrival the Lord has opened doors that were shut to us one year ago and since the D & RG [Denver and Rio Grande] and C & S [Colorado & Southern] Railroads have given us the use of their lines, it is possible that we will change our headquarters to Denver and work in the far west." Jacobs spelled out the reason for leaving Missouri: the churches had not contributed adequately toward the support of the car.

After just a few months in Pueblo, Colorado, *Messenger of Peace* was urged to return to Missouri. At Trenton, a desperate church wanted Jacobs to stay as pastor. At Worthington, a rapidly growing town, where the old Baptist church had died eighteen years before, a new church was in the works, 30 x 40 feet framed, weather boarded, and shingled, with a vestibule and cupola begun at the middle of the longest side.

Jacobs reported that the situation was most challenging. "It is my understanding that neither the lumber company nor the contractor has yet been paid anything. The professed Christians are for the most part Campbellites, Baptist, and modern Holiness people. The larger majority, by far, not claiming any religion at all." In April he hoped to put the car in the shops for extensive repairs, and he hoped that the people of Missouri would contribute liberally toward the shop bill.[17]

World's Fair Draws Crowds to Car

Celebrating the centennial of the Louisiana Purchase, the World's Fair was held in St. Louis in 1904. Covering fifteen acres, the Transportation Building looked like a majestic railroad station, and beneath its expansive roof were displayed all the modern methods of transportation together with historical exhibits of great interest. *Messenger of Peace* was displayed by the American Baptist Publication Society in the Transportation Building and remained in its place from opening day until its close.

According to several accounts, the Baptist chapel car tied for first-place honors with a coach exhibited by the Anheuser Busch Brewing Company that was parked next to it. According to a somewhat biased Baptist writer, the judges gave the decision to the chapel car because of its more worthy purpose — that of uplifting humanity.[18]

On one day alone more than ten thousand people passed through the car, including a couple who were married on the car, the first such event on the grounds, reported by the *St. Louis Daily Globe-Democrat* on May 26, 1904. After the brief ceremony, the bride and her groom were escorted to a special Pullman car where a reception area was provided by a representative of the Pullman Company. (A few days later a Baptist seminary student married another couple three hundred feet in the air, on the Monster Observation Wheel.)[19] The church on wheels elicited universal praise as more than a wedding chapel, and a large quantity of literature was distributed, and donations were received.[20]

It was at the 1904 fair that Jacobs had several important visitors: Bishop William David Walker of the first American chapel car, the Episcopal Cathedral Car of North Dakota, and Father Francis Kelley of the Catholic Church Extension Society. As a result of Father Kelley's enthusiastic impressions of that visit, the Catholic Church Extension Society would build three chapel cars in the coming years.

While the Reverend and Mrs. J. H. Webber, who had come to the car in 1906, were trying to adjust to life on the chapel car, Baptists in San Francisco were trying to rebuild after the great earthquake that had devastated the city in April. Dr. Henry L. Morehouse of the home mission society sent this first-person report.

Twice last week I stood on Nob Hill and looked upon such a scene of desolation as no spot in the civilized world has ever afforded. The exact area burned over is as yet a matter of estimation being somewhere from eight to fifteen square miles. There were not to exceed one dozen buildings standing within these limits, and ruin, desolation, ascending smoke, tottering walls everywhere. Back of me a mile or two, in the public squares and parks, on the military reservation, and even in the cemeteries, were gathered nearly two hundred thousand homeless, hungry, mostly helpless men, women, and children. Relief, so far as distribution of food, clothing and shelter is concerned, is being provided and the people are being cared for, all the circumstances considered, remarkably well. Seven of the nine Baptist churches in the city were either destroyed or badly damaged, and other churches as far away as Santa Rosa and Santa Clara, were also destroyed.[21]

From August 1906 through the spring of 1909, the Reverend and Mrs. J. S. Davis shepherded the car. Much of the chapel car work was among immigrants, for as a Missouri Baptist report pointed out in 1908, "We have in our borders peoples from almost every nation, kindred and tongue under heaven. Germans, Swedes, Bohemians, Danes, Italians, Russians, and Greeks — in all, about one million, making nearly one-third of our population. This brings to our doors a gracious missionary opportunity, from which we may not turn away except at our peril."[22]

After many months at Santa Rosa and Nashua, Missouri, and other towns in the southern part of the state, the car was turned over to the Reverend and Mrs. Thomas Gale. The Gales would stay on *Messenger of Peace* through a ministry with the YMCA and into the years of World War I.

For a number of years the American Baptist Publication Society had wanted to have one of the chapel cars work with the Railroad YMCA, and in 1910 *Messenger of Peace* was the car chosen for that opportunity. The Railroad Y, organized April 14, 1872, in Cleveland, Ohio, by evangelist George Myers, was a vital part of the Christian witness to rail workers as well as a means of making railroad life and passage safer and more efficient for all Americans.

In the 1800s, particularly before rail unions, "life on the rails was cheap." Crews suffered impossibly long hours, unfit food, and infested beds. Many of the frequent train wrecks could be linked directly to excessive duty and unhealthy "rest" periods when alcohol, gambling, wenching, and brawling were favorite pastimes. As a result, thousands of railroaders were killed or maimed.[23] The Railroad Ys provided a safe, wholesome home for thousands of railroad men across America, a place where they could find clean beds, good food, reading material, healthy physical activity, and spiritual guidance.

Among the earliest religious activities of the Railroad Y associations were the gospel trains, usually composed of a Christian engineer, fireman, conductor, and brakeman, all men of outstanding character and fervor, gifted with simple and homely speech. Services were conducted in churches and railroad association buildings. The gospel trains visited railroad communities where no railroad association existed, promoting interest in and sometimes organization of a Y branch. The service was simplicity itself — singing of old-time hymns, Scripture, and prayer, followed by thrilling recitals of personal experiences. Then would come an invitation to the audience "to entrain with the gospel crew as the train sped on toward the City of God."[24]

But in March 1909, Rail Y secretary A. G. Knebel reported about a real train car fitted for service:

My work during the month of March has been somewhat varied. The opening days of the month were spent at Proctor, Minnesota, and vicinity, in company with Secretary Davis taking a trip in the new Y.M.C.A. Car, visiting two or three of the points where groups of men are employed.

The car represents a most unique feature of railroad work. It has been turned over to the Proctor Association by the Company [Duluth, Missabe & Northern

Railway][25] and is splendidly fitted up with tables, reading matter, stationery, etc. It will accommodate from 80 to 90 men and the Association expects to conduct religious and social services for the men at outlying points.

On two days during the week the car is shifted in front of the shop and a noon meeting is held. The Association furnished coffee and sandwiches for 10¢ for quite a few of the men who ordinarily go home to dinner.[26]

International YMCA secretary F. H. Day in May 1910 reported that he made a visit to the Pullman Company at West Pullman, Illinois, and discussed with the superintendent the possibility of a gift from Pullman of such a car for the association's work. "The matter is still pending," Day concluded.

Whether a car was given by Pullman is not known, but it is known that several Railroad Y cars were in operation. Jacobs, now the missionary secretary, reported to the publication society in June 1911, "So great is the demand of chapel-car work that the Catholics have now two cars in the field, and the Railroad Young Men's Christian Association is using cars constantly. The railroads have reaffirmed their appreciation of them by continued free transportation, and even the Interstate Commerce Commission has commended them to the favorable consideration of the railroads."[27]

The social, spiritual, and physical services offered by the Railroad Y were important not only in the early days of railroading. In 1915 a study was conducted on the need for the Railroad Ys as opposed to other types of clubhouses set up by individual railroad companies.

Unfortunately most of the railroad terminals are located in the most undesirable parts of the community and usually the district is more or less thickly infested with saloons and other places of vice. Unless some special provision is made, the men who come in from their runs and are in need of refreshment and rest have great difficulty in securing good accommodations at any reasonable price, or any price, and are driven to the saloon, where they will at least be sure to find companionship and a certain amount of recreation. The result is that they are often far from fit when the time comes for them to take their trains out.

When we consider the complications in making up and getting the trains over the road and the possibilities for preventing damage to goods, and accidents to life and limb, if keen, bright men are in charge, it is not hard to see where railroads can make big savings by doing their part to keep the men in a fit condition.[28]

Messenger of Peace Works for Railroad Y

In the spring of 1910, the work was begun with the International Railroad YMCA on the Frisco system in Missouri, and E. L. Hamilton, secretary of the International Y, reported, "Have completed arrangements for the work of Reverend Thomas R. Gale in the Chapel Car on the Wabash lines. He will begin in the State of Missouri."[29]

Gale's first stop was at the Brooklyn yards just outside of East St. Louis, and from there he went to Decatur, Illinois, where he set up Bible classes and gospel meetings. He and Mrs. Gale, who was just as effective in the work as her husband, worked with the Horace, Kansas, and Helper, Utah, railroad associations with much success.[30]

It may have been during this time that the Gales stopped at Montpelier, Idaho, to work with the men in the railroad shops. Gale reported,

. . . the Montpelier work has been unique in its great moral influence upon the men, even where they have not been definitely born again. . . . The wife of a car inspector had got to the end of things and finally had taken out papers for divorce. She sent down to the car as her last hope. Could we convert the husband? We pointed out the supreme difficulty — the consent of the man himself to be converted. We undertook to do our

best, but do not know the final end yet. . . . A mother, whose son is in the yards at Detroit, gives his name and his weakness, and hopes much concerning the boy when we get there. The wife of the electrician is in dire distress; the husband's entanglements threaten to bring disaster to the home. Could we speak to him without letting him know who sent us?[31]

As *Messenger of Peace* traveled toward Boston to take its place in the exposition of "The World in Boston," representing both the publication society and the International Y, it worked at railroad points on the Wabash and the Canadian Grand Trunk.[32]

On the chapel car's return trip along the lines of the Chesapeake & Ohio, it made an exciting side trip to West Virginia and Thurmond Station, a mining town in the dangerous but beautiful New River Gorge, where the only way in was by the railroad that crawled along the cliffs of the gorge.

West Virginia missionary A. B. Withers said of Thurmond: "It has long held the unenviable reputation of being the wickedest county in the State, in recent years sharing this record with McDowell, however. Its record of crime of all kinds is written in the books of the State Penitentiary, to which institution it makes the greatest contribution. To the credit of Fayette County, however, it must be said that its citizens of the original stock are among the best people on earth. It is the alien element, the drifting, shifting population, and the vile wretches that prey on them, and use them to accomplish their political schemes who are responsible for Fayette County's reputation."[33]

Thurmond, incorporated in 1903, was at its prime in October 1911 when *Messenger of Peace* pulled into the station that saw more than two hundred people a day disembark. The good people of Thurmond of whom Withers spoke were the 150 townspeople gainfully employed, with more than 60 of those railroaders. There were also retail clerks, barbers, bookkeepers, and insurance agents, among others, at work in town. Due to the strict moral code of the town's founder,

Captain William Dabney Thurmond, there were no saloons in the town limits of Thurmond.[34]

But Thurmond was an island of sanity in a sea of surrounding immorality *(see fig. 10.3)*. There, amid hostility from saloon owners, especially in the Ballyhack district across the river from Thurmond, home to the notorious Black Hawk, Stackalee, South Side, and other watering holes of questionable repute,[35] a work was accomplished in cooperation with the Railroad Y.

At that time there was no Y association or building at Thurmond, but one was in the planning. Taking a little time off from the Railroad Y duties, *Messenger of Peace* and the Gales wound their way up the steep grades of the Chesapeake and Ohio Loup Creek Branch to the small mining community of Red Star and organized a church.

Withers described Gale's effect on the railroad men in West Virginia. "I am sure that I have never found a man who had more wonderful influence over men than he. It was a constant marvel to this writer — his power and skill in dealing with men. They love him — would die for him, we believe, if it were necessary. He has shaken Thurmond to its foundations. More than fifty people here have been converted, most of them railroad men. . . . There have been up to this writing over one hundred and fifty conversions in meetings held by these workers in the state. Brother Gale says this is a greater field for such work than that in which he has been working hitherto. We hope to have them many months in West Virginia."[36]

Messenger of Peace was not to stay many months as had been hoped, but several years later, *Herald of Hope* would come to the state for an extended service.

Returning from its concentrated tour with the Railroad Y, *Messenger of Peace* went back to work in Missouri, at Emmise, a new lumber town. At Christmas 1912, the car was packed with mothers and children decorating a Christmas tree,[37] a bit of a change from the pace of witnessing to railroaders in noisy engine shops or settlers in wild mountain towns.

Chapel Car Heads to West Coast

After a year along Colorado lines, the car was moved to the West Coast in 1913. The move was not accomplished without difficulty and took many letters and meetings. George L. White wrote in August to the Southern Pacific traffic manager, "We desire to do two types of work: the first is a general religious and moral work at division stations especially with the railroad men and their families. The second is in new towns where there are no churches and often where no religious work at all is being done. In such cases it is often possible to leave the car for a considerable time until a church is organized and a chapel erected and that, of course, is helpful to the town. Good people are influenced to settle there with their families and all concerned are benefited. Experience proves that the net results are helpful to the railroad company."

No response came, so White took the matter up with C. J. Millis, assistant to the president of the Southern Pacific, a Baptist. Millis was encouraging but said that he was not able to do much for them and suggested several courses of action. Several letters later, *Messenger of Peace* was on the way to

Fig. 10.3 For one year, starting in 1901, *Messenger of Peace* was assigned to the International YMCA, where it worked with the Railroad Ys. At Thurmond, West Virginia, the car faced opposition but succeeded in strengthening the Railroad Y branch and building a church. (From the Chesapeake & Ohio Historical Society Collection, Clifton Forge, Virginia)

Sacramento, not on the Southern Pacific, but on the Western Pacific Railroad.

Because of the extreme August heat in California, Gale was advised to stop first in the cooler elevation of Nevada, at Wells, a railroad town, then Deeth, Carlin, and Elko. Since the Western Pacific was a new road, frequently its stops were a distance from the town, which was probably located on the Southern Pacific line. The fresh possibilities for worship in the new towns along this young line offset some of the inconveniences.[38]

Another plea went to the Southern Pacific in a letter to Charles S. Fee, passenger & traffic manager: "As you probably know, most of the larger railroads in the country have for years transported free of charge the [chapel] cars operating on their lines, and we urgently request the Southern Pacific Company to grant the same courtesy within Northern California. As you also know, a large number of communities are growing into places of considerable prominence, and many of them have little or no gospel privileges. We are seeking as a missionary society to lay foundations in these communities that will make for the largest moral and spiritual development of all our citizens."[39]

At Oroville, California, a few week later, the Gales continued "our daily hunt of lost and discouraged Baptists,"[40] and became discouraged themselves in a difficult situation. But while there, they finally received the long-awaited response from Southern Pacific Company. "I am pleased to advise that this company, while discontinuing the practice of issuing annual passes for such cars, will be very glad to move your chapel car 'Messenger of Peace' on trip passes between points on our line as and when necessary in the conduct of the Missionary Society's business."[41] The letter was signed C. J. Millis.

After Oroville, the Gales wanted to go to Marysville, but because they were still on the Western Pacific, the car would have been sided too far from town to be effective.[42] The rice harvest prevented meetings at Richvale and Biggs, California, from being better attended and supported, but the work at

Antelope was successful. A widowed farmer who first came to the chapel car drunk finally accepted Christ, brought his children to see him baptized, and then married a widow who also had been baptized by the Gales. The whole community came to the wedding in the chapel car.

The Baptists of Roseville, California, had already been organized into a Sunday school, but on February 24, 1914, *Messenger of Peace* came to town to organize a church and start a building program of several months.[43]

In the fall of 1914 *Messenger of Peace* again was in need of painting, varnishing, and repairs, but publication society officials did not feel they could afford to have the work done. From the Philadelphia office, Guy C. Lamson wrote, "So far as platforms and gates were concerned, of course, we demanded that they should be put in perfect shape; but if the repairs which he [Gale] contemplated called for steel underframe, etc., such as been put on Hermiston's car [*Emmanuel*] and we refused to allow the thing to be done. If there is any question about the matter at all and the continuance of the car, we should immediately remove the car from the State of California, as we expect to remove the car immediately anyway when the new car [*Grace*] is finished."[44]

While his superiors talked about what was to be done on the car, Gale had it in the shops, and estimates were made as to what was necessary to keep it in service under interstate commerce rulings. White came from his office in Los Angeles to see the chapel car and evaluate the work that needed to be done. He wrote to Lamson:

> I found the exterior of the car in very bad condition, evidently the shoddiest kind of work was done when it was painted the last time. There are many places where nearly all of the paint has peeled off . . . as a matter of fact, the car does need to have all of the paint remaining on it burned off and it needs to be properly repainted and varnished. It takes seven coats, if properly done. If the car is then revarnished once a year at a cost of $50 or $60 it should not need to be repainted again for ten

years. We must, however have our cars varnished once a year. It will save us thousands of dollars in expense in the long run.[45]

Regardless of the fact that White felt the work needed to be done, Lamson was outraged at the $850 estimate by the Southern Pacific shops. "Gale would be surprised to know that the charges for the upkeep of his car during its lifetime have been two and a half times as great as those for any other car, and have been greater than those of any other two cars put together. . . . Two years ago we spent over $1700 on his car when we started out to spend $500."[46]

In April *Messenger of Peace* was in the Southern Pacific's Sacramento shops having a face lift: burn off paint, paint and varnish outside; clean and oil off inside, paint floor and seat foot rests; repair linoleum, renew defective screens, repair sink; tighten up trucks and paint; tighten up draft rigging and platforms; paint roof and blacken all iron work underneath,[47] the work done at cost for $479.93.

White wrote Lamson that the car looked first-class and that the railroad did several repairs for which they did not charge. "In the West there is considerable alkali dust and when that remains on the car it soon eats up the paint. About once a month, after wiping off the dust, the car should be gone over a second time with a very small amount of oil on a rag. The car may be kept looking well and preserved somewhat by the missionary himself if he paints the steps occasionally and paints exposed iron parts black so that they will not become rusty."[48]

Chapel Cars in a Game of Musical Rails

Confusion reigned during the summer of 1915 as officials in Philadelphia tried to decide what to do with *Messenger of Peace* and *Emmanuel* as a result of the new car *Grace* being put into service in California. A car needed to stay in California; one was go to Washington, Oregon, and Montana; and one was to go to West Virginia.

It was a game of musical rails. The missionaries on board never knew where they were going next. Letter and telegram conversations posed quandaries such as "*Emmanuel* has an iron underframe which is required by law in some of the Pacific Coast states, but the Baker heater has been taken out of *Emmanuel* and it has single windows. This would make it impossible to use in Montana, but *Messenger of Peace* has no steel underframes. How do we get *Emmanuel* to Spokane by way of Salt Lake? Would it be better to take *Messenger of Peace* by way of Salt Lake to Butte, Montana, instead of by Portland; or should we go to Helena?"

As for *Grace*, which had started all this trouble, questions flew: When is that car to be moved? Is it to go north from Frisco, or east, or south, or is it to go into Arizona before the end of the year or remain in California?"

Messenger of Peace made the first move. From Eagle Point, Oregon, Gale, patiently trying to keep his frustration under control and also care for Mrs. Gale, who was not in good health, wrote that they were busy helping a pastor who was much discouraged. In a week or so, they planned to go to Grants Pass for a few days. "I expect to hear from you or one of the secretaries in regard to future movements of the car, in the meanwhile we are heading for Portland."[49]

A Western Union telegram delivered to Jacobs, secretary in charge of the Montana district, from White made some points in the problem clear but posed an interesting question. "LAMSON SAYS GALE WILL STAY IN WASHINGTON AND EMANUEL WILL GO TO MONTANA WHERE IS EMMANUEL I WANT TO GO TO IT AT ONCE TO LOOK IT OVER AND GET IT INTO BUTTE AS SOON AS POSSIBLE WIRE ME AT ONCE PALMER LAKE COLO MUST HEAR FROM YOU TOMORROW AFTERNOON."[50]

The weather and the Baker heater were the main topics from Pasco, Washington, where the Gales spent January 1916.

We expressed the hope in our last letter that better weather would prevail in January than December, instead of this the opposite has been experienced. It is the hardest and strangest weather we ever have experienced on the Car, and having no hard coal or Coke worthwhile you can imagine the difficulty of keeping the Car from freezing and incidentally ourselves also. Work had to [be] suspended on the building and few meetings were possible owing to both snow and dust storms, and weather below Zero . . .

I am inclined to think that a stove in the chapel like Hermiston [on chapel car *Grace*] had is better than the Baker heater and not near the trouble. The price of hard coal is prohibitive in these parts, and the soft coal is out of the question for continuous service. I see that you are having floods in your district with loss of life and we are having the trains in the snow with loss of life also. I guess it has been hard all over.[51]

From Spangle, Washington, the Gales hoped to proceed to Opportunity and work along the Great Northern, "providing they do not charge for trackage. We have to pay full fare for transportation — $60 per 100 mile and $15 minimum."[52] Problems with transportation would continue to hamper the work along eastern Washington lines. Then in October 1916, the car was delayed while on a return trip to Pasco because the end sill was condemned, and they were switched onto the rip track for emergency repairs so the car could continue.

Many of the International Y secretaries had gone to work for the war effort in the fall of 1916, and the Canadian Ys were short of help. There was an effort to send *Messenger of Peace* to British Columbia and Alberta, Canada, in connection again with the International Committee of the YMCA. Gale very much wanted to go, but the transportation for that project never materialized.

Messenger of Peace was having trouble paying its way. Gale's report for November showed they had traveled 356 miles, held thirty-two meetings, visited 120 families, distributed more than a thousand papers and tracts, baptized five, and had ten confessed conversions. The costs for oil and fuel were $9.40, transportation $14.50, and expressage 35 cents. The collection was $20.76. Result, great gains for the Lord, but a ledger loss of $3.49. Many ledger losses were now creating a serious financial problem.[53]

Gales Spend War Years in Washington

In January 1917, the chapel car came to the Issaquah and Superior Coal Mine town of Issaquah, Washington. *Messenger of Peace* was not the messenger that mine president Count Von Albensleben had hoped for. He had planned to make a fortune with the construction of a chemical plant in town. When his German backers, including, some said, the kaiser himself, tried to bring money into town for the investment, something had happened along the way. World War I made German investors unwelcome.

Not long after *Messenger* began meetings in town, the federal alien property custodian arrived on the scene to take over Count Von Albensleben's holdings. But there was nothing left to claim — only deserted buildings and rusty machinery, because the Seattle bank that held the mortgage had failed.[54] The townspeople of Issaquah were discouraged as a result of the mine layoff and the failed chemical plant, but the chapel car meetings revived not only the Baptist church but the Methodists as well, even though services were plagued by rain and snow.[55]

At Kent, the chapel car went in to pour oil on the troubled waters of the Baptist church. They had invited a Congregationalist preacher of German stock to supply for them, and he preached antigovernment remarks that roused the temper of his people and almost ended in violence. Gale, who thought the man was just a pacifist who didn't think before he spoke, was able to quiet the storm.[56]

In Dryad, Gale again helped in the war cause by giving the "Flag Address" for a Liberty Loan effort that brought new people into the chapel car.[57]

One small but important item was frequently mentioned in chapel car correspondence, although it was generally couched in delicate terms — a toilet. Presumably the toilet installed on the cars (and shown on blueprints) was a railroad-type hopper, just a seat on a hole, probably with a container underneath. This was located in an area with a washbasin and some storage space in the living area. The unpleasant and unhealthy difficulties of such a setup in a long-term living situation in many different climates and locales can be imagined.

In the spring of 1917 the Gales wanted an improvement on the toilet situation in the car. "A toilet is a must," they wrote, not quite so delicately. Whether they meant the hopper system was unsatisfactory or something more drastic had happened is not known. White writes on April 17, 1917, "It is possible that a toilet closet may be built on one side of the platform at the living end of the car. It is not satisfactory in any other place. We would not want anything built there, however, which is not finished as well as the rest of the car. The new car *Grace* has such an arrangement."

Mrs. Gale had been suffering from poor health for several years, and the toilet situation did not help. In January 1918 she had to be admitted to a St. Louis sanitarium. Her husband had to send her to St. Louis by herself, as they did not have the money for both of them to go. A young man was assigned to help Gale, but that arrangement did not prove very successful.

Gale missed his wife. In spite of war concerns, transportation problems, and concerns about his wife's health, he continued to work in Washington towns and to strengthen and build churches. Because of the victory bond and other war efforts, community events and meetings were not well attended, and that made things even more difficult.

Then the Spanish influenza struck in the fall of 1918, and no public meetings could be held. In the United States alone 550,000 people died in ten months.[58] Everywhere the chapel cars went there was much sorrow. Gale, like the other chapel car missionaries, tried to comfort and minister, even if meetings could not be held.

During the war, the twenty-year-old *Messenger of Peace* needed to go into the shops for renovation, but the federal and local officials of the Northern Pacific Railroad told Gale that the work on the chapel car could not be scheduled because of pressing government work. So Gale wrote to Mr. Currie at the St. Paul Shops of the Northern Pacific Railroad, and Currie arranged to work the car into the South Tacoma shops.

In October 1918, Gale wrote White, "You would be pleased with the appearance of the car, it looks like a new one; indeed it appears to be in better shape now than when we took charge of it nearly ten years ago. The men have certainly treated us fine, and put a good deal of work both inside and out that is not mentioned in the statement."[59]

War continued to bring problems for the chapel cars. *Messenger of Peace* was stranded on a depot siding at Renton, Washington, in January 1919 because of the McAdoo tariff regulating rates and prohibiting private car movement. A Western Union telegram from Gale to White alerted: "NEW RATE ISSUED BY MCADOO OPERATIVE JANUARY FIRST MAKES MINIMUM MOVEMENT CHAPEL CARS FIFTY DOLLARS AND TRACKAGE THREE DOLLARS DAILY COMPELLED REMAIN RENTON PENDING REPLY NORTHERN PACIFIC OFFICIALS ST PAUL WHAT DO YOU ADVISE."[60]

The advice from the home office was not what Gale wanted to hear. "Please advise Mr. T. R. Gale that there is nothing that we can do except to observe strictly the tariff which became effective January 1st governing such cars, that is, on all movements he will have to purchase 30 tickets with a minimum revenue covering such movement of $50." But three months later the problem was resolved when intercessions and concessions had been made, and the Northern Pacific hauled the car back to Seattle for a minimum haul of five dollars and transportation at the rate of about twenty cents per mile.[61] There the car sat in the Seattle yards, waiting for a war to be over.

Status of Chapel Cars Uncertain

The stalemate over the movement of the chapel cars created the need for a questionnaire to be sent out by the publications society. One of the questions asked was, "If in your judgment the day of the chapel car has passed, will you state briefly why,

Fig. 10.4 Summer's heat, which sent temperatures soaring inside the chapel car, would cause the missionaries to put up the awnings. (American Baptist Historical Society, Valley Forge)

and also state what you would have to take its place."

Arizona Baptist state officials felt that the day of the chapel car was "by no means" past and that there were more opportunities than ever before for the work. South Dakota wasn't sure but would give the chapel cars another try. North Dakota felt it was "the MAN and not the Car" that made the difference. California was confident, "There is still a great need for Chapel car work, in fact, greater than ever before. Large number of small places where no religious work is being done." The Colorado state secretary wrote, "I do not think it is passed, providing you can secure reasonable transportation charges and trackage."

Montana's secretary felt that "high-typed men equipped with Ford cars would be less expensive," and Minnesota Baptist officials thought maybe a small boat would be of more use to them. Michigan, the automobile center of the world, was confident that cars were easier and cheaper but was convinced "a Chapel Car in the upper end of the State could be of great advantage because of its novelty."

The Washington secretary's cautious answer was, "I am not prepared to say that the day of the usefulness of the Chapel car is passed but I do believe the day of its largest usefulness is in the past."[62]

Messenger of Peace was not done with its work. In May 1919 Gale was excited about going to Seattle to "have the Car washed outside and cleaned inside, as she has become rather dusty looking lying in the depot so long." By June the Gales were in Port Angeles, Washington, still without the car. The Pacific salt air of Port Angeles and the "open conditions of this delightful place" benefited Mrs. Gale greatly, but they were both looking forward to when they could be back on *Messenger of Peace*.[63] When they did return, it was for a few weeks, as Mrs. Gale became very ill again, and "the noise of the car" bothered her.

As a result of Mrs. Gale's health, in March 1920 new missionaries were on the car. The Reverend Robert Gray, who was to receive fifteen hundred dollars per annum with some expenses,[64] almost found himself preaching in the dark on his first night in the chapel car at Sandpoint. "The lights began to go out on us Sunday night and I had to close the meeting early on that account," and in addition to work on the electric system, the Grays wrote they could use "a little more bedding: a comforter and some sheets, as this country is much colder than Western Washington where the car has been for several years. In fact, it freezes hard every night, and we have only one comforter and one light blanket."

Other than that, they were enjoying the work at Sandpoint.[65] Gray had no official stationary yet, and the letterhead on his next report read Duncan Brothers Grocery.

From Sandpoint, still in March, Gray wrote about a familiar theme. "Bro Gale informed me that the purchase of the Sanitary Chemical Closet was allowed by the society more than a year ago, but for some reason was never purchased." In Gray's financial report he shows the purchase of a sanitary chemical closet for 15 dollars, chemicals for $2.50, and installation for 5 dollars.[66] Mrs. Gray's life would be a little more pleasant than Mrs. Gale's had been.

Much of 1921 was spent in Kittitas, where the Grays were working with a community church, a seemingly pleasant mix of Baptists, Presbyterians, and Methodists. The Presbyterians and Methodists had tried keeping buildings and churches going but had not had much success,[67] so they had pretty much turned the town over to the Baptists. For a few months, while the Grays worked at Kittitas, the car was in the Northern Pacific shops at Tacoma being repainted and varnished.

The writing was on the wall for the chapel cars in the form of "fine paved highway" and "cars," in Gray's letter from Parker, Washington. "[T]he Baptists here, who were also busy in the hay and fruit harvests, began to move away on the fine paved highway which was built into Yakima only eight miles away, and what few Baptists were left in the community bought cars and joined the 1st church in Yakima, leaving the work here without any responsible people to care for it."[68]

Washington State was still feeling the effects of the railroad strike of 1921–1922 when Gray wrote that the church in Cowiche was going to build on schedule, although it might be slow because of the fruit situation. "The strike on the Railroads has kept buyers from the valley and the wholesaler or middleman is afraid to buy not knowing whether he will be able to move the fruit."[69]

Baker Heater, Fire, and Multicolored Car

At Cle Elum, the Grays helped in the absence of a pastor and built a strong children's program. Then an all too familiar telegram came to White, December 6, 1922: BAKER HEATER OUT OF ORDER RAILROAD MEN HERE WORKED TWO DAYS ON IT WITHOUT RESULT THEY SAY OLD STYLE NEEDS THOROUGH OVERHAULING AND SOME TROUBLE WITH IT EVERY WINTER HAVE HAD TO LET WATER OUT TO AVOID FREEZING SHALL I TAKE IT TO SHOPS ADVISE ME.

The answer came the next day: HAVE HEATER REPAIRED PENDLETON OR LA GRANDE DIVISION SHOPS ENROUTE IDAHO.[70]

Gray's troubles were not over. The Baker heater was repaired in the Portland shops, and Gray discovered from conversation with a Northern Pacific official that one of the Catholic Church Extension Society chapel cars had been in the shops for a similar problem. He also discovered that the Catholic cars were getting a better deal from the railroad. Perturbed and somewhat indignant, Gray reported to White, "He further told me they paid only $1 for transportation and that was to comply with some rule of regulation."[71]

Gray wasted no time in investigating the matter, and as a result *Messenger of Peace* also received a better rate for its next journey.

Off the Grays went toward their next stop in Idaho. It had been so mild in Portland, although drenching rain, that they had not needed to start the Baker heater. A little distance down the line, the temperature dropped and the heat was switched on. But there was no heat. More than dismayed, they carried on with many sweaters and coats until they reached La Grange and the shops there.

Sounding more like Job in every letter, Gray wrote, "They found a big hole in the coils and said no water had been in the heater for sometime although there was plenty of water in the pipes. The foreman's explanation was that when they put water in the pipes in the South Tacoma shops, they forced it in from below instead of pouring it in through the boiler (called in the shops a 'pig') on the top of the car."

Not willing to believe that railroad workers, who had always been so good with the cars, would do such a thing, Gray writes, "But it does not seem reasonable that they would do that . . . however they said that they could do nothing with the old coil and sent it to Portland to have a duplicate made, and we are waiting today for a new coil to be installed and living on the car in the shops."[72]

While they were in La Grange, the Grays held meetings with the local Baptist church and then set off again to Haines.

A fire on the car sent the car back to Portland shops, and Gray tried to explain the case of the multicolored *Messenger of Peace* to his boss, White:

> A year ago I got word from Dr. Neil to have lettering changed running the whole length of car, over windows, to read for both Societies. I hunted everywhere for a local painter and got a man from Topponish (the car was then at Buena) and this man and his assistant spent much time trying to match the olive green of the car — however it has never looked the same as the rest of the car; neither the body nor the lettering matching.
>
> Then when we had the fire at Haines, the firemen tried to get at the fire by breaking thro the side and the little painting done at La Grande shops over the new panels turns out to be another shade of green. So that now we have three shades of green and two shades of gold.[73]

It would cost 685 dollars to restore *Messenger of Peace* to one shade of green and one shade of gold.

At Melba, Idaho, in June, still with their multicolored chapel car, the Grays began an ambitious program that put new life and more members in the church over a period of several months.[74] In spite of their success there, the Grays left the chapel car ministry to serve as auto car colporters in the new car *The Overland Champion* in December 1923. The Reverend and Mrs. E. F. Hawes came to the rail car.

In September 1924, Gray sent a wistful note to White. "I often think of Bro and Sister Hawes on 'Messenger of Peace' and wonder if they are enjoying their work. We certainly miss the Chapel Car and sometimes think we made a mistake in leaving it, but may be, God had a purpose in it all."[75]

It seemed that God's purpose was for Hawes to be called to the pastorate of the First Baptist Church of Miami, Arizona, and for the Grays to return to their beloved if sometime beleaguered chapel car. The first problem they had to deal with was the Baker heater. When the coils were replaced in the shop, the wrong coil had been installed, a single instead of a double, so it was back to the shops again. When the temperature hit 32 degrees below zero in Idaho in January 1915,[76] the heater worked.

After years of faithful and difficult service, the Grays again left the car in June 1929, and the Reverend and Mrs. C. W. Driver came to the car.

About this time secretary Sam Neil felt his chapel car missionaries needed a lesson on personal appearance. "Many a time we all have seen a handsome woman tastily garbed but the lip stick, powder puff, and belladonna had wrecked her personal appearance, robbing her of that which we all should hold dear — the adornment and beauty of Nature's handiwork. We may be a little old fashioned but we have strong convictions on this point. This illustration has no direct bearing on chapel car and colporter missionaries, yet its counterpart is found in the unshaven face, soiled linen, mourning finger nails and unblackened shoe appearance that so many men in various walks of life present."[77]

Obviously "someone" had been observed as being less than tidy, certainly not Mr. Driver, who had not been on the car long enough. Chapel car missionaries had to be multitalented indeed — able to wipe down the sides of their chapel car with oil waste, tinker with the Baker heater, fill the oil lamps, walk and ride their bikes down muddy or dusty roads, wash themselves and their clothes without benefit of tub or machine, and still have immaculate fingernails and clothing.

Back in his tidy office in Philadelphia, it was easy for Neil to give such directives. Maybe he had forgotten what chapel car life was like when he was on *Messenger of Peace* twenty years earlier, or maybe attention needed to be called to points of real concern. Neil wanted nothing but the best for the chapel car program, and to the Scots taskmaster, appearances were important.

Unexpectedly, while he was on a mission trip in September 1932 to Glasgow, Scotland, Neil developed pneumonia and passed away on his native soil. His love and devotion for the chapel car work, his evangelistic zeal, and his wise, if not always welcome, advice to his workers were the marks of his tenure.

Cutlers Bring New Enthusiasm to Work

The Cutlers had dual duties in July 1934 as they lived on the chapel car at Willits, Washington, where they were having tremendous success rebuilding a congregation while working and residing at the town of Fort Bragg. They also served the little church at Caspar, the C. C. Camp at Russian Gulch, and the C. W. A. Camp at Marwadell, sometimes reaching nine hundred people a week in their rounds.[78]

Instead of starting and building churches, the chapel cars now spent much time in rebuilding and recharging churches. Cutler reported, "Our work in Oregon has combined with the priestly office, the work of both doctor and lawyer. At least three of the field we have served were tangled in legal difficulties, crippled up with church rows, near enough dead that some of the brethren said with Martha [Lazarus's sister], "By this time he stinketh,"... but work of this kind must be carried on quietly. It would be unjust and unChristian-like to get credit for ourselves by reporting other people's mistakes and failures."

On one field, the chapel car itself helped solve a problem. Two denominations were quarreling over a building. "We just locked up the building and used the chapel car. In four months they baptized thirty people and the problems were solved."[79]

At Elma, Washington, once a lumber town, now generally a farming area, the newspaper reporter was impressed with the chapel car, which was parked near the Northern Pacific depot.

Near the back of the chapel by the door is a good-sized circulating heater on the left and a portable organ on the right. On either side of the long aisle are seats, three-deep on the right and two-deep on the left. We noted book racks on the back of each seat, and numbered supply boxes under each seat, as we followed Rev. Cutler to the front of the chapel which serves as the reception room, slightly set apart from the rest of the auditorium by high valanced drapery across the ceiling of the car, forming a homey archway. The windows are curtained.

At the front of the auditorium are an Estey reed organ, a beautifully carved brass lectern or pulpit, a beautiful, large silk American flag with a spread eagle crest and an equally large Christian flag crested with a golden cross. In front of the organ are leather upholstered davenports where we were seated. On a glass window above the organ at the front of the chapel, in large gold letters are inscribed the words, "God is Love." On the front of the organ we read, "Is Christ your present Savior?"

Then Mrs. Cutler gave her the tour of the parsonage section of the car.

The main living room, which serves as bedroom, study, parlor and dining room, is about nine feet square. Here we found a Pullman berth, upper and lower, a studio couch, circulating heater, dining table, rolled-top desk, library of 500 religious books including 60 reference volumes, radio, carpeted floor, floor lamp, electric sewing machine and everything to make the life of the missionaries as comfortable and efficient as possible.

In the kitchen area were a clothes hamper, master mixer, sandwich toaster and other kitchen utensils. Joining the kitchenette is the wash room, shower and built-in clothes closets. Every nook and cranny throughout the car is used for built-ins and storage of books, bedding, supplies, literature, tools, etc. as every available space must be utilized.[80]

Although Mrs. Cutler was an ordained minister and a graduate of Kansas Bible Seminary, the Great Northern Railroad was not impressed when the publication society requested a pass for her. Their unqualified reply was that they did not give passes to women.[81]

Cutler made an interesting observation while they worked at Okanogan, within a few miles of the Canadian line, where locals touted the motto "Okanogan, Where God Makes

Apples." The Baptist church there was the only one in eighty miles in any direction.

It has had the usual ups and downs of pioneer churches. It has had good pastors, bad pastors, and just preachers. It has had its revivals. It has had its recessions. Right here we would stress a peculiar characteristic of Far Western Baptist Churches. They can be "up and coming" one day, and "down and out" the next. They may be a beehive of activity, energetic, praying, working, appealing to the crowds today and tomorrow nothing but an empty church building. One reason for this peculiar tendency is that Western people will not fuss over a difference, they just quit and stay home until the storm is past. The Okanogan Church stands out for this tendency, plus a very interesting characteristic, and that is its readiness to forgive and forget.[82]

The crowds continued to pour into the meetings at Okanogan, and there was the desire to put up a building, but the town was very poor. "We are doing as Jesus commanded, 'Preaching the Gospel to the poor.' Going into their homes, having folk pull out bills showing that they still owe for last Winter's groceries, finding they had had but a few days work in six months, having ranchers tell of losing from $1000 to $5000 on last year's crops, seeing abject poverty makes it almost impossible to ask folk to do more than what they may think is their best."

Even the eighteen dollars the electric company wanted for putting in a new switch box was hard to come by. The Cutlers had been putting in much of their own money in the needs of the Okanogan church. Cutler wrote John Killian for help. "The car is located near the packing sheds. In a few weeks the town will begin to fill up with itinerants, and since there has been considerable demand for Chapel Car services, it looks like, with your consent, we had better spend the $18."

From Sequim, Washington, Cutler reports that the chapel car was nicely located on a main highway with hundreds of tourists passing by every day and with many stopping to look

over the car. "Frankly we cannot help but believe that, if you brethren at headquarters could only see the deep interest being manifested by the tourists in this Baptist Home Missions Project you would be led to make an investment in new carpets and furnishings to make the interior of the Car as attractive as possible."[83]

In the summer 1941, *Messenger of Peace* was placed on a railroad barge and made the journey across salt water as it headed back to Port Angeles, and to Port Townsend, Sequim, Joyce, and Blyn on the Olympic Peninsula. In November 1942 the chapel car was moved to a rural community called Joyce where, even though they knew the community was largely Lutheran, they hoped to find an open door.

Joyce opened a field forty miles long by about ten miles wide in which there was no church and no religious work. Then, early in 1943, a defense project opened up within three miles of *Messenger of Peace*. A large camp was erected that was to house several hundred workmen. Every house and cabin in the community was filled with families of the workmen, and several trailers moved on vacant lots. Cutler reported, "For one time, we Baptists are in 'on ground floor.' At the present writing your missionaries have been granted the only passes into the project and have the only religious contact with the men and women working behind carefully and closely guarded gates."[84]

Cakes and Carroms for the Soldiers

The Cutlers also worked at Blyn, Gardiner, and Leland. They found themselves ministering not only to the local citizens but also to many soldiers who were stationed in that district.

What impresses us is not the uncertainty of conditions as much as the absolute certainty that we have a big and thrilling job on our hands as long as we are permitted to remain on the scene. It is difficult to estimate how many soldiers are on the Peninsula. Estimates run from 30,000 to 100,000. But what is thrilling to us is that we

Fig. 10.5 *Messenger of Peace*, with the Cutlers aboard, spent many months stopping at mountain hamlets like Sappho, Washington, two miles from Pleasant Lake. (American Baptist Historical Society, Valley Forge)

are making some fine contacts with the many camps that surround us and are finding some wonderful opportunities for service.

Our very limited knowledge of medicine and yet more extensive knowledge of First Aid has made it possible for us to open up First Aid Classes under the Red Cross in Blyn. In so doing we are contacting some we would never reach otherwise. Our contact with doctors, with whom we have always been friends, has opened the doors at an army field hospital to us in a very gracious manner and again we are meeting many of the boys we would never meet in any other way . . . we have given away all of our stock of Testaments to the boys and we can give away many more.[85]

One way the Cutlers got the soldiers to come to the chapel car for preaching was what they called "Cakes and Carroms." They filled the car two or three nights a week with soldiers who listened carefully to the preaching of the gospel. Then Cutler's "good Southern Cook" was able, before sugar rationing, to serve homemade cakes several times a week.

Along with the cakes was Carroms. Carroms was a game board about two feet square with corner pockets and little wooden disks that are shot with one's fingers. As Cutler explained, "It may be obtained at the mail order houses with an average cost of about $5. There is just enough science and just enough of the element of chance to make it interesting

and yet not too difficult. It appeals especially to men and boys. Yet the women and girls also enjoy it." The soldiers played Carroms in the chapel car, took the Carrom board to their camp, and seemed never to tire of the game.[86]

After serving for a while in a defense project at Vancouver, *Messenger of Peace*, with the Cutlers, was transferred to an area of South Tacoma, there to be used in urban mission work. The chapel car had traveled to Washington, Oregon, and Idaho and back to Washington for the last three decades. During this time, the mission of the chapel car had changed from frontier life to cities, "with teeming multitudes living in defense housing projects, with its terrible juvenile crime wave, with its frightful unconcern, and with the combined efforts of all religious organizations not reaching one tenth of the itinerant people."[87]

After almost fifty years in eleven states — Kansas, Missouri, Arkansas, Colorado, West Virginia, Utah, Nevada, California, Washington, Oregon, and Idaho — this last Baptist chapel car in active service, *Messenger of Peace*, was relocated by the Washington Baptist Convention to an area south of Everett in 1946. It was used to start a mission church of the First Baptist Church of Everett, the Memorial Baptist Church, until 1948, when Rev. Cutler suffered a stroke and the chapel car was put out of service.

Eventually sold to an individual in Washington State, the chapel car became a roadside diner along the Snohomish Highway. When highway construction forced the removal of the car, it came into the hands of a man who trucked it to his property to be used for storage *(fig.10.6)*.

Messenger of Peace still exists on private property on the shore of the Olympic Peninsula. Despite attempts to salvage it, the car is in deplorable condition. Stuffed with junk, its sides patched, its windows broken, the Ladies Car, which was described at its dedication as "the largest, the loveliest, the lightest, and brightest of them all," still has its mark of dignity and honor. The words *Messenger of Peace* can still be seen on the paint-peeled side, the gilded letters faded but not forgotten.

Sweep on, O car of light,
Roll o'er the mountain's height,
Roll o'er the waters bright,
The distant sea;
Visit the lonely vale,
Out fly the wintry gale —
Thy errand will not fail,
God moves with thee.[88]

Notes

[1] Samuel G. Neil file, "A Prince Has Fallen," obituary, ABHS, VF.

[2] Anniversary Report of the American Baptist Publication Society, Rochester, N.Y. , 1899, 14.

[3] Scott D. Trostel, *The Barney & Smith Car Company: Car Builders* (Fletcher, Ohio: Cam-Tech Publishing, 1993), 101.

[4] "Chapel Car at Argentine," *Ottawa Evening Herald*, June 17, 1898, colporter records, newspaper clippings, ABHS, VF.

[5] Speech from Samuel G. Neil file, ABHS, VF.

[6] *The Colporter*, March 1900, 6.

[7] John C. Pollock, *Moody: A Biographical Portrait of the Pacesetter in Modern Mass Evangelism* (New York: Macmillan, 1963), 314–15.

[8] Ibid., 315. The account of the train engineer is verified by the reply from the superintendent, Wabash Railway Company, Peru, Indiana, to W. R. Moody, November 24, 1899, acknowledging his letter of appreciation.

[9] Jackie McKeon, *If That Don't Beat the Devil* (self-published), 34. Also Colporter Files, John Killian, 1940, ABHS, VF.

[10] *The Colporter*, August 1900, 7.

[11] *The Colporter*, July 1900, 7.

[12] Ibid.

[13] J. Gordon Kingsley, *Frontiers: The Story of the Missouri Baptist Convention* (Jefferson City, Mo.: Missouri Baptist Historical Commission, 1983), 25.

[14] Joe P. Jacobs, "Remarkable Conversion of an Infidel in Chapel Car "Messenger of Peace"" (Philadelphia: American Baptist Publication Society, n.d.).

[15] *The Word and the Way*, May 14, 1903, Oklahoma Baptist Archives.

[16] *The Word and the Way*, June 11, 1903, Oklahoma Baptist Archives.

Fig. 10.6 *Messenger of Peace* was sold, and its owner turned it into a roadside diner. Now on private property on the Olympic Peninsula, the chapel car still proclaims its name. (Bud Carroll)

17 *The Word and the Way*, February 18, 1904.

18 Mrs. D. A. Ross, "Chapel Car is located in Elma," blue book in large flat box file, ABHS, VF.

19 *The Word and the Way*, June 2, 1904, 9.

20 Anniversary Report of the American Baptist Publication Society, Cleveland, Ohio, 1904, 86.

21 Letter from Henry L. Morehouse to editors of Baptist publications, April 19, 1906, Morehouse files, ABHS, VF.

22 Kingsley, 100.

23 *Encyclopedia of North American Railroading*, ed. Freeman Hubbard, "YMCAs, Railroad" (New York: McGraw-Hill Book Company, 1981), 365.

24 John F. Moore, *The Story of the Railroad "Y"* (New York: Association Press, 1930), 108.

25 *Railroad Association Magazine*, November 15, 1911, 30.

26 Report of A. G. Knebel, March 1909, secretary files, YMCA of the USA Archives, St. Paul, Minn.

27 Anniversary Report of the American Baptist Publication Society, Philadelphia, 1911, xx–xxi.

28 "Is the Railroad Y.M.C.A. Really Worth While?" *Railway Age Gazette*, February 26, 1915, Indiana State Library, Indianapolis, Ind., 358.

29 Report of E. L. Hamilton, September 1910, files of the International YMCA archives.

30 Hamilton report, October and November 1910, files of the International YMCA archives.

31 Thomas R. Gale, "Helping Railroad Men," tract of the American Baptist Publication Society, n.d., George L. White files, ABHS, VF.

32 Letter to J. M. Dudley, Montreal, Canada, from George L. White, December 6, 1916, George L. White files, ABHS, VF.

33 A. B. Withers, tract, "A Day on Board Messenger of Peace" (Philadelphia: American Baptist Publication Society, n.d.).

34 Ken Sullivan, *Thurmond: A New River Community* (Oak Hill, W. Va.: Eastern National Park & Monument Association, 1989), 15.

35 Ibid., 11.

36 Withers.

37 "Chapel Car Missions," pamphlet (Philadelphia: American Baptist Publication Society, n.d.).

38 Letter from George L. White to Thomas Gale, August 6, 1913, George L. White files, ABHS, VF.

39 Letter to Charles S. Fee, passenger & traffic manager, Southern Pacifc Railroad, San Francisco, Calif., from George L. White, August 8, 1913, George L. White files, ABHS, VF.

40 Letter from Thomas R. Gale to George L. White, George L. White files, October 3, 1913, ABHS, VF.

41 Letter from C. J. Millis to George L. White, October 11, 1913, George L. White files, ABHS, VF.

42 Letter from Thomas R. Gale to George L. White, October 30, 1913, George L. White files, ABHS, VF.

43 Letter from D. S. Coad to Russell Orr, American Baptist Churches of the West, June 27, 1971.

44 Letter from Guy C. Lamson to George L. White, October 30, 1914, George L. White files, ABHS, VF.

45 Letter from George L. White to Guy C. Lamson, March 31, 1915, Guy C. Lamson files, ABHS, VF.

46 Letter from Guy C. Lamson to George L. White, April 7, 1915, Guy C. Lamson files, (October 29 L), ABHS, VF.

47 Letter from J. P. Brendel to T. R. Gale, April 24, 1915 (October 22 K), ABHS, VF.

48 Letter from George L. White to Guy C. Lamson, July 3, 1915 (October 29 M), Guy C. Lamson files, ABHS, VF.

49 Letter from Thomas R. Gale to George L. White, July 19, 1915 George L. White files, ABHS, VF.

50 A Western Union telegram, July 26, 1915, to Joe P. Jacobs from George L. White, George L. White papers, ABHS, VF.

51 Letter from Thomas R. Gale to George L. White, January 1916, George L. White files, ABHS, VF.

52 Letter from Thomas R. Gale to George L. White, May 1, 1916, George L. White files, ABHS, VF.

53 Gale's report for November 1916, George L. White files, ABHS, VF.

54 Edwards R. Fish, *The Past at Present in Issaquah* (Seattle: Facsimile Reproduction, 1972), 83.

55 Letter from Thomas Gale, Issaquah, Wash., March 1, 1917, to George L. White, George L. White files, ABHS, VF.

56 Letter from Thomas Gale, Kent, Wash., July 30, 1917, to George L. White, George L. White files, ABHS, VF.

57 Letter from Thomas Gale, Dryad, Wash., October 24, 1917, to George L. White, George L. White files, ABHS, VF.

58 "The American Experience," PBS special.

59 Letter from Thomas Gale to George L. White, October 30, 1918, George L. White files, ABHS, VF.

60 A Western Union telegram from Gale at Renton, Washington, to White, January 15, 1919, George L. White files, ABHS, VF.

61 George L. White files, ABHS.

62 Survey on chapel cars, March 1919, American Baptist Publication Society, February 5, 1996, "C."

63 Letter from Thomas Gale to George L. White, August 27, 1919, George L. White files, ABHS, VF.

64 Letter from Samuel G. Neil to George L. White, February 3, 1920, George L. White files, ABHS, VF.

65 Letter from Robert Gray to George L. White, Sandpoint, Ida., February 11, 1920, George L. White files, ABHS, VF.

66 Letter from Robert Gray to George L. White, Sandpoint, Ida., March 19, 1920, George L. White files, ABHS, VF .

67 Letter from Robert Gray to George L. White, Kittitas, Wash., March 22, 1921, George L. White files, ABHS, VF.

68 Letter from Robert Gray to George L. White, Parker, Wash., October 17, 1921, George L. White files, ABHS, VF.

69 Letter from Robert Gray to George L. White, Cowiche, Wash., September 4, 1922, George L. White files, ABHS, VF.

70 Ibid.

71 Letter from Robert Gray to George L. White, November 12, 1922, George L. White fiiles, ABHS, VF.

72 Letter from Robert Gray to George L. White, La Grande, Ore., January 17, 1923, George L. White files, ABHS, VF.

73 Letter from Robert Gray to George L. White, Portland, Ore., February 22, 1923, George L. White fiiles, ABHS, VF.

74 Lemuel Call Barnes, *Pioneers of Light* (Philadelphia: American Baptist Publication Society, 1925), 107.

75 Letter from Robert Gray to George L. White, Seattle, Wash., September 4, 1924, George L. White files, ABHS, VF.

76 Letter from Robert Gray to George L. White, Portland, Ore., January 21, 1925, George L. White files, ABHS, VF.

77 Memo to missionaries, Samuel G. Neil files, ABHS, VF.

78 Letter to John Killian, July 11, 1934, John Killian file, ABHS, VF.

79 Report from Cutler, July 12, 1934, John Killian file, ABHS, VF.

80 Elma newspaper article, by Mrs. D. A. Ross, January 31, "O."

81 Letter from John Killian to C. W. Cutler, Okanogan, Wash., January 27, 1939, ABHS, VF.

82 Ibid.

83 Letter to Luther Wesley Smith from C. W. Cutler, Sequim, Wash., July 30, 1941, ABHS, VF.

84 Letter from C. W. Cutler, Joyce, Wash., February 12, 1943, ABHS, VF.

85 Anniversary Report of the American Baptist Publication Society, 1942.

86 Letter to G. Pitt Beers, New York, from C. W. Cutler, Joyce, Wash., December 20, 1942, Cutler files, ABHS, VF.

87 Annual report, Colporter Missionary Division, May 1, 1943–April 30, 1944, colporter files, ABHS, VF.

88 Hymn written for the *Messenger of Peace*.

CHAPTER 11

Baptist Car 6:
Herald of Hope, Roll On,
Roll On

Early in 1910 *Herald of Hope* came to Shawneetown, the oldest town in Illinois, where the early Baptist missionary John Mason Peck and his family had been storm-bound seventy years before. There Peck was threatened by ruffians and told that "the Bible would never cross the Mississippi." Missionary Walter J. Sparks tells the story of what happened to *Herald of Hope* at Shawneetown.

"This was a right smart town oncet," Old Man Winters said as he sat smoking on his porch. "But it's a flood town now and many of the folks is done gone. When the levee broke through last in 1898 and drowned twenty-eight of 'em, they moved away, and ain't come back yit. . . ."

A few old residents who can remember its better days sit dreaming of the past. They show with pride the place where McClellan found inspiration for his future greatness, the office where "Bob" Ingersoll began to study law, and the little house behind the levee where John A. Logan courted pretty Molly Cunningham. But the greatest relic of its faded glory is the place where Lafayette landed and was escorted "on a white sheet" stretched from the boat to the little brick hotel.

They do not know that at this self-same spot another hero landed; but it was here that John Mason Peck marched over the muddy levee to begin his great work for God in the Middle West. As "Old Man Winters" says, "All them times are done gone."

Into this district the chapel car comes. . . . The meetings open with such a medley as only the chapel car can get together — river-men, fishermen, pearl hunters, factory hands, loafers, "those who work every day, those who work oncet a week and those who never work at all. There are the moral, the immoral and the simply unmoral. In they come till the car is packed and the lights burn dim. . . ."

"When were you in church before?" I ask them.

One man say he went to church "to a funeral, fourteen years ago." Another that he was at church "oncet" when he was a boy, "over to Cave-in-Rock." Most of them will say they have not gone to church since they lived in this town but used to go sometimes "away back." They are a motley crowd, faces so lined and seamed by care and weariness and sin will reflect something of the peace which passes understanding. Among these poor souls are gems which at the touch of God are destined to become more beautiful than the pearls

Fig. 11.1 When the Walter Sparkses found themselves in New Boston, Ohio, in January 1913, the flood waters were high and life was not easy in this railroad shop town along the Ohio River. Before the Sparkses left, they had organized a Sunday school and church. (American Baptist Historical Society, Valley Forge)

grappled from the depths of their own muddy river.

"Can we sing a song or two we used to sing 'way back in old Kentucky?' So with many queer little turns and quavers, the swaying of bodies and nodding of heads, there swells forth,

"O Father, won't you meet me,
O Father, won't you meet me,
O Father, won't you meet me,
On Canaan's happy shore?"

Here comes Johnnie Gifford, roughened and hardened by years of river life. "Yes," he says, "I want to be a Christian, though I never thought much on't till tonight. It means such a change in the habits of yer life that a feller kind o'hesitates. Why, I ain't been to church since my brother was shot."

"Your brother shot in church?"

"Yes, but he waren't in the shootin' gang. It was this-away. We lived back in the hills acrost the river. The preacher was new and got sassy about the wrong-doin's. The boys 'lowed they'd tar an' feather him. The next night they went to church and kotched hold o'him to pull him off the platform, but he was a fighter and before they knowed it five of 'em was down on the floor. Then they-all shot out the lights, so there should be nary witness, and started in at the preacher. We-all crawled under the seats, but my brother got hit and was hurted bad."

"Did the preacher get hit?"

"Well, I should say! They-all piked seventeen holes inter him."

"No, he didn't die, but I heared he didn't preach no more. He just got discouraged and done quit."

"Yes, I want to be a Christian. I'm goin' to be, but a feller has to get used to the idee."

Here are two women coming out. They are notorious characters but they rose for prayer tonight. The missionary stops them at the door, but they look defiant and desperate. "We rose for prayer because God knows we need it," and they step outside on the platform.

"O Mothers, won't you meet me," rings out from the car.

The women stop as though touched by an electric current; their eyes dilate, their faces twitch, and out there in the dark they join with the people inside in the old mountain song. The strong voices ring out over the dark waters of the river, bringing to two hearts memories of a better past. Then, the song ended, they look at each other and walk away, the younger sobbing and wringing her hands. . . .

When mistletoe on the old oak on the levee begins to hide 'neath the newborn leaves of spring, the first baptismal service is held at the old Ferry where John M. Peck landed some seventy years ago.[1]

Dove Descends on Dedication

Eleven years before *Herald of Hope's* visit to Shawneetown, a remarkable incident occurred during the chapel car's dedication in Detroit, Michigan, on May 27, 1900. While Dr. Wayland Hoyt was offering the prayer of dedication, a dove was seen flying toward the car. As it reached a point directly over where Hoyt stood upon the platform, the dove made several circles in its flight. The few who saw it said it was a thrilling sight.[2]

Called the Young Men's Car, this sixth and last wooden car was a project of the young men of the Woodward Avenue Church. They had made a contribution of the first thousand dollars in the form of fifteen hundred five-dollar shares a year earlier. In the week before the dedication, shares were frantically being sold for the cost of the car, since some gentlemen who had pledged did not honor their agreements. But on the day of dedication, *Herald of Hope* was free of debt with almost every state and territory represented in giving.

Echoing the words of its dedication hymn, *Herald of Hope* was ready to "roll on, roll on, glad messages of light to bear." Like its five sister cars, this dazzling new Barney & Smith church on wheels, which was longer by ten feet than *Evangel*, had been built nine years earlier but was still a novelty. People who would not normally go to a church would flock to it.

Dr. Robert Seymour, missionary and Bible secretary, wrote to thank the Sunday school of the Emmanuel Baptist Church of Brooklyn, New York, one of hundreds that donated to the building of the car. "These wheels are like the wheels Ezekiel saw in the vision. The living spirits moving within the wheels, and the money the schools contribute, keep the wheels in motion."[3]

The car would begin its travels in Michigan, and the Michigan Baptist Convention superintendent of missions was to be consulted as to where the car could best do its threefold mission: in places wholly destitute of religious privileges, with struggling interests, and among railroad men at rail centers.

To provide the finishing touches, the women of the Detroit Woodward Avenue Church furnished the car with linens, bedding, dishes, and other household items, and the men of First Baptist Church of Galveston, Texas, purchased a handsome brass lectern. On the rear platform of the car, providing a whimsical touch, was a shiny new bicycle — a Rambler, for use in chapel car work. "Herald of Hope" was printed on the frame of the wheel in gold matching the gilded name on the car's side.

Hard Hearts Discourage Young Rosecrans

Grindstone City was the first stop for the new car after its dedication. In the summer of 1900, on the Pere Marquette line, the first railroad built into Grindstone City from Port Austin, *Herald of Hope* came into town and was put on a siding near the depot. At the tip of the thumb of Michigan, facing Lake Huron, Grindstone City was one of the most extensive grindstone quarries in the United States, a boom town since being purchased by the Cleveland Stone Company in 1888. Grindstones were used for polishing or sharpening tools and were in great demand until carborundum took their place after World War I.

In 1887 the first gristmill and elevator were built of

grindstone rock by Robert Wallace, who also built the first boarding house in town. Grindstone City was not without amenities. Town historian Mabel Cook collected business cards that advertised the Grindstone City Hotel, boasting about a new house and everything first class; a hardware store with mowers and farm implements; and W. J. Herrington, physician and surgeon, who answered calls promptly at all hours. Attorney D. E. Spencer was principal of the high school, organized in 1865 — a frame building 45 x 50 feet and one story high, one large room with two cloak rooms, two rows of seats on each side of a cordwood stove. A post office validated the town, along with several stores and saloons.[4]

At this town people did not flock to the chapel car at first. The town was not churchless. In 1871 the Presbyterian church was organized, and sometime in the 1890s, the Methodist church was built. Reports were that the Presbyterians and Methodists were not happy to see the fancy Baptist rail car come into town, and so the reception was cool if not hostile.

Fledgling missionaries Charles Rosecrans and his wife, native Nebraskans and recent graduates of the Gordon

Fig. 11.2 According to the young Reverend Rosecrans, the hearts of the people at Grindstone City, Michigan, were as hard as the grindstones they manufactured. (Grindstone City Historical Society)

Training School in Boston, surveyed Grindstone with trepidation *(fig. 11.2)*. What they found was a town of 450 inhabitants, "almost as hard as the stony products of the quarries there; nevertheless," Rosecrans reports, "we found that the hammer of the word of God was able to break the hearts of stone there as elsewhere."

A lawless, scoffing spirit controls among them, especially with regard to religious matters. . . . As an illustration of the disregard for education, it is a fact that no young man has ever graduated from the school here; not at high school either. At a recent graduation only one, a girl, was graduated. The youth have been known to make disturbances at revival meetings but their behavior in our services has been admirable, . . . yet not one person made a public desire to accept the Saviour. Many of the churchgoing people of the place have from the start bitterly opposed meetings . . . some of the Presbyterians are fighting us, and even encouraged their children to do so.[5]

On July 13, 1900, Seymour wrote Boston Smith, "I didn't get a Hallelujah letter from Rosecrans, only a doleful one. Wish I could get a good letter from him I could print."[6] After several weeks of meetings and visitations, the young workers began to see encouraging results, and Rosecrans cheerily reported, "We even broke up a dance because all the young women were at the chapel car. There were not young ladies enough present to carry on the dance."[7]

Mrs. Rosecrans organized a mission band of twenty young women, many of whom were those markedly absent from the town dance several weeks earlier. The young swains of the town shunned not only the appeals of a good education but also those of the missionaries and their preacher-helper the Reverend E. S. Wilson.

One piece de resistance for the young missionary was related with obvious glee although not much Christian charity. "We made trouble for the saloon keeper too. That's one thing we plan to do, God helping us, wherever we go. This fellow was on his infernal business without a license, violating the laws of both God and man. We made such warfare on him that he got frightened and took out a license; we felt sorry to hear that, for we were planning to send him to prison, if possible. He was heard to lay all his troubles on those Baptists in the chapel car."[8]

One day Rosecrans overheard two men talking in town. "I understand they talk of building a church," said one, who had visited the chapel car.

"Humph!" responded the other. "Where'd they get the money?"

"Where did they get the money to build that car?" was the reply, to which there was no answer.[9]

Plans for a church building were underway. The Grindstone Company offered stone for the foundation of the new church free of charge. Rosecrans reported that a splendid lot was donated by deacon-elect Wallace, one of the town's prosperous businessmen, and that four hundred dollars could be raised on the field, and he was raising some money with chalk-talk lectures. Pastor Howell of the nearby Port Austin Church was called to minister to the new fellowship, and *Herald of Hope* and its crew left Grindstone perhaps not quite so hard-hearted.

September found the chapel car on the Pere Marquette line, sidetracked in Melvin, where harvesting kept many from coming to the car. Meetings were well attended, although the Rosecranses again seemed easily discouraged by the work. Then Rosecrans developed throat problems and called in Brother Van Dorn of the Baptist church at Holly to help. Van Dorn had his own hands full, as Holly was the first railroad junction in the state and a major industrial center in the late 1800s. The south end of Saginaw Street downtown was known as Battle Alley due to the bloody fights that took place along the taverns and brothels. With Van Dorn's help, a baptistry was built in the church at Melvin, and membership doubled.[10]

Two months later, the chapel car witness of the Rosecranses ended, and officials reported that the couple was compelled to give up their work on account of Rosecrans's illness. The Reverend E. S. Wilson, formerly district missionary in the Bay district, who had been helping the Rosecranses, took charge of the car.

Work Overwhelms Young Workers

Unlike the rather naïve Rosecrans, Wilson knew that turn-of-the-century Michigan was a state of great extremes. From Detroit with a population of over 285,000,[11] where Henry Ford was creating his motor company, to rowdy mine operations to bucolic fishing villages and dairy farms, and to hamlets like Farmington just outside Detroit, where the chapel car stopped, culture was as varied as the crops grown in Michigan's fields and orchards.

All across the nation, enthusiasm for railroads reached a higher point during the quarter-century following the Civil War than ever before or since. Every town and hamlet sought a railroad, for it was universally believed that without one, a community had little hope for growth. Towns that had grown to considerable size in pioneer days withered and died when the railroad bypassed them.

Herald of Hope arrived at Brown City mid-November of 1901 with the intent of encouraging the congregation, organized in 1897 and now meeting in a storefront building. When Scotsman William Brown heard the railroad was going to come through his farm, he platted 275 lots for a town, which then took his name. The Port Huron and Northwestern Railroad, a narrow gauge, began operation December 1880, and in 1889 the Flint and Pere Marquette Railroad also entered the town proper.

With the trains came people, salesmen, merchants, and a connection with the outside world. By 1900 the town had eight churches, a bucket brigade fire department, a newspaper, a horse track, and an active Blue Lodge of Free and Accepted Masons. Fifty-candlepower electric street lights had replaced the old gas lights, and electricity was available for two hundred houses and businesses.[12]

The *Brown City Banner* described the chapel car as "really a portable palace, beautifully finished off on both inside and out. . . . Rev. Wilson is one of the leading young pulpit orators of the state and though young in years he is experienced in evangelical work and has already begun a grand work in Brown City. Though the weather has been inclement, the car which will comfortably seat over 100 people, has been full and there have been three conversions on Wednesday evening and many more are under conviction. All Christian people of whatever denomination are cordially invited, as well as all people of the world. Services every evening at 7:30 p.m."[13]

Michigan Baptist officials were concerned about the decrease in numbers of country churches and its import for social conditions in cities. "The tide is still, and is likely to continue to be, from the country to the city. The city church is maintained largely at the expense of the country church. Again the young life coming to the city is likely, if unsaved, to be swept by the strong currents there sweeping worldward beyond; for their own sake, they should be reached by the Gospel before they leave their country home."[14]

However, chapel car life was taking its toll on *Herald of Hope*. Like Rosencrans before him, Wilson was not feeling well. The difficulties of chapel car work were exacerbated by the August heat and his own ill health, and in October 1901, he resigned. In November the Reverend W. W. Dewey and his wife, who were well known throughout Michigan, were appointed to have charge of the car. Seymour wrote Smith optimistically that he had seen Dewey at the Michigan State convention and was delighted with him. "He will make a go of it I am sure."[15]

From Cement City, Dewey sent glowing reports, and in January 1902 the chapel car came to a hamlet south of Jackson-Clark Lake, where a church had been organized in 1868. The Clark Lake Church felt the first effects of industrial progress at a meeting of the board of trustees in 1895. Right-of-way men for the Cincinnati Northern Railroad were present to seek the right to lay their tracks closely adjacent to the church. There was much bartering on price for the right of way, and through the effort of an attorney hired by the church, a price finally was agreed upon. The tracks were laid and service began. From then on, the quiet meditation or morning sermon was frequently interrupted by the din of passing trains.

Herald of Hope was placed on the side track just south of the Clark Lake depot. The Deweys endeared themselves to the community and left a lasting impression on the youth and their elders. Ironically, a spark from a passing railroad train was later to cause a fire that destroyed the church.[16]

In spite of his personal success, Dewey seemed to be having some difficulties handling the logistics of chapel car work and received a rather curt response to a letter from Seymour on January 31, 1902. "You ask as to what you should do about transportation. Now we have chosen you because we think you have good judgment, and we are going to let you exercise that as to what to do."[17]

In the next few weeks, it was not just transportation Dewey became disgruntled about. His book order was wrong. The car needed work. He and his wife did not like the kitchen range; in fact, the whole tiny galley kitchen was not to their liking. Seymour responded more than curtly to their complaints, "If you ordered one book and they sent you two, send one back. . . . If the car needs repainting of course it must be painted. . . . About a new kitchen, I do not know. We have never had any complaint about the kitchen ranges. They have been first class in every respect. . . . You say this is no use. Now we cannot allow gasoline stoves. It would violate the insurance. You will have to work out that problem the best you can."[18]

On June 1, 1902, the Deweys accepted a call to a Chicago church. Chapel car life was not for everyone.

McDonald Brings Stability and Success

Seymour and Boston Smith, who was still managing the chapel cars, were beginning to wonder if they would ever find the right missionaries for *Herald of Hope*. The Reverend A. P. McDonald, formerly northern district missionary, came to the chapel car June 1, 1902, and he seemed to be the answer

to their prayers. Smith describes how McDonald soon discovered the dangers and victories of his new vocation.

Herald of Hope was sidetracked in the center of a northern Michigan village. It was Saturday night. There was a free dance in a nearby hall, under the auspices of a saloon. A large crowd was in attendance. About 1 a.m. Mr. McDonald heard a crash. A drunken rowdy had thrown another down the stairs. This was the signal for a free-for-all fight which lasted until morning. However, at 10 a.m. the Car was filled with people for Sunday service. The Missionary informed them of the occurrences of the night.

Under his leadership the congregation induced the Common Council to close the saloons at 10 p.m. every weekday and to keep them closed every Sunday. Moreover special police were appointed to keep order. After which the work of the Car proceeded successfully, remaining several weeks. The town now has a Baptist church with a good meeting house located but a few rods from where the midnight brawl took place.[19]

One of the nation's leading lumber producers at the turn of the century, Michigan had many mill towns, and McDonald related their experiences as the car visited several of these towns. The car rolled into one mill town of three thousand people, where Baptists were but little known. One of the first converts was a young man of unusual ability. When McDonald explained to him New Testament teaching, he requested baptism. In the absence of a baptistry, one was made in the ground by the side of the car. Men in a nearby sawmill helped fill the makeshift baptistry by means of a hose nearly eighty rods long, the water being forced through by a steam pump.[20]

In one mill town of five hundred inhabitants, the people would not enter the car, so McDonald sent to the publication society for one hundred Bibles. Upon their arrival, he took a Bible and going from house to house and from mill to mill announced that every boy or girl under eighteen years of age who came to the car the next morning at ten o'clock would receive a present of a Bible. Before the appointed hour, seventy-five children were in the car. After a lively meeting, each child carried away a Bible. That night parents came to the car, and within three days the car could not accommodate the crowd.[21]

In the 1902 minutes of the Michigan Baptist Convention, the work of *Herald of Hope* was praised, but concern was voiced as to how this good work would be sustained. "These churches [started by *Herald of Hope*] must be cared for. They need pastors, and that means additional appropriations. They also need meeting houses, and hence need appropriations from a Church Edifice Fund. But your Board has no such fund. The creation of such a fund is imperative."

At that same meeting, a plea was made for chapel car work in the Upper Peninsula, and the progress of the work of other denominations was reported. In the report was a mention of the second Episcopal chapel car in upper Michigan.[22]

The chapel car continued to start and support congregations hoping that pastors would be found to continue the work. In Evart, Michigan, on the Muskegon River and the Pere Marquette Railroad in January 1907, McDonald and his helper, Edward L. Killam, came to help the church that had been organized at Beeman's Opera House in 1884. McDonald wrote, "When our beautiful car *Herald of Hope* was sidetracked in the very heart of town, and the glad message proclaimed in the very business center of the town, it was a new thing, and the people began to flock to the car to hear the gospel preached and sung."[23]

Many members of the Evart church were still suffering from a tragedy that occurred on January 11, 1904, when the boiler at Marsh and Kennan's sawmill exploded and seven men lost their lives and many were injured. But the town was growing, and Saturdays were great trading days. A citizen counted 139 farmers' vehicles on Main Street one Saturday, and increasing numbers of freight cars were dispatched at the station. The Knights and Lady Maccabbees had recently built their new hall.[24]

The town saloons were not so busy. In Michigan and across the United States, the work of the Anti-Saloon League was making its mark. Two stanzas from "The Evart Saloon Keeper's Soliloquy" tell how effective the work of the Temperance Lodge was in Evart, even before the chapel car came.

> "Business is getting awful dull,
> I haven't got a cent,
> And here's last month's grocery bill —
> No cash to pay my rent.
> I haven't sold a drink to-day.
> One chap bought a cigar,
> If things don't brighten up next week
> I'll have to close my bar."[25]

McDonald, who served faithfully, later added, "As we eat and sleep on the car, we have some experiences which are not so pleasant; for instance, when we are thrown out of bed by coming in contact with a live engine. However, we rejoice in the work, and praise God for his goodness and protection."[26]

By the close of 1907, as *Herald of Hope* prepared to leave the state, several of the churches visited were no longer active as a result of the lack of a building, a pastor, or support. Michigan Baptists took a hard look at what was happening to their churches, and a Committee on Decadent Churches included this comparison of denominational work in their report.

The Baptists, Presbyterians and Methodists were on the field in 1836; all few in numbers but of about equal strength. The future was before them, and each denomination had an equal chance in the same field and in the same environment. The Congregationalists do not appear until 1846. Two years ago, after seventy years of history, these denomination numbers follow: Congregationalists, 336 churches, 32,403 members; Presbyterians, 263 churches, 34,507 members; Baptists, 453 churches, 45,709 members; and Methodists, 1135 churches and 110,393 members.[27]

After much discussion, the conclusion was "the proper explanation of this disparity is to be found, not in doctrine or contributions, but in the fact that, unlike ourselves, they [the Methodists] are able to keep all their churches, large and small, nearby and remote, supplied with pastors all the time." Michigan Baptists were not alone. The problem of keeping churches open was facing Baptists and other denominations nationwide.

Sparkses Cover Illinois, Iowa, Ohio

The day after Christmas in 1907, *Herald of Hope* arrived in Illinois, with the Reverend Walter J. and Katherine Sparks aboard. Sparks was known preeminently as a church builder, and his wife was an outstanding children's worker. From the last week in December to February 17, 1908, the Sparks worked in Streator, an important clay-producing area along the Vermilion River. Coal mining began there in 1872, and the importance of the enterprise was reflected in the fact that the city soon changed its name from Unionville to Streator in honor of the coal company's president.[28] One of the main goals at Streator was to establish a chapel at Mine No. 3, a point three miles outside of town in Livingston County, which would be a mission of the Streator Church.

But the work at Streator was not very successful. It was hoped that a mission might be organized and a chapel built, but the weather was cold and the missionaries had to learn by experience how to care for and heat the car, and there were other maintenance problems. Transportation and even side-track room were difficult to secure. After forty-three days, though, thirty-two persons made a profession of faith, resulting in sixteen baptisms.

After a short stay at Tonica the car went on to Oglesby, a town of about four thousand people, two thousand of them English-speaking. As there was not one Baptist family in the city and not a church nearby to give support, the car was there for six months, resulting in a church organized and a building fund started.[29]

In May 1909 Sparks challenged Illinois Baptists, "On almost every line of railroad in Illinois, new towns are springing up and becoming cities in a day. They need churches. With the chapel car to get there as soon as the saloon, what an opportunity for Baptists! With a little help from the funds of the State Convention to take care of the work after the church is organized and the house erected, we can take these cities for God. Are there funds sufficient to make it possible?"[30]

Delegates to the Illinois Baptist State Convention, held October 18–20, 1909, at Galesburg, were a few blocks away from the tiny Third Street childhood home of poet and storyteller Carl Sandburg. Sandburg's Swedish father worked as a blacksmith's helper at the Chicago, Burlington & Quincy shops, and *Herald of Hope* was sided near the depot where Carl loved to hang out as a boy.

Sandburg wrote in his autobiography, *Always the Young Strangers*, that when he was a youngster in the mid-1880s, he

Fig. 11.3 *Herald of Hope* was the one chapel car that did most of its work east of the Mississippi. From 1900 until the 1920s, Michigan and Illinois were considered the northern frontier, and Ohio and West Virginia still had many railroad towns without churches. The Reverend Walter Sparks, who served with his wife in Illinois, Iowa, and Ohio, is seen here on the car. (American Baptist Historical Society, Valley Forge)

could remember attending revival services at the Galesburg Baptist Church, where the Reverend W. H. Geistweit, a Baptist of national renown who wrote the hymn for chapel car *Evangel*, would hold forth on the evils of drink. The Baptist pastor would mention in his pulpit information of when certain saloons — like the White Elephant or Danny Flynn's — were open after hours or on Sunday. Reporters would attend the services to hear the tips, the newspapers would print them, and the police would swing into action or sometimes forget them. Because of Geistweit's eagle eye, saloons became careful about the word saloon. Instead, they called their businesses "sample rooms."

When Geistweit left Galesburg to preach in other, larger cities, like Minneapolis and Dayton, and more prominent churches, there must have been rejoicing in the sample rooms of the town.

Sandburg's heroes were not crusading preachers like Geistweit. They were railroad men. Like the chapel car missionaries, Sandburg learned that railroaders were a special breed of people with a special kind of profession. "No two trips alike," Sandburg wrote. "Some trips would 'scare the living daylights' out of any but a good railroad man. They have to make quick decisions. They expect the unexpected. They have the gift of humor — they kid each other and have their own slang. Their standard answer to those who asked, 'Why did they put this depot so far from town' was 'They wanted it next to the railroad.'"[31]

H. T. Cunningham, a Centralia layman, spoke to Illinois Baptists about his view of railroad men. "There are all kinds of men on the railroad. The characteristic attitude is indifference. As a class they have great insight. They are good judges of human nature. There must be no sham. They see through it at once. I believe that men are called to work on the railroad as well as called to the ministry. I cannot tell how to reach them. We must not depend too much on church buildings."[32]

A railroad church on wheels like *Herald of Hope* seemed to be the perfect answer for these railroad men.

At the same convention, attention was not on the towns like Galesburg but on the city of Chicago. Delegates passed several resolutions.

Whereas, There is now in the city of Chicago a great moral awakening resulting in the curbing of the forces of evil and arousing the good people to the many dangers that threaten them in the spreading social vice, the open lawless Sunday saloons, the public promiscuous dance halls and their resultant crime and sin, and the unspeakable white slave traffic with its kindred evils;

and Whereas, The appalling spread of cheap show houses, lurid pictures to the daily papers, and other vicious attractions, have drawn many of our young people into paths of sin and shame;

Resolved, That we urge upon the Attorney General of our state immediate, full and insistent co-operation with the lawful authorities of Cook County and the city of Chicago, consistent with his constitutional powers to the end that in the gigantic task of making our great city law respecting and law abiding, Illinois shall have done her full share.[33]

Another resolution was passed at the gathering to thank the Illinois Central, the North Western, the Wabash, the Eastern Illinois, Milwaukee and St. Paul railroads for their friendly and practical demonstration of sympathy and interest in the support of the chapel car work.

Wherever the railroads went, new towns were established along the lines. The need for churches in those growing towns was still great in Illinois after the turn of the century. While in many areas in Illinois the absence of a church would not be a matter of great concern, this was not the case in Champaign-Urbana, home of the University of Illinois and a Big Four shop. In the summer of 1909 the missionary committee of the First Baptist Church of Urbana drove over a part of Urbana lying north of the Big Four railroad to see the needs of that field. They found no church or Sunday school north of the track. More than one thousand people were living in the northwest part of Urbana, many of them children. Many residents worked for the Big Four Railroad. The committee was unanimous that something needed to be done.

In October a Reverend Meigs was in attendance at the convention at Galesburg. He telegraphed F. C. Hubbard that the chapel car, with the Sparkses in charge, would be in Champaign the next Saturday and to make arrangements to sidetrack in Urbana.[34] So *Herald of Hope* came to these cities, split by the controversial site of the Illinois Central Railroad depot, surrounding the newest state university in the Old Northwest Territory. Since its inception, the university had connected the cities, both physically and economically.

Arrangements were made to place the chapel car at Romine Street, and meetings opened in the chapel car on Sunday, October 24, 1909. From the first the mission was successful, and the Sunday school of the Herald of Hope Baptist Church, later changed to Pennsylvania Avenue Baptist Church of Urbana, was organized.

Sparks was working among the Big Four car shop people at Urbana, holding noon meetings in the shops, and officials seemed pleased with the meetings. One day in November 1909, Sparks offered to give a copy of John's Gospel to each rail worker who would read it. The supply of fifty was taken eagerly.[35] The car remained in the Urbana area for ten weeks because of the success of the work.

The Wildest Town in the West

From the civilized seat of learning of Champaign-Urbana to Grape Creek was a rail trip in a *Herald of Hope* time machine. When the Sparkses came to Grape Creek, Illinois, in 1909, it was the Grindstone City of Illinois, and it was once called the busiest and roughest mining town in the Middle West (*see fig. 11.4*).

"Where are you going next?" inquired two burly policemen as they watched the coal bunkers under the car being filled, preparatory to a move for *Herald of Hope*.

"To Grape Creek," brought a great laugh from the policemen and the advice, "Then you'd better take half a dozen of our men with you."

The idea of the Chapel Car going to Grape Creek appealed to everyone's sense of humor. Even the conductors were shaken out of their gravity. "What you got there, Billy?" called out one, as the train pulled from the platform and our conductor shouted, with a grin, "A carload of preachers for Grape Creek." This brought a chorus of laughter from the platform.

But we found that Grape Creek was living largely upon its past reputation . . . gained when it was the roughest mining camp in the Middle West, and the wild orgies of its bad men made people fear even to pass through on the train. Business had decreased, the roughest of the element had moved on, and empty "company houses" falling to ruins gave the town a desolate look. Saloons flourished on every corner and were sprinkled in between, but though Grape Creek was fifty years old, it had never had a church.

For some years the good agent of the C & E I Railroad, his wife and his father's family, had been the only influences for righteousness in the whole place, and they found it hard to leaven such a lump. But a few months previous, a section man had been converted, and gathering up a few others he organized a Baptist church. The deacon met us with a shovel. He had been shoveling out the slack that covered up the sidetrack. People lounged on the platform and stared, wondering what had "come to town."

At the meeting that night some forty men crowded the back seats or stood around the door. Others who could not get in listened outside. Most of them had been drinking and occasionally there would be an exodus of half a dozen who would presently come in again. "Where'd they go?" I asked.

"To get a drink," said the deacon; "when the sermon begins I'll stop 'em."

The only interruption to the sermon was a dialogue

between the deacon and a big miner whom drink had made drowsy. It was carried on in tones rather above the regulation stage whisper. "Here, Jimmie, this ain't no place to sleep. If you can't keep awake, git out."

"What's yer jumpin' onto me fer? I ain't the only one that's sleepin'!"

"Well, yer the only one snorin'. You kin sleep but you can't snore."

Sunday afternoon there were over one hundred men present, among them only five professing Christians. Some confessed they had not been inside of a church for thirty years. A few had never been at religious service within their recollection. That day a poor man stood outside the car . . . too outcast to sit among the men. A saloon keeper told me that he was "nothing but a haunt" [a saloon loafer]. He sat on the slack beside the car and listened to the sermon, a prodigal in a far country, living in shame.

The following Tuesday evening the sermon was on "The Tragedy of Sin." When the invitation was given for men to turn from the sinful life, the door opened and as the people sang, "I've wandered far from God, now I'm coming home," that miserable "Haunt" made his way to the platform. He stretched out one hand and, wiping away his tears with the other, sobbed out, "You hit me hard tonight and so you did on Sunday. Every word of those sermons was for me. I heard it all outside."

"And what do you want?" I asked.

"I want God! I want God!"[36]

Many miners were eager to give to build a church in Grape Creek, but they had little money for there was no work. After some weeks of weary tramping, the Sparkses had the money raised, money enough to put up a suitable building on lots that had been donated by the mining company. The building would provide a basement with reading room and gymnasium for the many young men who had no place but the saloon for recreation after their hard day's work. The contract was let at thirty-one hundred dollars.

Meanwhile, the work of the chapel car and missionaries was not going unheralded. "*Herald of Hope*, in charge of Rev. W. J. Sparks and wife, is now in Illinois in cooperation with the Illinois State Convention. The car has only been in one other state since it was built. It is the most complete car in construction, and the present missionaries have proved most excellent workers. When mileage has been paid the State Convention has paid it."[37]

Shawneetown, Grape Creek Revisited

January 1910 found *Herald of Hope* at Shawneetown, where it would stay many weeks. (Sparks's inspiring story of what happened at Shawneetown introduced this chapter.) Shawneetown was a railroad terminal of the Springfield branch of the Baltimore and Ohio Railroad, but it also had a branch of the Louisville and Nashville Railroad. With that north and south rail system, it was inevitable that the

Fig. 11.4 *Herald of Hope* pulls into the station at Grape Creek, Illinois, called the wildest town in the West by some, where people came to greet the car. (American Baptist Historical Society, Valley Forge)

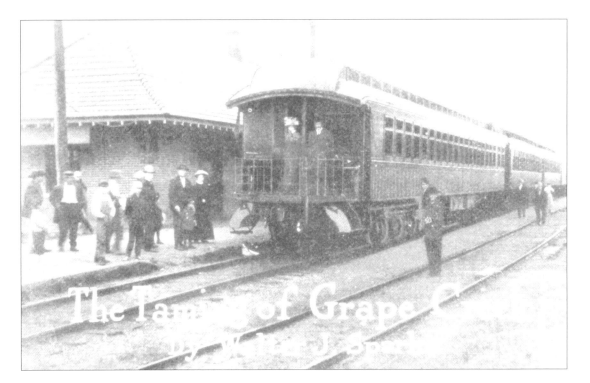

picturesque town along the riverbanks and bold rugged bluffs, blessed with magnolia and mistletoe, poplar and oak, cypress and vine, should prosper by its location as a river shipping point. Mills, foundries, machine shops, good schools, newspapers, churches, and banks were all part of the early success of the town,[38] as was the allure of riverboat travel.

Shawneetown had suffered greatly as a result of the ravages of Ohio River floods — 1883, when only twenty-eight out of six hundred homes survived; 1898 — with a loss of twenty-five lives; then 1913, when government boats blasted the levee banks to give additional protection to the historic city on the Ohio banks. The oldest church in Shawneetown, the First Methodist, had been built in 1842, stood through repeated floodings, finally fell, and was rebuilt in the new town.

What was the fate of the first Baptist church in Shawneetown, the town the Sparkses tried so hard to win and the church they tried so hard to build? After the flood of 1912, there was no record of a Baptist church in the new Shawneetown, which had been moved to higher ground.

In 1996 no churches could be found in Old Shawneetown. The only buildings left in the deserted original townsite were the towering, majestic First State Bank of Illinois, a few old homes, the historic law office of Robert Ingersoll, a small cafe, and four vacated saloons — beer-brand signs still dangling.

The site of the railroad depot where Herald of Hope *was sided in 1911 was no longer evident. But the mighty Ohio River was still there, flush with the joining of the Wabash, where Walter Sparks immersed those few "found souls" and where pioneer Baptist missionary John Mason Peck began his journey in 1841 to carry the gospel westward across the broad Mississippi.*

The next work of the chapel car was at Highland, east of Vandalia. This is a town of about four thousand people and almost no English spoken in the place. "We desired to make a test of the field, and especially as we had a few French Baptists living there." But it was impossible to establish a Baptist Church there at this time. There was much opposition

from a local church. A man requested Brother Sparks to visit his father who was sick. This he did, and shortly afterward the following unsigned notice appeared in the local paper. "NOTICE: Visiting evangelists are requested to remain away from homes of sick members of my congregation. Up to the present time I am in no need of outside assistance." It was thought best not to keep the car longer on that field.[39]

Back at Grape Creek, in July 1911, a splendid brick building was dedicated, the only church in a community that supported a busy mill and brick plant, a large company store, and eight saloons, once as many as nineteen.[40] But by 1913 Grape Creek was pastorless and struggling. On July 2, 1961, more than fifty years later, a report was filed in the office of the Illinois Baptist State Convention. The "splendid building" that the faithful in Grape Creek had prayed and worked so hard for was now a "brick building that is falling to pieces." The church and members had come on hard times and dissent between pastors, although seventy-five were present for evening service and excellent singing was enjoyed.[41] Not too long after, the Grape Creek Baptist Church was dropped from Illinois Baptist Convention work. But Grape Creek Baptist Church was not dead.

It was late on a 1997 January afternoon when we approached the community of Grape Creek. We had been given directions and a map in South Danville, although the gentleman at the appliance store looked a bit surprised that strangers would be wanting to go to Grape Creek.

"Yep, there is a church over there," he said in response to our question. "Just one."

The road curved down among hills that once housed mine shafts and tunnels, past mobile homes and houses and horses in a field. After we dropped into a valley, we could see the old Chicago & Eastern Illinois (C & EI) rail right of way, sometimes on our left and then switching to our right. At the T road a tavern stood, lights visible in the increasing dusk, encircled by cars.

We followed the winding road and rippling Grape Creek, named after the bountiful clusters that used to grow on its banks, and then we saw the steeple and the church on the hill. Probably not, *we thought,* the building is too new.

We pulled up behind a car parked in front of the church and got out, my husband pointing to a second cornerstone. It read, "Built in 1909," and we smiled. The church door was unlocked, and encouraged, we ventured in and found Pastor Jim Whittenburg in his office. He was not surprised when we talked about a chapel car — he knew from whence the church had come.

"Yes, Grape Creek did have a rough reputation, and people around here have not forgotten it." The pastor laughed, remembering. "Not too long ago one of our local youth group boys who works in Danville met up with some rough characters who had plans to see how tough he was. When they found out where he was from, one said, 'Hey, we won't mess with you. We've heard about Grape Creek."

The legend may stand, but the five coal mines, Kyger's Mill, the old brick plant, the company store on which ground the new church sits, the original church, the nineteen saloons, and three thousand people have disappeared from Grape Creek.[42]

Up on the hill, Grape Creek Baptist Church is still there. Oh yes, and one saloon. The odds are definitely better now.

Smallpox or diphtheria, according to conflicting reports, broke out at Panama in Bond County, a coal mining town where there was no church and no meeting house in a community of twelve hundred people, and prevented the Sparkses from continuing the meetings. It was during July and August, and the chapel car was unbearably hot, so it seemed to be a good time to take the car in for repairs[43] before it left Illinois on its way to Ohio, skipping over Indiana, which had made no requests for the use of the chapel cars.

Herald of Hope Comes to Ohio

After being put in good order in the shops of the Barney & Smith Car Company in Dayton, Ohio, *Herald of Hope* was rededicated in Dayton on November 28, 1911. Guy C. Lamson and Samuel G. Neil, who now had responsibilities for chapel car work, led the service. Also present was the Reverend William F. Newton, who had little knowledge that he would spend the last fifteen years of his life serving on *Herald of Hope.* Neil describes the rededication ceremony.

A visitor chancing to be around the Union Railway Station in Dayton, Ohio on Saturday afternoon, November 28th might well have been puzzled by the sight that met his eyes. The redecorated chapel car *Herald of Hope* was on a siding adjoining the station and looked bright and beautiful in its new coat of paint and varnish. It was a splendid advertisement of the missionary work of the Publication Society, as it seemed to say to all who passed by, "There is nothing too good, or swift, or modern, or convenient for the use of Christ in the winning of America's unsaved millions." Here was an attractive crowd of Dayton's best-known Baptists, young and old, all keenly interested . . . By three o'clock we settled down to the business of the afternoon. Amid the blowing of steam, the clang of bells and the shrieking of whistles. . . .[44]

Late in 1911 *Herald of Hope* came to Ohio, largely supported by generous Baptist laymen who urged its coming.[45] In the early 1900s, Ohio with its population of 4,448,677[46] ranked fourth in numerical strength among the states and had several growing centers of industrial power — Cleveland, Cincinnati, Columbus, Toledo, Dayton, and Springfield. Exploding populations in the large cities posed many problems for Ohio's country churches. In 1910, of 475 white Baptist churches in the state, about 250 were rural and about 150 were pastorless.

According to Richard H. Clossman, in his study of Ohio Baptists, there was an admission that the influence of the city had been detrimental to the rural churches. One rural church committee report observed, "the city population is rapidly overtaking the rural population. The city is a sort of dead sea into which the fresh waters of the Jordan flow and stagnate."

There was not even a country church in sight when *Herald of Hope* found itself lost in the darkness, seeing only the ghostly outline of trees, when it was sidetracked one Saturday night in 1911 near a small Ohio town. It was not where the car was supposed to be. After hunting up the depot to wire ahead the news of their delay, the Sparkses went to bed frustrated, wondering what would evolve from this hitch in their plans.

Morning came, and we had just planned an expedition down the track when we heard shots. Two young men carrying rifles came out of the woods and stood staring at the car in amazement. We invited them in. Our new-found friends thought *Herald of Hope* was a fine car and said there were some houses down the track. Two young sportsmen became two earnest chapel-car workers armed with literature and intent on bringing others back to hear the gospel. Not long afterward, faces peered shyly through the door and children filled the chapel car. As they ran home with cards, papers and the "Gospel of John" clasped tightly in eager hands, we felt

Fig. 11.5 Tracts like these telling the stories of the chapel car work were widely distributed across the nation in an effort to raise funds to keep the cars in service. (Norman T. Taylor)

there was little doubt about seeing their parents at the evening service.

Walter looked into faces filled with interest and curiosity and gave a simple gospel message. "My friends, I see but few in the car tonight who were born in America. Now, we want to get acquainted, and it will help us to know the country from which each of you came. As you tell me where you were born, I will write it on this blackboard. How many from Germany? I see five hands. Some came from Poland, I know. Yes, three born in Poland. In Ireland? Two in Ireland. In North Italy? and quite a number were born in South Italy. How many?"

At this point the section foreman became so excited that he roared out in Italian, "All you from south Italy hold up your hands!" When those who were born in America were asked to respond, the children swelled the number considerably, then he went over it all from the board and presented the message that whatever our earthly birthplace, we must be born again.[47]

Brewster, a village of about seven hundred and growing, was the location of the new shops of the Wheeling and Lake Erie Railway Company. About a million and a half dollars had been invested in the new facility, making that point the terminal between Cleveland and Toledo on the north and Zanesville and Pittsburgh on the south. The road belonged to the Wabash Company and offered the shortest route by eight hours between Chicago and New York.[48] No church or Sunday school was in the town until *Herald of Hope* and the Sparkses came in November 1911.

The Sparkses found children with no apparent moral or religious influence about them. The saloons and pool rooms were open to them night and day, Sundays included. "Young men had no place but these places of evil to spend a social hour. Young girls and women were subjected to these conditions of low morals. To sum up the conditions, it was a place of absolute religious and moral destitution."[49] Businessmen testified to the change that had come over the town since the car had arrived there, the church organized, and religious services begun.

From Brewster the chapel car went to the Hildreth Church in Columbus, where it was sided at Twentieth Street near the viaduct for the month of April. Meetings were well attended, including the children's meetings and the special sessions at 6:30 P.M. for newsboys. "A number of the boys have taken the pledge to abstain from the use of cigarettes." Nearly one hundred were reported to be converted during the meetings.[50]

In November 1912, Sparks brought *Herald of Hope* to the struggling Ohio congregation at New Boston, outside Portsmouth, on the banks of the Ohio River. The *Portsmouth Daily Times* reported on Friday, November 22, 1912, "The Baptist Chapel car, located on the Chillicothe Pike, near the cement plant, is crowded every night with men and women who are deeply interested in the evangelistic services being conducted by Mr. and Mrs. Sparks . . . who expect to remain in New Boston to help with the completion of the new church for 'maybe two months.'"

Also published in the *Times* of that day was a report that "salaries of the clerks in the Norfolk & Western offices are to be increased six percent from their $155 a month wage," at least fifty dollars more than the chapel car missionaries made, and that "a movement of West End grocers plan to keep their stores closed all day Sunday." Not only were stores to be closed on the sabbath, but in the December 26 issue, local ministers were also threatening "to oppose Sunday Picture Shows."

Two days before Christmas, when good crowds were still filling *Herald of Hope*, the Norfolk and Western Railroad ordered sixty-five new steel coaches, to be placed in passenger service immediately upon their arrival. The *Times* reported, "Eventually it is said that all wood coaches will be abandoned by this railroad. There is only one complaint made about the steel cars, and that is that it is almost impossible to keep them warm in extreme cold weather. But this is soon forgotten when it is figured how much safer these cars are than the old

style, which in a serious wreck are reduced to kindling wood."

Herald of Hope was the sign of those times; it was the last wooden chapel car to be built.

In January 1913, according to *Times* accounts, Sparks was making himself a favorite of the local Rail Y, whose members were expected to donate to a wedding gift fund for Helen M. Gould. The daughter of the infamous rail tycoon Jay Gould, Miss Gould established many branches of the Railroad Y.

Then the floods came, and the rains began, and people's thoughts were concerned with other things than weddings. Page one news was that at 3 o'clock on January 11, the Ohio River at Portsmouth was 52.2 feet and rising steadily at the rate of 2 inches an hour. Although the flooding subsided, that lead story was a portent of things to come months later — not on the cresting Ohio but on the roiling rivers called the Miami and the Mad.[51]

The governor of Ohio from 1909 to 1912 had been Judson Harmon, a Baptist known as an honest man.[52] His father, a noted pastor of the Walnut Street Baptist Church in Cincinnati for many years, named him after Adoniram Judson, the missionary to Burma. But in the spring of 1913, it was Governor James M. Cox who placed the city of Dayton under martial law and who faced the insurmountable task of dealing with the flood of 1913.[53]

In the path of the flood sat the Barney & Smith Car Company, which, unlike the Norfolk and Western Railroad, waited too long to switch to steel passenger cars. The choice oak and mahogany from the production of Barney & Smith's carefully crafted private wooden cars like the *Herald of Hope* floated, along with their future, down the river toward New Orleans.[54] (See chapter 14 for more on the Barney & Smith Car Company and the flood of 1913.)

During this time of flooding, *Herald of Hope* was still at New Boston. The congregation was so pleased with the work that they proposed making the front window of the new church a memorial to the chapel car. A local businessman, Mr. Peebles of the brick plant, donated thirty thousand bricks, enough for the inside of the Sunday school structure.[55]

Westward across the Mississippi to Iowa

The problem of transportation had become increasingly serious for the six Baptist chapel cars. In former years, the railroad companies had been glad to transport the cars without charge. Legislation against all free service made it impossible for most companies to continue. Now chapel cars had to pay for transportation, and as a result the operative expense had considerably increased. *Herald of Hope* still had work to do, and its missionaries hoped the Iowa railroads would be kind.

Herald of Hope moved to Iowa, where *Glad Tidings* had visited in 1900 and 1901, and began its work at Dubuque in the fall of 1913. At Carroll, which was laid out by the town lot department of the Chicago & North Western Railroad in August 1867, the congregation was encouraged.[56]

At Manly, after weeks of hard, sacrificial labor by the chapel car workers, a new church was started in a community that was growing rapidly. During the summer of 1912 construction work was started on the new Rock Island terminal and many trainmen, shop workers, and other maintenance men from other points moved into Manly, and by early summer of 1913 the new terminal was in full operation. It was considered one of the most modern railroad shops in the United States at this time.[57]

Before *Herald of Hope* left Iowa, it scheduled a stop at Clinton, on the west bank of the Mississippi. Three of the largest railway systems passed through Clinton: the Chicago, Milwaukee and St. Paul; the Chicago Burlington and Quincy; and the Chicago, Rock Island and Pacific, in addition to the Chicago and North Western, which built and maintained extensive shops and yards in the city. This made the stop attractive for the Sparkses, because of their desire to work with the railroad men as well as support the Clinton Baptist Church.

However, the meetings at Clinton did not turn out as the missionary workers and the Baptist congregation of Clinton would have wished. In fact, one church historian wrote that the visit was badly mismanaged.

. . . the Denomination sent a Chapel Car to Clinton, which was rather a mistake, for there was no place to locate it anywhere near our church. It was located on the corner of Railroad and Harrison Streets, a block from Chancy Chapel. The minister and his wife in charge of the car were faithful hard workers, but the people of our church [First Baptist Church of Clinton] were asked not to attend the meetings because of lack of room, and the services at Chancy Chapel were discontinued during the time the car was in Clinton. Although some professed conversion, we received very few, if any, additions, and the services at the Sunday School in the Chapel, when resumed, never reached their former proportions.[58]

Herald of Hope left Iowa in August 1914, and the Iowa Baptist Convention recorded that it had been promised another car after the expiration of another year. That was not to be. As far as records show, a chapel car did not return to Iowa after 1914, although an Iowa Baptist layman left money in his will for a chapel car to be built specifically for use for Iowa. Iowa's need was great, but there were too few chapel cars for the demand.

After leaving Clinton, the chapel car crossed the Mississippi and headed southeast to Dayton, Ohio, and the Barney & Smith Car Shops for refitting. Across the great Ohio and then down the ancient Kanawha River, West Virginia called.

Newtons Witness to West Virginia

Refitted in a new coat of paint and varnish and carrying new missionaries, *Herald of Hope* came to the valley and hills of West Virginia in early 1915. In those same lovely yet stormy hills the chapel car would be retired from service about seventeen years later.

Roscoe Keeney, a West Virginia Baptist historian, writes that *Herald of Hope* was an answer to prayer for West Virginia needs. "Isolated from one another by mountains, winter snows and heavy rains, West Virginians wanted help. The minutes of the 1904 Kanawha Valley Association report a request for a colporter missionary to work among unreached people in their area and in the Hopewell Association areas. The chapel car, which came a few years later, was a perfect response."[59]

The Reverend and Mrs. William F. Newton were transferred for a six-month assignment to *Herald of Hope* in West Virginia beginning in January 1915. A native of Rhode Island, Newton had worked in the Indian missions of the West and as an auto colporter in Connecticut before coming to West Virginia. Newton began his chapel car work at Point Pleasant and then went to Henderson, where a score or more accepted Christ.

At St. Mary's, Newton started a preaching tradition of witnessing in the pool halls of the towns. "The first evening we went into one place every cue was laid down and the balls put in the rack. The men sat and stood around the walls. They remained as quiet and listened as attentively as any congregation I have ever seen. Indeed, much better than the average conduct of some churches. This was repeated on several occasions. When we were absent for a few evenings, we were asked why we had not been back. When we said we did not like to abuse the privilege, we were told to come often, for we were welcome."[60]

The men employed by the B & O showed great courtesy to the Newtons. They also gave *Herald of Hope* the best place on the siding. Even the mayor gave his support to the work.[61]

On they went to Wheeling, where "God moved upon hard hearts," even though Billy Sunday had been there in 1912; and to Cameron, to give support to a young church organized in 1913. The car came to Wallace, an oil town on the Short Line Railroad, on April 8, 1915. After securing the poolroom, Newton organized a Sunday school with forty-five members. *Herald of Hope* left Wallace on May 17 for Lumberport, in the shadow of the huge Harrison Power Company, and then went to Clarksburg.

It was "seed-sowing time" at Industrial, and Wilsonburg where the "church was blessed," and Haywood, and Burnsville, where "many boys in Sunday School accepted Christ."

The Baptist Banner of November 11, 1915, reported that in the summer of 1915 the weather was too hot to hold services in the car, so the Newtons were given vacation time. As was their custom, they spent their vacation at Northfield, attending Dwight L. Moody's conference. They did not plan to return to *Herald of Hope*, as the Sparkses were to assume management of the car after their stay in Illinois. The decision was made to send the Sparkses elsewhere, and the Newtons returned to work on *Herald of Hope*.

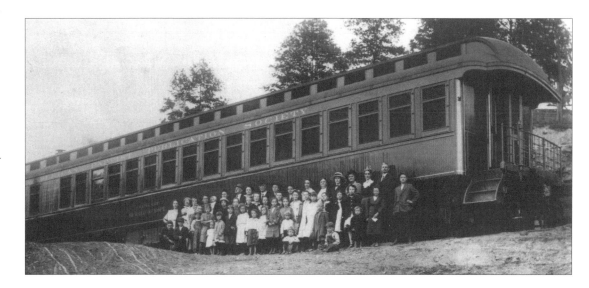

Fig. 11.6 Great meetings were held at the oil town of Wallace, West Virginia, and a church was organized. (American Baptist Historical Society, Valley Forge)

The *Banner* explained, "It is the policy of the Publication Society, with all their cars to place them under the direction of the State Mission Boards. In pursuance with this custom, our State Board appointed Rev. B. F. Caudill, Dr. D. B. Purinton and Rev. A. B. Withers to arrange for the car. Although it has not yet been definitely decided by the committee, it is thought that the car will operate in southern West Virginia during the coming year in the great coal fields that are opening up so rapidly."

From 1915 to 1918, *Herald of Hope* visited the central West Virginia towns of Gassaway and Clay, Hurricane,

Pisgah Mines, and the Kanawha Valley communities of Smithers (Cannelton), Gauley Bridge, Boomer, Cedar Grove, and Belle, as well as Ronda, about two miles up Cabin Creek, an area they would come to know well. The Cabin Creek area suffered from a ravaging flood August 9, 1916. Flood waters reached Cane Fork and Eskdale and other valley communities and finally flooded the whole valley from hill to hill.[62] These conditions only worsened the tensions caused by mine union troubles, making it more difficult to achieve success along the Cabin Creek line.

The Newtons and *Herald of Hope* came to Gassaway February 24, 1916. The Valley Hotel next to the track was a busy place. Mrs. Clara Thorne, organist at the Gassaway church for fifty years, whose father owned the hotel, remembers that the rail yards were the center of town activity. Many came to see the car and attend the meetings.[63] Gassaway was named for Senator Henry Gassaway Davis, who in 1906 purchased the Charleston, Clendenin & Sutton Railroad, which he renamed Coal and Coke Railroad.[64]

In 1917, a year after *Herald of Hope*'s visit to Gassaway, the C & C was purchased by the Baltimore & Ohio Railroad. The chapel car would travel many miles on the old Coal and Coke along the Kanawha Valley.

Newton organized the Hope Baptist Church at Frametown on March 17. Newton noted, "This new church has in it good material and starts with a good prospect of permanency. It is located at a common center where the people come to transact business."

In Otter, Newton "was reminded of St. Paul on his missionary journeys where there was no kindly spirit, but before we left they could not do enough for us personally and wanted us to stay longer."

Clendenin was still experiencing boom town status, which started with the discovery of oil and gas deposits in 1900 and continued with the building of the Elk Refining Company in 1911 and the Cobb Compressor Plant about 1917. At Clendenin the Sunday school was revived and grew in number.

On May 8, 1917, *Herald of Hope* was placed at Dunbar and ended its work there Sunday evening, June 11. Newton was impressed with Dunbar. "Dunbar is an important industrial community and promises to play a large part in the business of the Kanawha Valley. Already a population of a thousand or more are there and housed in exceptionally good class homes. But Baptists have been scarce there. More than once the Charleston pastors looked at the situation and sought for an opening for the establishment of a Baptist enterprise there."[65]

In June the Newtons held meetings at Malden and Dana (now Port Amherst), six miles above Charleston. Because of hot weather, the Newtons held many services in the open air near the Kanawha and Michigan Railroad station, where large numbers of men would meet from night to night. The work was mainly with railroad men at Dana, at the mouth of Campbell's Creek.[66]

Newton was disappointed that he did not make it to Putney. "It was hoped that the car could come to Putney, at the head of Campbell's Creek, but the railroad [Kanawha & Michigan] had such short curves the car should not make them."[67] The only way to get to Putney was by train, without the too-wide-sided *Herald of Hope*.

At the Dickinson Coal and Coke Railroad shops in the late summer of 1916, a large number accepted Christ. At the closing service, there were not seats for the great crowd. Two young railroad men were so eager to follow their Lord that "the night before I left the place they went from the shop in their working clothes and were baptized and returned to finish the day's work. That night I gave them the right hand of fellowship, and organized a B.Y.P.U. Morris, their pastor, will baptize the other candidates in August, providing the river is suitable."[68]

The Quincy area, perched above the Kanawha River, was a coal mining and railroad center as early as the 1880s. Stan Cohen, author of *Kanawha County Images: A Bicentennial History, 1788–1988*, writes that the Kanawha and Michigan Railroad Company, which evolved from the Kanawha and Ohio Railroad Company and operated independently in 1922, started mining in Quincy Hollow about 1890.

At Quincy, once home of the large K & M yards, then NYC and now the Conrail Car shop and yards, the chapel car found a home and was the site for services, resulting in the reorganization of the Naomi Baptist Church. J. G. Dickinson and his son gave the lot and agreed to level the site and build a road to the new church for one hundred dollars. The lumber was bought at Chelyan, across the river; a boat loaded with the wood was hauled across the river, through the locks, and down to the landing. On Thanksgiving Day a cornerstone was laid by the Knights of Pythias.[69]

The cornerstone of the Judson Baptist Church of Belle, like that of many churches in West Virginia, is marked with the Masonic symbol, and it shows the dates 1921 and 1936. During World War I the government started construction of a mustard gas plant, which metamorphosed into the huge Dupont Belle Chemical Plant,[70] and many church members worked for Dupont.

At Boomer, near the Elkem Metals Chemical Plant, Newton worked at carpentering, closing in the basement of the mission house and doing other things to make Miss Barber, the missionary he had baptized, comfortable during cold weather.[71] Newton also boarded in the basement of the church built by the Reverend Antonio Gigliotti for Hungarian and Italian workers, who had been brought to work in the mines.

At Clay meetings were held among the faithful miners. "One sister was so determined to serve Christ that she stepped out of the seat over a man with a wooden leg that was held up against her like a fence. He proved to be her husband. God can help people over any kind of obstacles."[72]

World War I Sidelines Car in Nitro

During World War I, the government halted movement of all private cars, including *Herald of Hope*. Newton found himself in the Dunbar/Nitro area during this time. He would say of this period of his work, "The object of the Chapel Car is to go to the people but it has been reversed here and they come to us."[73]

A local newspaper wrote, "Brother W. F. Newton, of the Chapel Car, *Herald of Hope*, is now at Lock Seven, and unusual interest is manifested in the work. At the first meeting Brother Newton spoke to more than a thousand men. Rev. Newton wrote back to headquarters, 'People are moving into area by the thousands. The great powder plant being constructed at Crawford City, now called Nitro, is drawing workmen from far and near. Our little church at Lock Seven is practically destroyed by the coming in of this great Government plant. The members of the church have nearly all moved away from the community.'"[74]

The government first revealed it had purchased the land and buildings in and around the village of Lock Seven, now Nitro, and gave the word it planned to build a powder plant in that area in November of 1917. In 1918 *Herald of Hope* was located in the Nitro area, where the new ninety-five-million-dollar power plant was under construction (Monsanto) with a potential work force of thirty-five thousand people.[75]

After the land at Nitro was purchased by the government, it was fenced, and armed guards were placed around the reservation. Membership loss and attendance for the Lock Seven Baptist Church was immediate and disastrous, since access to the reservation made it difficult to attend services. Construction work commenced immediately, and most of the members of the Lock Seven Baptist Church had been forced to move to other neighborhoods. The Lock Seven Baptist Church held its property in fee simple, and although they were within the boundary of land purchased for the plant site, the church lots were not included in the transfer of land.[76]

Herald of Hope's ministry in the Nitro/Dunbar area was bittersweet for the Newtons. "The three years we have been here have been much of a revival spirit though it has been difficult to harvest the results because of unsettled conditions."[77] In July 1921, *The Baptist Banner* reported that the chapel car was moved from Dunbar. Newton said of his wartime tenure there, "It was not possible to move from here to reach other points . . . but it has made no real difference, however, for

Fig. 11.7 This picture of the Reverend W. F. Newton hangs in Newton Memorial Baptist Church, the church he left money to build. (Parchment Valley, West Virginia, Historical Society)

thousands have come to us. It has been the greatest opportunity of our lives."[78]

Ministering to miners was central to the chapel car's West Virginia tenure, and the car could not have come at a more crucial time, with strikes and floods occurring up and down the creeks and hollows. Baptist leaders recognized this special mission and its requirement for a special minister. Sam Neil wrote in 1924:

> There are 1200 mining centers in West Virginia. Three hundred of these centers have no churches nearer than two miles. Our missionaries are finding a rich soil and plenteous harvest in the hearts and homes of the mining towns. Miners and Loggers need preaching that is simple, direct, picturesque and passionate. Straight from the shoulder. To meet the men face to face, and to speak to them in the bunkhouse or in the mess-hall, as opportunity offers, is no job for a lazy man or weakling. These men belong to one of the most radical groups in the entire United States. They have been rolling-stones, often with bad habits, earning freely and spending prodigally. Prohibition has been a great blessing.[79]

During a period of their service in the Nitro/Dunbar area, the Newtons and *Herald of Hope* ventured down the Cabin Creek area several times, probably with permission granted for movement of the car by the friendly Coal and Coke Railroad management. Here they ran into some angry miners. Someone at Eskdale tried to dynamite the chapel car. This was understandable, since this was looked on as a time of great unrest and mine wars in the area when all outsiders were suspect.

In *Missions*, the not-easily-intimidated Newton wrote that he walked up Cabin Creek about two miles and found a place as needy as anywhere. He stopped at a logging camp's two sawmills, met the superintendent, and had supper with him, and as a result of Newton's visit among the logging and coal camps, relations in the Cabin Creek area were improved. Partitions were removed in one of the coal company houses, a stove was put in, and seats were installed. Newton went from house to house inviting people to church. "I made over twenty calls, got my organ and singing books, and we had the house filled," he wrote.[80]

In another incident, Newton told that as they pulled into town with the car attached to the train, "the devil put up a great howl. Men stood in their store doors with clinched fist, telling us to go right on through. That afternoon I went from store to store, bought a little here and there and invited my knockers to come to the meeting that night. Some came; others followed."[81]

The chapel cars were classic studies of compactness and efficiency. It was one thing to tour the cars and another to live in them. Fanny Newton, who lived in *Herald of Hope* from 1915 to 1935, could have written the book on chapel car living. But life could not have been unpleasant, because she insisted on living in the car for several years after her husband's death, against the wishes of Baptist officials. According to those who visited the living quarters of the car, Mrs. Newton made them homey.

The Newtons had been down Cabin Creek before when times were tense. This trip to Ronda proved to be profitable, even though tension was still running high after the United Mine Workers' march of 1921, when federal troops, including air power, were called in to quiet the area.

> We left 3 a.m. the next morning (from Huntington) for Ronda, up Cabin Creek. We were soon side-tracked on as it is said "Hell's half acre, and the Devil's playground," where the men and boys congregate to play cards, gamble and drink. At our first meeting the car was crowded, we organized a Sunday school with 67 the first Sunday. The following Friday night we organized a temporary church with 15 members. On Sunday I baptized 5, one an old lady seventy-two years old, who is testifying for Christ every night, and others are seeking. We are planning to build or remodel a building for future days.
>
> Anyone desiring to help on this mining town it will be greatly appreciated by this little band of Christian

workers. Last Sunday was our third Sunday and the Sunday school had 89, so you can see we are in need of a building. Ronda is a busy town working when many coal towns are idle. These are great fields that will furnish men labor for 100 years.[82]

Through the Kanawha & Michigan Railroad Company, they received a special rate and had free parking, which would have been $3.60 per day.[83] The *Baptist Banner* reported that a church (the Dry Branch Baptist Church) and Sunday school had been organized in Ronda, and a building had been provided. Through the generosity of John Q. Dickinson of Charleston and his coal company, the Ronda church came into possession of property that had been used as a schoolhouse and later as a pool room. Several hundred dollars were spent on the building in remodeling and equipping it for a church. Newton reported, "The dedication was set for Sunday, April the 9th. The completion of the building has been much delayed by the financial situation in this coal field on Cabin Creek. Many have been without work."[84]

Herald of Hope Comes to Quinwood

On September 15, 1922, *Herald of Hope* came to Quinwood, a new mining town near Rainelle, in the western part of Greenbrier County. Newton probably had little knowledge that this was to be the end of his life's journey and the final station for the car. He commented that the town was about twenty-five hundred feet above sea level and would soon be a great town.[85]

The work at Quinwood went well. Families, most of them with miner fathers who worked for the Imperial Colliery Company (sometimes called the Imperial Smokeless Coal Company), came to the growing Sunday school. Lucille Pomeroy Fox became a favorite of Mrs. Newton, corresponding with her after Newton had died and Mrs. Newton had returned to her home in Massachusetts.

My dad, who worked for another company than the local Imperial Smokeless Coal Company, would tell me when I was very small [she was born in 1921] how he would tuck me under his arm and carry me across the snow to the chapel car. I remember it was Mrs. Newton who taught me how to keep myself neat and presentable as I grew older. She always stressed the importance of appearance. She taught my older sister, who was the first person baptized in the new church, how to play the piano, and she and Mr. J. Wade Bell, the owner of the coal company, bought a beautiful Baldwin piano for my sister and had it shipped from up north somewhere to our home.[86]

At the 1923 Hopewell Association, Newton, who had become known as "the chapel car man," made one of his talks on "Door Step Evangelism" and sang his favorite song, "Honey in the Rock." The hymn was requested many times and became his trademark. His full, rich voice would boom out F. A. Graves's old hymn, "O my brother, do you know the Savior, Who is wondrous kind and true? He's the Rock of your salvation; There's Honey in the Rock for you." Then the particularly appropriate last verse, "Then go out thro' the streets and byways, Preach the word to the many or few; Say to ev'ry fallen brother, There's Honey in the Rock for you."

The Quinwood congregation grew, and the January 17, 1924, *Baptist Banner* reported, "A church lot, finely located, will soon become the property of the First Baptist Church of Quinwood. It is fully expected that a splendid $8000 church house will be erected during the spring and summer."

In Mrs. Fox's cherished and worn *Herald of Hope* scrapbook there is an article about Newton from the *Beckley Post Herald* of February 1, 1960. The writer reports that after he was born, Newton's father enlisted in the Union army and never returned. When he was five, he was placed in an orphanage in Providence, Rhode Island, but was reunited with his mother for a short time. When he was twelve, his stepfather drove him from home, and as he left the house, his mother said, "Willie, be a good boy. Keep good company, and it will come out all right in the end." He always said, "My mother's prayers have followed me the whole world through." As a young man, he felt the call to the ministry and supported himself as a barber while he worked his way through classes offered by Dwight L. Moody at Moody's Northfield conference grounds. Moody also bought him a barber chair to help his efforts.[87]

One of Newton's last communiques to Neil dealt with the bane of all chapel car missionaries — the heating system.

> Dear Bro. Neil, You remember a year ago I asked for a new heater for the Chapel Car, costing $180 and it was granted not to cost more than that installed. The heater was put in and you sent me One Hundred Dollars as a first payment. At last I have had the plumber to do the rest of the job and I am ready to pay the balance $80 for the finish. I shall be pleased to make this payment. We like the Arkola heater, it keeps such a good fire with the soft coal. My coal has cost me nothing all the time I have been here, and Mr. Bell wants me to stay on the field until I am 70 years. Then according to your ruling I am to give way to another brother. I have held special meetings this fall. I paid our premium on Church building insurance and the slack run, only one day of work several weeks has made our offering very small. We will do better later.[88]

On June 4, 1931, Newton passed away while on vacation. The *Baptist Banner* included in his obituary that he died at Baltimore, Maryland, following an operation performed the day before. The *Banner* also reported that all Quinwood business places were closed during the funeral. He was buried at Orange, Massachusetts, his wife's hometown.[89]

Newton Memorial Baptist Church at Charmco was Newton's memorial to himself (*fig. 11.7*). According to the Reverend Homer Clinton Piercy, "Brother Newton had an insurance policy that matured and, perhaps sensing his mortality, he used the money to have the church and parsonage erected." This apparently preceded the organization of the church, since Newton told Piercy that he was going on vacation. "If I don't get back, I want you to organize a Baptist church."[90]

The events in the last years of *Herald of Hope* are somewhat difficult to follow. But they seem to be determined by Mrs. Newton's resolve not to leave her chapel car home, where she was comfortable, and her church family, where she was loved.

Fanny Newton Refuses to Leave Car

In the 1932 report of the American Baptist Publication Society, it was announced that after thirty-one years of constant service, chapel car 6 had been turned over to the board of the West Virginia Baptist State Convention, to be taken off the tracks, placed on a solid foundation, and used as a Baptist church and parsonage at MarFrance, West Virginia.[91] This seemed easier said and written than done.

According to correspondence between Neil and West Virginia state secretary A. S. Kelley, between June 17, 1931, and September 30, 1931, the problem with the disposal of *Herald of Hope* rested with Mrs. Newton's reluctance to leave the car and the understandable reluctance of Baptist leaders to force her to leave, especially when she was surrounded by a community that had high regard for her.

Kelley to Neil (9/10) said that he had decided MarFrance was the best place for the car, and he could get it moved without much expense. "I am somewhat embarrassed about Mrs. Newton's desire to continue on the car until spring. In my judgment the car should be moved this fall."

Neil responded (9/14): "We will count the matter settled; Chapel Car 'Herald of Hope' will go to MarFrance. The final decision for the moving of the car is left in your hands. . . ."

Neil asked Kelley to send one dollar and "the names of the brethren" who would hold the title of the car for the West Virginia Convention. "When I receive this I will forward to you full title as owners of the car. Of course, it is understood that the car will only be used for church purposes and it is hoped that the greater part of the material of the car will be finally worked into a new church building at MarFrance."

Kelley responded (9/18) and sent the names of the Reverend A. B. Withers of Parkersburg and the Reverend J. L. Forren of Rainelle. "If you think it wise to use my name that will be satisfactory. . . . I am not able to say just when the car will be moved. I cannot give it attention until after our State Convention in October. I am enclosing $1.00 for title, etc. The only embarrassing element connected with the matter is Mrs. Newton. I have the notion that she will want to stay on the Car until Spring and will perhaps want the Car to remain where it is. If you think it wise to yield to her request in that matter, I shall be glad to have you say so and we will follow your advice."

On September 30 Neil sent the title and said: "I do not think it will be advisable to let Mrs. Newton stay on the car until the spring. I think you ought to take immediate steps to have the car moved to its permanent location. This will enable the work to be thoroughly launched in MarFrance before the real cold winter weather sets in."[92]

Fanny Newton won out and continued to live in the chapel car at Quinwood until 1935, when she moved to Massachusetts. She returned to Quinwood in November 1952 for the thirtieth anniversary of the church. At that time she was eighty-six years old. Mrs. Newton died March 12, 1959.[93]

During Mrs. Newton's last days on the car, she gave away many of its furnishings to people she loved and who had connections to Herald of Hope's ministry. Among the items were two portable organs from the chapel car, given to the family of the Reverend Gordon Withers. That family has donated one organ to Parchment Valley, the home of the West Virginia Baptist Historical Society, and one to the American Baptist Historical Society, which also has a pew from Herald of Hope. A small model of a chapel car, silverware, and a Book of Matthew used in the chapel car are all on display at Parchment Valley.

In the newsletter of the West Virginia Baptist Historical Society of March 1994, the Reverend Earl Ted Wall, pastor emeritus of Winfield Baptist Church, reminisced about his Herald of Hope experience:

I think it was back in 1938 or '39 I was asked to come to MarFrance, a little community just out of Quinwood to conduct a revival service. I took with me a good friend, Wilson Mitchem, a good pianist and worker with young people. When we arrived, we learned the meetings were to be in a railroad car named Herald of Hope. I remember there was a pump organ. If you didn't pump, you didn't play. Although it was in the winter, Wilson would perspire as he pumped and played that organ. I didn't have a very wide audience, but I surely had a long one.

The fate of Herald of Hope was somewhat confirmed in a December 31, 1947, letter from Julian C. Cobb, from Ronceverte, West Virginia, to Mark Rich, chapel car secretary. "Enclosed is a picture of 'Herald of Hope' taken October 19, 1947. . . . The old car minus its wheels now, served as a shop and office for a coal tipple. The location is in Quinwood, Greenbrier County, about 40 miles from the celebrated White Sulphur Springs."[94]

Lucille Pomeroy Fox, oldest member of the Quinwood Baptist Church, looks down at a picture of Herald of Hope *pasted in her scrapbook, the one with the smiling people gathered outside, taken more than seventy years ago. She pats the worn book with its yellowing paper memories. "When Mrs. Newton moved back to her home east, Mr. Bell had the car moved to the coal company and used it as an office. I'm sure they tried to keep an eye on it, because Mr. Bell thought a lot of that car. One time someone got in and set fire to it. Then I think they used it for storage or something."*

Mrs. Fox begins to turn the pages of the scrapbook again, her eyes bright with sweet memories. She doesn't want to forget anything. "Did I show you this letter Mrs. Newton sent me after she went back to Massachusetts?"

There it was, the sixty-year-old note signed "Mrs. Fanny Newton."

"I never will forget that car. You know I spent most of my early years there. Mrs. Newton taught me how to act and dress. Almost everything I learned about my faith, I learned there… and I can remember all the books, and the lights from all the

Fig. 11.8 *Herald of Hope* remained in the valley between the communities of Quinwood and MarFrance, West Virginia, used as an office and storage shed by the Imperial Smokeless Coal Company until the company closed and cleared the area sometime in the early 1950s. (Julian C. Cobb, Ronceverte, West Virginia)

lamps . . . and the music . . . and Mr. and Mrs. Newton."

The muddy valley that once housed the Imperial Smokeless Coal Company is barren of all but trees and brush in 1995. If one looks carefully from the Quinwood ridge above, the indentations where rail tracks once rested can still be seen because of rain water puddling. Across that valley, no more than a mile, high on the opposite ridge, is the town of MarFrance.

A woman who lives along the Quinwood ridge related to the two of us inquisitive strangers, "Yes, I can remember that old chapel car down there by the coal tipple. It was used as an office or something, I think. But it's all gone now. Everything's gone. The company had everything cleared away . . . can't remember when. But I can remember seeing that old car. I can remember the older people telling me about it. But it's all gone now." She looks down in the valley, shaking her head, thoughtfully (see fig. 11.8).

Daylight is fading. You can see the lights from the homes in MarFrance through the trees on the hill and hear the bustle on the darkening streets of Quinwood. From the night shadows of the valley below, you can almost smell oil lamps and see their glow through art-glass window trim. If you listen carefully, you can almost hear on the autumn breeze blowing — the sound of a hymn, vigorously, lovingly pumped out on an Estey organ.

Herald of Hope, roll on, roll on,
Glad messages of light to bear
Where sin and night have reigned too long.
And wake the song of victory there.[95]

Notes

[1] *Missions*, May 1911, 302–6.

[2] *The Colporter*, July 1900, 3.

[3] Letter from Robert Seymour to Kate L. Garmond, Brooklyn, New York, May 18, 1900. Seymour files, ABHS, VF.

[4] Mabel Cook, updated by May Whalen, *History of Grindstone City* (self-published, 1977), 8–19, authors' collection.

[5] *The Colporter*, October 1900, 7.

[6] Letter from Robert Seymour to Boston Smith, July 23, 1900, Seymour files, ABHS, VF.

[7] *The Colporter*, October 1900, 7.

[8] Ibid.

[9] Ibid.

[10] *The Colporter*, December 1900, 8.

[11] *Encyclopedia Britannica*, "Michigan," 1968, vol. 15, 372.

[12] "History of Brown City," Brown City, Mich., Public Library.

[13] BSP, *Brown City (Michigan) Banner* article, date cut off clipping.

[14] Sixty-sixth annual meeting report, Michigan Baptist Convention, May 1901, 34.

[15] Letter from Robert Seymour to Boston Smith, October 21, 1901, Seymour ledger, ABHS, VF.

[16] Gordon Hiatt, *"Through a Glass Darkly," 100 Years and the Clark Lake Church* (Parma, Mich.: Lee Printing, n.d.), 7.

[17] Letter from Robert Seymour to W. W. Dewey, January 31, 1902, Seymour ledger, ABHS, VF.

[18] Letter from Robert Seymour to W. W. Dewey, February 12, 1902, Seymour ledger, ABHS, VF.

[19] M. E. D. Trowbridge, *History of Baptists in Michigan* (Michigan Baptist Convention, 1909), 173.

[20] Ibid., 174.

[21] Ibid.

[22] Minutes of the 1902 Michigan Baptist Convention.

[23] "Fresh from the Firing Line," tract, American Baptist Publishing Society, 15.

[24] "A History of Evart, Michigan," 73–76, Port Huron Public Library, Port Huron, Mich.

[25] Ibid., 31.

[26] Ibid., 16.

[27] Seventy-third annual meeting, Michigan Baptist Convention, 1908, 27–28.

[28] *Illinois: A Descriptive and Historical Guide*, Federal Writers Project (Chicago: A. C. McClure & Co., 1947), 444.

[29] Sixty-fourth annual session of Illinois Baptist State Convention, 1908, 40.

30 *Illinois Baptist Bulletin*, May 1909, 6.

31 Carl Sandburg, *Always the Young Strangers* (New York: Harcourt, Brace & World, 1952), 306–7.

32 Sixty-third annual session of Illinois Baptist State Convention, 1907, 48.

33 Sixty-sixth annual session, Illinois Baptist State Convention, 1910, 71.

34 "75th Anniversary History of the First Baptist Church of Urbana, Illinois," written in 1913, American Baptist Association Files, Green Lake, Wisconsin.

35 *Illinois Baptist Bulletin*, November 1909, 85.

36 "Grape Creek, An Illinois Town," tract, American Baptist Publication Society, ABHS, VF.

37 *Missions*, February 1910, 280.

38 Stella Pendleton Lyles, "History of Shawneetown," *Journal of Illinois State Historical Society*, 1929, 181–85.

39 *Illinois Baptist Bulletin*, April 1910, 164.

40 Sixty-sixth annual session, Illinois Baptist State Convention, 1910, 53.

41 American Baptist Churches of the Great Rivers Region, Springfield, Ill., files.

42 "Grape Creek," in *The Heritage of Vermilion County*, spring 1970, 3.

43 *Illinois Baptist Bulletin*, July 1910, 47.

44 Report of the American Baptist Publication Society to the Northern Baptist Convention, 1911.

45 *Missions*, June 1912, 449.

46 Richard H. Clossman, "A History of the Ohio Baptist Convention, 1907–1976" (unpublished doctoral dissertation, August 1976), 1, courtesy of the Ohio Baptist Convention Office, Granville, Ohio.

47 Katherine Sparks, "God's Plan and Ours," tract, American Baptist Publications Society, ABHS, VF.

48 *The Ohio Baptist Bulletin*, June 1912, 10.

49 *The Ohio Baptist Bulletin*, November 1912, 8.

50 *The Journal and Messenger*, April 11, 1912, 14, Samuel Colgate Baptist Historical Library, Colgate-Rochester Divinity School, Rochester, N.Y.

51 The *Portsmouth Daily Times*, issues as indicated in text, microfilm viewed at the Portsmouth, Ohio, Public Library, March 17, 1996.

52 Clossman, 19.

53 Charlotte Reeve Conover, *The Story of Dayton* (The Greater Dayton Association, 1917), 400, Wright State University Archives, Paul Laurence Dunbar Library, Dayton, Ohio.

54 Michael W. Williams, "The Barney & Smith Car Company," *Timeline*, October/November 1991, 34.

55 *Missions*, August 1914, 604.

56 Paul Maclean, *History of Carroll County, Iowa* (S. J. Clarke Publishing Company, 1912), 225–27.

57 *Worth County Heritage, 1853–1976*, Worth County Historical Society, Iowa Historical Society, 290.

58 "History of the First Baptist Church of Clinton," files of Pastor Stephen L. Petro, Clinton, Iowa.

59 Roscoe Keeney, "Chapel Car Ministry in the Mountains and Mining Camps," *American Baptist Quarterly*, March 1991, 37.

60 *Baptist Bulletin*, 1915; also Missions, n.d., 520.

61 Truett Rogers, *West Virginia Baptist History 1865–1965* (Terra Atta, W.Va.: West Virginia Baptist Historical Society, Headline Books, 1994), 74.

62 Stan Cohen, *Kanawha County Images* (Charleston, W.Va.: Pictorial Histories Publishing Co., 1987), 280.

63 Conversation with Mrs. Clara Thorne at the Gassaway Baptist Church, October 1995.

64 Cohen, 122.

65 *The Baptist Banner*, June 1916, 5.

66 *The Baptist Banner*, August 3, 1916, 8.

67 Cohen, 122.

68 Ibid.

69 *Missions*, October 1916, 677–78.

70 Cohen, 427.

71 *The Baptist Banner*, April 14, 1921, 10.

72 Ibid.

73 Ibid.

74 Letter from W. F. Newton to Samuel G. Neil, November 13, 1918, Samuel G. Neil papers, ABHS, VF.

75 *Missions*, 1918, 696.

76 Ninetieth anniversary program, Nitro First Baptist Church, May 19, 1991, American Baptist Assembly, Green Lake, Wisc.

77 *The Baptist Banner*, April 14, 1921, 10.

78 Ibid.

79 Samuel G. Neil, "A New Century of Colporter Missionary Work," tract for American Baptist Publications Society, 1924.

80 *Missions*, 1918, 433.

81 A. B. Withers, "Sunday School and Youth Work," *The Baptist Banner*, February 13, 1919, 12.

82 *The Baptist Banner*, November 17, 1921, 2.

83 Ibid.

84 *The Baptist Banner*, March 30, 1922, 11.

85 *The Baptist Banner*, October 5, 1922, 8.

86 Interview with Lucille Pomeroy Fox at Quinwood, W.Va., October [?], 1995.

87 Shirley Donnelly, *Beckley (West Virginia) Post Herald*, February 1, 1960, "Yesterday and Today" column.

[88] Letter from W. F. Newton to Samuel G. Neil, October 14, 1930, files of Samuel G. Neil, ABHS, VF.

[89] The Baptist Banner, July 12, 1931, 20.

[90] Homer Clinton Piercy, *Memories of a Country Preacher* (Charmco, W.Va.: Specific Goshen, 1980), n.p.

[91] Anniversary report of the American Baptist Publications Society, 1932.

[92] Samuel G. Neil file, ABHS, VF.

[93] An informal history of the Quinwood Baptist Church, West Virginia Baptist Historical Society, Parchment Valley, W. Va.

[94] Letter from Julian C. Cobb to Mark Rich, December 31, 1947, Mark Rich file, ABHS, VF.

[95] Written by E. N. Stephenson, sung to the tune: *Missionary Chant*.

CHAPTER 12

St. Anthony:
If the Baptists Can Do It,
So Can the Catholics

The Baptist chapel car ministry did not go unnoticed by the Catholic church, or at least by one man — Father Francis Clement Kelley *(fig. 12.2).* Kelley saw the Baptist chapel car *Messenger of Peace* at the St. Louis World's Fair in 1904. The Reverend Joe Jacobs, missionary on the car at the fair, recalled Kelley's visit.

Messenger of Peace was in the Transportation Building at the World's Fair at St. Louis from opening to closing. I do not remember the day nor the date but I clearly recall that one evening, just about the time for close, just as I was about to shut the door to go home, a man came up very anxious to see in the car and learn all he could about it. I answered many questions — he even took dimensions and inquired the expenses and several other things. One remark he made was why would this not be good for Catholics if it is good for Baptists? He thanked me for my kindness, slipped a bill in the free will offering box and went his way.[1]

As a young priest, Kelley experienced the same kind of epiphany as had Wayland Hoyt, the Baptist minister who traveled the rails in Minnesota and was heartsick to see town after town without churches. Kelley, a Canadian by birth —

his father was a Prince Edward Island sea merchant and his mother was the daughter of an Irishman whose ill health prevented him from entering the priesthood — was trying to raise funds to build a decent church in place of the "dry goods box with a cross on it"[2] of his first parish at Lapeer, Michigan. On a cross-country rail lecture trip in 1893, he was shocked as he saw few cross-topped steeples through the train windows. "Alas! how few there were — not one for every ten towns! There was certainly something wrong. By this time there were tears in my eyes."[3]

The Spanish-American War prevented Kelley from following up quickly on his discovery. He volunteered as a chaplain in the 32d Regiment from Michigan in May 1898,[4] but after the war he returned to the Lapeer parish and his fundraising lecture circuit. One night after his lecture at Argonia, Kansas, he discovered there was no Catholic church in town, in fact not one within twenty miles. On his way to Wichita the next day, Kelley thought, "Why not establish an organization to solicit funds to help build Catholic churches in places like Argonia?" When he talked the matter over with Bishop John J. Hennessey of Wichita, the bishop suggested that Kelley create such an organization that would collect money for needy parishes.[5] He further advised that he use as his guide the idea of church extension society from the

Fig. 12.1 At the dedication of the first Catholic Church Extension Society chapel car, *St. Anthony*, June 16, 1907, dignitaries gather around the car at the Chicago LaSalle Street Station. (Loyola University, Cudahy Library Archives, Chicago)

Methodists and other Protestant denominations.

Kelley gathered data from Protestant sources that indicated, among other things, that the unchurched West had been discovered by the Protestants and was rapidly being filled with churches of several denominations, the most successful of which were the Baptists and the Methodists. According to his findings, religion in the United States gained 582,878 communicants in 1904 with 2,310 churches. Catholics gained 241,955 of these communicants and 226 churches. The Baptists gained 85,040 communicants but built 469 churches. The Methodists gained 69,244 communicants but built 178 churches. What were these groups doing that the Catholics were not?

Of special interest to Kelley was the extension board of the Methodists, which had a standing offer of $250 as a gift to aid the building of a Methodist church in any of the frontier states and territories, the only condition being that each church must cost not less than $1,250 above the value of the lot. In 1904 the Methodist Extension Board aided 388 churches, and up to the close of 1904, it aided 13,914 churches. The fact that it also gave loans to poor churches, held annuity funds, and received from all its funds in 1904 the sum of $429,150.81, plus the $450,000 received by the home mission board annually, amazed and excited Kelley. He was determined to sell the home mission concept to influential archbishops.

His efforts failed until he reached Archbishop James E. Quigley of Chicago. Father Wilfred P. Schoenberg describes the scene in his history of the Catholic church in the Pacific Northwest. "While his Grace smoked peacefully into the twilight of a warm evening, the desperate priest bombarded him with facts and figures of Protestant success, of the crying need for a home mission society, of the plight of priests in the West who had no homes for providing rest after their labors in scattered churchless missions."[6] Kelley's pleas touched Archbishop Quigley's heart, for he too had experienced such a concern as a young priest.

With Archbishop Quigley's support and the backing of other prominent Catholics, the Catholic Church Extension Society was founded October 18, 1905, and Kelley became its first president. Eventually the society moved from the quiet country town of Lapeer to the bustling metropolis of Chicago.

Second in command to Kelley in the young society was Emmanuel B. Ledvina, an Indianapolis priest of Czech descent who, like Kelley, had given up a parish for extension work.[7] His excellent managerial skills and his honesty and steadfastness kept the chapel car program on an even keel when Kelley was not in the office.

Baptist Car Results in *St. Anthony*

During 1907 a young priest named William D. O'Brien was assigned to the society to serve as an acting president. His job was to conduct business while Kelley was on the road asking for funds. One of his first projects was the creation of the Order of Martha, local chapters of women who promoted missions and sewed vestments and altar linens for the chapel cars and mission chapels. Another project was the Child Apostles department, which involved children in the home missions effort.[8] Genial O'Brien, in the mold of Boston Smith, soon discovered the devotion that the little ones could bring to the missions' cause.

Kelley had not forgotten the Baptist chapel car he had seen in 1904. In a 1906 issue of *Extension*, which he created to promote the cause of missions, he described the appeal of the unique gospel car. He explained how its novelty would draw non-Catholics to hear a missionary. Literature could be carried in quantities in the car, which at the same time would be the home of the missionary. He also wrote that the railroads pulled chapel cars free of charge and they cost little to maintain, opinions that he would have cause to retract in the years to come. He concluded by asking, "If the Baptists can do it, why not the Catholics? Who will give us a chapel car to place in the service of the scattered ones of the flock?"[9]

Ambrose Petry Answers the Call

Someone did answer Kelley's call. Ambrose Petry *(fig. 12.3)*, president of the Ambrose Petry Company of New York and Detroit, a streetcar advertising firm, saw the public relations potential for such a car. In 1906 Petry, a Knight Commander of the Order of St. Gregory and a member of the extension society board of managers, moved his operations to Chicago's Rookery Building. The extension society was also housed in the Rookery, due to the kindness of two officials of the Pullman Company.

Petry and Richmond Dean, a vice president of Pullman and also a board member of the extension society, furnished the society's office. Petry had expensive taste,[10] and this look and feel of luxury would pose problems later for Kelley, as many visitors did not think it appropriate for a society for the poor to look so rich.

Pullman was disposing of the old Wagner cars, and Kelley approached Dean about buying one of the older sleepers. Petry offered to contribute two thousand dollars for the

project. Pullman records show that on July 7, 1907, Petry bought Wagner Palace Car Mentone #187, Plan 3049, Lot 1205, built in September of 1886 *(see fig. 12.4)*.[11] Dean, sometimes also described as a Pullman general manager, had the interior of the car reconstructed for chapel car use.[12]

Kelley described Petry as a man who could sell anything, a nervous bundle of enthusiasm. Half French and half German, Petry had no great knowledge of his faith yet an ardent love for it. "He missed Mass only twice in a life that was chiefly spent on trains and in hotels. Once he wired the pastor of a busy parish in Indiana to hold a congregation ten minutes, so that he could get there in time for Mass. Alas, the train was

Fig. 12.3 Ambrose Petry, of the Ambrose Petry Advertising Company of New York, donated *St. Anthony*, and the car was named after Petry's patron saint. (Loyola University, Cudahy Library Archives, Chicago)

later than ten minutes, and Mr. Petry lost Mass that day."[13] The other occasion was when Petry was in a hospital. His favorite devotion was to St. Anthony of Padua; he had a special life of the saint written and published, and he distributed it widely.

According to Kelley, Richmond Dean was a convert to the Catholic church and had never taken any interest in church affairs until he was approached about the chapel car project. Then his enthusiasm was evident. How much Dean paid for the renovation or how much work was done gratis as a result of his influence and position at Pullman is not recorded.

President of the Pullman Company at the time of *St. Anthony's* reconstruction was Robert Todd Lincoln, the only living son of President Abraham Lincoln. A successful corporate attorney, Robert Todd Lincoln first served as legal counsel for Pullman. After George Pullman's death in 1897, he ran the Pullman Company as acting executive and then as president.

In the summer of 1907, when the Wagner car was being transformed into a chapel car, Robert Lincoln was not in the best of moods or health. Beleaguered over the disposition of his father's personal papers, which were then boxed up in his office in the Pullman Building in Chicago, and concerned over the emotional and physical state of his mother,[14] he was becoming less active in the daily affairs of the company. He retired in 1911, although he continued to serve on the board of directors. It is unlikely that he would have paid any attention to this special project of one of his vice presidents.

Named appropriately by Petry in honor of the gentle saint of Padua, also patron saint of lost things, this first Catholic car — *St. Anthony* — was officially blessed June 16, 1907, at the Chicago LaSalle Street Station (*see fig. 12.1*), three days after Kelley was awarded an honorary doctor of laws degree by the University of Notre Dame.[15] Archbishop Quigley hoped to be present for the dedication but was unable to attend. He sent in his place Bishop Peter J. Muldoon.

The Reverend John W. Melody, associate professor of moral theology at the Catholic University of America, gave the address, and said, "The ceremony in which we are participating today marks a new era of missionary effort — not indeed a new era in the nature of this effort, but in the matter of its method. May God's blessing attend it upon its way. May it realize the mission upon which we send it forth. May it ever be the harbinger of grace to those to whom it shall come. May it finally augur propitiously for the new manner of missionary spirit which today it doth usher in."[16]

St. Anthony, seventy feet long with a normal seating capacity of fifty, was capable of holding sixty-five persons. The altar was so constructed that in its many drawers could be stored the sacred vessels and vestments. In the center of the altar was a painting of St. Anthony (*see fig. 12.7*). The candlesticks and an ivory crucifix, carved in the eleventh century and donated by Count Santa Eulalia, the Portuguese consul in Chicago,[17] were held in place by screws. The movable communion railing could be converted into a confessional. Two small rooms for the chaplain and attendants, a kitchen, and a dining room completed the arrangement.

The *New World* newspaper reported, "The car left the LaSalle Street Station at 6:30 Sunday evening [June 16, 1907] for Wichita, Kansas, where it will be at the service of Bishop Hennessey until next December. During this time the Bishop or a missionary priest will tour the branch lines of the railroads running through Kansas, stopping at towns where there are no Catholic Churches to administer the sacraments and bring the consolation of religion to the isolated members of the Faith."[18] The Soo Line was the first railroad to offer free transportation.

St. Anthony Heads to Kansas Mission

Especially adapted to the western and southern sections of the country, where Catholics were few and where small congregations could be housed during services, *St. Anthony* served in Kansas and South Dakota from 1907 to 1909. On board and in charge was layman George Hennessey, a jovial, red-headed Canadian Irishman who was a first cousin of Father Kelley. As superintendent of the cars, he received the "princely sum of $100 a month and his room and board."[19]

According to Kelley, Hennessey was gifted for chapel car work. He had been an altar boy when he was young, knew the ceremonies and everything that goes with their proper movement, had a beautiful tenor voice, could play the organ, and was the friend of "every unreconstructed backslider who comes along. . . . He does not preach, for that is the province of the Chaplain, but he talks to everybody without preaching, and somehow — God knows how — the talk is as good as a sermon for one man or woman." And the children loved him.[20]

After stopping at Kansas City and at St. Louis on June 17 and 18, where crowds visited the car, *St. Anthony* left on the Frisco and Missouri Pacific Railroad[21] for Wichita, where, because of the rush to have the car dedicated, certain adjustments had to be made: movable articles on the altar screwed down, screen doors, an electric light plant, and ventilation installed, and the apartment put into first-class order.[22]

The car arrived at its first mission at Wellington, Kansas, where the bishop said a low Mass in private for the donor of the car. According to George Hennessey, this was the first Mass offered in the car. Then Father T. A. McKernan, rightly called the first chaplain of the Catholic chapel cars, although Bishop Hennessey had the honorary title, celebrated Mass for the throng that filled the car. In the afternoon two children were presented by their parents for baptism; one of them was named Anthony in honor of the car's patron saint.[23]

At Castleton, Kansas, came the first results of a *St. Anthony* visit, when 3,100 dollars were subscribed for the building of a church, with a non-Catholic making the first subscription of 19 dollars and other non-Catholics adding 500 dollars toward the total amount. The next stop was Liberal, where another church was in the planning.[24]

A freight train pulled into the siding at Larned while the *St. Anthony's* black porter, Horace, was sweeping the platform. The fireman called out, "Hello, there, what you got there?"

"Church," replied Horace.

"Say what you givin' us?"

"It's a fact, complete Catholic Church."

"Well, say, don't that beat the limit!" was the exclamation of the fireman as *St. Anthony* pulled away.[25]

Opponents Attack Chapel Car Concept

As was true with the Episcopalians and Baptists, there were those in the Catholic church who did not agree that the chapel cars were a great idea. As early as fall 1907, opponents of the chapel car were heard and quickly rebutted by Bishop Hennessey in *Extension*.

Some crooked minded Judases raise their hands in hypocritical amazement and exclaim, "To what purpose is this waste?" Could not that Chapel Car be sold and the money given to poor churches? Why is the Chapel Car criticized and a handsome, costly parish church not? What is the difference in the object of both? Both have the same use — a suitable place to administer the Sacraments and in which to offer the Most Holy sacrifice of Mass. But a Chapel Car has the advantage of the parish church in that it can be brought into places where there are no churches, and the few that are found in these places are given every convenience that would have if they possessed a church. If a Chapel Car can be substituted for an empty grocery store, an Odd Fellow's hall, or a vacant woodshed, for the sacrifice of Mass, where is the objection?

The car itself is a teacher and a suggester by its neatness and the costliness of its appointments. In the experience which six weeks use of the Chapel Car in the diocese of Wichita has given, we include the education of young persons especially who never saw a church, and have been accustomed to hear Mass now and then in a farm house with a grunting pig doing duty for a choir. They see a neat holy water font at the door — they do not know its use! They see a beautiful altar, bright candlesticks bigger than they ever saw before, beautiful vestments of gold, not the conventional hand-me-downs which are found in the traveling bags of most missionaries, beautiful gold chalices and ciboriums — everything handsome, precious and suggestive of Him for whom they do honor.[26]

Bishop Hennessey was not done with his counterattack. "Our critics might say that all this could be done and is done by ordinary missionaries everywhere without a chapel car. Perhaps it could if conditions were favorable, if a suitable hall could be rented, and an organ provided, and an organ player imported, and a convenient dry goods box could be borrowed for an altar, and a codfish box for a credence table, and a couple of empty beer or catsup bottles for candlesticks, but we believe those who are listening to us will still be persuaded that the Chapel Car is away ahead in every respect, and that it is worth all the money that was paid for it."

Perhaps the most adamant foe of the chapel cars and the extension society was Archbishop Diomede Falconio, O.F.M., the apostolic delegate. Falconio had welcomed the society when it was established but reversed his position when it began operating chapel cars. He had been a Franciscan missionary in Newfoundland and had ideas about the way missionary work should be done. They did not include what he considered luxurious travel for missionaries; and a chapel car, he was sure, meant luxurious travel. "When I was a missionary," he snapped, "I went out with my pack on my back, slept in huts, and ate salt herring and dried cod. This Dr. Kelley wants to send missionaries out in a private Pullman with parlor, bedroom, and bath."

What His Excellency forgot, according to Kelley, was that a chapel car, unlike the lone missionary "with a pack on his back," could stay for weeks and months. It could also carry a temporary pastor fully equipped with his books and all the literature he needed for distribution during a course of lectures that the old-style missionary could not stay long enough to give. "He forgot likewise that the first chapel car — like its successors — cost us nothing, not even railroad fares; that the railroads welcomed it, especially on the new branch lines they

were building and along which churchless towns and settlements were springing up. We had no thought of denying credit to the old missionary. Chapel cars could never replace him."[27]

James P. Gaffey, in *Francis Clement Kelley and the American Catholic Dream*, tells of the elevated war of wills between Falconio and Kelley.

At one point, when Kelley had heard of the vocal attacks of Archbishop Falconio on the extension society and the chapel cars, he determined to go to Washington and clear the air in person. Prepared to find Falconio mildly unsympathetic to extension, he encountered an angry churchman. Given no opportunity to defend the society, Kelley was battered by a torrent of misinformation — mainly obtained from Archbishop John Farley, who was opposed to bringing extension into New York City.

Upon returning to Chicago, Kelley related his experience to his confidant, champion, and superior, Archbishop Quigley, who calmed him and advised him to reserve his defense for the appropriate moment. In 1910 Falconio again attacked not only the society and the chapel cars but also the character and ability of Kelley. Quigley responded by having the society board pass a series of resolutions expressing confidence in Kelley, the chapel car program, and the veracity of the report of chapels that were built by the chapel car work. An angry Archbishop Quigley challenged Falconio and declared, "This nagging at the President has to stop. . . . If this thing continues, we are going to fight. The Bishops of the West have some rights."[28]

Although by its success the extension society weathered much of its earlier opposition and obtained the position of a pontifical institute with its own clear channel to the Holy See, it still had its protesters in the East. In spite of the protected status of the society, Archbishop Falconio continued his attack on the chapel cars. When Archbishop Alexander Christie of Portland, Oregon, lauded the program, Falconio retorted, "Does the Archbishop think I am a child? I do not approve of the Chapel Car. I condemn it." Falconio was not content with carrying his grudge to other archbishops; he took his acrimony to the White House and managed to denounce the chapel car program during a public event where President William Howard Taft was to appear.[29]

Oblivious to the clouds on the future of the chapel cars, the *St. Anthony* crew on the Kansas mission was still early in the journey. At Bucklin on July 1, 1907, they found only two or three families, and those families were moving to Pratt, which was growing to be a large town on account of the change of the Rock Island division. Most of the railroad men were Catholic, and so with the planned increase, a larger church was going to be started at Pratt after the harvest.

St. Anthony would not be the only and last chapel car the people at Galena would see, as *Evangel*, with the Reverend and Mrs. John Thomas on board, would arrive in town for a stay the following spring. For a few years *St. Anthony* and several of the Baptist cars would share the Kansas rails, frequently visiting the same towns.

Later in the month at Chautauqua, George Hennessey and Father McKernan were surprised to find a number of Indians with Irish names, "all intelligent Catholic people."[30] That was not their only surprise. During the stay in Chautauqua, a group known as Fire Brand Baptists kept everyone awake with their groaning, praying, exhorting, and singing, which continued from dark to dawn. The *Michigan Catholic*, which kept track of the chapel car probably because of the extension beginnings in that state, reported, "The car has had strange company in its wanderings; among others, a traveling minstrel company from Wichita to Augusta, the John Robinson shows to Cherryvale and to Coffeyville, and in Chautauqua the Fire Brand Baptists."[31]

At Hanston the car was sided in company with a car of coal. Hennessey commented, "The farmer who owned the coal evidently considered the temporal comfort piled in the coal car superior to the eternal spiritual consolation typified by the Chapel Car, for he went at it with such a vim the following morning that Father Hull was obliged to expend much lung and pedal power at the organ to overcome this

din. . . . The population of Hanston is thoroughly Catholic, staunchly Teutonic, thrifty but solidly prudent in matters of progress."[32]

Hennessey especially enjoyed the times when train passengers would visit the chapel car. "As usual on the night trains, passengers from the cars ahead paid cosmopolitan respects to *St. Anthony* en route. On these occasions, Father McKernan often discovers one in whose bosom faith has grown cold, but the sight of the altar, the statue of St. Anthony, etc., revives the smoldering embers and the individual will linger over his adieus long enough to remark, 'Father, this visit has been more than an incident of travel. It has been years since I approached the sacraments, but I intend to do better henceforth.'"[33]

When the car arrived at Dodge City, the running gear was tested as usual by men assigned to that duty, and they discovered one of the brake rods all but falling; the bolt was secured by the final thread only. The discovery no doubt prevented a

Fig. 12.4 While on tour, *St. Anthony*, with the Reverend Tilesphore Plante, Father John J. O'Neill, and Father P. Monaghan, stopped in the Sioux Falls diocese at Sioux City, Iowa. (Sioux City Public Museum, Sioux City, Iowa)

serious mishap. Hennessey reported that that was the second time such an accident had been narrowly averted.[34]

While *St. Anthony* labored in Kansas, the National Eucharistic Congress was held at Pittsburgh, Pennsylvania, starting October 16, 1907, with church dignitaries from all parts of the country present. The cooler weather of harvest time brought relief to Chaplain McKernan. "With the coming of frost, life has become more bearable than it was during the warmer season, when the temperature in the chapel remained about 100 degrees, soaring sometimes to 106 degrees. Whenever we had Vespers in the various places, the car was crowded to the limit, and this together with the heat of the lamps and candles and a weighty cope made it rather uncomfortable for the priest in charge."

But McKernan said that *St. Anthony's* comfort level was high with the railroads. They were treated with courtesy and consideration everywhere, "in fact, railway men take a particular interest in the car because of its character as a chapel on tracks. . . ." The question of provisions was also satisfactorily solved by the contributions made to the larder whenever they had occasion to stop. The car was iced and watered while in transit with the same care and attention as were the cars in commission on the regular trains.[35]

Upon ending his term on the chapel car, McKernan said that more than four or five thousand people to date had visited the car, and many were travelers and tourists, belonging to different sects and representing nearly every avocation in life. "It was interesting to observe the effect of the chapel car on such visitors as were not of the Faith. The impression made will last; they departed with new ideas regarding the true character of the church, thus fostering respect for her ministers and children."[36]

Chaplain T. E. O'Sullivan, on board in 1908, described his reaction to western Kansas as they traveled from the chapel car to an outpost of Catholic farmers via a farm wagon.

As our party proceeded across the plains, at times the only moving thing in sight, the mirage unfolded its deceptive splendors before the eye. To a certain extent it seemed to typify the splendid hopes which had animated the hearts of the settlers when they came to this part of the West to build a home and provide for their families. It seemed to taunt the settlers — this image of water, — all that Western Kansas needs to make it "blossom as the rose." It is a monotonous country, beautiful in its lonesomeness and sense of immensity. The journey done — a short rest, and dinner was served at a farmhouse. These people are not in need of the necessities of life. They live well, but they lack the conveniences and the encouragement which come with prosperous times. The kitchen was of sod, and but few substantial improvements were upon the place. . . . The church, out by itself upon the prairie, lifted its wooden spire into the sky, a landmark for miles. The Sacrament of Confirmation was administered, words of advice and encouragement were spoken; and then almost at sunset, the party turned back over their long road to where the chapel car awaited them.[37]

Fig. 12.6 Hundreds lined up to tour *St. Anthony* when it visited Philadelphia and was sided at 32nd and Market Street Pennsylvania Railroad yard, October 26, 1908. (Loyola University, Cudahy Library Archives, Chicago)

Sioux Falls Offers Ecumenical Variety

After more than a year in Kansas, the car left Chicago on February 20 for the Sioux Falls, South Dakota, diocese, beginning at Beresford, February 28, 1908. On St. Patrick's Day, Hennessey wrote from Lake Preston that there was no porter on board, so he had to make the beds himself. He and Father Plante said Mass and went out to look up Catholics and to obtain a choir. "A quiet St. Patrick's day for a French man and an Irish man,"[38] but the meetings there were a success — they heard thirty-four confessions, and some of those were fifteen years away from the sacraments. The evening lectures were held in the Grand Army of the Republic hall, and 250 people attended. They were urged to stay another week, even by the non-Catholics.

The Reverend J. J. O'Neill and Father Monaghan were also on board throughout much of the mission. In Vienna, South Dakota, O'Neill reported that three hundred attended the meeting in the Grand Army of the Republic hall. They converted three, straightened four marriages, baptized five children, and heard ninety confessions. The local group of

Catholics would begin a parish, having Mass in the hall.[39] Many churches were started this way by the chapel cars.

The situation was not quite as successful in Northwestern, South Dakota, where a dispirited O'Neill wrote: "The 'non-Catholics gave us the cold shoulder and a delegation of twelve ministers who were attending a prohibition convention nearby came to the car,' but in Mobridge down the line, in a more victorious report, forty confessioners, mostly railroad men, had the opportunity to go to the Sacraments for the first time since they came to this country eighteen months ago."[40]

O'Neill described how they made their services as attractive as possible. ". . . we always call upon local musical talent. Some towns have much; others less; others again, none at all. At times the Methodist choir volunteers to sing hymns such as 'Nearer, My God, to Thee,' and 'Lead, Kindly Light.' Should there happen to be a Catholic teacher in the place, she generally brings several of the school children, Catholic and non-Catholic and has them sing more or less religious songs from the school song-book . . . when no singer is to be found, the chaplain, having no confidence in the musical power of his vocal chords, contents himself with playing the organ."[41]

Not all towns were alike, as O'Neill pointed out:

Ministers in some towns, honor us with a visit, while in others they never come near us. . . . At certain towns we have been invited to the minister's house, and, upon going, have been received in a very friendly and cordial manner.

Our Catholic people all approach the Sacraments, that is, all who can, for in some towns we find that the lodges have captured some of our people. Business reasons are what they give you, when asked the reason why. It is extremely difficult to get them to withdraw

altogether. They will come to Mass, send us coal, get us provisions, bring their non-Catholic friends to the car or hall, but will hardly step out of their lodge. They seem to leave that to the future.

As regards financing the car, we have little or no difficulty. Our good people will not let us starve. Every morning, they bring bread, butter, eggs, chickens, etc. and tell us to be sure to let them know should we be short in anything. Then, before we leave, they always take up a collection among themselves and present us with a few dollars.

Fig. 12.7 The altar in *St. Anthony* was much admired and appreciated by the thousands who visited the car but seldom if ever received the sacraments or attended Mass in the beauty of an appropriate worship setting. (Loyola University, Cudahy Library Archives, Chicago)

During Easter week, while the priests on the car were busy attending to parochial duties, the car was given a thorough spring cleaning at the shops of the Chicago & North Western Railroad, under the charge of Mr. Moulton, the local superintendent.

The non-Catholics at Eureka the first week of June 1908 were all Lutherans who took a great interest in the chapel car, and the question box was popular with them. The priests gave away many copies of "Faith of Our Fathers," written by James Cardinal Gibbons. Missions were given at Canistotal, Preston, and other villages until the car headed back to Chicago; then it went to Indianapolis, where it was on display during the convention of the Ancient Order of Hibernians. From Indianapolis it went to Boston for the American Federation of Societies. It was estimated by the Boston press that twenty-five thousand people visited the car on August 15 and 16. *St. Anthony* returned via Albany, Syracuse, Utica, Rochester, Buffalo, Erie, Cleveland, Toledo, and South Bend, and crowds came everywhere.[42]

Father William D. O'Brien, the acting president of the society, who would become a bishop and an archbishop, served as chaplain on occasion on several of the chapel cars. He explained the method used by *St. Anthony*. "Usually the nearest pastor where we were to stop was on hand to greet us when we rode into a little town, and he had already advised his people of our coming. Besides that, a notice was put up in the railroad station and in the local post office, saying that the *St. Anthony* Car accompanied by a chaplain would be at the home track for a few days and evenings, or a whole week, and everybody was invited to attend. The car was always crowded with good people."[43]

While the car was in Rochester, a doubting Thomas came to the car. O'Brien, who was known for his quick wit, described what happened.

He had been all through the car that morning, but discussing the church on wheels with one of his cronies, he returned in the afternoon to tell us he had come to the conclusion that the car was not just right, inasmuch as we did not have the approval of the Pope. Handing him the Extension Magazine of August, 1907, containing the letter of our Holy Father, approving and blessing Church Extension, we asked him what he thought of it, and glancing hurriedly over it, he remarked: "Well, this is all print and I think this car is only a fake."

The words hadn't left his mouth before the heavy brass lamp in the vestibule of the car fell with crushing force on his unprotected head. "My God," he exclaimed, "I'm cut, I'm killed," and catching him in my arms I beheld a bleeding wound fully an inch long on his head. I told him he had better hurry away to the doctor and the poor old fellow could not get away fast enough to have the wound attended to, and no doubt, offered up a little prayer in reparation for doubting good *St. Anthony*.[44]

In Erie, Pennsylvania, the crowd was so enormous that they had to close the car until the police arrived to help in handling the people. At Cleveland, O'Brien complained that the Union Station was one of the dirtiest and most miserable of all depots in the States, and the Lake Shore Railroad officials shunted the car away down in the freight yards where the people could not find it, although they had been very courteous in other places. At Sandusky every priest in the city came to see the car.[45]

Mississippi Mission Follows Eastern Tours

After a short Wisconsin tour, in October 1908 *St. Anthony* headed back east, stopping at Ft. Wayne, Cincinnati, Dayton, Columbus, Wheeling, Pittsburgh, Altoona, Harrisburg, Philadelphia, Trenton, Wilmington, Baltimore, Washington, Richmond, Louisville, and Lafayette. It then went back to Chicago for the first American Catholic Missionary Congress, exhibiting during the day and traveling by night. In Cincinnati the crowd was so large that the station master closed the gates, and he refused to reopen them on his own authority. The chaplain then assumed charge and, standing upon the fence, prevented crowding and controlled people in their eagerness to see *St. Anthony*.[46]

By January 16, 1909, the chapel car had gone back to work in the South — first to New Orleans, accompanied by the Reverend Alex P. Landry, field secretary of the extension society, where in three days of exhibition more than fifty-five hundred persons saw the car and marveled at its compactness, its chapel, living quarters for the crew, the kitchenette, library, and other facilities.[47]

Then the car traveled to Mississippi, over the Yazoo and Mississippi Valley Railroad to Clarksdale, and the first stop, with the Reverend Walter Polk, C.SS.R., a native Orleanian, on board. Polk was one of the many members of The Congregation of the Most Holy Redeemer, better known as Redemptorists, who served on the chapel cars. The purpose of the order is the sanctification of its members through the imitation of Jesus Christ and the preaching of the Word of God, especially to the poor, particularly through parish missions.

The population of the town was about fifteen hundred. George Hennessey reported, "When you ask the population of a town in this State or any of the southern states, the colored inhabitants are never included in the answer, regardless of the fact that they usually out-number, two to one, the white dwellers."[48]

St. Anthony crossed into Louisiana under the enthusiastic support of Archbishop James Hubert Blenk, S.M., with the

Reverend John Handley, and worked at the newly established lumber town of Bogalusa, and Franklinton, the county seat, on the New Orleans and Great Northern line. It then went back to Gloster, Woodville, and Redding, Mississippi.

The question box was always popular with visitors to the car, and in Gloster, where the Presbyterian and Baptist ministers tried to discourage their members from attending the public lectures, one gentleman put the question, "Who did Cain marry?" in the box. The next day he surprised his friends by announcing that he would not attend the lecture that night. "Why?" he was asked. "Are you not going to hear the answer to that question?" "Oh, I know the answer," he replied. "I just want to see if the priest knows it."

At Gloster, as in many of the other towns, people had some strange ideas about the priests. During one of Polk's lectures, a man whispered to his neighbor, "Say, do you see him touching that little black thing on the table there? I wonder what that is?" To which the neighbor replied, "Why, you fool, that's his watch!"[49]

Red Lick, Mississippi, on the Yazoo and Mississippi Valley Railroad, was a primitive settlement — two stores, three dwellings, and a railway station. Some thirty Catholics in the vicinity, mostly children of old soldiers who were con-verted by example of the sisters of the Southern battlefields, were devout but desperately poor. At Red Lick, Father John Handley baptized Catherine, daughter of James F. McCaleb and Undine Florence Byrnes, born at Cold Springs Plantation, Claeborne County, Mississippi, January 8, 1908. The godfather was William Howard McCaleb; the god-mother, Marie Idalie McCaleb. Records of baptisms were almost daily occurrences during chapel car missions. Because of the chapel car visit, a church was built in Red Lick.[50]

At Water Valley, Mississippi, on the Illinois Central, attendance was poor due to the earnest warnings against the church in the local Methodist conference, counter meetings each night, and the personal efforts of town clergy against the mission.

Due to the heat in the South, *St. Anthony* traveled in the Midwest and East for public appearances and exhibitions in the summer of 1909, leaving Chicago on July 2, visiting Clinton, Des Moines, and Council Bluffs, Iowa; Lincoln, Nebraska; Denver, Colorado; Cheyenne, Wyoming; and Salt Lake and Ogden, Utah.

St. Anthony, described as the "magnificent car, which is as complete in every detail as any Catholic church," and pro-claimed in *The Catholic Messenger* as being the only Catholic

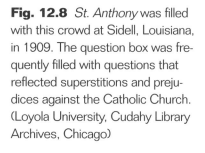

Fig. 12.8 *St. Anthony* was filled with this crowd at Sidell, Louisiana, in 1909. The question box was frequently filled with questions that reflected superstitions and prejudices against the Catholic Church. (Loyola University, Cudahy Library Archives, Chicago)

mission car in the world, arrived in Des Moines for the Fourth of July, 1909, from Clinton, and the next stop was Council Bluffs.[51] At Denver, on July 10, the car was side-tracked near Union Station. According to the *Denver Catholic Register*, it was on its way to the Alaska-Yukon-Pacific Exposition, where it would be placed on a track inside the fairgrounds.[52]

O'Brien and Doran Suffer Bugs, "Fools"

The first mission of the chapel car after it reached the Northwest was at Oxford, Idaho, July 17, 1909, with Father Alvah Doran, a former Episcopal minister, and the Reverend A. P. Doyle, a Paulist known for his preaching, in charge. In Oxford there was not one Catholic in the Mormon town, but on Sunday, July 18, Michael Casey, a foreman of the section gang at Swan Lake, was present at Mass. Doran and Doyle hopped on a handcar with Casey and went up the track to Swan Lake to "look up some stray sheep." On their way back, four sturdy Japanese pumped the handcar.

Summer missions were rare because of the tremendous heat in the chapel cars. O'Brien also described another problem summer brought: ". . . cockroaches, swarms of bedbugs and hungry mosquitoes made it impossible for us to live in the car in summer. Well do I remember a maintenance man using a blow torch to burn up the bedbugs around our berths and in the kitchen. Brunettes such as Fathers Fleming and Doran didn't suffer so much, but tenderskins like George and myself were simply eaten alive! The result was that we devised the idea of exhibiting the Chapel Cars to Catholic people throughout the settled parts of the country, especially in the larger cities."[53]

After the exhibition tour, *St. Anthony* stopped in many towns along the Idaho section of the route to Oregon. O'Brien explained, "In every town that the Chapel Car worked we always had more non-Catholics than our own, for the simple reason that our own were always in the minority. Some of these good people came to see if the lies told about the priests and the Church were true. Most of them were anxious to learn about the Church, and all of them, especially the Mormons in southern Idaho, were most neighborly."

Every morning Mass was said at 8:00 and a little talk given to the people who attended. Every evening at 7:30 the services would consist of fifteen minutes of the question box, followed by five decades of the rosary, and Benediction of the Blessed Sacrament. In *St. Anthony* there was no confessional, and the priest heard confessions just behind the altar. After services, the chaplains had the opportunity to talk with many of those who visited the car. "Volumes could be written on the life stories told by many of our own people to the chaplain, many of whom had not had the services of a priest for many years, not because they did not go to Church, but simply because there were no churches for them in or near the places where they lived,"[54] O'Brien wrote in his story of chapel car work.

A small circus was in town at McCammon, Idaho, and the circus cars on the same Oregon Short Line track as *St. Anthony*, contained animals, including an elephant and pinto horses. A Mormon visitor to the chapel car wanted to know if the circus was part of the chapel car show. Doran told the man no, they had attractions enough without the animals. In McCammon, *St. Anthony* followed the Baptist car *Emmanuel*, which had been there a few months earlier.

Doran did not suffer those he considered prejudiced "fools" gladly. Sometimes in his reports to the extension society, he displayed quite a degree of intolerance himself, whether the bias was directed toward Methodists, Baptists, Mormons, or people like those in the town of St. Anthony. "The honor of our patron Saint constrained us to preach his religion to a community largely as ignorant of it as they were to how there [sic] town got so good a name."[55]

But his devotion was marked by passion if not compassion. At American Falls, Idaho, Doran confessed that the main reason he had asked to be the chaplain on the Idaho mission was the chance to see his brother, not yet a convert, and his parents, recent converts, who were visiting his brother. A highlight of the American Falls mission was that thirty persons received the sacraments, and among them were the "dear father and mother" of Doran.

From American Falls the chapel car went on to Gooding on the Union Pacific, a town only a year and one-half old — 125 houses and 115 tents and no hall adapted for lectures, so the meetings were in the car, where a switch engine moved the congregation and the missionary during one evening sermon. At Gooding they hoped to see the Baptist chapel car *Emmanuel* and missionary E. R. Hermiston.

> We expected *St. Anthony* Chapel Car to have its first glimpse of a similar piece of rolling stock at Gooding but it was not to be. The Baptist Chapel *Emmanuel* (No. 2.) (they have seven in operation all told) had been there several months but moved on, strange coincidence! a few days before we arrived. As it was only twenty-five miles away at Jerome on the Idaho Southern railroad, Mr. Hennessey and I made the trip on Tuesday and visualized what we had so often heard about. After meeting the Catholics of Jerome we strolled down to the last rail laid on the Idaho Southern, found Mr. Hermiston, whose wife and daughter compose the crew of "Emmanuel", and had a pleasant hour swapping experiences with him. He assured us that the reports we had heard of his attacking the Catholic Church in his sermons was not true and agreed with our suggestion that it was better to live in peace and harmony than to abuse one another.[56]

The Catholic presence had been felt in Montana, Idaho, and Oregon as early as 1742, when a Canadian Jesuit, Father Claude Coquard, was assigned to visit trading posts of the West in the voyage of Pierre and Francois Chevalier La Verendrye, but his presence was not felt for long as he quickly left the party. Three decades later Spanish explorers continued the presence, and then the voyageurs, the boatmen, who transported the furs for the Canadian Fur Companies — the Hudson's Bay and Northwest and the American John Jacob Astor's Pacific Fur Company — continued spreading the faith among the Indians. In 1838 two Canadian priests became the first resident missionaries in Oregon: Francis Norbert Blanchet and Modeste Demers, followed by the revered Father Peter DeSmet in October 1858.[57]

McDonald, Polk Visit Oregon Towns

St. Anthony's presence in western Oregon in 1909 was mainly at the insistence of Archbishop Alexander Christie and Father H. J. McDevitt. McDevitt, formerly a vice president of the Catholic University of America, chose to return to mission work and was placed in the diocese of Baker City, Oregon, with responsibilities for mission stations. He built the first church in the town of Burns, and while doing so, he lost the sight of his right eye in helping to mix the mortar for the building. Many times he served on *St. Anthony* and later on *St. Peter*.[58]

The first mission held in the Archdiocese of Portland was at Rainier, commencing October 3, 1909, with Father E. K. Cantwell, C.SS.R., in charge. According to the accounts of the Reverend Francis P. Leipzig, the third bishop of Baker and author of *Extension in Oregon*, the first child to receive communion at Rainier would become a missionary priest — Father Ambrose Gallagher, a Columban Father of Massachusetts.[59]

At Sheridan, on the Southern Pacific line, October 17, the public lectures were given in the Woodman's Hall. His Grace the archbishop gave a lecture on "The Church and the Sacraments." After the lecture on the Bible, a non-Catholic who had been present said to one of his neighbors, "I am glad I heard that lecture for I heard something new about the Bible. I always thought that when Christ came down from Heaven that he brought the Bible with him." Father D. McDonald, C.SS.R., was the missionary on board and reported, "This is typical of the religious ignorance that prevails in many places in the West."[60] Extension granted a thousand-dollar gift to build the Good Shepherd Church after McDevitt conducted the mission there.[61]

Father Walter L. Polk was one of many who served on the chapel cars from the Redemptorists. One pleasant duty Father

Polk had at Falls City was to baptize a girl who had been born in "a real modern flat not of stone or pressed brick but of canvas 8 x 16 erected in a most poetic spot overlooking the picturesque Falls and rapids. Her home has all the modern conveniences, telephone electric light and water. When I called later I found her in a novel cradle — a new wash-basket — yet she seemed most happy and more contented than most babies of the same age, for during my visit she was most pleasant and continually smiled at me."[62]

One of the most unusual places visited by *St. Anthony* in Oregon was at Blackrock, a logging camp in the heart of one of the densest fir forests in the Willamette Valley. A special engine was sent by Mr. Gerlinger, the general manager of the Salem Falls City & Western Railroad, to bring the chapel car into the camp. "One hour after we found ourselves in the most desolate and God-forsaken spot we had yet visited. There were some two hundred huts spread out on the sides of the mountain. Trails from one house to the other were the only thoroughfare in the place, the railroad track serving as the main street of the camp."

Hennessey took *St. Anthony* to the Southern Pacific shops at Yoncalla to have the heating apparatus and the roof repaired over the Christmas holidays. McDonald, who had not been well, went to spend some time at home in Seattle at the Redemptorist house, and Hennessey was invited to stay with the Redemptorists in Portland. The new year opened with a stop at Oakland, where the local Baptist minister became so angry at his members because they came to the chapel car instead of their own church for midweek services that he left town the following day, and the Baptists were obliged to take up a subscription to pay his way to Portland.[63]

At Grants Pass, Oregon, where a few years earlier the area had been flooded by gold speculation, the local paper announced the chapel car's arrival on February 19 and mentioned that the week-long mission was offered to all without any discrimination of religious denominations.[64] *St. Anthony*'s priests had sixty confessions but found the Protestants of the town unfriendly and the few Catholics in town unhappy.

Supposedly the businessmen would not give employment to Catholics. The ex-mayor said publicly while he was still mayor that he would rid the town of Catholics. After the car left the place, he again said publicly that if he had been mayor the car would never have come to Grants Pass. In spite of the opposition, meetings were well attended,[65] with Hennessey and his rich tenor voice entertaining at the organ. But at Cottage Grove they found more opposition and prejudice waiting for them.

McDonald had worked hard during his tenure on the car, and he loved his work. Hennessey described how McDonald loved to preach. "And how the people loved him, Catholic and non-Catholic alike! The little children would run to him, won by his childlike simplicity and humble manner." Just before Easter 1910, McDonald left the car and returned to his home in the Canadian Northwest, where he died.[66]

When O'Brien made a visit to *St. Anthony* in 1910 and opened his first mission at Lyons July 10, the great majority of his overflow audience were non-Catholics, as there were only twenty-five Catholics living in town.

In Dallas, Oregon, with a population of about two thousand, there were about twenty-five Catholics in town. McDonald discovered that in this town, as in many others, the non-Catholics had strange ideas about the Catholic church. "Some of them think that if the Catholic Church becomes powerful enough, she will put to death all those who are not Catholics. They are strongly convinced that Catholics are obliged to pay to have their sins forgiven. They believe that Catholics may commit all the crimes they wish, and that the Priests are always ready to forgive them provided they have the money to pay for the Absolution."[67] A non-Catholic woman told him that she was surprised when he spoke to her, for she said that one of her neighbors told her that priests never speak to Protestants.

In Junction City, Oregon, July 26, *St. Anthony* was almost consumed by a fire that destroyed a neighboring warehouse. O'Brien, who was serving as chaplain on the car, reported, "It was with great difficulty that we had the car removed from its siding and only then in time to save it. As it was, the car bears several large blisters as a souvenir of its remarkable preservation."[68]

St. Anthony Called to Tour in East

From Harrisburg later in the summer, O'Brien was called back to Chicago for an assignment in Montreal. In September at the Eucharistic Congress in Montreal, when His Eminence the Cardinal Legate Vincenso Vanutelli visited the chapel car, he was met at the door by Archbishop Christie of the Oregon Archdiocese, who told him of the work the chapel car had done in Oregon. "This car has been the providential means of starting five churches which have been built and opened for Divine Services during the past eleven months. Five more are now under construction. There have been thirty-five missions given from the car. In fifteen of these thirty-five places there never was a Catholic service until the car came and went into towns comprising six hundred to one thousand people."[69]

Archbishop Christie further praised the work of the chapel car.

Persons who have never done pioneer missionary work have absolutely no conception of what it means to go to a town where there is no church and there, against great odds, make a start — say Mass in places which are unsuitable and board and lodge in quarters that are at times, to put it mildly, simply miserable. In marked contrast to all of this is the chapel car, where everything is decently and even beautifully arranged for the worthy oblation of the Most Holy Sacrifice of the Mass and for the administration of the Sacraments.

How anyone who has an honest desire to see the light of our glorious Faith spread amongst the people in lonely places can find any valid objection to the chapel car is entirely beyond my comprehension. I have seen for myself what the Chapel Car is doing and I am unalterably convinced that it is the most effective means yet devised for bringing the blessings of our Holy Religion to places where there are no churches.[70]

From Chicago the car went on the Grand Trunk Railroad to the Eucharistic Congress in Montreal, where more than forty thousand people toured the car. After the congress, *St. Anthony* visited St. John and Moncton, New Brunswick; Sydney, Glace Bay, Antigonish, and Halifax, Nova Scotia; and Ottawa, Peterboro, Toronto, and London, Ontario, all along the Canadian Pacific line. The chapel car visited South Bend, Indiana, where the *South Bend Tribune* inaccurately reported that the car was "the only house of worship of its kind in the United States." The Baptists were operating six cars at the time, one of them, *Herald of Hope*, as close as Grape Creek, Illinois.[71]

Back to Oregon and Baker City Diocese

After repairs in the Pullman shops at Chicago, *St. Anthony* returned to eastern Oregon late in 1910. On board were Father Kelley, Father Austin Fleming, chaplain, and George Hennessey. Along the way, exhibition stops were at Salt Lake City, Utah, and Oakland, Berkeley, San Francisco, San Jose, and Sacramento, California. After a brief visit at Baker City with Bishop O'Reilly, Kelley returned to Chicago.

Baker City was the supply center for all the mines in eastern Oregon and part of Idaho. Miners, promoters, gamblers, drummers, saloon keepers, Chinese, peace officers, army people, preachers, circuit judges, and scarlet women rushed to Baker City in the early days of the gold rush, and the transcontinental railroad came in 1884. By 1900, ten thousand people were living in Baker City,[72] and the growth had spread to surrounding towns in the diocese.

The Baker City diocese mission began at Ontario, where the superintendent of schools invited the students of the higher grades to listen to a sermon by Father Fleming on "Respect for Authority." The result of the Ontario mission was the completion of a church, which had been long in the building.

In Ontario, a town along the Snake River, the parish priest, Father Raymond Jarboe, explained in 1996 that one of the reasons he hosts an annual open house at the rectory is that non-Catholics used to have wild ideas about what went on in the rectory. This openness is especially important in Oregon, where 60 percent of the population shuns membership in any church and where some anti-Catholic sentiment still exists.[73]

The chapel car workers took collections at each stop, and expenses were carefully kept. These included the salary for a porter, who did the cooking and housecleaning on the car. Porters usually were changed frequently according to dioceses or local arrangements.

> The financial report for December 1910:
> Balance on hand 218.15
> Collection at Ontario 11.25
> Collection at Vale 25.50
> Collection at Brogan 27.00
> Collection at Huntington 7.80
> Collection at Baker City 15.00
> Check from office for expenses . . . .50.00 . . . 354.70
> Expenses:
> Porter for supplies 54.35
> Stamps 1.00
> Telegram to office 75
> Paid chaplain's salary 50.00
> Coal and wood 12.00
> Paid porter's salary to Jan 18 . . . . . .50.00 . . . 168.10
> Balance on hand 186.60

In addition, Hennessey had collected five subscriptions for *Extension* at one dollar a subscription.

In a memo attached to the report, Hennessey told O'Brien, acting general secretary of the society, "It has been very cold for the last couple of weeks and we were obliged to buy coal and wood. It is very hard to get hard coal here and when we can get it we have to pay One Dollar per sack. The heater we have in the car will burn hard coal only."[74]

The stop at Huntington, the terminal for the Oregon Railway Navigation Company of Portland and for the Oregon Short Line to Pocatello, Idaho, was brief, as it was planned to have the chapel car at Baker City for Christmas. Besides, Fleming was not happy with the reception. "The Catholics, mostly Railway employees in this Junction Town are a careless and indifferent crowd. There is a Church but the people do not seem to appreciate the blessing. When I return I intend to let forth a storm of spiritual thunder and lightning, for the softer melodies of Christ's message don't seem to reach the typanum of their organs of spiritual hearing."[75]

The chaplain's mood was improved by Christmas week, when he "had a good bath in the Episcopal bath room (an unknown luxury on the car). I feel renewed in spirit to go out again and face the foe." The foe that day as they left Baker City was a snowstorm.[76]

At Durkee, a Portuguese town, Fleming was also displeased:

> The Catholic people were foolish enough to be inveigled into giving money to build a Church called the "Union" to be used by all denominations, so they do not seem much inclined to subscribe a second time to build one for themselves. In conversation a good many of the men told me that they belonged to the "Knights of Pythias" and had not been to the Sacraments for a number of years, but they were willing to amend and they did. One man was brought in from the mountains and after persuasion was brought to his knees. Three children age seven, five, and three were baptized. Four others were left behind, unregenerated because of the objection of the husband, a Baptist by descent.[77]

In his frustration Fleming exploded, "The Baptist Church is a damnable creed."

Haines, with a population of about eight hundred, had only one Catholic family, but the car was crowded every evening. It was the first time a priest had said Mass at Haines in eight years.[78]

At Cove, Oregon, in the winter of 1911, this report came from Fleming on *St. Anthony*: "The engine on this line is one that was originally used for driving a chaff cutter. On the journey from Union to Cove it broke loose from the Chapel Car three times, refusing to drag such a load of truth." In the same town, Fleming admits, "We did not feel very elated at the large attendance for the people assured us that they patronized everything that came along."[79]

Hot Lake, Oregon, was a health resort for patients suffering from rheumatism and kindred disorders. Father Fleming and George Hennessey thought it curious to see snowclad hills surrounding a boiling lake, and they enjoyed their free rooms and "monthly bath" and use of the entertainment hall for lectures for the patients. *St. Anthony* and its crew left Hot Lake at the right time, for "an hour after our departure two freight cars turned turtle in the wind at the spot where we had been switched."[80]

In May 1911 Hennessey reported that repairs had to be made to *St. Anthony*.

> Both platforms were repaired besides being raised. From the jolting they had lowered somewhat and it was difficult sometimes to couple. When the car was put in the shops at Pullman last time they varnished it. However, they did not scrape the observation end that had been through the fire at Junction City a few months previous and the result was that it blistered again and the paint fell off showing the wood. I had this all burned off entirely and the whole rear end painted new. I also had the sisters at La Grande repair all the Vestments for me. The Gold Cope [a long, capelike garment] and Chasuble [an outer garment worn by the priest during celebration of the Mass] needed lining and all the other vestments strings, etc.

The extension society also thanked J. P. O'Brien, the general manager of the Oregon Railway and Navigation Company, in providing free transportation for the chapel car, and Mr. Buckley, superintendent, and James Corbett, assistant superintendent at La Grande, who later became a Southern Pacific Railway vice president at San Francisco.[81]

When *St. Anthony* got to Hermiston, Oregon, in June they found a large Baptist church there, and they remembered that when they talked to E. R. Hermiston of *Emmanuel*, he had told them the town was named after him. "The preacher of the Baptist car told us that the town was called after him, but we found out different when we reached there. It was called Hermiston before he was ever thought of."[82]

Klan, Rome, Heater Present Problems

Soldiers crowded the car at Fort Stevens, where Colonel Foote, the commandant, allowed the car to remain upon the government reservation, and many of the soldiers from the fort followed *St. Anthony* to the nearby town of Warrenton for services.[83]

Anti-Catholic propaganda flooded many of the towns visited by the chapel car, much of it spawned by the Ku Klux Klan.

> The hooded Kluxers had their turn a few years ago. In our time out on the Chapel Car it was the scurrilous sheet called, *The Menace*. We saw it advertised in every backhouse along the railroads! In one of the towns in Oregon I was asked the question, "Have priests hoofs like cows?" Believe it or not, I took off my shoes and stockings to show them a cleaner, less cornful or calloused foot than any of those present. In another town they asked, "Has a priest to kill four people before he is ordained?" My answer was, "Haven't been convicted of murder yet, but if people are so dumb as to believe such things, it wouldn't hurt much to knock off a few of you tonight!"[84]

O'Brien remembered when his path crossed with one of the Baptist chapel cars in the Northwest. As was the case with Doran in Gooding, Idaho, in 1909, the Baptist car was *Emmanuel*, and the missionary was Hermiston. "A Baptist Chapel Car was coupled onto ours in a railroad yard, and in a few minutes the minister [Hermiston] and I were comparing notes on Chapel Car operations. That night Mr. Hermiston and I had dinner in his car, cooked by his wife who traveled with him, together with their daughter, about fifteen years of age who played the organ at their services."[85]

The most consoling results of the years of chapel car work, O'Brien, now a bishop, wrote, "are the requests which still come in to the Society for baptismal certificates of the children of thirty and forty years ago who were baptized on the Chapel Cars and now want their baptismal record so that they might be married in the Church, or scores of our young men who wanted records of their birth when they were about to enter the armed services of our country. Only last year a woman wrote in to say: 'My mother told me I was baptized in a church car by a redheaded priest.' We sent her the certificate."

Back in Chicago, Kelley may have felt that he had been "turned turtle in the wind" when his petition for a national collection for the extension failed in October 1911. When the announcements were made of the new American cardinals, Kelley received a second blow. Bishop Quigley, who had been such a good friend of the society and the chapel cars, was not named as expected; instead, two archenemies of extension had been honored, bishops Farley and Falconio. It seemed obvious to Kelley and *St. Anthony* donor Ambrose Petry that in the eyes of Rome, Catholic America was still centered along the Atlantic seaboard. As Petry put it, there were now "Four Red Hats all within 500 miles in a North 7 South line."[86] Kelley knew what the problem was. "At the bottom of everything," he remarked bitterly, "is the fact that the Society is new and comes out of the West."[87]

In December 1911 Hennessey, who was having his own problems on *St. Anthony*, gave up on trying to buy and feed hard coal into the difficult Baker heater and bought an oil stove.[88] Like the Baptist cars, the Catholic cars had constant trouble with the Baker heaters, but unlike the Baptist cars, the stoves in the kitchens of the Catholic cars were wood-burning.

Hennessey was constantly amazed at the vast frontier of Oregon. "From the main line of the Harriman system the branch goes out from Deschutes Junction, and from 1:30 p.m. until 5:45 that evening, you do not strike a town. All this time it is one continuous climb of three thousand four hundred feet above sea level. It is one hundred and eighteen miles from the main line to Madras — the first town of any size — and until reaching this town you are surrounded at all times with mountains and pass through not a few tunnels. Previous to the railroad coming to this part of Oregon, these missions were attended by driving, by stage, and on horseback, from sixty to one hundred miles at one time."[89]

On the way from Medford to Talent, Oregon, in February 1912, *St. Anthony* almost derailed a whole passenger train as a result of an air-brake failure. Repairs had to be made before proceeding to Jacksonville in the Rogue River Valley;[90] a month or so later, the car was placed in the Towhey Brothers shops at Portland for overhauling.

New Siblings Reduce *St. Anthony*'s Image

In June 1912 *St. Anthony* received a little brother — really a big little brother, a fancier sibling, one made of steel. Chapel car *St. Peter*, built at the Barney & Smith Car Company in Dayton, Ohio, became the second car in the Catholic fleet, and as soon as it was on the road, *St. Anthony*, the older, wooden, less commodious car, lost respect. Not only did *St. Peter* upstage *St. Anthony*, but also the old car lost the undivided attention of its best friend, George Hennessey, who now had to share his time between the two cars. This resulted in *St. Anthony* not being in service as much, as the chaplains who were on board, mainly the Reverend Charles M. Smith, pastor of the Corvallis church, had to return to their parishes several days a week. The last straw was that another new member of the family, also named *St. Peter* — a motor chapel car — was now in service in the South and receiving praise for its mobility, much easier maintenance, and appearance. Even the pope liked the concept of the motor chapel cars better, as Kelley would discover on one of his trips to the Vatican.

St. Anthony needed a facelift, and this was done in the late summer of 1913 at the Corvallis and Eastern Railroad Company shops.

> In regard to repairs to Chapel Car, St. Anthony's. This car will be stripped and cleaned thoroughly inside and out, paint and varnish removed from outside of car, body of car to be painted six coats Flood & Conklin's paint. All holes filled with hard putty and surface rubbed with Eureka stone. Will apply three coasts Pullman color and two coats varnish. Lettering to be all renewed with gold leaf. Inside of car will be cleaned, varnished and rubbed where necessary. All pews varnished one coat. Sash and doors to be removed, repainted and varnished, all broken glass renewed, embossed glass to be touched up where needed. Cement floor to be patched where necessary and light repairs made to body of car where needed, trucks removed, repaired and painted two coats. Costs will be approximately, labor for painting $150.00, carpenter, $140.00, material such as paint, lumber, glass, gold leaf, etc. $99.00, making a total of $380.00. Signed J. Taylor, Master Mechanic.[91]

After work had started on *St. Anthony*, problems that were not in the original estimate needed attention. The platform and vestibule timbers on the kitchen end of the car were so badly decayed that they must be replaced; the vestibule diaphragm was worn out and must be renewed or discarded. Some of the embossed glass in the side windows and colored lights in the deck sash were broken, about fourteen in all. It was recommended by the master mechanic at Corvallis and Eastern that the lights be sent ahead to Povey Brothers in Portland to finish, that the vestibule diaphragm be left off, a cupboard be built on the platform for the cook, and the lower part be lined with galvanized iron and used for an ice chest.[92]

When the work was done, *St. Anthony* looked like a new car, but its mission now was to serve as a church in areas where there was no church or while a church was being built.

At Alpine, Oregon, in 1913, on one of *St. Anthony*'s less frequent missions, Smith reported:

> There are about sixty Catholics, most of them French Canadians. Here also a small chapel is a crying necessity. Mass is being celebrated there once a month in a hall over a billiard room, which is a very unsatisfactory arrangement. . . . The Catholics there are poor, and a considerable portion of them are young children who will be lost to the church completely if unusual efforts are not made in their behalf. While the Chapel car was at Alpine, Rev. Father Lane of Albany, who speaks French with great fluency, gave instructions in that language, to the delight of some of the good old people to whom our faith and our language, "notre foi et notre langue," are rightfully their most cherished possession.[93]

One of the favorite porters who traveled on the chapel cars in the Northwest was See Hung Joe, a Chinese cook. *St. Anthony* was left in Wallowa, Oregon, for the summer and used by the priest of a new church there. Joe brought twelve other Chinese to the car, and they were baptized. "During the administration of the Sacrament, Joe would explain to them in the Chinese language the meaning of each ceremony. Nearly all of these men are in business in La Grande."[94]

Comparisons were being made not only between the older chapel car and the newer cars but also between the Catholic and Baptist cars and missionary methods. In a letter Ledvina, vice president of the society and general secretary, mentioned the new Baptist chapel boat and car:

> The Motor boat chapel of the Baptists is certainly a novel affair. They are certainly losing no time to be up-to-date. I met Bishop Hennessey at Bishop Janssen's funeral in Belleville last week, and he was telling me about one of the Baptist chapel cars that he saw a short time ago. He said that he was astounded at the general appearance outside and inside. He said that there were fine carved pews in the car, and the pulpit or lectern arrangement was very handsomely embellished. It looks

like we have been setting the pace, and our rivals are not slow to catch up.

The mission to southern Oregon began January 1914 at Divide, and in spite of rain all week, the chapel car was filled, the people coming in on handcars from points three and four miles distant. At Drain, although there were only fifteen Catholics in the town, they could not accommodate the numbers, with many standing outside the car. A group of Socialists attended the meetings at Roseburg, and at Glendale, the music for the services was provided by the Presbyterian choir and the Sunday evening lecture was held in the Presbyterian church. Grants Pass was one of the most progressive towns *St. Anthony* visited in southern Oregon, and their most southern mission was at Ashland, twelve miles from the California line.

Father William J. Kane, chaplain on this mission, discovered that people would attend the chapel car in cases when they would not attend service held in a church or chapel. Curiosity prompted their first visit, and this frequently gave way to interest in the topics discussed. Kane relates an incident that occurred as the car was lying in the north end of the Roseburg yard, waiting for the northbound train, which was due about midnight:

> Being in Roseburg, and not being an Elk, I retired early. The car was in darkness and my bedroom window was raised. I heard some people approaching, and when they drew near I heard one read the inscription on the car. His comment was, "Too much church." Without any ado I answered, "Not too much, but too many." Nothing further was said, and I presume that in certain localities it's being whispered about that the nefarious Chapel Car has been known to speak.[95]

The second funeral held on the chapel car was at Glenns Ferry, Idaho, in October 1914, when the two-year-old son of the storekeeper in town passed away. (The first funeral took place in Wallowa earlier.) As early as April 1915, when Brady

was on *St. Anthony* at Juntura, Oregon, arrangements were being made to spruce up *St. Peter*. Hennessey, who was on *St. Peter*, was told by Ledvina, "With regard to the painting and repairs on the 'St. Anthony;' under the circumstances, there is nothing else to be done but to go ahead with that too. So, you need not write again for permission, but just use your best judgment to have all the necessary work done with a view of putting the car in such condition that it will serve its purpose decently."[96]

Again *St. Anthony* was going to take a back seat to another chapel car — *St. Paul*, the last of the Catholic fleet. Like *St. Peter*, *St. Paul* was donated by Peter Kuntz, built at the Barney & Smith shops, and put into service in New Orleans in the spring of 1915. It was a state-of-the art car.

Brady was planning to keep *St. Anthony* at Riverton, Oregon, his next stop after Juntura, where a chapel was being built, for quite some time, and Ledvina was glad to hear that news. "That will be all right with us. Old 'St. Anthony' comes in very handy for that kind of work."[97]

Fire Damages Car; Future Uncertain

On October 9, 1915, Brady reported that *St. Anthony* had suffered damage in a fire in the railroad yards of Riverside, where the car was being stored. The fire destroyed a chair car, two stock cars, and the water tower. "The chapel car was only twenty feet away from the burning tower and was saved from utter destruction only by the hard efforts of the town people. The outside is all scorched and blistered from the intense heat, and moreover the panes of glass are broken. It seems the car should be sent to the shops for the necessary repairs."

The ensuing letter from extension vice-president Ledvina to George Hennessey about the fire damage matter had a somewhat different tone. "Now regarding the future of that car; you expressed in your letter just what Monsignor Kelley expressed when he was told about the car being near a fire. He, too, remarked that it is a pity the whole thing did not go up. The remark plainly indicted that the poor old 'St. Anthony'[98] has gotten now to the 'pension age,' and it will prove more of a burden than a blessing."

Ledvina confided that the perfect plan would be to bring the car back to Chicago and install it as a shrine. The problem was that the society did not presently have ground for that, and church politics were indefinite as to the naming of a successor to Archbishop Quigley, who had died July 10, 1915. The final agreement was that the car should be put into presentable condition in case it could be used as a shrine somewhere.

George Hennessey, who was the heart and soul of the chapel cars, traveled from chapel car *St. Peter* in Oregon to Idaho to care for the shop arrangements and other needs related to *St. Anthony*, and his expense account reflected the mounting costs of keeping the older car in service: Hotel expenses for 90 days at $1.50 per day, $135; meals at $1 a day, $90; telegrams, $2; trips to Salt Lake and Portland, $10; and laundry, $5.50.[99]

In December of 1916, *St. Anthony* was put in good condition with hopper and wood toilets removed, all carpets cleaned, rolltop desk repaired along with kitchen hopper and seats, metal work polished, platforms and draft gear changed from wood to steel, steps and board platforms renewed, all battens and aprons under windows sills renewed, and fresh interior and exterior paint done at the shops of the Oregon Short Line for $1,000.[100] The resuscitated car was placed at Dietrich, Oregon, where there was no Catholic church and where *St. Peter* had just finished a mission.[101] Mass was said in the car twice a month, and the car was cared for by some of the women in the parish.

St. Anthony's work in Oregon resulted in forty-three missions in the Archdiocese of Portland and forty-one in the Diocese of Baker. It had seen completion of eleven churches in the archdiocese and nine in the Baker diocese, with several others under construction.

A severe blow was given to the mobility of the Catholic cars, as it was with the Baptist cars, in April 1917 with the country's entry into World War I. The extension society offered the chapel cars to the government to be used as hospital cars or to be used in Red Cross work, but the offer was declined on the ground that there were sufficient cars for the required purposes.

St. Anthony served as a chapel in 1918 while the new St. Anthony's Church in Portland was being built,[102] and then at Fairfield, Idaho, until July, when it was removed to the Pocatello shops for an overhaul and exterior painting. In September 1918 Ledvina, himself now a monsignor, wrote to Hennessey on *St. Peter* to tell him that *St. Paul*, the last extension society chapel car to be built, would soon be put into storage. That decision was a result of the Federal Railroad Administration at New Orleans declaring it to be a private car and not to be hauled if it would interfere with traffic crucial to war efforts. It was hoped that George Hennessey would be able to continue the work on the northwest lines with *St. Peter*, unless he decided to enlist, as he was considering. As for *St. Anthony*, it was hoped that it could be placed somewhere as a chapel during the war.[103]

In October 1918 Hennessey reported that he had placed *St. Anthony* at Pleasant Valley, Oregon, where there were seven or eight Catholic families and where the missionary priest could use it for services. The railroad stored the car on a special spur so that it would not be touched as long as it would be there.[104] The influenza struck Hennessey in October, and his scheduled stops were delayed as a result of his illness.

When Ledvina wrote on January 27, 1919, the news was not good, although Hennessey's health was better. Ledvina was surprised and disappointed that the chapel cars would be charged for all movement at twenty-five passenger fares or seventy-five cents per mile when he had been promised by John Barton Payne, who was connected with the legal department of the railroad administration, that the status of the Catholic cars would not be changed. "Accordingly, there must be some mistake . . . but if the rulings stand, I see nothing else to do but simply put the Chapel Cars up somewhere as best we can, and go out of business as far as Chapel Cars are concerned. But I think this is only a temporary excitement, and it will all come out in the washing."[105]

In February Ledvina expressed his distress at the thought of giving up the chapel car work but did not see anything else to do under the circumstances. The cost of moving the cars would be prohibitive. As an afterthought, Ledvina wondered what the Baptists were going to do.[106] In a letter the next week, he suggested that Hennessey be thinking about his own future, in case the chapel car work was over.

Contrary to Ledvina's hopes, the rule stood. But the status of the chapel cars was changed to that of agricultural, demonstration, educational, exhibition, fish commission, hospital, medical laboratory, mine resource, public health, and Red Cross cars — ten fares or the equivalent of 30 cents per mile on lines where the one-way passage fare was 3 cents per mile, or 40 cents per mile in states where the one-way passenger fare was 4 cents per mile. The minimum charge for each movement would be 15 dollars, and parking and storage charges would be waived.[107]

The donor of *St. Anthony*, Ambrose Petry, whose lifestyle had soon reduced him to penury and forced him into hiding, one step ahead of creditors,[108] was in business in South America. Although he was many miles away, he still felt that his chapel car could be of service, so extension society officers were careful to try and find a suitable home for the eldest Catholic chapel car.

St. Anthony was taken under the wing of the Oregon Central Railroad, where it was stored on a siding near Union, Oregon. It remained there for some time, and in the fall of 1919 the car was moved free of costs by the Oregon Central and then the Oregon Trunk Railroad and the Southern Pacific and Spokane to Fallbridge, Washington, described by Schoenberg as "a desolate looking village below barren cliffs on the north bank of the Columbia."[109]

One story that appears in the files at Loyola University's Cudahy Library archives, written by T. A. Edwards, former pastor of the church at Fallbridge, is that the parishioners of Fallbridge (later Wishram), who had no church, concocted a scheme to get the car on their side of the river so they could use it as their place of worship. The wife of one of the passenger engineers persuaded her husband to kidnap the car by taking it across the river to the Washington side. As the railway men were on strike and not working, they laid tracks from the main line of the railroad to a lot in the center of town, and soon the car was resting on its new foundation.[110] There was no reference to such a crime in Hennessey's accounts, as he only reported that he saw to the movement of the car to Fallbridge.

Whether the story is true or not, the fact stands that the people of Fallbridge loved *St. Anthony*. In January 1920 there was an urgent request for *St. Anthony* at a new railroad town, Crane, but Hennessey wrote Ledvina, "I told him [the local priest] I could not possibly give him the *St. Anthony* at present because it was being used regularly and there would be an open riot if I even mentioned taking it away from Fallbridge."[111]

Houses, trees, and lawns soon blocked *St. Anthony*'s way back to the railroad, as the town grew up around the car.[112] For almost a decade it remained the only center of worship in that locality, until it was replaced by a small chapel called House of God and Gate of Heaven,[113] and then later by the Church of St. James. It may have been one of the last Wagner sleeping cars in existence.[114] The altar, pews, vestments, sacred vessels, and the leaded glass were used in the new church, and the altar from *St. Anthony* is presently being used in St. Paul's School in Yakima, Washington.

According to Edwards, then pastor of St. James, *St. Anthony* was left like the ship of the desert, the camel, to bleach its bones on the sands of the Columbia River . . . "for it was made of wood and in time, it disintegrated and disappeared."[115]

Forerunner of the dawn of Faith,
Pent 'tween two bands of steel,
O, Chapel Car "St. Anthony,"
We hear thy flying wheel
As o'er the roaring stream below,
Or through the fields of gold,
Drawn by the prisoned steam ahead,
Thou seek'st the wandering fold.[116]

Notes

1 Letter from Joe Jacobs to John Killian, January 17, 1940, Colporter Department, Archives, ABHS, VF.

2 George Lundy, "The Story of Extension," *Extension*, March 1976, 4.

3 Pete Kelly, "Chapel Cars, Pioneers Blaze Trail for the Church in Oregon," *Extension*, July 1996, 8.

4 "Kelley, Francis Clement," *New Catholic Encyclopedia* (Washington, D.C.: Catholic University of America, 1967), vol. 8, 144–45.

5 Timothy F. Wenzl, "The Extension Society's Chapel Car," from an interview with Father Tom McKernan, assistant to Bishop Hennessey during a Kansas tour of *St. Anthony* in 1907, *The Centennial of Sacred Heart Parish: Mission to Cathedral, 1882–1982, Dodge City, Kansas*, 1982, 25.

6 Wilfred P. Schoenberg, S.J., *A History of the Catholic Church in the Pacific Northwest: 1743–1983* (Washington, D.C.: The Pastoral Press, 1987), 443–45.

7 James P. Gaffey, *Francis Clement Kelley & The American Catholic Dream* (Bensenville, Ill.: The Heritage Foundation, 1980), 89.

8 The Right Rev. Francis C. Kelley, D.D., LL.D., The Story of Extension (Chicago: Extension Press, 1922), 100.

9 *Extension*, 1906.

10 Gaffey, 129.

11 Newberry Library, Chicago, Ill., Pullman Collection.

12 Francis P. Leipzig, *Extension in Oregon* (St. Benedict, Ore.: The Benedictine Press, 1956), 34.

13 Kelley, *The Story of the Extension*, 71–72.

14 David C. Mearns, *The Lincoln Papers* (New York: Doubleday, 1948), vol. 1, 92–93.

15 Gaffey, xx.

16 Leipzig, 34.

17 "St. Anthony's Chapel Car," *Michigan Catholic*, July 4, 1907, 2, Hesburgh Library, the University of Notre Dame, South Bend, Ind.

18 Leipzig, 35.

19 Ibid., 36.

20 Kelley, *The Story of Extension*, 88.

21 Report from George C. Hennessey, Monday, June 17, 1907, LUCA.

22 Report from George C. Hennessey, Wednesday, June 19, 1907, LUCA.

23 Report from George C. Hennessey, June 23, 1907, LUCA.

24 Report from George C. Hennessey, June 26, 1907, LUCA.

25 "A Week with the Chapel Car," *Extension*, November 1907, 10.

26 An Observer, "The Mission of the Chapel Car," *Extension*, September 1907, 11.

27 Francis Clement Kelley, *The Bishop Jots It Down* (New York: Harper & Brothers, 1939), 141.

28 Gaffey, 106–11.

29 Ibid.

30 Report from George C. Hennessey, July 13, 1907, LUCA.

31 "Adventures of the Catholic Chapel Car," *Michigan Catholic*, August 22, 1907, 5, Hesburgh Library, the University of Notre Dame, South Bend, Ind.

32 Report from George C. Hennessey, September 25, 1907, LUCA.

33 Report from George Hennessey, October 1907, LUCA.

34 *Extension*, November 1907, 10.

35 T. A. McKernan, "The Chapel Car and Its Mission," *Extension*, January 1908, 9.

36 Ibid.

37 T. E. O'Sullivan, "With the Chapel Car in the West," *Extension*, February 1908, 23.

38 Report from George C. Hennessey, March 17, 1908, LUCA.

39 Father O'Neill, journal, March 28, 1908, LUCA.

40 Ibid., April 7, 1908.

41 J. J. O'Neill, "The Chapel Car en Route," *Extension*, June 1908, 10.

42 *Extension*, October 1908, 14.

43 O'Brien, "Memoirs of a Beggar," 56.

44 William D. O'Brien, "The 'Church on Wheels' in the East," *Extension*, October 1908, 15.

45 Ibid.

46 A. P. Landry, "A Word from the Chapel Car," *Extension*, January 1909, 21.

47 Roger Baudier Sr., K.S.G., official chronicler of the Archdiocese of New Orleans, "The Chapel Cars of the Catholic Church Extension Society in the Louisiana Dioceses," February 1956, 2.

48 George C. Hennessey, "The Chapel Car in the South," *Extension*, July 1909, 9.

49 Ibid., 15.

50 Report of John Handley, April 11, 1909, LUCA.

51 "Chapel Car Through Iowa," *The Catholic Messenger*, July 8, 1909, 7, Hesburgh Library, the University of Notre Dame, South Bend, Ind.

52 "Mission Car in Denver," *Denver Catholic Register*, 5, Hesburgh Library, the University of Notre Dame, South Bend, Ind.

53 O'Brien, "Memoirs of a Beggar," 23.

54 Ibid., 58.

55 Report of Alvah W. Doran, St. Anthony, Idaho, July 25 to 31, 1909, LUCA.

56 Report of Alvah W. Doran, Gooding, Idaho, August 23 to 24, 1909, LUCA.

57 Schoenberg, 26.

58 O'Brien, "Memoirs of a Beggar," 22.

59 Leipzig, 42.

60 Report of D. McDonald, Sheridan, Ore., October 17 to 23, 1909, LUCA.

61 Schoenberg, 478.

62 Report of Walter L. Polk, Falls City, Ore., October 31 to November 6, 1909, LUCA.

63 Report of D. McDonald, Oakland, Ore., January 1 to 10, 1910, LUCA.

64 Church announcements, *Rouge River Courier*, February 18, 1910, 8, Grants Pass, Ore.

65 Report of D. McDonald, Grants Pass, Ore., February 20 to March 4, 1910, LUCA.

66 George C. Hennessey, "Missions and the Chapel Car," *Extension*, December 1910, 15.

67 "The Chapel Car in Oregon," *Extension*, July 1910, 5.

68 Report of William D. O'Brien, Junction City, Ore., July 22 to 28, 1910, LUCA.

69 Leipzig, 50.

70 Ibid.

71 "Church on Wheels Visits South Bend," *The South Bend (Indiana) Tribune*, Saturday, October 22, 1910, n.p., Hesburgh Library, the University of Notre Dame, South Bend, Ind.

72 Miles F. Potter, *Oregon's Golden Years: Bonanza of the West* (Caldwell, Idaho: Caxton Printers, 1976), 99.

73 Pete Kelly, "Chapel cars, pioneers blaze trail for the Church in Oregon," *Extension*, July 1996, 8.

74 Report of George C. Hennessey, Baker City, Oregon, ending December 31, 1910, LUCA.

75 Report of Austin Fleming, Huntington, Ore., December 21 to 24, 1910, LUCA.

76 Report of Austin Fleming, Baker City, Ore., December 25 to January 1, 1911, LUCA.

77 Report of Austin Fleming, Durkee, Ore., January 4 to 9, 1911, LUCA.

78 Schoenberg, 479.

79 Report of Austin Fleming, Cove, Ore., January 29, 1911, LUCA.

80 Report of Austin Fleming, Hot Lake, Ore., February 2 to 4, 1911, LUCA.

81 Leipzig, "Churches on Wheels Delivered Faith," *Oregon Catholic History Newsletter*, 1984, 6.

82 Report of Austin Fleming, Hermiston, Ore., June 5 to 10, 1911, LUCA.

83 Report of Austin Fleming, Warrenton, Ore., September 4 to 9, 1911, LUCA.

84 O'Brien, "Memoirs of a Beggar," 57.

85 Ibid., 58.

86 Gaffey, 118.

87 Ibid., 120.

88 Report from George C. Hennessey, Baker City, Ore., from October 31 to December 31, 1911, LUCA.

89 George C. Hennessey, "The Chapel Car in the West," *Extension*, June 1912, 9.

90 Report of D. L. Barrett, Jacksonville, Ore., March 5 to 11, 1912, LUCA.

91 Letter to George C. Hennessey from J. Taylor, Corvallis and Eastern Railroad Co., July 11, 1913, LUCA.

92 Letter to George C. Hennessey from J. Taylor, Corvallis and Eastern Railroad Co., July 22, 1913, LUCA.

93 Report of Charles Smith to the Catholic Church Extension Society, LUCA.

94 George C. Hennessey, "With the Chapel Car St. Peter," *Extension*, May 1913, 11.

95 William J. Kane, "'St. Anthony' — The Pioneer 'Church on Wheels,'" *Extension*, August 1914, 11.

96 Letter from E. B. Ledvina to George C. Hennessey, Pocatello, Idaho, April 27, 1915, LUCA.

97 Ibid.

98 Letter from E. B. Ledvina to George C. Hennessey, November 22, 1915, LUCA.

99 Letter from George Hennessey, Wasco, Ore., to E. B. Ledvina, May 1, 1916, LUCA.

100 Work Order Authority of Oregon Shore Line, Pocatello, Idaho, July 14, 1916, LUCA.

101 Letter from George C. Hennessey to E. B. Ledvina, December 1916, LUCA.

102 Schoenberg, 334.

103 Letter from E. B. Ledvina to George C. Hennessey, Wheeler, Ore., September 17, 1918, LUCA.

104 Letter from George C. Hennessey to E. B. Ledvina, Bay City, Ore., October 1, 1918, LUCA.

105 Letter from E. B. Ledvina to George C. Hennessey, Portland, Ore., January 27, 1919, LUCA.

106 Letter from E. B. Ledvina to George C. Hennessey, Portland, Ore., February 12, 1919, LUCA.

[107] Letter from the United States Railroad Administration, Director General of Railroads, Washington, to E. B. Ledvina, March 7, 1919, LUCA.

[108] Gaffey, 88.

[109] Schoenberg, 479.

[110] An account supposedly written by T. A. Edwards of Yakima, Washington, LUCA.

[111] Letter from George C. Hennessey to E. B. Ledvina, Portland, Ore., January 31, 1920, LUCA

[112] "The Last Days of the Chapel Car of St. Anthony," a draft in the files, with note at bottom, See Correspondence Rev. T. A. Edwards, Yakima, Wash., LUCA.

[113] Schoenberg, 382.

[114] Robert P. Burghardt, "Chapels on steel wheels: How Catholic missionaries used railroad car to serve their flocks," *Trains*, December 1992, 80.

[115] Edwards.

[116] Kelley, *The Story of Extension*, first stanza of a poem written in honor of St. Anthony by T. A. McKernon, 105.

CHAPTER 13

St. Peter:
The First Steel Apostle
and Peter Kuntz

During a stop in Dayton, Ohio, before *St. Anthony*'s mission to the Northwest, a wealthy Dayton businessman, Peter Kuntz, visited the car. After examining the renovated Wagner car, Kuntz, who was never a man to mince words as the extension society would discover, said to the chaplain on board, "Why doesn't your society build a good chapel car, instead of this old thing?"

It was likely that Kuntz had seen the new Baptist cars coming out of the nearby Barney & Smith shops and had made some comparisons. So in 1912 the Catholic Church Extension Society turned to the Barney and Smith Car Company, the Baptist chapel car builder, to build their second car — a steel *St. Peter*, with a twenty-five-thousand-dollar donation from Kuntz.[1]

Head of the mammoth Kuntz lumber enterprises, Peter Kuntz was known for his charitable giving and his deep religious convictions (*see fig. 13.2*). "Eccentric he was to a degree, but a more practical man never devoted himself to any industry," wrote one biographer, "and he gave without attracting public attention."[2]

Father Francis C. Kelley described his first impression of Kuntz, whom he met at a lecture Kelley gave in Dayton. Even in the packed house, Kelley had no difficulty in spotting Kuntz, a small, oldish gentleman sitting in a box to his left, with very long side whiskers and a skullcap. "One glance sufficed. I knew that Mr. Kuntz was present, and launched out with a bit of the Story of Extension. The audience thought that I was talking for the benefit of all; but, truth to tell, I was talking only to Peter Kuntz. When I glanced at him, as I did now and then, I rather fancied that his twinkling eye was trying to tell me that Peter Kuntz was 'wise to me'; and Peter Kuntz was."[3]

Kuntz wanted people to think him a bit odd; no one ever knew what he would do, according to Kelley.

He dressed like a poor man, but he had three automobiles. He lived in a rented house, but could easily have bought ten city blocks. He was crusty, and could say "No" to anyone; but year after year he took hundreds of poor children out into the country and gave them a gala time at his expense. He gave in his own way, and at his own time. He was really the greatest "bluff" I ever met, for he systematically went about disguising the fact that he had the softest and most loving old heart in the world; trying to make people think him a crank and a skinflint, making enemies who liked him, and friends who wondered why they thought so well of him as to be

Fig. 13.1 A special Mass was said during the dedication of *St. Peter*, the first steel chapel car, at Dayton, Ohio, the home of the Barney & Smith Car Company, June 30, 1912. (Loyola University, Cudahy Library Archives, Chicago)

Fig. 13.2 *St. Peter's* donor, Peter Kuntz, was a wealthy Dayton lumberman and generous Catholic Church Extension Society benefactor. Having his own ideas as to what he wanted on the chapel cars and where he wanted them to be used, Kuntz also endowed the building of the last Catholic chapel car, *St. Paul.* (Loyola University, Cudahy Library Archives, Chicago)

his friends. He always refused with his lips, and consented in his heart. He was a wonderful father and husband, a Catholic who practiced his religion, who feared no man and no devil, but who certainly feared God.[4]

The agreement entered between Kuntz and the extension society specified that the car be used only for religious purposes, and if the society either no longer existed or did not want the car, it should be returned to the ownership of Kuntz. Part of the contract was that from "all priests celebrating Mass in the car, that the donor and his family, both living and dead, shall have a memento; and, further, that on one day during each week, that said car is in actual missionary work, a Mass, the stipend for which it is understood shall be taken from the offerings given on board the car, shall be offered for the donor and his family, both living and dead."[5]

St. Peter, a modern car compared to *St. Anthony*, was dedicated by the Right Reverend Monsignor John B. Murray, Vicar General of the Diocese of Cincinnati, June 30, 1912, in Dayton *(see fig. 13.1)*. *St. Peter* would serve in Oregon, Washington, Idaho, Utah, Kansas, and North Carolina. Said to be one of the longest cars in the world at that time, just as Baptist car *Emmanuel* had been in 1893, the overall length was eighty-four feet with the part set aside for the chapel measuring forty-three feet *(fig. 13.4)*.

Finished in a rich St. Jago mahogany, with dark green ceilings touched with graceful designs, the sanctuary platform, elevated six inches above the car floor, had a storage area underneath. A handsome communion railing in the English fashion — a rood screen of scroll nature on which was mounted the rood, or the cross, separated a neat altar and a permanent confessional from the nave *(fig. 13.7)*.[6] Stations of the cross were built in to form a part of the car's interior decoration *(fig. 13.3)*, and an organ, built by the Hinners Organ Company of Pekin, Illinois, was installed near the entrance.

Remaining space, including a shower bath and adequate toilet facilities, was used as living quarters by the chaplains, managers, and porters. The compartments included a study

that could also be used as a dining room, a library, or an office, a sleeping compartment, and a kitchen. Storage areas were located throughout the car, which was lighted with acetylene gas and heated by the notorious Baker system.

From Dayton, with chapel car superintendent George Hennessey and Father Emmanuel B. Ledvina, the extension society's vice president, aboard, the new cathedral on wheels made its apprentice exhibition journey to Chicago on the Big Four lines, dropping down to Cincinnati and Hamilton, Ohio. It then went through Indiana, stopping at Lawrenceburg, Evansville, Vincennes, Princeton, Washington, Loogootee, Seymour, North Vernon, and Terre Haute. On Illinois tracks it traveled to Mt. Carmel and finally Chicago.[7]

While it was in Chicago, *St. Peter* was sided on the Illinois Central Railroad tracks in Grant Park, opposite the Blackstone Hotel, which was, according to Father Edward L. Roe, who was in charge of transportation for the chapel cars, "the most advantageous site in Chicago." This feat was accomplished by the courtesy of Illinois Central officials, Judge Payne, the president and superintendent of the South Park Commissioners, and Dolese and Shepard, contractors.

The matter of passes for the car and its missionaries soon brought up an unintentional deceit that sometimes turned into an intentional advantage. Hennessey was a layman. The railroad policy was that to get a clergy pass, a person had to be an ordained minister or priest, and sometimes even ordained persons did not get a clergy pass. For example, Mrs. Cutler, a Baptist missionary wife, was an ordained minister but could not get a pass because she was a woman.

Roe wrote to Ledvina on August 14 that he had secured a time pass, good until September 30, 1912, on the Chicago, Milwaukee & St. Paul Railroad for Hennessey under the mistaken impression that he was a priest. "This wrong impression came to them from seeing passes issued on western roads to him as Rev. Geo. C. Hennessey. I would advise that any communications had with the C. M. & St. P. Ry., be on the official stationery of the Society and not on that of the Chapel Car, on which his name does not appear as Rev., for I am sure the pass would be recalled if this road found out he was only a layman." Roe also obtained passes on the Chicago, Milwaukee and Puget Sound Railroad, the Tacoma Eastern Railroad, and the Idaho and Western Railroad for the chapel car and "Rev." Geo. C. Hennessey, under the same camouflage.[8]

Hennessey Was Heart of Chapel Cars

Hennessey was the lay heart of the extension society chapel cars. Born in Prince Edward Island, Canada, as a boy he was brought to assist his cousin, the young Father Francis Kelley, founder of the extension society, in his work in Lapeer, Michigan. Among Hennessey's duties were altar boy, sexton, organist, and horse driver. When the first chapel car became a reality, Hennessey was named superintendent, "a natural for the job," his cousin would brag. "Brimful of personality, a splendid speaker, a fine singer, he was a magnet to Catholics and non-Catholics alike."[9]

Hennessey was a man who knew how to get things done, with his jovial manner, Irish wit, and sometimes a few cigars. Ledvina joked, on hearing about the Baptist chapel car missionary who was shocked when he received his repair bill from the shops. "I have no worry about your getting that kind of treatment; but then, of course, there is a reason — you are no Baptist minister, and you know how to handle situations of that kind diplomatically. A box of cigars goes a far way at times."[10]

St. Peter's first trip was not to the West but to the East: Boston, where it made its debut at the First Missionary Congress, visited by thousands of people eager to see a church on rails. When the car finally started on its westward journey, with Hennessey and Father William O'Brien on board, the trip followed almost exactly the schedule of towns visited by the first Baptist chapel car, *Evangel*, twenty-one years earlier — Davenport, Iowa, where the local paper reported that hundreds visited the car; St. Paul, Minneapolis, Aberdeen, St. Cloud, Fargo, Bismarck, Glendive, Miles City, Billings, Helena, and Missoula.

The financial report for September 4 to October 19

showed $100 received from the office for expenses; collections of $421 for income; and expenses of four hundred pounds of carbide at $3.50 per; a cot for $3.50; living expenses for chaplain and Hennessey, $175; for the cook $50; oil stove $5.50; four months laundry $2.75; charcoal, incense, candles, sanctuary oil, floats, etc. $10.50; and transportation for Father O'Brien on an Idaho trip, $25, leaving a balance of $224.80.[11]

From Portland the car went to La Grande, Oregon, where the older *St. Anthony* and the new *St. Peter* were together, in order to transfer literature and other necessaries onto the new car. After the transfer, *St. Anthony* returned to Willowa, Oregon, and *St. Peter* set out for the Boise diocese, first stopping at Haines, in the Baker City diocese, with Father J. F.

Fig. 13.3 The chapel of *St. Peter* was finished in St. Jago mahogany with a Gothic design. Although the car was steel, the wood interior trim still reflected the craftsmanship of the Barney & Smith builders. In the foreground can be seen two auxiliary upper berths. (Loyola University, Cudahy Library Archives, Chicago)

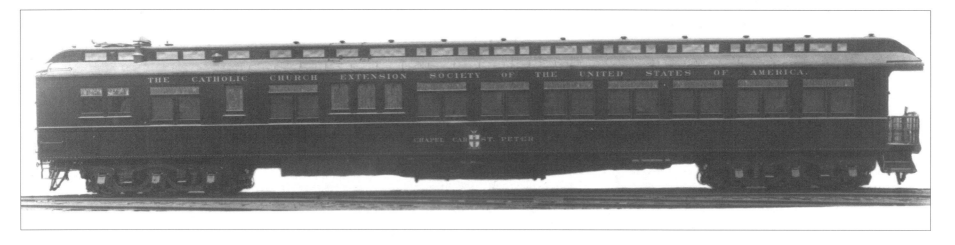

Fig. 13.4 At the time *St. Peter* was built, it was considered to be one of the longest railroad cars in the world. (Loyola University, Cudahy Library Archives, Chicago)

Murphy and Father P. L. Barrett, C.SS.R., in charge.[12] At Weiser, Idaho, more than 150 people approached the sacraments, among them several who had been away from their duty for years.

At New Meadows, a town only eighteen months old with a population of about four hundred, the car was filled for the week, not withstanding bad weather and roads. Council, a town of about five hundred, was warring with New Meadows over the honor of being county seat, and at the last election, Council won. The present three Catholics in town might be joined by some new residents as a result of the election. At Midvale, the Church of Christ had the town sewed up, as the saying goes. Barrett reported, "They really believe it is the only true church and the majority of its members, which include some of the businessmen of the town are firmly convinced that their church was founded by Christ." In spite of the Church of Christ monopoly, "a couple of renegades returned and one forsook the Odd Fellows and promised to be a good catholic from henceforth."[13]

In May 1913 the introduction of a new motor chapel car, also called *St. Peter*, in Texas proved a rival for the Catholic rail chapel cars *(fig. 13.5)*. Motor chapels, which were being used by the American Baptist Publication Society as well as most major denominations, had some advantage over rail cars, mainly that they could go many more places for less expense.

Some important officials in the Catholic church favored the growing trend toward motor chapels. Kelley pointed out, "Pope Pius X was always a devoted admirer of 'these modern missionary innovations,' but he was more interested in motor chapels than in chapel cars, and Monsignor Diomede Falconio, afterwards Cardinal, 'could not abide the thought of them [rail chapel cars].' His Excellency was always cordial until he had brought the talk round to his bete noire. After that there was no peace, for I couldn't destroy the cars and wouldn't if I could; and His Excellency would never rest until they were 'all burned up.'"[14]

Baker Heater Plagues Hennessey

It did not take long for an old and familiar problem to surface on *St. Peter*. Chaplain Alvah W. Doran reported from Montpelier, Idaho, on January 5, 1913:

> The temperature of Jan. 5th and 6th, twenty eight-degrees below was too much for the heating plant of the car which together with the water system was completely frozen. The railroad men took pity on the crew and moved the car alongside the round-house where a fine pressure of steam made things comfortable. We had expected to complete the line of missions in charge of Fr. De Stoop but on account of this severe weather and

the lack of getting steam compelled us to postpone till the warmer season.[15]

After having repairs made on the steam pipes, the car moved on the Oregon Short Line to Blackfoot, where three-and-a-half years earlier *St. Anthony* had stopped for a week. At Idaho Falls more than 350 people, including a Mormon apostle, attended the lecture "Why I Became a Catholic."[16]

Hennessey received the news that Sister Mary Catharine of Jesus was making purple tabernacle curtains at the Holy Rosary Hospital of the Dominican sisters in Ontario, Oregon, and she would send them as soon as she was finished. "The purple is not ready yet as I had great delay in getting the right shade."[17]

Doran especially enjoyed the visit at Pocatello, where *St. Anthony* had stopped in 1909. "It is not often the chapel cars get to work in such a large community as our time is so largely spent in small places which have no church. However the car showed its usefulness on this occasion. Pocatello is a hustling railroad centre and many Catholics are train-men or work in the shops or yards. Week-day Mass was said for them at 6:30 A.M. so that they could come in their working clothes and get to work before the whistle blew." The Knights of Columbus secured a public hall for the closing lecture, and an audience of over twelve hundred listened to Father Doran again give his lecture on "Why I Became a Catholic."[18]

From Adams, Oregon, in May 1913, Father R. J. Murphy reported that most of the Catholics in town were half-breed Indians who had come under the influence of a Jesuit priest, Father Ball, on the reservation twelve or fifteen miles north. The chapel car proved to be a great attraction, and many non-Catholics came to the services. A church building plan was started.[19]

Hennessey lost his cool in the frosty March of 1914 when the pipes of the Baker heater, which were to have been repaired at the Parsons shops of the Missouri, Kansas & Texas rail lines (MK&T), leaked in the very spot that was supposed to have been fixed: "The water ran all over the floor in the

chapel and I was obliged to drain the water entirely from the pipes and it has not been used since. Today we are suffering with the cold on this account for it is blowing a fierce Kansas gale here at this moment, using four oil stoves to keep this little room warm. Now that's the way the repairing was done. Do you think a job like this is worth the bill?"[20]

The response from the MK&T office was that they were not responsible for the problems, as all tested well when the car left the shops and their best man did the work. Hennessey replied, "I suppose the poor 'Katy' will go out of business if this bill is not paid. I am enclosing check for Thirty-three dollars and forty cents ($33.40). Thirty-three dollars as a donation and forty cents for the work done during the four days the car was in the shops at Parsons."[21]

From the northwest to the southwest, *St. Peter* took its mission to the Mexicans of Kansas. The first Mexican mission was at Hutchinson, where daily attendance averaged 75; 72

Fig. 13.5 The advent of Catholic Church Extension Society motor chapel cars, like motor chapel *St. Peter*, introduced in Temple, Texas, provided formidable competition for the aging chapel car. This was also true with the American Baptist Publication Society chapel cars. (Loyola University, Cudahy Library Archives, Chicago)

received the Sacrament of Penance, and 120 received Holy Communion. Eighteen children made their first Holy Communion on the last day, the children from the Catholic school singing during the Mass. At Florence even more people attended, and at Augusta, Arkansas City, and Woodward, short missions were held for the bands of Mexicans living in poverty in those areas.

The last town visited on this mission was Pratt, where one of the Mexicans who came to the car told of a black Protestant pastor who on several instances had extended a cordial invitation to attend services in his church, assuring them that he was also a Catholic. As proof he produced a medal of Our Lady of Guadalupe that he wore around his neck. Father R. Serrano, C.M.P., Spanish-speaking chaplain for the mission, was upset over what he felt was a perverted attempt to proselytize Catholics.[22]

When Serrano arrived at Hutchinson with the chapel car, the sound of his "velvety Castilian tongue" caused a train of precious memories that struggled for expression in the souls of the Mexicans of the town. "Some of them cried and some of them laughed, and in their glee some had the light-hearted gaiety that made them shout." From Mass with instruction in the morning to catechism for the children after dinner, to meetings with the rail workers in the evening, the car was full. Little groups would depart for their cottages only to return in an hour or more. These same groups would go and come half a dozen times in a day.

> There was a score or more of daily communions. All approached the Sacraments at least once. There were marriage kinks untwisted, and at the closing service tawny faces peered through the windows from the observation platform, half envious of these who occupied the seats or crowded in the aisles. When we moved away, it was very gently. The engine seemed to understand the sorrow of these poor neglected Catholics and fairly crawled. Every one had to kiss the missionary's hand and say good-by.

There were many tears on the sturdy faces of those sun-bronzed trackmen. Here and there a woman sobbed. Children kissed their finger-tips to say an "Adios." The people were saying many things in Spanish, which of course we could not understand. And we wanted to know, so we asked Father Serrano. "They are saying that I am going," he answered, "and that I will never come again. 'We are orphans!' they are crying." And as the engine slipped around a bend, we realized in part the sorrow that had come into the lives of that little group of exiles from poor old war-scarred Mexico, for their beloved Padre had gone.[23]

Father P. J. MacCorry related the rocky trip *St. Peter* took on the tail end of a freight from Dodge City to Elkhart, the end of the Kansas line. They went swinging, swaying, and bumping down the rail, which had been laid just a year and now sagged desperately until "one could close his eyes and believe he were on the heaving billows rather than railroading across the plains of Kansas. The way we plunged and pitched and pirouetted made mad pandemonium among our pots and pans, and not infrequently the monotony of 'the song of the rails' was punctuated by the crash of a lamp-globe or a precious plate hurtling to destruction in the depths of the kitchen."

According to MacCorry, three times the engine broke its dry bar and romped alone giddily across the sand dunes. Twice the car seemed to poise an instant on its left-side wheels, as though undetermined whether to return to its jerky job or flop over on the green and give up the attempt to finish it. But they finally landed at Elkhart, where Baptist chapel car *Evangel* had been pulled on one of the first trains into town a year earlier. From Hugoton, where anti-Catholic material had been distributed, "a hog-train" bumped them on to Copeland, where a tiny Catholic Russian-German settlement nearby provided most of their audience.[24]

Following the Mexican mission, the car spent several weeks in western Kansas. At Bazine, there was not one

Catholic in town, but several families, half Irish and half German-Russians, lived about eight miles from the railroad tracks. The newspaper commented favorably on the presence of *St. Peter* at Ness City, and believers and unbelievers came to see the ingeniously constructed "roaming" missioner.

Heavy rains formed large lakes at Dighton, but crowds overflowed the chapel car into the Baptist church. Father Andrew felt that longer stays were needed to "really make non-Catholics reflect seriously on the truths of our religion, and enable them to grasp what the Church is and teaches." Scott City was the last stop, and a disappointing one, for even with a Catholic chapel in town, there seemed to be little interest.[25]

Anti-Catholic Sentiment Follows to Idaho

From July 4 to October 25, 1914, *St. Peter* worked in the Diocese of Boise, Idaho, on the Oregon Short Line, starting with Rupert, where Doran and Hennessey found the town in the middle of a Fourth of July celebration with games of all kinds. At Burley, which Doran described as "over-boomed," they found that although a chapel had been built with extension society assistance, many Catholic families had moved from the predominantly Mormon town, leaving only a handful.[26]

St. Peter was the first chapel car to travel over the Oregon Short Line, Montana Division Victor branch line, as it had been in operation only one year, and Doran had seen no finer country than this valley along the Teton Mountains. Their congregation at Victor was "truly Catholic," with fourteen present distributed among six nationalities: Italian, Mexican, Chinese, French, Belgian, and Irish American.[27] Finishing the mission in the Boise diocese, *St. Peter* was left in Pilot Rock, Oregon, a mission town of the Capuchin Fathers, to be used as a chapel for several months while Hennessey went east to prepare the new *St. Paul* for dedication.

After being painted and revarnished at Pocatello in April 1915, *St. Peter* continued on working in the Boise diocese along the Bend branch of the Oregon Short Line, where there were many new towns although not many Catholics. Some of the towns, like Murphy, consisted of not more than six dwellings, two saloons, three general stores, and a hotel and restaurant combined with a post office.[28]

Frequently there were clashes between the priests and non-Catholics, but in August 1915 there was a problem with the parish priest at Harrison, Idaho. He insisted that Hennessey change his schedule, which the bishop of Boise had set, to accommodate his wishes, and when Hennessey refused to do so, the planned mission for Harrison was canceled.

Fig. 13.6 A First Communion class at Helper, Utah, poses with the chaplains on board *St. Peter*. The chaplains mostly enjoyed the work with children who came to the car. (Loyola University, Cudahy Library Archives, Chicago)

St. Peter Joins Baptist Car at Exposition

There had been some doubt whether the extension society would send a car to the San Francisco Panama-Pacific Exposition. What caused Kelley, now the Right Reverend Monsignor Kelley, to decide to send *St. Peter* to San Francisco was that the new Baptist car *Grace* was there. Kelley wrote Ledvina that *Grace* was a fine car with a good appearance inside and out. He thought that the pews were not as nice looking but more practical for the reason they were reversible. Also, Kelley was quite taken with the brass bedstead in the sleeping quarters, which gave it a homelike appearance. Kelley had talked with E. R. Hermiston on board *Grace*, who said he would be pleased to see chapel car *St. Peter* join them and again see Hennessey.[29] Hermiston and Hennessey had become good friends.

With new carpet in the sanctuary and replated cross, candelabra, and chimes, *St. Peter* was on exhibition at the Southern Pacific depot by Sunday, September 19. Hennessey had been instructed by Ledvina to "take special note of all the points on the new Baptist Chapel Car. Take your time to give me a sketch of any point or feature that strikes you as very practical, and which might be applied to any possible future Chapel Car of our own. Mr. Kuntz is still anxious to give us another car for Florida, provided we can get the transportation. . . ."[30]

This was not difficult for Hennessey to do; *St. Peter* was coupled onto *Grace*. He took careful notes and wrote that he was not that impressed with the Baptist car. Ledvina replied that he was glad, for according to Monsignor Kelley's description, "It had us beat. I now feel very much satisfied that we are still 'on top.'"[31]

Unlike lines in the South, where *St. Paul* was having serious transportation problems, the railroads in the Northwest were generous to the chapel cars. They seemed to realize the usefulness of the cars in helping the development of their colonization enterprises, and realized, according to Ledvina, that Catholic settlers feel more contented if they see that their spiritual wants are looked after.[32]

Like the Baptist cars, the Catholic cars had lighting problems, and they also found the solution in Coleman lamps. "As for the selection of lights for the car . . . go ahead with the installation of 'The Coleman System,'" Ledvina instructed Hennessey, when problems occurred on *St. Peter*.

Baptist and Catholic car workers over the years had certain areas, generally of creed and practice, where they could not agree, but some bonds tied them — such as the Baker heater. "We see that the Baptist Car, *Emmanuel*, is in the shops, and has been there for a couple of months. Those Baker Heaters seem to give everybody trouble, if they are not watched closely. I see that Baptist heaters freeze just as quickly as Catholic heaters."[33]

In spring 1916 *St. Peter* was busy along the Oregon Western Railroad and Navigation Company lines in the Baker City diocese under Archbishop Alexander Christie. Father Thomas Brady was again chaplain, and although many of the towns along the line contained more than two hundred souls, he delighted in the few Catholics who were found, including an Irish boy working on a ranch about three miles from Kent, Oregon.[34]

Brady was not treated so well at Shaniko, the end of the branch line, as the parish priest and the bishop, for some reason not stated, ordered the car out of town.[35] Brady expected trouble from those along the line who had read the poison pen of *The Menace*, an anti-Catholic publication that followed the Catholic cars wherever they traveled, but to have this kind of treatment from fellow priests was an upsetting experience.

Riverside, a railroad town that had a history of only two years, "peopled by that class of people who follow railroads into new territory and as a consequence few care for religion," had poor attendance. At the Oregon Western Railroad and Navigation Company's construction camps, though, the *St. Peter* crew found thirty Catholic men who came into the car and another forty or so who thought their working clothes did not become the interior of a chapel car and who remained outside, still participating in the services.[36]

Someone else was thinking of building a chapel car, for in the summer of 1916, Ledvina received a letter from a Cincinnati law firm asking how much it would cost to fit up a railroad chapel car, such as the extension cars. Ledvina thought the request was prompted either by someone who wanted to give another chapel car or by someone trying to get information for the building of a Protestant chapel car.[37]

While *St. Peter* was being repainted and revarnished in the Pocatello shops, Hennessey was teased by Ledvina that the reason George always requested Murphy's varnish on the chapel cars was because George's mother was a Murphy. "Your mother varnished you all right; but, I have no doubt, that your old daddy helped too, at least in the 'rubbing down' act."[38]

One concern voiced by Ledvina was that *St. Peter*'s crews might not be spending enough time in one place. He used the Baptist cars as an example, citing that they worked their field more thoroughly, and he urged Hennessey to slow down a bit. "There is no question about it but that when our cars are in operation, they work and they work hard, and everybody on board does likewise; but that does not mean that we shall close our eyes to any improvement, if we get still better results."[39]

Come spring 1917, Father William D. Cronin was on the car, and at Scappoose, Oregon, they found a Bohemian settlement where the Catholic services were preached in Bohemian and the children instructed in Bohemian. On this account, English-speaking people did not attend Mass. Cronin was busy instructing children after school and gathering up those Catholics who had been absent from the Mass.

At Oak Grove the mission was difficult, even though they had gone to great trouble to get there, first on the electric line of the Portland Railroad Light and Power, next on the Spokane, Portland and Seattle Road, then on the Southern Pacific, and finally on the Portland Railroad Light and Power Company. The problem at Oak Grove was that the town was made up of ex-ministers: the store man, the butcher, the postmaster, even the man who peddled the papers.[40] Too many Protestant ministers spoiled the Catholic chapel car broth.

The first wedding on the extension society cars was at Richfield, Idaho, where a local rancher and a New York City woman, who had known each other since childhood, were married in *St. Peter*. At the same stop seven married children who had not spoken to each other in two years were reconciled, much to the joy of their Irish mother.

Chaplain Jerome B. Donegan thought that *St. Peter* was the first chapel car that people at Myrtle Point, Oregon, had seen, but he soon discovered that the Baptists had been there first and had worked all the towns along the line. "However we are not bothered by what they have done so far and the difference in 'Class' of the cars has also helped us. They had one of their wooden cars [chapel car 4, *Good Will*] and did not draw the crowds that we are having all along the lines."[41] At Powers, Donegan saw some of the results of the Baptist car's visit, as a new Baptist church was being built next to the new Catholic church, and the Baptist minister came to several of the lectures.[42]

Oregon's beauty was not wasted on Donegan. "Nature has been partial to the south Western part of Oregon. The sombre fir and hemlock — the tender myrtle — the gorgeous rhododendron — the brilliant scotch bloom — the quiet white lilies in the sheltering leaves of green, combine here to make it a wonder[fully] attractive place."[43]

Hennessey, facing his tenth year of chapel car work, thought that he may have been on the car long enough. He was hearing glowing reports of the work of layman Michael Cousins on *St. Paul*, and perhaps he was feeling a little unappreciated. He also was hearing reports that some chaplains who served on the cars felt that he was getting too much salary, as much as they were, and resented that. With World War I heating up, maybe he should join the army? Ledvina was relieved to hear a few letters later that Hennessey had changed his mind and would stay for a while longer on the car.[44]

Those second thoughts may have arisen after the close-up view of army life Hennessey got during July and August 1917 when the car was at Clackamas, Oregon, for the benefit of the soldiers encamped there. While there were only a few Catholic soldiers in the camp, still the archbishop wanted to do all in his power to assist them and look after their spiritual welfare. While the car was at Clackamas, the archbishop visited the car, along with Kelley.[45]

St. Peter, which had served as a wedding chapel, now became a funeral car as it bore the body of Bishop Alphouse J. Glorieux, an unwavering supporter of the chapel car work in his diocese, to Boise. There *St. Peter* remained until after the funeral, and then it carried the archbishop and his party back to Portland, where it was used as a chapel at Arleta Station.

Ledvina was confident that the society cars would have no problem in transportation, even with the wartime government control. He wrote to the president of the Portland Railway Light & Power Company, expressing thanks for their courtesies to the chapel car.

We have on our Executive Board, prominent men in the business world. One of them is the Vice-President of the Pullman Company, and the other is the President of the Haskell & Barker Car Co., formerly General Manager of the American Car and Foundry Co., and at present associated with Mr. Hurley, at Washington, with the transportation problem for the war activities of our country. We likewise have among the members of our Board, some prominent Railway men of the country. We mention this, just by way of substantiation of our confidence that we may have opportunities to evidence our appreciation of courtesies, in one or another way, that may prove welcome and acceptable, when opportunity may present itself in the future.[46]

In spite of the government regulations, *St. Peter* continued to move along the Idaho lines, revisiting many of the towns where it had stopped earlier. At Hailey local non-Catholics said they would close the businesses in town for a couple of hours if Chaplain Austin Fleming would give a talk on the position of the Catholic church on Americanism. The largest theater in town was filled, and the lecture was well received.[47]

Utah Mission Starts at Salt Lake

April 1918 found *St. Peter* parked at the Union Depot in Salt Lake City, ready for a Utah mission, with Austin Fleming as chaplain. Permission had been denied by the Los Angeles & Salt Lake Railroad (L.A. & S.L.R.R.) as well as the Coast lines, but the Denver and Rio Grande had permitted movement on its lines to Murray and Midvale and to Eureka, a silver and lead mining town of about four thousand, at an elevation of more than seven thousand feet. Fleming noted that the town was undermined from the drives from the mine shafts and it was no unusual thing to be awakened at night with the loud report of blasting underneath the priest's house where they were lodging. In their services was a Mormon bishop and many of his congregation.[48]

St. Peter had the honor of being the first and last chapel car to visit Thistle, Utah, population 150, a roundhouse railroad town in the middle of a barren mountain district. Fleming reported that for smoke and dust, it equaled Pittsburgh. It would not equal Pittsburgh for long, for Thistle would soon be removed from the map, as the Denver and Rio Grande Railroad was moving the roundhouse to Summit. Observing "the cloud of Mormanism" over the town, Fleming quipped, "America is known over as the land of invention and discovery, as it is sure the home of new modes of getting to heaven."[49]

At Helper, which was so called for being the station where the big engines, the helpers, were hooked on to drag the trains over the mountains, mainly Italian children were rounded up to form a First Communion class *(fig. 13.6)*. Their Catholic mothers who had married outside the church could not be remarried, as their husbands were at some far-off construction point, but they promised they would remarry in the Catholic church in town when "the first chance presents itself."[50] The reception at Park City, a mining town and one of the oldest parishes of the diocese, was quite different, where Fleming was asked to speak at the Fourth of July celebration and the chapel car was full.

According to a letter from Ledvina, Hennessey might still wear the uniform of his country. "If the new draft includes men of forty-five I can see our genial Superintendent of Chapel cars keeping step to the tune of 'It's a Long Way to Tipperary.'" Ledvina also cautioned Hennessey to be careful with the new kerosene gas machine purchased for *St. Peter*. "Be sure however, to have the different cans properly marked for gasoline and kerosene. You might happen to get the contents switched and you might have a typical war trench disaster."[51]

War, Flu Discouraged Hennessey in Oregon

In the fall of 1918, *St. Peter* was working along the Southern Pacific lines in Oregon. At Tillamook, one of the oldest towns in the state, famous for its cheese, the Catholic population was about 120 families, mostly Swiss, who could not come to the scheduled services because of morning and evening milkings.[52] After leaving Banks, down the Tillamook branch of the Southern Pacific, the car returned to Portland because of the Spanish influenza, which had caused all churches, theaters, and public gatherings to be closed by the state board of health. This was just as well, for Hennessey was still suffering from his own battle with the flu.[53]

By December the chapel car was back on the Southern Pacific and after a rather circuitous ride on the end of a freight train arrived at Tigard, Oregon. There the crew found, as they had in many of other towns, that a woman described as "the infamous and shameless ex-nun Lucretia of Portland" had visited the town with her well-rehearsed story of the supposed vice of priests and nuns. She had succeeded in stirring up prejudice against anything Catholic.[54]

As early as January 1919, with all the problems with transportation, war, and influenza, Monsignor Kelley had expressed his preference to bring the chapel car program to an end. February found Hennessey sleeping in a sidetracked *St. Peter*, temporarily out of service.

> I am sleeping on the St. Peter and believe me it is some cold in the morning and also at night. The only heat I have is oil stoves and as for water I have to carry it about half a mile. The car is a long way from the street and down behind a lot of freight cars and when it comes to carrying oil and gasoline I sometimes wonder if the people are not a little suspicious of me because now they see me and now they don't.
>
> At night when I come in here I am always looking for some guy to say "hands up" or suddenly get hit with a club in the back of the head. When I'm inside the car

Fig. 13.7 This altar view of *St. Peter* shows the confessional screen protected by curtains that could be drawn for privacy. The art-glass door to the right leads to the living area of the car. (Loyola University, Cudahy Library Archives, Chicago)

> I breath a deep breath and say "safe again. . . ." The charge for living expenses — I am taking it for granted that I am allowed this amount as heretofore when there is no mission work going on. Of course no white man can live on two dollars a day and live at restaurants etc. but by taking two meals a day one can get along fairly well.[55]

Hennessey was not the only one discouraged about the future of the chapel cars. Ledvina wrote to console him in his uncomfortable situation. "This Chapel Car business is certainly coming to an inglorious end; but we certainly cannot help it, nor can anyone criticize us for it. If conditions were favorable, we certainly would keep it up; but under the circumstances, there is nothing else left for us to do but to play quits. Too bad that it is so!"[56]

Even in his discouragement, Ledvina felt that they must do everything possible to keep the cars in operation, as long as the donors held out the hope that they would pay for the transportation and parking charges. He asked Hennessey to send him an itinerary and an estimate of transportation and parking charges for *St. Peter* and *St. Paul*. Ledvina would forward it to the Kuntz estate for consideration. "If we can give them an idea what it would cost, I feel that we have to meet them at least half way."[57]

Ledvina was surprised to get a bill for altar wine, as *St. Peter* was not in service, but Hennessey explained, "I got tired even trying to beg wine, so thought it best to order some for future use. The subject of altar wine out here, in this bone dry state is becoming very serious. There are places where the district attorney had taken it upon himself to say just how much the priest in charge is allowed. To ask for a bottle of Altar wine out here is like asking for a loan of a thousand dollars. If you offer to pay them for a bottle or two they'll think you are lacing them in the bootleggers class — so they would just as soon you wouldn't ask them at all."[58]

Sale Plans Fail As *St. Peter* Gets New Life

Bad news came in April, as the Kuntz heirs decided to have *St. Peter* and *St. Paul* sold and to record the proceeds in the books of the society to the credit of the Kuntz estate. Hennessey was instructed to inventory the contents of the car, which were strictly ecclesiastical and which properly ought to be excluded from the sale, and to provide other details that would be of interest to a potential buyer. He was not to mention the anticipated sale to anyone, especially railroad men. Then Ledvina writes of Hennessey's tenure with the chapel cars.

Coming back to the regretful development of our Chapel Car work; I want to express in the name of the Society, even at this advanced date, my deep regret that this climax of the Chapel Car work, at least according to present indications, means the severance of the pleasant relations between Mr. Geo. C. Hennessey and The Catholic Church Extension Society; unless something turns up or develops that may open some position for the continuation of this relation. At this writing, I do not see anything of that kind; but perhaps when Monsignor Kelley returns, his vision may be better than mine, and he might see a place now obscured from my vision. I hope so.[59]

Something happened on the way to the sale barn for *St. Peter* and *St. Paul*. The Northwest federal manager of the United States Railroad Administration, J. P. O'Brien, wrote Bishop Christie of the Portland diocese, "It has been decided that for the present we will continue former practice of transporting your chapel car free over lines under my jurisdiction. If you will re-submit request for transportation same will be granted."[60]

Confusion reigned, or as the perplexed Ledvina said, "Now, this whole Chapel Car matter is, indeed, in a muddle; and I cannot understand how your Federal Director in the Northwest can issue orders diametrically opposite to those which have been settled upon definitely by the headquarters at Washington. Either the Federal Director in the Northwest has taken it on his own responsibility to go ahead granting free transportation, or the Washington office doesn't know what it is doing, or at least has taken an arbitrary stand which Regional Directors, or Federal Directors may feel privileged to differ."

Ledvina cautioned Hennessey to proceed carefully: "move slowly; for we might get tripped-up, and might have a fine big bill presented to us at the end of an itinerary, demanding pay for the transportation."[61]

Hennessey was tired of sitting in a cold chapel car in a spooky back rail yard in Portland, and he did not go slowly. He quickly got the car ready, called his favorite porter, Joe, back to the car, and with Chaplain J. B. Donegan, C.SS.R, on board took off for the state of Washington. On the Spokane Portland and Seattle road in the Diocese of Seattle, they opened the mission Sunday morning, April 27, at Goldendale, with an inspiring view of mounts Adams and Hood. Even though the flu still had its grip on many members of the community, the car was crowded.[62] The car visited Centreville, Fallbridge, White Salmon, and Stevenson, Washington, before ending the mission.

As Ledvina feared, April 30 found federal manager O'Brien writing to Bishop Christie of Portland again, regretfully stating their previous stance was wrong and that the chapel car would be charged according to existing tariffs.[63]

June found St. Peter at Parkrose, Oregon, a settlement outside the parish of St. Rose, where the bishop requested that it remain for a period to help start a parish[64] until matters of transportation could be more stable. In late September the car was moved to the shops of the Oregon Western Railroad and Navigation Company at Albina for a general overhauling with exterior and interior painting. Ledvina felt that if the car was to be overhauled it would be just as cheap to have the work done in Albina, Oregon, than to bring it back to the Barney & Smith Car Shops in Dayton, Ohio.

The beleaguered vice president lamented, "You know, our old friends at that place have all been ousted. We would meet none but strange faces there now. I don't know where our different acquaintances have gone. I know that when I wanted to get a full copy of the blue Print of the 'St. Peter', they wanted to charge us $300, whereas before I could have gotten a set for the mere asking. That will plainly indicate how the wind blows there."[65]

What Ledvina did not realize was that Barney & Smith was undergoing desperate times and was in receivership, and for the first time in the history of the company, an outsider, Willard Sullivan, had been hired as general manager. A group of Cincinnati stockholders had assumed control in an attempt to reorganize the business but had failed, and much of the machinery had been sold to meet debts.[66] The company could no longer afford to give away prints. It was having great difficulty keeping the doors open.

With the lifting of governmental controls in 1920, the car was ready to continue its missions. After spending nearly all of its tenure in the Northwest, St. Peter headed to North Carolina. For six years the car, still drawing attention and admiration, visited one hundred towns in North Carolina, mainly along branch lines over which the newer, larger, and more imposing coaches rarely passed.

In May 1920 free transportation was again granted St. Peter, and it resumed its missions with Father Doran aboard, along the Oregon Western Railroad (O.W.R.R.) between Vancouver and Seattle, in charge of the Franciscan Fathers of Cowlitz Prairie. Father O'Hara, who would become archbishop of Kansas City, was on the car in January 1921 along with Father Eugene McGuinness, who would become bishop of Oklahoma — Tulsa. At Oakridge, in the depths of the Cascade range, McGuinness had been leading a Mass, and a non-Catholic commented to a Catholic friend, "I have listened to this young orator from Chicago, but all he speaks is Latin and I do not understand the Italian language."[67]

Before St. Peter would leave the Northwest, 268 missions would be completed: 108 in the Oregon City archdiocese, 64 in the Baker City diocese, 73 in the Boise diocese, 10 in the Salt Lake diocese, and 13 in the Seattle diocese.

The message and financial statement from Hennessey at Warrenton, Oregon, in December 1921 to William D. O'Brien, who was now vice president and general secretary of the society, was to the point. "Please send the balance due as soon as possible for I need the money for Christmas and besides I cannot put up any more for the running of this institution because I haven't any. So hurry."[68]

Lack of Support Disheartens Hennessey

Hennessey, discouraged and feeling much neglected and abused by the lack of financial support and direction on the part of extension society officials, was not comforted by the outlook for the chapel cars. Even O'Brien's jokes did not make the situation palatable. Although he continued to keep *St. Peter* in service in 1922, Hennessey was discouraged at the lack of interest of Irish families and lapsed Catholics who had become members of the forbidden societies such as the Masons and the Odd Fellows.

Although the car was busy in the prosperous farming community of Dayton, at Waitsburg, a visiting lecturer, Three-Fingered Jack, had visited and lectured on the dangers of the Catholic faith and frightened the people. At Starbuck, on the Oregon Western Railroad & Navigation Company, many Catholics would not attend Mass as it was held in the Masonic Hall, the only available place in town.[69] Once-genial George seemed to have lost his knack for fun and his optimism.

Cold weather in Idaho in November 1922 caused Hennessey to explain that expenses would be higher as they were obliged to keep five oil stoves going both day and night so the car would be warm in the morning for the people.[70] At Harrison, on the north bank of Lake Coeur d'Alene, on the Union Pacific branch, they gave two missions, one in English and one in Italian. Because it had been so long since the Italians had a priest who used their language, there were thirty-six confessions, forty-eight communions, and five marriages rectified.

Chaplain McDevitt, whose fluent Italian was so much appreciated, was delighted with the scenery. "The old saying regarding Naples 'Un pezzo di Cielo caduto' — a piece of Heaven fallen down, may be applied very aptly to Lake Coeur d'Alene and the majestic parts of Kootenai County, Idaho, which surround it."[71]

In February 1923 O'Brien jestingly reminded Hennessey that he needed to file his income tax return for his yearly salary of fifteen hundred dollars, "or he would go to jail where he should have gone long ago."[72] After filing his taxes, Hennessey and crew traveled the beautiful routes through the evergreen-covered mountains and along the sparkling rivers of Washington State to the Canadian line. Among that scenery George pondered his future with the chapel cars and without the chapel cars.

Jumpoff, Washington, was not a town, just a colony of Austrians and a few Germans. According to legend, many years ago there had been a stage driver whose name was Joe. At the steepest part of the road, between Valley and Jumpoff, Joe had the habit of shouting to his passengers "Everybody jump off," and the passengers did jump off and walked up the steep grade so as to lighten the load for the horses.

The mission opened with Mass on Sunday morning, June 10. On Monday this written request was found in the question box. "Please Father dont holler so loud like you did Sunday night. Some people are very nervous in this church God blessed you with to loud a voice." O'Brien read this request verbatim to the fine congregation assembled Monday evening and expressed regret if he had shocked the nerves of any of his hearers by speaking too loudly.

Then I reminded them that my poor little human voice, no matter how loud it might be, was as nothing, compared to the way in which Almighty God speaks to us His children at times in the storm winds, the thunder and the lightning, even though these make many of us nervous. He had his own divine purpose.

When the services were ended that evening and

those good people had begun to leave the church, a terrific storm verified what had been said in reply to that rather amusing request: "Please Father dont holler so loud" — Awe-inspiring lightning flashed again and again followed by peal after peal of frightful Thunder. Rain came down in torrents followed by a destructive hail-storm. Fortunately the people returned to their pews in the church for safely. Many were in tears not knowing what might happen.

Then took place a most edifying episode. Spontaneously those dear people fell on their knees, and led by the women, in their native tongue, they implored our Dear Lord and His Heavenly Mother to protect them. And their supplications ceased not until the storm had passed. It was a scene never to be forgotten.[73]

The chapel car program seemed to lose its heart when, in October 1923, after sixteen years as manager, Hennessey resigned and entered the mortuary business, the trade practiced by his father. He felt quite at home remaining in Portland after serving so long in the diocese of Archbishop Alexander Christie, who had him honored as a Knight of the Holy Sepulcher.

But *St. Peter* was not done with its work, although without George's direction a confusion occurred that would haunt the extension society in the form of Peter Kuntz's words.

Kuntz had insisted that *St. Peter* was to be used mainly in the North, and *St. Paul* was "never" to go north but was to work in the South. When the two cars were in storage in Chicago, there was a mix-up in orders, and *St. Paul*, which had been brought up from the South, was sent north. *St. Peter*, which was to have gone north, was sent south — the opposite of what Kuntz had in mind. If Hennessey had been around, this never would have happened.

Ill Father Albert Starts Mission

Father Stephen Sweeney, the first of four Passionist missionaries to serve on the car in North Carolina, had taken *St.*

Paul to Chicago and returned to work on *St. Peter*. Then the work was taken over by Father Egbert J. Albert, C.P., who conducted a twelve-week mission in the towns along the eastern side of North Carolina.

Named after the English monk who crossed the Irish Sea during the Anglo-Saxon period to acquire sanctity and learning in Ireland and who influenced the monks of Iona to follow the Pope Gregory's Roman calendar,[74] Father Albert was described as always ready with sparkling wit or a flash of delightful repartee. His fellow priest Charles J. Gable said of him, "He was loved not because he played to the popular whims of men, but because he spoke to them in a most buoyant, irresistible cheerfulness of God."[75]

In January 1926, *St. Peter* rolled into Morehead City with Father Egbert Albert on board. Not well, the young priest worked hard to establish a church at that town, which jutted into the waters of the North Carolina coast. Three years later, after a strenuous tour of mission stops, he passed away on February 7, 1929, while he was at a retreat at the Passionist monastery in Springfield, Massachusetts. The physical demands of his missions in the South and pernicious anemia, which developed into pneumonia, were the cause of death.[76] The church at Morehead City was named after Father Albert, and when that building was replaced, a devotional area in the new church was given the name of the young priest.

After the death of Father Albert, Passionist Father Luke Hay, a Massachusetts native, served his first mission on *St. Peter* in 1930 in a town outside New Bern, where no more than a hundred people lived. It was not an auspicious beginning for the young priest. Very few came to the car. After preaching for about an hour, he stopped and inquired if anyone had any questions. No questions. "I then asked one man if he had ever heard about the Catholic Church, and to my surprise he answered 'No.' I asked another man and he said that he had heard about the Pope and he believed that the Pope was a Catholic, but since he knew very little about him he never paid much attention to what he had heard. He guessed the Catholics were all right and about as good as anyone else."[77]

The other stops of Father Luke's mission were somewhat better, and he reported that all to whom he talked told him it was the first time they had ever heard a Catholic priest or had ever seen what the inside of a Catholic church looked like. "When the many things were explained to them, they not only saw the reasonableness of it all, but likewise much of its beauty."[78]

For many months the car worked along the Atlantic coast section of North Carolina, a section barely two or three feet above sea level, a district under the supervision of Father Charles J. Gable. Over a period of seven years they received into the Catholic church almost one hundred converts, most of whom could be traced either directly or indirectly to the visits of the chapel car. Many of the converts were black, members of the St. Joseph's Colored Mission at New Bern.

Near Easter 1931, the car made its way to the heart of the state, a place of mill towns and small farms. At one such mill town, Father Hay was interrogated by a man about whether the wine Jesus turned from water contained alcohol. When Hay told him that all wine contains some alcohol, the man replied, "Well, I know that Christ ain't the kind of a fellow that would make such wine, and if you believe that wine had alcohol in it, then I don't believe anything you have to say."

At High Point, Meb, the black porter on board, was told by a woman, when she discovered that he was a Catholic, "When you joined that Church, surely your poor mother must have turned over in her grave."

"If she did," replied Meb, "she turned over with joy."[79]

On February 23, 1933, while *St. Peter* was in storage in Raleigh, news came that Hennessey had passed away. He would have been distressed to know that the car had been broken into and some damage done. But he would have been relieved to know that none of the sacred vessels were harmed. They were then removed to the cathedral at Raleigh for safe keeping.[80]

St. Peter's Last Station in Oxford

In 1939 the car was given to the Diocese of North Carolina, and in 1940 the car was sent to Oxford, North Carolina, to serve as the parish church. An article in the Oxford, North Carolina, paper reported, "Recently the Seaboard Air line Railroad deposited a Chapel Car on their siding near Military street in southeast Oxford. This car will serve the Catholic people of Oxford until a church is erected."[81]

Most of the Catholics who attended the car were assigned to duty at Camp Butner, where no chapels were yet completed. In March 1941 the car was still being used as a church with Lenten services announced in the paper. Father Cletus J. Helfrich of Henderson was the pastor in charge.[82] Mass was still being said in the chapel car in July 1944 on Sunday,[83] but soon after the car sat unused on a siding for ten years.

Oxford, North Carolina, is a quiet town, and in the public library on a quiet afternoon, we had a pleasant surprise in store for us. We had come to town looking for information about the demise of chapel car St. Peter. *The librarian directed us to a small room where several people were quietly at work on an Oxford church history project. One gentleman glanced up from his research as we told the librarian about our interest in the chapel car, and as soon as we settled down with some local church history material at the table, he told us that he knew about* St. Peter — *in fact had had a close encounter with the chapel car.*

As a child, he had played in the chapel car while it sat deserted, unsupervised, and unlocked on the siding on Military Street. When he was told that I was a retired schoolteacher, he laughed and said, "You probably would not want to know how roughly we played in that old car. You know how little boys are." But he remembered that St. Peter *still had the beautiful wood paneling; the green window-glass trim, although some panes were broken; the beautiful rolltop desk and the bookcases in the study. In their boyish games of hide and seek in the chaplains' rooms, the washroom, and the kitchen, they could still sense the difference of this adapted playroom on wheels.*

We climbed in his van, and he took us to the spot where the rail car had sat, past the regal grounds of the old military school, past the lovely old homes, past the Catholic church that had been built with the funds from the dismantled St. Peter, *the same church that would stand empty, abandoned, when the parish moved to Henderson.*

He obviously enjoyed his recollection of the chapel car and those boyhood days. He enjoyed sharing his memories with strangers, and we enjoyed hearing them. We stepped from the van and stood looking at a field of weeds — imagining, recreating the form of Peter Kuntz's gift, the once-beautiful St. Peter. *Our guide stood quietly too — looking, calling up, and cherishing his childhood memories.*

As we climbed back into the van for our return trip to the library, the thought occurred to me that St. Peter *would not have minded little boys playing within its mahogany walls. For didn't Jesus say, "Suffer the little children to come unto me, for of such is the kingdom of Heaven" (Matthew 19:14, KJV)?*

In April 1953, young people of the parish working with axes and wrecking bars tore apart the interior mahogany-finished panels to prepare for the steel-cutter's torch that reduced the car to metal junk *(fig. 13.9)*. It was reported that about one thousand pounds of copper, stripped from the top of the car, had been sold for $169. Another one hundred thousand pounds of iron and steel brought about $1,500, and the proceeds were used for the new church.[84]

Peter Kuntz's car that was never to have gone South sacrificed itself to support a Southern church, but on its journey to Oxford it left behind hundreds who had come to a new relationship and acceptance of the Catholic faith.

> Holy God! We praise Thy name!
> Lord of all, we bow before Thee!
> All on earth Thy sceptre claim
> All in Heaven above adore Thee;
> Infinite Thy vast domain
> Everlasting is Thy reign.[85]

Notes

[1] Correspondence from E. B. Ledvina to George C. Hennessey, at New Meadows, Idaho, November 4, 1912, LUCA.

[2] *Memoirs of the Miami Valley*, ed. John C. Hover et al. (Chicago: Robert O. Law Company, 1919), vol. 3, 360–63.

[3] Francis C. Kelley, *The Story of Extension* (Chicago: Extension Press, 1922), 93.

[4] Ibid.

[5] Agreement between Peter Kuntz and The Catholic Church Extension Society of the United States of America, LUCA.

[6] *Dayton (Ohio) Daily News*, "Splendid New Chapel Car Completed at Dayton Plant for Catholic Extension," June 27, 1912.

[7] Financial report of George Hennessey, July 16, 1912, LUCA.

[8] Report of Edward L. Roe, in regard to chapel car *St. Peter*, transportation, August 14, 1912, LUCA.

[9] *Oregon Catholic History Newsletter*, vol. 6, 1984, 10.

[10] Correspondence from E. B. Ledvina to George C. Hennessey, December 12, 1919, LUCA.

Fig. 13.9 In 1953 *St. Peter* was stripped, the materials sold for salvage, and the profits used to help build the Catholic church at Oxford, North Carolina. That parish would move to Henerson years later, leaving the town of Oxford without the church *St. Peter* was sent to start. (Loyola University, Cudahy Library Archives, Chicago)

11 Report of George Hennessey, October 19, 1912, LUCA.

12 Report of George Hennessey, September 4, 1912, LUCA.

13 Reports from P. L. Barrett, November 2 to November 30, 1912, LUCA.

14 Francis P. Leipzig, *Extension in Oregon* (St. Benedict, Ore.: The Benedictine Press, 1956), 102–3.

15 Report of Alvah W. Doran, Montpelier, Idaho, January 5, 1913, LUCA.

16 Report of Alvah W. Doran, Blackfoot, Idaho, February 13, 1913, LUCA.

17 Letter from Sister Mary Catharine of Jesus, Holy Rosary Hospital, Dominican Sisters, Ontario, Ore., February 15, 1913, LUCA.

18 Report of Alvah W. Doran, Pocatello, Idaho, March 1, 1913, LUCA.

19 Report of J. F. Murphy, Wallowa, Ore., June 12, 1913, LUCA.

20 Letter from George Hennessey, Turon, Kan., to J. P. Seymour, chief clerk, MK&T line, Parsons, Kan., March 19, 1914, LUCA.

21 Letter from George Hennessey, Wichita, Kan., to W. H. Maddocks, MK&T, Parsons, Kan., April 8, 1914, LUCA.

22 R. Serrano, C.M.F., "The Mexican Missions on the Chapel Car — 'St. Peter,'" *Extension*, June 1914.

23 P. J. MacCorry, "Covering Missions with the Chapel Car 'St. Peter,'" *Extension*, July 1914, 11.

24 Ibid.

25 Father Andrew, O.M.Cap., "'St. Peter' Chapel Car in Western Kansas," *Extension*, August 1914.

26 Report of Alvah W. Doran, Burley, Idaho, July 12, 1914, LUCA.

27 Letter from Alvah W. Doran, Victor, Dreggs, Tetonia, and Ashton, Idaho, August 16–21, 1914, LUCA.

28 Report of Michael P. Seter, Murphy, Idaho, July 8, 1915, LUCA.

29 Letter from E. B. Ledvina to George C. Hennessey, Pendleton, Ore., August 23, 1915, LUCA.

30 Letter from E. B. Ledvina to George C. Hennessey, San Francisco, Calif., September 13, 1915, LUCA.

31 Letter from E. B. Ledvina to George C. Hennessey, San Francisco, Calif., October 15, 1915, LUCA.

32 Letter from E. B. Ledvina to Joseph S. Glass, bishop of Salt Lake City, Utah, October 13, 1915, LUCA.

33 Correspondence between E. B. Ledvina and George C. Hennessey, January 14, 1916, LUCA.

34 Report of Thomas J. Brady, Kent, Ore., May 17, 1916, LUCA.

35 Report of Thomas J. Brady, Shaniko, Ore., May 21, 1916, LUCA.

36 Report of Thomas J. Brady, Riverside, Ore., June 11, 1916, LUCA.

37 Letter from E. B. Ledvina to George C. Hennessey, Vale, Ore., June 27, 1916, LUCA.

38 Letter from E. B. Ledvina to George C. Hennessey, Pocatello, Idaho, August 14, 1916, LUCA.

39 Letter from E. B. Ledvina to George C. Hennessey, Hailey, Idaho, November 20, 1916, LUCA.

40 *Extension*, May 1918, 29, LUCA.

41 Report of Jerome B. Donegan, Myrtle Point, Ore., May 28, 1917, LUCA.

42 Report of Jerome B. Donegan, Powers, Ore., June 3, 1917, LUCA.

43 Report of Jerome B. Donegan, North Bend, Ore., June 17, 1917, LUCA.

44 Letter from E. B. Ledvina to George C. Hennessey, Marshfield, Ore., June 11, 1917, LUCA.

45 Report from George C. Hennessey to E. B. Ledvina, Arleta Station, Portland, Ore., September 10, 1917, LUCA.

46 Letter from E. B. Ledvina to Franklin T. Griffith, president, Portland Railway Light & Power Company, Portland, Ore., February 7, 1918, LUCA.

47 Report of Austin Fleming, Hailey, Idaho, March 20, 1918, LUCA.

48 Report of Austin Fleming, Eureka, Utah, May 12, 1918, LUCA.

49 Report of Austin Fleming, Thistle, Utah, June 3, 1918, LUCA.

50 Report of Austin Fleming, Helper, Utah, June 9, 1918, LUCA.

51 Letter from E. B. Ledvina to George C. Hennessey, Portland, Ore., August 20, 1918, LUCA.

52 Report of Jerome B. Donegan, Tillamook, Ore., September 22, 1918, LUCA.

53 Report of George C. Hennessey, Banks, Ore., October 14, 1918, LUCA.

54 Letter from J. B. Donegan, C.SS.R., Tigard, Ore., December 15, 1918, LUCA.

55 Report of George C. Hennessey, Portland, Ore., February 5, 1919, LUCA.

56 Letter from E. B. Ledvina to George C. Hennessey, February 12, 1919, LUCA.

57 Letter from E. B. Ledvina to George C. Hennessey, March 1, 1919, LUCA.

58 Report from George C. Hennessey, Portland, Ore., March 31, 1919, LUCA.

59 Correspondence from E. B. Ledvina to George C. Hennessey, April 9, 1919, LUCA.

60 Letter from J. P. O'Brien to A. Christie, Portland, Ore., April 1, 1919, LUCA.

61 Letter from E. B. Ledvina to George C. Hennessey, April 15, 1919, LUCA.

62 Report of George C. Hennessey, Goldendale, Washington, April 27, 1919, LUCA.

63 Letter from J. P. O'Brien to A. Christie, April 30, 1919, LUCA.

64 Report of George C. Hennessey, Parkrose, Ore., June 7, 1919, LUCA.

65 Letter from E. B. Ledvina to George C. Hennessey, Portland, Ore., October 23, 1919, LUCA.

66 Scott D. Trostel, *The Barney & Smith Car Company: Car Builders* (Fletcher, Ohio: Cam-Tech Publishing, 1993), 166–67.

67 Leipzig, 68.

68 Letter from George C. Hennessey to William D. O'Brien, Warrenton, Ore., December 2, 1921, LUCA.

69 "A Chapel Car Report," *Extension*, October 1922.

70 Report from George C. Hennessey to William D. O'Brien, Worley, Idaho, November 6, 1922, LUCA.

71 Report of H. J. McDevitt, Harrison, Idaho, November 12, 1922, LUCA.

72 Letter from William D. O'Brien to George C. Hennessey, February 10, 1923, LUCA.

73 Report of H. J. McDevitt, Jumpoff, Wash., June 10, 1923, LUCA.

74 Anne Sargent, *Carteret (North Carolina) News-Times*, March 19, 1995, 1.

75 Charles J. Gable, "The Martyr of the Chapel Car," *Extension*, May 1929, 13.

76 Ibid.

77 Luke Hay, C.P., "Good Soil," *Extension*, September 1929, 26.

78 Ibid.

79 Luke Hay, C.P., "Preparing the Way," *Extension*, May 1931, n.p.

80 Letter from Arthur R. Freeman, diocese of Raleigh, chancery office, to Richard R. St. John, Catholic Church Extension Society, May 3, 1933, LUCA.

81 *Maxwell Ledger*, "Catholic Services to be Held in Chapel Car Near Military Street," August 2, 1940, Oxford Public Library, Oxford, North Carolina.

82 *Maxwell Ledger*, April 11, 1941, Oxford Public Library.

83 *Maxwell Ledger*, July 28, 1944, Oxford Public Library.

84 "Church on Wheels Goes to Scrap Pile," *Raleigh News Observer*, April 5, 1953.

85 "Holy God, We Praise Thy Name," an English paraphrase of the *Te Deum*, translation by Clarence A. Walworth, chapel car song sheet.

CHAPTER 14

Barney & Smith Car Company and the Flood of 1913

After struggling through years of financial troubles resulting from the panic of 1893 and the reluctance to give up the construction of their wooden cars, the Barney & Smith Car Company finally went to steel production in 1905. Barney President Arthur M. Kittredge insisted the public would never favor all-steel cars over the woodworker's art. The decision to delay conversion of their passenger cars to steel would eventually prove to be a fatal mistake by the Barney management.[1]

The fact soon became obvious: they no longer needed nor could afford those skilled workers who had labored to make the wooden Baptist cars beautiful. In order to insure cheaper labor for the production of steel cars, Barney & Smith engaged J. D. Moskowitz, a labor contractor who had created a Hungarian colony around the Malleable Iron Works on Dayton's west side and another colony in Pennsylvania. Barney & Smith wanted him to create a workers' colony for them like the one George M. Pullman had built at Pullman, Illinois. This colony would be different, however. The Barney employees would own their own homes and receive credit at the company store, even during layoffs, whereas Pullman colony employees rented their homes at high prices, even when laid off.

Moskowitz, not the Barney management, would receive the profits from colony businesses, he purchased the land and built a four-square block area now known as North Dayton — bounded by Notre Dame and Mack Avenues and by Baltimore Street and surrounded by a high fence. Within those boundaries, he erected forty doubles with five rooms to a side for $800 each (*fig. 14.2*). He named the colony Kossuth, in honor of a Hungarian hero.

Two hundred men could sit at the Kossuth clubhouse bar that Moskowitz built for the workers — the biggest bar in Dayton. Also in the building were a bank, a massive grocery and general store, and a travel agency, so the colony residents could bring relatives over from Hungary. Barney & Smith gave employees brass script to make purchases in the company store; purchases outside that store were prohibited. For a 55-hour work week, the company paid the workers about nine dollars, slightly less than the U.S. average. Room, board, and laundry were only eight to ten dollars monthly.[2]

In spite of the "I owe my soul to the company store" concept, life in the colony flourished. For these immigrants, life had probably never been better. Families were close-knit and frugal, continuing to observe their native customs and prepare traditional foods. The entire community participated in lavish and ritualistic Christmas, Easter, and wedding celebrations. Church services for the predominantly Roman Catholic residents were held in one of the houses set aside for that purpose[3] until a Roman Catholic Church was built.

"Each day the workers walked a mile to and from the colony and the car works. One man who operated a clothing store in North Dayton said 'the men looked like a flock of geese trailing by my store in the evening.'"[4]

Fig. 14.1 The surging waters of the Mad River devastated the city of Dayton, as well as the Barney & Smith Car Company. The great flood of 1913 left many citizens dead and more without homes or jobs. (Special Collections and Archives, Paul Laurence Dunbar Library, Wright State University, Dayton, Ohio)

Fig. 14.2 When Barney & Smith changed to producing steel cars, many of their wood craftsmen were no longer needed. Jacob Moskowitz was hired to bring workers from Hungary to live in a company community, the Kossuth Colony. This is a street of original workers' homes in the colony, which is still a pleasant community. (Norman T. Taylor)

Not everyone in Dayton thought the Kossuth Colony was a good idea. The editor of the Dayton paper launched a vigorous denunciation of the colony and of Jacob D. Moskowitz. Its chief accusation was that the colony with its high fence was contrary to the ideals of America. The furor created by the *News* was so great that the state sent a labor investigator down from Columbus to inspect the community. Probably to the dismay of the newspaper, the investigator found no infraction of labor laws and cleared Moskowitz of the charges.[5]

Steel *St. Peter* Leaves Plant before Flood

In 1912 the Kossuth Colony workers built Catholic Church Extension Society's chapel car *St. Peter*, the first steel chapel car constructed by the Barney & Smith Car Works. When the company had finally produced its first steel passenger car in 1905, it was suffering through its third straight year

of losses. By 1912, the company showed a modest profit, and the year 1913 looked more promising yet[6] — until March 25 and the Great Flood of Dayton.

. . . bells rang and whistles blew, utterly failing to rouse people to a sense of their danger; . . . a brown wave of water, six feet high, rolled its foaming crest westward on the streets and meeting at each corner a similar wave from the north, piled the water into a raging torrent which filled the streets with foam and wreckage . . . and women who had sipped their breakfast coffee in serene ignorance that anything more momentous than ironing day was ahead of them found themselves a few hours later, feeding half-drowned babies or identifying bodies brought in by rescue corps.[7]

The surging waters of the Mad River obliterated restraining levees and poured into the Barney & Smith Car Company, inundating the plant under fourteen feet of water. Precious hoards of rare wood for car interiors were swept away. Pieces of teak and mahogany were pulled out of the water as far downstream as New Orleans.[8]

The flood caused more than a million dollars worth of damage to the car works, dealing the already fragile company a blow from which it would never recover.

Allan W. Eckert's account of the flood, *A Time of Terror*, illustrates in a touching way the personal and corporate losses suffered by E. J. Barney, the Baptist layman who had done so much to further the cause of rail evangelism by his support of the chapel cars, his fine construction, and his charitable discounts.

March 30, 11 a.m. — The relief line stretched for blocks along K Street to the side door of the National Cash Register Company. A gangly, scraggly-whiskered laborer with rotten teeth and sour breath scratched himself under the arm of his filthy coveralls and complained bitterly to the man behind him in line.

"It's them damn' millionaires caused all this!" he said

passionately. "They got all the money an' coulda prevented this from happenin', but they ain't about to give up none of that money."

"That so?" asked the other man, a short, rather bland-looking older individual. He, too, wore coveralls of the type given out at NCR.

"Hell, yes, it's so! You k'n bet you won't find them lousy buggers wantin' food or clothes or losing anything they got. No siree! By God, it's them millionaires. They'll make a fortune on this flood an' it'll be at our expense."

They reached the head of the line, each receiving three small loaves of bread and a sack of potatoes. . . . The whiskered man slapped his companion on the shoulder and grinned. "Ummm, thought I'd never see fresh bread again. Looks like you could use a little, too."

"I have been a little hungry," the other admitted.

"Your home is in pretty good shape?"

"Oh, yeah, water dint even touch it. We made out pretty good, 'cept we ain't been able to get no bread nowhere till now. You lose much in the flood?"

"Yes." the older man said softly, "just about everything."

". . . Mebbe I'll see you again. My name's Roal Rupert. What's yours?"

"Barney. Eugene J. Barney," the older man said simply, turning away.[9]

Oak and mahogany from the production of Barney & Smith's carefully crafted private wooden interiors floated, along with their future, down the river toward New Orleans.[10] That high wooden wall around the Kossuth Colony, which was considered so un-American, was torn down to make rafts to rescue victims of the raging waters of the Miami and Mad. It would never be built up again.

Fig. 14.3, 14.4 These views of Barney & Smith buildings M-7 and M-8 show the damage the flood caused to the plant, the last blow to a failing company. The Catholic Church Extension Society chapel car *St. Peter* had left the plant in the spring of 1912, but the company would build two more chapel cars, the extension society's *St. Paul* and the American Baptist Publication Society's *Grace*. (Special Collections and Archives, Paul Laurence Dunbar Library, Wright State University, Dayton, Ohio)

The company would rise again to build two more chapel cars — great arks, not of gopher wood covered inside and out with pitch, as Noah was instructed (Genesis 6:14), but of steel and great interior panels of polished mahogany and oak — the Catholic Church Extension Society *St. Paul* and the American Baptist Publication Society *Grace*.

Notes

[1] Michael W. Williams, "The Barney & Smith Car Company," *TIME-LINE* (Ohio Historical Society, 1991).

[2] Bruce W. Ronald and Virginia Ronald, *Dayton: The Gem City* (Tulsa: Continental Heritage Press, Inc., 1981), 59.

[3] Elizabeth Zimmerman, *Dayton (Ohio) Daily News*, Sunday, March 31, 1974, 15.

[4] Stanley R. Cichanowicz, "The Kossuth Colony and Jacob D. Moskowitz — An Experiment in the Settlement of Hungarian Immigrants in Dayton, Ohio," an unpublished thesis for the University of Dayton, December 3, 1963, 26, Dayton Public Library, Dayton, Ohio.

[5] Cichanowicz, 26.

[6] Williams, 25.

[7] Charlotte Reeve Conover, *The Story of Dayton* (Dayton, Ohio: The Greater Dayton Association, 1917), 196–98.

[8] Williams, 25.

[9] Allan W. Eckert, *A Time of Terror* (Boston: Little, Brown and Company, 1965), 324–25.

[10] Williams, 34.

CHAPTER 15

St. Paul: The Great Steel Ark of the Apostle

Peter Kuntz did not attend the dedication of his first extension society chapel car, *St. Peter*. It was not because he did not care but because he cared too much. He did not want to be pointed out as the donor. According to those who knew him well, he did what he did not for the glory of men but for the glory of God. When *St. Peter* had been working for some months, Kuntz dropped into the Chicago extension office. "How is the *St. Peter* doing?" he asked Father Kelley.

"Splendidly," Kelley replied. "Do you want me to show you some of the chaplain's reports?"

"Never mind," Kuntz said, as he started for the door. "I'll build you another." And he did.[1]

Kuntz paid thirty-five thousand dollars for *St. Paul*. He was adamant that *St. Paul* was never to go north. In June 1914 Barney & Smith Car Company delivered to Father Emmanuel B. Ledvina the proposed plan for the new car. Certain ecclesiastical sections were to be fashioned by a professional designer of interior Gothic decorations.

The floor plan was an improvement over that of *St. Peter*. The kitchen ran the full end of the car, and the refrigerator inside of the kitchen instead of out on the platform, a much better arrangement for the cooks and porters. There would be no dragging of oils or anything else through the car since all cabinets for oils and for the lighting system would be accessible from the outside of the car, from the platform. In the toilet room as well as in the kitchen, provisions were made for filling the tanks for water supply both by hand and by force. Proper consideration was taken for the water service, inasmuch as, most of the time, the car was in places where water work facilities were not readily available.

The study would be much the same, with a lower and an upper berth on one side, but a folding table would be used in the study to provide more flexibility (*fig. 15.3*). Pigeonholes in the desk would be arranged like drawers and the shelves made much heavier in order to receive heftier volumes. Instead of two berths in the rear of the chapel, there would be one. Attending priests had requested that the confessional be made in the folding style so the prie dieu could be attached and folded.

As for the dreaded Baker heater, Coleman Company officials thought they could improve on it. It was their opinion that the Baker system troubles resulted from the fact that people tampered with the tanks by trying to fill them by hand, which couldn't provide the necessary pressure to force the water into every part of the pipe and prevent air pockets. Such air pockets were almost always the cause of defective service.[2]

Kuntz would heed none of this advice and would have none of the Baker heater. Ledvina, obviously frustrated, wrote in July, "The old gentleman has put his foot down on that positively. That Car is going to be built for the South, and the

Fig. 15.1 The children leaving *St. Paul* at Egan, Louisiana, in 1917 have just had their catechetical instruction. Much of the work of the chapel cars was done with children, although at Egan prominent leaders of the town welcomed the car and crowds came for services. (Loyola University, Cudahy Library Archives, Chicago)

South only! Mr. Kuntz would not hear to putting in any electric wires. . . . He had even decided to omit the Baker Heating system all together and to run no steam pipes through the car, but under the car. . . . I think however he will be agreeable to the suggestion to put in some kind of a heating system anyway."[3]

The contract between the Catholic Church Extension Society and Kuntz for the transfer of possession of *St. Paul*, which was in its final stage of construction, was signed December 17, 1914, with the same stipulations as for *St. Peter* — that if the society determined not to use the car for its intended missionary purposes, it would be returned to the original owners; that all priests celebrating Mass in the car, and the donor and his family, both living and dead, should have a memento on one day during the week that the car was in missionary operation; and that the stipend be taken from the offerings given on board the car.[4]

New Orleans Celebrates Dedication

St. Paul, with all the improvements and carefully designed Gothic touches, headed south to New Orleans on January 12, on the Louisville and Nashville Railroad (L & N). Information about the car and its arrival at certain points — Louisville, Owensboro, Henderson, Evansville, Nashville, Birmingham, Montgomery, Pensacola, Mobile, Biloxi, Bay St. Louis, Pass Christian, and New Orleans — had been forwarded, and it was hoped that crowds, including schoolchildren, would be at stations to greet the car.[5]

Kuntz grudgingly relented, and the car did have portable oil stoves and steam pipes that could be connected with outside steam connections on storage tracks.[6]

Visitors to the chapel car had been reading disturbing news: the British and French fleets in the Dardanelles were being bombarded; the British had decided to make contraband all food destined for Germany in retaliation against the German declaration that British waters were to be regarded as a war zone; and German troops had crossed over the East Prussian border. Catholics were also concerned about the news that half a million dollars ransom was being demanded for the release of all the native Catholic clergy in Mexico City, where conditions were dire with little flour, bread, or water in the city as fighting continued.[7]

Local news was also disturbing to the chaplains heading South. Night riders were active along the border of Kentucky and Tennessee;[8] although most of the trouble focused on blacks, the priests knew that hatred was also being spread about "Papists." The decade of the 1920s was dominated by the rise of the Knights of the Ku Klux Klan. In 1915 William Joseph Simmons resurrected the post–Civil War Klan in Georgia, which became the new Ku Klux Klan.[9]

At Atlanta, the car was parked at the terminal station and drew a good crowd on Sunday, February 21, but most of the railroaders of a religious bent were at the "Railroad Night" revival of Dr. J. Wilbur Chapman on Monday night. The sermon was one of the strongest preached by Chapman, and there were tears in the eyes of hundreds of his hearers.

According to the *Atlanta Constitution*, "Big strong engine men, who are wont to face all sorts of danger and 'tight' places in their daily work along the tracks, bowed their heads in silent prayer and sobbed." He pleaded especially with the railroad men, declaring them to be the class that needed to make peace with God so they could be properly guided in their care of the thousands of passengers who entrusted themselves to the engineers.[10]

St. Paul left Atlanta for Birmingham and its display at the Louisville and Nashville Railroad Station, and then it would go to Montgomery. The Chapman revival blazed on in Atlanta.

The day of the dedication came in New Orleans, Sunday, March 14, 1915 *(fig. 15.2)*. *St. Paul* was placed on the siding at the foot of Canal Street, the city's main thoroughfare, close to the Mississippi River and the L & N station. A special platform, decked with bunting, was constructed in front of the chapel on wheels. Archbishop James H. Blenk, though ill, was determined to participate in the ceremonies, so he had Mr. Fabacher, K.S.G., take him to Cardinal James Gibbon's home, where a procession of automobiles bearing the cardinal and the visiting prelates was formed.

The cavalcade moved down Canal Street, and near the chapel car it was met by Knights of Columbus units, uniformed ranks of the Holy Name Society, cadet corps of various schools, bands, and drum corps. The cardinal, a striking figure in his scarlet robe, the archbishops and bishops, Mayor Behrman, Chief Justice O'Neill, the chief of police, and the heads of religious orders in the city took their places on the platform under a sunny sky. Facing them was a throng estimated by the New Orleans *Morning Star* at ten thousand.[11]

Bishop John E. Gunn, S.M., of Natchez, Mississippi, delivered a masterly address, according to the *Morning Star*, stressing the need for educating others about the true nature of the Catholic church.

Seeds of bigotry are sown; prejudice is rooted; a fear of the Church is engendered, and when the bigot and fanatic canvass the country voters to penalize Catholic

consciences, to inspect convents, to hamper even the saying of Mass, we are sadly familiar with the results obtained as evidenced by the legislative acts of some of our nearby States. I attribute much of the violence of recent and present anti-Catholic intolerance, first to plain ignorance, and secondly to manufactured ignorance, and both kinds flourish only where the Catholic Church has never had a hearing. Our commission is to carry the Gospel message outside Judea and Samaria, even to the uttermost bounds of the earth. I am pleading to carry it at least to the neglected, deserted spots of our own American Continent. If it is true that an honest peasantry is a nation's pride, and when once destroyed can never be supplied, it is equally true that if we let the taint of bigotry and intolerance take root in our country it will never be eradicated.[12]

At the close, the bishop voiced gratitude for the munificence of the donor of the car and lauded his spirit, which he said should be an inspiration to them on behalf of mission work. During Gunn's address, the donor himself, Peter Kuntz, was seated alone in the pews of *St. Paul*. He had declined to appear on the platform and desired that his name not be used.[13]

This last 86-foot steel ark would travel the rails of Louisiana from 1915 to 1918, under the direction of Archbishop Blenk, devoting its work to the mixture of people located there — black, French Creoles, Irish, German, French, lumberjacks, shrimpers, cotton farmers, and rail workers — as well as serving in Texas, North Carolina, and Oklahoma.

St. Paul's First Mission Begins at Bunkie

After the dedication, the first stop for *St. Paul* was Bunkie, a growing town on the Texas and Pacific Railroad in central Louisiana, in a section called Avoyelles. Populated mainly with descendants of the Acadian exiles, it was a network of meandering bayous and swampy areas and roads of sticky clay spotted by quagmires. Father Alvah W. Doran was the chaplain, and interest in the mission grew so much that it was soon impossible to accommodate all who came in the car. And so the meetings were moved to the local chapel.

By means of the question box, Doran tried to dissipate false notions about the Catholic church. Two hundred Catholics took Communion, twenty-four children were given instruction and made their First Communion, and two converts were received into the church. Many Italians received the sacraments, being able to make their confessions in their own tongue, as Doran knew the language.[14]

The chapel car congregation was made up of Italians, Mexicans, French, Irish, Creoles, and blacks at Cheneyville, but Doran reported, "The Italians preponderate and it is only fair to say that along this line of railroad they are the finest of their race the Chapel Cars have found, zealous, affectionate, industrious and 'practical.' They pushed forward the building of the church, have fenced it in and laid out a garden with their own hands. Socialism and secret societies have not touched them. They claimed the missionary as their own because he spoke a little of their mother tongue. They are mostly from Palermo."[15]

At Secompte, Doran was becoming used to the indifference of Catholic and non-Catholic alike, and "the last night rush" of visitors.[16] At Boyce, a rail division point on the Red River, Mr. Smith Texada and Mrs. Annie Ryan became converts and "were as good Catholics as the rest of us" before *St. Paul* left town.[17]

Doran commented that floods and poor crops had held the French Catholics in Aloha in poverty and ignorance. Although they were mostly Catholic in name only, two hundred came out for the evening lecture, and three men agreed to abandon forbidden secret societies. Two civil marriages were validated and another repaired.[18]

At Powhatan, on the Louisiana River and Navigation Company Railroad, the local priest, N. Gudermanns, who was more accustomed to the hardships of southern missionary work, enjoyed the chapel car luxuries:

I lost no time in adapting myself to my new surroundings. How easy it is to fit oneself into luxuries! I was rather timid at first. How was I, who now had a study, a private room, a dining-room, kitchen and so forth, to act, but like a king in his royal car? I thought it well to pretend not to have any surprise at my new surroundings, and acted as if it was natural to me to be so well fixed. My! I thought, I will have a fine time on my vacation!

And just then the work began. The first sermon of my "vacation series" was preached to a "crowded house," with a considerable overflow on all kinds of benches and chairs on the outside. The Car had been placed close to several stores, the roofs and windows of which were galleries filled with well-disposed and serious people who listened attentively. That night it was hot, 102 degrees in the car, and so I did not preach on hell; if I had, I am sure I would have dispersed the crowd. For the next four days I said Mass and preached twice a day. I had the pleasure of baptizing one grown person. My vacation was becoming more strenuous; in fact, I had lost sight of the element of rest, which, theory says, plays an important role in vacations.[19]

Chaplain Owen A. McGrath had seen many outrageous sights in his ministry, but he was "somewhat shocked" when he discovered in late October that in Winnfield the Baptists, who had absolute control, had a large open pavilion on the main street where not only men but also women preached.[20]

Town Receptions Sometimes Threatening

Already *St. Paul* was experiencing problems. Although the Dallas diocese wanted the car, because of its lack of heating facilities it was feared it could not take the cold sometimes experienced in that city. More of a problem was the difficulty of getting free transportation. The Rock Island had refused any concessions, saying that it had gone into the hands of a receiver and could not afford to make any concessions. Ledvina responded, "Poor excuse!"[21]

Jena, Louisiana, was notorious through the state as a murder town, and McGrath found it deserved its reputation. Killings had been numerous and convictions unknown. The week before he arrived the town marshal shot and killed the ex-marshal, and the day he left one man cut another's throat with a pocket knife. According to McGrath, the people generally were merciless and unforgiving, revengeful and untouched by any refinement of Christianity. He realized from the start that he was unwelcome, for he could get but a few people to accept his handbills. The Masons were in control, and McGrath felt the town reflected their influence. Trouble was outside the windows of the chapel car the last three nights, as men taunted the visitors to the car and waited outside. One Catholic woman told McGrath that she was afraid they would shoot in through the windows. However, they were able to leave town unharmed.[22]

At Goodpine, between Trout and Talltimber, the reception was kinder, even with the strong influence of the Baptists and Methodists, and the car was filled every night. McGrath reported that the black people were eager to come, but the white people told them to stay away, which they did. However, several ventured to come and stand outside the windows.[23] St. Paul closed the year at Ruston, a city of five thousand, where although five hundred handbills were distributed, only a few people came to the car.

The second year of service for St. Paul began with the car sided on the Vicksburg, Shreveport & Pacific (V.S. & P) tracks at Shreveport in care of the porter, Wendell Walker. The effort was being made to find a shop where the car could be painted and varnished. Originally it was planned to take the car to the Texas and Pacific shops at Marshall, Texas, but that became impossible when those shops were destroyed in a storm. The next approach was to try the one of the shops of the Queen and Crescent,[24] but the car ended up at the Southern Pacific shops at Houston. At the shops St. Paul, just a year old, was painted and revarnished and had every window and door removed and adjusted. One of the platforms was also pushed out of shape, indicating that the car had been in some kind of wreck.[25]

While Ledvina was in Texas caring for the work done on St. Paul and motor chapel car St. Peter, a shocking crime occurred in Chicago. Someone with anarchistic tendencies, who had enough dynamite to "blow up Chicago" in his apartment, poisoned the soup served at the banquet for the new archbishop of Chicago, the Most Reverend George William Mundelein, February 10, 1916, at the University Club.

Many of the priests at the banquet who partook of the soup were ill, including Monsignor Kelley, the extension society's president, and Father O'Brien, vice president. Mundelein, the new archbishop, did not partake of the soup. In a letter informing Ledvina of the event, extension society clerk G. M. Johnson concluded, "It is almost unbelievable that there are men in this world with such perverted minds; and when the consequences are considered, had his plot been successful, it makes one cold with apprehension."[26]

Wendell Walker, the black porter who had been caring for St. Paul while it was out of service and who had been a favorite of the chaplains, resigned. He was replaced with Michael Cousins, an Irish seminary student who decided that he was not fitted for the priesthood but would like a lay position in the church. Like George Hennessey, long-time chapel car superintendent serving on St. Peter, Cousins could sing and play the organ and quickly became a valued part of the chapel car program.

For the next year the car crisscrossed the state, visiting towns like Eros on the Tremont & Gulf Railroad; the old town of Bastrop on the V.S. & P Railroad; Monroe, Shreveport, and small interior sawmill towns where there were few Catholics and no churches. In Rochelle, on the Iron Mountain Railroad, visitors found the stations of cross, arranged between the windows in the chapel area, a great attraction apparently new to them.

In 1916, the Redemptorist Fathers from New Orleans took charge of the car. At Turkey Creek in April Father E. L. Mattingly borrowed a horse and rode many miles through the piney woods and across the prairies looking up scattered Catholics. He soon became lost. A Protestant man volunteered to be his guide back to the chapel car and became an enthusiastic worker during the mission, which was quite successful.[27]

Chaplains Find God-forsaken Places

Oakdale — which Mattingly described as the most God-forsaken place he had ever met, the place on Satan's route where the devil had turned back and said the rest was safe — was a haven of Presbyterians, Baptists, and Hard-Shelled Baptists. They made the chaplain's situation difficult by blocking a move to larger accommodations and forbidding their

Fig. 15.3 The study/dining/living area in *St. Paul* features a desk with bookcase, comfortable chairs, and, under a berth, seats with a table. To the right of the desk is the confessional door, with a small table and chair for the priest. (Loyola University, Cudahy Library Archives, Chicago)

members to come to the meetings. Even when the Mattingly went out to witness to some Choctaw Indians, a Baptist minister was waiting to refute his message.[28]

Father John Diederich, C.SS.R., was on the car in late 1916 and early 1917, and his routine in towns like Egan, Lacassine, and the parishes of Jeff Davis and Acadia included 7 A.M. Mass, catechism for the children at 4 P.M., and a lecture mainly for non-Catholics at night.

Although other Louisiana railroads handled its transportation differently, in October 1916 the Southern Pacific refused to handle *St. Paul* for no charge. A distressed Ledvina wrote, "Seems that this part of the S.P. is in hands of bigots. Seems strange anyway, after they handled the Car free down here before."[29]

In spite of the injunction, the car traveled to DeRidder in October to begin its autumn itinerary. The Hudson River Lumber Company had one of its largest mills at DeRidder, and the Vizard Company turpentine stills were also located there. The Catholic children who came to the car were "woefully ignorant of everything pertaining to religion. We found boys and girls from eight to fourteen years of age who did not know a prayer — did not even know how to make the sign of the cross, and the non-Catholics in town had never seen a priest, their knowledge of the Catholic faith mainly from the vile sheets as 'The Menace' and 'Tom Watson' magazines."

But when the car prepared to leave, the children, who had been instructed and received Holy Communion, came bearing gifts of fruit, flowers, cakes, and other presents as tokens of their gratitude. Their parents shed tears of joy.[30]

At Sulphur in December 1916, the problem was arranging services so that the men who worked in the mines could attend. Once the shaft was sunk and the mine began operation, they had to work day and night and never stop until the mine was exhausted. Then a dance held by the Woodmen of the World kept those who should have been at the car for Mass, and when the priest found out what had taken place at the dance, he preached a sermon in which he could not find language strong enough to denounce those who had been at the event. The high point of the mission was when the mine superintendent invited Mattingly to visit the mines and speak to the men.[31]

It was Christmastime and Vinton was the last stop on the Southern Pacific. The *St. Paul* crew determined to have a crib for the infant Jesus. Most of the children had never seen a crib and waited excitedly. Cousins built the crib, and a set of figures was rushed from Finney and Company of New Orleans for fifteen dollars, donated by the women of the parish. On Christmas morning Mattingly sang a High Mass and then a Low Mass around the crib of the infant Jesus.[32]

The year 1917 started at Lake Arthur, where Father John Diederich took over the work and the people were most receptive. At Hayes the people, mostly French, were very poor and illiterate, and although they were Catholic, many had never learned any prayers and had never gone to confession. Before *St. Paul* left, more than 134 people had taken communion, and eight marriages were revalidated. In country districts there were many couples whose marriages were never blessed by the church. One reason was a lack of priests, another the inconvenience and hardship connected with calling on a priest, if he was miles away and there was no transportation, or in this situation, a swamp in the way.[33]

On April 20, 1917, when *St. Paul* was working in the area north of Baton Rouge, Archbishop Blenk, the great friend of the chapel car work in Louisiana, died at New Orleans. Father Jeanmard, chancellor, had been designated to take over the duties of administrator and decisions about the chapel car, with the continued assistance of Father Gassler, one of the vicars general.

The fall mission in 1917 included towns along the Gulf Coast lines from Palmetto in St. Landry Parish, through Pointe Cupee Parish, and to Port Allen in West Baton Rouge Parish. In October, at Krotz Springs, a sawmill town east of Opelousas, there were ten Catholic families out of a population of seventy-five. Father Bernard Kalvelage, C.SS.R., reported, "There was a little prejudice among those who had

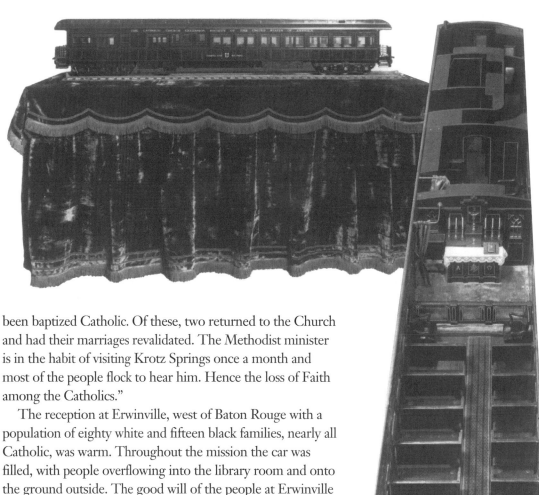

been baptized Catholic. Of these, two returned to the Church and had their marriages revalidated. The Methodist minister is in the habit of visiting Krotz Springs once a month and most of the people flock to hear him. Hence the loss of Faith among the Catholics."

The reception at Erwinville, west of Baton Rouge with a population of eighty white and fifteen black families, nearly all Catholic, was warm. Throughout the mission the car was filled, with people overflowing into the library room and onto the ground outside. The good will of the people at Erwinville was also shown by their calls with food for the priest and his helpers.[34]

At Oscar Crossing, most of the people were Italians, and so the chaplain on board called on a nearby Italian priest to help them. The car moved down the Texas and Pacific Railroad to Morrows, Louisiana, where it stayed nine days. "Fr. Girven and the staff were amazed upon arriving at Morrows to behold a great array of autos, buggies and saddle horses, but they were soon informed by natives that the large gathering was not for the chapel car. They pointed out three saloons, two for whites and one for Negroes. The number of people was explained by the fact that surrounding towns

Fig. 15.4, 15.5 The Pullman Company made this model of *St. Paul* for the Vatican Museum in Rome, where it is on display. The cutaway view details the layout of the car. (Loyola University, Cudahy Library Archives, Chicago)

were 'dry,' so folks made the trek to this town to satisfy their thirst."[35]

Right before Christmas Father James H. Dreis, C.SS.R., replaced Girven as chaplain, and the car was moved to Melville where a priest from Lebeau offered Mass once each month to the residents, including twelve Catholic families. Dreis decided to postpone opening the mission until after Christmas because of the family gathering and other holiday events, but the day after the car's arrival, a circus set up quarters near the chapel car and remained for the holidays.

It was at Melville that a woman who had been a Methodist from birth came for instruction. She was convinced of the Catholic church as the true church and asked for admission. Wednesday at 3 P.M. was set as the time for conditional baptism. At 2 P.M., word was sent to the chaplain that the convert's mother had swallowed poison when she heard of her daughter's action. The convert did not come again to the car.

There was an unusual occurrence at the farming town of Fordoche, where about ten Catholic families lived — it snowed! Although many children had come for instruction, the thermometer dropped to 4 degrees, and very few attended the closing exercises.[36]

In January 1918, *St. Paul* continued along the Texas & Pacific line to Addis, a rail center, where the two hundred Catholics in town eagerly awaited the car and longed for a chapel of their own. As a result of the chapel car's visit, a lot was donated and money raised to begin building.

Torras, a plantation site near the junction of the Red and Mississippi rivers, was not such a good experience. The postmaster had not received the advance handbills, so the arrival of the chapel car was quite a surprise. Only four adults appeared on the first night. At Lettsworth attendance was also small. The town was predominantly Presbyterian, and not one of them came near the car, according to Dreis, not even to inspect it. But at the last stop on the line, Chamberlin, crowds came to the car. A Methodist judge was baptized, received his First Communion, and invited the crew of *St. Paul* to his birthday celebration at his home.

Father Prats Awakens *St. Paul*

Due to war restrictions and the refusal of Louisiana railroads to permit free transportation for the chapel car, *St. Paul* was stored in a railroad yard at New Orleans. Any plan for putting the car back into operation was postponed because of the influenza epidemic in the winter of 1918 and 1919, which took the life of the black cook serving the car. Cousins, who had been exempted from the draft and was now married, had also suffered from the flu, but he patiently waited for the time when the chapel car could be put back into service.

Ledvina, concerned about not using *St. Paul*, wrote, "We naturally feel in honor bound to keep the Chapel Cars operating, since the donors gave them in good faith." He had recently received reminders from the Kuntz family of the original assurance that the cars would be used for the purpose for which they were built. In the spring of 1919, the Kuntz family had decided to sell *St. Peter* and *St. Paul* and give the money to the extension society for other mission uses. Because the railroads in the Northwest were lenient in permitting *St. Peter* to continue movement, the sale of the cars was put on hold, and *St. Paul* was put in storage in New Orleans.

St. Paul would have continued to "sleep in its wraps, tucked away on that siding," in 1920, if it were not for Father Vincent Prats, who had just received his credentials as pastor of the newly created parish of St. Leo the Great . . . but all he had in his immense new parish were "a few houses here and there" and the huge Mylam-Morgan Mill.

Prats suddenly remembered *St. Paul*, now peacefully sleeping but "suddenly to be awakened by a Macedonian call," and he rushed to the streetcar line that would take him to Archbishop John Shaw's residence. He was so excited that he hummed the jubilant *Te Deum*, but he soon sobered down, forgot the exultant *Laudate Pueri Dominum*, and switched to the penitential *Miserere*, as he realized his project was not yet won.

Roger Baudier, the official chronicler of the Archdiocese of New Orleans, describes the scene. "Archbishop Shaw placidly raised incredulous eyebrows while he rocked at the usual measure of 12 times per minute, in his comfortable episcopal rocking chair, as Fr. Prats knelt and kissed the episcopal ring while blurting out: 'Your Grace, I have a church for next Sunday — that is, if you say so. All I have to do is to roll it in place.'"

After anxious moments getting permission to use a siding at the mill for the chapel car, on Sunday, February 13, 1920, Prats offered Mass for the first time in the new parish of St. Leo the Great, and that great event took place in *St. Paul*. The car was jammed to capacity, and many more people stood outside.

Prats occupied the living quarters of the car, and he discovered, like the other missionaries who would serve on *St. Paul*, that during the summer the car was an oven and in winter it was an icebox. But the devoted young priest stayed on with his chapel car for nine months while funds were raised and a frame church built.[37]

It was finally determined that *St. Paul* could not be placed back in service in Louisiana, and the extension society decided to use the car for promotion purposes in an exhibition tour of the East. At the end of the Louisiana mission, Father Kriger, the chaplain on *St. Paul*, wrote:

> While in most localities, the chapel car and the missionary Fathers were received joyously and enthusiastically, and shown every mark of esteem and courtesy by the townspeople, non-Catholics as well as Catholic, in some instances the priest had to contend against the most aggressive bigotry. The car and the missionary were cursed outright; the services were disturbed and food had to be ordered from places as distant as 30 miles, because the fanatics refused to sell to the hated priest and his car . . . sometimes, bigotry was so rife and so wild, that the protection of parish officials had to be sought. Examples of this kind may make interesting reading, but they proved rather uncomfortable for those who had to submit to them.[38]

Kriger stressed that those situations were the exception rather than the rule. In most places non-Catholics who came to hear the discourses through curiosity became attentive listeners, and even if they were not converted, they went away less prejudiced against their Catholic fellow citizens; and thus the spirit of bigotry and intolerance was greatly allayed.

During 1922 *St. Paul* covered the East from Chicago to New York on the Erie Railroad, from New York to Washington on the Philadelphia and Reading and Baltimore and Ohio, from Washington toward Harrisburg on the Pennsylvania, and then on the Pennsylvania and Harrisburg to Altoona.[39]

When *St. Paul* traveled to Pittsburgh and parked in the Pennsylvania freight yards in May 1923, it was not in the best shape. Women from St. Patrick's Church visited the car and were dismayed at its grime and dust. Feeling that it should be as spotless as their own church, they asked and received permission to clean the car, and, according to the Pittsburgh Catholic paper, after their labor of love it surpassed in appearance even the private car of President Rea of the Pennsylvania system.[40]

St. Paul moved south again in 1923 to work in North Carolina. At an early stop, around four o'clock in the afternoon of December 3, the priest saw children were leaving the local school. They saw Number 62 start from the depot, stop, and back down to the switch.

> This was unusual. The old passenger train, made up of a baggage car and one coach, had been familiar to them from infancy. It had passed out of the town at this time every day without stopping or backing down on the switch. Today it left an elegant car on the siding, proudly puffed back to the main track, and went on to the terminal in New Bern. Filled with curiosity, the children hurried to the car. They read the words audibly, "Chapel Car St. Paul." Seeing me, their astonishment increased. Before I had finished my invitation to come into the Car, two dozen breathless boys and girls rushed up the steps and into the Church on Wheels, unable to suppress or conceal their emotions.

Fire and Klan Threaten Chapel Car

Sometime during the winter of 1924, the kitchen of *St. Paul* was damaged by fire that resulted from the explosion of a gasoline tank. The man who had been acting as cook and filling several other positions on board sustained painful burns. It took several months for the car to be put back in service after repairs were made.[41]

At Maysville, Chaplain Alexis Cunneen, C.P., was curious. Where were the people? From the platform of the car he noticed the garage, store, hotel, post office, and a few dwellings. To the west he saw trees — nothing but tall, fresh, verdant pines. Their tops were being lighted by the golden rays of the setting sun, like candles burning on God's western altar, and the glories of that scene made him for the moment forget the indifference of the people. It was as if God had placed his benediction on the town.

Not long after the town awakened in its interest of the chapel car, and a lot was given and plans made to build a church. One of the local leaders was warned that if they built a Catholic church in town, it would be burned down. After arrangements had been made with the local agent for *St. Paul* to be moved to the next town, Cunneen received a letter.

> Dear Sir:
>
> We would be glad if you will notify the leaders of the Catholic Extension Society that they have been here long enough, and ask that they move on from Jones County. A word to the wise is sufficient.
>
> K.K.K. of Jones County
> The "Night Shirts."

Cunneen said that it was regrettable that the letter from the "Kluckers" came late, because the "Night Shirts" might have thought the car's departure was hastened by the letter.[42]

Father Stephen Sweeney, C.P., had a frightening experience at Plymouth, North Carolina, in the spring of 1924.

> We were told by a colored boy that all was arranged by the K.K.K. to drive us out of town. But we were not the least afraid of this threat because similar ones had been made before. I received the following letter the day after entering the town, and about half an hour before the afternoon train left:

> *The Catholic Coast Line Station,*
> *The Catholic Church on Wheels,*
> *Plymouth, N.C.*
>
> *Sir:*
>
> *This is to notify you that your presence in this city is not desired, and I would advise that you get the 3:55 train of this date to carry you away safely. A hint to the wise is sufficient.*
> *Plymouth Klan 140.*

> I dismissed my man, Mr. Stephen McLaughlin, insisting upon him leaving the car until the threat of the Klan would die a natural death. I was all alone in the car, and in a neighborhood most hostile to the Church. There is not a Catholic in Plymouth. There was not as much as a person to whom I could appeal if any violent measures were taken. But I had the Blessed Sacrament in the car, and my unfailing refuge would not allow any harm to come, unless it would be for a greater good, so I placed all my confidence in the Heart of the Prisoner of love. Nothing happened. Our friends of the Invisible Empire did not so much as burn a cross. But do not let it be supposed that the people of the South are much in sympathy with the K.K.K. I am told that they number now in North Carolina, 2,800 whereas a short time ago they numbered 32,000. Nothing can thrive upon hatred.[43]

St. Paul Leaves Louisiana for Storage

In May 1924 *St. Paul*, through the courtesy of Daniel Willard, president of the Baltimore and Ohio Railroad, was used to carry Cardinal Mundelein home to Chicago from New York on his return from Rome. Mass was offered on the car by Cardinal Mundelein, who had as his congregation nearly all the distinguished clergy of Chicago.

Arriving in Chicago, *St. Paul* was turned over to the Right Reverend Thomas W. Drumm for mission work in the diocese of Des Moines, Iowa,[44] where it exhibited in Des Moines and visited Corydon, Allerton, Humeston, Davis City, Kellerton, Mt. Ayr, New Market, Clarenda, Sydney, Bedford, and Gravity.[45]

Drumm and his assistant, Father William Appleby, soon discovered that the Klan's activities were not confined to the South, when at Bedford, Iowa, he reported, "The weather, rainy and unsettled, interfered greatly yet there was on average attendance of 80 or more about an average of 50 non-Catholics. This was considered very good due to the fact that Bedford is strongly entrenched with Protestantism, and the K.K.K.s are predominant in everything. No disturbance however and some of their leaders attended the lectures before the car traveled on to Gravity"[46] and southwestern Iowa.

In the fall of 1924, the chapel car was in Oklahoma, first at Elk City, where the crowds flowed into a local theater. From Grandfield they went to Carnegie for three weeks of services. Albert A. Ille, a nineteen-year-old in his first job, was supposed to stay with the chapel car at Carnegie and keep the batteries charged for the Kohler Plant electric system while the priest, Father Huff, went to spend the Christmas holidays at Oklahoma City. Albert did not stay with the car, and he too went to Oklahoma City. The weather got very cold. The batteries froze and broke, and Albert was fired from his first job.[47]

Catholic Church Uses Other Rail Cars

The Catholic church in 1926 and 1927 used church rail cars in several ways other than the chapel cars. In Arthur D. Dubin's *Some Classic Trains*, he tells about the cars of the International Eucharistic Congress.

On June 16, 1926, at 10 a.m. a most extraordinary train departed from Grand Central Terminal in New York city bound for Chicago and the XXVIII International Eucharistic Congress, the first such event to occur in the United States. Delegates, both clergymen and laymen, came from all parts of the world to attend. To accommodate the Cardinals and their party on their journey from New York to Chicago, the New York Central Railroad and the Pullman Company supplied the Cardinals Train as their contribution to the national welcome extended to the distinguished visitors.

This amazing operation was known as the Cardinals Train. It consisted of seven stunning cars newly painted in cardinal red trimmed with gold. There were six Pullmans and a New York Central-operated dining car, each appropriately named for the occasion.[48]

Dubin writes that the cars' new names and their original names were the Eagle Cliff, the club car renamed the Charles Carroll of Carrollton; the Sunderland (ten compartments), renamed Cardinal Bonzano; the Glen River (six compartments, three drawing rooms), renamed Cardinal Hayes; the Glen Flora (six compartments, three drawing rooms), renamed Bishop Quarter; the Glen Ellyn (six compartments,

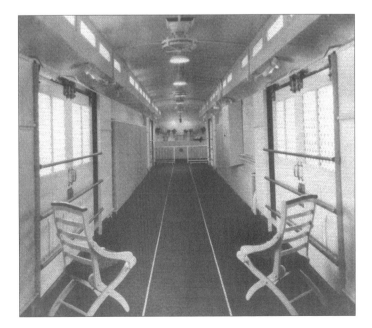

Fig. 15.6 Another chapel car put into service by the Catholic Church was this converted baggage car that was used for the Notre Dame football team and guests to celebrate Mass on the way home from the Navy game at Baltimore in 1927. (Herb Juliano)

three drawing rooms), renamed Father Marquette; and the Superb, the observation car assigned to the papal legate to the congress, Cardinal Bonzano, was renamed Pope Pius XI. The New York Central dining car was renamed for the seminary at Mundelein, St. Mary of the Lake.

Fig. 15.7 The kitchen in *St. Paul* was usually tended by a Chinese or a black cook or porter who did the shopping and cleaning in the car. Frequently these cooks would stay on the car for quite a length of service and become attached to the mission work of the chapel car. According to reports, the cooks could prepare excellent meals with this small stove and oven. (Norman T. Taylor)

Not only ecclesiastic dignitaries would be honored guests carried on special rail cars. The Notre Dame football team used a car that was similar but not as elaborate on their way back from the Notre Dame/Navy game, played in Baltimore in 1927. From pictures of the car, it was originally a baggage car refitted as a chapel car, with an elaborate altar installed at one end and other lights and fixtures added.

Herb Juliano, a sports researcher, writes in *Notre Dame Odyssey*, "Priests, altars, communion rails and pews ordinarily are not included in the equipment of traveling football teams, but the Notre Dame boys had them in mobile form. The car supposedly was built for the Baltimore and Ohio Railroad by the Pullman Company for the use of the road's ecclesiastical

guests, but it was attached to the Notre Dame special train at Willard, Ohio, for the team and staff and other fans to attend mass on their way home from the game."[49] It must have been a celebratory worship, as in usual Knute Rockne style the Irish beat Navy 19–6.

Confusion Sends Cars Wrong Ways

It took the 1933 Chicago World's Fair to get *St. Paul* out of storage, where it had been since completing its western tour. More than a million and a half people had passed through the gates of the Century of Progress grounds before the formal opening. One of the sights they could see there was *St. Paul*, on display on a track between the Chinese Temple and Soldiers Field Memorial Stadium, for what might have been its last formal appearance. "Soon it will be only a memory," *Extension*'s June issue pointed out, "but it will ever be a happy memory to those whom it has served, those whom it brought back or those whom it attracted to the Church."[50]

In 1936, due to a misunderstanding at the Pullman Shops in Chicago, where *St. Paul* and *St. Peter* were in storage, the Most Reverend Edwin O'Hara, bishop of Great Falls, Montana, procured the *St. Paul* for use in his diocese. And *St. Paul* went north, against the orders of the now deceased Peter Kuntz, in a move that was to be the beginning of its end.

The car was stationed in Bear Creek, Montana, a mission of Red Lodge, for more than a year. Then it was moved to Gardiner, an entrance to Yellowstone Park,[51] where it served the people as a parish church until 1954, when the new St. William's Church was built.

In 1960, scrubbed, polished, and proudly wearing a new coat of paint, all work that had been donated by the Northern Pacific Railroad and done at their Livingston shops, *St. Paul* was to be moved to the entrance to Glacier National Park for the winter season. It was moved again by the Northern Pacific and Great Northern railroads to Summit for the summer season. After just a year or so, it was determined that the car was too hot in the summer, too cold in the winter, and too small in general to fill the parish needs of that area.

After the Great Northern was told by the Reverend Joseph A. Cusack, general secretary of the Catholic Church Extension Society, "to dispose of the Chapel Car in any way you see fit," *St. Paul* was sold at a token price to Montana state senator Charles Bovey in 1967. Senator Bovey wanted the car for his railroad museum and restored gold-rush town at Nevada City.[52]

The move from East Glacier to Nevada City was not without problems. The East Glacier to Alder leg was smooth. From Alder to Nevada City movement was slower and more involved. Since terminal transfer had to be made over state highway 287, it was necessary to obtain special permission. The car was placed on a low-boy with sixty pneumatic tires and moved fifteen miles by Zion Building Movers of Great Falls, Montana, with no apparent mishap.

The car then rested on a short section of track in a conspicuous place close to Highway 287 in Nevada City and was open to visitors during the summer months *(fig. 15.8)*. According to Vincent T. J. Lenth, M.D., in his letter of April 3, 1970, to the Most Reverend John L. May of the Catholic Church Extension Society, the cost of the move was eight hundred dollars, supposedly paid by Mr. Bovey.[53]

On September 29, 1985, in celebration of the eightieth anniversary of the Catholic Church Extension Society, Mass was again said in *St. Paul*. Bradley Collins of *Extension* wrote of the occasion: "Mass at the old chapel car looked almost exactly as it had 70 years ago. Local residents, dressed in frontier costumes, arrived by horseback and wagons. A bright Montana sun gleamed through the car's green-and-white stained glass windows as an overflow crowd filled its narrow pews. . . . Extension President Fr. Edward J. Slattery offered Mass for Extension donors, past and present."[54]

In the late fall of 1996, Ford Bovey of Nevada City, Montana, and John Larkin, owner of the Escanaba–Lake Superior Railroad in Wells, Michigan, traded four Soo Line cars and a steam engine in Nevada City for a restored 1911 Baldwin steam locomotive and three railroad cars from Michigan. Included in that trade was chapel car *St. Paul*.

St. Paul is being renovated at the shops of the Escanaba–Lake Superior Railroad at Wells, Michigan, with the expectation that it will be put on display at the Lake Superior Museum of Transportation in Duluth, Minnesota.

When Peter Kuntz died, a friend was with Father Kelley when he heard the news. The friend had heard of Kuntz, though not favorably.

I gently told him the story of the real Peter. "Impossible," he said. "He had no heart." Then I thought of something, an event that had happened at the dedication of the "St. Paul" in New Orleans. Alongside the car was a platform erected for the ceremonies. An Archbishop had just blessed the car, and a Bishop was preaching out there on the platform. Thousands of people were listening. I slipped into the car. Alone on a seat in a little room sat the old man to whom the Church owed that Car and another. He was hiding. When I looked through the door at him, I saw the tears dropping down from his eyes. They had fallen on his queer side whiskers, and the sun made them

Fig. 15.8 From 1967 to 1996, *St. Paul* was included in a collection of vintage railroad cars in Nevada City, Montana, in a restored gold mining town owned by the Bovey corporation. In 1996 the car was traded and is now being restored in Wells, Michigan. (Norman T. Taylor)

glisten like diamonds. The tears were to me a revelation of the soul of Peter Kuntz. No heart? He was all heart.[55]

Somewhere in the great beyond, the voice of crusty Peter Kuntz can probably be heard grumbling to the real St. Peter and St. Paul: "I said that car was never to go north!"

> Hark! The loud celestial hymn,
> Angels' choirs above are raising,
> Cherubim and Seraphim,
> In unceasing chorus praising;
> Fill the heavens with sweet accord;
> Holy, Holy, Holy Lord.[56]

Notes

[1] Francis C. Kelley, *The Story of Extension* (Chicago: Extension Press, 1922), 92–93.

[2] Correspondence to George C. Hennessey from E. B. Ledvina, June 10, 1914, LUCA.

[3] Correspondence to George C. Hennessey from E. B. Ledvina, July 6, 1914, LUCA.

[4] Contract between Peter Kuntz and the Catholic Church Extension Society, December 17, 1914, LUCA.

[5] Correspondence from E. B. Ledvina to Alvah W. Doran, December 31, 1914, LUCA.

[6] Correspondence to Alvah W. Doran from E. B. Ledvina, December 19, 1914, LUCA.

[7] *Nashville Banner*, February 20, 1915, 1.

[8] Ibid., 14.

[9] "Birmingham, the Magic City: A Sense of Mission," *The Birmingham News* publication, 1929, Birmingham Public Library.

[10] *Atlanta Constitution*, February 23, 1915, 7.

[11] Roger Baudier Sr., *The Chapel Cars of The Catholic Church Extension Society in the Louisiana Dioceses*, 1956, 9, the Catholic Church Extension Society archives (hereafter CESA), 9.

[12] The New Orleans *Morning Star*, March 20, 1915, 1.

[13] Francis P. Leipzig, *Extension in Oregon* (St. Benedict, Ore.: The Benedictine Press, 1956), 64.

[14] Roger Baudier Sr., "Journey of St. Paul," in *Cross, Crozier and Crucible: A Volume Celebrating the Bicentennial of a Catholic Diocese in Louisiana*, ed. Glenn R. Conrad (New Orleans: Archdiocese of New Orleans, in cooperation with the Center for Louisiana Studies, n.d.), 237.

[15] Report of Alvah W. Doran, Cheneyville, La., April 6, 1915, LUCA.

[16] Report of Alvah W. Doran, Secompte, La., April 11, 1915, LUCA.

[17] Report of Alvah W. Doran, Boyce, La., April 17, 1915, LUCA.

[18] Report of Alvah W. Doran, Aloha, La., May 2, 1915, LUCA.

[19] "How I Spent My Vacation," *Extension*, October 1915, 20.

[20] Report of Owen A. McGrath, Winnfield, La., October 24, 1915, LUCA.

[21] Letter from E. B. Ledvina to George C. Hennessey, October 25, 1915, LUCA.

[22] Report of Owen A. McGrath, Jena, La., November 1, 1915, LUCA.

[23] Report of Owen A. McGrath, Goodpine, La., November 7, 1915, LUCA.

[24] Letter from E. B. Ledvina to George C. Hennessey, January 26, 1916, LUCA.

[25] Letter from E. B. Ledvina to George C. Hennessey, May 2, 1916, LUCA.

[26] Letter from B. M. Johnson to E. B. Ledvina, February 12, 1916, LUCA.

[27] Report of E. L. Mattingly, Turkey Creek, La., April 3, 1916, LUCA.

[28] Report of E. L. Mattingly, Oakdale, La., May 15, 1916, LUCA.

[29] Letter from E. B. Ledvina to George C. Hennessey, October 5, 1916, LUCA.

[30] Report of E. C. Mattingly, DeRidder, La., October 16, 1916, LUCA.

[31] Report of E. L. Mattingly, Sulphur, La., December 7, 1916, LUCA.

[32] Report of E. L. Mattingly, Vinton, La., December 27, 1916, LUCA.

[33] Report of John Diederich, Hayes, La., January 13, 1917, LUCA.

[34] Baudier, in *Cross, Crozier, and Crucible*, 241.

[35] Ibid., 250.

[36] Ibid., 243.

[37] Ibid., 36, 37, 38.

[38] Ibid., 15, 16.

[39] D. Letter from William O'Brien to George C. Hennessey, Tigard, Ore., April 7, 1923, LUCA.

[40] "Who Said 'Smoky Pittsburgh'? Chapel Car Is Cleaned Here," *Pittsburgh Catholic*, June 10, 1913, 18, Hesburgh Library, the University of Notre Dame, South Bend, Ind.

[41] *Extension*, April 1924, 31.

[42] *Extension*, July 1924, 15.

[43] "Three Months on the Chapel Car," *Extension*, June 1927, 32.

[44] *Extension*, July 1924, 25.

[45] *The Catholic Messenger*, Thursday, May 22, 1924, 10, Hesburgh Library, the University of Notre Dame, South Bend, Ind.

[46] Report of Cornelius Lalley, Gravity, Iowa, June 30, 1924, LUCA.

47 Note from Albert A. Ille to his brother, V. John Ille, December 11, 1973, Diocese of Great Falls archives.

48 Arthur Dubin, *Some Classic Trains* (A Kalmbach Publication, 1964), 380.

49 Correspondence from Herb Juliano to Norman Taylor and Wilma Taylor, January 22, 1997, about Notre Dame chapel car, material from his *Notre Dame Odyssey*.

50 *Extension*, June 1933, n.p.

51 Correspondence to A. M. D. Gillen of the Church of the Little Flower in Browning, Mon., from the presidents of the Northern Pacific and Great Northern Railroads, St. Paul, Minn., December 23, 1959, CESA.

52 Correspondence from Emmett Kelley, vice chancellor of the diocese of Helena, to Vincent T. J. Lenth, M.D., of Jacksonville, Ill., September 26, 1968, CESA.

53 Letter from Vincent T. J. Lenth, M.D., to Most Reverend John L. May, April 3, 1970, CESA, Chicago.

54 Bradley Collins, *Extension*, November 1985, n.p.

55 Kelley, 94.

56 *Te Deum*, a German choral, printed on a song sheet in the Catholic chapel cars.

CHAPTER 16

Baptist Car 7: Amazing *Grace*, the Last of the American Fleet

Like a bride on her way to her wedding, chapel car *Grace*, on its way to its dedication at the Los Angeles Convention in 1915, was accompanied by a jubilant bridal party of four Pullman cars full of Eastern Baptists. All along the line the burnished Pullman Green steel car, trimmed with gilded letters announcing its name and owners, was met by Baptists bearing gifts — like the Nebraska Baptists of Lincoln and Fairbury, who turned out in force at their stations bearing lovely baskets of roses.[1]

Stenciled on the side of the car near the chapel end vestibule, Ephesians 2:8 (KJV) could easily be read: "For by Grace are ye saved through faith; and that not of yourselves; it is the gift of God."

Two and three services were held in the car each day for en route passengers — from Chicago, on the Rock Island Railroad, to Los Angeles, via the Denver and Rio Grande and Southern Pacific lines. The whole train resounded with hymns and voices singing, "Amazing Grace, how sweet the sound that saved a wretch like me, I once was lost and now am found, was blind but now I see." Passengers on the non-Baptist cars would have had problems not being involved in the fellowship and festivities.

As early as 1913, plans had been set in motion for soliciting gifts toward a new chapel car, this one of necessity made of steel. Thirteen years had passed since the last Baptist chapel car, *Herald of Hope*, had left the Barney & Smith Car Company at Dayton, Ohio. Although a new chapel boat, the *Lifeline*, costing about five thousand dollars, and several new motor chapel cars had recently been put into service, the American Baptist Publication Society still felt there was a need for churches on rails.

The Conaway/Birch Oil family of Orange County, California, agreed to donate twenty thousand dollars for a chapel car in memory of their daughter and sister Grace. Thus *Grace*, the seventh Baptist car and the last of the great fleet of American chapel cars, was contracted with the Barney & Smith Car Company at a price of $21,150 (the contract was signed September 12, 1914).[2] *Grace* cost five times more than did the first chapel car, *Evangel*.

Grace's construction had barely begun when a battle brewed over which chapel car missionary would live and work on the new car. Guy C. Lamson, the publication society's missionary and Bible secretary, presented the situation to George White, his western district supervisor. It was clear he was not happy with E. R. Hermiston, presently serving on *Emmanuel*.

Fig. 16.1 The designers at Barney & Smith Car Company were asked by the American Baptist Publication Society officials to make *Grace*, the last of the fleet of American chapel cars, more "churchy." This was done by using Gothic arches instead of the inset block feature that had been a part of the design of earlier Baptist cars. In this view of the chapel, the repetition of arches can be seen clearly. This picture was taken at a Chicago stop as the car was en route to Green Lake, Wisconsin, to be removed from active service. (American Baptist Historical Society, Valley Forge)

I have just this morning received a long telegram from Hermiston containing seventy-four words, concerning the man who is to be put upon the new Chapel Car. If Hermiston has allowed the general impression to be that he was to go on the new chapel car he has acted wholly without any encouragement from anybody, and the fault is his own and not ours. We cannot very well give one man a preference above another. If the car was to be given to the oldest Chapel Car missionary, in point of service, who has asked for the same, we should have to give it to Sparks. Sparks [presently on *Herald of Hope*], Hermiston, Killian [presently on *Evangel*], have all asked for the car, and we cannot give it to one and deny all the others, unless we have a valid reason for so doing.[3]

But persistent and insistent Hermiston ingratiated himself in person and by correspondence with the Conaway/Birch families, who had not failed to notice his stellar reputation for soul winning in southern California churches. White conveyed to Lamson that Mrs. Birch "spoke to me very earnestly on behalf of Mr. and Mrs. Hermiston urging that they be appointed for the new car," and the publication society could not afford to displease the Conaways and the Birches.[4] Lamson reluctantly conceded and transferred Hermiston to the new car, but he wondered how much influence Hermiston had been bringing to bear to produce this result.[5]

To the delight of the Hermistons and to the envy of all the other chapel car missionaries, including Father Kelley of the Catholic Church Extension Society, chapel length on *Grace* had been reduced to include a separate bedroom with a full-size brass bed *(fig. 16.2)*. The priests and assistants on the three Catholic cars generally had to sleep in berths, as did the other Baptist chapel car missionaries, except for those who had modified their sleeping arrangements with couches and fold-up beds.

At 134,000 pounds, 85 feet, 6 inches long, having an observation platform 4 feet, 4 1/2 inches long at one end and a closed vestibule platform at the other, standing 13 feet tall, and 10 feet 8, inches wide, *Grace* was not dainty! But it was "churchier" than the other Baptist chapel cars.

It was the desire of publication society officials that this car emphasize a more churchy look, and the golden oak interior with arch repetitions in ceiling vaults, panels, and pews was executed in subtle Gothic lines while honoring and preserving the less embellished traditions of the Baptist concept of worship *(fig. 16.1)*. No doubt some of the Gothic touches were the same as those installed in *St. Paul*, which was in the finishing stages while *Grace* was being started in the shops. The diamond-motif stained-glass door panel leading into the living quarters, the green leaded-arch art glass window trim in the upper sashes and clerestory windows, and the gold-lettered "God Is Love" window over the pulpit platform added a cathedral touch.

Thousands Visit *Grace* at Exposition

One of *Grace's* first stops after Los Angeles was at the 1915 Panama-Pacific International Exposition in San Francisco. Nearly nineteen million tourists flocked to see the post-earthquake, newly rebuilt San Francisco for this celebration of the completion of the Panama Canal.[6] President Woodrow Wilson sent by wire the spark that triggered the colors to be flown, salutes to be fired from the cannons in the bay, the fountain of energy to leap upward, and all the whistles in the city and harbor to bellow. The main door of the Palace of Machinery swung open, disclosing exciting exhibits in motion. White doves of peace were released into the sky.

Salvos of artillery from the batteries on both sides of the Golden Gate and from warships anchored in the bay ushered in the opening day. A parade of tens of thousands — in societies; in fraternities; in civic, neighborhood, and business organizations — marched through the entrance to the concourse fronting the Tower of Jewels and down the Avenue of Palms. On the grounds more than four hundred national and international conventions and many sporting events, including the Vanderbilt Cup race, entertained the crowds.[7]

Thousands passed through *Grace* at its location outside the

Transportation Building and admired its churchly beauty, and some were converted.[8] Hermiston told of their experience. "We have had a delightful and profitable work of grace on the Exposition grounds at San Francisco in the chapel car 'Grace.' It has been one of the religious centers on the fair grounds, and while we were there on exhibition, yet we made good use of the time to hold services. From 300 to 1,500 people went through the car daily. At times on special days the number was greater. We scattered 50,000 pages of tracts, and some days I held as many as seven services in the car. Of course, they had to be short as it was hard to hold the people very long."[9]

Much of the work at the fair was in keeping *Grace* shiny and beautiful for the visitors. The rest of the day was spent with car tours, distributing tracts, and holding services for those at the fair. The exposition officials put in free plumbing, furnished water and garbage pickup, and helped in every way possible to make the car a religious center and to make life pleasant for the Hermistons.[10]

As *Grace* was getting ready to leave the exposition, a new neighbor pulled in: *St. Peter*. For several days, visitors could see and compare the cars. Relations between Hermiston and George Hennessey, manager of the Catholic car, were cordial, although in private correspondence to their bosses, both would boast of having the more beautiful car.

In many ways the two men were twins, although one was redhaired and the other balding, one an Irishman and the other a Canadian Scotsman. Both were affable jokesters with a wide streak of melodrama, softened by a warm heart and fired by abiding religious zeal. In private they would brand each other with the label *nonbeliever*, but the logistics of life on the chapel cars — heating systems, fuel, federal regulations, transportation, shop considerations, vandalism, official opposition — bound them in many ways as brothers.

The Hermistons, transferred from the much older *Emmanuel*, were excited about the new car, especially since the lighting problems had been corrected. During the exposition, Hermiston had asked W. C. Coleman, president of the Coleman Lamp Company and a prominent Baptist layman,

to look at the lighting system on the car, which he did, and Hermiston commented on the improvements.

Chapel Car 'Grace' is a 'Beauty' and I like it more and more. I think it is arranged perfectly. The lighting system could not be better. . . . We have a Coleman gasoline lighting plant and I consider it better than electricity. We are delighted with the fine large sleeping room with full sized bed, the bathroom and the kitchen with modern equipment. Our free circulating library is a great help to the work. The people enjoy coming to the car and I notice that the railroad men appreciate it, especially. An engineer told me the other day that he considered it the finest car he had ever seen.[11]

Missions Begin at St. Helena, California

After the exposition, the first series of evangelistic meetings in the car started at St. Helena, California, on the Southern Pacific, where the car was crowded every night. Hermiston inspired the membership, helped them improve the property, and raise a budget.[12] "The people are really kind also in supplying provisions for our table," Hermiston wrote his supervisor, "and they surprised us recently with an abundance of good things including canned fruit, chickens, fruit cake, etc. We are expecting large results in Northern California through the use of this splendid equipment."[13]

From St. Helena they traveled up the Napa Valley to Calistoga, where they complained about the November chill and planned to put the Baker heater to good use. Backtracking down the line, the chapel car was crowded at Yountville every night despite stormy weather, which Hermiston described as "terrible" with floods knee deep.[14] There they counted twenty-five confessions, among them residents of the California Veterans Home and many children. The parents of the children wanted them to make a public decision but balked at baptism, because most were not desirous of membership in the Baptist church, the only church in town.[15]

At Napa, with the weather still against them, they had an

excellent response; and at Vallejo, the headquarters for the navy men at Mare Island, so many made confessions that the church decided to build a larger building. At Santa Rosa, in the Sonoma Valley, where the congregation was much discouraged and many had left the church to "go into a Holiness organization," and at nearby Petaluma, Hermiston had great success in church reviving and soul saving.[16] He was living up to the expectations of the Conaway/Birch family, even though northern California had been reported to be a difficult district in which to do religious work.

September was housecleaning time for Mrs. Hermiston. She had grown tired of the dingy curtains in the living area and coaxed her husband to purchase new ones, plus a new cover for the "coveted" brass bed and some less decorative but essential new garbage cans. In addition, the Estey organ had to be tuned, as a glass of liquid had been upset on it.[17]

Meetings were crowded out of *Grace* into a huge tent at Calexico in southern California's Imperial Valley. Only five years old, the town had a population over five thousand, including soldiers from Camp Beacom. Mrs. Hermiston's ministry among the young soldiers was reported "phenomenal,"[18] although it no doubt helped that daughter Marjorie, an attractive young woman, provided much of the music for the services. Hermiston reported, "Just across the Mexican border and practically a part of the same city is Mexicali, one of the toughest places to be found anywhere. One of the worst gambling dens on the continent is located there and every form of vice is practiced openly."[19]

In the spring of 1917, *Grace* was requested in the East for a denomination program, but the request was canceled because of a German submarine blockade. According to reports from Baptist headquarters, the railroad yards from Chicago east were blockaded with trains of freight that could not be unloaded. None of the larger vessels were venturing to sea, and most of the smaller ones were careful about going. It was thought that the factories in the East would have to shut down because their output could not be transported.

During 1917 *Grace* came to the port of San Pedro, called the harbor city of Los Angeles, where two railroads, the Southern Pacific and the Salt Lake, maintained terminals. The population, stated at fifteen thousand, was probably more than twice what it was five years ago before annexation and development, and many more than when *Emmanuel* had visited thirteen years previously with the Hermistons on board.

Now San Pedro was a busy town: railroad shops, lumber suppliers, fishery and canning industries, oil pipeline terminals, a new ship-building plant, plus five hundred soldiers, revenue cutter men, a submarine flotilla base, and a naval reserve training station. The diversity of the population reflected the typical California pattern: Mexican common laborers, Japanese truck farmers and fishing workers, and mainly Swedish, German, and Italian longshoremen and lumber handlers. The railroad men, storekeepers, town officials, and policemen were Americans from all parts of the country, with a sprinkling of the old Spanish families who owned some of the original ranches. Once a wild railroad town, San Pedro had a more wholesome ratio now of just six saloons to five churches — Catholic, Presbyterian, Methodist, Baptist, and Episcopal.

But the Baptists were struggling. The church membership of the town was stated at 500, of which the Baptists had approximately 110, but no adequate building. The recent pastor had left convinced that his efforts had been unsuccessful. *Grace* was sidetracked on Front Street near the Southern Pacific station and the steamer landings, and in front of the six saloons. An observer who reported on the work of the car for *Missions* said that the need for *Grace* at San Pedro was threefold: first, the general lack of churchgoing traditions; second, the diversity of people living in the area, a transient population to a great extent; and third, the fact that few if any people of financial or directing ability were interested in the churches.[20] Everywhere they could think of, the Hermistons held services — on the chapel car, in the church, on one of the battleships, at the fort, and on the streets. Their work reaped great rewards in San Pedro.

After spending a month in the oil field camps at Taft, and

at East Bakersfield, where many meetings were held with the railroad men, Hermiston hoped to go to Reward, but the railroad was a mile and half from town and the work probably could not be very effective.[21] Instead, from San Lucas in February 1918, the Hermistons traveled into the Santa Lucia Range mountain valleys of Plato, Lockwood, and Peachtree to witness to "cow punchers" and "mountaineers."

War Finds *Grace* at Camp Fremont

During the war, Hermiston particularly enjoyed the work at Camp Fremont near Palo Alto. June 1918 found the Hermistons working with the soldiers in cooperation with the YMCA and the chaplains' program. They would have a service in the chapel car and then go to one of the big tents and hold another service; double work, but they met many of the soldiers they knew and some they had baptized.[22] They tried to provide support for all the chaplains.

Camp Fremont was much cleaner morally than Hermiston thought it would be. He found the "moral squad" made it almost impossible for prostitutes to frequent the camp, and "boot-leggers" found it difficult to reach any of the soldiers because of the close watch kept on their movements.[23]

Hermiston particularly had a great time with the army engineers. "People said they were a hard bunch to handle, but we got on fine with them. I made a straight appeal to the boys and told them to come up and talk with me. I said, 'If you want to get married, or borrow money, or talk on religion, come,' and they did come. One gunner said, 'I am not religious, but I tell you the nearer I get to the front, the nearer I feel the need of knowing Jesus Christ.'"[24]

Putting *Grace* into the shops at the Oakland yards in July 1918, Hermiston took the time to work with A. P. Brown, a labor missionary, who told him "because of the war, things are lively now at the big shops."

Hermiston wrote that at Vacaville, where they were working in the fall of 1918, "the flu is so bad they don't want us to call. Many are down with it, and it is the dangerous kind, as many have already died. They are using the Presbyterian

church as a hospital."[25] In January the Hermistons came down with the flu, but they recovered after many weeks of convalescence.

Although many of the Baptist cars were forced to halt movement after the government shut-down of private rail cars in January 1919, the Southern Pacific still granted *Grace* free movement on its California lines. The Hermistons, now at Chico, still recovering from the effects of the flu, wrote that they had accepted a call to "a very important church [the

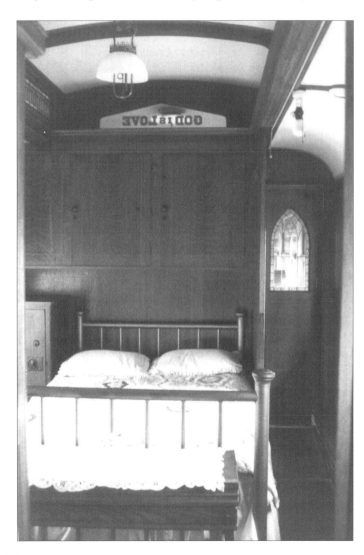

Fig. 16.2 Mrs. Hermiston was envied by the other missionary wives because she had a separate bedroom with a brass bed, a feature only on *Grace*. (Norman T. Taylor)

Chico church]" and would be leaving chapel car work. But by April, after urgings from railroad officials as well as many others, plus a three-hundred-dollar raise to his fifteen-hundred-dollar-a-year salary, Hermiston decided to stay on the chapel car only if he could be assured that the new administration, a combination of the publication and home mission societies, would still keep the "old workers" on the cars.[26]

Land Speculation Bug Bites Hermiston

The land speculation bug bit Hermiston in the fall of 1919 at Gerber, California, and that bite might have contributed to his demise. According to all letters and reports, the infatuation seemed to take his focus off the gospel work that had seemed so important to him since his conversion as a young baseball player many years before.

Plotted six years earlier, by 1916 Gerber was established as a fourth-class post office, and construction had begun on businesses of all kinds, homes, churches, and schools. Investors built many hotels to accommodate the train crews and passengers. Most of the town residents were employees of the Southern Pacific, which had moved its operations from Red Bluff, with a twice-monthly payroll of a hundred thousand dollars. Lumbermen, cattlemen, and farmers composed the rest. Many families, traveling in immigrant cars filled with all their belongings, were still arriving in Gerber, coming to seek their fortunes.

Hermiston first visited the town in 1916 and fired up the young people. Baptists in the community gathered under a tree that year to organize a church. In March 1919, the Hermistons returned to Gerber to help build a church. What they found at Gerber was the beginning of a boom town. A repair shop was to be built, as were other buildings and facilities, including an icing plant to service refrigerator cars, livestock yards, close to twelve miles of tracks, and freight and passenger stations. Many trains were now stopping at the busy depot.[27]

In July, Hermiston wrote to White, "I have been able to get some reliable information that it [Gerber] will have big

shops and other interests. If you want me to get you a close in Business lot let me know and I will do so."[28]

Less than a month later, the recently widowed White responded with a request for Hermiston to purchase for him several lots in town on the main street, one-half block east of the Pacific Highway [California State Highway 99]. He thought he might use them for a garage business. "West fifty foot of lots one and town, block sixteen, subdivision A, and the West fifty foot, lots three and four, block sixteen, subdivision A, all in the town of Gerber, California, for $1000.00 less $62.50 discount, for cash, making the total cost to me $937.50."[29]

White was assured by Hermiston, "I secured you a real bargain in your lot. I would not of sold it to any one but you as I did not want to be guilty of putting you in wrong. You cant get any cheap lots now as they have come up on everything. If you keep your lot for three years you will receive a fine increase for as soon as the labor and railroad troubles are adjusted you will see some big improvement here."[30]

After many delays because of the high price of lumber, the church in Gerber was finally finished, and Hermiston appeared ready to move on with *Grace*, leaving the investments to grow along with the hopes of the town.

After spending the summer at Orland building a parsonage, Hermiston finally realized that the chapel car was in need of serious repair work, repainting, and revarnishing. None had been done since the car's dedication five years earlier. The bill from the Southern Pacific shops in Los Angeles was $1,390.02, but Hermiston reported "it looks good," as the work resumed at Hughson.

White learned that Hermiston had supposedly sold out his interests in Gerber, leaving White on his own. "I turned over the big contract I had on Gerber to a Big Millionare [.] He bought 21 houses and will build 15 more and put in a bank and take over the water system [,] so I am free now to continue the Car work — I feel better and I am sure I have done the best thing although I am sure I could of made big money If I had gone into Gerber."[31]

But Hermiston was not to do "the best thing," for in December he wrote from Sacramento, "A big Banking Co is coming into Gerber and they just received the charter here at the Capitol. They will have one hundred thousand dollars to begin with and they have not asked any one to buy any stock [.] The Bay Miller Land Company here is back of it and they will put a building on my corner. If everything I hear is o. k. Anyway they will build a $10,000 building and the R. R. folks will spend a barrel of money there at least $3000.00. Right away it is announced. If you want the corner at $1100, let me know — $3.40 down [this might be $340] — write me at Waterford, Calif [.] I want to get the other piece of land before [it] rise[s]."

There was no news of the chapel car work progress at Waterford.[32]

In March 1921, Charles White of the home mission society, now co-managing the chapel car work with the publication society, informed George White that Hermiston had not sent in any of his collection money for seven months.[33] When White asked him about the matter, Hermiston explained that because of the type of church building he was doing, he could not raise any money on the field. This seemed strange to George White, but after sending a list of his concerns about the money to Hermiston, he accepted him at his word but warned him about keeping careful records.

Besides building a church now at Chowchilla, a progressive town of mostly Easterners, and officiating at the wedding of their daughter, Marjorie, in a ceremony on *Grace*, other issues had been keeping Hermiston occupied. In May, Hermiston, still at Chowchilla, asked White for a loan of two hundred dollars, because "my brother has had a serious operation." A concerned but cautious White replied that he regretted that he was unable to grant that request.[34]

There would be no more correspondence in the files for several years about Hermiston's investment interests in Gerber, but that did not mean that the matter had been dropped. Seemingly with his mind more on chapel car work

at Chowchilla, Hermiston completed a large church of Moorish design that would seat 350.[35]

While he was at Auberry, in the foothills of the Sierra near the San Joaquin River, Hermiston received instructions to have the car relettered with the names of the home missions and publication societies in equal size. He wanted to have the chapel car ready to travel to their new assignment at Las Vegas, Nevada. He and Mrs. Hermiston, not enthusiastic about leaving California, knew the call to Las Vegas had been long and urgent.

Grace Answers Long Call to Las Vegas

It was not until eight months after the crews of the San Pedro, Los Angeles, and Salt Lake Railroad spiked the last sections of track to create the first rail line between Los Angeles and the East, May 15, 1905, that Las Vegas was platted as a town. A promotional brochure around 1910 boasted: a population of 1250, a handsome business block, First State Bank, Ice Factory, six good Hotels and several lodging houses, Opera House, numerous Fraternal Societies, modern telephone exchange, a grade school and high school, ten miles of graded and curbed streets, pure spring water piped to every lot, moving picture show, two churches — the Methodist and the Episcopal — and eleven bars and saloons.[36]

What the brochure did not mention was Block 16. It was the most notorious neighborhood in early Las Vegas, a neighborhood where liquor could be served without any restrictions and prostitution flourished. Block 16 would continue to operate until after World War II, when threats to place Las Vegas off limits to military personnel forced the town to clean up.[37]

Plans had been in the making since 1921 to send *Grace* and the Hermistons to Las Vegas, but they did not reach there until 1924, when financial conditions of the home and publication societies stabilized enough to be able to support the building of a church. The delay was probably just as well, because in 1921 in Las Vegas, Union Pacific employees called a strike to protest firing practices, and soon the strike became

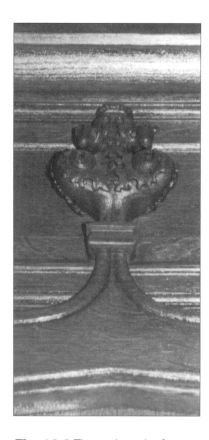

Fig. 16.3 The trademark of Barney & Smith's oak cars was the oak motif above the door. The design and the surrounding trim echo the Gothic arch and flying buttress details that gave *Grace* a more churchy look than the earlier cars. (Norman T. Taylor)

part of a nationwide strike of four hundred thousand rail workers fighting a wage cut. The strike was settled in 1922, but then the Union Pacific decided to shut down the Las Vegas repair shops, and hundreds of workers left town to find jobs elsewhere.[38]

The town had not quite recovered from those hard times when the front page of the Las Vegas *Review* announced the chapel car's arrival. "The Rev. and Mrs. E. R. Hermiston, the noted chapel car evangelists, will hold services in the chapel car at the Union Pacific depot Sunday evening at 7:30. These workers have been very successful, winning many converts."[39] On page 4 of the same issue, under "Chapel Car Service," "Don't fail to hear Mrs. E. R. Hermiston at the chapel car next Sunday evening at 7:30 o'clock on 'Can We Know Each Other in Heaven?' She is a high-class reader and elocutionist and you will enjoy hearing her preach. The chapel car is located at the foot of Bridger Street south of the Union Pacific depot."[40]

It did not take the Hermistons long to get a church organized. The *Review* reported on April 20, "A very pleasant social time was enjoyed at the chapel car Thursday evening. The car was crowded and nearly one hundred participated in the organization of a Baptist Church." The new officers were named, refreshments were served, and a program was presented. It was announced that on the next Sunday evening, Hermiston would preach on "A Larger Las Vegas," and Mrs. Hermiston would recite "The Apron Corner." The service would be in the car, and all boosters were invited.[41]

On March 2 Hermiston reported to White that they were hard at work canvassing the town. "This is a wonderful town and I wonder we were never able to get in before. But there may be reasons [.] It is different from the work we have done as the town is 20 years old and other churches established and yet if the damm [Hoover Dam, or Boulder Dam] goes through it will mean a town of 30000." He is looking at several lots for a church, and the services in the chapel car are "interfered with by the trains," but he is going to get a better location."[42]

Investments, Dam Distract Hermiston

Then, on March 6 the old problems reappeared. White wrote Hermiston; "Mr. B. F. Conaway has spoken to me several times relative to the $300 which you borrowed from him. He says about three years ago. He said today that you had not repaid it and had not said anything about the matter for a couple of years. I hope that it may be returned right away. Mr. Conaway has been very generous with our society. We hope to receive further gifts from him and are anxious to retain his hearty good will."[43]

In response to White, Hermiston wrote about his find of sixteen Baptists in town, but he was more excited about the forty senators from Washington who were also in town, investigating the prospects for a government dam. He scrawled, "things are looking lively." He told White he would need twelve hundred dollars for a lot and twenty-five hundred dollars to build the kind of church he has in mind, a plant they would not be ashamed of. Then he mentioned the owed money. "I wrote Conaway today about $300.00. He let me have it and said to keep it until I could pay and as I am going good again or will be good soon for 25 or $30,000.00 I wrote him I would clear it up soon."[44]

On March 15, 1923, Hermiston described an exciting day. "We are hard at it here [and] we went to the Damm yesterday with 40 senators and we also attended big Banquet in evening and heard some fine speeches I guess they intend to put over some big stuff here and it is a wise thing for the denomination to get in now."[45]

A week later, Hermiston and Bruce Jackson of the home mission society made the decision to purchase a lot at 6th and Fremont, just outside the business district but in the heart of the new residential section. Jackson wrote White, "I wired the office in New York the recommendation to send Mr. Hermiston a draft to cover purchase, $3150.00 for seventy-five feet and [if desired] $1600.00 for an additional fifty. The price seems terribly high but the lot on the other corner of that block is held at $10,000.00. One of the conservative bankers there estimated that that lot would be worth

$20,000.00 in ten years."[46] In regard to the new lot, Hermiston boasted, "I got it at a bargain price."[47]

Sometime in the late summer, since it was too hot to stay in *Grace*, the Hermistons left Las Vegas and the chapel car and traveled to Ohio, where he had family, and then in August came back to Modesto, California, where Mrs. Hermiston's sister lived, for a rest. By September they had not returned to the work or *Grace* at Las Vegas.

News of Hermiston's Unexpected Death

A shocking telegram arrived for White September 2, 1923, from Mrs. Hermiston. "MR HERMISTON PASSED AWAY THIS EVENING FUNERAL SATURDAY AFTERNOON IN MODESTO."[48]

According to Mrs. Hermiston, and the facts were never known, her husband had rapidly developed a case of uremic poisoning. At the time of Hermiston's death they lacked but nine days of rounding out twenty years of chapel car service. They had been instrumental in erecting about thirty-five churches and in organizing many churches and Sunday schools. Baptists in the West would sorely miss Hermiston.[49]

Because she did not have enough savings and retirement benefits to live on, Mrs. Hermiston went on the speaking circuit and became a popular preacher in her own right. She was called upon by many churches who remembered fondly the work she and her husband had accomplished. Whether she ever preached it again or not, she no doubt remembered frequently, and perhaps tearfully, the sermon she preached their first week in Las Vegas, "Can We Know Each Other in Heaven?"

Grace sat unused and unoccupied in Las Vegas until the late summer of 1924. Then bricklayer turned chapel car missionary A. C. Blinzinger, like Hermiston, transferred from chapel car *Emmanuel* to continue the work.

We came here beginning the hot season and found it 110 in the car and the lighting system needed repair. A man from Utah came here and wanted to hold meetings in the car and trying out the lights the car caught fire and so you see everything was against us and so we took the car in for repairs and expect to start the work when we feel we can go on unhampered. If there is any town that needs the Gospel it is Las Vegas. The work will be hard under the best conditions.

Railroad towns are the hardest towns to labor as there is a constant change and people come and go. The M.Es having begun a new church building also makes it harder for us yet in the face of everything we need a testimony in this town for the Baptists. . . . Expect to get pledges for a new church and go right ahead with the building project. There is a hand full of Baptists here and they will bring others. I feel that we ought to stick here and see the work through and build a memmorial for Brother Hermiston and call it, "The Hermiston Memmorial Baptist Church." A man who has put in 20 years in Chapel Car work deserves a memmorial dont you think so?[50]

After taking the car to Los Angeles for repairs, the Blinzingers got busy. They put posters in every home; they went to the high school and talked to students. On Saturday nights they took an express car to the Union Pacific Depot, put the baby organ on it, and held services in front of the worst gambling hells, where they sang, played, and gave a message. Most of the time they had from fifty to seventy-five men and women listening to the message. Twice a week they would go to the Union Pacific Railroad shops with the organ during the noon hour and hold services after the men were through eating. Blinzinger explained, "Well, the fact is the people wouldn't come to the car very much, and so we took the message where the people were."[51]

On November 2, 1924, the Baptist church in Las Vegas was organized, for the second time, formally with fourteen members. Blinzinger had said that he was never able to find the group that the Las Vegas *Review* wrote about that organized when Hermiston came to the town. Construction began in December and services were held in the new church March 1, 1925.[52]

Completing the church for which Hermiston had laid the groundwork, Blinzinger was not unhappy to be leaving Las Vegas in the spring of 1925. His exit report would never be included in a Chamber of Commerce brochure. "The leading business was gambling, next came bootlegging and next the Red Light District."

Back in California, at the mining community of Oroville, the Blinzingers built another church. In his "no-monkey-business" style, Blinzinger reported to White, "Well, we will be here for some months and like other places [we will] finish the work here and establish same and put everything on a good basis and then leave. We don't believe in spasms but do thorough work and stay long enough to see the work through."[53] Lots were bought, a Sunday school unit built, and the membership grew to fifty-two in a town where Blinzinger said 90 percent attended no church.

During much of 1926, *Grace* worked in California and in the Salt Lake City, Utah, area. In 1927 they traveled to Nevada towns like Contact and Winnemucca to attempt to revive flocks that had been started by previous chapel car missionaries and to make additions to buildings or build parsonages.

A first for Blinzinger, an old hand at church building, was helping to work *Evangel* into the structure of the First Baptist Church of Rawlins, Wyoming. Beginning in October 1929, *Grace* served as the chapel and parsonage for the growing Rawlins membership. *Evangel* was literally cut in half and incorporated into the new church as *Grace* stood by to help.

Work in the Wind River Canyon

By February 1931, the Blinzingers had moved on through the majestic Wind River Canyon to Thermopolis, Wyoming, the location of the largest hot springs in the United States. At the beginning they faced great indifference from the community, but finally they gained the support of the people and constructed a building for the Baptists. It would be acclaimed as one of the finest in the Big Horn Basin, constructed out of scrapped stone and rock from a nearby quarry and a lot of volunteer labor.

The project received much attention and praise but was not without problems from within the church fellowship and without. Blinzinger had the tendency to leave a church before all the bills were paid and in some cases before all the construction was completed. Although the exterior of the building was handsome, there were no seats, no furnace, and no money to hire a minister. Blinzinger received fourteen pews from the now encapsulated *Evangel*, donated by the Rawlins church to use in the Thermopolis church.[54] The Ladies Aid raised money with bake and needlework sales to purchase at one dollar each 140 chairs, paid for by the month, plus a stove for five dollars.

As a result of being pastorless for a number of years and with failing finances, the Thermopolis church could not pay its bills, including some left by Blinzinger. In August 1934 the church was in danger of closing. Much of what happened to the church at Thermopolis was not Blinzinger's fault — the Depression was a major factor, as well as general lack of support. Struggling through the next few years, the church finally managed to survive and grow.

Whether it was another result of the Depression or thievery, before the chapel car was moved from Thermopolis and while the Blinzingers were on vacation, *Grace* was broken into. Almost all their clothes were taken, even Blinzinger's Sunday suit, plus blankets, canned goods, silver, and other items. Blinzinger wrote to Samuel G. Neil, the Bible and field department secretary of the publication society, from Powell, Wyoming, to ask for blankets and also to inform him about the deteriorating condition of the outside of the chapel car.

There were other problems to report at Powell. There was no place to park the car "as the beets will be moving right along and we are on the beet track and it won't be long before we will have to move. Then there is the potatoes and other things to move and the parking situation is the worst we have ever seen and so we will have to spur the car out to get it out of the way. . . ."[55] On September 12, Blinzinger wrote Neil again, laying out another long list of concerns.

Neil would never read those lists, for on September 8, while in Scotland on a preaching mission, he died. The Reverend John Killian, a former chapel car missionary on *Evangel*, took his place as general secretary of the American Baptist Publication Society. Boasting a bit on his own behalf, Blinzinger laid out his approach to chapel car work for Killian: "We have been busy about real things and have not wasted any money, nor run over our allowance and have always added a letter each month stating what we have been doing and what we are up against and you folks always knew all about us and there never was any question mark about us and hence no misunderstanding."[56]

Not only had Blinzinger been an efficient manager of the publication society's money; he had also spent much of his own funds in the building of the churches, even taking the savings he and his wife had made from selling their furniture when they first went into chapel car work. The amount was over two thousand dollars,[57] money that it seemed as if he would never see again, money that was their life savings.

Blinzinger Known as Church Builder

During this time of church building, *Grace* had gone without much-needed repainting and revarnishing. Blinzinger asked for and received permission to purchase the paint and do the painting and varnishing himself, something that most other chapel car men could not do. With his years of building experience, he was able to complete the work so that *Grace* looked decent again, but the job was not as well done as it would have been at a large shop. A touch-up was not as adequate as a good sanding, repair and preparation of the wood, several coats of paint, fresh gilt on the lettering, several coats of varnish, and a linseed rub down. But money was scarce. It was the best they could do, and better than nothing.

Blinzinger learned that the Catholic Church Extension Society chapel car *St. Peter* had been on display at the Chicago World's Fair and that no Baptist chapel car had been sent. With a rush of a 181-word run-on sentence, he told Killian how he felt about that.

Well, I read this article in the "Time" [magazine] and no doubt it was due to the fact that this Chapel Car Peter is the only car displayed at the Century exposition at Chicago and of course people that know nothing about Chapel cars think the catholic church is the only one that has such cars and most of our Baptist folks do not know that Baptists have been the Pioneers in chapel Car work and are still doing the impossible, in establishing churches, Sunday schools, quickening and reviving discouraged churches, putting up church buildings and meeting the Spirit of the day by preaching an unadulterated Gospel, setting forth a sane, live Evangelistic fervor and setting an example of the Gospel of the Grace of God wherever they go. . . .

Our car was at the Panama Exposition and when fixed up is still as fine a car as there is on the Track and if our car had been at Chicago the people would have seen the contrast between Car Peter and ours and we would have greatly advertised our work.[58]

Although he was brusque and quick to complain about the work of others at times, Blinzinger was an effective minister. Luella Mowry, who was baptized by Blinzinger at Powell, on Easter Sunday, April 16, 1933, remembers him fondly. "He was a brick mason by trade, he had learned it in the old country. He came from Germany with no more than a 4th or 5th grade education. He completed high school, then went on to seminary [Colgate]. He had a portable organ. In the summer on Saturday nights, he would go down town, park it in front of the only saloon at that time and play and sing. The first time that I ever heard 'His Eye Is On The Sparrow,' was by him."[59]

The Blinzingers completed building their twelfth church at Riverton, where the people had been worshiping "in some shacks that were joined together." Again the task seemed impossible at first. Blinzinger, much discouraged, wrote Killian.

This is a mess and a half and the church divided into factions. Of course Dr. Palmer and the Board expect us to do the same wonders at Riverton as at other places and somehow they just take it for granted that we undertake such impossible tasks and work ourselves to a frazzle but Mrs. Blinzinger and Myself are just about filled up with such stuff.

We have talked matters over and we are about ready to quit Chapel car work. Why work like beavers and wear ourselves out, give all our money and get nothing but empty words. Thats the way we feel. We can go

Fig. 16.4 The rolltop desk with the leaded-glass bookcase had a roll-up shelf underneath for a typewriter, a tool needed by the missionaries for reports and correspondence. The books on the shelf are a complete set of Bible study guides. (Norman T. Taylor)

back into the regular pastorate and have much more money than now, have a car, much easier living and not be worn to a frazzle. All we do is work, give, build up and we have built up everything we have ever tackled.[60]

But when the church was finished, with bricks hauled from an old building thirty miles away, and the people were in a stirring revival, Blinzinger was praised for his accomplishment by his superiors. "It took vision, plus inspiration, plus perspiration to accomplish this most wonderful piece of work."[61]

At Torrence, Wyoming, where the church had been organized by an earlier visit of *Glad Tidings* and the building constructed by Blinzinger, the children had special fun on the chapel car. Meetings for the children were not only on Sunday but also many days after school, usually conducted by the chapel car wife. "Some places we do not have a spur for the car and so some times we are switched aside while the children's meeting is going on, and some of the youngsters would say to Mrs. Blinzinger, whom they called 'Mrs. Chapel Car,' 'Well the best thing about it [the brief ride], we don't have to pay for it.'"[62]

Leaving their thirteenth project completed at Torrence, the Blinzingers finished similar work at Buffalo, again hauling brick from an abandoned theater ninety miles away to build the church and leaving fifty-three new members to the church roll; Sheridan, where a basement was renovated for service; and Lander, where they improved the building and built an annex out of railroad ties.

Future of Remaining Cars Questioned

Before he left chapel car service, Blinzinger was asked for advice about the prospects for the future of the three remaining chapel cars, *Emmanuel*, *Messenger of Peace*, and *Grace*.

If you are going to maintain a car then [the] car to be considered is Chapel Car Grace, or our car. It will last for another generation and there will be no question as to transportation and of the railroad companies.

The other two cars are about finished and the

railroad companies hesitate to transport them and under the best condition have to be transported by freight as they will not pass inspection or interstate commerce act.

Next, the cars are an expensive proposition these days as we have to pay first class transportation and now fares are rising and so will cost even more and if one travels distances it is quite an expense. Years ago, before the last world war we traveled free but all has been changed.

Now, as we are not organizing and establishing new churches, the cars simply serve as a living quarter and so at best cannot be located where one would like them located and under present condition a missionary could have a trailer outfit and locate in a most convenient place and do the work of building up or reviving a church and make repairs etc, and so be more comfortable with less expense to the society.

No, you need not expect that the railroads will give you anything for the other two old cars for the railroad companies have plenty of these kind and use them for bridge gangs.

Now as to the use of these cars in case that some little church would like to have them. Well, the car Evangel at Rawlins which I turned into the church, the Railroad company, or the U.P. took the trucks, which is the most costly and vital part of a car and hauled the rest up to the church lot and so did not cost us anything. . . . If I were to handle another car and work it into a church, I would build an Episcopal style church. Cut the car through the center and separate it, fill in between, and this would give me the whole frame work of the church and then brick veneer it and put on the roof etc.[63]

Blinzinger Retires; Parry Years Begin

Upon his retirement in 1942, Blinzinger received a pension of $213.84 per year. "I wish it might be larger but the very heavy deficits which we have been compelled to meet in the missionary budget for the past several years have made it necessary for us to revise our pension benefits," the treasurer of the home mission society wrote.[64] At a rate of fifty-nine cents a day, the Blinzingers, no doubt with heavy hearts, wished it might be larger too.

It was decided to remove *Emmanuel* from active duty and to keep *Grace* and *Messenger of Peace* in service. As a result of that decision, in 1943, after *Grace* had again been put into good mechanical and physical shape at the Denver and Rio Grand shops, the Reverend and Mrs. Howard Parry were transferred to *Grace* from *Emmanuel*.

Parry had cleaned up affairs for the retirement of *Emmanuel* and then served as a colporter for a period in Colorado and Utah in defense housing projects. A philosophical, quiet man, Parry had also followed Hermiston and Blinzinger on *Emmanuel*.

The three men were a trinity of differing personalities and missionary styles: Hermiston, a bombastic, Billy Sunday–style huckster who touched many hearts for Christ; Blinzinger, a roll-up-your-sleeves man who boasted of his abilities yet labored faithfully through great difficulties; Parry, a gentle scholar and loving pastor with a need for order, who kept a diary every day of his dedicated ministry. The last stage of *Grace*'s ministry would be more suited to the nature of Howard Parry.

The world in 1943 was very different from the world of the first Baptist car, *Evangel*, in 1891. Towns were no longer so isolated, churches were much more common, the railroads were no longer in their heyday, and in some ways World War II was the only thing keeping the railroads in the center of the nation's transportation system. *Grace* still had work to do — work in strongly Mormon southern Utah in the town of Orem, with a mixture of war plant employees, ranchers, Mexican farm workers, and non-Mormons.

The site of the huge Geneva Steel plant at Orem presented unique problems for Mary and Howard Parry.

Indifference, long working hours, inconveniences connected with trailer camp life for the women with

Fig. 16.5 The congregation of the Grace Baptist Church at Orem, Utah, was mainly composed of workers at the Geneva Steel plant, military personnel, local ranchers, and workers, many from the American Indian population. (American Baptist Historical Society, Valley Forge)

families all effect the ability and willingness to attend services despite any kind of approach. However, in time with patience, response will come. Uncertainty of residence for the construction workers still on the project creates a feeling and attitude of unwillingness to get into church work or community work. The native Mormons frankly are antagonistic toward the defense workers as you can well understand in as much as this is ZION, their promised land. When the permanent element, operating skilled workers get settled the prospects will begin to clarify.[65]

Getting settled into *Grace* was an adjustment for the Parrys. They acknowledged that *Grace* was much better equipped, and Mary Parry liked the separate bedroom and brass double bed, but they still missed *Emmanuel*, now retired at Swan Lake Baptist Camp in South Dakota. After three weeks, they still did not have an electrical connection; and coal, which the Baker heater required, was impossible to obtain in Orem. So they purchased a distillate stove secondhand for the chapel and in the living quarters continued to use a Coleman heater given them by Mr. Coleman himself.

Parry's Diary Records Ministry

In his diary, Parry noted on Sunday, February 20, 1943, that at Sunday school four Indian teenagers made first confession responses, and after Parry preached on "How Big Is My World," Bill and Ronald Fuller, of Comanche Miami blood, and Muriel and Freeman Walker of Comanche Miami blood, came forward. Their parents had come from Oklahoma to work at the Geneva Steel Plant.

On Tuesday, June 6, 1943, Parry printed in his diary in big letters: "INVASION. LANDED 3:32 A.M. U.S. TIME. NORMANDY COAST. Cherbourg: 83 miles from English Coast. AIR ARM STRUCK SHORTLY BEFORE MIDNIGHT." In a little box targeted with arrows on each side, Parry wrote, "Invasion came 6th Hour, 6th Day, 6th Month." On the next day, the items were more mundane: "Cleaned chapel car, washed seats and mopped floor." He had made three calls and started to study his Sunday school lesson. The weather was "Very Warm."

On Easter Sunday, April 9, 1944, the neat program printed by Parry was crammed with scholarly scriptural references regarding Easter, and poetry, as well as the order of worship.

At the bottom of the page was the instruction for the Russian greeting on Resurrection Day: "As the devout Christians greet each other one says 'He is Risen.' The one addressed replies: 'He is Risen indeed.'" The program also included the assurance that "The Chapel Car and its workers will remain at the service of the Christian people of Orem indefinitely. . . . You may with confidence continue to invite your friends to the ministry of the Chapel Car."[66]

Mormon Church Had Early Church Car

Grace was not the only church on rails to travel in Utah. The Mormon church also had a form of church car in the 1870s when they were given sixty thousand dollars worth of equipment for their contract labor in the construction of the Union Pacific Railroad across Utah. Lucius Beebe in *Mansions on Rails* described the car.

> One of the first things the Mormons did on receipt of the rolling stock was to rebuild the most available coach into a private car suitable to Brigham Young. . . . Angels were painted on the ceiling, so folklore holds, and gilt and scrollwork appeared in wildest profusion. When finished the car combined the best features of business office and episcopal palace. Aboard it the bearded patriarch traveled extensively and splendidly over the then existing railroads of Utah surrounded by his wives, bishops of the church, elders and other peers in saintliness until his death in 1877.[67]

The car disappeared from view toward the turn of the twentieth century, although some claims were made about the car being seen in secular service. But by the 1940s the only chapel car in Mormon country was *Grace*, with no angels painted on its ceiling, just a delicate, tasteful design stenciled in the corners.

One day Parry, who had organized a father-and-son banquet in San Juan County, found attendance gathered from as far as twenty miles distant, and people attending had traveled on rural roads ankle deep in mud in places. It was no small reason for

Fig. 16.6 The living area of *Grace* was a comfortable, if cramped, home for Mary and Howard Parry and their pet, a big cat. The radio behind Mrs. Parry was much enjoyed by her husband, who had quite an interest in national affairs during World War II. (American Baptist Historical Society, Valley Forge)

satisfaction that forty-five men and boys had gathered. "Despite restrictions and regulation there is a constant shifting of families from farm to factory and back to farm, from the local plant to more favorable wage earning jobs. In addition labor organizing keeps the morale unstable, which effects the stability of people with whom the colporteur must work."

In addition to his many other duties, Parry had a radio program over KOVO in Provo, a first for a chapel car missionary. Beside his chapel car duties, a frequent notation on his diary pages for most of his years of service was "Headache today."

On May 8, 1945, the diary read, "EUROPEAN WAR ENDS (GERMAN SURRENDER)." In the face of such a momentous event, Parry made his pastoral calls, went to see the doctor about his headache, and worked on his convention sermon (*fig. 16.6*).

On August 14 — "2ND WORLD WAR ENDS, Japan Surrenders Official 5:00 PM, 7 P.M. E.W. Time."

Parry went to see the doctor again, made his calls, received corn, onions, parsnips, beans, kohlrabi, and lettuce from a member, picked apricots to take to a member, and cut down the weeds around the chapel car. The news of the world he acknowledged, absorbed, and recorded, but he steadfastly went about ministry — headache and all.

After the war, the Geneva Steel Plant closed its operations, and hundreds of employees set forth to find other jobs and other homes. The pews in *Grace* became empty, and the Parrys knew it was time to move on. They also knew, as did the publication and home mission societies, that the time of the chapel cars had probably come to an end. Only *Messenger of Peace* was still serving in a defense project in upper Washington State. *Grace* was not needed now in Orem, but it was wanted at the Northern Baptist Assembly (now the American Baptist Assembly) at Green Lake, Wisconsin.

Grace Heads to Final Stop at Green Lake

In May 1945, Parry went to visit the Conaway/Birch family, the donors of *Grace*. Mr. Conaway had passed away, and Mrs. Conway was ninety-three years old, but she and her daughter were still vitally interested in the chapel car and its future. She said that she would like to see the car

Fig. 16.7 This is one of the last services held in *Grace* at Orem, Utah, before the car was taken out of service and sent to the American Baptist Assembly at Green Lake, Wisconsin. (American Baptist Historical Society, Valley Forge)

stationed in the West but would also be in favor of it being taken to the Northern Baptist Assembly grounds at Green Lake. She agreed Green Lake would be a fitting memorial place for it.

Using money that had been given to him and Mrs. Parry personally, Parry was going to have the car touched up so it would still be in good condition for service, as long as that might be. Unlike Blinzinger, he would not attempt to do the work himself. Frequently the Parrys used their own money to support the work of the chapel cars and other missionary interests, never calling attention to the fact.[68]

When the Parrys first transferred to *Grace*, their first love had been *Emmanuel*. Now their hearts were with *Grace* as they looked toward the move to retirement at Green Lake. "Tomorrow with mingled emotions we close eleven years of service in Railroad Chapel Car service. We love the car, what its ministry has meant to us and our predecessors with their distinctive ministries," Parry wrote Green Lake business manager John Clark.[69]

The Salt Lake and Utah Railroad would move *Grace* from Orem to Provo, Utah, and from there to the shops of the Denver and Rio Grande Western Railroad (D & RGW), where the chapel car would be put back in good order for its new future. Parry, like a father sending a child off alone on a journey, requested of the D & RGW that the car be handled with care and the courtesy of putting it in a place that would not inconvenience the necessary movement of their own stock yet close enough to supervise, "for there are many valuable personal effects of my own as well as our society equipment inside."[70] On the bill of lading that traveled with *Grace* was this description: One Railway Chapel car. Passenger car, Unoccupied — Handle with care.

While the chapel car was in the shops Parry went on a speaking trip, and he also made an appointment with the Leahy Clinic in Boston. He was still seeking relief from his headaches. The doctor gave him advice: eat all foods, take medication with meals, change work, and get a real rest. Parry would not rest long, for in the fall of 1946, just a few months after leaving *Grace* at Green Lake, he was assigned to Lodge Grass, Montana, where he worked with the ministry of the Little Brown Church, until exhaustion caused him to retire in 1950.

On Easter Sunday, April 21, 1946, *Grace* was on a Chicago, Burlington & Quincy Railroad passenger yard siding in Chicago, Illinois, at 12th Street near Canal, waiting to be feted and inspected again after thirty-one years of service. Present railroad rules did not permit the stops at depots where Baptist friends could honor the car's long service. It traveled humbly in a line of rumbling freight cars, but glittering on its sides was still the worthy and holy name *Grace*.

Although still beautiful as a result of a recent renovation at the Denver and Rio Grande shops, this time the car was not a shining bride setting forth on her honeymoon but a senior citizen heading to her retirement home. No jubilant cars of Baptist conventioneers singing hymns followed in its stead, just some quiet visitors with sedate psalms and prayers, although a photographer from the Associated Press took pictures.

When the chapel car arrived at Green Lake via the Chicago and North Western Railroad, the journey became more jubilant. Townspeople followed *Grace*'s every move with interest and excitement. According to eyewitness Herman Schultz, a gardener at the assembly, the car arrived at the depot, there to be moved to the American Baptist Assembly grounds by the Shea-Matson Company of Milwaukee at a cost of 1,500 dollars. The task required three and a half days.

Probably the greatest difficulty was in removing the car from the railroad tracks at the depot. The tracks there were above the roadbed and thus stood four feet higher than the moving trucks. It was necessary for the crew to skid the car sideways for more than one hundred feet in order to ease it onto the trucks. This required more than a day to accomplish. Two sixteen-wheelbase trucks were used, placed back to back, one truck proceeding and the other backing all the way. The rate of speed was one-fourth mile per hour.

The next day, followed by fascinated crowds of residents,

the trucks and *Grace* proceeded as far as the western city limits of Green Lake. On the third day, they reached the designated spot on the assembly grounds, near the Abbey Barn area, not far from the front gate *(fig. 16.8)*. The following morning, the car was lowered back onto it trucks and then onto the rails that had been laid by assembly workmen.[71]

On August 4, 1946, *Grace* was dedicated in ceremonies in the car. Luther Wesley Smith, executive secretary of the board of education and publication, gave the address. The crowd gathered in the chapel car joined in dedicating the car to the memory of those whose vision, leadership, and sacrifice provided this car as a method of carrying the gospel to the unreached communities of America, to those who served in this car as our missionaries of the gospel, and to the memory and blessing of those who by the thousands have found Christ in chapel car *Grace*. It was hoped that many who would visit the car would draw inspiration from the story of its glorious ministry in the service of our Christ.[72]

Several volunteer projects and the continued support of the assembly staff have preserved *Grace*. In the spring of 1968, the car was repainted inside and out (Pennsylvania Railroad

Fig. 16.8 *Grace* was delivered to the depot of Green Lake, Wisconsin, from Chicago, via Denver and Salt Lake, loaded on two trucks, and moved slowly from the town to the Abbey area grounds of the Northern Baptist Assembly. (American Baptist Assembly, Green Lake, Wisconsin)

Fig. 16.9 In November 1982, *Grace* was moved from the Abbey area to a more prominent place on the lakefront near the conference center. The move, done with truck and hydraulic cranes, was difficult because of a narrow, winding bridge along the only possible route. (American Baptist Assembly, Green Lake, Wisconsin)

Tuscan Red) by a crew of senior high students and their leaders from the First Baptist Church of Waukegan, Illinois, led by the Reverend Mason L. Brown.

During Senior High Week in 1981, delegates under the direction of the Reverend Eldon Elmore of West Side Baptist Church, Wichita, Kansas, along with other central region young people, gave the car's interior a thorough cleaning and began to scrape the exterior paint. The project was completed in June 1982 with the stripping and refinishing of the pews and other repairs.

In 1982, because of the influence of Harold Mitchell, director of operations at that time, and the support of new American Baptist Assembly president Paul LaDue, the L & H Gyr Trailer Services of Fond du Lac moved *Grace* from the Abbey area to the Luther Wesley Smith Conference Area. Mitchell's wife, Ardis, recalled that her husband was

concerned about the future of the car where it was, rather out of sight and mind in the Abbey area. Mitchell and LaDue both agreed it needed to be in a spot where it could be a more visible symbol and thus more likely to be preserved.

When Dave Elsinger and his partner Allen Stream, young employees of the L & H Gyr Company first came to the assembly to see the car and its proposed route — via a twisting one-lane bridge lined by two-foot stone walls — to the lakefront site, Elsinger told Mitchell, "I don't know how we can do it. It can't be done." Mitchell, who had already been told that by other Ohio and Indiana moving companies, told Elsinger, in a wild moment of desperation, "Money is no object."

After four or five trips on their own time to study the possibilities, Elsinger and Stream finally came up with a plan. They would use two fifty-ton cranes, a semi trailer with a fifth wheel, a bucket hydraulic caterpillar, plus spreaders and a dolly system. The key to the success of the project would be the weather. It had to be dry.

When the September day for the journey to the lake front site came, it rained. The decision was made to bring the cranes into position and see if the weather would change to permit the move, as every hour the cranes were there, Elsinger said, "the meter was running."

After an hour or so the rain stopped, and *Grace* was lifted by the two cranes off its sets of multiple wheels and strapped with half-inch chains on an eighty-foot flatbed trailer (*fig. 16.9*). Just as the dollies and truck came off the grassy plot at the edge of the Lawsonia Golf Course where the car had been standing, the car began to tilt. Hearts stopped. Workers moved quickly to plank under the truck wheels, and the car righted itself.

Moving at a crawl, someone, later discovered to be not a member of the moving crew, yelled "Stop!" The driver stopped, and the behemoth of truck and chapel car sunk into the soft soil and could not move. Even with the second loader and a one-and-one-half-inch cable pulling, the wheels spun on the blacktop road.

The driver of the caterpillar's hydraulic bucket saved the day, finally pulling them free, and *Grace*, perched on its patient beast of burden, crawled the rest of the 1.7-mile trip between the rolling greens of Lawsonia Golf Course, under the arches of great honey locust, maples just starting to turn red, and tall sentinels of pine, by vistas of valley and lake, and past curious deer.

At the bridge, bleachers had been set up for anxious staffers to watch the caravan maneuver the dreaded one-lane stone bridge, one of many built by Victor Lawson, owner and publisher of the Chicago *Daily News* at the turn of the century. Oh so slowly, *Grace* started through the narrow serpentine opening, but the angle was quite not right, and the drivers decided to back up and try again. This time — by just one inch, swinging on the dolly over the natural stone walls — *Grace* made it through. The crowd on the bleachers stood up and clapped with relief and thanksgiving.

The drama was not yet over. At the destination site, as the workers were preparing the cranes to swing the car back onto its trucks, which had been placed on sections of rail, one of the cranes blew its hydraulic line. When he was told that it would take another day to repair the line, Mitchell became very concerned. His rash words, "Money is no object," came back to haunt him. He did not see how they could afford the added costs of keeping the equipment for another day. "Isn't there something that you can do?" he begged Elsinger.

"We had just one option, at that point." Elsinger, who said he and his partner will never forget this first big challenge and who with their own company has moved many railroad cars and engines since, went to the remaining crane operator and asked if he thought he could move the car onto its trucks by himself. He thought he could. One crane, one end at a time, moved the chapel car onto its trucks."[73]

The cost for the move was 6,500 dollars. Mitchell was convinced that *Grace* was worth it.

Shortly after the move was completed, the car was restored from the Tuscan Red of its 1968 painting to its original Pullman Green, and other repairs were made by a dedicated

Fig. 16.10 Now protected by a shelter built by volunteers and staff, *Grace* still is a place of worship visited by thousands every year. (Norman T. Taylor)

volunteer group from the First Baptist Church of Pittsburg, Kansas.

In 1990 volunteer staff members raised the money to have a shelter built over the chapel car to protect it from the elements. Several years later, John L. "Bud" Carroll, former denominational youth leader and assembly board member, started an endowment fund to help maintain and preserve the chapel car. For many years, Harriet Dowdy, an assembly volunteer, regularly has given tours and talks to visitors of the chapel car.

One of the authors of this book, Norman Taylor, a railroad shop employee, began a new restoration project on the car in 1991.

Without the support and interest of past and present leaders of the assembly, *Grace* probably would have gone the route of other chapel cars, forgotten, neglected, and abandoned. But leaders from Luther Wesley Smith and J. L. Kraft to Paul LaDue and Ken Giacoletto have preserved the car and honored its history.

Thousands of visitors to the pastoral grounds at Green Lake will tell you that *Grace* is not out of service. The familiar strains of "Amazing Grace" from the Estey organ can still be heard through an open window on a summer day, and worshipers frequently fill the pews for services. Light filters through lace curtains and sprinkles across the bright quilt on the prized brass double bed, as a photo of Mary and Howard Parry looks down from a bedroom shelf. An open Bible rests on the brass podium in the chapel waiting to be read, and the glow of *Grace's* green stained-glass window trim mirrors the rippling waters of Green Lake.

> O God of grace, this Chapel speed,
> Wherever sin is found
> Display thy light, thy love, thy life,
> Till grace much more abound.
>
> Go forth, go forth to all mankind;
> Go preach my gospel true.
> All pow'r is mine; go forth, go forth!
> I am with you, I am with you![74]

Notes

[1] *Watchman Examiner*, May 20, 1915, 625, American Baptist Seminary of the West, Berkeley, Calif.

[2] Contract/Blueprint file, Colporter File-Historical, ABHS, VF.

[3] Letter from Guy C. Lamson to George L. White, Los Angeles, Calif., December 23, 1914, 36.1, Box 36, ABHS, VF.

[4] Letter from George L. White to Guy C. Lamson, Philadelphia, Pa., January 6, 1915, 35.12, Box 35, ABHS, VF.

[5] Letter from Guy C. Lamson to George L. White, Los Angeles, Calif., January 13, 1915, 36.1, Box 36, ABHS, VF.

[6] *Our Times: Multimedia Encyclopedia of the 20th Century*, CD, "In the United States: 1915," Vicarious, Inc., 1996.

[7] *Atlanta Constitution*, February 20, 1915, 1.

[8] "Chapel Car Grace," *The Standard*, October 30, 1915, Box G. Pitts Beers, ABHS, VF.

[9] Ibid.

[10] Report from E. R. Hermiston on his stay at the Panama Exposition, 27.12, Box 27, ABHS, VF.

[11] "Chapel Car Grace," *Missions*, December 1915, 122.

[12] Letter from E. R. Hermiston to George L. White, St. Helena, Calif., October 25, 1915, Box 27, ABHS, VF.

[13] Ibid.

[14] Letter from E. R. Hermiston to George L. White, Yountville, Calif., December 13, 1915, Box 27, ABHS, VF.

[15] Letter from E. R. Hermiston to George L. White, Yountville, Calif., December 8, 1915, Box 27, ABHS, VF.

[16] Material sent from E. R. Hermiston to George L. White, "Soul Winning Work on Chapel Car Grace," 27.13, Box 27, ABHS, VF.

[17] Letter from E. R. Hermiston to George L. White, Burlingame, Calif., September 29, 1916, 27.13, Box 27, ABHS, VF.

[18] "A Battle Down the Border," *Missions*, November 1917, 752.

[19] Ibid.

[20] "A Stranger's View of the Practical Value of Chapel Car Work," *Missions*, November 1917, 757.

[21] Letter from E. R. Hermiston to George L. White, East Bakersfield, California, December 5, 1917, ABHS, VF.

[22] Letter from E. R. Hermiston to George L. White, Menlo Park, Calif., June 17, 1918, ABHS, VF.

[23] *Missions*, September 1918, 634.

[24] Material for *Missions*, "Chapel Car Grace in Camp Fremont," 27.13, Box 27, ABHS, VF.

[25] Letter from E. R. Hermiston to George L. White, Vacaville, Calif., November 5, 1918, 27.13, Box 27, ABHS, VF.

[26] Letter from E. R. Hermiston to George L. White, Redding, Calif., April 4, 1919, 27.13, Box 27, ABHS, VF.

27 Inez M. Borror, "Trains All Stopped at Gerber in Busy Bygone Years" (David Louis Harter, California Technologies, 1996).

28 Letter from E. R. Hermiston to George L. White, Gerber, Calif., July 3, 1919, 27.13, Box 27, ABHS, VF.

29 Letter from George L. White to E. R. Hermiston, Los Angeles, Calif., August 13, 1919, 27.13, Box 27, ABHS, VF.

30 Letter from E. R. Hermiston to George L. White, Gerber, Calif., August 24, 1919, 27.13, Box 27, ABHS, VF.

31 Letter from E. R. Hermiston to George L. White, Hughson, Calif., November 17, 1920, 27.14, Box 27, ABHS, VF.

32 Letter from E. R. Hermiston to George L. White, Sacramento, Calif., December 9, 1920, 27.14, Box 27, ABHS, VF.

33 Letter from Charles L. White to George L. White, New York, N.Y., March 30, 1921, 69.1, Box 69, ABHS, VF.

34 Letter from George L. White to E. R. Hermiston, Los Angeles, Calif., May 25, 1921, 27.14, Box 27, ABHS, VF.

35 "Railroad Evangelism," *Missions*, March 1922, 156.

36 Stanley W. Paher, *Las Vegas: At it began — as it grew* (Las Vegas: Nevada Publications, 1971), 118.

37 Ralph J. Roske, *Las Vegas: A Desert Paradise* (Tulsa: Continental Heritage Press, 1986), 62.

38 Ibid., 70.

39 *Las Vegas Review*, Friday, March 2, 1923, 1.

40 Ibid., 4.

41 *Las Vegas Review*, April 20, 1923, 4.

42 Letter from E. R. Hermiston to George L. White, Las Vegas, March 2, 1923, 27.14, Box 27, ABHS, VF.

43 Letter from George L. White to E. R. Hermiston, Los Angeles, Calif., March 6, 1923, 27.14, Box 27, ABHS, VF.

44 Letter from E. R. Hermiston to George L. White, Las Vegas, March 12, 1923, 27.14, Box 27, ABHS, VF.

45 Letter from E. R. Hermiston to George L. White , Las Vegas, March 15, 1923, 27.14, Box 27, ABHS, VF.

46 Letter from Bruce E. Jackson to George L. White, Salt Lake, March 21, 1923, Box 40, ABHS, VF.

47 Letter from E. R. Hermiston to George L. White, Las Vegas, April 5, 1923, 27.14, Box 27, ABHS, VF.

48 Telegram from Mrs. E. R. Hermiston to George L. White, Modesto, Calif., September 27, 1923, 27.14, Box 27, ABHS, VF.

49 *Missions*, September 1923, 687.

50 Letter from A. C. Blinzinger to George L. White, Las Vegas, September 12, 1924.

51 Ibid.

52 History of the First Baptist Church of Las Vegas.

53 Letter from A. C. Blinzinger to George L. White, Oroville, Calif., December 31, 1925, 5.17, Box 5, ABHS, VF.

54 Letter from Will Gordon to A. C. Blinzinger, Rawlins, Wyo., April 21, 1931, Colporter Box, ABHS, VF.

55 Letter from A. C. Blinzinger to Samuel G. Neil, Powell, Wyo., September 8, 1932, Colporter Box, ABHS, VF.

56 Letter from A. C. Blinzinger to Miss Linda DeArmond, Powell, Wyo., December 5, 1932, Colporter Box, ABHS, VF.

57 Letter from A. C. Blinzinger to John C. Killian, Powell, Wyo., April 25, 1933, Colporter Box, ABHS, VF.

58 Letter from A. C. Blinzinger to John C. Killian, Powell, Wyo., July 13, 1934, Colporter Box, ABHS, VF.

59 Letter from Luella Mowry to Leroy Shikles, Limon, Colo., Samuelson Collection, ABHS, VF.

60 Letter from A. C. Blinzinger to John C. Killian, Riverton, Wyo., September 13, 1935, Colporter Box, ABHS, VF.

61 "Old and New Trails in the Colporter Mission," American Baptist Publication Society pamphlet, Chapel Car Literature Box, ABHS, VF.

62 Letter from A. C. Blinzinger to John C. Killian, Torrence, Wyo., March 12, 1938, Colporter Box, ABHS, VF.

63 Letter from A. C. Blinzinger to Mark Rich, Lander, Wyo., March 15, 1942, Mark Rich Box, ABHS, VF.

64 Letter from ELR, treasurer of American Baptist Home Mission Society, to A. C. Blinzinger, June 25, 1942, Dorothy Martin Correspondence, Grace Article Request, ABHS, VF.

65 Letter from Howard Parry to Luther Wesley Smith, Orem, Utah, October 18, Chapel Car Records, Howard Parry Collection, Box 2, ABHS, VF.

66 Grace Baptist Church program, Orem, Utah, Easter 1944, Colporter Box, Howard Parry Collection, ABHS, VF.

67 Lucius Beebe, *Mansions on Rails: The Folklore of the Private Railway Car* (Berkeley, Calif.: Howell-North, 1959), 101.

68 Letter from Howard Parry to Luther Wesley Smith, Orem, Utah, May 30, 1945, Colporter Box, Howard Parry Collection, ABHS, VF.

69 Letter from Howard Parry to J. C. Clark, business manager, Green Lake, Wisc., from Orem, Utah, February 2, 1946, Green Lake files, American Baptist Assembly, Green Lake, Wisc.

70 Letter from Howard Parry to Mr. Sagstetter, Master Mechanics Office, D & RG, Orem, Utah, February 1, 1946, Colporter Records, Howard Parry Collection, ABHS, VF.

71 Green Lake newspaper article in American Baptist Assembly files, Green Lake, Wisc.

72 Copy of dedication ceremony, Green Lake files, Green Lake, Wisc.

73 Personal interview with Dave Elsinger of Fond du Lac, Wisc., May 9, 1998.

74 From the song written by E. M. Stephenson for the dedication of Baptist chapel car *Grace*.

CHAPTER 17

The End of the Chapel Car Era

The last American chapel car still mobile was the Catholic Church Extension Society's *St. Paul*, which was used as a seasonal chapel at Browning and Summit, Montana, near the entrance to Glacier National Park until 1962. Although it has "lost its go," chapel car *Grace* still serves as a house of worship.

But the spirit of the chapel cars lives on in many different forms.

Along a busy highway near the Wisconsin/Illinois line, a truck lot is jammed with eighteen-wheelers, engines idling, drivers eating hot meals in the nearby restaurant, talking to bosses on table side phones. Both drivers and bosses are eager for the rigs to get quickly on the road again and safely to their destination. A message comes over the public address system, "Meeting at the mobile chapel in half an hour. Everybody welcome."

It is not difficult to find the mobile chapel, even in the midst of the rows of brightly designed trucks. A red neon cross beckons from on top, and from the side can be read clearly "Mobile Chapel, Transport for Christ." Across the back, the words of John 3:16 (KJV) loom large: "For God so loved the world, that he gave his only begotten Son, that whosoever believeth on him should not perish, but have everlasting life" (fig. 17.2).

The same Scripture was printed on the side of many of the chapel cars. The message is the same. The Spirit is the same. Only the wheels are different.

For a story in the *New York Times*, journalist Pam Belluck interviewed Howard E. Jones, former trucker and president of Transport for Christ International, which sponsors twenty-one eight-foot-wide, twenty-four-hour-a-day chapels (fig. 17.1).

"There's close to six million drivers in the United States and Canada," Jones said. "They're the largest unreached group, unreached by Jesus. . . . There are all kinds of temptations for truckers—sex and drugs and pornography. They're away from the home four to six weeks at a time."

Transport for Christ International is not the only group witnessing to truckers. Others, among them Truckers for Christ, Truck Stop Ministries, and the Association of Christian Truckers hold meetings and cruise the two thousand truck stops on the interstate to bring the gospel to these men and women who seldom go where the gospel is being preached.[1]

In some Third World countries, missionaries, like the Swiss colporters of long ago, still bravely carry their Gospels in bags slung around their necks, venturing into areas where God's Word has never traveled.

Many religious denominations still use cars, trucks, vans, buses, and boats to reach the hard-to-reach territories of their ministries, although it seems that some mainline denominations no longer have the emphasis on evangelism they once had. One administrator of a leading denomination offered his opinion: "Evangelism has been more or less left to the 'evangelicals.'"

Fig. 17.1 The spirit of the chapel cars lives on in projects like Transport for Christ International, which sponsors twenty-four-hour-a-day chapels that cruise the two thousand truckstops on the interstate to bring the gospel to men and women who seldom go where the gospel is being preached. (Norman T. Taylor)

Fig. 17.2 The Scripture on the back of this truck chapel, John 3:16, was the same Scripture inscribed on the sides of many chapel cars during their era. (Norman T. Taylor)

The United Methodist Church, which has been a forerunner in evangelism from the days of their circuit riders, has not forgotten that heritage. Their General Board of Global Ministries is promoting new ventures in missions, including a fly-in ministry into Trapper Creek, Alaska, and adjacent areas, where several hundred families are scattered in areas without churches or other forms of religious services.[2] The Catholic Church Extension Society also has an aviation ministry in Alaska.

In cyberspace, a random search will discover web sites by the thousands of faiths and denominations, reaching out to whomever will make a hit on the Internet.

In their beginning, the chapel cars were the fastest, most exciting, state-of-the-art, high-tech way "to go." For that was and is the command to the church. Christ said to his disciples, "Go therefore and make disciples of all the nations, baptizing them in the name of the Father and the Son and the Holy Spirit, teaching them to observe all that I commanded you; and lo, I am with you always, even to the end of the age" (Matthew 28:19, NASB).

Few people question that the coming of the railroad to the West brought many advantages and perhaps realized the concept of America's proclaimed Manifest Destiny. Agricultural commodities, minerals, lumber, and manufactured goods of all kinds, along with passengers from all parts of the world, were able to be carried to the harbors and towns and cities from coast to coast.

The transcontinental railroads no doubt helped make America *great*. At their beginnings, they did little to help America be *good*.

From 1890 to 1946, thirteen chapel cars made spiritual journeys across America's West, Northwest, South, and Southeast. They brought faith, morality, and hope to the faithful and faithless alike. The end of the line for the chapel car era had come. Behind, along shining rails of steel, thousands of Americans had found God, and communities had been changed for the better.

Notes

[1] Pam Belluck, "Drivers Find New Service at Truck Stops: Old-Time Religion," *New York Times*, Sunday, February 1, 1998, 1, 14; also from authors' visit to Rochelle, Ill., truck stop in summer 1996.

[2] Correspondence from Barbara J. Campfield, General Board of Global Ministries, The United Methodist Church, 475 Riverside Drive, New York, N.Y. 10115, August 14, 1998.

Floor Plans of the Chapel Cars

Cathedral Car of North Dakota: *Church of the Advent*
Episcopal Missionary District of North Dakota

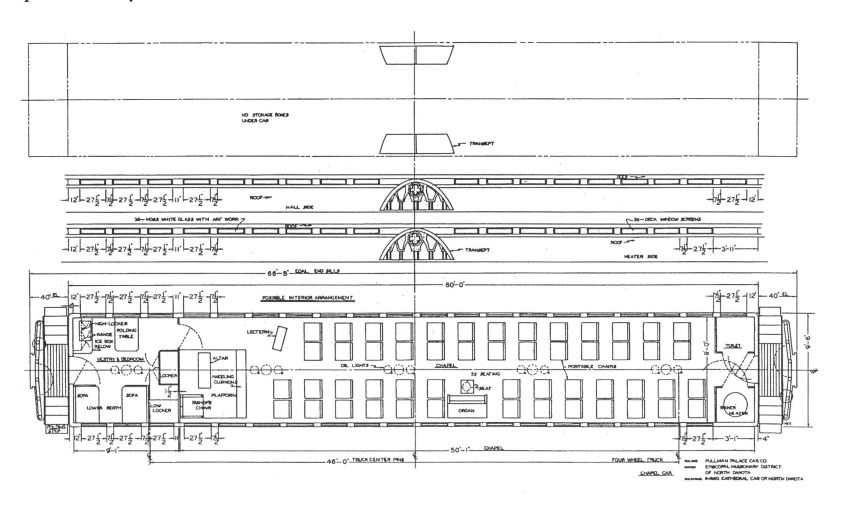

Baptist Chapel Car #1: *Evangel*
American Baptist Publication Society

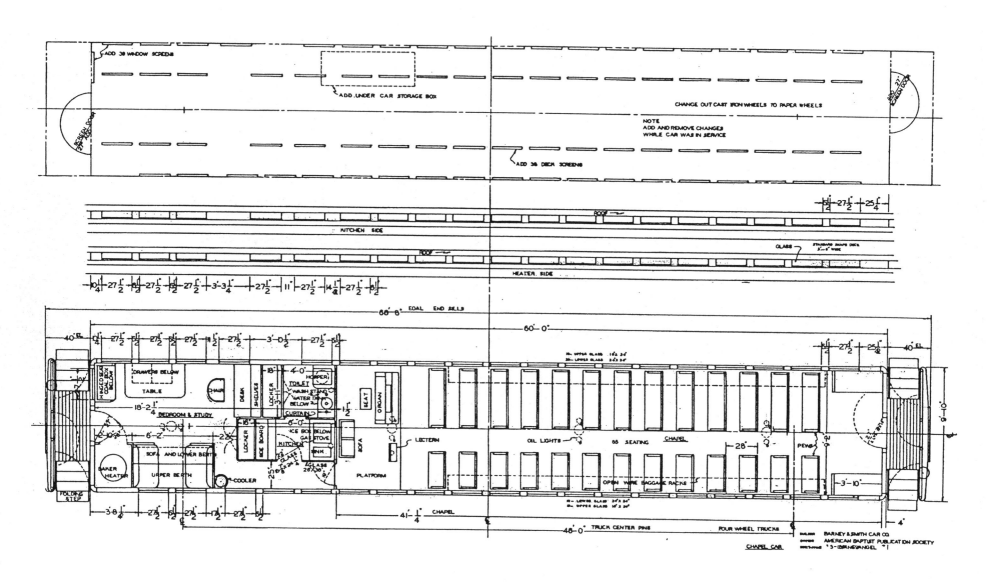

Episcopal Car of Northern Michigan
Episcopal Missionary District of Northern Michigan

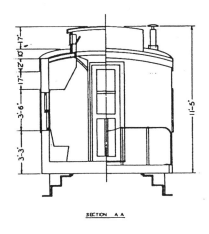

SECTION A A

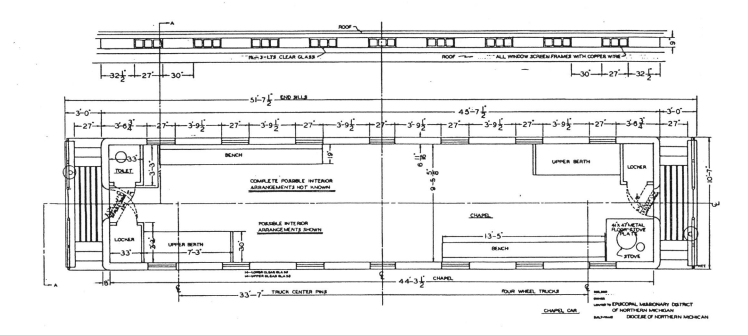

CHAPEL CAR

Baptist Chapel Car #2: *Emmanuel*
American Baptist Publication Society

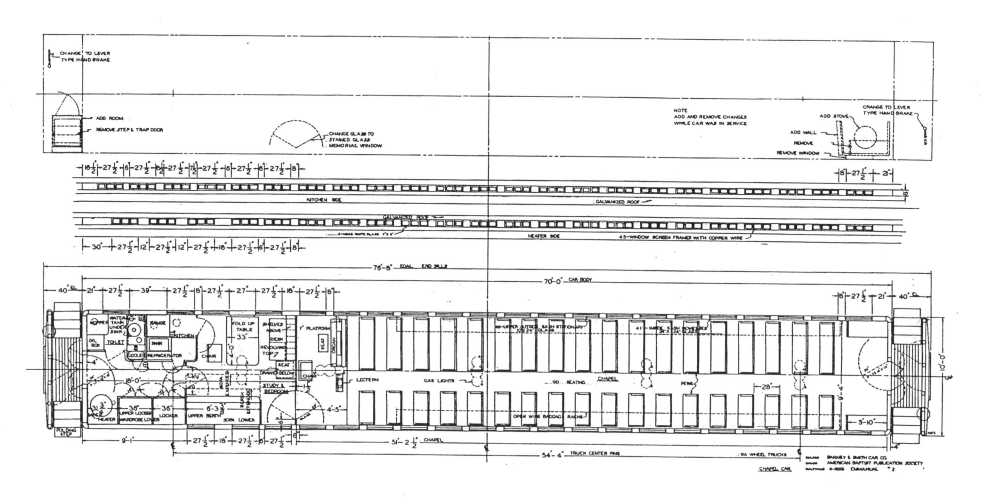

Baptist Chapel Car #3: *Glad Tidings*
American Baptist Publication Society

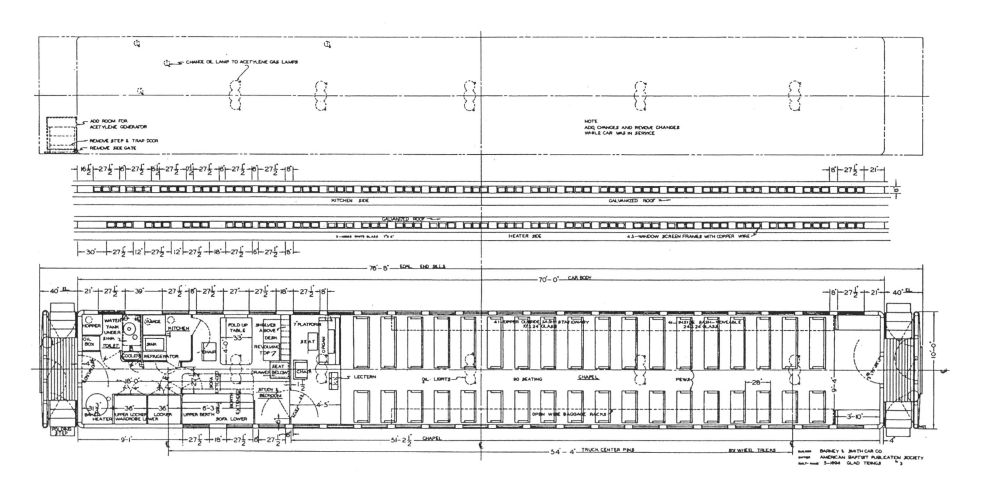

Baptist Chapel Car #4: *Good Will*
American Baptist Publication Society

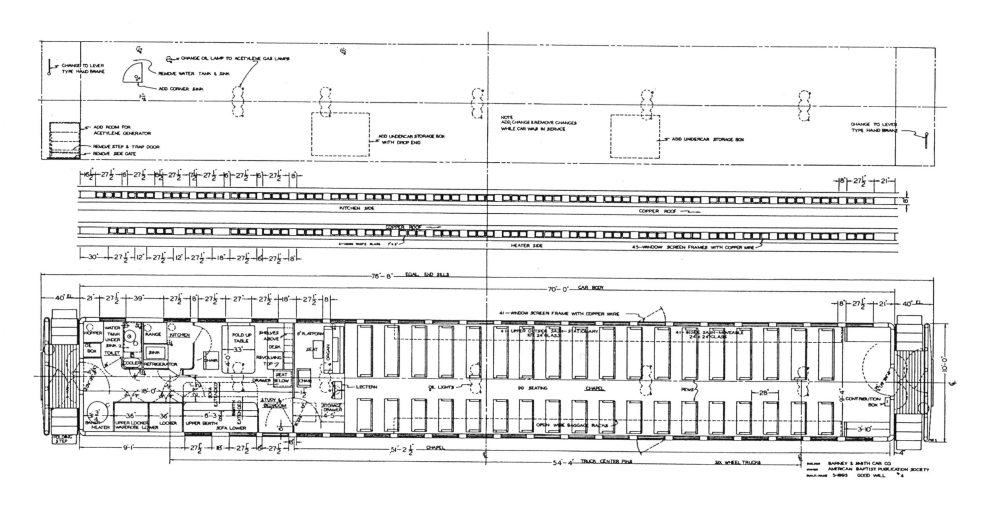

Baptist Chapel Car #5: *Messenger of Peace*
American Baptist Publication Society

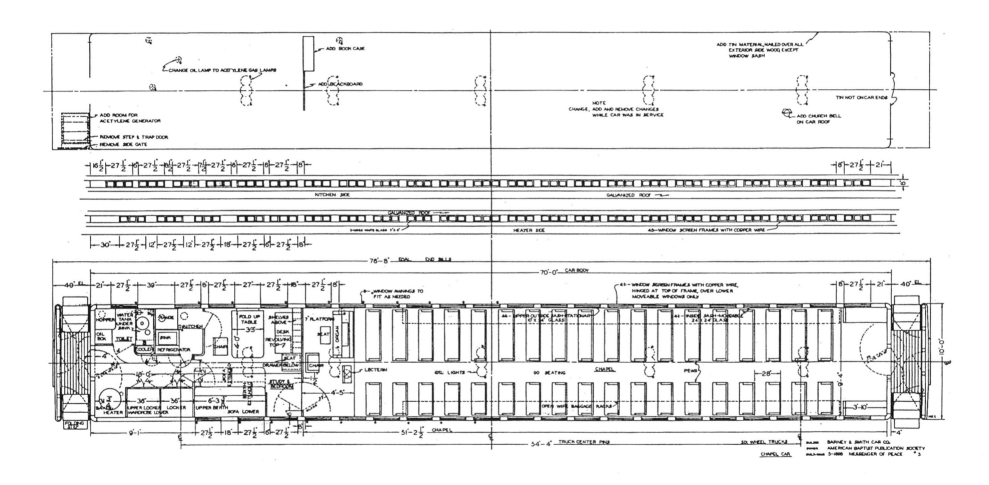

Baptist Chapel Car #6: *Herald of Hope*
American Baptist Publication Society

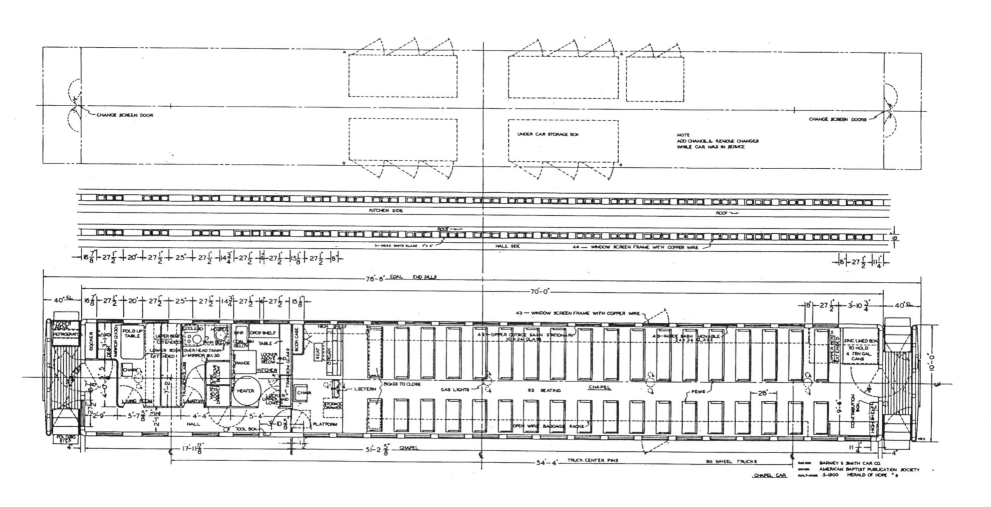

St. Anthony
Catholic Church Extension Society of the United States of America

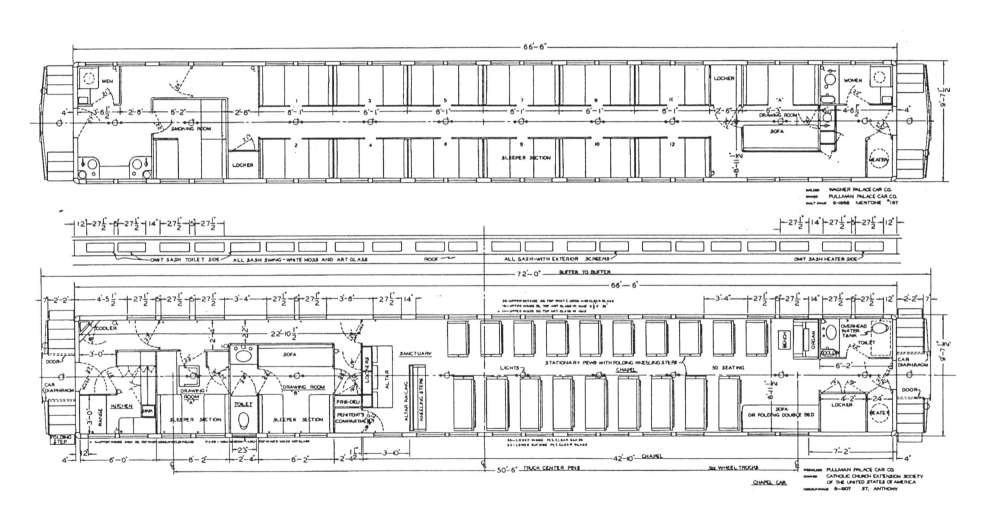

St. Peter
Catholic Church Extension Society of the United States of America

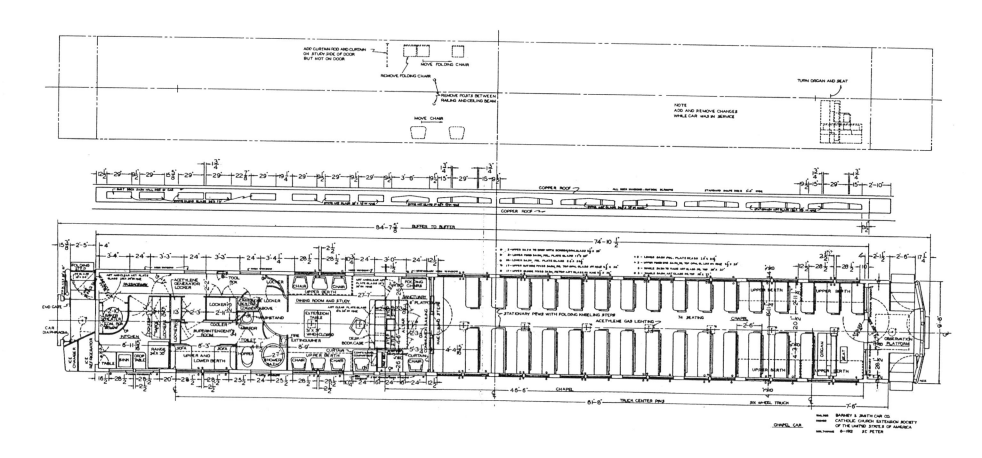

St. Paul
Catholic Church Extension Society of the United States of America

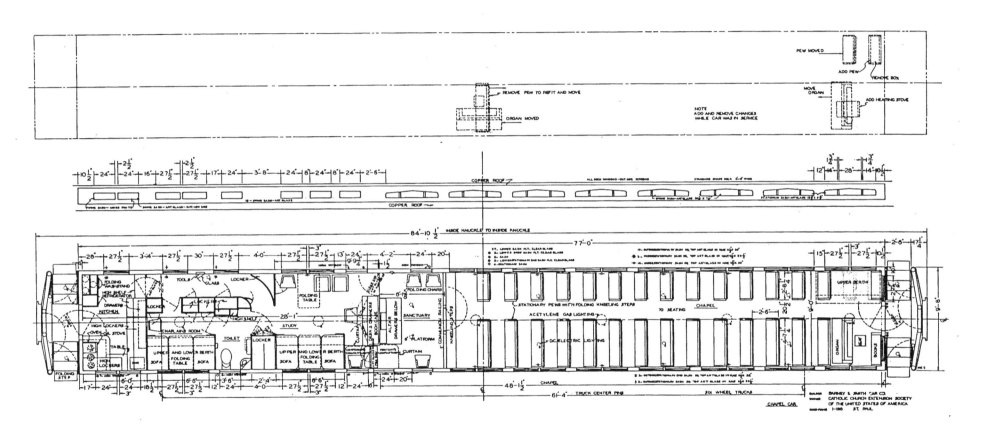

Baptist Chapel Car #7: *Grace*
American Baptist Publication Society

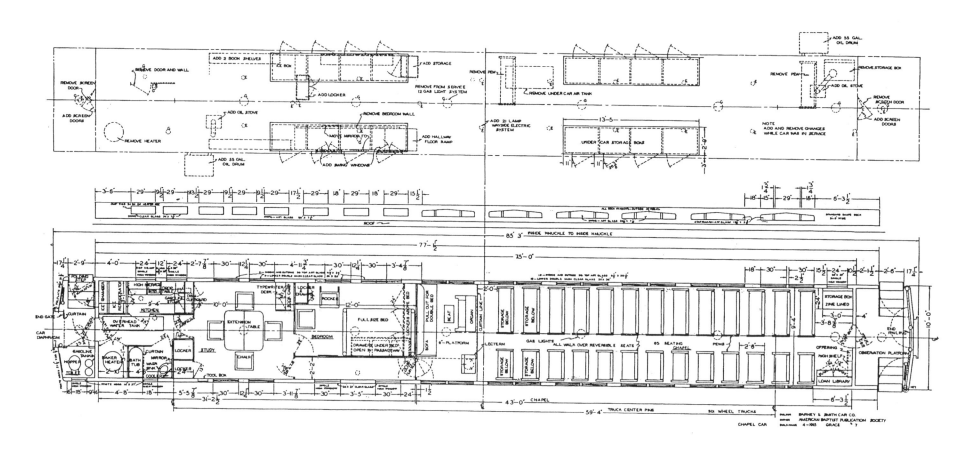

Logs of Cars' Journeys and Missionaries

CHAPEL CAR LOGS

NOTE: These are recorded towns where chapel cars stopped. The cars visited more towns than listed. Most dates are arrival dates. Due to lack of verifiable information, dates and places may be in error. Numbers in parenthesis in the Missionary Column relate to numbered information in the Comment Column. Railroad abbreviations are identified in a section following the logs.

PERSONNEL SERVING ON CARS	Y	M	D	TOWN	ST	COMMENTS FROM ACCOUNTS, LETTERS	R R
THE CATHEDRAL CAR OF NORTH DAKOTA							
THE CHURCH OF THE ADVENT						THE EPISCOPAL DIOCESE OF NORTH DAKOTA	
Bishop W. D. Walker (1)	1889	04	14	Fargo	ND	Approached Cornelius Vanderbilt II and friends in the East for funds to build chapel car	—
Bishop W. D. Walker	1890	04	28	Chicago	IL	Contract signed with Pullman Palace Car Company for building car at $4215	—
Bishop W. D. Walker	1890	10	17	Pullman	IL	Car finished ready to ship, waiting on Bishop W. D. Walker	IC
Bishop W. D. Walker	1890	11	08	Pullman	IL	Paid total cost of car, $4224.16	IC
Bishop W. D. Walker	1890	11	11	Pullman	IL	Car shipped from car builder, Pullman Palace Car Company	IC
Bishop W. D. Walker	1890	11	12	Chicago	IL	Exhibit, 1 day, Lv 11-13-1890	CM&SP
Bishop W. D. Walker	1890	11	17	Minneapolis	MN	Exhibit, 1000 people inspected car, 2 days	CM&SP
Bishop W. D. Walker	1891	11	20	Fargo	ND	First TOUR, POSSIBLE TOWNS, DATES ESTIMATED, 13 PLACES IN 3 MONTHS	CM&SP
Bishop W. D. Walker	1891	12	04	Grand Forks	ND	(1) Bishop of missionary district of North Dakota	GN
Bishop W. D. Walker	1891	12	11	St. Thomas	ND		GN
Bishop W. D. Walker	1891	12	18	Walhalla	ND		?
Bishop W. D. Walker	1891	12	25	Larimore	ND		GN
Bishop W. D. Walker	1892	01	02	Valley City	ND		NP
Bishop W. D. Walker	1892	01	09	Jamestown	ND		NP
Bishop W. D. Walker	1892	01	16	Bismarck	ND		NP
Bishop W. D. Walker	1892	01	23	Wahpeton	ND		NP
Bishop W. D. Walker	1892	01	30	Grafton	ND		NP
Bishop W. D. Walker	1892	02	06	Forest River	ND	Note : In the Episcopal District of North Dakota in 1892, 18 churches plus	?
Bishop W. D. Walker	1892	02	13	Cresy	ND	35 missions equal 53 towns, not all are railroad towns	GN
Bishop W. D. Walker	1892	02	20	Devil's Lake	ND		NP
Bishop W. D. Walker	1892	02	27	Lisbon	ND		NP
Bishop W. D. Walker	1892	03	06	Dickinson	ND	NOTE: 2ND TOUR, POSSIBLE TOWNS VISITED, ALL DATES ESTIMATES	NP
Bishop W. D. Walker	1892	03	13	Pembina	ND	NOTE: BISHOP WALKER PLANNED 6 DAYS AT EACH TOWN PLUS 1 DAY TRAVEL	NP
Bishop W. D. Walker	1892	08	02	Unnamed village	ND		?
Bishop W. D. Walker	1892	08	09	Milton	ND		GN
Bishop W. D. Walker	1892	08	16	Park River	ND		GN
Bishop W. D. Walker	1892	08	23	Minot	ND		GN
Bishop W. D. Walker	1892	08	30	Devils Lake	ND		GN
Bishop W. D. Walker	1892	09	06	Carrington	ND		NP
Bishop W. D. Walker	1892	09	13	Valley City	ND		NP
Bishop W. D. Walker	1892	09	20	Jamestown	ND		NP
Bishop W. D. Walker	1892	09	27	Bismarck	ND		NP
Bishop W. D. Walker	1892	10	05	Mandan	ND		NP
Bishop W. D. Walker	1892	10	12	Dickinson	ND		NP
Bishop W. D. Walker	1892	10	19	Oberon	ND		GN
Bishop W. D. Walker	1892	10	26	Lakota	ND		GN
Bishop W. D. Walker	1892	11	02	Rolla	ND		GN
Bishop W. D. Walker	1892	11	09	Churchs Ferry	ND		GN
Bishop W. D. Walker (4)(5)	1892	11	16	Larimore	ND		GN
(5)(6)	1892	11	23	Northwood	ND		GN
Bishop J. D. Morrison (5)(7)	1892	11	30	Mayville	ND		GN
Bishop J. D. Morrison (5)(8)	1892	12	07	Casselton	ND		GN
Bishop S. C. Edsall (5)(9)	1892	12	14	Ardock	ND		GN
Bishop S. C. Edsall (5)	1892	12	21	Fort Totten	ND	Sioux mission	GN
(2)	1892	12	28	Canton	ND	(2) Car vacant and stored, Bishop at Oxford, Oxford University for his D.D.	NP
(3)	1893			Fargo	ND	(3) Car vacant and stored, Bishop at Dublin, Trinity College for his L.L.D.	NP
Bishop W. D. Walker	1894			Fargo	ND		?
Bishop W. D. Walker	1895	01	01	Other towns	ND	(4) Transferred to New York, NY, 01-01-1897	NP
Bishop W. D. Walker	1896	04	10	Drayton	ND		?
Bishop W. D. Walker	1895	05	01	Other towns	ND	(5) Episcopal Church Conference	NP
Bishop W. D. Walker	1895	08	11	Minneapolis	MN	(6) Car vacant and car may be retired from RR service, 38 months ?	?
Bishop W. D. Walker	1895	09	01	Other towns	ND	(6) Car vacant, 14 months	NP
Bishop W. D. Walker (4)(5)	1896			Fargo	ND	(7) Temporary in charge of missionary district North Dakota	NP
(5)(6)	1897	01	01	Fargo	ND	(8) Returned to be Bishop of Duluth (Northern half of MN)	NP
Bishop J. D. Morrison (5)(7)	1897	09	27	Fargo	ND	(9) From 11-01-1896	NP
Bishop J. D. Morrison (5)(8)	1896	10	31	Fargo	ND	(10) Car vacant during winter, 4 months	NP
Bishop S. C. Edsall (5)(9)	1896	11	01	Fargo	ND	Car inspected in car shed, needs repairs	NP
Bishop S. C. Edsall (5)	1899	02	11	Fargo	ND	Used as a stationary chapel for mission, lay reader in charge for Sunday services	NP
Bishop S. C. Edsall (5)	1899	03	01	Carrington	ND	(11) Car vacant during winter, 4 months	NP
(10)	1899	11	01	Carrington	ND	Used as a stationary chapel for mission, lay reader in charge for Sunday services	NP
Bishop S. C. Edsall	1900	11	01	Carrington	ND	(12) Car sold for $1,000, which was applied to the mortgage of bishop's house	NP
(11)	1900	11	01	Carrington	ND	Used as a stationary chapel for mission, lay reader in charge for Sunday	NP
Bishop S. C. Edsall	1901	03	01	Carrington	ND	(13) To missionary district of Minnesota 10-03-1901	NP
Bishop S. C. Edsall (12)(13)	1901	09	06	Carrington	ND		?
	1902				ND	Car dismantled	?
	1903			McHenry	ND	Furniture from dismantled car used in St. Michael's mission	—
	1904			Fargo	ND	Car shed dismantled and lumber used for a barn	—
	1919	09	21	Guelph	ND	Carved eagle lectern and font from car used at St. Mary's Church at Guelph, ND	—
	1998			Fargo	ND	Two gas ceiling chandeliers now wall mounted electric in Gethsemane Church, Fargo, ND	—
	1999	01		Oakes	ND	Some items still in use in St. Mary's and St. Mark's Episcopal Church in Oakes, ND	—

EPISCOPAL CAR of NORTHERN MICHIGAN

EPISCOPAL FIRST CHAPEL CAR of MICHIGAN U.P.

PERSONNEL SERVING ON CARS	Y	M	D	TOWN	COMMENTS FROM ACCOUNTS, LETTERS	ST	RR
Archdeacon G. M. Williams (1)	1891			SEE NOTES	Car loaned to G. M. Williams by CN&W Railroad, date not known	MI	—
Archdeacon G. M. Williams	1892				(1) Archdeacon of Missionary District Northern Michigan	MI	DSS&A
Archdeacon G. M. Williams	1892	09	20	Newberry	* NOTE: THESE ARE POSSIBLE TOWNS VISITED	MI	DSS&A
Archdeacon G. M. Williams	1892	10	01	Seney	** NOTE: ALL TOWNS AND DATES ARE ESTIMATES ONLY	MI	DSS&A
Archdeacon G. M. Williams	1892	10	10	Trout Creek		MI	DSS&A
Archdeacon G. M. Williams	1892	10	20	Trout Lake		MI	DSS&A
Archdeacon G. M. Williams	1892	11	01	L'Anse		MI	DSS&A
Archdeacon G. M. Williams	1892	11	10	Pequaming		MI	?
Archdeacon G. M. Williams	1892	11	20	Kitchi		MI	DSS&A
Archdeacon G. M. Williams	1892	12	01	Ewen		MI	DSS&A
Archdeacon G. M. Williams	1892	12	10	Bessemer		MI	DSS&A
Archdeacon G. M. Williams	1892	12	20	Rockland		MI	M&NR
Archdeacon G. M. Williams	1893	01	01	Flint Steel		MI	?
Archdeacon G. M. Williams	1893	01	10	Baraga		MI	DSS&A
Archdeacon G. M. Williams	1893	01	20	Chassell		MI	DSS&A
Archdeacon G. M. Williams	1893	02	01	Portage Entry		MI	?
Archdeacon G. M. Williams	1893	02	20	Segola		MI	M&NR
Archdeacon G. M. Williams	1893	03	01	Republic		MI	M&NR
Archdeacon G. M. Williams	1893	03	10	Michigamme		MI	DSS&A
Archdeacon G. M. Williams	1893	03	20	Spurr		MI	DSS&A
Archdeacon G. M. Williams	1893	04	01	Norway		MI	C&NW
Archdeacon G. M. Williams	1893	04	10	Hermansville	* Lumber town	MI	C&NW
Archdeacon G. M. Williams	1893	04	20	Stephenson		MI	C&NW
Archdeacon G. M. Williams	1893	05	01	Ingalls		MI	C&NW
Archdeacon G. M. Williams	1893	05	10	Thomaston		MI	DSS&A
Archdeacon G. M. Williams	1893	05	20	Whitney	* Lumber mill town	MI	C&NW
Archdeacon G. M. Williams	1893	06	01	Dollarville		MI	DSS&A
Archdeacon G. M. Williams	1893	07	01	Sault Ste. Marie	*NOTE: POSSIBLE TOWNS, SOME VISITED A NUMBER OF TIMES	MI	DSS&A
Archdeacon G. M. Williams	1893	07	10	Brimley (Bay Mills)	**NOTE: DATES ESTIMATES ONLY	MI	DSS&A
Archdeacon G. M. Williams	1893	07	20	St. Ignace	***	MI	DSS&A
Archdeacon G. M. Williams	1893	08	01	Manistique	**	MI	MSP&SSM
Archdeacon G. M. Williams	1893	08	10	Gladstone	**	MI	MSP&SSM
Archdeacon G. M. Williams	1893	08	20	Wilson	**	MI	C&NW
Archdeacon G. M. Williams	1893	08	30	Escanaba	**	MI	C&NW
Archdeacon G. M. Williams	1893	09	01	Stephenson	**	MI	C&NW
Archdeacon G. M. Williams	1893	09	10	Menominee	**	MI	C&NW
Archdeacon G. M. Williams	1893	09	20	Iron Mountain	**	MI	C&NW
Archdeacon G. M. Williams	1893	10	01	Iron River	**	MI	C&NW
Archdeacon G. M. Williams	1893	10	10	Crystal Falls	**	MI	C&NW
Archdeacon G. M. Williams	1893	10	20	Ironwood	**	MI	WC
Archdeacon G. M. Williams	1893	11	01	Ewen	**	MI	DSS&A
Archdeacon G. M. Williams	1893	11	10	Sidnaw	**	MI	CM&SP
Archdeacon G. M. Williams	1893	11	20	Rockland	**	MI	CM&SP
Archdeacon G. M. Williams	1893	12	01	Ontonagon	**	MI	CM&SP
Archdeacon G. M. Williams	1893	12	10	L'Anse	**	MI	DSS&A
Archdeacon G. M. Williams	1893	12	20	Pequaming	**	MI	?
Archdeacon G. M. Williams	1894	01	01	Houghton	**	MI	DSS&A
Archdeacon G. M. Williams	1894	01	10	Hancock	**	MI	H&C
Archdeacon G. M. Williams	1894	01	20	Lake Linden	**	MI	H&C
Archdeacon G. M. Williams	1894	02	01	Calumet	**	MI	MR
Archdeacon G. M. Williams	1894	02	10	Ishpeming	**	MI	DSS&A
Archdeacon G. M. Williams	1894	02	20	Negaunee	**	MI	DSS&A
Archdeacon G. M. Williams	1894	03	01	Cherry Creek	**	MI	?
Archdeacon G. M. Williams	1894	03	10	Onota	**	MI	DSS&A
Archdeacon G. M. Williams	1894	03	20	Rock River	**	MI	DSS&A
Archdeacon G. M. Williams	1894	04	01	Republic	**	MI	DSS&A
Archdeacon G. M. Williams	1894	04	10	Au Train	**	MI	DSS&A
Archdeacon G. M. Williams	1894	04	20	Munising	**	MI	DSS&A
Archdeacon G. M. Williams	1894	05	01	Seney	**	MI	DSS&A
Archdeacon G. M. Williams	1894	05	10	Shingleton	**	MI	DSS&A
Archdeacon G. M. Williams	1894	05	20	Newberry	**	MI	DSS&A
Archdeacon G. M. Williams	1894	06	01	Detour	**	MI	?
Archdeacon G. M. Williams	1894	07	01	Marquette	Possible retired date of car, date, place and conditions not known	MI	DSS&A

EPISCOPAL CAR OF NORTHERN MICHIGAN

EPISCOPAL SECOND CHAPEL CAR OF U.P.

PERSONNEL SERVING ON CARS	Y	M	D	TOWN	COMMENTS FROM ACCOUNTS, LETTERS	ST	RR
	1893				Ordered a new or rebuilt car, a gift from C&NW ?	MI	—
	1894	02			Chapel car may have been a business car for the railroad	MI	—
Archdeacon G. M. Williams (1)	1894	10		Marquette	Chapel car may have been received for service about this time	MI	DSS&A
Archdeacon G. M. Williams	1894	12	01	Other towns	(1) Archdeacon of the missionary district of Northern Michigan	MI	LS&I ?
Archdeacon G. M. Williams	1895	01	06	Thomaston	* NOTE: POSSIBLE TOWNS VISITED, DATES ESTIMATES ONLY	MI	DSS&A
Archdeacon G. M. Williams	1895	01	10	Ballentine		MI	DSS&A
Archdeacon G. M. Williams	1895	01	15	Matchwood	* NOTE : 7 churches, 27 missions in Upper Peninsula	MI	DSS&A
Archdeacon G. M. Williams	1895	01	20	Three Lakes		MI	DSS&A
Archdeacon G. M. Williams	1895	01	25	Humboldt		MI	DSS&A
Archdeacon G. M. Williams	1895	02	06	Champion		MI	DSS&A
Archdeacon G. M. Williams	1895	02	10	Crystal (Crystal Lake)		MI	DSS&A
Archdeacon G. M. Williams	1895	02	15	Kenton		MI	DSS&A
Archdeacon G. M. Williams	1895	02	20	Ewen		MI	DSS&A
Archdeacon G. M. Williams	1895	02	25	Munising		MI	DSS&A
Archdeacon G. M. Williams	1895	03	05	Eagle Mills		MI	LS&MS

PERSONNEL SERVING ON CARS	Y	M	D	TOWN	ST	COMMENTS FROM ACCOUNTS, LETTERS	R R
Archdeacon G. M. Williams	1895	03	10	Wetmore	MI		DSS&A
Archdeacon G. M. Williams	1895	03	15	Detour	MI	** NOTE: OCCASIONAL CHURCHES, DATES ARE ESTIMATES ONLY	?
Archdeacon G. M. Williams	1895	03	20	Flint Steel (Flintsteel)	MI		?
Archdeacon G. M. Williams	1895	04	05	Quinnesec	MI		C&NW
Archdeacon G. M. Williams	1895	04	10	Spalding	MI		C&NW
Archdeacon G. M. Williams	1895	04	15	Ford River	MI		C&NW
Archdeacon G. M. Williams	1895	04	20	Seney	MI		DSS&A
Archdeacon G. M. Williams	1895	04	25	Deer Park	MI		?
Archdeacon G. M. Williams	1895	05	05	Osceola	MI		MR
Archdeacon G. M. Williams	1895	05	10	Eagle River	MI		?
Archdeacon G. M. Williams	1895	06	15	Bruce Crossing	MI		DSS&A
Bishop G. M. Williams (2)	1896	11	14	Marquette	MI	(2) Bishop Elect of Diocese of Marquette	DSS&A
Bishop G. M. Williams (3)	1896	05	01	Marquette	MI	(3) Bishop of Diocese of Marquette	DSS&A
Rev. Mulligan (4)	1896	09	01	Ontonagon	MI	Car placed near depot after town and church was destroyed by fire 08-25-1896	CM&SP
(5)	1897	01	01	Ontonagon	MI	(4) From Ontonagon, MI, to NE; resigned due to health of wife, Lv 12-31-1896	CM&SP
Rev. E. Warren (6)	1898	02	01	Ontonagon	MI	(5) Car vacant, 4 weeks	CM&SP
Rev. W. Poyser (7)	1898	10	03	Marquette	MI	(6) Car left after church was rebuilt, LV 09-01-1898	DSS&A
(8)	1899	01	08	Stephenson	MI	(6) Former rector returned 02-01-1897, Lv 12-31-1897	C&NW
Bishop G. M. Williams (9)	1899	05	10	Munising	MI	Car used for church building	MUN
Rev. A. H. Brook (9)	1899	10	05	Ishpeming	MI	Lv 10-01-1899	DSS&A
Bishop G. M. Williams	1900			Other towns	MI	Iron mines	?
Bishop G. M. Williams	1901	02	10	Sault Ste. Marie	MI	Car in the railway suburb	MSP&SSM
Bishop G. M. Williams	1902			Other towns	MI	(7) Past situation unknown	?
Bishop G. M. Williams	1903			Other towns	MI	(8) Car vacant, 3 months	?
	1903	02	06	Date unknown	MI	(9) Past situation unknown	?
	1903	02	06	Date unknown	MI	Car sold to LS&I Railroad for bridge and building maintenance bunk car	LS&I
	1905	06	12	Date unknown	MI	Sold to Munising Railroad	MUN
	1905	08	10	Date unknown	MI	Car had side doors and air brakes added	MUN
	1907	03	10	Date unknown	MI	Car sold to LS&I, car renumbered XB111	LS&I
	1907	10	10	Date unknown	MI	LS&I used car as a boarding car and car exterior painted red	LS&I
	1961	03	06	Marquette	MI	Car stored in train yard	LS&I
	1960			Marquette	MI	Car sold to Clint Jones, car in west yard	--
	1962	06	10	Negaunee	MI	Car sold to Marilyn Mutch to use as a gift shop near DSS&A-C&NW depot	--
	1968	10	03	Elk Grove	IL	Car sold to J. B. Sanfilippo for museum private railroad use	--
A.B.P.S. CAR 1, EVANGEL						**AMERICAN BAPTIST PUBLICATION SOCIETY**	
	1890	05			MN	Chapel Car Syndicate formed to purchase first Baptist Chapel Car	--
	1890	07			MN	Sketched design for Chapel Car	--
Boston W. Smith (1)	1891	06	15	Dayton	OH	Car shipped from builder Barney & Smith Car Company	CH&D
Boston W. Smith	1891	05	21	Cincinnati	OH	Dedication 05-23-1891, A.B.P.S. Anniversary Meeting, Grand Central Depot	CH&D
Boston W. Smith	1891	06	30	St. Paul	MN	Car waiting for interior furnishing	WC
Boston W. Smith	1891	06	03	Minneapolis	MN	Ladies of Minneapolis/St. Paul churches furnished interior of car	WC
Boston W. Smith	1891	06	18	Minneapolis	MN	Car in shop, wire screens applied to windows	WC
Boston W. Smith	1891	06	30	Chicago	IL	(2) Played organ, 12-year old girl was first woman to serve on chapel cars	WC
Boston W. Smith & daughter Mabel	1891	07	07	Brainerd	MN	Church asked Boston W. Smith to find a good man for their pastor	NP
Boston W. Smith & daughter Mabel (2)	1891	07	08	Brainerd	MN	Starts Northwest tour	NP
Boston W. Smith & daughter Mabel	1891	07	12	Fargo	ND	Three days, a non-church-going town	NP
Boston W. Smith & daughter Mabel	1891	07	15	Jamestown	ND	Car stopped for 3 meetings	NP
Boston W. Smith & daughter Mabel	1891	07	19	Bismarck	ND	(1) Minnesota State Baptist Colporteur Missionary	NP
Boston W. Smith & daughter Mabel	1891	07	21	Mandan	ND	Town stirred up by the visit of car	NP
Boston W. Smith & daughter Mabel	1891	07	24	Dickinson	ND	Car visited 88 places in the first year in service	NP
Boston W. Smith & daughter Mabel	1891	07	27	Miles City	MT	Church asked Boston W. Smith to serve on chapel cars	NP
Boston W. Smith & daughter Mabel	1891	07	30	Billings	MT	Montana cowboys came to car	NP
Boston W. Smith & daughter Mabel	1891	08	02	Livingston	MT	Good resulted from car services	NP
Boston W. Smith & daughter Mabel	1891	08	03	Livingston	MT	In shop, changed car cast iron wheels to paper wheels	NP
Boston W. Smith & daughter Mabel	1891	08	15	Steele	ND	Car packed full for every meeting, much joy to church	NP
Boston W. Smith & daughter Mabel	1891	08	19	Lisbon	ND	Three days	NP
Boston W. Smith	1891	08	23	Bemidji	MN		GN?
Boston W. Smith (3)	1891	08	29	Battle Lake	MN	(3) To superintendent of chapel car evangelism	NP
Boston W. Smith	1891	09	01	Little Falls	MN	On car 5 months, Boston W. Smith visited 60 places	NP
Boston W. Smith	1891	09	09	Minneapolis	MN	End Northwest tour	NP
Boston W. Smith	1891	10	02	Lisbon	ND	ND Baptist State Convention	NP
Boston W. Smith (3)	1891	12	01	Minneapolis	MN	Lv for coast to turn car over to Rev. & Mrs. Wheeler	NP
Rev. E. G. Wheeler (4) & wife	1891	12	05	Portland	OR	Car stocked with provisions, Lv 12-09-1891	SP
Rev. E. G. Wheeler & wife	1891	12	09	Woodburn	OR	(4) From A.B.P.S. general sunday school missionary 12-01-1891	SP
Rev. E. G. Wheeler & wife	1891	12	11	Oregon City	OR	Pleasant meetings	SP
Rev. E. G. Wheeler & wife	1891	12	13	Albany	OR	Meetings well attended	SP
Rev. E. G. Wheeler & wife	1891	12	15	Salem	OR	Yew Park Church, First Sunday school organized in car	SP
Rev. E. G. Wheeler & wife	1891	12	20	Harrisburg	OR	First church organized in car 12-22-1891	SP
Rev. E. G. Wheeler & wife	1892	01	10	Cottage Grove	OR	Church organized 01-16-1892	SP
Rev. E. G. Wheeler & wife	1892	01	11	Creswell	OR	Car visited 40 places in 5 months of service	SP?
Rev. E. G. Wheeler & wife	1892	01	12	Eugene	OR		SP
Rev. E. G. Wheeler & wife	1892	01	13	Junction City	OR		SP?
Rev. E. G. Wheeler & wife	1892	01	14	Oakland	OR		SP
Rev. E. G. Wheeler & wife	1892	01	15	Wilbur	OR		SP
Rev. E. G. Wheeler & wife	1892	01	16	Gold Hill	OR		SP
Rev. E. G. Wheeler & wife	1892	01	17	Roseburg	OR		SP
Rev. E. G. Wheeler & wife	1892	01	18	Dillard	OR		SP
Rev. E. G. Wheeler & wife	1892	01	19	Riddles	OR		SP
Rev. E. G. Wheeler & wife	1892	01	21	Grants Pass	OR		SP
Rev. E. G. Wheeler & wife	1892	01	22	Medford	OR		SP
Rev. E. G. Wheeler & wife	1892	01	23	Ashland	OR		SP

PERSONNEL SERVING ON CARS	Y	M	D	TOWN	ST	COMMENTS FROM ACCOUNTS, LETTERS	RR
Rev. E. G. Wheeler & wife	1892	01	27	Independence	OR	Church organized 02-03-1892	SP
Rev. E. G. Wheeler & wife	1892	02	01	Merlin	OR	Church organized 02-06-1892	SP
Rev. E. G. Wheeler & wife	1892	02	03	Corvallis	OR		SP
Rev. E. G. Wheeler & wife	1892	02	07	Portland	OR	Also west side towns ?	NP
Rev. E. G. Wheeler & wife	1892	02	26	Centralia	WA		NP
Rev. E. G. Wheeler & wife	1892	02	28	Napavine	WA	Church organized	NP
Rev. E. G. Wheeler & wife	1892	03	02	Anacortes	WA	Church organized	S&N
Rev. E. G. Wheeler & wife	1892	03	05	Castle Rock	WA		NP
Rev. E. G. Wheeler & wife	1892	03	08	Wooley	WA	Church organized	NP
Rev. E. G. Wheeler & wife	1892	03	10	Edison	WA		NP
Rev. E. G. Wheeler & wife	1892	03	12	Tacoma	WA		NP
Rev. E. G. Wheeler & wife	1892	03	15	Seattle	WA		NP
Rev. E. G. Wheeler & wife	1892	03	20	Fremont	WA	Church organized 03-21-1892, Lv 03-24-1892	NP
Rev. E. G. Wheeler & wife	1892	04	04	Snohomish	WA	Church organized in car 04-07-1892	GN
Rev. E. G. Wheeler, wife & B. W. Smith (5)	1892	04	11	Everett	WA	Church organized in car 04-17-1892, Lv 04-25-1892	GN
Rev. E. G. Wheeler & wife	1892	04	25	South Westminster	BC	Canada	GN
Rev. E. G. Wheeler & wife	1892	04	26	Blaine	WA		GN
Rev. E. G. Wheeler & wife	1892	04	27	Custer	WA		GN
Rev. E. G. Wheeler & wife	1892	04	28	Ferndale	WA		GN
Rev. E. G. Wheeler & wife	1892	04	29	Ballard	WA		GN
Rev. E. G. Wheeler & wife	1892	04	30	West Seattle	WA		GN
Rev. E. G. Wheeler & wife	1892	05	02	Tacoma	WA		NP
Rev. E. G. Wheeler & wife	1892	05	06	Walla Walla	WA		UP
Rev. E. G. Wheeler & wife	1892	05	07	Colfax	WA		UP
Rev. E. G. Wheeler & wife	1892	05	08	Garfield	WA		UP
Rev. E. G. Wheeler & wife	1892	05	09	Spokane	WA		NP
Rev. E. G. Wheeler & wife	1892	05	10	Kootenai	ID		NP
Rev. E. G. Wheeler & wife	1892	05	13	Coeur d'Alene	ID		NP
Rev. E. G. Wheeler & wife	1892	05	16	Helena	MT	(5) Superintendent of chapel car evangelism	NP
Rev. J. M. Sawers (7), son & Rev. E. B. Edmunds (8)	1892	05	19	Minneapolis	MN	(6) To A.B.P.S. missionary and financial agent 08-01-1892	NP
Rev. J. M. Sawers & Rev. E. B. Edmunds	1892	05	28	Philadelphia	PA	A.B.P.S. Anniversary Meeting, Lv 05-31-1892	PRR
Rev. J. M. Sawers & Mr. Johnson (9)	1892	07	01	Hanford	CA	Church organized 07-17-1892	SP
Rev. J. M. Sawers & wife	1892	07	19	Caruthers	CA	in CA 5 weeks, 25 towns	SP
Rev. J. M. Sawers & wife	1892	07	21	Pinole	CA	(7) From MN state Baptist missionary 08-01-1892	SP
Rev. J. M. Sawers & wife	1892	07	24	San Francisco Bay	CA	(8) From A.B.P.S. WI state Baptist missionary	SP
Rev. J. M. Sawers & wife	1892	07	27	Bade Palo Alto	CA	(9) From Swedish colporter work	SP
Rev. J. M. Sawers & wife	1892	08	01	Little Falls	MN	Church organized 08-18-1892, Lv 12-16-1892 ?	NP
Rev. J. M. Sawers & wife	1892	10	10	St. Paul	MN	MN Baptist State Convention, Lv 10-16-1892	NP
Rev. J. M. Sawers & wife	1893	01	01	Other towns	MN	Car in ND, SD, and MN	?
Rev. J. M. Sawers & Rev. F. Sprague (10)	1893	01	01	Barker	MN	(10) No information	NP
Rev. J. M. Sawers & Rev. F. Sprague	1894	02	01	Wheeler	WI	(11) Destination unknown	WC
Rev. J. M. Sawers (11) & Rev. F. Sprague (12)	1894	03	02	Greenwood	WI	(12) Destination unknown	WC
Rev. J. S. Thomas (13)	1894	07	03	Argenta	AR	AR Baptist State Convention, without car	—
Rev. J. S. Thomas & Elder J. G. Doyle (14)	1894	08	01	Newport	AR	Suburb of Little Rock, AR, meeting with railroad men	SLIM&S
Rev. J. S. Thomas & Elder J. G. Doyle	1894	09	02	Little Rock	AR	(13) From TN colporter, 09-21-1894 on car 09-21-1894	SLIM&S
Rev. J. S. Thomas & Elder J. G. Doyle	1894	10	03	Griffithville (Griffith)	AR	(14) From Argenta, AR, church elder	SLIM&S
Rev. J. S. Thomas & Elder J. G. Doyle	1894	10	26	Lonoke	AR	Started work with AR Baptist State Convention	SLIM&S
Rev. J. S. Thomas & Elder J. G. Doyle	1894	11	01	Bald Knob	AR	Church organized with AR Baptist State Convention, Elder W. P. Kime spoke on car	SLIM&S
Rev. J. S. Thomas & Elder J. G. Doyle	1894	11	05	Fulton	AR	Meetings a failure	SLIM&S
Rev. J. S. Thomas & Elder J. G. Doyle	1894	12	07	Vincent	AR	Meetings a failure	SLIM&S
Rev. J. S. Thomas & Elder J. G. Doyle	1895	01	18	Earle	AR	Church reorganized	SLSW
Rev. J. S. Thomas & Elder J. G. Doyle	1895	02	12	Sherrill	AR	Church organized, building built, result of car	SLSW
Rev. J. S. Thomas & Elder J. G. Doyle	1895	02	01	Bradford	AR	Church organized	SLSW
Rev. J. S. Thomas & Elder J. G. Doyle	1895	03	15	Gurdon	AR	Building built result of car	SLSW
Rev. J. S. Thomas & Elder J. G. Doyle	1895	03	29	Keo	AR	Church organized, building built result of car	SLSW
Rev. J. S. Thomas & Elder J. G. Doyle	1895	04	16	Clarendon	AR	Church organized, building built result of car	AM
Rev. J. S. Thomas & Elder J. G. Doyle	1895	04	25	Judsonia	AR	Church organized, building built, result of car	SLIM&S
Rev. J. S. Thomas & Elder J. G. Doyle	1895	05	01	Vincent	AR	Church reorganized	W&BRV
Rev. J. S. Thomas & Elder J. G. Doyle	1895	05	26	Marvell	AR	Building built result of car	W&BRV
Rev. J. S. Thomas & Elder J. G. Doyle	1895	06	05	Garner	AR	Building built result of car	W&BRV
Rev. J. S. Thomas & Elder J. G. Doyle	1895	06	26	Cotton Plant	AR	A place of no religious interest before car came	?
Rev. J. S. Thomas & Elder J. G. Doyle	1895	08	22	Sawdust	GA	Wedding on car, Etta Doyle, daughter of L. G. Doyle, married to Mr. Scott	?
Rev. J. S. Thomas & Elder J. G. Doyle	1895	10	20	Little Rock	AR	Car full, Little Rock to AR Baptist State Convention	S&WP
Rev. J. S. Thomas & Elder J. G. Doyle	1895	11	21	Monticello	AR	Both have been sick with fever	SLSW
Rev. J. S. Thomas & Elder J. G. Doyle	1895	12	11	Searcy	AR	Visited 25 places, staying 4 days to 3 weeks in 1895	SLIM&S
Rev. J. S. Thomas & Elder J. G. Doyle	1895	12	22	Higginson	AR	Beautiful little church house	SLIM&S
Rev. J. S. Thomas & Elder J. G. Doyle	1896	01	01	Vincent	AR	Church reorganized	SLSW
Rev. J. S. Thomas & Elder J. G. Doyle	1896	02	12	Clarendon	AR	Church organized	CO&G
Rev. J. S. Thomas & Elder J. G. Doyle	1896	03	28	Casa	AR	Church reorganized	SLSW
Rev. J. S. Thomas & Elder J. G. Doyle	1896	04	24	Sherrill	AR	Building built result of car	SLIM&S
Rev. J. S. Thomas & Elder J. G. Doyle	1896	05	30	Gurdon	AR		CO&G
Rev. J. S. Thomas & Elder J. G. Doyle	1896	06	16	Nehemyer	AR	Help building of church	?
Rev. J. S. Thomas & Elder J. G. Doyle	1896	07	17	Perryville	AR		CO&G
Rev. J. S. Thomas & Elder J. G. Doyle	1896	08	08	Houston	AR	Help building of church	SLIM&S
Rev. J. S. Thomas & Elder J. G. Doyle (15)	1896	09	30	Garner	AR	(15) To become secretary of AR Baptist state Sunday school board	HS
Rev. J. S. Thomas & Mr. C. Bedford (16)	1896	11	20	Forest Hill	LA	(16) Singer for Rev. J. S. Thomas	KCW&G
Rev. J. S. Thomas & Mr. C. Bedford	1897	01	15	Keo	AR	(17) Future situation unknown	SLSW
Rev. J. S. Thomas & Mr. C. Bedford	1897	03	21	Sedgwick	AR	(18) From AR Baptist state Sunday school Missionary	KCFS&M
Rev. J. S. Thomas & Mr. C. Bedford	1897	07	12	Imboden	AR	(19) LV 09-01-1898	KCFS&M

PERSONNEL SERVING ON CARS	Y	M	D	TOWN	S T	COMMENTS FROM ACCOUNTS, LETTERS	R R
Rev. J. S. Thomas & Mr. C. Bedford	1897	09	05	Woodworth	LA	Small pox quarantine	KCW&G
Rev. J. S. Thomas & Mr. C. Bedford	1897	11	16	Palestine	AR	(20) Daughter of Ora Thomas	LR&M
Rev. J. S. Thomas & Mr. C. Bedford (17)	1897	12	07	Donaldsonville	LA		T&P
Rev. J. S. Thomas & Rev. W. P. Kime (18)(19)	1898	01	22	Argenta	AR	Sawmill town, baptized in Castor River, 2 weeks	SLIM&S
Rev. J. S. Thomas, wife & daughter (20)	1898	02	08	Olla	LA		SLIM&S
Rev. J. S. Thomas, wife & daughter	1898	09	02	Griffinville	AR	Church organized	S&DA
Rev. J. S. Thomas, wife & daughter	1898	11	09	St. Louis	MO	First Chapel Car Conference near St. Louis, without car	—
Rev. J. S. Thomas, wife & daughter	1899	06	01	Alexandria	LA	While waiting for Boston W.Smith, ordained Brother Cole	KCW&G
Rev. J. S. Thomas, wife & daughter	1899	09	01	Woodworth	LA	Mill ran extra time to keep men from attending meetings	KCW&G
Rev. J. S. Thomas, wife & daughter	1899	11	18	Jonesboro	AR	AR Baptist State Convention, without car	KCW&G
Rev. J. S. Thomas, wife & daughter	1899	12	01	Forest Hill	LA	Sunday school organized, car received light damage	KCW&G
Rev. J. S. Thomas, wife & daughter	1899	12	20		MO	Car in shop for light damage repairs	?
Rev. J. S. Thomas, wife & daughter	1900	02	02	Other towns	AR	Fifty miles west of Little Rock, on Choctaw Route	?
Rev. J. S. Thomas, wife & daughter	1900	02	02	Searcy	AR		S&DA
Rev. J. S. Thomas, wife & daughter	1900	05	08	Hot Springs	AR	AR Baptist State Convention, without car	—
Rev. J. S. Thomas, wife & daughter	1900	05	19	Ola	AR	(21) From AR Baptist state Sunday school missionary	CO&G
Rev. J. S. Thomas, wife & daughter	1900	05	24	Detroit	MI	A.B.P.S. Anniversary Meeting, without car, Lv 05-26-1900	—
Rev. J. S. Thomas & W.P. Kime (21)	1900	06	01	Perryville (N. Perryville)	AR	Rev. J. S. Thomas sick	CO&G
Rev. W. P. Kime & family	1900	06	27	Casa	AR	Rev. J. S. Thomas sick and on vacation	CO&G
Rev. J. S. Thomas & W. P. Kime	1900	07	16	Houston	AR		CO&G
Rev. J. S. Thomas & W. P. Kime (22)	1900	08	17	Ola	AR	(22) To AR Baptist state school missionary 09-01-1900	S&DA
Rev. J. S. Thomas	1900	09	10	Griffinville	AR		SLIM&S
Rev. J. S. Thomas	1900	11		Little Rock	AR	AR Baptist State Convention	?
Rev. J. S. Thomas	1901	01	30	Other places	AR	May be in AR and/or iTOK to 03-01-1902	SLIM&S
Rev. J. S. Thomas	1902	02	20	Fort Smith	AR	Rev. Thomas, severe illness	SLIM&S
Rev. J. S. Thomas	1902	05	01	Sallisaw	iTOK	Meeting over filled the car, one week	SLIM&S
Rev. J. S. Thomas	1902	05	27	Fort Gibson	iTOK	Second Chapel Car Conference, without car, Lv 10-06-1902	?
Rev. J. S. Thomas & wife	1902	10	06	Kansas City	MO		KCS
Rev. J. S. Thomas & wife	1902	10	07	Milan	MO	RR meeting, all chapel car missionaries, without car	MK&T
Rev. J. S. Thomas & wife	1902	10	08	Novinger	MO	Church dedication, all chapel car missionaries, without car	CO&G
Rev. J. S. Thomas & wife	1902	10	10	Green City	MO	Church dedication, all chapel car missionaries, without car	?
Rev. J. S. Thomas & wife	1902	10	10	Others Places	MO	May be in MO or KS to 07-01-1902	—
Rev. J. S. Thomas	1903	07	01	?	MO	Car out of shop	?
Rev. J. S. Thomas	1903	09	28	Oklahoma City	iTOK	OK Baptist State Convention, Lv 10-01-1903	AT&SF
Rev. J. S. Thomas	1904	01	04	Spiro	iTOK	Church building built, 3 months	KCS
Rev. J. S. Thomas	1904	02	21	Coweta	iTOK	While at Spiro, Indian Territory Oklahoma	MK&T
Rev. J. S. Thomas	1904	03	02	Howe	iTOK	Helped finish church building	MK&T
Rev. J. S. Thomas	1904	04	17	Adamson	iTOK	Church organized	?
Rev. J. S. Thomas	1904	04	27	Pryor (Pryor Creek)	iTOK	Church building built and Rev. Thomas rejoiced with the people	MK&T
Rev. J. S. Thomas	1904	05	17	Okemah	iTOK	Church building built	FS&W
Rev. J. S. Thomas	1904	05	30	Oktaha	iTOK	Church organized but failed	?
Rev. J. S. Thomas	1904	06	20	Crowder (City?)	iTOK	Church organized and a fine success	MK&T
Rev. J. S. Thomas	1904	07	05	Savanna	iTOK	Church building built and many conversions	MK&T
Rev. J. S. Thomas	1904	09	02	Porter	iTOK	Church organized but failed	MK&T
Rev. J. S. Thomas	1904	09	25	Broken Arrow	iTOK	Church organized and success and progress	MK&T
Rev. J. S. Thomas	1904	10	15	Boynton	iTOK	Church organized with great struggle	FS
Rev. J. S. Thomas	1904	11	25	Morris	iTOK	Church organized with nice satisfactory meetings	FS
Rev. J. S. Thomas	1905	01	05	Bristow	iTOK	Plans materialized into a glorious success	FS
Rev. J. S. Thomas	1905	03	20	Ringwood	iTOK	Church organized, securing a good man to take over	CRI&P
Rev. J. S. Thomas	1905	04	28	Okeene	iTOK	Storm blew down stone walls, hard work but happiest time	CRI&P
Rev. J. S. Thomas	1905	06	08	Fort Cobb	iTOK	Interest was good	MK&T
Rev. J. S. Thomas	1905	06	11	Parsons	KS	Church organized and building is moving along	MK&T
Rev. J. S. Thomas	1905	10	15	Other towns	iTOK	KS Baptist State Convention	?
Rev. J. S. Thomas	1905	10	20	South McAlester	iTOK	Car may be in iTOK and/or KS to 01-01-1907	MK&T
Rev. J. S. Thomas	1907	01	16	Atoka	iTOK	Thomas wrote urging a new OK Baptist state school to be built	MK&T
Rev. J. S. Thomas	1907	01	19	Denison	TX	RR YMCA shop meetings	?
Rev. J. S. Thomas	1907	01	24	Other towns	KS	Maybe in iTOK, OK, AR, TX, or KS	MK&T
Rev. J. S. Thomas	1907	04		McPherson	KS	KS Baptist State Convention	MK&T
Rev. J. S. Thomas	1907	10	13	Parsons	KS	Starting in KS	MK&T
Rev. J. S. Thomas, wife & daughter (23)	1907	10	20	Pittsburg	KS	(23) Daughter of Mrs. Thomas	KCS
Rev. J. S. Thomas, wife & daughter	1908	01	21	Council Grove	KS		MK&T
Rev. J. S. Thomas, wife & daughter	1908	02	11	East Pittsburg	KS		KCS
Rev. J. S. Thomas, wife & daughter	1908	02	22	West Pittsburg	KS		KCS
Rev. J. S. Thomas, wife & daughter	1908	03	02	Mound Valley	KS		FS
Rev. J. S. Thomas, wife & daughter	1908	03	19	Galena	KS		FS
Rev. J. S. Thomas, wife & daughter	1908	04	01	Pittsburg	KS		KCS
Rev. J. S. Thomas, wife & daughter	1908	04	12	Kansas City	MO	Third Chapel Car Conference, without car	—
Rev. J. S. Thomas, wife & daughter	1908	04	21	Parsons	KS	Car full from Parsons with singers for A.B.P.S. Anniversary Meeting	FS
Rev. J. S. Thomas, wife & daughter	1908	05	14	Oklahoma City	OK	A.B.P.S. Anniversary Meeting	AT&SF
B. W. Smith (24) & Rev. J. S. Thomas	1908	05	21	Oklahoma City	OK	Eight interpreters interpret for Boston W. Smith as he talked to eight Indian tribes	AT&SF
Rev. J. S. Thomas, wife & daughter	1908	05	22	Herington	OK	Southside meetings	AT&SF
Rev. J. S. Thomas, wife & daughter	1908	05	28	Topeka	KS	(24) Superintendent of chapel evangelism	CRI&P
Rev. J. S. Thomas, wife & daughter	1908	05	29	Caldwell	KS	Car in shop	AT&SF
Rev. J. S. Thomas, wife & daughter	1908	06	18	North Topeka	KS		AT&SF
Rev. J. S. Thomas, wife & daughter	1908	07	01	Labette	KS		AT&SF
Rev. J. S. Thomas, wife & daughter	1908	07	18	La Harpe	KS		MK&T
Rev. J. S. Thomas, wife & daughter	1908	09	06	Smith Center	KS		MK&T
Rev. J. S. Thomas, wife & daughter	1908	10	08		KS		CRI&P
Rev. J. S. Thomas, wife & daughter	1908	10	19		KS		MK&T
Rev. J. S. Thomas, wife & daughter	1908	11	10		KS		MK&T
Rev. J. S. Thomas	1909	01	02	Norman	OK	Speaking invitation, state university town, without car	CRI&P

PERSONNEL SERVING ON CARS	Y	M	D	TOWN	ST	COMMENTS FROM ACCOUNTS, LETTERS	R R
Rev. J. S. Thomas, wife & daughter	1909	02	03	Junction City	KS	Church organized, 2 weeks	UP
Rev. J. S. Thomas, wife & daughter	1909	04	01	Blaine	KS	Church organized	SJ&Gi
Rev. J. S. Thomas, wife & daughter	1909	04	22	Severance	KS		CRI&P
Rev. J. S. Thomas, wife & daughter	1910	05	15	Lebanon	KS	Also car may have been in AR, MO, OK for 1910	AT&SF
Rev. J. S. Thomas (25), wife & daughter	1910	09	25	Iola	KS	(25) Resigned 10-01-1910	FS
Rev. J. C. Killian (26) & wife	1910	10	05	Parsons	KS	Ladies' Aid societies of KS refurnished car interior needs	--
Rev. J. C. Killian & wife	1910	10	05	Wichita	KS	Mission work in town, without car	FS
Rev. J. C. Killian & wife	1910	10	08	Wichita	KS	Mr. W. C. Coleman installed his new wire gas lights on car	CRI&P
Rev. J. C. Killian & wife	1910	11	20	Wellington	KS	A special help to church	CRI&P
Rev. J. C. Killian & wife	1911	02	04	Herington	KS	Church and RR round house meetings	CRI&P
Rev. J. C. Killian & wife	1911	02	15	Plains	KS	(26) Was pastor in Trenton, NJ, 10-01-1910	MP
Mrs. Killian & Rev. J. C. Killian	1911	02	26	Lyons	KS	Rev. Killian called to the East, mother died	MP
Rev. J. C. Killian	1911	03	20	Frederick	KS		MP
Rev. J. C. Killian & wife	1911	04	05	Hoisington	KS		FS
Rev. J. C. Killian & wife	1911	04	23	Ellsworth	KS		KCS
Rev. J. C. Killian & wife	1911	06	01	?	KS	Car repairs, vacation and conventions, Lv 07-02-1911	--
Rev. J. C. Killian & wife	1911	06	11	Philadelphia	PA	A.B.P.S. Anniversary Meeting, without car	--
Rev. J. C. Killian & wife	1911	06	18	Philadelphia	PA	Baptist World Alliance, without car, Lv 06-26-1911	--
Rev. J. C. Killian & wife	1911	07	04	Neodesha	KS	RR meetings	FL
Rev. J. C. Killian & wife	1911	09	06	Lenexa	KS	Helped build church building, 2 months	FL
Rev. J. C. Killian & wife	1911	10	08	Garden City	KS	KS Baptist State Convention, without car	AT&SF
Rev. J. C. Killian & wife	1911	11	01	Arkansas City	KS	Interest is deep and a prayerful group	CRI&P
Rev. J. C. Killian & wife	1912	01	03	Pittsburg	OK	Finished building first church in town	FL
Rev. J. C. Killian	1912	01	07	Norman	OK	Spoke about 1 hour to University of Oklahoma students, without car	FL
Rev. J. C. Killian & wife	1912	02	11	Fort Gibson	OK	Church need of a pastor was filled	CRI&P
Rev. J. C. Killian & wife	1912	03	04	Watonga	OK	Church needed a pastor, was answered, 2 weeks	KCM&O
Rev. J. C. Killian & wife	1912	04	05	Fairview	OK	Pastor found for the church	--
Rev. J. C. Killian & wife	1912	05	15	Kansas City	MO	Fourth Chapel Car Conference and churches, without car	--
Rev. J. C. Killian & wife	1912	05	21	Des Moines	IA	A.B.P.S. Anniversary Meeting, without car, Lv 05-30-1912	FL
Rev. J. C. Killian & wife	1912	06	01	Ames	OK	New pastor shared with Okeene, OK	FL
Rev. J. C. Killian & wife	1912	06	10	Okeene	OK	New pastor shared with Ames, OK	MV
Rev. J. C. Killian & wife	1912	06	20	Haskell	OK	Helped build church building, 2 months	MV
Rev. J. C. Killian & wife	1912	09	01	Muskogee	OK	Car repaired, RR shop meetings, and mission church	MV
Rev. J. C. Killian & wife	1912	10	12	Arkansas City	KS	KS Baptist State Convention	CRI&P
Rev. J. C. Killian & wife	1913	01	17	Liberal	KS	Church and RR meetings	AT&SF
Rev. J. C. Killian & wife	1913	03	09	Dodge City	KS	RR meetings	AT&SF
Rev. J. C. Killian & wife	1913	03	15	Rolla	KS	Chapel car on first train, built first church building in town	AT&SF
Rev. J. C. Killian & wife	1913	06	16	Elkhart	KS	Helped build first church building in town	AT&SF
Rev. J. C. Killian & wife	1913	07	05	Rolla	KS	Helped build first church building in town	KSC
Rev. J. C. Killian & wife	1913	08	01	Pittsburg	KS	Car repairs, painting, change of lettering on letter board	--
Rev. J. C. Killian & wife	1913	08	02	Pittsburg	KS	On New England speaking tour two months, without car	--
Rev. J. C. Killian & wife	1913	10	05	Pittsburg	KS	A very helpful series of meetings	KSC
Rev. J. C. Killian & wife	1913	11	12	Columbus	KS	Discouragement at first, but they changed for the better	FL
Rev. J. C. Killian & wife	1913	12	03	Weir	KS	Coal mining town had hard times	FL
Rev. J. C. Killian & wife	1913	12	27	Olathe	KS	Good solid work being done	FL
Rev. J. C. Killian & wife	1914	01	30	Galena	KS	Car was full in afternoon and church full at night	--
Rev. J. C. Killian & wife	1914	03	19	East Topeka	KS	Seward Avenue Baptist Church and RR meetings	AT&SF
Rev. J. C. Killian & wife	1914	10	11	Ottawa	KS	KS State Baptist Convention, Lv 10-15-1914	AT&SF
Rev. J. C. Killian & wife	1914	11	10	North Ottawa	KS	Church meetings	AT&SF
Rev. J. C. Killian & wife	1914	12	27	Gardner	KS	Best first night meeting we have had on car	AT&SF
Rev. J. C. Killian & wife	1915	02	10	Turner	KS		AT&SF
Rev. J. C. Killian & wife	1915	03	07	Lansing	KS		UP
Rev. J. C. Killian & wife	1915	03	21	Belleville	KS		MK&T
Rev. J. C. Killian & wife	1915	04	09	Council Grove	KS		C&S
Rev. J. C. Killian & wife	1915	05	01	Hasting	CO	Working in Cokedale, CO, mining camp, 2 weeks	--
Rev. J. C. Killian & wife	1915	06	17	Denver	CO	Helping on exhibit trip of chapel car 7, Grace, without car	AT&SF ?
Rev. J. C. Killian & wife	1915	05	18	Salt Lake City	UT	Helping on exhibit trip of chapel car 7, Grace, without car	CRI&P
Rev. J. C. Killian & wife	1915	05	27	Los Angeles	CA	A.B.P.S. Anniversary Meeting, without car	--
Rev. J. C. Killian & wife	1915	06	19	Los Angeles	CA	Chapel Car Conference, without car, Lv 05-28-1915	--
Rev. J. C. Killian & wife	1915	06	07	Englewood	CO	A very helpful series of meetings	C&S
Rev. J. C. Killian & wife	1915	07	05	Limon	CO	Church organized 06-12-1915, Lv 08-29-1915	--
Rev. J. C. Killian & wife	1915	07	19	Deertrail (Deer Trail)	CO	While working at Limon, CO, without car	--
Rev. J. C. Killian & wife	1915	07	25	Bijou	CO	While at Limon, CO, several nights of meetings, without car	FL
Rev. J. C. Killian & wife	1915	09	03	Cokedale	CO	Grand meetings	C&S
Rev. J. C. Killian & wife	1915	10	01	Hasting	CO	Formed church and raised money for part time pastor	C&S
Rev. J. C. Killian & wife	1915	10	10	Delagua	CO	Raised money for part time pastor	?
Rev. J. C. Killian & wife	1915	10	18	Greeley	CO	CO Baptist State Convention, Lv 10-22-1915	C&S
Rev. J. C. Killian & wife	1915	11	01	Berwind	CO	Hasting, Delagua, and Berwind, CO, will have the same pastor	C&S
Rev. J. C. Killian & wife	1915	11	10	Tobasco	CO	Meeting will be with Berwind, CO	C&S
Rev. J. C. Killian & wife	1915	11	11	Trinidad	CO	No meetings	C&S
Rev. J. C. Killian & wife	1915	11	15	Starkville	CO	Needed more time on this 1 night, without car	--
Rev. J. C. Killian & wife	1915	11	21	Sorpris	CO	Held a few meetings	?
Mrs. Killian	1915	12	12	Pueblo	CO	RR meetings	C&S
Rev. J. C. Killian	1915	12	12	Ordway	CO	Special meetings to 12-21-1915, without car	--
Mrs. Killian	1915	12	20	Pueblo	CO	Local pastors' wives meeting on car	C&S
Rev. J. C. Killian & wife	1916	01	01	Denver	CO	Bethany Church, 1 month	C&S
Rev. J. C. Killian & wife	1916	01	31	Denver	CO	Car in shop, Rev. Killian's father died in Philadelphia, PA, from auto wreck	C&S
Rev. J. C. Killian (27) & wife	1916	02	01	Denver	CO	On speaking trip to NH, MA, NY, NJ, and PA, without car	BR
Rev. A. V. Allen (28) & wife	1916	06	05	Whitman	NE	(27) Transferred to New England 02-10-1916	BR
Rev. A. V. Allen & wife	1916	07	02	Omaha	NE	(28) Previous situation unknown	BR
Rev. A. V. Allen & wife	1916	08	06	Hastings	NE	(29) To pastor at Columbus, NE, 04-16-1917	BR
Rev. A. V. Allen & wife	1916	09	02	Merna	NE	Church without pastor, 6 weeks	BR

PERSONNEL SERVING ON CARS	Y	M	D	TOWN	ST	COMMENTS FROM ACCOUNTS, LETTERS	RR
Rev. A. V. Allen & wife	1916	09	20	Cliff	NE	While at Merna, NE, without car	—
Rev. A. V. Allen & wife	1916	10	13	Grand Island	NE	Took people on car to NE Baptist State Convention	UP
Rev. A. V. Allen & wife	1916	10	14	Fremont	NE	NE Baptist State Convention Lv 10-20-1916	UP
Rev. A. V. Allen & wife	1916	10	20	Columbus	NE	Repaired building and organized Sunday school	UP
Rev. A. V. Allen & wife	1917	03	09	Aurora	NE	No support for building, 3 weeks	BR
Rev. A. V. Allen (29) & wife	1917	04	02	Ord	NE	Organized Sunday school, 2 weeks	BR
(30)	1917	04	16	Ord	NE	(30) Car vacant 2 weeks	BR
Rev. J. C. Killian (31)(32) & wife	1917	05	01	Ord	NE	(31) From superintendent of middle district A.B.P.S. 04-29-1917	BR
Rev. J. C. Killian (33) & wife	1917	05	17	Plattsmouth	NE	Car in Shop for painting and repairs	BR
Rev. J. C. Killian (33) & wife	1917	09	05	Falls City	NE	(32) Temporary on car for only 3 months	BR
Rev. W. M. Kennedy (34) & wife	1917	09	26	Philadelphia	PA	A.B.P.S. board of manager's meeting 09-27-1917, without car	—
Rev. W. M. Kennedy & wife	1917	09	29	Falls City	NE	To pick up car	BR
Rev. W. M. Kennedy & wife	1917	10	01	Superior	NE	(33) Returned to superintendent of middle district A.B.P.S. 09-30-1917	BR
Rev. W. M. Kennedy & wife	1917	10	20	Alma	NE	(34) From chapel car 3, Glad Tidings, 09-10-1917	BR
Rev. W. M. Kennedy & wife	1917	11	16	Oxford	NE	(35) Resigned 01-10-1918	BR
Rev. W. M. Kennedy & wife	1917	12	01	Atlanta	NE	Church revived, 4 weeks	BR
Rev. W. M. Kennedy (35) & wife	1917	12	28	Atlanta	NE	Vacation in the East due to Mrs. Kennedy's health	BR
(36)	1917	12	28	Atlanta	NE	Government takes over operation of railroads due to WWI	?
Rev. V. E. Clarke (37) & wife	1918	01	10	Atlanta	NE	(36) Car vacant 3-1/2 months	—
Rev. V. E. Clarke & wife	1918	05	01	Lodi	NE	(37) From AZ colporteur, appointed to car 04-20-1918	UP
Rev. V. E. Clarke & wife	1918	05	04	Wellfleet	NE	Discouraged church rescued	BR
Rev. V. E. Clarke & wife	1918	05	20	Wellfleet	NE	Church greatly revived and built up in many ways	UP
Rev. V. E. Clarke & wife	1918	06	12	Kearney	NE	Used by Omaha City, NE, missions for a church building, 9 months	UP
Rev. V. E. Clarke & wife	1918	07	19	Rockville	NE	(38) Resigned 09-01-1919	BR
Rev. V. E. Clarke & wife	1918	08	29	Norman	NE	1 month	BR
Rev. V. E. Clarke & wife	1919	01	10	Cairo	NE	Spiritual influence inspiring	BR
Rev. V. E. Clarke (38) & wife	1919	02	07	Ord	NE	Rev. Clarke first day of meeting had flu, flu epidemic stopped work on car	BR
(39)	1919	09	01	?	NE	(39) Car vacant 6 months	?
(39)	1920	03	01	?	NE	Government returned ownership to railroads	—
Rev. B. H. Ward (40) & wife	1920	03	05	Dannebrog	NE	(40) From UT-ID Baptist state field worker 03-05-1920	UP
Rev. B. H. Ward & wife	1920	03	21	Wellfleet	NE	(41) To pastor at Superior, NE, 06-01-1920	BR
Rev. B. H. Ward (41) & wife	1920	04	17	Stella	NE	(42) Car vacant 6 months	MP
(42)	1920	05	01	Omaha	NE	(43) Used by Omaha City, NE, missions for a church building, 9 months	?
(43)	1920	10	25	Omaha	NE	Church organized 11-20-1920, Lv 08-10-1921	PVT
Rev. F. I. Blanchard (44) & wife	1921	03	25	Rockville	NE	Church organized	PVT
Rev. F. I. Blanchard & wife	1921	08	12	Loup City	NE	(44) From chapel car 3, Glad Tidings, 08-10-1921	UP
Rev. F. I. Blanchard & wife	1921	09	04	Norfolk	NE	Three ladies converted, prepare for missionary service	—
Rev. F. I. Blanchard	1921	10	07	Wheatland	WY	NE Baptist State Convention, without car, Lv 10-14-1921	C&S
Rev. F. I. Blanchard & wife	1922	01	16	Other towns	WY	(45) From chapel car 3, Glad Tidings, 08-01-1921	?
Rev. F. I. Blanchard & wife	1922	01	28	Casper	WY	Revival meetings	C&NW
Rev. F. I. Blanchard & wife	1922	03	01	Evansville	WY	Membership doubled	?
Rev. F. I. Blanchard & wife	1922	03	24	Parkerton	WY	Church organized	C&NW
Rev. F. I. Blanchard & wife	1922	05	01	Lucerne	WY		BR
Rev. F. I. Blanchard & wife	1923	04	02	Sandspeed	WY		?
Rev. F. I. Blanchard (45) & wife	1923	04	29	?	WY		?
(46)	1923	09	01	?	WY	(46) Car vacant, 2 weeks	?
Rev. C. J. Bukoutz (47)	1924	04	01	Rawlins	WY	(47) From Dannebrog, NE, 04-15-1924	UP
Rev. H. M. Richmond (48) & wife	1924	04	15	Rawlins	WY	(48) From Collier, KS	UP
Rev. H. M. Richmond & wife	1924	06	15	Rawlins	WY	No meetings held	UP
Rev. H. M. Richmond (49) & wife	1924	10	06	Rawlins	WY	(49) Resigned due to Mrs. Richmond's illness 11-15-1924	UP
(50)	1924	11	07	Rawlins	WY	(50) Unknown minister on car for a few weeks	UP
(51)	1924	12	01	Rawlins	WY	(51) Car retired, car given to WY Baptist State Convention for a church	UP
	1925	03	25	Rawlins	WY	Rev. Smith severely burned due to oil stove explosion	UP
	1925	05	24	Rawlins	WY	Rev. C. Fisher organized Sunday school	—
	1925	06	07	Rawlins	WY	Rev. C. Fisher organized church 06-07-1925	—
	1925	06	08	Rawlins	WY	WY State Baptist Convention gave car to Rawlins Baptist Church	—
	1925	11	21	Rawlins	WY	Car body moved to church lots, without car building	—
	1929	10	05	Rawlins	WY	Chapel car 7, Grace, and Rev. Blinzinger arrived	—
	1930	10	05	Rawlins	WY	Car turned 90 degrees and incorporated in rear of church	—
	1930	11	01	Rawlins	WY	Some chapel cars pews used in Rawlins, WY, church	—
	1930	11	14	Rawlins	WY	Built education wing around 50 ft. of car body	—
	1954	05	14	Rawlins	WY	Fifty feet of car body within church building	—
	1955			Rawlins	WY	Built 2nd floor over educational wing and 50 ft. of car body	—
	1960			Rawlins	WY	Fifty feet of car body within church building	—
	1961			Rawlins	WY	Fire destroyed educational wing, but car unharmed	—
	1963	12	15	Rawlins	WY	Fifty feet of car body within church building	—
	1999			Rawlins	WY	Fifty feet of car body within church building	—
A.B.P.S. CAR 2, EMMANUEL						**AMERICAN BAPTIST PUBLICATION SOCIETY**	
	1892	05	22	Philadelphia	PA	Asked for free will car donors, $7500 total	—
	1892	06	30	Philadelphia	PA	A.B.P.S. Anniversary Meeting, $3071 given at this time	—
Rev. E. G. Wheeler	1892	08	10	Dayton	OH	Contract signed to start building car	CH&D
Rev. E. G. Wheeler (1) & wife	1893	04	27	Dayton	OH	Car shipped from builder Barney & Smith Car Company	CH&D
Rev. E. G. Wheeler & wife	1893	04	29	Dayton	OH	Car on exhibit at Dayton, OH, fair	CH&D
Rev. E. G. Wheeler & wife	1893	05	26	Denver	CO	Car dedication at A.B.P.S. Anniversary Meeting, Union Station	UP
Rev. E. G. Wheeler & wife	1893	06	18	Palo Alto	CA	Emmanuel Baptist Church organized 06-18-93	SP
Rev. E. G. Wheeler & wife	1893	06	16	Aromas	CA	(1) Transferred from A.B.P.S. special service 04-20-1893	SP
Rev. E. G. Wheeler & wife	1893	06	24	Morgan Hill	CA	Left a strong group	SP
Rev. E. G. Wheeler & wife	1893	07	15	Salinas	CA	Lv 07-26-1893	SP
Rev. E. G. Wheeler & wife	1893	07	26	Rodeo	CA	Sunday school and preaching	SP
Rev. E. G. Wheeler & wife	1893	08	04	Aptos	CA	Lumber station, no Protestant church in town	SP
Rev. E. G. Wheeler & wife	1893	08	13	Santa Cruz	CA		SP

PERSONNEL SERVING ON CARS	Y	M	D	TOWN	ST	COMMENTS FROM ACCOUNTS, LETTERS	R R
Rev. E. G. Wheeler & wife	1893	08	21	Watsonville	CA		SP
Rev. E. G. Wheeler & wife	1893	08	28	San Lucas	CA		SP
Rev. E. G. Wheeler & wife	1893	09	03	Santa Margarita	CA		SP
Rev. E. G. Wheeler & wife	1893	09	30	Kings City	CA		SP
Rev. E. G. Wheeler & wife	1893	10	12	Dixon	CA	CA Baptist State Pacific Association, Lv 10-15-1893	SP
Rev. E. G. Wheeler & wife	1893	11	02	Hanford	CA	Revival meetings, good work, 1 month	SP
Rev. E. G. Wheeler & wife	1893	11	09	Bakersfield (Sumner)	CA	Car filled	SP
Rev. E. G. Wheeler & wife	1894	01	04	Armona	CA	Church, Sunday school, and BYPU organized	SP
Rev. E. G. Wheeler & wife	1894	01	12	Pollasky	CA	Good done	SP
Rev. E. G. Wheeler & wife	1894	01	22	Mendota	CA	Church and Sunday school organized	SP
Rev. E. G. Wheeler & wife	1894	03	05	Herndon	CA		SP
Rev. E. G. Wheeler & wife	1894	03	15	Atwater	CA	Town has had a phenomenal growth	SP
Rev. E. G. Wheeler & wife	1894	03	24	Palo Alto	CA	Encouragement	SP
Rev. E. G. Wheeler & wife	1894	04	02	Bakersfield	CA		SP
Rev. E. G. Wheeler & wife	1894	05	01	Athlone	CA		?
Rev. E. G. Wheeler & wife	1894	05	05	San Luis Obispo	CA		SP
Rev. E. G. Wheeler & wife	1894	05	10	Ricklin	CA		SP
Rev. E. G. Wheeler & wife	1894	05	15	Ocean View	CA		SP
Rev. E. G. Wheeler & wife	1894	05	20	Lawrence	CA		SP
Rev. E. G. Wheeler & wife	1894	05	25	Castroville	CA		SP
Rev. E. G. Wheeler & wife	1894	05	30	Martinez	CA		SP
Rev. E. G. Wheeler & wife	1894	06	04	Port Costa	CA		SP
Rev. E. G. Wheeler & wife	1894	06	09	Hayward	CA	Many baptized with baptistry banked with flowers, 10 days	SP
Rev. E. G. Wheeler & wife	1894	06	14	Melrose	CA		SP
Rev. E. G. Wheeler & wife	1894	06	24	Decoto	CA		SP
Rev. E. G. Wheeler & wife	1894	06	29	Copa Valley	CA		?
Rev. E. G. Wheeler & wife	1894	07	02	Oakland	CA	Rev. Wheeler with pneumonia, Lv 08-05-1894	SP
Rev. E. G. Wheeler & wife	1894	08	06	Rutherford	CA		SP
Rev. E. G. Wheeler & wife	1894	08	10	Sacramento	CA	Car repair shops, 2 months	—
Rev. E. G. Wheeler & wife	1894	10	15	Lindsay	CA	Church organized, 2 weeks, without car	—
Rev. E. G. Wheeler & wife	1894	11	02	South Vallejo	CA	Church organized	SP
Rev. E. G. Wheeler & wife	1894	12	27	Camarillo	CA		SP
Rev. E. G. Wheeler & wife	1895	01	05	Chino	CA		SP
Rev. E. G. Wheeler & wife	1895	01	10	Banning	CA	Two weeks	A&P
Rev. E. G. Wheeler & wife	1895	01	25	Barstow	CA		A&P
Rev. E. G. Wheeler & wife	1895	03	10	Daggett	CA		SP
Rev. E. G. Wheeler, wife & H. E. Hills (2)	1895	03	13	El Paso	TX	(2) Assistant to Wheelers	PV
Rev. E. G. Wheeler, wife & H. E. Hills	1895	04	01	Roswell	TNM	West End Mission Sunday school and Chinese RR workers	PV
Rev. E. G. Wheeler, wife & H. E. Hills	1895	04	08	Carlsbad (Eddy)	TNM	Lv 04-08-1895	T&P
Rev. E. G. Wheeler, wife & H. E. Hills	1895	04	10	Pecos	TX	Eddy Baptist Church	T&P
Rev. E. G. Wheeler, wife & H. E. Hills	1895	04	13	Tucson	TAZ	Church reorganized, 3 weeks	NM&A
Rev. E. G. Wheeler, wife & H. E. Hills	1895	05	06	Nogales	TAZ		SP
Rev. E. G. Wheeler, wife & H. E. Hills	1895	05	08	Naco	TAZ		A&SE
Rev. E. G. Wheeler, wife & H. E. Hills	1895	05	10	Bisbee	TAZ		A&P
Rev. E. G. Wheeler, wife & H. E. Hills	1895	05	12	Gallup	TNM	Coal mining, Indian trading post	A&P
Rev. E. G. Wheeler, wife & H. E. Hills	1895	05	14	Holbrook	TAZ	No church in town until 1913	A&P
Rev. E. G. Wheeler, wife & H. E. Hills	1895	05	17	Winslow	TAZ		A&P
Rev. E. G. Wheeler, wife & H. E. Hills	1895	05	21	Flagstaff	TAZ	Lumber mills, Arizona Cattle Company headquarters	A&P
Rev. E. G. Wheeler, wife & H. E. Hills	1895	05	23	Williams	TAZ	Folks said never seen a car of this nature	A&P
Rev. E. G. Wheeler, wife & H. E. Hills	1895	05	28	Hackberry	TAZ		A&P
Rev. E. G. Wheeler, wife & H. E. Hills	1895	06	04	Valentine	TAZ		SP?
Rev. E. G. Wheeler, wife & H. E. Hills	1895	06	07	Needles	CA	Wanted car to return in fall or winter, car did not return	SP?
Rev. E. G. Wheeler (3) & wife	1895	06	11	Santa Monica	CA	(3) Rev. Wheeler killed in an A&P passenger train washout, while on vacation, not on chapel car	SP
Mr. H. E. Hills (4)	1895	06	15	Fillmore	CA	(4) Temporarily in charge of car 08-09-1895, without car	SP
Mr. H. E. Hills	1895	06	19	Santa Paula	CA		SP
Mr. H. E. Hills	1895	06	30	Norwalk	CA		SP
Mr. H. E. Hills	1895	07	05	Los Angeles	CA	Car in shop for repairs, and RR shop meetings	SP
Mr. H. E. Hills	1895	07	10	Aromas	CA		SP?
Mr. H. E. Hills	1895	07	15	Sacramento	CA	(5) Superintendent of Chapel Car Evangelism	SP
Mr. H. E. Hills	1895	07	20	Santa Paula	CA	Meeting too large for car	SP
Rev. E. G. Wheeler (3) & wife	1895	08	07	Grants	TNM		—
Mr. H. E. Hills	1895	08	09	Sacramento	CA	Car in shop for repairs, painting and other repairs, Lv 10-12-1895	SP
Mr. H. E. Hills	1895	09	01	Berkeley	CA	Stayed 4 days	—
Mr. H. E. Hills	1895	11	20	San Luis Obispo	CA	Few days	—
Mr. H. E. Hills	1895	12	01	Melrose	CA	Stayed 10 days	SP
Mr. H. E. Hills	1895	12	08	San Francisco	CA	Stayed 1 week	SP
Mr. H. E. Hills	1895	12	14	Corning	CA		SP
Mr. H. E. Hills	1896	01	02	Montague	CA		SP
Mr. H. E. Hills	1896	02	04	Yreka	CA		YR
Mr. H. E. Hills	1896	02	16	Wheatland	CA		SP
Mr. H. E. Hills	1896	02	20	Maxwell	CA		SP
Mr. H. E. Hills	1896	02	25	Williams	CA	RR meetings at River St. Station	SP
Mr. H. E. Hills	1896	02	28	Orland	CA		SP
Mr. H. E. Hills & B. W. Smith (5)	1896	03	01	San Francisco	CA	(6) From Lowell, MA 03-01-1896, on car 03-10-1896	SP
Rev. B. B. Jacques (6), wife & H. E. Hills	1896	03	10	San Francisco	CA	(7) Last day in charge of car, 03-10-1896	SP
Rev. B. B. Jacques, wife & H. E. Hills (7)	1896	03	12	Wheatland	CA		SP
Rev. B. B. Jacques, wife & H. E. Hills	1896	03	18	Los Angeles	CA		SP
Rev. B. B. Jacques, wife & H. E. Hills	1896	03	20	Covina	CA		SP
Rev. B. B. Jacques, wife & H. E. Hills	1896	03	24	Duarte	CA	Organized Sunday school	SC
Rev. B. B. Jacques, wife & H. E. Hills	1896	03	29	Colton	CA	Stayed 6 days	SP
Rev. B. B. Jacques, wife & Mr. Moffett	1896	04	03	Santa Ana	CA	Car near center of town	SP
Rev. B. B. Jacques, wife & H. E. Hills	1896	04	07	Whittier	CA		SP

PERSONNEL SERVING ON CARS	Y	M	D	TOWN	ST	COMMENTS FROM ACCOUNTS, LETTERS	RR
Rev. B. B. Jacques, wife & H. E. Hills	1896	04	12	Coalinga	CA	Oil town, Church organized	SP
Rev. B. B. Jacques, wife & H. E. Hills	1896	04	16	Van Nuys	CA		SP ?
Rev. B. B. Jacques, wife & H. E. Hills	1896	04	20	Camarillo	CA		SP
Rev. B. B. Jacques, wife & H. E. Hills	1896	04	26	Armoras	CA		SP
Rev. B. B. Jacques, wife & H. E. Hills	1896	04	30	Alta (Lake Alta)	CA		SP
Rev. B. B. Jacques, wife & H. E. Hills	1896	05	10	Colton	CA	Stayed 6 days	SP
Rev. B. B. Jacques, wife & H. E. Hills	1896	05	16	Los Angeles	CA		SP
Rev. B. B. Jacques, wife & H. E. Hills	1896	05	19	San Francisco	CA	(8) No information	SP
Rev. B. B. Jacques, wife & Mr. Moffett (8)	1896	05	23	Oakland	CA	RR shop meetings and town meetings	SP
Rev. B. B. Jacques, wife & Mr. Moffett	1896	06	25	Towles	CA	Church organized, 4 weeks	SP
Rev. B. B. Jacques, wife & Mr. Moffett	1896	07	27	Dutch Flat	CA		SP
Rev. B. B. Jacques, wife & Mr. Moffett	1896	08	21	Blue Canon	CA		SP
Rev. B. B. Jacques, wife & Mr. Moffett	1896	09	20	Truckee	CA	Visiting homes and saloons, great children's meetings, 16 days	SP
Rev. B. B. Jacques, wife & Mr. Moffett	1896	09	29	Verdi	NV	Sunday school organized 9-25-1896	SP
Rev. B. B. Jacques, wife & Mr. Moffett	1896	10	15	Reno	NV	Great influence on First Baptist Church young people, 2 weeks	SP
Rev. B. B. Jacques, wife & Mr. Moffett	1896	10	25	Wadsworth	NV	Church organized 11-07-1896, and RR shop meetings	SP
Rev. B. B. Jacques, wife & Mr. Moffett	1896	11	15	Hot Springs	NV	Sunday school organized in the depot, without car	—
Rev. B. B. Jacques, wife & Mr. Moffett	1896	11	16	Lovelock	NV		SP
Rev. B. B. Jacques, wife & Mr. Moffett	1896	12	18	Winnemucca	NV	RR town	SP
Rev. B. B. Jacques, wife & Mr. Moffett	1896	12	23	Sacramento	CA	Car in shop and memorial window for car interior door put in place	SP ?
Rev. B. B. Jacques, wife & Mr. Moffett	1896	12	26	Washington	CA		SP
Rev. B. B. Jacques, wife & Mr. Moffett	1897	01	03	Sacramento	CA	Emmanuel Baptist Church meetings	SP
Rev. B. B. Jacques, wife & Mr. Moffett	1897	01	09	Gold Run	CA		SP
Rev. B. B. Jacques, wife & Mr. Moffett	1897	01	12	Towles	CA	Church organized	SP
Rev. B. B. Jacques, wife & Mr. Moffett	1897	01	18	Colfax	CA		SP
Rev. B. B. Jacques, wife & Mr. Moffett	1897	01	26	Clipper Gap	CA	Great sermons, 10 days	SP
Rev. B. B. Jacques, wife & Mr. Moffett	1897	02	08	Auburn	CA		SP
Rev. B. B. Jacques, wife & Mr. Moffett	1897	02	12	Penryn	CA		SP
Rev. B. B. Jacques, wife & Mr. Moffett	1897	02	15	Rocklin	CA		SP
Rev. B. B. Jacques, wife & Mr. Moffett	1897	02	19	Morgan Hill	CA		SP
Rev. B. B. Jacques, wife & Mr. Moffett	1897	03	13	Floriston	CA		SP
Rev. B. B. Jacques, wife & Mr. Moffett	1897	03	22	Duarte	CA		SP
Rev. B. B. Jacques, wife & Mr. Moffett	1897	04	01	Penryn	CA		SP
Rev. B. B. Jacques & wife	1897	04	05	Tulare	CA	Stayed 2 weeks	SP
Rev. B. B. Jacques, wife & Mr. Moffett	1897	04	09	Lindsay	CA		SP
Rev. B. B. Jacques, wife & Mr. Moffett	1897	04	16	Porterville	CA		SP
Rev. B. B. Jacques, wife & Mr. Moffett	1897	04	22	Monson	CA	Few days	SP
Rev. B. B. Jacques, wife & Mr. Moffett	1897	04	28	Penryn	CA		SP
Rev. B. B. Jacques, wife & Mr. Moffett	1897	05	02	Rocklin	CA	Good harvest	SP
Rev. B. B. Jacques, wife & Mr. Moffett	1897	05	07	Clovis	CA		SP
Rev. B. B. Jacques, wife & Mr. Moffett	1897	05	12	Sacramento	CA	CA Baptist State American River Association, Lv 05-16-1897	SP
Rev. B. B. Jacques, wife & Mr. Moffett	1897	05	19	Pittsburg	PA	A.B.P.S. Anniversary Meeting, without car, Lv 05-22-1897	—
Rev. B. B. Jacques, wife & Mr. Moffett	1897	05	31	Sacramento	CA		SP
Rev. B. B. Jacques, wife & Mr. Moffett	1897	06	01	Exeter	CA		SP
Rev. B. B. Jacques, wife & Mr. Moffett	1897	06	13	Lindsay	CA		SP
Rev. B. B. Jacques, wife & Mr. Moffett	1897	06	27	Oakland	CA		SP
Rev. B. B. Jacques, wife & Mr. Moffett	1897	07	10	Cottonwood	CA		SP
Rev. B. B. Jacques, wife & Mr. Moffett	1897	07	19	Willows	CA	Mrs. Jacques ill and in hospital in San Francisco, CA	SP
Rev. B. B. Jacques, wife & Mr. Moffett	1897	07	30	Redding	CA	RR shop meetings	SP
Rev. B. B. Jacques, wife & Mr. Moffett	1897	08	05	Anderson	CA	RR shop meetings	SP
Rev. B. B. Jacques, wife & Mr. Moffett	1897	08	08	Sacramento	CA	Car repairs and shop meetings	SP
Rev. B. B. Jacques, wife & Mr. Moffett	1897	08	22	Mountain View	CA	Church organized, 2 weeks	SP
Rev. B. B. Jacques, wife & Mr. Moffett	1897	09	04	Hollister	CA		SP
Rev. B. B. Jacques & Mr. Moffett	1897	09	18	San Jose	CA		SP
Rev. B. B. Jacques & Mr. Moffett	1897	10	16	Los Gatos	CA	CA Baptist State Association and young people's meeting, Lv 10-31-1897	SP
Rev. B. B. Jacques, wife & Mr. Moffett	1897	10	25	Sacramento	CA		SP
Rev. B. B. Jacques, wife & Mr. Moffett	1897	11	02	Oakland	CA	Church reorganized, Lv 11-29-1897	SP
Rev. B. B. Jacques, wife & Mr. Moffett	1897	11	10	Anderson	CA		SP
Rev. B. B. Jacques, wife & Mr. Moffett	1897	11	10	Ashland	OR		SP
Rev. B. B. Jacques, wife & Mr. Moffett	1897	12	10	Talent	OR		SP
Rev. B. B. Jacques, wife & Mr. Moffett	1897	12	17	Central Point	OR		SP ?
Rev. B. B. Jacques, wife & Mr. Moffett	1898	01	20	Medford	OR	Aroused the people	SP
Rev. B. B. Jacques, wife & Mr. Moffett	1898	01	31	Tolo	OR	Sunday school organized	SP
Rev. B. B. Jacques, wife (9) & Mr. Moffett	1898	02	19	Grants Pass	OR	(9) Mrs. Jacques is ill and left car	SP
Rev. B. B. Jacques & Mr. Moffett	1898	02	28	Fort Stevens	OR	Army servicemen's meetings	A&CR
Rev. B. B. Jacques & Mr. W. Dimock (10)	1898	03	07	Merlin	OR	(10) Mr. Wilfred Dimock, assistant 8 - 1/2 months.	SP
Rev. B. B. Jacques & Mr. W. Dimock	1898	03	20	Leland	OR	People would not come, 3 days	SP
Rev. B. B. Jacques & Mr. W. Dimock	1898	03	23	Wolf Creek	OR	People wholly indifferent	SP
Rev. B. B. Jacques & Mr. W. Dimock	1898	04	09	Glendale	OR	Sunday school organized	SP
Rev. B. B. Jacques & Mr. W. Dimock	1898	04	11	Riddles	OR		SP
Rev. B. B. Jacques & Mr. W. Dimock	1898	04	30	Dillard	OR	Stayed 2 weeks	SP
Rev. B. B. Jacques & Mr. W. Dimock	1898	05	11	Wilbur	OR		SP
Rev. B. B. Jacques & Mr. W. Dimock	1898	05	25	Oakland	OR		SP
Rev. B. B. Jacques & Mr. W. Dimock	1898	05	31	Cottage Grove	OR	Church organized, first in OR	SP
Rev. B. B. Jacques & Mr. W. Dimock	1898	06	03	Yoncalla	OR		SP
Rev. B. B. Jacques & Mr. W. Dimock	1898	06	07	Creswell	OR		SP
Rev. B. B. Jacques & Mr. W. Dimock	1898	06	16	Drain	OR		SP ?
Rev. B. B. Jacques & Mr. W. Dimock	1898	06	19	Portland	OR	OR Baptist State Willamette Association, without car, Lv 07-01-1898	—
Rev. B. B. Jacques & Mr. W. Dimock	1898	06	27	Irving	OR		SP
Rev. B. B. Jacques & Mr. W. Dimock	1898	07	08	Shedd (Shedds)	OR		SP

PERSONNEL SERVING ON CARS	Y	M	D	TOWN	ST	COMMENTS FROM ACCOUNTS, LETTERS	R R
Rev. B. B. Jacques & Mr. W. Dimock	1898	07	29	Eugene	OR		SP
Rev. B. B. Jacques & Mr. W. Dimock	1898	08	05	Astoria	OR	City being built on piles, modern Venice, 2 weeks	A&CR
Rev. B. B. Jacques & Mr. W. Dimock	1898	08	19	New Astoria	OR	End of railroad, near Fort Stevens, soldier boys, 1 week	A&CR
Rev. B. B. Jacques & Mr. W. Dimock	1898	08	27	Harrisburg	OR		SP
Rev. B. B. Jacques & Mr. W. Dimock	1898	08	29	Knappa	OR	Church organized	A&CR
Rev. B. B. Jacques & Mr. W. Dimock	1898	09	03	Westport	OR		A&CR
Rev. B. B. Jacques & Mr. W. Dimock	1898	09	16	Portland	OR	Terminal yards, RR meetings	SP
Rev. B. B. Jacques & Mr. W. Dimock	1898	10	05	Halsey	OR		SP
Rev. B. B. Jacques & Mr. W. Dimock	1898	10	17	Brownsville	OR	OR Baptist State Convention, Lv 10-23-1898	SP
Rev. B. B. Jacques & Mr. W. Dimock (11)	1898	11	02	Springfield	OR	(11) Leaves car	SP
Rev. B. B. Jacques & wife (12)	1898	11	19	St. Louis	MO	First Chapel Car Conference near St. Louis, without car	–
Rev. B. B. Jacques & wife	1898	12	03	Coburg	OR	(12) Returns to car from being ill	SP
Rev. B. B. Jacques & wife	1898	12	19	Lebanon	OR		SP
Rev. B. B. Jacques & wife	1899	01	04	Corvallis	OR	Church organized	SP
Rev. B. B. Jacques & wife	1899	02	06	Wells	OR	Wells Station	SP
Rev. B. B. Jacques & wife	1899	03	01	Amity	OR		SP
Rev. B. B. Jacques & wife	1899	04	22	Corvallis	OR		SP
Rev. B. B. Jacques & wife	1899	06	13	San Dimas	CA	A.B.P.S. Anniversary Meeting, without car, Lv 05-27-1899	–
Rev. B. B. Jacques & wife	1899	05	24	San Francisco	CA		SP
Rev. B. B. Jacques & wife	1899	06	07	Buckhorn	CA		SP
Rev. B. B. Jacques & wife	1899	07	04	Verdi	NV		SP
Rev. B. B. Jacques & wife	1899	08	20	Wadsworth	NV	RR center	SP
Rev. B. B. Jacques & wife	1899	09	24	Lovelock	NV		SP
Rev. B. B. Jacques	1899	10	16	Portland	OR	OR Baptist State Convention, without car, Lv 10-23-1899	SP
Rev. B. B. Jacques	1899	11	02	Winnemucca	NV	Railroad town, 3 weeks	SP
Rev. B. B. Jacques	1899	11	26	Golconda	NV	First Sunday that a preaching service was held in town	SP
Rev. B. B. Jacques & wife	1899	12	24	Camarillo	CA	(13) Mrs. Jacques sick, leaves car	–
Rev. B. B. Jacques & wife	1900	01	10	Los Angeles	CA	Speaking tour in the East, without car	SP
Rev. B. B. Jacques & wife	1900	02	23	Oxnard	CA	Car on side track outside of new town, 3 weeks	SP
Rev. B. B. Jacques & wife	1900	03	08	Los Angeles	CA	Speaking tour at Los Angeles churches	SP
Rev. B. B. Jacques & wife (13)	1900	04	17	San Francisco	CA	Rest and vacation	SP
Rev. B. B. Jacques	1900	06	24	East Oakland Shops	CA	Car repairs and paint, national couplers, Lv 09-19-1900	SP
Rev. B. B. Jacques, wife & Mr. T. Moffat (14)	1900	09	01	Pasadena	CA	Without car	–
Rev. B. B. Jacques & Mr. T. Moffat	1900	09	19	Pasadena	CA	(14) From 09-01-1900	SP
Rev. B. B. Jacques & Mr. T. Moffat	1900	10	20	San Pedro	CA	Church organized	SP
Rev. B. B. Jacques & Mr. T. Moffat	1900	11	07	Santa Clara	CA		SP
Rev. B. B. Jacques & Mr. T. Moffat	1900	12	09	Monte	CA	Organized Sunday school, 16 days	SP
Rev. B. B. Jacques & Mr. T. Moffat	1901	04	01	Arizona towns	TAZ		?
Rev. B. B. Jacques & Mr. T. Moffat	1901	04	11	Tempe	TAZ	AZ Baptist State Convention, Lv 04-15-1901	M&P&SRV
Rev. B. B. Jacques & Mr. T. Moffat	1901	04	20	Guadalupe	M	Mexico, car traveled 791.6 miles to boys and girls meetings	MC
Rev. B. B. Jacques & Mr. T. Moffat (15)	1901	05	01	Arizona towns	TAZ	(15) Leaves car 10-15-1901	?
Rev. B. B. Jacques & Mr. T. Moffat	1901	06	11	Los Angeles	CA	Car repairs Los Angeles Car Company, Lv 09-06-1901	SP
Rev. B. B. Jacques & wife (16)	1902	01	03	Novinger	MO	Church dedicated 01-24-1902	BR
Rev. B. B. Jacques & wife	1902	01	08	Green City	MO	Church dedication, all chapel car missionaries, without car	?
Rev. B. B. Jacques & wife	1902	01	13	Omaha	NE	Church dedication, all chapel car missionaries, without car	?
Rev. B. B. Jacques & wife	1902	01	25	King City	MO	(16) Mrs. Jacques returns to car 10-15-1901	?
Rev. B. B. Jacques & wife	1902	03	01	?	CO	With friends, without car	SP ?
Rev. B. B. Jacques & wife	1902	03	01	Denver	CO	Minister's meeting, without car	SP
Rev. B. B. Jacques & wife	1902	07	10	?	NV	Church organized, without car	–
Rev. B. B. Jacques, wife & Mr. T. Moffat	1902	07	10	San Francisco	CA	Vacation and rest, 2 months	SP
Rev. B. B. Jacques & Mr. T. Moffat	1902	09	19	San Francisco	CA	Car repairs $200	SP
Rev. B. B. Jacques & Mr. T. Moffat	1902	09	21	Reno	NV	Leaves for Chapel Car Conference in MO, without car	?
Rev. B. B. Jacques & Mr. T. Moffat	1902	09	24	Palisade	CO	Without car	–
Rev. B. B. Jacques & Mr. T. Moffat	1902	09	27	Kansas City	MO	Pulpit supply, without car	–
Rev. B. B. Jacques & Mr. T. Moffat	1902	10	06	Milan	MO	Second Chapel Car Conference, without car, Lv 10-06-1902	–
Rev. B. B. Jacques & Mr. T. Moffat	1902	10	07	Novinger	MO	RR meeting, all chapel car missionaries, without car	–
Rev. B. B. Jacques & Mr. T. Moffat	1902	10	08	Green City	MO	Church organized	–
Rev. B. B. Jacques & Mr. T. Moffat	1902	10	11	Wadsworth	NV		SP
Rev. B. B. Jacques & Mr. T. Moffat	1902	10	14	Fallon	NV		SP
Rev. B. B. Jacques & Mr. T. Moffat	1902	10	17	San Pedro	CA		SP
Rev. B. B. Jacques, wife & Mr. T. Moffat	1902	10	20	Other towns	CA		SP
Rev. B. B. Jacques (17) & wife	1903	05	07	Merlin	OR	(17) To pastor Santa Clara Baptist Church, 10-01-1903	SP
Rev. E. R. Hermiston (18), wife & daughter	1903	10	01	Portland	OR	(18) From Presbyterian Evangelistic Association, Shiloh, OH 10-01-1903	SP
Rev. E. R. Hermiston, wife & daughter	1903	10	15	Halsey	OR	Assisted in church dedication	SP
Rev. E. R. Hermiston, wife & daughter	1904	01	02	Tallman	OR	Highland church	SP
Rev. E. R. Hermiston, wife & daughter	1904	01	07	Verdi	NV	Church organized	SP
Rev. E. R. Hermiston, wife & daughter	1904	01	13	Sparks (East Reno)	NV	Baptist church, first service from flat car, without car	–
Rev. E. R. Hermiston, wife & daughter	1904	03	05	Wadsworth	NV	RR shops and town moved to Sparks, NV, without car	SP ?
Rev. E. R. Hermiston & wife	1904	10	01	Fallon	NV	Mining town, church reorganized	SP
Rev. E. R. Hermiston & wife	1904	12	13	San Pedro	CA		SP
Rev. E. R. Hermiston & wife	1905	01	01	Orland	CA	Revival	SP
Rev. E. R. Hermiston & wife	1905	01	10	Shasta Springs	CA		SP
Rev. E. R. Hermiston, wife & daughter	1905	02	16	Red Bluff	CA	Prize-fighting saloon keeper saved, RR meetings, 2 weeks	SP
Rev. E. R. Hermiston, wife & daughter	1905	05	04	Anderson	CA	Three weeks	SP
Rev. E. R. Hermiston, wife & daughter	1905	12	16	Central Point	OR		SP
Rev. E. R. Hermiston & wife	1906	01	07	Roseberry ?	OR		UP ?
Rev. E. R. Hermiston & wife	1906	01	28	Wilbur	OR		SP
Rev. E. R. Hermiston, wife & daughter	1906	02	10	Eugene	OR	RR men	SP
Rev. E. R. Hermiston, wife & daughter	1906	02	20	Halsey	OR	Car repairs	SP
Rev. E. R. Hermiston, wife & daughter	1906	04	01	Albany	OR		SP
Rev. E. R. Hermiston, wife & daughter	1906	05	02	Baker City	OR		OR&N
Rev. E. R. Hermiston, wife & daughter	1906	05	07	San Pedro	CA	Without car	SP
Rev. E. R. Hermiston, wife & daughter	1906	05	14	Coalinga	CA	Without car	–

PERSONNEL SERVING ON CARS	Y	M	D	TOWN	ST	COMMENTS FROM ACCOUNTS, LETTERS	R R
Rev. E. R. Hermiston, wife & daughter	1906	05	25	?	OR	Visit churches, without car	–
Rev. E. R. Hermiston & wife	1906	06	27	Los Angeles	CA	Without car	–
Rev. E. R. Hermiston & wife	1906	07	15	?	OR	Visit churches, without car	?
Rev. E. R. Hermiston & wife	1906	07	29	Santa Cruz	OR	Twin Lakes Assembly	SP
Rev. E. R. Hermiston & wife	1906	08	11	Corvallis	OR		SP
Rev. E. R. Hermiston & wife	1907	01	20	Highland	OR	Sunday school reorganized	?
Rev. E. R. Hermiston & wife	1907	03	17	McMinnville	OR		SP
Rev. E. R. Hermiston & wife	1907	03	17	Hermiston	OR	Church organized 04-07-1907, saloon girl story, 9 months	OR&N
Rev. E. R. Hermiston	1907	06	19	Ashland	OR	OR Baptist State Rogue River Association, without car	–
Rev. E. R. Hermiston	1907	10	14	Salem	OR	OR Baptist State Convention, without car	OR&N
Rev. E. R. Hermiston & wife	1907	12	25	Hermiston	OR	Rev. Hermiston officiated laying of cornerstone	OR&N
Rev. E. R. Hermiston & wife	1908	02	03	Payette	ID		OSL
Rev. E. R. Hermiston & wife	1908	02	18	Boise	ID	Stayed 10 days	OSL
Rev. E. R. Hermiston & wife	1908	03	05	Emmett	ID		IN
Rev. E. R. Hermiston & wife	1908	04	06	Nampa	ID		IN
Rev. E. R. Hermiston & wife	1908	04	29	Caldwell	ID		OSL
Rev. E. R. Hermiston	1908	05	14	Kansas City	MO	Third Chapel Car Conference, without car	–
Rev. E. R. Hermiston & wife	1908	06	26	Mountain Home	ID		OSL
Rev. E. R. Hermiston & wife	1908	06	20	Hermiston	OR	Dedication of building	OR&N
Rev. E. R. Hermiston & wife	1908	06	23	Shoshone	ID		OSL
Rev. E. R. Hermiston & wife	1908	08	06	Pocatello	ID	Car repairs, RR YMCA, shop meetings, Lv 10-06-1909	OSL
Rev. E. R. Hermiston & wife	1908	10	20	Twin Falls	ID	Raising money for building, 3 months	OSL
Rev. E. R. Hermiston & wife	1909	01	10	Jerome	ID	Built building	IS
Rev. E. R. Hermiston & wife	1909	01	31	Willard	ID		?
Rev. E. R. Hermiston & wife	1909	02	23	Emmett	ID	No pastor	IN
Rev. E. R. Hermiston & wife	1909	03	16	Hailey	ID		OSL
Rev. E. R. Hermiston & wife	1909	03	24	Rupert	ID	Started movement for building	OSL
Rev. E. R. Hermiston & wife	1909	04	07	Emmett	ID		IN
Rev. E. R. Hermiston & wife	1909	04	27	Caldwell	ID		OSL
Rev. E. R. Hermiston & wife	1909	06	15	McCammon	ID	Church organized	OSL
Rev. E. R. Hermiston & wife	1909	06	02	Buhl	ID		OSL
Rev. E. R. Hermiston & wife	1909	06	29	Gooding	ID	No pastor	OSL
Rev. E. R. Hermiston & wife	1909	07	07	Buhl	ID	Built building, Lv 09-15-1909	OSL
Rev. E. R. Hermiston & wife	1909	08	14	Pocatello	ID	Without car	–
Rev. E. R. Hermiston & wife	1909	08	20	Black Foot	ID	Without car	OSL
Rev. E. R. Hermiston & wife	1909	09	16	Arco	ID	No pastor	OSL
Rev. E. R. Hermiston & wife	1909	09	26	Darlington	ID	Church organized	UP ?
Rev. E. R. Hermiston & wife	1909	10	28	Hollister	ID		UP ?
Rev. E. R. Hermiston & wife	1909	11	07	Moore	ID		OSL
Rev. E. R. Hermiston & wife	1909	11	14	American Falls	ID		OSL
Rev. E. R. Hermiston & wife	1909	12	18	Du Bois	ID	Church organized	OSL
Rev. E. R. Hermiston & wife	1910	01	10	Boise	ID		OSL
Rev. E. R. Hermiston & wife	1910	02	07	Milner	ID	No pastor	OSL
Rev. E. R. Hermiston & wife	1910	02	13	Spencer	ID		OSL
Rev. E. R. Hermiston & wife	1910	04	06	Picabo	ID		OSL
Rev. E. R. Hermiston & wife	1910	04	27	Shoshone	ID		OSL
Rev. E. R. Hermiston & wife	1910	05	18	Caldwell	ID		OSL
Rev. E. R. Hermiston & wife	1910	06	04	Twin Falls	ID		OSL
Rev. E. R. Hermiston & wife	1910	06	26	Payette	ID		OSL
Rev. E. R. Hermiston & wife	1910	07	20	Nampa	ID		OSL
Rev. E. R. Hermiston & wife	1910	08	12	Kimberly	ID		OSL
Rev. E. R. Hermiston & wife	1910	08	19	Oakley	ID		M&N
Rev. E. R. Hermiston & wife	1910	09	24	Bellevue	ID	No pastor	OSL
Rev. E. R. Hermiston & wife	1910	10	17	Minidoka	ID		OSL
Rev. E. R. Hermiston & wife	1910	10	24	Wendell	ID		OSL
Rev. E. R. Hermiston & wife	1910	12	19	Downey	ID		OSL ?
Rev. E. R. Hermiston & wife	1911	01	08	Prosser	WA	Church organized 01-20-1911	NP
Rev. E. R. Hermiston & wife	1911	01	20	Parker	WA	Church organized, built building	NP
Rev. E. R. Hermiston & wife	1911	02	02	Garfield	WA		CM&PS
Rev. E. R. Hermiston & wife	1911	02	10	Ellensburg	WA	Near town of Opportunity, WA, 2 weeks	CM&PS
Rev. E. R. Hermiston & wife	1911	02	16	Tekoa	WA	Church organized	NP
Rev. E. R. Hermiston & wife	1911	02	23	Wapato	WA	Hillyard Shops, light car repairs, shop and town meetings	GN
Rev. E. R. Hermiston & wife	1911	02	28	Hillyard	WA	Working with 2 or 3 churches, without car	–
Rev. E. R. Hermiston & wife	1911	03	05	Spokane	WA	Church organized, without car, 5 weeks	–
Rev. E. R. Hermiston & wife	1911	03	09	Yacama (Yacama City)	WA	Stayed 10 days, without car	SP&S
Rev. E. R. Hermiston & wife	1911	04	18	Yakima (No. Yakima)	WA		SP&S
Rev. E. R. Hermiston, wife & daughter	1911	04	30	Hermiston	OR		SP&S
Rev. E. R. Hermiston, wife & daughter	1911	05	06	Portland	OR		CM&PS
Rev. E. R. Hermiston, wife & daughter	1911	05	06	Astoria	OR	Church organized, built building, RR meetings, 4 months	SP&S
Rev. E. R. Hermiston & wife	1911	05	16	Malden	WA	Church complained about car not staying longer	NP
Rev. E. R. Hermiston & wife	1911	09	03	Washougal	WA		CM&PS
Rev. E. R. Hermiston & wife	1911	09	05	Kittitas	WA	Building repaired	NP
Rev. E. R. Hermiston & wife	1911	09	12	Ellensburg	WA	Mining town	–
Rev. E. R. Hermiston & wife	1911	09	28	Cle Elum	WA	(Kennewick)	SP&S
Rev. E. R. Hermiston & wife	1911	10	11	Lyle	WA		SP&S
Rev. E. R. Hermiston & wife	1911	10	14	White Salmon	WA	Car near depot, successful meetings	SP&S
Rev. E. R. Hermiston & wife	1911	10	17	Stevenson	WA	ID Baptist State Convention, without car	–
Rev. E. R. Hermiston & wife	1911	10	20	Goldendale	WA	Car inventory of equipment at $140 and car at $6500, Lv 11-20-1911	SP&S
Rev. E. R. Hermiston & wife	1911	10	25	Twin Falls	ID	Church organized, 3 weeks	SP&S
Rev. E. R. Hermiston & wife	1911	11	02	Camas	WA	Wants to hear evangelist Gypsy Smith, 2 or 3 weeks	SP&S
Rev. E. R. Hermiston & wife	1911	11	08	Parker	WA		NP
Rev. E. R. Hermiston & wife	1911	11	28	Vancouver	WA		NP

PERSONNEL SERVING ON CARS	Y	M	D	TOWN	ST	COMMENTS FROM ACCOUNTS, LETTERS	R R
Rev. E. R. Hermiston & wife	1911	12	17	Pasco	WA	Church organized, RR meetings	NP
Rev. E. R. Hermiston, wife & daughter	1911	12	22	Latah	WA		OWR&N
Rev. E. R. Hermiston, wife & daughter	1911	12	27	McMinnville	OR		SP
Rev. E. R. Hermiston & wife	1911	12	28	Brawley	CA	May be a Nazarene chapel car in service, Lv 01-22-1912	SP
Rev. E. R. Hermiston & wife	1912	01	04	Pocatello	ID	ID Baptist State Convention, without car	--
Rev. E. R. Hermiston & wife	1912	01	12	Santa Barbara	CA	CA Baptist State Convention, without car	HIU
Rev. E. R. Hermiston & wife	1912	02	01	Holtville	CA	Moves too fast, needed to stay longer, does not finish work	HIU
Rev. E. R. Hermiston & wife	1912	02	17	El Centro	CA	Temple Baptist reorganized, no Nazarene chapel car	SP
Rev. E. R. Hermiston & wife	1912	03	14	Thermal	CA		SP
Rev. E. R. Hermiston & wife	1912	03	28	San Bernardino	CA	Shop and town meetings	SP
Rev. E. R. Hermiston & wife	1912	04	24	San Bernardino	CA	Car in shop, repairs and paint, Lv 09-25-1912	SP
Rev. E. R. Hermiston & wife	1912	04	25	El Monte	CA	AT&SF wanted to charge full fares, without car	--
Rev. E. R. Hermiston & wife	1912	05	08	Kansas City	MO	Speaking tour, MO, IA, OH, and vacation at Cleveland, OH	--
Rev. E. R. Hermiston & wife	1912	05	15	Kansas City	MO	Fourth Chapel Car Conference and churches, without car	--
Rev. E. R. Hermiston & wife	1912	06	22	Des Moines	IA	A.B.P.S. Anniversary Meeting and churches, without car, Lv 10-05-1912	--
Rev. E. R. Hermiston	1912	08	22	Los Angeles	CA	Occidental Heights, infantile paralysis scare, without car	--
Rev. E. R. Hermiston	1912	08	28	Pasadena	CA	Helping Rev. Jacques at mission, without car	SP
Rev. E. R. Hermiston	1912	09	25	San Bernardino	CA	Picked up car at shop	SP
Rev. E. R. Hermiston & wife	1912	09	27	Banning	CA		SP
Rev. E. R. Hermiston & wife	1912	10	12	Yuma (Yuma City)	AZ		AE
Rev. E. R. Hermiston & wife	1912	10	31	Safford	AZ		AE
Rev. E. R. Hermiston & wife	1912	11	17	Globe	AZ	Lv 12-11-1912	AE
Rev. E. R. Hermiston & wife	1913	01	03	Miami	AZ	Great mining camp	AE
Rev. E. R. Hermiston & wife	1913	01	06	Redlands	CA		AT&SF
Rev. E. R. Hermiston & wife	1913	01	11	San Diego	CA	CA Baptist State Southern Convention, Lv 01-16-1913	AT&SF
Rev. E. R. Hermiston & wife	1913	01	19	Tucson	AZ		SP
Rev. E. R. Hermiston & wife	1913	02	11	Phoenix	AZ	Arizona celebrated first birthday of statehood, 02-14-1913	AE
Rev. E. R. Hermiston & wife	1913	03	11	Buckeye	AZ		AE
Rev. E. R. Hermiston & wife	1913	03	25	Mesa	AZ		AE
Rev. E. R. Hermiston	1913	04	02	Prescott	AZ		AE
Rev. E. R. Hermiston & wife	1913	04	07	Mesa	AZ	Spinal meningitis, had to leave, to Los Angeles, CA, for a while	AE
Rev. E. R. Hermiston & wife	1913	04	11	Los Angeles	CA	Raising money for Wilshire Baptist, without car	--
Rev. E. R. Hermiston & wife	1913	04	23	Mesa	AZ	Returned from Los Angeles, CA, after spinal meningitis outbreaks	AE
Rev. E. R. Hermiston & wife	1913	05	03	Tempe	AZ	Prison witnessing, without car	AE
Rev. E. R. Hermiston & wife	1913	05	18	Naco	AZ	Car needs steel vestibule platforms	EP&SW
Rev. E. R. Hermiston & wife	1913	06	08	Douglas	AZ	Stayed 10 days	EP&SW
Rev. E. R. Hermiston & wife	1913	06	18	Clifton	AZ	Town meetings, car repaired and painted exterior, $65.50	A&NM
Rev. E. R. Hermiston, wife & daughter	1913	06	23	Los Angeles	CA	Working at Emmanuel mission 10 days and vacation	SP
Rev. E. R. Hermiston, wife & daughter	1913	08	07	Long Beach	CA		SP
Rev. E. R. Hermiston, wife & daughter	1913	09	06	Downey	CA		SP
Rev. E. R. Hermiston, wife & daughter	1913	09	21	Compton	CA		SP
Rev. E. R. Hermiston & wife	1913	10	14	Chino	CA	Stayed 2 weeks	SP
Rev. E. R. Hermiston & wife	1913	11	04	Santa Paula	CA		SP
Rev. E. R. Hermiston & wife	1913	11	19	Oxnard	CA		SP
Rev. E. R. Hermiston & wife	1914	01	18	Santa Barbara	CA	Meeting very successful	SP
Rev. E. R. Hermiston & wife	1914	06	04	Lompoc	CA	So many people, moved to church, then to opera house	SP
Rev. E. R. Hermiston & wife	1914	06	10	Boston	MA	A.B.P.S. Anniversary Meeting, without car, Lv 06-26-1914	--
Rev. E. R. Hermiston & wife	1914	06	11	Los Angeles	CA	Car in heavy repair shop $908.12, Lv 08-31-1914	SP
Rev. E. R. Hermiston & wife	1914	06	20	?	CA	Speaking tour in East, without car, Lv 09-30-1914	SP
Rev. E. R. Hermiston & wife	1914	10	20	Los Angeles	CA	Car in for shop for light steam line repairs, $56.58	SP
Rev. E. R. Hermiston & wife	1914	10	26	Lancaster	CA	Car north of depot	SP
Rev. E. R. Hermiston & wife	1914	12	01	Van Nuys	CA	Church organized 12-17-1914, built building, 3 months	SP
Rev. E. R. Hermiston & wife	1915	05	18	Los Angeles	CA	A.B.P.S. Anniversary Meeting, without car	SP
Rev. E. R. Hermiston & wife	1915	05	27	Los Angeles	CA	Chapel Car Conference, 2 days, without car, Lv 05-28-1915	--
Rev. E. R. Hermiston (19) & wife	1915	05	31	Los Angeles	CA	(19) Transferred to chapel car 7, Grace, 07-01-1915	SP
(20)	1915	07	02	Los Angeles	CA	Car vacant, storage, 1 month	SP
(20)	1915	08	03	Butte	MT	Car in shop, installed a used Baker Heater $49.46	LA&SL
Rev. G. L. White & wife	1915	08	15	Butte	MT	On car during transfer of car from Los Angeles, CA, to Butte, MT	LA&SL
(20)	1915	08	17	Butte	MT	Car vacant, storage, 4 months	OSL
(20)	1915	12	12	Pocatello	ID	Car in shop	UP
Rev. F. I. Blanchard (21) & wife	1916	02	06	Butte	MT	(20) Storage and shops, 7 months total	UP
Rev. F. I. Blanchard & wife	1916	02	13	Anaconda	MT	Car in heavy repair shop, 4 weeks	BA&P
Rev. F. I. Blanchard & wife	1916	03	16	Missoula	MT	Very anxious to have the car, 4 weeks	NP
Rev. F. I. Blanchard & wife	1916	04	18	Victor	MT	(21) From Pontiac, MI, 02-01-1916	NP
Rev. F. I. Blanchard & wife	1916	05	17	Darby	MT		NP
Rev. F. I. Blanchard & wife	1916	08	21	Hamilton	MT		NP
Rev. F. I. Blanchard & wife	1916	09	16	Belt	MT	1 month	GN
Rev. F. I. Blanchard & wife	1916	10	11	Lewistown	MT	Had to close for a while due to the election, Lv 11-19-1916	CM&SP
Rev. F. I. Blanchard & wife	1917	04	09	Roundup	MT	Church organized, 6 months	CM&SP
Rev. F. I. Blanchard & wife	1917	10	24	Wyola	MT		BR
Rev. F. I. Blanchard & wife	1917	11	03	Lodgegrass	MT		BR
Rev. F. I. Blanchard & wife	1917	12	28	Sheridan	WY		--
Rev. F. I. Blanchard & wife	1918	01	02	Sheridan	WY	Government takes over operation of railroads due to WW I	BR
Rev. F. I. Blanchard & wife	1918	02	06	Carneyville	WY		BR

PERSONNEL SERVING ON CARS	Y	M	D	TOWN	ST	COMMENTS FROM ACCOUNTS, LETTERS	R R
Rev. F. I. Blanchard & wife	1918	03	02	Laurel	MT	Church was without a pastor	NP
Rev. F. I. Blanchard & wife	1918	03	28	Livingston	MT	(22) Transferred to chapel car 3, Glad Tidings, 08-01-1918	NP
Rev. F. I. Blanchard & wife	1918	05	03	Manhattan	MT		NP
Rev. F. I. Blanchard & wife	1918	05	28	Lodgegrass	MT	Also worked with Crow Indians	BR
Rev. F. I. Blanchard & wife	1918	06	15	Flagler	CO	Church organized 06-30-1918	CRI&P
Rev. F. I. Blanchard & wife	1918	07	02	Belgrade	MT	Rev. Blanchard sick, short stay	NP
Rev. F. I. Blanchard (22) & wife	1918	07	05	Bozeman	MT	Rev. Blanchard in hospital 1 month with acute bronchitis, Lv 09-28-1918	NP
Rev. A. C. Blinzinger (23) & wife	1918	08	02	Stevensville	MT	(23) From pastor, Holyoke,CO, 08-02-1918	--
Rev. A. C. Blinzinger & wife	1918	10	07	Bozeman	MT	MT Baptist State Convention, without car, Lv 10-12-1918	--
Rev. A. C. Blinzinger & wife	1918	10	21	Pueblo	CO	CO Baptist State Convention, without car, Lv 10-25-1918	--
Rev. A. C. Blinzinger & wife	1918	11	02	Boone	CO	Church organized, built building	SF
Rev. A. C. Blinzinger & wife	1919	01	02	Simla	CO	Built building	CRI&P
Rev. A. C. Blinzinger & wife	1919	04	05	Limon	CO	Built building	CRI&P
Rev. A. C. Blinzinger & wife	1920	02	07	Eastlake (East Lake)	CO	Church organized	UP
Rev. A. C. Blinzinger & wife	1920	03	01	Other towns	CO	Government returned ownership to railroads	--
Rev. A. C. Blinzinger & wife	1920	06	20	?	CO	Car repairs $2106.85	?
Rev. A. C. Blinzinger & wife	1920	10	01	Brighton	CO	Church organized 11-14-1920, built building	UP
Rev. A. C. Blinzinger & wife	1921	02	16	Fort Lupton	CO	Reorganized church 03-13-1921, built building	UP ?
Rev. A. C. Blinzinger & wife	1921	06	09	?	WY	West NE and East in WY, maybe 8 months	?
Rev. A. C. Blinzinger & wife	1921	10	17	Canon City	CO	CO Baptist State Convention, without car, Lv10-21-1921	D&RGW
Rev. A. C. Blinzinger & wife	1922	01	22	Littleton	CO	Church organized 04-23-1922, built building, 1 year	--
Rev. A. C. Blinzinger & wife	1922	05	01	?	CO	New instructions, exterior lettering on chapel cars	--
Rev. A. C. Blinzinger & wife	1922	10	16	Colorado Springs	CO	CO Baptist State Convention, without car, Lv 10-21-1922	UP
Rev. A. C. Blinzinger & wife	1922	12	06	Iliff	CO		UP
Rev. A. C. Blinzinger & wife	1923	02	01	Other towns	CO	(24) Transferred to chapel car 7, Grace, 04-01-1924	--
Rev. A. C. Blinzinger (24) & wife	1924	04	01	Denver	CO	Car repairs, Burnham shops, Lv 04-02-1924	D&RGW
Rev. F. I. Blanchard (25) & wife	1924	04	01	Denver	CO	(25) Transferred from chapel car 1, Evangel, 04-01-1924	D&RGW
Rev. F. I. Blanchard (26) & wife	1924	04	02	Denver	CO	(26) Picked up car at Burnham shops 04-02-1924	D&RGW
Rev. F. I. Blanchard & wife	1924	04	21	Cheyenne	WY	WY Baptist Southern State Association, without car, Lv 04-25-1924	UP
Rev. F. I. Blanchard & wife	1924	06	01	Ovid	CO		UP
Rev. F. I. Blanchard & wife	1924	09	05	Craig	WY	While at Ovid, CO, without car	--
Rev. F. I. Blanchard & wife	1924	10	30	Greybull	WY	While at Ovid, CO, without car	BR
Rev. F. I. Blanchard & wife	1925	01	01	Julesburg	WY	Revival meetings	--
Rev. F. I. Blanchard & wife	1925	05	25	Gebo	WY	Coal camp, built building, without car	--
Rev. F. I. Blanchard & wife	1926	03	28	Steamboat Springs	CO	Organized church, built building, Lv 03-27-1926	D&SL
Rev. F. I. Blanchard & wife	1926	05	05	Clark	CO		GW
Rev. F. I. Blanchard & wife	1926	06	05	Bear River	CO	Church organized, Lv 06-13-1926	D&SL
Rev. F. I. Blanchard & wife	1926	06	14	Denver	CO	Car in Burnham shops, on vacation in MI	D&RGW
Rev. F. I. Blanchard & wife	1926	11	08	Ovid	WY	Organized church 12-05-1926, built building, Lv 08-28-1927	UP
Rev. F. I. Blanchard & wife	1927	01	05	Sedgwick	CO	Without car, Lv 04-12-1938	--
Rev. F. I. Blanchard & wife	1927	03	05	Craig	CO	Built building	--
Rev. F. I. Blanchard & wife	1928	01	01	Winnemucca	NV	Church reorganized 04-08-1928, built building	SP
Rev. F. I. Blanchard & wife	1928	06	25	Padroni	CO	Burnham shop repairs $607.16, Lv 12-17-1928	BR
Rev. F. I. Blanchard & wife	1928	11	18	Denver	CO	Church reorganized 01-13-1929, built building, Lv 06-02-1929	D&RGW
Rev. F. I. Blanchard & wife	1928	12	20	Agate	CO	Organized church 12-29-1929, built building	UP
Rev. F. I. Blanchard & wife	1929	06	14	Phippsburg	CO	In shop car repairs $110.25, Lv 04-12-1930	D&SL
Rev. F. I. Blanchard & wife	1929	10	16	Phippsburg	CO	(27) Car not used, stored and shopped for repairs, 10 months total	D&SL
Rev. F. I. Blanchard & wife	1929	10	17	Phippsburg	CO	Stayed 6 months	D&SL
Rev. F. I. Blanchard & wife	1930	04	24	Bijon	CO	Lighting struck chapel car at depot on 08-03-1930	BR
Rev. F. I. Blanchard & wife	1930	07	01	Yampa	CO	Car out of service, without car	D&SL
Rev. F. I. Blanchard & wife	1930	08	04	Yampa	CO	Burnham shop car repaired $1380.86, Lv 11-10-1930	D&SL
Rev. F. I. Blanchard & wife	1930	08	21	Denver	CO	Car returned to service	D&RGW
Rev. F. I. Blanchard & wife	1930	11	14	Yampa	CO	Built building, Lv 08-31-1932	D&SL
Rev. F. I. Blanchard & wife	1931	04	05	Bennett	CO	While at Bennett, CO, without car, Lv 08-31-1932	UP
Rev. F. I. Blanchard & wife	1932	05	03	Watkins	CO	Car not used, car stored	--
Rev. F. I. Blanchard & wife	1932	09	01	Denver	CO	Helping at Mt. Hermon Baptist, without car	UP
Rev. F. I. Blanchard & wife	1932	09	12	Bennett	CO	Burnham shop car repairs $304.13, Lv 04-12-1933	--
Rev. F. I. Blanchard & wife	1933	02	02	Denver	CO	(27) Car not used, stored and shopped for repairs, 10 months total	UP
Rev. F. I. Blanchard & wife	1933	04	12	Denver	CO	While at Deer Trail, CO, without car	D&RGW
Rev. F. I. Blanchard & wife	1933	07	18	Deer Trail (Deertrail)	CO	Stayed 6 months, Rev. Blanchard very ill	D&RGW
Rev. F. I. Blanchard & wife	1934	02	17	Byers	CO	Lv 06-09-1935	UP
Rev. F. I. Blanchard & wife	1934	09	10	Littleton	CO		CRI&P
Rev. F. I. Blanchard, wife & Rev. A. J. Morris (28)	1934	12	01	Peyton	CO	(28) Temporary for 6 months, starting 12-01-1934	CRI&P
Rev. F. I. Blanchard (29), wife & Rev. A. J. Morris	1934	12	10	Peyton	CO	Lv 01-31-1935	CRI&P
Rev. A. J. Morris (30)	1935	02	03	Peyton	CO	From another position 01-31-1935, Lv 02-11-1935	CRI&P
Rev. H. Parry (31)(32) & wife	1935	06	03	Peyton	CO	(32) On car 02-03-1935	CRI&P
Rev. H. Parry & wife	1935	06	10	Colorado Springs	CO	A.B.P.S. Anniversary Meeting, Lv 06-26-1935	AT&SF
Rev. H. Parry & wife	1935	06	26	Peyton	CO	Lv07-02-193	CRI&P
Rev. H. Parry & wife	1935	07	02	Denver	CO	Burnham shop car repairs $560.81, Lv 08-19-1935	CRI&P
Rev. H. Parry & wife	1935	08	08	Denver	CO	RR shop meeting car full and many outside	D&RGW
Rev. H. Parry & wife	1935	08	20	Briggsdale	CO	Car truss rod broke 10-25-1935 due to minus 19 degrees, 9 months	D&RGW
Rev. H. Parry & wife	1936	04	01	Peyton	CO	Speaking tour in NY and NJ, 1 month, without car	UP
Rev. H. Parry & wife	1936	05	19	St. Louis	MO	A.B.P.S. Anniversary Meeting, Lv 05-26-1936, without car	--
Rev. H. Parry & wife	1936	06	27	Crowley	CO	High cost of anthracite coal, 9 months, Lv 12-26-1937	MP
Rev. H. Parry & wife	1936	12	27	?	CO	Speaking tour in AZ and NM, also on vacation, without car	--
Rev. H. Parry & wife	1937	03	07	Ordway	CO	While at Crowley, CO, without car, Lv 12-26-1937	UP
Rev. H. Parry & wife	1938	01	09	Deer Trail (Deertrail)	CO	Two hundred miles, 20 hour trip, spotted car 1 week, then to site, 10 months	--
Rev. H. Parry & wife	1938	01	10	Byers	CO	Related ministry with Deer Trail, CO, without car	UP
Rev. H. Parry & wife	1938	03	13	Pueblo	CO	Speaking tour in NE and IA, 23 towns, Lv 04-03-1938, without car	--
Rev. H. Parry & wife	1938	10	04	Denver	CO	CO Baptist State Convention, need car repairs funds	--
Rev. H. Parry & wife	1938	11	11	Denver	CO	Burnham shop, car repairs $548.42, Lv 12-25-1938	D&RGW
Rev. H. Parry & wife	1939	01	02	South Fork	CO	Lumber camp, built building, Lv 03-15-1941	D&RGW

PERSONNEL SERVING ON CARS	Y	M	D	TOWN	ST	COMMENTS FROM ACCOUNTS, LETTERS	RR
Rev. H. Parry & wife	1939	01	10	Del Norte	CO	Related ministry with South Fork, CO, without car	—
Rev. H. Parry & wife	1939	01	15	Ordway	CO	Related ministry with South Fork, CO, without car	—
Rev. H. Parry & wife	1939	01	20	Mancos	CO	Related ministry with South Fork, CO, without car	—
Rev. H. Parry & wife	1939	01	25	Del Norte	CO	Related ministry with South Fork, CO, without car	—
Rev. H. Parry & wife	1939	10	03	Denver	CO	CO Baptist State Convention, without car	—
Rev. H. Parry & wife	1940	04	16	Philadelphia	PA	Speaking tour and A.B.P.S. headquarters, without car, Lv 05-15-1940	—
Rev. H. Parry & wife	1940	09	16	?		Speaking tour in IN and OH, and vacation in Ohio, without car, Lv 10-15-1940	—
Rev. H. Parry & wife	1941	02	12	South Fork	CO	Moved belongings out of chapel car, for storage at Monticello, UT	D&RGW
Rev. H. Parry & wife	1941	03	15	Del Norte	CO	Car stored and out of service at Del Norte, CO	D&RGW
Rev. H. Parry & wife	1941	03	20	Lakewood	CO	Has ammunitions plant, organized church, without car	D&RGW
Rev. H. Parry & wife	1941	05	12	Del Norte	CO	Without car, Lv 02-01-1942	—
Rev. H. Parry & wife	1941	06	17	Philadelphia	PA	A.B.H.M.S. committee voted for permanent location for car	—
Rev. H. Parry (33)(34)(35) & wife	1942	02	01	South Fork	CO	Last chapel car church service in chapel car 2, Emmanuel	D&RGW
Rev. H. Parry	1942	07	23	Swan Lake	SD	(33) Supervised car movement to Swan Lake, SD, $642.84	D&RGW
Rev. H. Parry	1942	07	26	Sioux Falls	SD	On RR depot siding near Kiwanis Ave. and 10th ST	CMSP&P
Rev. H. Parry	1942	07	27	Viborg	SD	Near depot, chapel car trucked to Swan Lake	GN
Rev. H. Parry	1942	08	16	Swan Lake	SD	Baptist young people's camp assembly grounds	—
Rev. H. Parry	1942	08	18	Swan Lake	SD	Car retired 08-18-1942	—
	1943	01	27	Swan Lake	SD	Car sold to SD Baptist State Convention for $1	—
	1944			Swan Lake	SD	Car used for church services and lodging for missionaries	—
	1945			Swan Lake	SD	(34) Transferred to chapel car 7, Grace, 09-01-1942	—
	1946			Swan Lake	SD	(35) Lv in auto 09-01-1942 for Monticello, UT, as colporter	—
	1950			Sioux Falls	SD	Car used as a house	—
	1955			Sioux Falls	SD	Baptist assembly grounds and to Mennonites	—
	1956			Sioux Falls	SD	Car sold for $400 to 2 men, salvage business, in Sioux Falls, SD	—
	1967			Sioux Falls	SD	Car in junk yard	—
	1968			Sioux Falls	SD	Sold to Brandt Engineering Company for storage building	—
	1971	02	08	Sioux Falls	SD	In Brandt Engineering Company storage yard	—
	1972	07		Sioux Falls	SD	Car given to First Baptist Church young people to use in Norton Froehlich addition	—
	1972	10	16	Prairie Village	SD	Church and Brandt Engineering Company moved car to Prairie Village, west of Madison, SD	—
	1976	09		Prairie Village	SD	Car eligible for National Register of Historic Places	—
	1979	06		Prairie Village	SD	Car restoration starts	—
	1983			Prairie Village	SD	Car shed roof placed over chapel car	—
	1999			Prairie Village	SD	Car on exhibit and undergoing restoration	—
A.B.P.S. CAR 3, GLAD TIDINGS						**AMERICAN BAPTIST PUBLICATION SOCIETY**	
Car named by Mrs. W. M. Hills	1893	05	24	Denver	CO	Mr. W. M Hills donates car	—
	1893	05	25	Denver	CO	If money collected for car 4 before 01-1895, Mr. Hills will build chapel car 3, Glad Tidings	—
	1894	03	03		CO	Mr. Hills requested A.B.P.S. to have Barney & Smith Car Company start building car 3, Glad Tidings	CCC&SL
Rev. E. B. Edmunds (1)	1894	03	20	Dayton	OH	Car shipped from builder Barney & Smith Car Company	D&H
Rev. E. B. Edmunds	1894	05	24	Saratoga	NY	Mount Morris Church NY, NY, furnishing car interior needs	D&H
Rev. E. B. Edmunds (2)	1894	05	26	Saratoga	NY	Car dedication 05-25-94, A.B.P.S. Anniversary Meeting	NP
(3)	1894	06	12	Minneapolis	MN	(1) WI Sunday school missionary temporarily assigned, 05-24-1894	NP
	1894	06	13	Minneapolis	MN	(2) Return to WI Sunday school missionary position	NP
Rev. C. H. Rust (4)(5) & wife	1894	06	12	Minneapolis	MN	MN Baptist State Convention, Lv 10-17-1894	NP
Rev. C. H. Rust & wife	1894	10	18	Crookston	MN	(3) Car vacant 4-1/2 months, waiting for missionaries	NP
Rev. C. H. Rust & wife	1894	10	25	Brainerd	MN	(4) From Warren Avenue Baptist Church, Boston, MA, 10-12-1894	NP
Rev. C. H. Rust & wife	1894	11	04	Staples	MN	(5) On chapel car in freight yard	NP
Rev. C. H. Rust & wife	1894	11	15	St. Paul	MN	Como shop, storm windows, shop meetings, 2 weeks	NP
Rev. C. H. Rust & wife	1894	12	03	Staples	MN	Without car	NP
Rev. C. H. Rust & wife	1895	01	18	Frazee	MN	Stayed 02-01-1895 to 09-01-1896 ?	NP
Rev. C. H. Rust & wife	1895	02	01	Other towns	MN	Stayed 3 weeks	?
Rev. C. H. Rust & wife	1895	09	06	Breckenridge	MN	Gunney Baptist Church, 10 days	NP
Rev. C. H. Rust & wife	1895	09	29	Wahpeton	ND	Car in shop for general repairs, 2 weeks	NP
Rev. C. H. Rust & wife	1895	10	16	St. Paul	MN	Helping pastor follow up, without car, 1 week	NP
Rev. C. H. Rust	1895	10	23	Breckenridge	MN	Helping pastor follow up, without car, 1 week	—
Rev. C. H. Rust & wife	1895	10	30	Wahpeton	ND	Picked up car at Como shop, exterior paint & repairs	NP
Rev. C. H. Rust & wife	1895	11	04	St. Paul	MN	Meeting house would not hold the crowds, 3 weeks	NP
Rev. C. H. Rust & wife	1895	11	06	Philbrook	MN	Stayed 4 weeks	NP
Rev. C. H. Rust & wife	1895	12	03	Fairmount	ND	Heater pipe froze up and burst at minus 24 degrees, repaired at no cost	NP
Rev. C. H. Rust & wife	1896	01	12	Cooperstown	ND	Business men of town petition for car	NP
Rev. C. H. Rust & wife	1896	01	23	Wheaton	MN	Car full, had to use church for services	NP
Rev. C. H. Rust & wife	1896	03	22	Bismarck	ND	Stayed 05-01-1996 to 12-31-1896	?
Rev. C. H. Rust & wife	1896	05	01	Other towns	ND	WI Baptist State Convention, Lv 10-05-1896	WC
Rev. C. H. Rust & wife	1896	10	01	Milwaukee	WI		WC
Rev. C. H. Rust & wife	1896	12	07	Other towns	WI		?
Rev. C. H. Rust, wife & Mr. C. W. Meacham (6)	1887	05	19	Pittsburg	PA	A.B.P.S. Anniversary Meeting, without car, Lv 05-22-1887	—
Rev. C. H. Rust, wife & Mr. C. W. Meacham	1897	06	08	Wheeler	WI	(6) From Moody Bible Institute, Chicago, IL	WC
Rev. C. H. Rust, wife & Mr. C. W. Meacham	1897	07	10	Thorp (Thorpe)	WI	RR shop meetings about 50 men every noon, Lv 01-17-1898	NP ?
Rev. C. H. Rust, wife & Mr. C. W. Meacham (7)	1897	08	20	Silver Lake	WI	Officiate funeral, 3 weeks	WC
Rev. C. H. Rust & Mr. C. W. Meacham	1897	09	18	Spencer	WI		WC
Rev. C. H. Rust	1897	10	17	?	WI	Church dedication	?
Rev. C. H. Rust & Mr. C. W. Meacham	1897	11	21	Brule	WI	(7) Future situation unknown	NP ?
Rev. C. H. Rust & Mr. C. W. Meacham	1897	12	26	Waukesha	WI	RR shop meetings about 50 men every noon, Lv 01-17-1898	WC
Rev. C. H. Rust & Mr. C. W. Meacham (7)	1898	01	18	Wheeler	WI	Officiate funeral, 3 weeks	WC
Rev. C. H. Rust & Rev. Leland (8)	1898	03	04	Thorp (Thorpe)	WI	(8) From Cumberland, WI	WC
Rev. C. H. Rust & Rev. Leland	1898	03	30	Abbotsford	WI	Swedes	WC
Rev. C. H. Rust & Rev. Leland	1898	05	07	Ogema	WI	(9) To Cumberland, WI	WC
Rev. C. H. Rust & Rev. Leland	1898	06	08	Prentice	WI		WC
Rev. C. H. Rust & Rev. Leland	1898	06	08	Stevens Point	WI	Stayed 10 days	WC
Rev. C. H. Rust & Rev. Leland	1898	10	07	Plainfield	WI	Stayed 2 weeks	WC
Rev. C. H. Rust & wife	1898	11	19	St. Louis	MO	First Chapel Car Conference near St. Louis, without car	—

PERSONNEL SERVING ON CARS	Y	M	D	TOWN	ST	COMMENTS FROM ACCOUNTS, LETTERS	R R
Rev. C. H. Rust & wife	1899	01	19	St. Paul	MN	Como shop meeting most pleasant and profitable	NP
Rev. C. H. Rust & Rev. Leland	1899	04	29	Lake Nebagamon	WI	Stayed 3 weeks	DSS&A
Rev. C. H. Rust & Rev. Leland (9)	1899	05	21	Superior	WI	(also called West Superior), Swedes	DSS&A
Rev. C. H. Rust & wife	1899	05	24	San Francisco	CA	A.B.P.S. Anniversary Meeting, without car, Lv 05-27-1899	—
Rev. C. H. Rust & Mr. A. I. Tipton (10)	1899	06	03	Silver Lake	MN	(10) Previous position unknown	GN
Rev. C. H. Rust & Mr. A. I. Tipton (11)	1899	08	23	Bemidji	MN	(11) Also Rev. W. Francis from Minneapolis, MN, Lv 10-21-1899	GN
Rev. C. H. Rust & Mr. A. I. Tipton	1899	10	26	Frazee	MN	Mr. Tipton met his future wife here, Lv 11-20-1899	NP
Rev. C. H. Rust & Mr. A. I. Tipton (12)	1899	11	22	Golconda	MN	First Sunday preaching in town	NP
Rev. C. H. Rust & wife	1899	12	05	Detroit	MN	Mrs. Rust received money for a gold watch from church members	NP
Rev. C. H. Rust & wife	1900	01	07	Brainerd	MN	RR shop and RR YMCA meetings, evening service at church	NP
Rev. C. H. Rust & wife	1900	01	24	Brainerd	MN	Car repairs and exterior paint, Lv 03-07-1900	—
Rev. C. H. Rust & wife	1900	01	29		MN	Speaking tour to PA, MA, NY, MD, NJ, and DC, without car	—
Rev. C. H. Rust & wife	1900	03	07	Brainerd	MN	Picked up car, Lv 03-07-1900	NP
Rev. C. H. Rust, wife & daughter	1900	03	30	Jordan	MN	Preaching at a funeral, large crowd	M&SL
Rev. C. H. Rust & wife	1900	05	30	Jordan	MN	(12) Future situation unknown	M&SL
Rev. C. H. Rust & wife	1900	06	04	Minneapolis	MN	Vacation at home	NP
Rev. C. H. Rust & wife	1900	06	20	Corwith	IA	Addition to building and church was helped	M&SL
Rev. C. H. Rust & wife	1900	07	15	Iowa Falls	IA		BCR&N
Rev. C. H. Rust & wife	1900	07	18	Holmes	IA	Holmes Baptist Church organized 09-12-1900, built building, 2 months	BCR&N
Rev. C. H. Rust & wife	1900	09	20	Bemidji	MN	Lv 10-21-1900	GN
Rev. C. H. Rust & wife	1900	10	23	Minneapolis	MN	At home	NP
Rev. C. H. Rust & wife	1900	11	03	Valley Junction	IA	Addition to building	CRI&P
Rev. C. H. Rust & wife	1901	01	06	Woolstock	IA	Church organized	C&NW
Rev. C. H. Rust & wife	1901	03	02	Greenville	IA		BR
Rev. C. H. Rust & wife	1901	04	03	Goldfield	IA		BCR&N
Rev. C. H. Rust & wife	1901	04	24	Livermore	IA	Testified to the good work	BCR&N
Rev. C. H. Rust & wife	1901	05	11	Langdon	IA	Built building	M&SL
Rev. C. H. Rust & wife	1901	06	12	Frazee	MN	At home	NP
Rev. C. H. Rust & wife	1901	09	05	Montgomery	IA		BCR&N
Rev. C. H. Rust & wife	1901	10	20	Cedar Falls	IA	IA Baptist State Convention, Lv 10-26-1901	BCR&N
Rev. C. H. Rust & wife	1901	11	30	Spirit Lake	IA	Addition to building, meetings with great success	BCR&N
Rev. C. H. Rust & wife	1902	01	02	Mason City	IA	A few weeks	CM&SP
Rev. C. H. Rust & wife	1902	02	04	Clinton	IA		CM&SP
Rev. C. H. Rust & wife	1902	02	13	St. Paul	MN	Car may be in shop	NP
Rev. C. H. Rust, wife & Rev. E. A. Spear (13)	1902	02	15			East speaking trip to MA, NY, PA, and MD, without car	—
Rev. C. H. Rust & Rev. E. A. Spear	1902	05	21	St. Paul	MN	A.B.P.S. Anniversary Meeting, Lv 05-24-1902	NP
Rev. C. H. Rust & Rev. E. A. Spear	1902	05	29	Ormsby	MN	Church organized, built building	M&SL
Rev. C. H. Rust & Rev. E. A. Spear	1902	06	19	Monterey	MN	(13) Also called Professor Spears	M&SL
Rev. C. H. Rust & Rev. E. A. Spear	1902	07	03	Bemidji	MN	Built building	GN
Rev. C. H. Rust & Rev. E. A. Spear	1902	07	13	Little Falls	MN		NP
Rev. C. H. Rust & Rev. E. A. Spear	1902	07	21	Battle Lake	MN		NP
Rev. C. H. Rust & Rev. E. A. Spear	1902	12	08	Milwaukee	WI	Church organized, built building, Lv 12-07-1902	NWL
Rev. C. H. Rust & Rev. E. A. Spear	1903	01	01	Portage	WI	South Baptist Church, preaching at church until new pastor arrives	NWL
Rev. C. H. Rust & Rev. E. A. Spear	1903	03	02	Other towns	MN	12-1902 to 03-1903	—
Rev. C. H. Rust & Rev. E. A. Spear	1903	03	02	Stevens Point	WI	Church services held for several months	—
Rev. C. H. Rust & Rev. E. A. Spear	1903	09	26	Kansas City	MO	Second Chapel Car Conference, without car, Lv 10-06-1902	WC
Rev. C. H. Rust & Rev. E. A. Spear	1903	10	06	Wisconsin Rapids	WI	Town previously called Grand Rapids	WC
Rev. C. H. Rust & Rev. E. A. Spear	1903	10	07	Milan	MO	RR meeting, all chapel car missionaries, without car	—
Rev. C. H. Rust & Rev. E. A. Spear	1903	10	08	Novinger	MO	Church dedication, all chapel car missionaries, without car	—
Rev. C. H. Rust & Rev. E. A. Spear	1903	09	10	Green City	MO	Church dedication, all chapel car missionaries, without car	—
Rev. C. H. Rust & Rev. E. A. Spear	1903	09	21	Milwaukee	WI	South Baptist Church, evangelistic services	NWL
Rev. C. H. Rust & Rev. E. A. Spear	1903	10	05	La Crosse	WI	First Baptist, evangelistic services	CM&SP
Rev. C. H. Rust & Rev. E. A. Spear	1903	10	01	Milwaukee	WI	WI Baptist State Convention, Lv 10-09-1903	CM&SP
Rev. C. H. Rust & Rev. E. A. Spear (14)	1903	11	27	Wisconsin Rapids	WI	Church organized 11-19-1903, raised money for building	CM&SP
Rev. C. H. Rust & Rev. E. A. Spear	1903	12	25	Wausau	WI	Town previously called Grand Rapids	CM&SP
Rev. C. H. Rust & Rev. E. A. Spear	1904	01	02	Merrill	WI	(14) Future situation unknown	NWL
Rev. C. H. Rust & wife	1904	01	10	Milwaukee	WI	First Baptist Church, special services, 2 weeks	WC
Rev. C. H. Rust & wife	1904	01	25	Minocqua	WI	Evangelistic services, 2 weeks	CM&SP
Rev. C. H. Rust & wife	1904	02	01	Bancroft	WI	Evangelistic services	CM&SP
Rev. C. H. Rust & wife	1904	02	10	Arbor Vitae	WI	South Baptist Church, evangelistic services	CM&SP
Rev. C. H. Rust	1904	03	01	Star Lake	WI	Rev. Rust at church dedication	NWL
Rev. C. H. Rust & wife	1904	03	11	Milwaukee	WI	First Baptist Church, evangelistic meetings, 2 weeks	CM&SP
Rev. C. H. Rust & wife	1904	04	20	Hudson	WI	First Baptist Church, evangelistic meetings	NWL
Rev. C. H. Rust & wife	1904	07	01	Scottsbluff	NE	Evangelistic meetings, several weeks	BR
Rev. C. H. Rust & wife	1904	09	05	Clear Lake	SD	Church greatly helped and strengthened	CRI&P
Rev. C. H. Rust & wife	1904	10	04	Watertown	SD	SD Baptist State Convention, Lv 10-10-1904	CM&SP
Rev. C. H. Rust	1904	10	12	Elkton	SD		NWL
Rev. C. H. Rust & wife	1904	12	01	Crookston	MN		NP
Rev. C. H. Rust & wife	1905	03	08	Carroll	NE	Stayed 3 weeks	NWL
Rev. C. H. Rust	1905	03	31	Omaha	NE	NE Baptist State board meeting 1 day, without car	—
Rev. C. H. Rust & wife	1905	04	02	Bancroft	NE	Found religious life at low ebb	NWL
Rev. C. H. Rust & wife	1905	04	25	Oakland	NE	Rev. Rust may have had a total of 8 assistants	NWL
Rev. C. H. Rust & wife	1905	05	21	St. Louis	MO	A.B.P.S. Anniversary Meeting, without car, Lv 05-24-1905	—
Rev. C. H. Rust (15) & wife	1905	05	28	Tekamah	NE	(15) To A.B.P.S. New England District Secretary, 07-01-1905	NWL
Rev. C. H. Rust (15) & wife	1905	06	17	Herman	NE	Lv 07-15-1905	NWL
(16)	1905	07	01	?		(16) Car vacant 3 months	MP
Rev. G. L. White (17), wife & son	1905	11	20	Louisville	NE	Church organized	NWL
Rev. G. L. White, wife & son	1906	01	02	Hartington	NE	Stayed 3 weeks	NWL

PERSONNEL SERVING ON CARS	Y	M	D	TOWN	ST	COMMENTS FROM ACCOUNTS, LETTERS	RR
Rev. G. L. White, wife & son	1906	01	17	Ponca	NE	(17) Pastor from NE. 10-01-1905	NWL
Rev. G. L. White, wife & son	1906	02	03	Wayne	NE		NWL
Rev. G. L. White, wife & son	1906	02	16	Randolph	NE	Church reorganized	NWL
Rev. G. L. White, wife & son	1906	03	06	Carroll	NE		NWL
Rev. G. L. White, wife & son	1906	03	17	Emerson	NE		NWL
Rev. G. L. White, wife & son	1906	04	24	Springfield	NE	Church organized	MP
Rev. G. L. White, wife & son	1906	05	21	Louisville	NE		MP
Rev. G. L. White, wife & son	1906	06	18	Wabash	NE		MP
Rev. G. L. White & wife	1906	07	13	Lorton	NE		MP
Rev. G. L. White & wife	1906	07	26	Auburn	NE		BR
Rev. G. L. White & wife	1906	08	15	Nebraska City	NE		BR
Rev. G. L. White & wife	1906	08	22	Waterloo	NE	Evangelistic services	UP
Rev. G. L. White & wife	1906	10	04	Albion	NE	Church pastorless	UP
Rev. G. L. White & wife	1906	10	15	Valparaiso	NE		UP
Rev. G. L. White, wife & Rev. J. S. Davis (18)	1906	11	20	Wellfleet	NE	Church organized, raised some money for building	BR
Rev. G. L. White, wife & Rev. J. S. Davis	1906	12	18	Stanton	NE	Attendance small but their faith is growing	NWL
Rev. G. L. White, wife & Rev. J. S. Davis	1907	01	26	Pilger	NE	(18) Past situation unknown	NWL
Rev. G. L. White, wife & Rev. J. S. Davis	1907	02	18	Plainview	NE	Church and parsonage repaired, 4 weeks	NWL
Rev. G. L. White, wife & Rev. J. S. Davis	1907	03	27	Creighton	NE	(19) Transferred to A.B.H.M.S. general secretary, UT and WY 06-01-1907	NWL
Rev. G. L. White, wife & Rev. J. S. Davis	1907	04	30	Tilden	NE	Blessing in the chapel car services	MP
Rev. G. L. White, wife & Rev. J. S. Davis	1907	06	02	Springfield	NE	Church organized	NWL
Rev. G. L. White, wife & Rev. J. S. Davis	1907	07	12	Lincoln	NE	(20) Future situation unknown	NWL
Rev. G. L. White, wife (19), & Rev. J. S. Davis (20)	1907	07	18	Albion	NE	Special effort to build-up BYPU	NWL
Rev. L. A. Drumwright (21) & wife	1907	09	04	Albion	NE	(21) From pastor Aurora, MO, on car 09-04-1907	NWL
Rev. L. A. Drumwright & wife	1907	10	14	Valparaiso	NE	Only 8 church members in good standing	UP
Rev. L. A. Drumwright & wife	1907	12	03	David City	NE		UP
Rev. L. A. Drumwright & wife	1907	12	26	Polk	NE		UP
Rev. L. A. Drumwright & wife	1908	01	10	Central City	NE		UP
Rev. L. A. Drumwright & wife	1908	02	16	Grand Island	NE		?
Rev. L. A. Drumwright & wife	1908	03	20	Cotesfield	NE		UP
Rev. L. A. Drumwright (22) & wife	1908	05	11	Maxwell	NE		--
(23)	1909	04	11	Laurel	MT	Third Chapel Car Conference, without car	BR
Rev. E. A. Spear (24) & wife	1909	05	01	Kansas City	MO	Few days	BR
Rev. E. A. Spear & wife	1909	06	17	Huntley	MT	Car in shops, Rev. L. A. Drumwright sick and on vacation.	BR
Rev. E. A. Spear & wife	1909	07	10	Billings	MT	RR man first in town to accept on faith, without car	--
Rev. E. A. Spear & wife	1908	07	05	Forsyth	MT	Bible given to a sheep herder, 8 1/2 months	GN
Rev. E. A. Spear & wife	1908	06	18	Laurel	MT		GN
Rev. E. A. Spear & wife	1908	09	07	Laurel	MT		GN
Rev. E. A. Spear & wife	1909	04	11	Billings	MT		GN
Rev. E. A. Spear & wife	1909	05	01	Helena	MT	Without car	--
Rev. E. A. Spear & wife	1909	07	10	Torrington (Torrence)	WY	(24) From Worland, WY, 05-01-1909	BR
Rev. E. A. Spear & wife	1910	02	10	Manderson	WY	Stayed 5 weeks	BR
Rev. E. A. Spear & wife	1910	03	15	Laurel	MT	Terrible wind from north, but car was full	NP
Rev. E. A. Spear & wife	1910	04	05	Basin	WY	(25) To 01-01-1911	BR
Rev. E. A. Spear & wife	1910	06	03	Garland	WY	Fourth Chapel Car Conference, without car	FS
Rev. E. A. Spear & wife	1910	05	13	Des Moines	IA	Later voted to disband and join with Powell, WY, church	BR
Rev. E. A. Spear & wife	1910	06	18	Powell	WY	Irrigation project, church organized 07-10-1910, 4 weeks	BR
Rev. E. A. Spear & wife	1910	08	01	Powell	WY	On vacation	BR
Rev. E. A. Spear & wife	1910	08	30	Thermopolis	WY	WY Baptist State Convention, Lv 09-05-1910	BR
Rev. E. A. Spear & wife	1910	09	07	Cheyenne	WY	Revival meetings	BR
Rev. E. A. Spear & wife	1910	10	02	Greybull	WY	Revival meetings	BR
Rev. E. A. Spear (25) & wife	1910	10	28	Lovell	WY	Revival meetings, poor rail service, only 1 train each day	BR
Rev. A. S. Sangston (26) & wife	1911	01	08	Lucerne	WY	Church organized 01-17-1911, 30 people with engine and car	CRI&P
Rev. A. S. Sangston, wife & son	1911	08	10	Worland	WY	WY Baptist State Southern Conference, LV 08-13-1911	D&IM
Rev. A. S. Sangston, wife & son	1912	04	10	Grey Bull	WY	(26) From PA 01-01-1911	D&RG
Rev. A. S. Sangston, wife & son	1912	05	13	Kansas City	MO	Fourth Chapel Car Conference, without car	CRI&P
Rev. A. S. Sangston, wife & son	1912	06	03	Garland	WY	A.B.P.S. Anniversary Meeting, without car	D&RG
Rev. A. S. Sangston, wife & son	1912	06	18	Des Moines	IA	Church revived, organized Sunday school	D&RG
Rev. A. S. Sangston & wife	1912	07	20	Bridgeport	NE	Church reorganized, and on vacation, 4 months	D&RG
Rev. A. S. Sangston & wife	1912	10	08	Scottsbluff	NE	Helped church very greatly	D&RG
Rev. A. S. Sangston	1912	10	20	Alliance	NE		UP
Rev. A. S. Sangston	1913	03	03	Vona	CO	Church organized, picnic lunch in car, worked on building	UP
Rev. A. S. Sangston (27) & wife	1913	11	08	Barnum	CO	Church greatly strengthened and built up	UP
(28)	1913	12	22	Monte Vista	CO	Built building, much interest being manifested	D&RG
Rev. J. S. Davis (29) & wife	1914	01	03	Del Norte	CO	Strong opposition to Baptist, a very difficult place	D&RG
Rev. J. S. Davis & wife	1914	01	22	Del Norte	CO	Had a glorious revival in car and most encouraging	UP
Rev. J. S. Davis & wife	1913	10	16	Ault	CO	(27) Resigned ill health 10-31-1913, to Russell, IA	UP
Rev. J. S. Davis & wife	1913	11	08	Ault	CO	(28) Car vacant 16 days	UP
Rev. J. S. Davis, wife & son	1913	11	08	Lafayette	CO	(29) Pastor from KC, MO, on car 11-01-1913, served on chapel car 5, Messenger of Peace	D&RG
Rev. J. S. Davis & wife	1913	12	22	Alamose	CO	Happy over the revival, 4 weeks	D&RG
Rev. J. S. Davis & wife	1914	02	23	Deer Trail	CO	Charles Davis, missionaries youngest son, sang and preached	UP
Rev. J. S. Davis & wife	1914	03	02	Crestone	CO	May have organized church, Lv 03-30-1914	D&RG
Rev. J. S. Davis & wife	1914	04	03	Fort Morgan	CO	Car at south end of Main St. and tracks	D&RG
Rev. J. S. Davis & wife	1914	06	18	Wiggins	CO		BR
Rev. J. S. Davis & wife	1914	07	01	Gilcrest	CO	Russian-German church revival services, start English-speaking services	UP
Rev. J. S. Davis & wife	1914	07	10	Kansas City	MO	Baptist Young Peoples Union convention, without car	UP
Rev. J. S. Davis & wife	1914	10	20	Holyoke	CO	Revival services	BR

PERSONNEL SERVING ON CARS	Y	M	D	TOWN	ST	COMMENTS FROM ACCOUNTS, LETTERS	R R
Rev. J. S. Davis & wife	1914	11	07	Sterling	CO	Work was greatly appreciated	UP
Rev. J. S. Davis & wife	1914	12	15	Iliff	CO		UP
Rev. J. S. Davis & wife	1915	01	07	Douglas	WY	Organized church 03-25-1915, Lv 07-20-1915	BR
Rev. J. S. Davis & wife	1916	08	05	Lucerne	WY	Church organized, built building, 6 weeks	BR
Rev. J. S. Davis & wife	1916	09	27	?	WY	Car in shop for repairs cost about $650	?
Rev. J. S. Davis & wife	1916	11	09	Douglas	WY	Returned to help them with troubles, Lv 01-10-1917	BR
Rev. J. S. Davis (30) & wife	1917	01	12	Dwyer	WY	(30) Resigned poor health 02-28-1917	C&S
(31)	1917	03	01	Dwyer	WY	(31) Car vacant, 1 month	C&S
Rev. W. M. Kennedy (32) & wife	1917	04	01	Dwyer	WY	(32) Pastor from Millville, NJ, 04-01-1917	C&S
Rev. W. M. Kennedy & wife	1917	04	08	Rock Springs	WY		UP
Rev. W. M. Kennedy (33) & wife	1917	07	01	Chugwater	WY	Church organized, vacation in the East 5 weeks	C&S
Rev. E. E. Barnhart (34)	1917	08	29	Chugwater	WY	Transferred to chapel car 1, Evangel, due to altitude 09-10-1917	C&S
Rev. W. J. Bell (35) & wife	1917	09	27	Chugwater	WY	From SD, ND director of Sunday school, temporary 1 month	C&S
Rev. W. J. Bell & wife	1917	09	29	Dwyer	WY		C&S
Rev. W. J. Bell & wife	1917	10	14	Superior	NE	(35) From Pipestone, MN, 09-27-1917	BR
Rev. W. J. Bell & wife	1917	10	22	Alma	NE		BR
Rev. W. J. Bell & wife	1917	10	31	Oxford	NE		BR
Rev. W. J. Bell & wife	1917	11	18	Brighton	CO	Hope of building a church	UP
Rev. W. J. Bell & wife	1917	12	28	Berthoud	CO	Government takes over operation of railroads due to WWI	--
Rev. W. J. Bell & wife	1918	01	07	Lafayette	CO	Great inspiration to the people	C&S
Rev. W. J. Bell & wife	1918	02	11	Arvada	CO		C&S
Rev. W. J. Bell & wife	1918	03	04	Louisville	CO	Resigned due to Mrs. Bell's health 07-01-1918	C&S
Rev. W. J. Bell (36), & wife	1918	03	27	Torrington	WY	Revival meetings. Church organized 05-19-1918 and Sunday school later	BR
(37)	1918	04	12			(37) Car vacant, 1 month	BR
Rev. F. I. Blanchard (38) & wife	1918	07	01	North Kansas City	MO	Stayed 6 months	BR
Rev. F. I. Blanchard & wife	1918	08	01	Other towns in MO	MO	From chapel car 2, Emmanuel, 08-01-1918	?
Rev. F. I. Blanchard & wife	1919	02	01	Little Blue	MO	Transferred to chapel car 1, Evangel, 08-01-1921	MP
Rev. F. I. Blanchard (39) & wife	1920	02	17	Armstrong	MO	Government returned ownership to railroads	--
(40)	1920	03	01	Armstrong	MO	Car in shop for repairs $416 and on vacation	C&A
Rev. A. B. Howell (41)(42) & wife	1920	06	28	Armstrong	MO	Car vacant at shop for 1 month, Lv 09-03-1921	C&A
Rev. A. B. Howell & wife	1921	09	03	Dallas	TX	Transferred from Puerto Rico 09-01-1921	C&A
Rev. A. B. Howell & wife	1921	09	04	Douglas	AZ	First stop for planning campaign	CRI&G
Rev. A. B. Howell & wife	1921	09	15	Bisbee	AZ	Picked up car at shop 09-03-1921	SP
Rev. A. B. Howell & wife	1921	09	21	Naco	AZ	Working with Mexicans in AZ 2 weeks	EP&SW
Rev. A. B. Howell & wife	1921	10	14	Nogales	AZ	Car stopped within 200 feet of Mexican line, 6 weeks	EP&SW
Rev. A. B. Howell & wife	1921	12	01	Tucson	AZ	Car on Main St. in front of court house, 6 weeks	EP&SW
Rev. A. B. Howell & wife	1922	01	13	Red Rock	AZ		SP
Rev. A. B. Howell & wife	1922	02	05	Case Grande	AZ	Without car	--
Rev. A. B. Howell & wife	1922	03	01	Phoenix	AZ		SP
Rev. A. B. Howell & wife	1922	04	29	Glendale	AZ		SF
Rev. A. B. Howell & wife	1922	05	01	Indianapolis	IN	New instructions, exterior lettering on chapel cars	SF
Rev. A. B. Howell & wife	1922	06	01	Phoenix	AZ	On vacation and in IN, 1 month	SF
Rev. A. B. Howell & wife	1922	08	15	Phoenix	AZ	A.B.P.S. Anniversary Meeting, without car, Lv 06-18-1922	SF
Rev. A. B. Howell & wife	1922	08	20	Phoenix	AZ		SF
Rev. A. B. Howell & wife	1922	09	01	Chandler	AZ	Lv 09-01-1922	SP
(44)	1922	11	01	Douglas	AZ	(44) Car vacant, 2 months	SP
Rev. W. C. Driver (45) & wife	1922	12	30	Chandler	AZ	Assisted local pastors	SF
Rev. W. C. Driver & wife	1923	02	15	Phoenix	AZ	Car painted for $117 or $150, not at a RR shop	SF
Rev. W. C. Driver & wife	1923	05	08	Nogales	AZ	Church organized 04-06-1923	SF
Rev. W. C. Driver & wife	1923	05	18	Douglas	AZ	AZ Baptist State Convention, without car	AE
Rev. W. C. Driver & wife	1923	06	01	Miami	AZ	Lv 05-31-1923	AE
Rev. W. C. Driver & wife	1923	07	10	Glendale	AZ	Car in shop for repairs and painting	--
Rev. W. C. Driver & wife	1924	02	21	Willcox	AZ	Church without pastor, without car	AE
Rev. W. C. Driver & wife	1924	03	08	Tucson	AZ	(45) From chapel car 4, Good Will, 11-01-1922	AE
Rev. W. C. Driver & wife	1924	05	06	Flagstaff	AZ	AZ Baptist State Convention, without car	EP&SW
Rev. W. C. Driver & wife	1925	02	01	Flagstaff	AZ	Lv 10-31-1925	AE
Rev. W. C. Driver & wife	1925	03	16	Flagstaff	AZ	Car retired and given to AZ Baptist State Convention for church and parsonage	--
Rev. W. C. Driver & wife	1925	03	25	Flagstaff	AZ		SP
Rev. W. C. Driver (46) & wife	1925	10	31	Flagstaff	AZ	(46) Resigned 10-31-1925	SP
	1926	02	10	Flagstaff	AZ	Chapel car at saw mill yard location for church services	SP
	1926	05	18	Flagstaff	AZ	Pastor Rev. V. A. Vanderhoof and wife from colporter missionary work	SF
	1926	06	01	Flagstaff	AZ	Car given to Glad Tidings Church	SF
	1927	02	18	Flagstaff	AZ	Car on RR siding near South Beaver St. and main track	SF
	1927	03	13	Flagstaff	AZ	Car on lot at South Beaver St. and Cottage Ave.	SF
	1928			Flagstaff	AZ	Car used for church and parsonage	SF
	1931					Glad Tidings Church purchased a church building	SF
	1932					Car dismantled, parts used in Glad Tidings Church building	SF
	1932					Glad Tidings Church moved into church building	--
	1960					Car parts removed from building and given to mission church	--
	1970					Mission church built new building and car parts not used	--

A.B.P.S. CAR 4, GOOD WILL

PERSONNEL SERVING ON CARS	Y	M	D	TOWN	ST	COMMENTS FROM ACCOUNTS, LETTERS	R R
	1893	06	01	Denver	CO	AMERICAN BAPTIST PUBLICATION SOCIETY — Asked for free will car donors, $8500 total	--
	1894	06	01	Dayton	OH	1700 shares @ $5 ea., paid before 06-01-1894	--
	1894	10	01	Dayton	OH	Barney & Smith Car Company now building car	--
	1894	12	25	Philadelphia	PA	Entire cost of car pledged	--
	1895	05	01	Dayton	OH	Car shipped from builder Barney & Smith Car Company	CCC&SL
Rev. E. S. Stucker (1) & wife	1895	06	01	Saratoga	NY	Car dedication A.B.P.S. Anniversary Meeting, Lv 06-04-1895	D&H
Rev. E. S. Stucker & wife	1895	06	05	Buffalo	NY	(1) From pastor Aurora, IL 06-01-1895	NYC&HR

PERSONNEL SERVING ON CARS	Y	M	D	TOWN	ST	COMMENTS FROM ACCOUNTS, LETTERS	RR
Rev. E. S. Stucker & wife	1895	06	11	Other town	KS	KS Baptist State Convention	UP
Rev. E. S. Stucker & wife	1895	06	15	North Topeka	KS	RR meeting, car between round house and machine shop	MK&T
Rev. E. S. Stucker & wife	1895	06	20	Denison	TX		MK&T
Rev. E. S. Stucker & wife	1895	06	30	Dallas	TX		?
Rev. E. S. Stucker & wife	1895	07	02	Other towns	TX	Frontier towns above Canadian river in the wild El Llano Estacado region	DT&FW
Rev. E. S. Stucker & wife	1895	08	11	Texline	TX	Church organized, RR town, everyone in town in all meetings in car, 2 weeks	T&P
Rev. E. S. Stucker & wife	1895	08	26	Fort Worth	TX		T&P
Rev. E. S. Stucker & wife	1895	09	07	Marshall	TX	RR shop meeting at noon and night meetings	MK&T
Rev. E. S. Stucker & wife	1895	10	10	Belton	TX	TX Baptist State Convention, Lv 10-12-1895	PVT
Rev. E. S. Stucker & wife	1895	11	10	Thurber	TX	Texas & Pacific Coal Company, owned town and church	T&P
Rev. E. S. Stucker & wife	1895	12	01	Big Sandy	TX	(2) To A.B.P.S. NW district secretary, 11-01-1896	MK&T
Rev. E. S. Stucker & wife	1896	01		Smithville	TX	Large meeting in opera house	SP
Rev. E. S. Stucker & wife	1896	02	13	San Antonio	TX	Near international depot and in the vicinity of other depots	?
Rev. E. S. Stucker (2) & wife	1896	03	01	Other towns	TX	03-01-1896 to 10-31-1896	SP
Rev. A. J. Diaz (3)	1896	05	06	Del Rio	TX	Church organized, car in local train yard, 4 weeks	SP
Rev. A. J. Diaz (4)	1896	11	01	San Antonio	TX	(3) From Cuba	SP
(5)	1897	11	01	Border towns	TX	(4) Resigned, returning to Cuba to fight in war as an officer	?
Rev. E. G. Townsend & wife (6)	1898	03	17	Tenaha	TX	(5) Car vacant 5 months	HE&WT
Rev. E. G. Townsend & wife	1898	04	05	Galveston	TX	(6) From pastor Dallas, TX, 03-20-1898	MK&T
Rev. E. G. Townsend & wife	1898	04	28	Galveston	TX	Second Baptist Church, building was later lost in 09-08-1900 storm	MK&T
Rev. E. G. Townsend & wife	1898	10	14	Abilene	TX	South Baptist Church, building was later lost in 09-08-1900 storm	MK&T
Rev. E. G. Townsend & wife	1898	11	19	Del Rio	TX	Central Baptist Church, speaking at his old church	T&P
Rev. E. G. Townsend & wife	1898	12	07	Comstock	TX	Preached at night in a tent and at 3 P.M. in car for men only	—
Rev. E. G. Townsend & wife (7)	1899	01	15	Dallas	TX	First Chapel Car Conference near St. Louis, Mo, without car	GH&SA
Rev. E. G. Townsend & B. W. Smith (8)	1899			Hearne	TX	Found church strengthened by the visit of Rev. Stucker	?
Rev. E. G. Townsend	1899	12	18	Somerville	TX	Less than 12 houses in town, but ranchers came from miles	H&TC
Rev. E. G. Townsend & Mr. V. C. Hart (9)	1900	01	03	Brownswood	TX	(7) Mrs. Townsend died while in childbirth in August 1899	H&TC
Rev. E. G. Townsend (10) & Mr. V. C. Hart	1900	01	11	Ft. Worth	TX	(8) Superintendent of chapel cars from Minneapolis, MN	GC&SF
Rev. G. B. Rogers (11)	1900	01	23	Houston	TX	Near RR round house, car full and all windows up for men outside	?
Rev. G. B. Rogers	1900	02	06	Cleveland	TX	(9) Mr. V. C. Hart, singer from Israel, TX, and returned	GC&SF
Rev. G. B. Rogers	1900	02	20	Livingston	TX	(10) Resigned 02-01-1900, pastor East Waco, TX	GC&SF
Mr. V. C. Hart	1900	02	20	Hot Springs	AR	(11) From pastor MS, LA, and TX	GC&SF
Mr. V. C. Hart	1900	03	16	Dallas	TX	Railroad meetings, 8 days	GC&SF
Rev. G. B. Rogers	1900	04	19	Summerville	TX	Railroad meetings, 4 days	GC&SF
Rev. G. B. Rogers	1900	05	08	Galveston	TX	Pastor had been discouraged but church revived, 10 days	GC&SF
Rev. G. B. Rogers & Mr. T. Moffat (12)	1900	06	03	Galveston	TX	(12) From St. Louis, MO, singer and organist	HE&WT
Rev. G. B. Rogers & Mr. T. Moffat	1900	06	10	Galveston	TX	Great storm 09-08-1900 and 09-09-1900, car light damage	LR&HW
Rev. G. B. Rogers & Mr. T. Moffat	1900	08	31	Galveston	TX	Received $725 car repair bill, A.B.P.S. has no money to pay	MK&T
Rev. G. B. Rogers & Mr. V. C. Hart (13)	1900	09	01	Galveston	TX	TX Baptist State Convention asked for donations, Glad Tidings, helps	GC&SF
Rev. S. G. Neil (14)(15) & Mr. V. C. Hart	1900	09	08	Galveston	TX	(13) Mr. V. C. Hart, starting 6 month trial with Rev. Roger 05-01-1900	GC&SF
Rev. G. B. Rogers & Mr. V. C. Hart	1900	09	08	Waco	TX	(14) Rev. Rogers sick, Rev. Neil from chapel car 3, Glad Tidings, helps	—
Rev. G. B. Rogers & Mr. V. C. Hart	1900	11	02	Dallas	TX	Also B. W. Smith, asked for repair funds, without car	—
Rev. G. B. Rogers & Mr. V. C. Hart	1900	11	08	Denison	TX	Also B. W. Smith, asked for repair funds, without car	GC&SF
Rev. G. B. Rogers & Mr. V. C. Hart	1900	12	03	Dublin	TX	Also B. W. Smith, asked for repair funds, without car	GC&SF
Rev. G. B. Rogers & Mr. V. C. Hart	1900	12	05	Denison	TX	Also B. W. Smith, asked for repair funds, without car	GC&SF
Rev. G. B. Rogers & Mr. V. C. Hart	1900	12	07	Plano	TX	Also B. W. Smith, asked for repair funds, without car	—
Rev. G. B. Rogers & Mr. V. C. Hart	1900	12	09	Whitewright	TX	(15) Returned to chapel car 3, Glad Tidings	—
Rev. G. B. Rogers & Mr. V. C. Hart (16)	1900	12	13	Brownswood	TX	Also Boston W. Smith, asked for repair funds	MK&T
Rev. G. B. Rogers & Mr. H.L. Heitt (17)	1900	12	22	Lancaster	TX		SL&SW
Rev. G. B. Rogers & wife (18)	1900	12	30	Greenville	TX	(16) Resigns 09-01-1901	MK&T
Rev. G. B. Rogers & Mr. H.L. Heitt	1901	02	09	Gainesville	TX	Car in shop for repairs	MK&T
Rev. G. B. Rogers (19), wife, Mr. H.L. Heitt (20)	1901	02	23	Denton	TX	(17) Previous situation of singer unknown, 10-01-1901	MK&T
Rev. T. S. Fretz & wife	1901	06	30	Waco	TX	A united band of 22 workers, car full, had to moved to hall	MK&T
Rev. T. S. Fretz (21) & wife	1901	08	05	Dallas	TX	Car in shops, 2 months	AT&SF
Rev. T. S. Fretz & wife	1901	10	28	Belton	TX	(18) Wife now on car	AT&SF
Rev. T. S. Fretz & wife	1902	02	14	Carthage	TX	Second Chapel Car Conference, without car, Lv 10-09-1902	?
Rev. T. S. Fretz & wife	1902	06	01	Other towns	TX	RR meeting, all chapel car missionaries, without car	—
Rev. T. S. Fretz (22) & wife	1902	06	10	Kansas City	MO	Church dedication, all chapel car missionaries, without car	—
(23)	1902	09	27	Milan	MO	Church dedication, all chapel car missionaries, without car	UP
Rev. L. T. Barkman (24), wife & son	1902	10	06	Novinger	MO	(19) To TX Baptist general missionary, 01-01-1904	C&S
Rev. L. T. Barkman, wife & son (25)	1902	10	07	Green City	MO	(20) Singer also leaves car	OO&KC
Rev. L. T. Barkman, wife & son	1903	01	04	East Texas	TX	Organized church, provided for it weekly services	C&S
Rev. L. T. Barkman, wife & son	1903	02	07	Waco	TX	Appreciated the honest and earnest efforts of people	GW
Rev. L. T. Barkman, wife & son	1904	01	05	Bennett	CO	Badly divided church but doubled membership	C&S
Rev. L. T. Barkman, wife & son	1904	02	27	Lafayette	CO	(21) From 01-01-1904	MP
Rev. L. T. Barkman, wife & son	1905	03	20	Pattonsburg	MO		D&RG
Rev. L. T. Barkman, wife & son	1906	01	08	Wellington	CO	Workers without a church home	D&RG
Rev. L. T. Barkman, wife & son	1906	02	14	Johnstown	CO	Church organized, 6 months	D&RG
Rev. L. T. Barkman, wife & son	1906	03	10	Arvada	CO		D&RG
Rev. L. T. Barkman, wife & son	1906	04	07	Ordway	CO	(22) Retired 07-01-1907 or 12-31-1907	D&RG
Rev. L. T. Barkman, wife & son	1906	11	13	Fruita	CO	(23) Car vacant 7 months	D&RG
Rev. L. T. Barkman, wife & son	1907	01	24	Johnstown	CO	Picked up car	AT&SF
Rev. L. T. Barkman, wife & son	1907	06	29	Denver	CO	Past situation not known	—
Rev. L. T. Barkman, wife & son	1908	03	01	Denver	CO		C&S
Rev. L. T. Barkman, wife & son	1908	03	03	Alamosa	CO		OO&KC
Rev. L. T. Barkman, wife & son	1908	04	07	Del Norte	CO	(25) Son Floyd T. of Rev. Barkman	D&RG
Rev. L. T. Barkman, wife & son	1908	05	11	Trinidad	CO		D&RG
Rev. L. T. Barkman, wife & son	1908	05	14	Kansas City	MO	Third Chapel Car Conference, without car, Lv 05-09-1909	AT&SF

PERSONNEL SERVING ON CARS	Y	M	D	TOWN	ST	COMMENTS FROM ACCOUNTS, LETTERS	R R
Rev. L. T. Barkman, wife & son	1908	06	16	Sopris	CO	In Las Animas County	C&S
Rev. L. T. Barkman, wife & son	1908	07	08	Cokedale	CO		?
Rev. L. T. Barkman, wife & son	1908	08	21	Colorado City	CO		D&RG
Rev. L. T. Barkman, wife & son	1908	09	27	Walsenburg	CO		D&RG
Rev. L. T. Barkman, wife & son	1908	10	11	Arvada	CO		C&S
Rev. L. T. Barkman, wife & son	1908	10	25	Boulder	CO	CO Baptist State Convention, Lv 10-30-1908	C&S
Rev. L. T. Barkman, wife & son	1908	12	29	Pueblo	CO	Lake Avenue Baptist Church	AT&SF
Rev. L. T. Barkman, wife & son	1909	02	03	Florence	CO		D&RG
Rev. L. T. Barkman, wife & son	1909	03	08	Golden	CO		C&S
Rev. L. T. Barkman, wife & son	1909	04	12	Johnstown	CO	In Weld County	GW
Rev. L. T. Barkman, wife & son	1909	05	19	Denver	CO	Mt. Olivet Baptist Church	D&RG
Rev. L. T. Barkman, wife & son	1909	07	27	Colorado Springs	CO	Mt. Olive Baptist Church	AT&SF
Rev. L. T. Barkman, wife & son	1909	08	17	Montrose	CO	Chapel building erected	D&RG
Rev. L. T. Barkman, wife & son	1910	01	12	Olathe	CO	Addition to building started	D&RG
Rev. L. T. Barkman, wife & son	1910	02	05	Fruita	CO		D&RG
Rev. L. T. Barkman, wife & son	1910	03	26	Austin	CO	Church organized 04-22-1910, Lv 06-18-1910	D&RG
Rev. L. T. Barkman, wife & son	1910	06	20	Hotchkiss	CO		D&RG
Rev. L. T. Barkman, wife & son	1910	09	05	Provo	UT	UT Baptist State Convention, Lv 09-09-1910	D&RG
Rev. L. T. Barkman, wife & son	1911	01	01	Springville	UT		?
Rev. L. T. Barkman, wife & son	1911	03	08	Rio Grande ?	NV	At mission and many RR workers from railroad shops	?
Rev. L. T. Barkman, wife & son	1911	05	15	McCammon	ID	Church organized	OSL
Rev. L. T. Barkman, wife & son	1911	07	09	?	ID	Car in shops for repairs	?
Rev. L. T. Barkman, wife & son	1911	08	10	New Plymouth	ID	ID State Baptist Convention gospel tent used, without car	--
Rev. L. T. Barkman, wife & son	1911	09	11	Salt Lake City	UT	UT Baptist State Convention, Lv 09-15-1911	OSL
Rev. L. T. Barkman, wife & son	1911	10	01	Salt Lake City	UT	Controversial Rev. Barkman manages to stay out of trouble	OSL
Rev. L. T. Barkman, wife & son	1911	10	05	?	ID	ID Baptist State Convention	?
Rev. L. T. Barkman, wife & son	1911	10	10	Elko	NV		SP
Rev. L. T. Barkman, wife & son	1911	11	01	Murray	UT	Rev. Barkman in trouble because of attacks on lodges	OSL
Rev. L. T. Barkman, wife & son (26)	1912	01	02	Winnemucca	NV	(26) Son Floyd stays temporarily as pastor	SP
Rev. L. T. Barkman & wife	1912	02	22	Imlay	NV	NV Baptist State Board does not want Rev. Barkman, 04-22-1912	SP
Rev. L. T. Barkman & wife	1912	03	06	Mason	NV	Rev. Barkman had trouble working with people	NCB
Rev. L. T. Barkman & wife	1912	03	15	Wabuska	NV		SP
Rev. L. T. Barkman & wife	1912	04	04	Tremonton	UT		OSL
Rev. L. T. Barkman & wife	1912	05	15	Kansas City	MO	Fourth Chapel Car Conference and churches, without car	--
Rev. L. T. Barkman & wife	1912	06	21	Des Moines	IA	A.B.P.S. Anniversary Meeting, without car, Lv 05-30-1912	OSL
Rev. L. T. Barkman & wife	1912	06	06	Arco	ID	East ID Baptist Association, Lv 06-10-1912	OSL
Rev. L. T. Barkman & wife	1912	06	12	Darlington	ID		--
Rev. L. T. Barkman & wife	1912	08	01	?	ID	Church organized, Lv 09-29-1912	OSL
Rev. L. T. Barkman, wife & son (27)	1912	09	29	Payette	ID	(27) Vacation in Southern CA for Mrs. Barkman's health, 1 month	OSL
Rev. L. T. Barkman, wife & son	1912	11	01	Spencer	ID	ID Baptist State Convention, without car Lv 10-04-1912	OSL
Rev. L. T. Barkman (28), wife & son	1912	11	29	Dubois	ID	(28) To pastor Los Angeles, CA, 01-01-1913	OSL
Rev. L. T. Barkman, wife & son	1912	12	26	Dubois	ID	Church organized	OSL
(29)	1913	01	03	Dubois	ID	(29) Car vacant waiting for missionary, 3 days	OSL
Rev. F. H. Farley (30)(31) & wife	1913	01	06	Pocatello	ID	Picked up car	OSL
Rev. F. H. Farley & wife	1913	01	06	Downey	ID	Light car repairs and car supplies	OSL
Rev. F. H. Farley & wife	1913	02	05	American Falls	ID	(30) Temporarily in charge of car 01-01-1913 to 05-01-1913	OSL
Rev. F. H. Farley & wife	1913	02	08	Milner	ID	(31) From Philadelphia, PA	OSL
Rev. F. H. Farley & wife	1913	02	26	Buhl	ID	(32) End service 05-01-1913, off car 05-11-1913	OSL
Rev. F. H. Farley & wife	1913	03	27	Filer	ID	(33) From evangelistic work Tacoma, WA, 05-01-1913	OSL
Rev. F. H. Farley (32) & wife	1913	04	21	American Falls	ID	Church building baptistry, 3 weeks	--
Rev. F. H. Farley (33) & wife	1913	05	01	Salt Lake City	UT	Large crowd in church, offering small	OSL
Rev. J. F. Day	1913	06	30	Pocatello	ID	Large attendance in car, coal mix up for car heating	OSL
Rev. J. F. Day	1913	07	02	Salt Lake City	UT	Helping English-speaking church	OSL
Rev. J. F. Day	1913	07	09	Salt Lake City	UT	Car waiting repairs, no repairs, 2 months Lv 07-01-1913	OSL
Rev. J. F. Day	1913	08	16	Picabo	ID	Without car	OSL
Rev. J. F. Day	1913	08	23	Shoshone	ID	ID Baptist State Convention, Lv 10-04-1913	OSL
Rev. J. F. Day	1913	08	28	Gooding	ID	Hard work	OSL
Rev. J. F. Day	1913	09	29	Boise	ID	Meeting with shop forces for repairing and painting car	OSL
Rev. J. F. Day & Mr. L. Crownover (35)	1913	09	30	Blackfoot	ID	Rev. Day home at McMinnville, OR, without car	--
Mr. L. Crownover	1913	10	07	Bellevue	ID	Working to have repairs started on car	OSL
Rev. J. F. Day & Mr. L. Crownover	1913	11	05	Bellevue	ID	Unable to get reasonable crowds or interest started	OSL
Rev. J. F. Day & Mr. L. Crownover	1913	11	13	Hailey	ID	Started car repairs and painting $500	D&RG
Rev. J. F. Day & Mr. L. Crownover	1913	11	25	Picabo	ID	Best crowds yet and with 6 inches snow and sub zero weather	D&RG
Mr. L. Crownover	1913	12	18	Shoshone	ID	Watch night service with good people	OSL
Rev. J. F. Day & Mr. L. Crownover	1913	12	23	Huntington	OR	Rev. Day home at McMinnville, OR, without car	OSL
Rev. J. F. Day	1913	12	31	Gooding	ID	Installed new Coleman tube type gas lights on car, very good lights	OSL
Rev. J. F. Day & Mr. L. Crownover	1914	01	12	Gooding	ID	Rev. Day at McMinnville, OR, for medical examination, without car	OSL
Rev. L. Crownover	1914	01	26	Glenns Ferry	ID	Very good beginning	OSL
Rev. J. F. Day & Mr. L. Crownover	1914	02	21	Nampa	ID	Great crowds and prayerful people	OSL
Rev. J. F. Day	1914	02	28	Ontario	OR	Full house with large results	OSL
Rev. J. F. Day	1914	03	06	Huntington	OR	RR town, Rev. Day sick and has lost 20 lbs.	OSL
Rev. J. F. Day	1914	04	06	Haines	OR	At 3500 ft. we had heavy snow 3 feet deep all around us	OSL
Rev. J. F. Day	1914	04	14	Salem	OR	OR Central Baptist Association, without car, Lv 04-18-1914	OSL
Rev. J. F. Day & Mr. L. Crownover (36)	1914	04	21	North Powder	OR	(36) Singer left	--
Rev. J. F. Day & Mr. W. Lickey (37)	1914	05	01	Enterprise	OR	(37) Singer from Gooding, OR, 31 days	OWR&N
Rev. J. F. Day (38) & wife (39)	1914	05	20	Elgin	OR	(38) Resigned to pastor at Carlton, OR, 07-01-1914	OWR&N
Rev. J. F. Day & Mr. W. Lickey	1914	06	03	La Grande	OR	(39) Assistant, 30 days	OWR&N
(40)(41)	1914	07	01	Portland	OR	(40) Car vacant, stored and car repairs, 4 months	OWR&N
(40)(41)	1914	07	22	Portland	OR	(41) Rev. Day checks on car at shop and held RR shop meetings	SP
(40)(41)	1914	08	06	Portland	OR	Car repairs and varnishing $191.09, Lv 11-04-1914	SP

PERSONNEL SERVING ON CARS	Y	M	D	TOWN	ST	COMMENTS FROM ACCOUNTS, LETTERS	R R
Rev. W. C. Driver (42)(43) & wife	1914	11	01	Portland	OR	Sunday school organized, without car	—
Rev. W. C. Driver & wife	1914	11	04	Portland	OR	Picked up car at shops, no meetings	SP
Rev. W. C. Driver & wife	1914	11	20	Adams	OR	Calvary and Tabernacle churches, 1900 attended in 1 month	PRL&P
Rev. W. C. Driver & wife	1914	12	21	Milton	OR	After leaving, 3 Sundays preaching while at Athena, OR	WWV
Rev. W. C. Driver & wife	1915	01	11	Freewater	OR	After leaving, 3 Sundays preaching while at Athena, OR	WWV
Rev. W. C. Driver & wife	1915	02	10	Athena	OR	(42) Offered car on 07-29-1914 to start 11-01-1914	OWR&N
Rev. W. C. Driver & wife	1915	02	26	Ione	OR	(43) Evangelist from Mt. Holly, VT, on car 11-04-1914	OWR&N
Rev. W. C. Driver & wife	1915	03	31	Arlington	OR	Poor half crop every other year and none between	OWR&N
Rev. W. C. Driver & wife	1915	04	04	Redmond	OR		OWR&N
Rev. W. C. Driver & wife	1915	04	26	Prineville	OR	Organ in bad shape, should not repair, need new one	UP ?
Rev. W. C. Driver & wife	1915	05	07	Portland	OR	OR Baptist Association, without car	—
Rev. W. C. Driver & wife	1915	05	18	Los Angles	CA	A.B.P.S. Anniversary Meeting, without car, Lv 05-27-1915	—
Rev. W. C. Driver & wife	1915	06	12	Gresham	OR		PRL&P
Rev. W. C. Driver & wife	1915	07	20	Pleasant Home	OR	Church dedication 08-05-1915, very successful	PRL&P
Rev. W. C. Driver & wife	1915	08	12	Hood River	OR	Most successful meetings	OWR&N
Rev. W. C. Driver & wife	1915	09	17	Portland	OR	Car repairs, painting and varnish inside, $90, Lv 10-06-1915	SP ?
Rev. W. C. Driver & wife	1915	10	08	Veneta	OR		SP
Rev. W. C. Driver & wife	1915	10	17	Eugene	OR	OR Baptist State Convention, Lv 10-23-1915	SP
Rev. W. C. Driver & wife	1915	11	20	Cottage Grove	OR	Rev. Driver sick but still worked for 2 weeks	SP
Rev. W. C. Driver & wife	1915	12	13	Portland	OR	Maple Lane, bad weather, sharp curve damaged hook on car	SP ?
Rev. W. C. Driver & wife	1916	02	10	Carlton	OR	Just built building no money left, hard times	SP
Rev. W. C. Driver & wife	1916	03	12	Cherry Grove	OR	Most people for miles around have been at the meetings	SP ?
Rev. W. C. Driver & wife	1916	04	22	McMinnville	OR	Just to get people interested in our car work, 2 days	SP
Rev. W. C. Driver & wife	1916	04	28	Amity	OR	Car roof leaks, needs to be fixed	SP
Rev. W. C. Driver & wife	1916	06	07	Wellsdale	OR	Baptized in Willamette River, 1 month plus 2 Sundays	SP
Rev. W. C. Driver & wife	1916	06	11	Newberg	OR	OR West Willamette Baptist Association, without car, Lv 06-15-1916	—
Rev. W. C. Driver & wife	1916	06	16	Lafayette	OR	County jail house meeting and church meetings on car work	SP
Rev. W. C. Driver & wife	1916	07	03	Portland	OR	Car in shops for roof repairs and on vacation	SP
Rev. W. C. Driver & wife	1916	07	24	Portland	OR	OR Baptist State Convention, Lv 10-21-1916	SP
Rev. W. C. Driver & wife	1916	10	16	Salem	OR		SP
Rev. W. C. Driver & wife	1916	10	22	Powers	OR	Logging town, church organized 10-29-1916	SP
Rev. W. C. Driver & wife	1916	11	01	Broadbent	OR	Started well, organized church 12-03-1916	SP
Rev. W. C. Driver & wife	1916	12	05	Coquille	OR		SP
Rev. W. C. Driver & wife	1916	12	11	Beaver Hill	OR		SP&S
Rev. W. C. Driver & wife	1917	01	14	Marshfield	OR	Show houses kept chapel car crowds down	SP
Rev. W. C. Driver & wife	1917	02	04	Hauser	OR	Some people walked 4 to 5 miles each night to be at car	SP&S
Rev. W. C. Driver & wife	1917	02	20	Lakeside	OR		SP&S
Rev. W. C. Driver & wife	1917	03	12	Springfield	OR	Car in Twohey Brothers shop for repairs and painting	SP
Rev. W. C. Driver & wife	1917	04	10	North Palestine	OR	People great to come forward and give on collections	—
Rev. W. C. Driver & wife	1917	04	16	Creswell	OR	OR Central Baptist Association, Lv 04-14-1917	SP
Rev. W. C. Driver & wife	1917	05	18	Albany	OR	Visits to grade and high schools to give talks to the children	SP
Rev. W. C. Driver & wife	1917	05	29	Clatskanie	OR	Clatskanie Junction	SP&S
Rev. W. C. Driver & wife	1917	06	07	Portland	OR	Shop for inspection and repair estimate $900.	SP
Rev. W. C. Driver & wife	1917	07	11	Astoria	OR	Government takes over operation of railroads due to WWI	—
Rev. W. C. Driver & wife	1917	08	16	Fort Stevens	OR	Soldier meetings, 2 weeks	P&ER
Rev. W. C. Driver & wife	1917	08	31	Portland	OR	Lv 01-27-1918	?
Rev. W. C. Driver & wife	1917	09	02	Portland	OR	Churches, Soldiers Pacific Home, without car	—
Rev. W. C. Driver & wife	1917	10	14	Talent	OR		SP
Rev. W. C. Driver & wife	1917	10	22	The Dalles	OR	Lv 04-28-1917	P&ER
Rev. W. C. Driver & wife	1917	11	17	Phoenix	OR	OR Central Baptist Association, Lv 10-27-1917	SP
Rev. W. C. Driver & wife	1917	12	09	Gold Hill	OR		SP
Rev. W. C. Driver & wife	1917	12	19	Klamath Falls	OR	Good meetings, 2 weeks	SP
Rev. W. C. Driver & wife	1917	12	28	Medford	OR	Very hot, in the 100s, 1 month	SP
Rev. W. C. Driver & wife	1918	01	04	Ashland	OR		—
Rev. W. C. Driver & wife	1918	02	02	Butte Falls	OR		SP
Rev. W. C. Driver & wife	1918	03	08	Jacksonville	OR		—
Rev. W. C. Driver & wife	1918	04	02	Grants Pass	OR		SP
Rev. W. C. Driver & wife	1918	05	21	Eagle Point	OR	OR Baptist Rogue River Association, without car, Lv 08-12-1918	—
Rev. W. C. Driver & wife	1918	06	07	Central Point	OR	While on vacation helping church, preaching and singing without car	—
Rev. W. C. Driver & wife	1918	07	09	Gold Hill	OR	While on vacation helping church, preaching and singing without car	SP
Rev. W. C. Driver & wife	1918	07	25	Rogue River	OR		SP
Rev. W. C. Driver & wife	1918	08	08	Klamath Falls	OR		SP
Rev. W. C. Driver & wife	1918	08	12	Butte Falls	OR	In the vicinity	SP
Rev. W. C. Driver & wife	1918	08	19	Eagle Point	OR		SP
Rev. W. C. Driver & wife	1918	08	26	Merlin	OR		PVT
Rev. W. C. Driver & wife	1918	08	30	Myrtle Creek	OR		SP
Rev. W. C. Driver & wife	1918	09	03	Roseburg	OR	Spanish flu health orders closed us down, 1 month	SP
Rev. W. C. Driver & wife	1918	10	13	Portland	OR	Helping a A.B.H.M.S. family and Mrs. Driver's tonsil operation	—
Rev. W. C. Driver & wife	1918	10	16	Portland	OR	Been collecting money for army and navy Bibles, Lv 11-31-1918	—
Rev. W. C. Driver & wife	1918	11	14	Lebanon	OR	Beaver Hill Coal Mine, coal and logging RR had bad tracks	PVT
Rev. W. C. Driver & wife	1919	01	01	Beaver Hill	OR	New orders on cost for car movement and track cost	SP
Rev. W. C. Driver & wife	1919	01	08	Portland	OR	Moved car to unused street car track, car stored due tariff 3 months	—
Rev. W. C. Driver & wife	1919	01	18	Portland	OR	With Mr. Hennessey, superintendent of Catholic chapel cars	PRL&P
Rev. W. C. Driver & wife	1919	01	24	Portland	OR	Helping at local churches in area and Hood River, without car	PRL&P
Rev. W. C. Driver & wife	1919	02	12	Portland	OR	Spoke at shipyard men's meeting and in Russian church, without car	—
Rev. W. C. Driver & wife	1919	03	10	Portland	OR	Working with local churches as Sunday supply, without car	—
Rev. W. C. Driver & wife	1919	04	03	Portland	OR	Received information as to free car transportation again	—
Rev. W. C. Driver & wife	1919	04	14	Portland	OR	Car damaged by fire from a live overhead trolley electric wire	PRL&P
Rev. W. C. Driver & wife	1919	04	15	Arleta	OR	Supply until new pastor comes 06-01-1919, without car	PRL&P
Rev. W. C. Driver & wife	1919	04	28	Gresham	OR	OR Baptist Willamette Association, without car, Lv 05-01-1919	—
Rev. W. C. Driver & wife	1919	06	08	Portland	OR	Car in shops for general repairs and fire damage repairs	SP

PERSONNEL SERVING ON CARS	Y	M	D	TOWN	ST	COMMENTS FROM ACCOUNTS, LETTERS	RR
Rev. W. C. Driver & wife	1919	07	02	Sellwood	OR	No pastor, will supply church until car is out of shop, without car	—
Rev. W. C. Driver & wife	1919	10	19	Portland	OR	OR Baptist State Convention, without car, Lv 10-24-1919	—
Rev. W. C. Driver & wife	1919	12	20	Portland	OR	Car out of shop, total time waiting shop and car repairs, 8 months	SP
Rev. W. C. Driver & wife	1920	01	03	Independence	OR		SP
Rev. W. C. Driver & wife	1920	03	01		OR	Government returned ownership to railroads	—
Rev. W. C. Driver & wife	1920	05	06	Lewisburg	OR	Car needs a new vestibule lantern	SP
Rev. W. C. Driver & wife	1920	07	01	Eddyville	OR	Baptized in Yaquina River	SP
Rev. W. C. Driver & wife	1920	09	02	Portland	OR	Rev. Driver not feeling well	SP
Rev. W. C. Driver & wife	1920	09	06	Corvallis	OR	OR State Baptist Convention, without car, Lv 09-11-1920	SP
Rev. W. C. Driver & wife	1920	09	09	Portland	OR	Repair estimate $1700, shop short men, work not done on car	SP
Rev. W. C. Driver & wife	1920	09	15	Summit	OR	Rev. Driver sick	SP
Rev. W. C. Driver & wife	1920	11	07	Veneta	OR	Wives no longer given official status as assistants on chapel cars, Rev. Driver angry	SP
Rev. W. C. Driver (44) & wife	1921	02	06	Salem	OR	(44) Rev. Driver sick, not working and car out of service	SP
Rev. W. C. Driver (44) & wife	1921	04	25	Portland	OR	Rev. Driver wants salary increase but he is not well	SP
Rev. W. C. Driver (44) & wife	1921	05	31	Salem	OR	Doctor orders Rev. Driver to full rest for 3 months	SP
Rev. W. C. Driver (44) & wife	1921	12	11	Portland	OR	Car in shop for repairs $735	SP
Rev. W. C. Driver (44) & wife	1922	03	11	Portland	OR	Car ready to leave shops but Rev. Driver is sick	SP
Rev. W. C. Driver (44) & wife	1922	03	12	Portland	OR	Car stored	SP
Rev. W. C. Driver (44) & wife	1922	05	01	Portland	OR	New instructions for exterior lettering on chapel cars	SP
Rev. W. C. Driver (44) & wife	1922	05	02	Portland	OR	Rev. Driver starts on half salary	SP
Rev. W. C. Driver (44) & wife	1922	10	16	Portland	OR	Car stored in Brooklyn yard, at no cost to 05-01-1923	SP
Rev. W. C. Driver (44) & wife	1922	10	23	Portland	OR	Rev. Driver home from an operation in hospital	SP
Rev. W. C. Driver (44) & wife	1922	10	30	Portland	OR	(45) Car out of service, sickness, funds and repairs, 21 months	SP
Rev. W. C. Driver (44) & wife (45)	1922	10	31	Portland	OR	(46) Transferred to chapel car 3, Glad Tidings, 11-01-1922	SP
(47)	1922	11	01	Portland	OR	(47) Car vacant 8 -1/2 months, no missionary	SP
Rev. J. B. Speed (48), wife & daughter	1923	06	13	Portland	OR	Picked up car in Brooklyn yard	SP
Rev. J. B. Speed, wife & daughter	1923	06	15	Swisshome	OR	(48) From Reno, NV, appointed 05-01-1923 on car 06-13-1923	SP
Rev. J. B. Speed, wife & daughter	1923	07	31	Columbia City	OR	OR Baptist State Convention, without car, Lv 08-08-1923	—
Rev. J. B. Speed (49), wife & daughter	1923	08	02	North Bend	OR	(49) To CA 10-20-1923, due to health	SP
Rev. J. D. Chappelle (50) & wife	1923	10	14	North Bend	OR	(50) From Alturas, CA, temporarily in charge 10-14-1923	SP
Rev. J. D. Chappelle (50) & wife	1926	03	05	Bandon	OR		?
Rev. J. D. Chappelle & wife	1926	04	20	Roseburg	OR	Added to the members of the church	SP
Rev. J. D. Chappelle & wife	1926	04	26	Grants Pass	OR	OR Baptist Umpqua Association, without car, Lv 04-24-1926	SP
Rev. J. D. Chappelle & wife	1926	11	01	Cottage Grove	OR	OR Rogue River Association, without car, Lv 04-29-1926	SP?
Rev. J. D. Chappelle & wife	1927	01	10	Prineville	OR	Built building	SP
Rev. J. D. Chappelle & wife	1927	01	18	Junction City	OR	Sunday school and mission organized	SP
Rev. J. D. Chappelle & wife	1927	02	02	Eugene	OR	Helped church get out of debt and revived	?
Rev. J. D. Chappelle & wife	1927	02	19	Eugene	OR	Finished building free of debt	SP
Rev. J. D. Chappelle (51) & wife	1927	01	16	Brookings	OR	Also may be in KS some part of year	?
Rev. J. D. Chappelle & wife	1927	04	08	Summer & Fall	OR	Evangelistic meeting	SP
Rev. J. D. Chappelle & wife	1927	04	21	Ashland	OR	Organized a church, purchased a Presbyterian building	?
Rev. J. D. Chappelle & wife	1927	06	01	McMinnville	OR	Evangelistic meeting, town and RR shop meetings	SP
Rev. J. D. Chappelle & wife	1927	07	12	Oroville	CA	Evangelistic meeting	?
Rev. J. D. Chappelle & wife	1927	07	26	Mt. Shasta	CA	Evangelistic meeting	—
Rev. J. D. Chappelle & wife	1927	08	07	Tracy	CA	New Natron cut-off, working with new churches organizations along new railroad	SP
Rev. J. D. Chappelle & wife	1928	01	10	Medford	OR	OR Baptist State Convention, without car, Lv 07-17-1926	SP
Rev. J. D. Chappelle & wife	1928	03	03	Modesto	CA	May have built building	NWP?
Rev. J. D. Chappelle & wife	1928	04	02	Tracy	CA	Built building, dedication 10-25-1931, Lv 10-28-1931	SP
Rev. J. D. Chappelle & wife	1929	01	16	Brookings	OR	Church organized, baptisms in swimming pool	SP
Rev. J. D. Chappelle & wife	1929	04	02	Modesto	CA	Car inspected and found in poor shape	SC
(52)	1929	08	05	Modesto	CA	(51) Left car 08-05-1929	NWP
Rev. A. C. McChesney (53)(54) & wife	1930	02	01	San Anselmo	CA	No church construction	SP
Rev. A. C. McChesney (55) & wife	1930	03	09	Tracy	CA	No church construction	SP
Rev. A. C. McChesney & wife	1930	12	31	Sonora	CA	(52) Car vacant 6 months	WP
Rev. A. C. McChesney & wife	1931	11	01	San Anselmo	CA	(53) Started 02-01-1930, resigned as former colporter	SP
Rev. A. C. McChesney & wife	1931	11	07	Merced	CA	Built building	SC
Rev. A. C. McChesney & wife	1932	01	01	Paradise	CA	CCC camp	NWP
Rev. A. C. McChesney & wife	1932	03	07	Martinez	CA	CWA camp	SP
Rev. A. C. McChesney & wife	1932	07	08	Others towns	CA	Also serving soldiers at Fort Bragg	SP
Rev. A. C. McChesney & wife	1933	01	01	Caspar	CA	Without car	SP
Rev. A. C. McChesney & wife	1934	02	06	Russian Gulch	CA	(55) Has 5 children, 9, 7, 5 -1/2, 4, 1-1/2 years of age	NWP?
Rev. A. C. McChesney & wife	1934	03	01	Marwedell	CA	Sunday school organized, Lv 05-21-1932	?
Rev. A. C. McChesney (56) & wife	1934	04	17	San Anselmo	CA	(56) Resigned 02-01-1935, without car	?
(57)	1934	07	08	Tracy	CA	(57) Car vacant, 3 months	NWP
Rev. I. M. Dryer & wife	1934	08	09	Willits	CA	Had baptismal service in San Francisco Bay	SP
Rev. I. M. Dryer & wife	1934	10	25	Willits	CA	Cleaning and repairing car	NWP
Rev. I. M. Dryer (58) & wife	1935	02	01	Willits	CA	(58) From colporter missionary, 05-01-1935	NWP
Rev. I. M. Dryer & wife	1935	03	01	Santa Rosa	CA	(59) Assigned to church as special ministry, without car	NWP
Rev. I. M. Dryer & wife	1935	03	01	Graton	CA	Survey and visitation, without car	SP
Rev. I. M. Dryer & wife	1935	05	02	Colinga	CA	Rally service, without car	SP
Rev. I. M. Dryer & wife	1935	06	05	Fowler	CA	Trying to realign church, without car	SP
Rev. I. M. Dryer & wife	1935	07	15	Fowler	CA	Car also connected to electric company for electricity	—
Rev. I. M. Dryer & wife	1935	08	08	Santa Rosa	CA	Rev. Dryer has been sick in bed	—
Rev. I. M. Dryer & wife	1935	12	20	Santa Rosa	CA	Last time car roof painted light green, now washing down on sides	SP
Rev. I. M. Dryer & wife	1936	02	07	Santa Rosa	CA		SP

PERSONNEL SERVING ON CARS	Y	M	D	TOWN	ST	COMMENTS FROM ACCOUNTS, LETTERS	RR
Rev. I. M. Dryer & wife	1936	03	04	Santa Rosa	CA	First Baptist Church, not started by chapel car 4, Good Will	SP
Rev. I. M. Dryer & wife	1936	06	05	Lakeport	CA	Visitation and preaching campaign, without car	—
Rev. I. M. Dryer & wife	1936	06	25	Santa Rosa	CA	Working to find a place for retired car off rails	SP
Rev. I. M. Dryer (59) & wife	1936	09	16	Santa Rosa	CA	(59) Left church assignment as special ministry	SP
Rev. I. M. Dryer & wife	1936	10	17	San Francisco	CA	Preaching mission, without car	—
Rev. I. M. Dryer & wife	1936	10	26	Oakland	CA	Preaching mission, without car	—
Rev. I. M. Dryer & wife	1936	11	12	Fowler	CA	Preaching mission, without car	—
Rev. I. M. Dryer & wife	1936	11	20	Fresno	CA	Preaching mission, without car	—
Rev. I. M. Dryer & wife	1936	12	15	Santa Cruz	CA	Trying to fine place to move car	SP
Rev. I. M. Dryer & wife	1937	03	11	Fowler	CA	Forward Move rally service, without car	—
Rev. I. M. Dryer & wife	1937	03	18	Colinga	CA	Forward Move rally service, without car	—
Rev. I. M. Dryer & wife	1937	10	15	Santa Rosa	CA	Rev. Dryer, operation at Modesto, CA, almost died	SP
Rev. I. M. Dryer & wife	1937	12	15	Santa Rosa	CA	Not working until 01-16-1938	SP
Rev. I. M. Dryer & wife	1938	01	30	Boyes Springs	CA	Car removed from rails, without car trucks and place on rented lot	SP
Rev. I. M. Dryer & wife	1938	02	16	Boyes Springs	CA	Chapel car body settled on concrete foundations	—
Rev. I. M. Dryer (60) & wife	1938	03	01	Boyes Springs	CA	(60) Return to colporter missionary 03-01-1938	—
(61)	1938	05	02	Boyes Springs	CA	(61) Car vacant 2-1 / 2 months	—
(61)	1938	05	17	Boyes Springs	CA	A.B.P.S. retired chapel car and gave car to CA Baptist State Northern Convention	—
	1938	09	01	Boyes Springs	CA	CA Baptist Northern State Convention headquarters	—
	1938	09	02	Boyes Springs	CA	Rev. Dryer and wife may be living in car	—
	1938	09	23	Boyes Springs	CA	CA Baptist State Northern Convention, car for home and Headquarters	—
	1940	09	25	Boyes Springs	CA	CA Baptist State Board and A.B.P.S. voted to sell car and lot for $275.	—
	1944			Boyes Springs	CA	May have been used by the navy for public relations	—
	1947			Boyes Springs	CA	May have been used as living quarters for Hot Springs Resort cooks	—
	1958			Boyes Hot Springs	CA	Car body and lot resold, used by owners in variety of ways	—
	1999			Boyes Hot Springs	CA	Car body used as a storage building	—
A.B.P.S. CAR 5, MESSENGER OF PEACE						**AMERICAN BAPTIST PUBLICATION SOCIETY**	
NICKNAME - THE LADIES CHAPEL CAR	1894	05	26	Saratoga	NY	Two ladies started donors fund for car	—
	1897	05				Asked for free will car donors, $7500 total, 75 Baptist women of NY @ $100 ea.	—
Boston W. Smith (1)	1898	05	18	Dayton	OH	Car shipped from car builder, Barney & Smith Car Company	CCC&SL
Rev. S. G. Neil (2), wife & B.W. Smith	1898	05	20	Rochester	NY	Car dedication 05-21-1898, A.B.P.S. Anniversary Meeting	NYC&HR
Rev. S. G. Neil, wife & B.W. Smith	1898	05	25	Buffalo	NY	Exhibit, 2 days	NYC&SL
Rev. S. G. Neil, wife & B.W. Smith	1898	05	27	Erie	PA	Exhibit, 2 days	NYC&SL
Rev. S. G. Neil, wife & B.W. Smith	1898	05	29	Cleveland	OH	Exhibit, 2 days	NYC&SL
Rev. S. G. Neil, wife & B.W. Smith	1898	05	31	Toledo	OH	Exhibit, 2 days	WAB
Rev. S. G. Neil, wife & B.W. Smith	1898	06	04	St. Louis	MO	Exhibit, 2 days	WAB
Rev. S. G. Neil & wife	1898	06	07	Kansas City	MO	Exhibit, 2 days	ATS&F
Rev. S. G. Neil & wife	1898	06	12	Argentine	KS	Car at station, RR workers thanked missionaries for the car services	AT&SF
Rev. S. G. Neil & wife	1898	06	17	Ottawa	KS	(1) From Minneapolis, MN, superintendent of chapel car evangelism	AT&SF
Rev. S. G. Neil & wife	1898	07	12	Osawatomie	KS	(2) From Salvation army	MP
Rev. S. G. Neil & wife	1898	08	18	Eureka	KS	Well attended, broke ground for building, 6 weeks	AT&SF
Rev. S. G. Neil & wife	1898	10	01	Hamilton	KS	People hungry for the gospel, 5 days	AT&SF
Rev. S. G. Neil & wife	1898	10	09	Newton	KS	KS Baptist State Convention, Lv 10-15-1898	AT&SF
Rev. S. G. Neil & wife	1898	10	17	Fredonia	KS	Church organized with excellent results, gave a 8' x 4' US flag for the car	MP
Rev. S. G. Neil & wife	1898	11	07	St. Louis	MO	Exhibit at station, 2 days	MP
Rev. S. G. Neil & wife	1898	11	09	St. Louis	MO	First Chapel Car Conference near St. Louis, Lv 11-15-1898	SL&KC
Rev. S. G. Neil & wife	1898	11	26	Carrollton	MO	Neil heard from car the comment about car, "If that don't beat the devil"	WAB
Rev. S. G. Neil & wife	1898	11	27	Kansas City	MO		WAB
Rev. S. G. Neil & wife	1899	02	20	Brownell	KS	Built building	MP
Rev. S. G. Neil & wife	1899	04	08	Manning	KS	Built building	MP
Rev. S. G. Neil & wife	1899	06	02	Dighton	KS	Built building	AT&SF
Rev. S. G. Neil & wife	1899	07	03	Garden City	KS	Secured lots	AT&SF
Rev. S. G. Neil & wife	1899	10	08	Ottawa	KS	KS Baptist State Convention, Lv 10-14-1899	AT&SF
Rev. S. G. Neil & wife	1899	10	15	Omaha	NE	NE Baptist State Convention, Lv 10-20-1899	MP
Rev. S. G. Neil & wife	1899	11	18	Kansas City	KS	Dr. Neil took Dwight L Moody's place for the last service	MP
Mrs. S. G. Neil	1899	11	27	St. Louis	MO	A mortally ill Dwight L Moody rode car to St. Louis, MO, transferred on home to die	WAB
Rev. S. G. Neil & wife	1899	11	28	Kansas City	KS		WAB
Rev. S. G. Neil & wife	1900	02	15	Birds Point	MO	American Car and Foundry repaired car, $649.09	SLIM&S
Rev. S. G. Neil & wife	1900	02	16		MO	Speaking trip to PA, MA, NY, MD, NJ, and DC, without car	—
Rev. S. G. Neil & wife	1900	03	17	St. Louis	MO	Preached in church, without car	—
Rev. S. G. Neil & wife	1900	03	20	Delta	MO	Built building	SLIM&S
Rev. S. G. Neil & wife	1900	04	25	St. Louis	MO	Bad case of fleas on car	SLIM&S
Rev. S. G. Neil & wife	1900	05	01	Ardeola	MO	Church and Sunday school organized	SLSW
Rev. S. G. Neil & wife	1900	05	08	Hot Springs	AR	AR Baptist State Convention, without car	—
Rev. S. G. Neil & wife	1900	06	02	Birds Point	MO	Mrs. Neil sick with malaria	SLIM&S
Rev. S. G. Neil & wife	1900	06	23	Charleston	MO		SLIM&S
Rev. S. G. Neil & wife	1900	07	01	Delta	MO	Dedication, church window has dove, symbol of chapel car, in it	SLIM&S
Rev. S. G. Neil & wife	1900	07	10	Charleston	MO		SLIM&S
Rev. S. G. Neil & wife	1900	07	23	St. Louis	MO		SLIM&S
Rev. S. G. Neil & wife	1900	08	01	St. Louis	MO	Car too hot, off car for month of August in IL & TX	SLIM&S
Rev. S. G. Neil	1900	08	02	Cairo	IL	Without car	—
Rev. S. G. Neil	1900	08	10	Galveston	TX	Helping on chapel car 4, Good Will, Neil left town before the great storm hit, without car	—
Rev. S. G. Neil & wife	1900	09	01	Other towns		In MO or KS	?
Rev. S. G. Neil & wife	1900	10	14	McPherson	KS	KS Baptist State Convention, Lv 10-20-1900	CRI&P
Rev. S. G. Neil & wife	1900	11	03	St. Joseph	MO		MP
Rev. S. G. Neil & wife	1900	11	20	Kansas City	MO	(3) To pastor in Philadelphia, PA, 05-31-1901	MP
Rev. S. G. Neil (3)& wife	1901	05	21	Springfield	MA	A.B.P.S. Anniversary Meeting, without car, Lv 05-27-1901	—
(4)	1901	06	01	Kansas City	MO	(4) Car vacant 1 month	MP
G. Sully (5)	1901	07	01	Kansas City	MO	(5) On car for a short time and resigned	MP
G. Sully	1901	07	12	Kansas City	MO	Car may have had exterior painting paid by insurance	MP
(6)	1901	09	05	Kansas City	MO	(6) Car vacant 1 month	MP

PERSONNEL SERVING ON CARS	Y	M	D	TOWN	ST	COMMENTS FROM ACCOUNTS, LETTERS	R R
Rev. J. P. Jacobs (7), wife & B. W. Smith	1901	10	13	Kansas City	MO	(7) From North Vernon, IN, 10-01-1901	MP
Rev. J. P. Jacobs & wife	1901	10	13	Kansas City	KS	KS Baptist State Convention, Lv 10-19-1901	MP
Rev. J. P. Jacobs & wife	1901	11	03	Green City	MO		OKC&E
Rev. J. P. Jacobs & wife	1902	01	02	Birds Point	MO	Car repairs, exterior painting and varnishing, American Car & Foundry	SLIM&S
Rev. J. P. Jacobs & wife	1902	02	07	Republic	MO		SL&SF
Rev. J. P. Jacobs, wife & T. Moffat	1902	02	15	Marshfield	MO		SL&SF
Rev. J. P. Jacobs, wife & T. Moffat	1902	02	26	Lebanon.	MO		SL&SF
Rev. J. P. Jacobs & wife	1902	03	04	Novinger	MO	Special sidetrack built for car, church organized, 3 months	OO&KC
Rev. J. P. Jacobs & wife	1902	07	09	Walsenburg	CO		D&RG
Rev. J. P. Jacobs & wife	1902	09	27	Kansas City	MO	Second Chapel Car Conference, in car, Lv 10-06-1902	OO&KC
Rev. J. P. Jacobs & wife	1902	10	06	Milan	MO	RR meeting, with all chapel car missionaries	OO&KC
Rev. J. P. Jacobs & wife	1902	10	07	Novinger	MO	Church dedication, with all chapel car missionaries	OO&KC
Rev. J. P. Jacobs & wife	1902	10	08	Green City	MO	Church dedication, with all chapel car missionaries	OO&KC
Rev. J. P. Jacobs & wife	1903	03	18	Brimson	MO	Built building and dedication, built parsonage	OO&KC
Rev. J. P. Jacobs & wife	1903	04	21	Republic	MO	New church, no pastor	FS
Rev. J. P. Jacobs & wife	1903	05	24	Buffalo	NY	A.B.P.S. Anniversary Meeting, without car Lv 05-27-1903	—
Rev. J. P. Jacobs & wife	1903	06	07	Novinger	MO	RR and mining town, no pastor	OO&KC
Rev. J. P. Jacobs & wife	1903	06	29	North Vernon	IN	Married friends at his former church, without car	—
Rev. J. P. Jacobs & wife	1903	07	10	Denver	CO	Took folks to the Christian Endeavor meeting in car	D&RG
Rev. J. P. Jacobs & wife	1903	08	19	Pueblo	CO	Stirring religious quickening, Lv 11-??-1903	D&RG
Rev. J. P. Jacobs & wife	1903	09	15	Trinidad	CO	Southern CO Baptist Association, Lv 09-19-1903	D&RG
Rev. J. P. Jacobs & wife	1903	10	01	Del Norte	CO	A little Baptist band was greatly encouraged	D&RG
Mrs. Jacobs	1903	10	25	?	CO	CO Baptist State Convention	?
Rev. J. P. Jacobs & wife	1904	01	02	St. Louis	MO	Waiting transportation for car	CRI&P
Rev. J. P. Jacobs & wife	1904	01	12	Trenton	MO	Railroad town, church and RR meetings	CRI&P
Rev. J. P. Jacobs & wife	1904	01	24	St. Joseph	MO	Pulpit supply	CRI&P
Rev. J. P. Jacobs & wife	1904	01	29	Worthington	MO	Helped build building	I&SL
Rev. J. P. Jacobs & wife	1904	02	16	Republic	MO	Church organized and built building	FS
Rev. J. P. Jacobs & wife	1904	02	26	St. Louis	MO	Car repairs by Pullman Car Company	?
Rev. J. P. Jacobs & wife	1904	04	15	St. Louis World's Fair	MO	St. Louis Baptist Missionary and Benevolent Union, without car	GOVT
Rev. J. P. Jacobs & wife	1904	06	25	St. Louis World's Fair	MO	St. Louis World's Fair Exposition grounds	GOVT
Rev. J. P. Jacobs & wife	1905	01	01	Other towns	MO	Wedding on car, members of Tower Grove Baptist Church	?
Rev. J. P. Jacobs & wife	1905	04	07	Connelsville	MO	Stayed 3 months	I&SL
Rev. J. P. Jacobs & wife	1905	05	18	Gifford	MO	Sunday school organized	I&SL
Rev. J. P. Jacobs & wife	1905	06	13	Connelsville	MO	Two towns 1/2 mile apart, no pastor, 3 weeks	I&SL
Rev. J. P. Jacobs & wife	1905	07	03	Livonia	MO	Church organized, no pastor, 2-1/2 weeks	I&SL
Rev. J. P. Jacobs & wife	1905	08	03	Del Norte	CO	New church, 3 weeks	D&RG
Rev. J. P. Jacobs & wife	1905	08	30	Novinger	MO	Rest and work, preached to cowboys on Clear Creek, 3 weeks	I&SL
Rev. J. P. Jacobs & wife	1905	09	06	Connelsville	MO	Few days	I&SL
Rev. J. P. Jacobs & wife	1905	09	10	Livonia	MO	Tent services, built building	I&SL
Rev. J. P. Jacobs (8) & wife	1906	01	01	St. Louis	MO	(8) To A.B.P.S. field secretary 05-31-1906	OO&KC
Rev. J. P. Jacobs	1906	05	16	Dayton	OH	A.B.P.S. Anniversary Meeting, without car, Lv 05-19-1906	—
(9)	1906	06	01	St. Louis	MO	(9) Car vacant 10 days	OO&KC
Rev. J. H. Webber (10) & wife	1906	06	11	St. Louis	MO	(10) Transferred from on 06-11-1906	OO&KC
Rev. J. H. Webber & wife	1906	07	01	Worthington	MO	Built building	I&SL
Rev. J. H. Webber & wife	1906	08	14	Livonia	MO	Built building	I&SL
Rev. J. H. Webber & wife	1906	10	01	Gifford	MO		I&SL
Rev. J. H. Webber & wife	1907	01	23	Milan	MO	RR shop	OO&KC
Rev. J. H. Webber & wife	1907	02	10	Santa Rosa	MO	Now building	OO&KC
Rev. J. H. Webber & wife	1907	04	02	Nashua	MO	Built building	OO&KC
Rev. J. H. Webber (11) & wife	1907	07	30	Kansas City	MO	(11) Transferred to 07-31-1907	OO&KC
(12)	1907	07	31	Kansas City	MO	(12) Car vacant 1 week	OO&KC
Rev. J. S. Davis (13) & wife	1907	08	06	Brimson	MO	(13) Transferred from 08-06-1907	OO&KC
Rev. J. S. Davis & wife	1907	10	01	Galt	MO		OO&KC ?
Rev. J. S. Davis & wife	1907	11	01	Milan	MO	RR car shop and church meetings, great works done	OO&KC
Rev. J. S. Davis & wife	1907	11	11	Santa Rosa	MO	Completed building	OO&KC
Rev. J. S. Davis & wife	1907	12	11	Pattonsburg	MO		OO&KC
Rev. J. S. Davis & wife	1908	01	08	Santa Rosa	MO		OO&KC
Rev. J. S. Davis & wife	1908	04	11	Osborn	MO		OO&KC
Rev. J. S. Davis & wife	1908	05	14	Kansas City	MO	Third Chapel Car Conference	OO&KC
Rev. J. S. Davis & wife	1908	05	26	Nashua	MO	Built building	OO&KC
Rev. J. S. Davis (14) & wife	1908	06	01	Santa Rosa	MO	(14) To pastor in Kansas City, MO	OO&KC
(15)	1908	07	16	Nashua	MO	(15) Car vacant 4 months	OO&KC
Rev. T. R. Gale (16) & wife	1908	09	01			(16) Previous situation unknown	?
Rev. T. R. Gale & wife	1909	03	01	Poplar Bluff	MO	Street meeting and RR shop meeting	FS
Rev. T. R. Gale & wife	1909	05	14	Lilbourn	MO	Car surrounded by water	FS
Rev. T. R. Gale & wife	1909	11	05	Erimise	MO	Lumber town, organized Sunday school	?
Rev. T. R. Gale & wife	1910	02	01	Other towns	MO	RR YMCA, several RR points	?
Rev. T. R. Gale & wife	1910	03	06	Montpelier	IA	RR YMCA	CRI&P
Rev. T. R. Gale & wife	1910	04	01	Other towns	IL	RR YMCA	?
Rev. T. R. Gale & wife	1910	10	01	East St. Louis	IL	RR YMCA, Brooklyn yards	TRESL
Rev. T. R. Gale & wife	1910	10	01	Decatur	IL	RR YMCA, very deep interest, 3 weeks	WAB
Rev. T. R. Gale & wife	1910	11	10	Springfield	IL	RR YMCA, organized Bible class	WAB
Rev. T. R. Gale & wife	1911	01	01	Other towns	IL	RR YMCA	?
Rev. T. R. Gale & wife	1911	08	01	Boston	MA	RR YMCA, The World of Boston Exposition	B&A
Rev. T. R. Gale & wife	1911	08	01	Other towns	WV	RR YMCA	C&O
Rev. T. R. Gale & wife	1911	10	09	Thurmond	WV	RR YMCA, Lv 11-09-1911	C&O
Rev. T. R. Gale & wife	1911	10	24	Red Star	WV	While at Thurmond, WV	C&O
Rev. T. R. Gale & wife	1911	12	01	Other towns	MO		?
Rev. T. R. Gale & wife	1912	03	16	St. Louis	MO	Railroad asked that car be part of train to Denver, CO	?

PERSONNEL SERVING ON CARS	Y	M	D	TOWN	ST	COMMENTS FROM ACCOUNTS, LETTERS	RR
Rev. T. R. Gale & wife	1912	04	08	Denver	CO	International Convention of Christian Endeavor	CRI&P
Rev. T. R. Gale & wife	1912	05	13	Kansas City	MO	Fourth Chapel Car Conference, Lv 05-20-1912	CRI&P
Rev. T. R. Gale & wife	1912	05	21	Des Moines	IA	A.B.P.S. Anniversary Meeting, Lv 05-30-1912	CRI&P
Rev. T. R. Gale & wife	1912	06	02	Milan	MO	Car in shop for repairs and vacation, 2 weeks	QO&KC
Rev. T. R. Gale & wife	1912	06	17	Milan	MO	RR shop meetings, Lv 06-20-1912	QO&KC
Rev. T. R. Gale & wife	1913	03	20	Milan	MO	Everybody discouraged, distrustful, and reluctant to work together	QO&KC
Rev. T. R. Gale & wife	1913	05	19	Kansas City	MO	RR wanted to use chapel car for Baptists to travel to Detroit, MI	WAB
Rev. T. R. Gale & wife	1913	05	21	Detroit	MI	A.B.P.S. Anniversary Meeting, car load from Kansas City, MO, Lv 05-29-1913	WAB
Rev. T. R. Gale & wife	1913	05	31	Kansas City	MO	Car adopted by ladies of First Baptist Church, Kansas City, MO	WAB
Rev. T. R. Gale & wife	1913	06	10	Denver	CO	Mission points near Denver, CO	?
Rev. T. R. Gale & wife	1913	07	04	Bennett	CO	Revival services	UP
Rev. T. R. Gale & wife	1913	07	16	Denver	CO	RR shop meetings, evenings at church	D&RG
Rev. T. R. Gale & wife	1913	07	30	Ogden	UT		D&RG
Rev. T. R. Gale & wife	1913	08	01	Salt Lake	UT	No services	OSL
Rev. T. R. Gale & wife	1913	08	03	Montpelier	ID	RR shop meetings	SP
Rev. T. R. Gale & wife	1913	08	06	Wells	NV		SP
Rev. T. R. Gale & wife	1913	08	09	Deeth	NV		SP
Rev. T. R. Gale & wife	1913	08	19	Carlin	NV	Car on track 1 mile from town	SP
Rev. T. R. Gale & wife	1913	08	23	Gerlach	NV	RR roundhouse and freight point, 3 days	WP
Rev. T. R. Gale & wife	1913	08	26	Portola	CA	Lumber town, meeting fairly well attended	WP
Rev. T. R. Gale & wife	1913	09	19	East Oakland	CA	CA San Francisco Baptist Association	SP
Rev. T. R. Gale & wife	1913	09	26	West Oakland	CA		SP
Rev. T. R. Gale & wife	1913	09	27	Oroville	CA	Rev. and Mrs. Gale not well, still holding car and street meetings	SP
Rev. T. R. Gale & wife	1913	11	10	Oakland	CA	Northern CA Baptist State Convention, Lv 11-15-1913	SP
Rev. T. R. Gale & wife	1913	11	16	Oroville	CA	Difficult situation, Lv 12-30-1913	SP
Rev. T. R. Gale & wife	1913	12	11	Other towns	CA	Revival meetings while at Oroville, CA, without car	—
Rev. T. R. Gale & wife	1913	12	21	Richvale	CA	Rice harvest interfered with attendance	SP
Rev. T. R. Gale & wife	1914	01	02	Biggs	CA	Very gracious work accomplished	SP
Rev. T. R. Gale & wife	1914	01	09	Antelope	CA	Dedication service	SP
Rev. T. R. Gale & wife	1914	01	10	Stockton	CA	Working in the suburbs	SP
Rev. T. R. Gale & wife	1914	01	17	Riverbank	CA	Assisting building plans, while at Stockton, CA, without car	—
Rev. T. R. Gale & wife	1914	01	20	Thermalito	CA	Very encouraging meetings	NE
Rev. T. R. Gale & wife	1914	02	21	Roseville	CA	Evangelistic meetings, helped start funds for building lots	SP
Rev. T. R. Gale & wife	1914	02	27	Marysville	CA	Car out of town and no church building for meetings	SP
Rev. T. R. Gale & wife	1914	03	01	Antelope	CA	Hopeful for a good future	SP
Rev. T. R. Gale & wife	1914	04	14	Roseville	CA	RR families and farmers came to car, Lv 05-03-1914	SP
Rev. T. R. Gale & wife	1914	05	23	Riverbank	CA	Swearing turned to praying and praising, Lv 06-20-1914,	SP
Rev. T. R. Gale & wife	1914	07	12	Roseville	CA	Building dedication service, without car	SP
Rev. T. R. Gale & wife	1914	08	21	Richmond	CA	RR shop meetings, depression in the shops	SP
Rev. T. R. Gale & wife	1914	09	18	Sacramento	CA	Car in shop for some light repairs to comply with ICC rules	SP
Rev. T. R. Gale & wife	1914	09	20	Richvale	CA	Without car	—
Rev. T. R. Gale & wife	1914	10	26	Waterford	CA	CA Baptist Association, without car	SP
Rev. T. R. Gale & wife	1914	11	03	Washington	CA	Dedication of new building, without car	SP ?
Rev. T. R. Gale & wife	1914	11	17	Roseville	CA	Without car	SP
Rev. T. R. Gale & wife	1914	12	18	Antelope	CA	Without car	—
Rev. T. R. Gale & wife	1915	01	02	Santa Barbara	CA		—
Rev. T. R. Gale & wife	1915	02	12	Broderick	CA	RR laid off, very hard times, Lv 04-23-1915	SP
Rev. T. R. Gale & wife	1915	04	24	Sacramento	CA	Car repairs, cleaning, exterior painting $479.93, Lv 07-06-1915	SP
Rev. T. R. Gale & wife	1915	04	25	Broderick	CA	Mrs. Gale not well, without car	—
Rev. T. R. Gale & wife	1915	05	19	Los Angeles	CA	A.B.P.S. Anniversary Meeting, without car	—
Rev. T. R. Gale & wife	1915	05	27	Los Angeles	CA	Chapel Car Conference, 2 days, without car, Lv 05-28-1915	—
Rev. T. R. Gale & wife	1915	06	12	Oakland	CA	Without car	—
Rev. T. R. Gale & wife	1915	07	01	San Francisco	CA	With chapel car 7, Grace, at San Francisco Exposition, without car	SP
Rev. T. R. Gale & wife	1915	07	07	Broderick	CA	Well attended	SP ?
Rev. T. R. Gale & wife	1915	07	07	Eagle Point	OR	Pastor discouraged due to loss of his best workers	P&ER ?
Rev. T. R. Gale & wife	1915	07	26	Grants Pass	OR	Colporteur on vacation, no one to work with, 1 day	SP
Rev. T. R. Gale & wife	1915	08	03	Portland	OR	Directed building the church	SP
Rev. T. R. Gale & wife	1915	08	12	Pasco	WA	Also while at Kennewick, WA, second time without car	NP
Rev. T. R. Gale & wife	1915	09	22	Richland	WA	Also while at Kennewick, WA, church organized, without car	NP
Rev. T. R. Gale & wife	1915	10	23	Kennewick	WA	3 weeks, Lv 11-09-1915	NP
Rev. T. R. Gale & wife	1915	11	10	Wallula	WA	A fusion of denominations but a church organized	NP
Rev. T. R. Gale & wife	1915	11	25	Pasco	WA	Chapel car at Pasco, WA, but Burbank, WA, may be able to help Pasco, WA, without car	NP?
Rev. T. R. Gale & wife	1915	12	04	Walla Walla	WA		NP
Rev. T. R. Gale & wife	1915	12	13	Burbank	WA		NP
Rev. T. R. Gale & wife	1916	03	09	Coeur d' Alene	ID	Gracious revival stirred the community	NP
Rev. T. R. Gale & wife	1916	04	01	Spangle	WA	Hard proposition, church nearly dead	GN
Rev. T. R. Gale & wife	1916	04	20	Spokane	WA	While at Spokane, WA, without car	GN
Rev. T. R. Gale & wife	1916	05	03	Opportunity	WA	Evangelistic services and helped build building, 3 weeks	GN
Rev. T. R. Gale & wife	1916	06	03	Deer Park	WA	WA Baptist ? Association, without car	S&IE
Rev. T. R. Gale & wife	1916	06	25	?	WA	No pastor and every thing is upside down	S&IE
Rev. T. R. Gale & wife	1916	07	05	Valleyford	WA	Most encouraging in every way	NP
Rev. T. R. Gale & wife	1916	08	03	Freeman	WA	Wheat district and most are away during the week	NP
Rev. T. R. Gale & wife	1916	08	16	Oakesdale	WA	Meetings were well attended	NP?
Rev. T. R. Gale & wife	1916	08	24	Moscow	WA	East WA and North ID Baptist Convention, without car	NP
Rev. T. R. Gale & wife	1916	10	01	North Yakima	WA	Car in shop for ICC repairs and varnishing, $190, shop meetings	NP
Rev. T. R. Gale & wife	1916	10	14	Pasco	WA	Town meetings, delighted with general uplift, without car	—
Rev. T. R. Gale & wife	1916	10	25	Winlock	WA	Little lumber mill center, need is apparent, 3 weeks	NP
Rev. T. R. Gale & wife	1916	11	04	South Tacoma	WA		NP
Rev. T. R. Gale & wife	1916	11	08	South Tacoma	WA		—
Rev. T. R. Gale & wife	1916	11	28	Wilburton	WA		NP?
Rev. T. R. Gale & wife	1916	12	14	Mid Lakes	WA	While at Wilburton, WA	NP?
Rev. T. R. Gale & wife	1916	12	23	Renton	WA	Mining camp, religious conditions deplorable, good finish	NP

PERSONNEL SERVING ON CARS	Y	M	D	TOWN	ST	COMMENTS FROM ACCOUNTS, LETTERS	RR
Rev. T. R. Gale & wife	1917	01	21	Issaquah	WA	Coal mining camp, snow storms affect meetings, 6 weeks	NP
Rev. T. R. Gale & wife	1917	03	04	North Bend	WA	A helpful time for the church, but very bad weather	NP
Rev. T. R. Gale (17)	1917	03	17	Arlington	WA	(17) Mrs. Gale had an operation and had to leave car	HE
Rev. T. R. Gale	1917	04	18	Granite Falls	WA	Pastor of church just resigned	NP
Rev. T. R. Gale & wife	1917	05	05	Wickersham	WA	Their renewal of energy and spirit gives them hope	NP
Rev. T. R. Gale & wife	1917	05	22	Sumner	WA	Pastor is very anxious to receive help	NP
Rev. T. R. Gale & wife (18)	1917	06	05	Seattle	WA	(18) No services, Mrs. Gale had appendicitis operation	NP
Rev. T. R. Gale & wife	1917	06	30	Kent	WA	An invited pro-German preacher has lead to a protest	NP
Rev. T. R. Gale & wife	1917	07	18	Moclips	WA	1 week	NP ?
Rev. T. R. Gale & wife	1917	07	23	Snohomish	WA	WA Baptist ? Association, without car	NP
Rev. T. R. Gale & wife	1917	07	27	Hoquiam	WA	Car helped get new people in touch with pastor	NP
Rev. T. R. Gale & wife	1917	08	22	Gate	WA	Small village and the young pastor needs help	NP
Rev. T. R. Gale & wife	1917	08	28	Pe Ell	WA	No pastor but the pastor from Dryad, WA, will help	NP
Rev. T. R. Gale & wife	1917	09	06	South Bend	WA	Mills idle in town and churches suffering commercially	NP
Rev. T. R. Gale & wife	1917	09	25	Raymond	WA		NP
Rev. T. R. Gale & wife	1917	10	01	Lebam	WA		NP
Rev. T. R. Gale & wife	1917	10	25	Dryad	WA	Red Cross, liberty loan, potatoes are matters of interest	NP
Rev. T. R. Gale & wife	1917	11	10	Chehalis	WA		NP
Rev. T. R. Gale & wife	1917	12	11	Puyallup	WA	Filled with hope as they now see how things can be done	NP
Rev. T. R. Gale & wife	1917	12	28		WA	Government takes over operation of the railroads due to WWI	—
Rev. T. R. Gale & wife	1918	01	03	Burlington	WA	Enforcing McAdoo tariff schedule, car holding at depot	NP
Rev. T. R. Gale	1918	01	18	Burlington	WA	To straighten out a tangle, 2 days, without car	—
Rev. T. R. Gale (19)	1918	01	21	Sumner	WA	(19) Mrs. Gale in St. Louis sanitarium, 03-07-1918	—
Rev. T. R. Gale	1918	03	23	Kent	WA	(20) From Medford, OR	NP
Rev. T. R. Gale & Mr. L. S. Cox (20)	1918	04	07	Kelso	WA	Helper not working out, WWI effects on wages	NP
Rev. T. R. Gale & Rev. E. C. Cofer (21)	1918	05	27	Kelso	WA	Talks about RR shop problem, Camp Lewis and YMCA work	NP
Rev. T. R. Gale & Rev. E. C. Cofer	1918	06	01	Kelso	WA	Waiting word that car can be moved, 8 weeks	NP
Rev. T. R. Gale & wife	1918	09	02	Kelso	WA	Waiting word to go to RR shops, 6 weeks	NP
Rev. T. R. Gale & wife	1918	10	12	Seattle	WA	Car given word to move in shops for repairs	NP
Rev. T. R. Gale & wife	1918	10	14	South Tacoma	WA	Car in shop for repairs, $151.51	NP
Rev. T. R. Gale & wife	1918	11	07	Tacoma	WA	Car at Union Depot waiting for permission to move	NP
Rev. T. R. Gale & wife	1919	01	01	Renton	WA	New tariffs on car movement and track space	NP
Rev. T. R. Gale & wife	1919	01	17	Burlington	WA	Railroad transportation and chapel car movement tariffs	GN
Rev. T. R. Gale & wife	1919	02	08	Seattle	WA	Problems with car movement tariffs	GN
Rev. T. R. Gale & wife	1919	03	10	Marysville	WA	Encouraging results	GN
Rev. T. R. Gale & wife	1919	03	21	Burlington	WA	(21) From Portland, OR	GN
Rev. T. R. Gale & wife	1919	05	17	Burlington	WA	Car movement tariff reduced and free trackage again	GN
Rev. T. R. Gale & wife	1919	05	28	Seattle	WA	interior and exterior car cleaning	NP
Rev. T. R. Gale & wife	1919	06	02	Port Angeles	WA	A problem to solve before church is back together	CM&SP
Rev. T. R. Gale & wife	1919	09	01	?	WA	Car air brakes cleaned, also car interior and exterior cleaned	CM&SP
Rev. T. R. Gale & wife	1919	09	22	Tenino	WA	Worked with them to link up with the Centralia, WA, church	NP
Rev. T. R. Gale & wife	1919	10	18	Napavine	WA	Elderly workers are about holding their own	NP
Rev. T. R. Gale (22)(23) & wife	1920	01	06	Kelso	WA	Church worse than before, again needs lots of help	NP
(24)	1920	01	07	Spokane	WA	(22) Transferred to East WA as Sunday school field worker 01-01-1920	UP
Rev. R. Gray (25) & wife	1920	02	04	Spokane	WA	(23) Left car 01-06-1920 and concerned about car	UP
Rev. R. Gray & wife	1920	02	07	Sandpoint (Sand Point)	ID	(24) Car vacant 1 month	NP
Rev. R. Gray & wife	1920	03	01		ID	(25) From Seattle, WA, 02-01-1920	NP
Rev. R. Gray	1920	03	06	Spokane	WA	Government returned ownership to railroads	—
Rev. R. Gray	1920	05	03	?	ID	Inter-Church Conference, without car	—
Rev. R. Gray & wife	1920	05	12	Newport	WA	East WA and North ID Baptist State Convention, without car, Lv 06-05-1920	—
Rev. R. Gray & wife	1920	06	01	Spokane	WA	ID ? Baptist Association, without car, Lv 05-05-1920	GN
Rev. R. Gray & wife	1920	08	31	Newport	WA	Car needs to be in RR shop, Grays want vacation, Lv 09-28-1920	GN
Rev. R. Gray & wife	1920	09	28	Tekoa	WA	East WA and North ID Baptist State Convention, without car, Lv 06-03-1920	CM&SP
Rev. R. Gray & wife	1920	10	14	Springston	ID	Car lighting parts replaced $47.25	UP
Rev. R. Gray & wife	1920	11	13	Oakesdale	WA	Stopped here due to railroad bridge washout and missionaries were welcomed by town	UP
Rev. R. Gray	1920	12	02	Moscow	ID	Milltown, night meetings in car, mill has laid off help	UP
Rev. R. Gray & wife	1920	12	16	Oakesdale	WA	Pastor left a divided church	UP
Rev. R. Gray & wife	1920	12	27	Hay	WA	Religious Education institute, 2 days, without car	NP
Rev. R. Gray & wife	1921	02	10	Kittitas	WA	Small fire in wall and behind range, repairs $104.67	CM&SP
Rev. R. Gray & wife	1921	05	13	South Tacoma	WA	Good meeting and interest, well attended, Lv 01-26-1921	NP
Rev. R. Gray & wife	1921	05	14	Kittitas	WA	Build or to buy a church building, need a pastor	—
Rev. R. Gray & wife	1921	07	07	South Tacoma	WA	Car in shop, repairs and painting	CM&SP
Rev. R. Gray & wife	1921	08	03	Parker	WA	Work very successful here, without car, Lv 07-11-1921	NP
Rev. R. Gray & wife	1921	09	15	Buena	WA	Car finished for $869.16, on vacation, Lv 07-28-1921	NP
Rev. R. Gray & wife	1921	11	20	Prosser	WA	Warm weather, good meetings and fine attendance, Lv 10-19-1921	NP
Rev. R. Gray & wife	1922	05	01	Spokane	WA	While at Parker, WA, only Baptist work is what we are doing, without car	NP
Rev. R. Gray	1922	06	07	Spokane	WA	New instructions, exterior lettering on chapel cars	NP
Rev. R. Gray & wife	1922	07	07	Buena	WA	Large group of people working as one, new car lettering	NP
Rev. R. Gray & wife	1922	07	07	Cowiche	WA	RR shop crafts strike problems in valley, church group planning to build	NP
Rev. R. Gray & wife	1922	10	17	Cle Elum	WA	Pastor had a burn accident from a boiler explosion and later died	NP
Rev. R. Gray & wife	1922	10	25	Cle Elum	WA	Mrs. Gray in Seattle, WA, hospital, for neck operation	NP
Rev. R. Gray & wife	1922	12	12	Cle Elum	WA	Problems with Baker heater and need RR shop to repair	NP
Rev. R. Gray & wife	1922	12	31	South Tacoma	WA	Car in shops for heater repairs, had personal belongings missing	NP
Rev. R. Gray & wife	1923	01	05	Spokane	WA	Information on Catholic chapel car transportation cost	UP
Rev. R. Gray & wife	1923	01	15	Pendleton	OR	Baker heater will not heat	UP
Rev. R. Gray & wife	1923	01	17	La Grande	OR	Car in shops for Baker heater coil replaced, $119.89	UP
Rev. R. Gray & wife	1923	02	02	La Grande	OR	Living in car at shops and working with church at night	UP
Rev. R. Gray & wife	1923	02	23	Haines	OR	Fire on car 02-10-1923, fireman needed to put fire out	UP
Rev. R. Gray & wife	1923	03	01	Portland	OR	Waiting for car space and fire insurance report	UP
Rev. R. Gray & wife	1923	03	01	Portland	OR	Inspected chapel car 4, Good Will, while stored in SP shop, without car	SP

PERSONNEL SERVING ON CARS	Y	M	D	TOWN	ST	COMMENTS FROM ACCOUNTS, LETTERS	RR
Rev. R. Gray & wife	1923	03	03	Portland	OR	Car in shop for fire damage repairs $685, Lv 03-23-1923	SP
Rev. R. Gray & wife	1923	03	05	Portland	OR	Working with local church, without car	--
Rev. R. Gray & wife	1923	03	23	Haines	OR		UP
Rev. R. Gray & wife	1923	06	04	Melba	ID	Evangelistic services	UP
Rev. R. Gray & wife	1923	07	24	Portland	OR	Rev. Gray had eye accident, went to Portland, OR, for special treatment, without car	--
Rev. R. Gray & wife	1923	09	17	Kuna	ID	Car moved day and night by trainmen with very rough handling	UP
Rev. R. Gray	1923	10	04	Weiser	ID	ID First Baptist Association, without car, Lv 10-08-1923	--
Rev. R. Gray & wife	1923	10	12	Ontario	ID	No services	UP
Rev. R. Gray (26) & wife	1923	10	13	Payette	ID	No track space here, car at Ontario, OR, no pastor at church, without car	--
(27)	1923	12	16	Ontario	OR	(26) Transferred to West WA colporter missionary 12-15-1923	UP
Rev. F. E. Hawes (28) & wife	1924	01	01	Ontario	OR	(27) Car vacant 2 weeks	UP
Rev. F. E. Hawes & wife	1924	01	04	Payette	ID	(28) From Mesa, AZ, 01-01-1924, without car	UP
Rev. F. E. Hawes & wife	1924	08	26	Caldwell	ID	ID First Baptist Association, without car, Lv 08-30-1924	SP
Rev. F. E. Hawes & wife	1924	09	01	Gooding	ID	ID Central Baptist Association, without car, Lv 09-04-1924	UP
Rev. E. E. Cox (29) & wife	1924	09	05	Wilder	ID	(29) To pastor Miami, AZ, 09-28-1924	UP
Rev. E. E. Cox (30) & wife	1924	09	28	Wilder	ID	(30) Temporarily on car from colporter missionary 09-28-1924	UP
Rev. E. E. Cox & wife	1924	10	01	Haines	OR		UP
Rev. R. Gray (31) & wife	1924	12	01	Haines	OR	(31) From colporter missionary Seattle, WA, 12-01-1924	UP
Rev. R. Gray & wife	1924	12	03	Buena	WA		UP
Rev. R. Gray & wife	1924	12	21	Jerome	ID	No pastor	UP
Rev. R. Gray & wife	1925	01	04	Portland	OR	Baker heater repairs $95.12	SP
Rev. R. Gray & wife	1925	02	04	Grandview	WA	Very difficult situation, many Baptist but members of other churches, 10 weeks	SP
Rev. R. Gray & wife	1925	04	20	Pomeroy	WA	Very difficult situation, church has been closed 4 years	UP
Rev. R. Gray & wife	1926	04	26	Other towns	OR	Also car could be in ID or WA	SP
Rev. R. Gray & wife	1926	09	02	Other towns	OR	Car in shop for repairs	SP
Rev. R. Gray & wife	1927	01	01	Other towns	OR	Also car could be in ID or WA	NP
Rev. E. E. Cox & wife	1927	01	05	Oakey	CA	Car near depot	?
Rev. R. Gray & wife	1928	01	01	Other towns	OR	Also car could be in ID or WA	--
Rev. R. Gray & wife (32)	1929	05	11	Haines	OR	Car in RR shops, tin may have been applied over exterior wood	SP
Rev. C. W. Cutler & wife	1929	07	01	Portland	OR	Car in shops for repairs, not ready to leave	SP
Rev. C. W. Cutler & wife (33)	1929	07	02	Other towns	OR	With their auto, without car	--
Rev. C. W. Cutler & wife	1929	07	10	Portland	OR	Picked up car at shops, $432.91	SP
Rev. C. W. Cutler & wife	1929	09	01	Marshfield	OR	Pastor of church during this time Lv 05-01-1930	SP
Rev. C. W. Cutler & wife	1930	01	07	Buena	WA	Built church	NP
Rev. C. W. Cutler & wife	1930	03	18	Cowiche	WA	Built church	--
Rev. C. W. Cutler & wife	1930	05	21	Portland	OR	OR Baptist State Convention, without car Lv 05-24-1930	SP
Rev. C. W. Cutler & wife	1930	06	02	La Grande	OR	(32) Transferred to west WA colporter missionary 06-30-1929	UP
Rev. C. W. Cutler & wife	1930	07	03	Hermiston	OR	(33) Transferred from NY and PA chapel auto missionaries 07-01-1929	UP
Rev. C. W. Cutler & wife	1930	09	29	Pendleton	OR		UP
Rev. C. W. Cutler & wife	1930	11	12	Columbia City	OR	Built church	?
Rev. C. W. Cutler & wife	1931	01	08	Medford	OR	One month	SP
Rev. C. W. Cutler & wife	1931	02	22	Ontario	OR		UP
Rev. C. W. Cutler & wife	1931	03	25	Hillsboro	OR		--
Rev. C. W. Cutler & wife	1931	01	29	Roundup	MT	Begin service	CMSP&P
Rev. C. W. Cutler & wife	1931	05	20	Blackfoot	ID		UP
Rev. C. W. Cutler & wife	1931	06	16	Junction City	OR		SP
Rev. C. W. Cutler & wife	1931	07	26	Grants Pass	OR		SP
Rev. C. W. Cutler & wife	1931	05	07	Lakeview	OR		SP
Rev. C. W. Cutler & wife	1931	05	22	Lewiston	ID		SP
Rev. C. W. Cutler & wife	1931	07	01	Burns	OR		UP
Rev. C. W. Cutler & wife	1932	03	01	Bend	OR	OR Baptist State Convention, without car, Lv 05-27-1932	--
Rev. C. W. Cutler & wife	1933	03	01	La Grande	OR	Easter egg hunt, new organ and heaters for car	PEP
Rev. C. W. Cutler & wife	1933	04	01	Eugene	OR	OR Baptist State Convention, without car, Lv 05-19-1933	?
Rev. C. W. Cutler & wife	1934	05	23	Klamath Falls	OR	Bible school and study, morning and evening worship, Lv 04-07-1938	UP
Rev. C. W. Cutler & wife	1934	03	01	Pleasant Home	OR	Enlistment and evangelism	?
Rev. C. W. Cutler	1934	02	15	Portland	OR	OR Baptist State Convention, without car, Lv 05-11-1934	NP
Rev. C. W. Cutler & wife	1934	01	29	Lents (Lents Junct.)	OR	Evangelistic campaign, 1 month	?
Rev. C. W. Cutler & wife	1935	04	08	Arleta	OR	Every night in car, Sunday in church, Lv 02-28-1935	NP
Rev. C. W. Cutler & wife	1935	11	07	Harper	OR		?
Rev. C. W. Cutler & wife	1935	06	05	Other towns	ID		NP
Rev. C. W. Cutler & wife	1936	06	18	Kooskia	WA	Fine prayer meetings and crowded chapel car, 2 months	NP
Rev. C. W. Cutler & wife	1937	09	01	Other towns	WA		NP
Rev. C. W. Cutler & wife	1938			Other towns	WA		NP
Rev. C. W. Cutler & wife	1938			Okanogan	WA	Only Baptist church within 80 miles, Lv 06-18-1940	GN
Rev. C. W. Cutler & wife	1939			Okanogan	WA	Installed wiring on car for the electric power company connection, $18	GN
Rev. C. W. Cutler & wife	1940			Snohomish	WA	Lv 04-30-1941	NP
Rev. C. W. Cutler & wife	1940			Snohomish	WA		NP
Rev. C. W. Cutler & wife	1941	06	17	Blyn	WA	Moved car, spurring car, water and electric hook up $225	CMSP&P
Rev. C. W. Cutler & wife	1941	06	19	Forks	WA	While at Blyn WA, without car	--
Rev. C. W. Cutler & wife	1941	06	20	Beaver	WA	While at Blyn WA, without car	--
Rev. C. W. Cutler & wife	1941	06	21	Pleasant Lake	WA	While at Blyn WA, without car	--
Rev. C. W. Cutler & wife	1941	06	22	Sappho	WA	While at Blyn WA, without car	--
Rev. C. W. Cutler & wife	1941	06	25	Joyce	WA	While at Blyn WA, without car	--
Rev. C. W. Cutler & wife	1941	06	26	Pysht	WA	While at Blyn WA, without car	--
Rev. C. W. Cutler & wife	1941	06	27	Neah Bay	WA	While at Blyn WA, without car	--
Rev. C. W. Cutler & wife	1941	07	02	Gardiner	WA	While at Blyn WA, without car	--
Rev. C. W. Cutler & wife	1941	07	03	Leland	WA	While at Blyn WA, without car	--
Rev. C. W. Cutler & wife	1941	07	22	Blyn	WA	Roof painted, interior varnishing and carpet	CMSP&P
Rev. C. W. Cutler & wife	1942	04	18	Blyn	WA	Received auto missionary trailer at car for repair and to use as a outpost	--
Rev. C. W. Cutler & wife	1942	08	10	Portland	OR	Vacation 1 month, without car	CMSP&P
Rev. C. W. Cutler	1942	10	20	Berkeley	CA	Meeting at Berkeley, without car	--

PERSONNEL SERVING ON CARS	Y	M	D	TOWN	ST	COMMENTS FROM ACCOUNTS, LETTERS	R R
Rev. C. W. Cutler & wife	1942	11	07	Joyce	WA	Only house is a county store, due to the WWII men are leaving area	CMSP&P
Rev. C. W. Cutler & wife	1942	11	08	Pysht	WA	While at Joyce, WA, without car	--
Rev. C. W. Cutler & wife	1942	11	09	Neah Bay	WA	While at Joyce, WA, without car	--
Rev. C. W. Cutler & wife	1943	01	10	Portland	OR	Evangelism, visitation, and working with pastor organizing church, without car	CMSP&P
Rev. C. W. Cutler & wife	1943	02	06	Joyce	WA	Defense project and army camp within 3 miles of car	CMSP&P
Rev. C. W. Cutler & wife	1943	08	20	Joyce	WA	Rev. Cutler painted exterior of car	CMSP&P?
Rev. C. W. Cutler & wife	1944	04	18	Walnut Grove	WA	Car is the church home for the church while the new building is built	CMSP&P?
Rev. C. W. Cutler & wife	1944	04	18	Walnut Grove	WA	New linoleum and kitchen improvements for car $30	CMSP&P?
Rev. C. W. Cutler & wife	1945	01	01	Barberton	WA		NP
Rev. C. W. Cutler & wife	1945	03	10	Barberton	WA	Replaced some car window blinds, $60	NP
Rev. C. W. Cutler & wife	1946	04	27	Green Lake	WI	NBA Third Green Lake Conference, without car	--
Rev. C. W. Cutler & wife (34X35)	1946	07	12	Barberton	WA	(34) Rev. Cutler had a stroke 08-18-1946 went to Portland, OR, for rest	NP
Rev. C. W. Cutler & wife (35)	1946	10	05	South Everett	WA	(35) Car out of service 10 months	CMSP&P
Rev. C. W. Cutler & wife (35X36)	1947	06	01	South Everett	WA	(36) Rev. Cutler retires 06-01-1947	CMSP&P
(37)	1947	06	02	South Everett	WA	(37) Car vacant 21 months	CMSP&P
(37)	1948			South Everett	WA	Car retired	CMSP&P
(37)	1949	03	01	South Everett	WA	Car sold in 1949 for $400, and used as a roadside diner	CMSP&P
	1949	06	01	South Everett	WA	Car body purchased by WA highway department	--
	1951			Everett	WA	Car body given away by highway department for moving the car body from highway	--
	1952			Everett	WA	Car body moved to new owner's back yard	--
	1953			Snohomish	WA	Car body moved to owner's front yard in West WA	--
	1954			Olympic Peninsula	WA	Car body without trucks and on blocking in front yard of owner, used as storage	--
	1999			Olympic Peninsula	WA		--
A.B.P.S. CAR 6, HERALD OF HOPE **NICKNAME - THE YOUNG MEN'S CAR**						**AMERICAN BAPTIST PUBLICATION SOCIETY**	
	1896	05	28		MI	A.B.P.S. Board asked for free will car donors	--
	1896	05	29		MI	Young men of Woodward Avenue Baptist Church gave first money	--
	1897			Detroit	MI	Raised $7500 total	--
	1898	05	21	Rochester	NY	Need 1500 shares @ $5 ea, to be paid before 07-01-1898	--
	1899	05	24	San Francisco	CA	Needed more free will car donors @ $5 ea	--
	1899	10	14	Dayton	OH	Car under construction	--
	1900	03	02			Short $1000 due before 04-01-1900	--
Rev. C. E. Rosecrans (1) & wife	1900	05	18	Dayton	OH	Shipped from car builder, Barney & Smith Car Company	CH&D
Rev. C. E. Rosecrans & wife	1900	05	20	Detroit	MI	Ladies of Woodland Avenue Baptist Church furnished interior needs	PM
Rev. C. E. Rosecrans & wife	1900	05	27	Detroit	MI	A.B.P.S. Anniversary Meeting car dedication near Woodward Ave.	PM
Rev. C. E. Rosecrans & wife	1900	06	02	Grindstone City	MI	(1) Training school graduates, started 05-18-1900	PM
Rev. C. E. Rosecrans (3), wife & Rev. E. S. Wilson (2)	1900	09	16	Melvin	MI	(2) Temporarily assigned 08-01-1900 for 2 months	PM
(4)	1900	10	01	Detroit	MI	(3) Resigned due to throat trouble 10-01-1900	PM
Rev. E. S. Wilson (5) & Rev. E. L. Killam (6)	1900	11	02	Unionville	MI	(4) Car in shop and vacant 1 month	ST&H
Rev. E. S. Wilson & Rev. E. L Killam	1900	11	02	Muskegon Heights	MI	(5) From MI district missionary 11-01-1900	PM
Rev. E. S. Wilson & Rev. E. L. Killam	1900	12	15	Farmington	MI	(6) From MI district missionary 11-01-1900	?
Rev. E. S. Wilson & Rev. C. Truby (7)	1901	08	03	Brown City	MI	(7) Singer from PA	PM
Rev. E. S. Wilson (8) & Rev. E. L. Killam	1901	09	01	Evart	MI	(8) Sick 07-1901, resigned due to illness 10-01-1901	PM
Rev. E. L. Killam (9)	1901	10	16	Grand Rapids	MI	MI Baptist State Southern Convention	PM
Rev. W. W. Dewey (10) & wife	1901	11	01	Saginaw	MI	(9) Returned to MI district missionary 11-01-1901	ON
Rev. W. W. Dewey & wife	1902	01	08	Tower	MI	(10) From MI northern district missionary 11-01-1901	ON
Rev. W. W. Dewey & wife	1902	01	08	Clarks Lake	MI	(11) Resigned to pastor Chicago church 06-01-1902	LS&MS
Rev. W. W. Dewey & wife	1902	02	03	North Adams	MI	Church organized	MCR
Rev. W. W. Dewey (11) & wife	1902	05	01	Gladwin	MI	(12) From MI district missionary 06-01-1902	MCR
Rev. A. P. McDonald (12) & Rev. E. L. Killam (13)	1902	06	02	Standish	MI	Church organized	MCR
Rev. A. P. McDonald	1902	09	27	Kansas City	MO	Second Chapel Car Conference, without car, Lv 10-06-1902	--
Rev. A. P. McDonald	1902	10	06	Milan	MI	RR meeting, all chapel car missionaries, without car	--
Rev. A. P. McDonald	1902	10	07	Novinger	MO	Church dedication, all chapel car missionaries, without car	--
Rev. A. P. McDonald	1902	10	08	Green City	MO	Church dedication, all chapel car missionaries, without car	--
Rev. A. P. McDonald & Rev. E. L. Killam	1902	11	02	Sterling	MI	Church organized, pleased with work	PM
Rev. A. P. McDonald & Rev. E. L. Killam	1903	03	03	Saginaw	MI	(13) From MI district missionary 06-01-1902	PM
Rev. A. P. McDonald & Rev. E. L. Killam	1903	05	14	Coleman	MI		GR&I
Rev. A. P. McDonald & Rev. E. L. Killam	1903	07	08	Millersburg	MI		PM
Rev. A. P. McDonald & Rev. E. L. Killam	1904	01	13	Shepherd	MI	Church revived, 6 months	D&M
Rev. A. P. McDonald & Rev. E. L. Killam	1904	06	08	Chippewa	MI	Church revived	D&M
Rev. A. P. McDonald & Rev. J. S. Collins	1904	08	20	Marion	MI		AA
Rev. A. P. McDonald & Rev. E. L. Killam	1905	01	14	Boyne City	MI		PM
Rev. A. P. McDonald & Rev. E. L. Killam	1905	05	22	Reed City	MI		AA
Rev. A. P. McDonald & Rev. E. L. Killam	1905	07	05	Loomis	MI		BC&SE
Rev. A. P. McDonald & Rev. E. L. Killam	1905	09	06	Herrick	MI		PM
Rev. A. P. McDonald (15) & Rev. E. L. Killam (14)	1906	01	10	Coleman	MI	(14) To pastor at Chippewa, MI, before 06-1907	PM
Rev. A. P. McDonald (15) & Rev. E. L. Killam (14)	1907	01	10	Evart	MI	(15) To pastor at Mt. Clements, MI, before 09-1907	GR&I
(16)	1907	09	08		MI	Stayed 8 months	PM
(16)	1907			Car in shops	MI	Car in shops about 2 months	PM
(16)	1907	11	01	Car in shops		(16) Car vacant and in shops about 4 months total	PM
Rev. W. J. Sparks (17) & wife	1907	12	28	Streator	IL	Secured a lot for building, Lv 02-17-08	WAB
Rev. W. J. Sparks & wife	1908			Mine No. 3	IL	Mine 3 miles from Streator, IL, without car, Lv 02-17-1908	IC
Rev. W. J. Sparks & wife	1908	02	18	Tonica	IL	Lv 03-02-08	IC
Rev. W. J. Sparks & wife	1908	03	05	Oglesby	IL	Mining community, church organized, 6 months	CM&SP
Rev. W. J. Sparks & wife	1908	05	14	Kansas City	MO	Third Chapel Car Conference, without car	IC
Rev. W. J. Sparks & wife	1908	10	01	LaSalle	IL	(17) From Shenandoah, IA, 12-26-1907	IC
Rev. W. J. Sparks & wife	1908	10	18	Decatur	IL	IL Baptist State Convention, Lv 10-22-1908	IC
Rev. W. J. Sparks & wife	1908	11	01	Rockford	IL		NWL
Rev. W. J. Sparks & wife	1909	01	02	Harvard Park (Harvard)	IL	Mission organized, 1 week	C&EI
Rev. W. J. Sparks & wife	1909	03	03	South Danville	IL	Church organized	C&EI
Rev. W. J. Sparks & wife	1909	04	25	Grape Creek	IL	Coal field, 10 weeks	C&EI

PERSONNEL SERVING ON CARS	Y	M	D	TOWN	ST	COMMENTS FROM ACCOUNTS, LETTERS	R R
Rev. W. J. Sparks & wife	1909	07	02	Hillery	IL	Secured a lot for building	NWL
Rev. W. J. Sparks & wife	1909	07	15	Zion City	IL	Sunday school organized	NWL
Rev. W. J. Sparks & wife	1909	08	05	Rondout	IL	Assisted pastor from Waukegan, IL, mission organized	CM&SP
Rev. W. J. Sparks & wife	1909	08	26	Milwaukee	WI	Car in repair shops, 3 weeks	CM&SP
Rev. W. J. Sparks & wife	1909	09	18	Blue Island	IL		CRI&P
Rev. W. J. Sparks & wife	1909	09	22	Joliet	IL		CRI&P
Rev. W. J. Sparks & wife	1909	10	03	Springfield	IL	Mission organized	WAB
Rev. W. J. Sparks & wife	1909	10	16	Galesburg	IL	IL Baptist State Convention, Lv 10-21-1909	AT&SF
Rev. W. J. Sparks & wife	1909	10	23	Urbana	IL	Town and shop meetings. Sunday school organized. Lv 01-01-1910	CCC&SL
Rev. W. J. Sparks & wife	1910	01	03	Shawneetown	IL	Church organized, 3 months	B&OSW
Rev. W. J. Sparks & wife	1910	04	17	Highland	IL	Almost no English religious services in town, 5 weeks	VA
Rev. W. J. Sparks & wife	1910	04	25	Mount Vernon	IL	IL Baptist State Southern Union, without car, Lv 04-26-1910	–
Rev. W. J. Sparks	1910	05	27	Panama	IL	Coal town, had to leave due to diphtheria or smallpox	TSL&W
Rev. W. J. Sparks	1910	06	27	Grape Creek	IL	Dedication 06-26-1910, building finances, without car	–
Rev. W. J. Sparks	1910	07	01	Shop	IL	Car hot, vacation and car in shop, 2 months	?
Rev. W. J. Sparks	1910	07	03	Urbana	IL	Working on building finances, without car	–
Rev. W. J. Sparks	1910	07	23	Oglesby	IL	Dedication 07-24-1910, building finances, without car	IC
Rev. W. J. Sparks, wife & wife's father	1910	09	02	Blue Island	IL		–
Rev. W. J. Sparks, wife & wife's father	1910	10	16	Urbana	IL	IL Baptist State Convention, without car, Lv 10-21-1910	CM&SP
Rev. W. J. Sparks, wife & wife's father	1910	10	23	Oglesby	IL		CRI&P
Rev. W. J. Sparks, wife & wife's father	1911	01	21	Rockdale	IL		CRI&P
Rev. W. J. Sparks, wife & wife's father	1911	04	28	Joliet	IL		IC
Rev. W. J. Sparks, wife & wife's father	1911	07	01	Havana	OH	New railroad shops being built, Lv 02-18-1912	W&LE
Rev. W. J. Sparks, wife & wife's father	1911	09	20	Brewster	OH	Town and shop meetings, Lv 06-02-1912	PRR
Rev. W. J. Sparks, wife & wife's father	1912	02	20	Columbus	OH	Fourth Chapel Car Conference and churches, without car	PRR
Rev. W. J. Sparks & wife	1912	05	15	Kansas City	MO	North Toledo,OH, mission, Lv 10- 30-1912	B&OSW
Rev. W. J. Sparks, wife & wife's father	1912	06	04	Toledo	OH	OH Baptist State Convention, without car, Lv 10-25-1912	–
Rev. W. J. Sparks, wife & wife's father	1912	10	20	Columbus	OH	Steel district, town and RR YMCA meetings	N&W
Rev. W. J. Sparks	1912	10	27	New Boston	OH	Church dedication 1-03-1912, without car	CGW
Rev. W. J. Sparks	1912	11	02	Brewster	OH	RR YMCA meetings	C&NW
Rev. W. J. Sparks & wife	1912	12	15	Portsmouth	OH		C&NW
Rev. W. J. Sparks & wife	1913	04	01	Dubuque	IA		CGW
Rev. W. J. Sparks & wife	1913	05	03	Clinton	IA		–
Rev. W. J. Sparks & wife	1913	05	19	Carroll	IA	(18) On loan 6 months to IL Baptist State Convention 08-31-1914	–
Rev. W. J. Sparks (18) & wife	1913	07	20	Manly	IA	Church organized 08-16-1914	PCC&SL
(19)	1914	09	05	Dayton	OH	Car repaired Barney & Smith Car Company, Lv 11-28-1914	–
(19)	1914	11	28	Dayton	OH	Car rededicated at Dayton, OH, Union Station	–
(19)	1914	11	29	Dayton	OH	(19) Car vacant, repaired and stored 4 months total	B&O
Rev. W. F. Newton (20) & wife	1915	01	01	Dayton	OH	Picked up car at Barney & Smith Car Company	B&O
Rev. W. F. Newton & wife	1915	01	03	Point Pleasant	WV	(20) On loan from CT Baptist State Convention 6 months 01-01-1915	–
Rev. W. F. Newton & wife	1915	01	14	Henderson	WV	It was reported that First Baptist Church adopted car, lead in providing salary	B&O
Rev. W. F. Newton & wife	1915	01	15	Dayton	OH	Two weeks	B&O
Rev. W. F. Newton & wife	1915	02	01	St. Marys	WV	Six weeks	B&O
Rev. W. F. Newton & wife	1915	02	10	Wheeling	WV		C&O
Rev. W. F. Newton & wife	1915	02	24	Cameron	WV		C&C
Rev. W. F. Newton & wife	1915	04	08	Wallace	WV	Sunday school organized, Lv 05-17-1915	C&C
Rev. W. F. Newton & wife	1915	05	19	Lumberport	WV	Few days	C&C
Rev. W. F. Newton & wife	1915	06	01	Haywood	WV		C&C
Rev. W. F. Newton & wife	1915	06	05	Clarksburg	WV		B&O
Rev. W. F. Newton & wife	1915	06	10	Industrial	WV	Industrial School	B&O
Rev. W. F. Newton & wife	1915	06	15	Wilsonburg	WV		B&O
Rev. W. F. Newton (21) & wife	1915	06	20	Burnsville	WV	(21) Return to CT chapel auto service, 08-01-1915	B&O
(22)	1915	06	01	Quincy	WV	(22) Car vacant, vacation and car repairs 4 months	K&M
Rev. W. F. Newton (23) & wife	1915	12	02	Quincy	WV	Dickinson shops, RR shop meetings, 2 weeks	–
Rev. W. F. Newton & wife	1915	12	15	Logan	WV	Factory town, without car	WV
Rev. W. F. Newton & wife	1915	12	21	Quincy	WV	(23) Reassigned to car 12-01-1915	K&M
Rev. W. F. Newton & wife	1916	01	05	Bower	WV		C&C
Rev. W. F. Newton & wife	1916	02	08	Gassaway	WV	All had Grippe	C&C
Rev. W. F. Newton & wife	1916	03	10	Frametown	WV	Church reorganized 03-17-1916	C&C
Rev. W. F. Newton & wife	1916	03	20	Otter	WV		C&C
Rev. W. F. Newton & wife	1916	03	25	Clay	WV		?
Rev. W. F. Newton & wife	1916	04	01	St. Marys	WV	Stayed 2 weeks	B&O
Rev. W. F. Newton & wife	1916	04	15	Wheeling	WV		K&M
Rev. W. F. Newton & wife	1916	04	17	Eagleville	WV	Oil and gas fields	–
Rev. W. F. Newton & wife	1916	04	20	Clendenin	WV	WV Baptist State Convention, car on exhibit	C&C
Rev. W. F. Newton & wife	1916	05	06	Charleston	WV	Church reorganized and built building	B&O
Rev. W. F. Newton & wife	1916	05	08	Dunbar	WV	Church organized 06-09-1916, Lv 06-11-1916	K&M
Rev. W. F. Newton & wife	1916	06	12	Port Amherst (Dana)	WV	Near station, town and RR meetings	K&M
Rev. W. F. Newton & wife	1916	06	15	Malden	WV	While at Dana, WV, without car	C&O
Rev. W. F. Newton & wife	1916	06	26	Hurricane	WV		C&O
Rev. W. F. Newton & wife	1916	07	03	Pisgah Mines	WV	Church organized and worked on mission building	K&M
Rev. W. F. Newton & wife	1916	08	22	Smithers (Cannelton)	WV	RR shop meetings and cottage meetings, 2 weeks	K&M
Rev. W. F. Newton & wife	1916	09	10	Dickinson	WV	Received word go back to Quincy, WV	C&O
Rev. W. F. Newton & wife	1916	09	27	Logan	WV	Church reorganized and built building	K&M
Rev. W. F. Newton & wife	1916	10	15	Quincy	WV		K&M
Rev. W. F. Newton & wife	1917	01	01	Belle	WV		K&M
Rev. W. F. Newton & wife	1917	03	03	Boomer	WV	Church organized and worked on mission building	K&M
Rev. W. F. Newton & wife	1917	04	04	Longacre	WV	Influenced town	K&M
Rev. W. F. Newton & wife	1917	05	05	Cedar Grove	WV	Church organized	K&M
Rev. W. F. Newton & wife	1917	07	07	Smithers(Cannelton)	WV	Influenced town	C&O
Rev. W. F. Newton & wife	1917	10	06	Gauley Bridge	WV	Lumber camp	K&M

A.B.P.S. CAR 7, GRACE

PERSONNEL SERVING ON CARS	Y	M	D	TOWN	ST	COMMENTS FROM ACCOUNTS, LETTERS	R R
Rev. W. F. Newton & wife	1917	11	01	Lock Seven	WV	Church building located inside restricted Government power plant area at Nitro, WV	K&M
Rev. W. F. Newton & wife	1917	12	28		WV	Government takes over operation of railroads due to WWI	—
Rev. W. F. Newton & wife	1918	03	01	Nitro (Lock Seven)	WV	Lock Seven Baptist Church, without car	—
Rev. W. F. Newton & wife	1918	06	01	Dunbar	WV	Church organized, without car	C&O
Rev. W. F. Newton & wife	1918	10	01	Ronda	WV	Lumber camp, attempt made to dynamite car	K&M
Rev. W. F. Newton	1919	01	01	Nitro (Lock Seven)	WV	Baptism in Kanawha River	K&M
Rev. W. F. Newton	1919	06	29	Wallace	WV	Church dedicated, without car, Lv 06-30-1919	—
Rev. W. F. Newton & wife	1920	01	01	Nitro (Lock Seven)	WV	Car at Nitro, car needs repairs, LV 04-14-1921	K&M
Rev. W. F. Newton & wife	1920	03	01		WV	Government return ownership to railroads	—
Rev. W. F. Newton & wife	1921	06	07	Dunbar	WV	Lv 08-02-1921	K&M
Rev. W. F. Newton & wife	1921	06	04	Hurricane	WV		K&M
Rev. W. F. Newton & wife	1921	09	03	Bower	WV		B&O
Rev. W. F. Newton & wife	1921	09	04	Belle	WV		K&M
Rev. W. F. Newton & wife	1921	09	05	Boomer	WV	Church organized	C&O
Rev. W. F. Newton & wife	1921	10	01	Huntington	WV	Car in shop, town meetings, Lv 11-17-1921	C&O
Rev. W. F. Newton & wife	1921	11	19	Ronda	WV	Building dedicated 04-09-1922, Lv 05-01-1922	C&O
Rev. W. F. Newton & wife	1921	12	04	Charleston	WV	Without car	—
Rev. W. F. Newton & wife	1922	05	01	Quinwood	WV	New instructions, exterior lettering on chapel cars	G&E
Rev. W. F. Newton & wife	1922	09	15	Quinwood	WV	Church organized 11-12-1922, Rev. Newton pastor	G&E
Rev. W. F. Newton & wife	1922	11	16	Coal River	WV	Alum Creek, without car	G&E
Rev. W. F. Newton & wife	1922	12	01	Quinwood	WV	Coal mining town	G&E
Rev. W. F. Newton & wife	1923			Quinwood	WV	Build building	G&E
Rev. W. F. Newton & wife	1923	12	05	Leslie	WV	Church organized, without car	—
Rev. W. F. Newton & wife	1924			Quinwood	WV		G&E
Rev. W. F. Newton & wife	1925			Quinwood	WV		G&E
Rev. W. F. Newton & wife	1926			Quinwood	WV		G&E
Rev. W. F. Newton & wife	1927			Quinwood	WV		G&E
Rev. W. F. Newton & wife	1928			Quinwood	WV		G&E
Rev. W. F. Newton & wife	1929			Quinwood	WV		C&O
Rev. W. F. Newton & wife	1930			Quinwood	WV	Car heating plant reworked	C&O
Rev. W. F. Newton (24) & wife	1931	06	04	Quinwood	WV	(24) Rev. Newton died after operation in MD	C&O
Mrs. Newton	1931	06	22	Quinwood	WV	Mrs. Newton using car as a residence	C&O
Mrs. Newton	1931	09	29	Quinwood	WV	Car retired 09-30-1931	C&O
Mrs. Newton	1931	09	30	Quinwood	WV	Car sold to WV Baptist State Convention for $1, 09-30-1931	C&O
Mrs. Newton (25)	1935			Quinwood	WV	(25) Mrs. Newton return to North New Salem, MA	C&O
	1938			Quinwood	WV	Car may have been at Marfrance, WV, for 1 week ?	C&O
	1940			Quinwood	WV	Car used for coal company office about this time	C&O
	1946			Quinwood	WV	Car interior car furnishings scattered	C&O
	1947			Quinwood	WV	Car without trucks on ties and ground in coal tipple yard	—
	1948			Quinwood	WV	Coal company office and shop	—
	1950			Quinwood	WV	Car dismantled when coal company and yard was vacated	—

Car named after Grace Lothian Conaway

AMERICAN BAPTIST PUBLICATION SOCIETY

PERSONNEL SERVING ON CARS	Y	M	D	TOWN	ST	COMMENTS FROM ACCOUNTS, LETTERS	R R
Rev. S. G. Neil (1) & wife	1913	06	02	Dayton	OH	Asked for cost estimate on a new steel chapel car	—
Rev. S. G. Neil & wife	1914	03	16	Dayton	OH	Barney & Smith Car Company steel chapel car estimate $20,000	—
Rev. S. G. Neil & wife	1914	03	17		CA	Car donors Mr. & Mrs. Conaway and Mr. & Mrs. Birch	—
Rev. J. P. Jacobs (2) & wife	1914	06	17	Boston	PA	Pledged gift of chapel car at A.B.P.S. Anniversary Meeting	—
Rev. J. P. Jacobs & wife	1914	07	27	Dayton	OH	Car builder has been on steel work for some time	—
Rev. J. P. Jacobs & wife	1914	09	17	Denver	CO	Signed car building contract with Barney & Smith Car Company	—
Rev. J. P. Jacobs & wife, Rev. J. C. Killian (3) & wife	1915	01	05	Los Angeles	CA	Rev. E. R. Hermiston and wife choice of car donors for car 7	—
Rev. J. P. Jacobs & wife, Rev. J. C. Killian & wife	1915	04	30	Dayton	OH	Car shipped from builder, Barney & Smith Car Company	CH&D
Rev. J. P. Jacobs & wife, Rev. J. C. Killian & wife	1915	05	01	Dayton	OH	Car dedication 05-21-1915 at A.B.P.S. Anniversary Meeting	CH&D
Rev. G. L. White (4), wife and daughter	1915	05	06	Toledo	OH	(1) District superintendent temporarily on car while in transit to Chicago and on exhibit	CH&D
Rev. G. L. White, wife and daughter	1915	05	11	Chicago	IL	Exhibit, Services each day in car on way to Los Angeles, CA, Lv 05-15-1915	CRI&P
Rev. G. L. White, wife and daughter	1915	05	15	Lincoln	NE	(2) District superintendent temporarily on car while car is in transit to CA and A.B.P.S. Anniversary	CRI&P
Rev. G. L. White, wife and daughter	1915	05	16	Fairbury	NE	Exhibit, greeted chapel car on train	CRI&P
Rev. G. L. White, wife and daughter	1915	05	17	Denver	CO	Exhibit, while at station on train	D&RG
Rev. G. L. White, wife and daughter	1915	05	18	Salt Lake City	UT	Exhibit, while at station on train	SL&LA
Rev. G. L. White, wife and daughter	1915	05	19	Los Angeles	CA	(3) From chapel car 1, Evangel, temporary on car in transit to CA and A.B.P.S. Anniversary Meeting	AT&SF
Rev. G. L. White (4), wife and daughter	1915	05	27	Los Angeles	CA	(4) District superintendent temporarily on car from Los Angeles, CA, to Seattle, WA, and return	AT&SF
Rev. G. L. White, wife and daughter	1915	05	28	Inglewood	CA	Exhibit	AT&SF
Rev. G. L. White, wife and daughter	1915	06	03	Seattle	WA	Exhibit	SP
Rev. G. L. White, wife and daughter	1915	06	06	Medford	OR	Exhibit, chapel car stopped 10 places on return trip from Seattle, WA, to San Francisco, CA	SP
Rev. G. L. White, wife and daughter	1915	06	07	Ashland	OR	Exhibit	SP
Rev. C. M. Gardner (5) & wife	1915	06	13	Oakland	CA	Exhibit	SP
Rev. C. M. Gardner & wife	1915	06	16	Oakland	CA	(5) Colporter from northern CA temporary on car while car is on exhibit at exposition	SP
Rev. T. R. Gale (6) & wife	1915	06	17	San Francisco	CA	(6) From chapel car 5, Messenger of Peace, temporarily on car while car is on exhibit at Exposition	SP
Rev. E. R. Hermiston (7), wife & daughter	1915	06	18	P.I.E. grounds	CA	To Panama-Pacific International Exposition	SP
Rev. E. R. Hermiston, wife & daughter	1915	06	23	P.I.E. grounds	CA	Panama-Pacific International Exposition, 1 week	SP
Rev. E. R. Hermiston	1915	07	03	P.I.E. grounds	CA	Panama-Pacific International Exposition, 1 week	SP
Rev. E. R. Hermiston	1915	07	10	P.I.E. grounds	CA	Panama-Pacific International Exposition, 3 months	SP
Rev. E. R. Hermiston	1915	08	16	Oakland	CA	Baptist Young Peoples Union special day at exposition and car	SP
Rev. E. R. Hermiston, without car	1915	08	23	Oakland	CA	Services at church, 1 morning, without car	SP
Rev. E. R. Hermiston, wife & daughter	1915	09	27	?	CA	Services at church, 1 morning, without car	SP
Rev. E. R. Hermiston, wife & daughter	1915	10	01	San Francisco	CA	CA Baptist San Francisco Association, without car	SP
Rev. E. R. Hermiston, wife & daughter	1915	10	03	St. Helena	CA	From Panama-Pacific International Exposition	SP
Rev. E. R. Hermiston, wife & daughter	1915	11	16	Calistoga	CA	First revival services on car, church has been revived	SP
Rev. E. R. Hermiston, wife & daughter	1915	11	22	Yountville	CA	(7) Transferred from chapel car 2, Emmanuel, 07-01-1915	GOVT
Rev. E. R. Hermiston, wife & daughter	1915	12	23	Los Angeles	CA	Veterans vacation, car out of service	GOVT
Rev. E. R. Hermiston, wife & daughter	1916	01	04	Napa	CA	Christmas vacation	GOVT
Rev. E. R. Hermiston, wife & daughter	1916	01	29	Vallejo	CA	Bad weather but great meetings, 10 days	GOVT
Rev. E. R. Hermiston, wife & daughter	1916	02	20	Santa Rosa	CA	Navy boys from Mare Island at services	SP
Rev. E. R. Hermiston, wife & daughter					CA	Church made from one Redwood tree	SP

PERSONNEL SERVING ON CARS	Y	M	D	TOWN	ST	COMMENTS FROM ACCOUNTS, LETTERS	R R
Rev. E. R. Hermiston, wife & daughter	1916	03	18	Petaluma	CA	Forks are interested	NWP
Rev. E. R. Hermiston, wife & daughter	1916	04	12	Healdsburg	CA	Great victory in this old town	SP
Rev. E. R. Hermiston, wife & daughter	1916	05	01	San Francisco	CA	Working with Tabernacle Baptist Church, a struggling church	SP
Rev. E. R. Hermiston, wife & daughter	1916	05	19	Sacramento	CA	Working to start a new east side mission	SP
Rev. E. R. Hermiston, wife & daughter	1916	06	23	Sacramento	CA	Car in shop for light car repairs, RR shop and RR YMCA meetings. Lv 07-30-1916	SP
Rev. E. R. Hermiston, wife & daughter	1916	06	28	Broderick	CA	Working with church, without car	--
Rev. E. R. Hermiston, wife & daughter	1916	06	30	Sacramento	CA	Meetings at Oak Park Baptist Church and other churches, without car	SP
Rev. E. R. Hermiston, wife & daughter	1916	07	27	Van Nuys	CA		SP
Rev. E. R. Hermiston, wife & daughter	1916	08	16	St. Helena	CA		SP
Rev. E. R. Hermiston, wife & daughter	1916	08	21	Napa	CA		SP
Rev. E. R. Hermiston, wife & daughter	1916	08	10	Vallejo	CA		SP
Rev. E. R. Hermiston, wife & daughter	1916	09	02	Roseville	CA	Fine meetings in both town and RR shop meetings	SP
Rev. E. R. Hermiston, wife & daughter	1916	09	17	Burlingame	CA	Purchased some interior furnishing for car, 2 weeks	SP
Rev. E. R. Hermiston, wife & daughter	1916	10	15	Redwood City	CA	Helped pastor raise money for repairs and held fine meetings	SP
Rev. E. R. Hermiston, wife & daughter	1916	10	30	Palo Alto	CA	Town meetings and worked with students at Stanford University	SP
Rev. E. R. Hermiston, wife & daughter	1916	11	12	San Jose	CA	Burbank mission	SP
Rev. E. R. Hermiston, wife & daughter	1916	12	07	San Jose	CA	Calvary Baptist Church mission, 10 days	SP
Rev. E. R. Hermiston, wife & daughter	1916	12	20	Los Gatos	CA	Good meetings and dedicated a new building	SP
Rev. E. R. Hermiston, wife & daughter	1916	12	28	Watsonville	CA		SP
Rev. E. R. Hermiston, wife & daughter	1917	01	16	Los Angeles	CA	CA Southern State Baptist Convention	SP
Rev. E. R. Hermiston, wife & daughter	1917	01	17	Los Angeles	CA	Clean, oil, test, and stencil, air brake triple valve, $.81	SP
Rev. E. R. Hermiston, wife & daughter	1917	01	18	Los Angeles	CA	Exhibit, car open house 12 noon to 2 P.M. at depot, 1 day	SP
Rev. E. R. Hermiston, wife & daughter	1917	01	19	Calexico	CA	Soldiers from Fort Beacom came to car, 4 weeks	--
Rev. E. R. Hermiston, wife & daughter	1917	02	25	Holtville	CA	Submarine blockade, Hermiston wrote "wish Kiser was in heaven"	HIU
Rev. E. R. Hermiston, wife & daughter	1917	03	14	Brawley	CA	A little fire on car due to gasoline lights, no serious damage to car	SP
Rev. E. R. Hermiston, wife & daughter	1917	04	06	Thermal	CA		--
Rev. E. R. Hermiston, wife & daughter	1917	04	30	Colton	CA	A great time in meeting with high school and young people	SP
Rev. E. R. Hermiston, wife & daughter	1917	06	04	San Pedro	CA	Busy harbor town	SP
Rev. E. R. Hermiston, wife & daughter	1917	07	10	Los Angeles	CA	Car in shop, repairs, exterior paint and varnish $107.45, Lv 08-25-1917	PE
Rev. E. R. Hermiston, wife & daughter	1917	07	12	Los Angeles	CA	Helped at eastside mission, 10 day, without car	--
Rev. E. R. Hermiston, wife & daughter	1917	11	06	Huntington Beach	CA		SP
Rev. E. R. Hermiston, wife & daughter	1917	11	05	Taft	CA	Open air services, visited camps, schools, house to house	SUN
Rev. E. R. Hermiston, wife & daughter	1917	12	03	East Bakersfield	CA	RR meetings and spoke to 600 at high school, Lv 12-24-1917	SP
Rev. E. R. Hermiston, wife & daughter	1917	12	28		CA	Government takes over operation of railroads due to WWI	--
Rev. E. R. Hermiston, wife & daughter	1918	01	04	McKitterick	CA	Oil camps	PE
Rev. E. R. Hermiston, wife & daughter	1918	01	10	Santa Monica	CA		PE
Rev. E. R. Hermiston, wife & daughter	1918	01	20	Hermosa	CA		?
Rev. E. R. Hermiston, wife & daughter	1918	01	25	San Pedro	CA	Services on battleship and fort, in town for Japanese and Spanish people	SP
Rev. E. R. Hermiston, wife & daughter	1918	05	08	Palo Alto	CA	Assist Rev. J. L. Sawyer at Camp Fremont with soldiers	SP
Rev. E. R. Hermiston, wife & daughter	1918	05	21	Morgan Hill	CA		PE
Rev. E. R. Hermiston	1918	06	07	Camp Fremont	CA	Working with army chaplains and YMCA in car and tent	GOVAT
Rev. E. R. Hermiston, wife & daughter	1918	06	26	Berkeley	CA	CA Baptist Pacific Coast Convention, without car, Lv 06-26-1918	SP
Rev. E. R. Hermiston, wife & daughter	1918	07	15	Oakland	CA	RR train yard meetings, car cleaned, air brake and flat wheel repairs	--
Rev. E. R. Hermiston, wife & daughter	1918	08	03	Oakland	CA	On vacation, car out of service	SP
Rev. E. R. Hermiston, wife & daughter	1918	08	16	Long Beach	CA		--
Rev. E. R. Hermiston, wife & daughter	1918	02	16	San Lucas	CA	While at San Lucas, CA, without car	--
Rev. E. R. Hermiston, wife & daughter	1918	02	18	Lockwood Valley	CA	Helped to reorganize church work and put it on a workable basis	SP
Rev. E. R. Hermiston, wife & daughter	1918	02	20	Plato Valley	CA	While at San Lucas, CA, without car	--
Rev. E. R. Hermiston, wife & daughter	1918	02	23	Peachtree Valley	CA	Cow punchers and mountaineers, while at San Lucas, CA, without car	--
Rev. E. R. Hermiston, wife & daughter	1918	03	12	King City	CA	While at San Lucas, CA, without car	--
Rev. E. R. Hermiston, wife & daughter	1918	03	16	Salinas	CA	Good families compelled the chapel car to remain another week	SP
Rev. E. R. Hermiston, wife & daughter	1918	03	19	Gonzales	CA	Having big crowds and grand success	SP
Rev. E. R. Hermiston, wife & daughter	1918	04	13	Bakersfield	CA	Had to close up due to dyptheria, school also closed	SP
Rev. E. R. Hermiston, wife & daughter	1918	04	24	Watsonville	CA	Railroad center	SP
Rev. E. R. Hermiston, wife & daughter	1918	04	24	Monterey	CA		SP
Rev. E. R. Hermiston, wife & daughter	1918	04	24	Aromas	CA	Baptismal service	SP
Rev. E. R. Hermiston, wife & daughter	1918	08	08	Pittsburg	CA	Problem when car left town without permission	SP
Rev. E. R. Hermiston, wife & daughter	1918	10	24	Vacaville	CA	Many have flu in town which makes it hard to call on people	SP
Rev. E. R. Hermiston, wife & daughter	1919	01	03	Sacramento	CA	Rev. E. R. Hermiston and wife both sick with flu	SP
Rev. E. R. Hermiston, wife & daughter	1919	01	13	Sacramento	CA	Railroad car transportation and chapel car parking problem may concern car	SP
Rev. E. R. Hermiston, wife & daughter	1919	01	23	San Francisco	CA	Rev. E. R. Hermiston threatens to leave car to be pastor here	SP
Rev. E. R. Hermiston, wife & daughter	1919	02	07	Chico	CA	Having big crowds and grand success	SP
Rev. E. R. Hermiston, wife & daughter	1919	02	24	Red Bluff	CA	Built building, Lv 01-15-1920	SP
Rev. E. R. Hermiston, wife & daughter	1919	03	28	Redding	CA	10 days	SP
Rev. E. R. Hermiston, wife & daughter	1919	04	09	Anderson	CA	They wanted chapel car back to help them	SP
Rev. E. R. Hermiston, wife & daughter	1919	05	10	Gerber	CA	Fine services	SP
Rev. E. R. Hermiston, wife & daughter	1920	01	16	Corning	CA	Government returned ownership to railroads	SP
Rev. E. R. Hermiston, wife & daughter	1920	01	27	Orland	CA	Car inspected for repairs and painting estimate, $2000.	SP
Rev. E. R. Hermiston, wife & daughter	1920	02	15	Arbuckle	CA	Built parsonage	SP
Rev. E. R. Hermiston, wife & daughter	1920	03	01	Grimes	CA	Car repaired, $1390.02 plus $.51 = $1390.53	SP
Rev. E. R. Hermiston, wife & daughter	1920	04	16	Sacramento	CA	Repaired church building and built parsonage	SP
Rev. E. R. Hermiston, wife & daughter	1920	05	05	Orland	CA	Settled pastor, improved property and meetings	SP
Rev. E. R. Hermiston, wife & daughter	1920	08	16	Hughson	CA	Church organized 04-12-1921 and built building, Lv 08-01-1921	SF
Rev. E. R. Hermiston, wife & daughter	1920	10	11	Waterford	CA		SF
Rev. E. R. Hermiston, wife & daughter (8)	1920	12	06	Chowchilla	CA	(8) Daughter Marjorie Hermiston married on car by her father, 03-??-1921	SP
Rev. E. R. Hermiston & wife	1921	11	16	Del Rey	CA		SF
Rev. E. R. Hermiston & wife	1922	01	02	Malaga	CA		SP
Rev. E. R. Hermiston & wife	1922	01	23	Lemoore	CA	Repaired car lamps $55	SP

PERSONNEL SERVING ON CARS	Y	M	D	TOWN	ST	COMMENTS FROM ACCOUNTS, LETTERS	R R
Rev. E. R. Hermiston & wife	1922	02	01	Chowchilla	CA	Built building ?	SP
Rev. E. R. Hermiston & wife	1922	02	05	San Joaquin	CA	Sometimes called San Joaquin City, built building, 10 months	SP
Rev. E. R. Hermiston & wife	1922	05	01			New instructions, exterior lettering on chapel cars	--
Rev. E. R. Hermiston & wife	1922	12	21	Auberry	CA	Moved building and held meetings, without car	--
Rev. E. R. Hermiston & wife	1923	03	03	Las Vegas	NV	Church organized 04-19-1923, car south of depot	UP
Rev. E. R. Hermiston (9) & wife	1923	08	01	Las Vegas	NV	(9) Rev. Hermiston died 09-27-1923 in Modesto, CA, while taking a rest, without car	UP
Rev. E. R. Hermiston (10)	1923	08	02	Las Vegas	NV	(10) Car out of service 7 weeks	UP
(11)	1923	09	18	Las Vegas	NV	(11) Car vacant 09-28-1923 through 04-01-1924, 6 months	UP
Rev. A. C. Blinzinger (12) & wife	1924	04	01	Las Vegas	NV	(12) Transferred from chapel car 2,Emmanuel, 04-01-1924	UP
Rev. A. C. Blinzinger & wife	1924	05	20	Los Angeles	CA	Car repairs, lights, fire damage, painting, varnishing	SP
Rev. A. C. Blinzinger & wife	1924	05	25	Las Vegas	NV	RR shop meetings, depot town meetings and visited homes, without car	UP
Rev. A. C. Blinzinger & wife	1924	09	14	Camarillo	CA	Meetings, without car	SP
Rev. A. C. Blinzinger & wife	1924	09	26	Los Angeles	CA	Picked up car from shop	SP
Rev. A. C. Blinzinger & wife	1924	09	28	Las Vegas	NV	First service in car 09-30-1924, out of service 6 months	UP
Rev. A. C. Blinzinger & wife	1925	04	25	Ortonville	CA	Build building, 12 months	SP
Rev. A. C. Blinzinger & wife	1926	06	01	Salt Lake City	UT	Also surrounding area	UP
Rev. A. C. Blinzinger & wife	1927	01	01	Winnemucca	NV	Built building invocation offered 10-10-1927	SP
Rev. A. C. Blinzinger & wife	1927	05	01	Sonora	CA	Without car	SP
Rev. A. C. Blinzinger & wife	1927	05	13	Contact	NV	Without car	--
Rev. A. C. Blinzinger & wife	1928			Other towns	NV		?
Rev. A. C. Blinzinger & wife	1929	06	15	Rawlins	WY	Built building, some pews from chapel car 1, Evangel, used in Sunday school, Lv 10-25-1930	UP
Rev. A. C. Blinzinger & wife	1930	11	19	Thermopolis	WY	Built building, some pews from chapel car 1, Evangel, used in church	BR
Rev. A. C. Blinzinger	1931	08	21	Cheyenne	WY	WY Baptist State Convention, without car	--
Rev. A. C. Blinzinger	1932	04	27	Lander	WY	WY Baptist Big Horn Association, without car	BR
Rev. A. C. Blinzinger & wife	1932	08	29	Thermopolis	WY	While on vacation car was broken into and items taken, Lv 06-30-1932	BR
Rev. A. C. Blinzinger & wife	1932	09	02	Powell	WY	Built building, 36 months, Lv 09-06-1935	BR
Rev. A. C. Blinzinger & wife	1933	04	26	Thermopolis	WY	WY Baptist Big Horn Association, without car	BR
Rev. A. C. Blinzinger & wife	1933	11	21	Chugwater	WY	Special meetings, without car	--
Rev. A. C. Blinzinger & wife	1934	05	02	Riverton	WY	WY Baptist Big Horn Association, without car	BR
Rev. A. C. Blinzinger & wife	1934	05	22	Rochester	NY	A.B.P.S. Anniversary Meeting and vacation, without car, Lv 05-29-1934	--
Rev. A. C. Blinzinger & wife	1934	05	30	Powell	WY	Received reduction in pay as of 05-01-1934 due to Home Mission Society budget reduction	BR
Rev. A. C. Blinzinger & wife	1934	10	14	Powell	WY	Painted car roof, trucks and exterior	--
Rev. A. C. Blinzinger & wife	1935	08	27	Powell	WY	WY Baptist State Convention, in church, Lv 09-07-1935	BR
Rev. A. C. Blinzinger & wife	1935	09	08	Casper	WY	Baker heater and car repairs	C&NW
Rev. A. C. Blinzinger & wife	1935	09	12	Riverton	WY	Built building and vacation, Lv 06-01-1937	C&NW
Rev. A. C. Blinzinger & wife	1937	06	07	Torrington	WY	Completed building, Lv 09-19-1938	BR
Rev. A. C. Blinzinger & wife	1938	07	05	?	WY	Car vacant, 1 month	?
Rev. A. C. Blinzinger & wife	1938	07	10	Buffalo	WY	Car repaired $650	WY
Rev. A. C. Blinzinger & wife	1938	09	10	Sheridan	WY	Built building and vacation, Lv 09-03-1940	BR
Rev. A. C. Blinzinger & wife	1940	09	04	?	WY	Lv 01-05-1941	?
Rev. A. C. Blinzinger & wife	1941	01	06	?	WY	Car air brake repairs $3.65	BR
Rev. A. C. Blinzinger & wife	1942	01	07	Lander	WY	Remodeled building, built educational unit	C&NW
Rev. A. C. Blinzinger & wife	1942	03	06	Lander	WY	Lv 09-30-1942	C&NW
Rev. A. C. Blinzinger & wife	1942	07	25	Billings	MT	Rev. A. C. Blinzinger in hospital for operation, without car	--
Rev. A. C. Blinzinger (13) & wife (14)	1942	10	01	Denver	CO	(13) Special service for repair funds 09-01-1942 through 11-30-1942, off car 10-01-1942	D&RGW
	1942	10	02	Denver	CO	(14) Left car 10-01-1942 and retired 11-30-1942	D&RGW
	1942	10	20	Denver	CO	Burnham shop car repair estimate $800	D&RGW
(15)	1943	09	12	Denver	CO	(15) Car vacant, 4 months	D&RGW
(16)	1943	06	29	Denver	CO	(16) Car in shop for exterior paint and heater repairs 5 months, $537.83	D&RGW
(17)	1943	07	29	Denver	CO	(17) Car vacant, 1 month	SL&U
Rev. H. Parry (18) & wife	1943	08	01	Orem	UT	Set car on spur track spot	SL&U
Rev. H. Parry & wife	1943	09	27	Orem	UT	(18) From pastor, Monticello, UT, 07-22-1943, picked up car, 07-29-1943	SL&U
(19)	1944	01	01	Orem	UT	(19) Out of service, waiting for Rev. H. Parry, 2 months	--
Rev. H. Parry (20) & wife	1944	05	08	Salt Lake City	UT	(20) On car, first service in car 10-08-1943	SL&U
Rev. H. Parry & wife	1944	07	31	Ogden	UT	UT Baptist State Convention, without car, Lv 05-09-1944	--
Rev. H. Parry & wife	1944	10	20	Denver	CO	UT Baptist Assembly, north fork of Ogden Canyon, without car, Lv 08-11-1944	D&RGW
Rev. H. Parry & wife	1945	01	20	Chicago	IL	Drives auto to Chicago while car is en route to Chicago	--
Rev. H. Parry	1945	10	07	Phoenix	AZ	AZ Baptist State Convention promotional conferences, without car, Lv 10-18-1945	--
Rev. H. Parry	1946	01	12	?	KS	KS state speaking trip returned 01-23-1946, without car	--
Rev. H. Parry	1946	02	03	Orem	UT	Last church service in car, car left 02-06-1946	SL&U
Rev. H. Parry	1946	02	13	Denver	CO	New England speaking trip IL, MA, PA, NJ, NY, OH, and IN, returns 03-31-1946, without car	D&RGW
Rev. H. Parry & wife	1946	04	14	Payton	CO	Burnham shops car in shop repairs and painting	D&RGW
Rev. H. Parry & wife	1946	04	15	Denver	CO	Church service, without car	D&RGW
Rev. H. Parry & wife	1946	04	18	Denver	CO	Burnham shops removed personal effects for storage	D&RGW
Rev. H. Parry	1946	04	20	Chicago	IL	Memorial service in car 04-22-1946 at 12th St. coach train yard	CB&Q
Rev. H. Parry	1946	04	23	Green Lake	WI	Began loading car body and car trucks on hi-way trucks, 04-24-1946	C&NW
Rev. H. Parry	1946	04	30	Green Lake	WI	Car retired from active service	C&NW
Rev. H. Parry	1946	05	01	NBA grounds	WI	Car body near car trucks and track, car move completed on 05-03-1946	--
Rev. H. Parry	1946	05	09	NBA grounds	WI	First use of car	--
Rev. H. Parry	1946	05	10	NBA grounds	WI	Car on section of track in Town & County Center, Abbey Area	--
Rev. H. Parry	1946	05	15	NBA grounds	WI	Exhibit, Third Green Lake Conference	--
Rev. H. Parry	1946	08	16	NBA grounds	WI	Exhibit car dedicated to all chapel car workers of the past	--
Rev. H. Parry	1947	01	01	NBA grounds	WI	Exhibit, car also used as living quarters for some time	--
Rev. H. Parry (21)	1948	01	01	NBA grounds	WI	(21) Transferred to Lodge Grass and Wyola, MT, 11-01-1946	--
	1983	06	25	ABA grounds	WI	Exhibit, car moved to section of track in conference area	--
	1999	12		ABA grounds	WI	Exhibit, car used for some church services, since 05-09-1946	--
C.C.E.S. FIRST CAR, ST. ANTHONY Car named by Mr. Ambrose Petry in honor of St. Anthony	1903					**THE CATHOLIC CHURCH EXTENSION SOCIETY OF THE UNITED STATES OF AMERICA**	--
Rev. Francis Clement Kelley, president of C.C.E.S.,	1904	06	01	St. Louis	MO	Rev. Francis Clement Kelley visits 1904 St. Louis, MO, World's Fair (exact date unknown)	--
originator of Catholic Church Extension Society chapel cars	1904	06	02	St. Louis	MO	Rev. Kelley sees chapel car 5, Messenger of Peace, at St. Louis World's Fair	--
	1906	12		Chicago	IL	After seeing Baptist chapel car, Rev. Kelley asks for Catholic Extension Society chapel car donors	--

Y	M	D	TOWN	ST	COMMENTS FROM ACCOUNTS, LETTERS	RR	PERSONNEL SERVING ON CARS
1907	01		Chicago	IL	Car donors, Ambrose Petry and Richmond Dean offer to give chapel car	—	
1907	02		Pullman	IL	Wagner Sleeping car in shop for alterations to chapel car	IC	
1907	06	14	Pullman	IL	Car shipped from Pullman Palace Car Company	IC	
1907	06	16	Chicago	IL	Car dedication in La Salle St. Station	CRI&P	Mr. G. C. Hennessey (1) & Rev. T. A. McKernan (2)
1907	06	17	Kansas City	MO	Waiting travel plans and railroad chapel car passes	MP	Mr. G. C. Hennessey & Rev. T. A. McKernan
1907	06	18	St. Louis	MO	Large crowds visited car at Union Station	MP	Mr. G. C. Hennessey & Rev. T. A. McKernan
1907	06	19	Wichita	KS	Pullman Car Company finishing car, large crowds go through car	CRI&P	Mr. G. C. Hennessey & Rev. T. A. McKernan
1907	06	23	Wellington	KS	First Mass offered in car on 06-23-1907	CRI&P	Mr. G. C. Hennessey & Rev. T. A. McKernan
1907	06	24	Wichita	KS	No mission	CRI&P	Mr. G. C. Hennessey & Rev. T. A. McKernan.
1907	06	25	Hutchinson	KS	Car stayed over night only	CRI&P	Mr. G. C. Hennessey & Rev. T. A. McKernan.
1907	06	26	Castleton	KS	(1) Superintendent of Catholic Church Extension Society chapel cars from MI	AT&SF	Mr. G. C. Hennessey & Rev. T. A. McKernan.
1907	06	27	Turon	KS	(2) First chapel car chaplain from KS	CRI&P	Mr. G. C. Hennessey & Rev. T. A. McKernan.
1907	06	29	Liberal	KS	Met with townsite company for land to build on	CRI&P	Mr. G. C. Hennessey & Rev. T. A. McKernan.
1907	06	30	Meade	KS	A committee called to start building church	CRI&P	Mr. G. C. Hennessey & Rev. T. A. McKernan.
1907	07	01	Bucklin	KS	Most of the town moving to Pratt, KS	CRI&P	Mr. G. C. Hennessey & Rev. T. A. McKernan.
1907	07	02	Pratt	KS	Used church, attendance low due to harvesting	AT&SF	Mr. G. C. Hennessey & Rev. T. A. McKernan.
1907	07	06	Girard	KS	Mr. Petry paid $2000 for car to Pullman Palace Car Company	FS	Mr. G. C. Hennessey & Rev. T. A. McKernan.
1907	07	06	Weir City (Weir)	KS	Dedication of church	FS	Mr. G. C. Hennessey & Rev. T. A. McKernan.
1907	07	07	Cherokee	KS	We visited several small towns for dedications	FS	Mr. G. C. Hennessey & Rev. T. A. McKernan.
1907	07	08	Scammon	KS	Laying corner stone of church building	FS	Mr. G. C. Hennessey & Rev. T. A. McKernan.
1907	07	10	Parsons	KS		?	Mr. G. C. Hennessey & Rev. T. A. McKernan.
1907	07	11	Galena	KS	Dedication of church	?	Mr. G. C. Hennessey & Rev. T. A. McKernan.
1907	07	12	Green Bush	KS	Mentioned that all Indians in town had Irish names	AT&SF	Mr. G. C. Hennessey & Rev. T. A. McKernan.
1907	07	13	Chautauqua	KS	Town of 5000 with no church	AT&SF	Mr. G. C. Hennessey & Rev. T. A. McKernan.
1907	07	14	Caney	KS	Car at depot, 2 days	CRI&P	Mr. G. C. Hennessey & Rev. T. A. McKernan.
1907	07	18	Hotwater	KS		AT&SF	Mr. G. C. Hennessey & Rev. T. A. McKernan.
1907	07	28	Herington	KS		AT&SF	Mr. G. C. Hennessey & Rev. T. A. McKernan.
1907	09	10	Wichita	KS	English tourists on train to Kingsley, KS, came in to see car	AT&SF?	Mr. G. C. Hennessey & Rev. T. A. McKernan.
1907	09	22	Kingsley	KS	Site selected for building church	AT&SF	Mr. G. C. Hennessey & Rev. T. A. McKernan.
1907	09	25	Hanston	KS	Coupled to a coal car, organ had to overcome the noise from unloading coal	AT&SF	Mr. G. C. Hennessey & Rev. T. A. McKernan.
1907	10	12	Dodge City	KS	Remained overnight, no mission, found truck brake rod bad	AT&SF	Mr. G. C. Hennessey & Rev. T. A. McKernan.
1907	10	15	Ingalls	KS	A very grateful and devout congregation	AT&SF	Mr. G. C. Hennessey & Rev. T. A. McKernan.
1907	10	18	Offerle	KS	Helped settled problem to build church building	AT&SF	Mr. G. C. Hennessey & Rev. T. A. McKernan.
1907	10	24	Belpre	KS	People not expecting car, we give night missions	AT&SF	Mr. G. C. Hennessey & Rev. T. A. McKernan.
1907	10		Lewis	KS		AT&SF	Mr. G. C. Hennessey & Rev. T. A. McKernan.
1907	11		Other towns	KS	No records for 11-1907 through 01-1908	?	Mr. G. C. Hennessey
1908	02	05	Chicago	IL		NWL	Rev. J. J. O'Neill (3)
1908	02	21	Bearsford	SD	(3) From Beresford, SD	NWL	Rev. J. J. O'Neill & Rev. Plante (4)
1908	02	24	Canistota	SD	(4) From SD	NWL	Rev. J. J. O'Neill & Rev. Plante
1908	02	28	Mc Cook	SD	Has interest in work beyond listening	NWL	Rev. J. J. O'Neill & Rev. Plante
1908	03	01	Sioux Point	SD		NWL	Rev. J. J. O'Neill & Rev. Plante
1908	03	07	Beresford	SD	No mission, chapel car porter sick, had to received care	NWL	Rev. J. J. O'Neill & Rev. Plante
1908	03	17	Lake Preston	SD	No chapel car porter, 13 Catholic families trying to build church	CM&SP	Rev. J. J. O'Neill & Rev. Cafferky (5)
1908	03	21	Aberdeen	SD	Used car but moved to hall for 300 in attendance	CM&SP	Rev. J. J. O'Neill & Rev. Cafferky
1908	03	23	Mobridge	SD	RR men at meeting, town less than 1 year old	CM&SP	Rev. J. J. O'Neill & Rev. Cafferky
1908	03	28	Vienna	SD		CM&SP	Rev. J. J. O'Neill & Rev. Cafferky
1908	03	30	Bryant	SD	(5) From Bryant, SD	CM&SP	Rev. J. J. O'Neill & Rev. Plante
1908	04	06	Manchester	SD	Guest of Rev. Cafferky's home town	MWL	Rev. J. J. O'Neill & Rev. Plante
1908	04	06	Wolsey	SD	Stayed 1 week	MWL	Rev. J. J. O'Neill & Rev. Plante
1908	04	07	Eureka	SD	Three Catholic women in town, cold non-Catholics	MWL	Rev. J. J. O'Neill & Rev. Plante
1908	04	11	Roscoe	SD	Fair attendance at lectures	NWL	Rev. J. J. O'Neill & Rev. Plante
1908	04	18	Wessington	SD	Car in shop, steam system repairs and cleaned car	NWL	Rev. J. J. O'Neill & Rev. Plante
1908	04	25	Westport	SD		NWL	Rev. J. J. O'Neill & Rev. Amirault (6)
1908	05	02	Wetonka	SD		NWL	Rev. J. J. O'Neill & Rev. Amirault
1908	05	09	Huron	SD	(6) From ND	NWL	Rev. J. J. O'Neill & Rev. Amirault
1908	05	11	Broadland	SD	First town visited that had a church building	NWL	Rev. J. J. O'Neill & Rev. Amirault
1908	05	24	Athol	SD		CM&SP	Rev. J. J. O'Neill & Rev. Amirault
1908	05	27	Northville	SD	Catholic population in great numbers	CM&SP	Rev. J. J. O'Neill & Rev. Amirault
1908	06	06	Aberdeen	SD	Large Catholic crowds	CM&SP	Rev. J. J. O'Neill & Rev. Amirault
1908	06	07	Hecla	SD	Everybody in town is German from Russia, car full	CM&SP	Rev. J. J. O'Neill & Rev. Amirault
1908	06	14	Leola	SD	Many Catholics went through car	M&SL	Rev. J. J. O'Neill & Rev. Amirault
1908	06	22	Cresbard	SD	(7) From Sioux Falls, SD	CCC&SL	Rev. J. J. O'Neill & Rev. O'Meara (7)
1908	07	19	Chicago	IL	(8) From Chicago, IL, vice president of C.C.E.S.	CCC&SL	Rev. W. D. O'Brien (8)
1908	08	15	Indianapolis	IN	Exhibit, reception, cordial and results encouraging	NYNH&H	Rev. W. D. O'Brien
1908	08	17	Boston	MA	First city on northeastern exhibition cities tour	NYNH&H	Rev. W. D. O'Brien
1908	08	18	Albany	NY	Catholic population in great numbers	NYC&HR	Rev. W. D. O'Brien
1908	08	19	Utica	NY	Large Catholic crowds	NYC&HR	Rev. W. D. O'Brien
1908	08	19	Syracuse	NY	Many Catholics went through car	NYC&HR	Rev. W. D. O'Brien
1908	08	22	Rochester	NY	Car in great location for all the city to see, 2 days	NYC&HR	Rev. W. D. O'Brien
1908	08	22	Buffalo	NY	Stayed 2 days	LS&MS	Rev. W. D. O'Brien
1908	08	24	Erie	PA	For safety, police helped handle the people, 2 days	LS&MS	Rev. W. D. O'Brien
1908	08	25	Cleveland	OH	One day in Union Depot, 1 day in a poor place in freight yard	LS&MS	Rev. W. D. O'Brien
1908	08	26	Sandusky	OH	Chaplains thought every priest in city came to see the car	LS&MS	Rev. W. D. O'Brien
1908	08	27	Toledo	OH	A hearty reception was extended to the car	LS&MS	Rev. W. D. O'Brien
1908	08	28	South Bend	IN	Last city on northeastern exhibition cities tour	LS&MS	Rev. W. D. O'Brien
1908	08	29	Chicago	IL	Car repairs, car sides weather-beaten and sun-blistered	IC	Mr. G. C. Hennessey
1908	08	30	Pullman	IL		IC	Mr. G. C. Hennessey
1908	09	18	Chicago	IL		WC	Mr. G. C. Hennessey
1908	09	20	Milwaukee	WI	Start short Wisconsin state exhibition tour	WC	Mr. G. C. Hennessey & Rev. W. D. O'Brien

PERSONNEL SERVING ON CARS	Y	M	D	TOWN	ST	COMMENTS FROM ACCOUNTS, LETTERS	R R
Mr. G. C. Hennessey & Rev. W. D. O'Brien (9)	1908	09	21	Green Bay	WI	Exhibit	NWL
Mr. G. C. Hennessey & Rev. A. P. Landry (9)	1908	10	01	Chicago	IL	(9) Previous situation unknown	WC
Mr. G. C. Hennessey & Rev. A. P. Landry	1908	10	09	Ft. Wayne	IN	First city on eastern exhibition tour	CH&D
Mr. G. C. Hennessey & Rev. A. P. Landry	1908	10	10	Cincinnati	OH	Large crowds, station master had to close track gates for safety	CH&D
Mr. G. C. Hennessey & Rev. A. P. Landry	1908	10	11	Dayton	OH	Car visited by Mr. Peter A. Kuntz Sr., donor of 2nd and 3rd car	CH&D
Mr. G. C. Hennessey & Rev. A. P. Landry	1908	10	12	Columbus	OH	Exhibit	PRR
Mr. G. C. Hennessey & Rev. A. P. Landry	1908	10	13	Wheeling	WV	Exhibit	PRR
Mr. G. C. Hennessey & Rev. A. P. Landry	1908	10	14	Pittsburg	PA	Exhibit	PRR
Mr. G. C. Hennessey & Rev. A. P. Landry	1908	10	15	Altoona	PA	Exhibit	PRR
Mr. G. C. Hennessey & Rev. A. P. Landry	1908	10	16	Harrisburg	PA	Exhibit, the whole town talked chapel car and came through car	PRR
Mr. G. C. Hennessey & Rev. A. P. Landry	1908	10	17	Philadelphia	PA	Exhibit, hard rain kept people away from chapel car	PRR
Mr. G. C. Hennessey & Rev. A. P. Landry	1908	10	18	Trenton	NJ	Exhibit	PRR
Mr. G. C. Hennessey & Rev. A. P. Landry	1908	10	19	Wilmington	DE	Exhibit	PRR
Mr. G. C. Hennessey & Rev. A. P. Landry	1908	10	20	Baltimore	MD	Exhibit	PRR
Mr. G. C. Hennessey & Rev. A. P. Landry	1908	10	21	Washington	DC	Exhibit	C&O
Mr. G. C. Hennessey & Rev. A. P. Landry	1908	10	22	Richmond	VA	Exhibit	C&O
Mr. G. C. Hennessey & Rev. A. P. Landry	1908	10	23	Louisville	KY	Exhibit	Cl&L
Mr. G. C. Hennessey & Rev. A. P. Landry	1908	10	24	Lafayette	IN	Last city on eastern tour	Cl&L
Mr. G. C. Hennessey	1908	10	25	Chicago	IL	No services	Cl&L
Mr. G. C. Hennessey	1908	11	14	Pullman	IL	Light repairs	IC
Mr. G. C. Hennessey	1908	11	20	Chicago	IL	Exhibit, First American Catholic Missionary Congress, 5 days	IC
Mr. G. C. Hennessey	1908	11	26	Pullman	IL	Car may be in shop for repairs or waiting next mission	IC
Mr. G. C. Hennessey & Rev. W. L. Polk (10)	1909	01	14	Chicago	IL	Car starts south (10) From Portland, OR	IC
Mr. G. C. Hennessey & Rev. W. L. Polk	1909	01	16	New Orleans	LA	Twenty thousand people visited car	Y&MV
Mr. G. C. Hennessey & Rev. W. L. Polk	1909	01	22	Memphis	TN	Five thousand people visited car	Y&MV
Mr. G. C. Hennessey & Rev. W. L. Polk	1909	02	01	Clarksdale	MS	Non-Catholic lectures held in courthouse	Y&MV
Mr. G. C. Hennessey & Rev. W. L. Polk	1909	02	01	Rosedale	MS	A deeply religious town	Y&MV
Mr. G. C. Hennessey & Rev. W. L. Polk	1909	02	09	Gloster	MS	Morning Mass in car, evening lectures in town hall	Y&MV
Mr. G. C. Hennessey & Rev. W. L. Polk	1909	02	13	Woodville	MS	Three or four Jewish families at lectures	Y&MV
Mr. G. C. Hennessey & Rev. J. W. Handly (11)	1909	02	22	New Orleans	LA	(11) From Winchester, TN	NO&GN
Mr. G. C. Hennessey & Rev. J. W. Handly	1909	02	27	Bogalusa	LA	Company sawmill town, mill runs 24 hour 7 days a week	NO&GN
Mr. G. C. Hennessey & Rev. J. W. Handly	1909	03	06	Franklinton	LA	Morning Mass in car, evening lectures in court house	NO&GN
Mr. G. C. Hennessey & Rev. J. W. Handly	1909	03	13	Slidell	LA	Lectures in Red Men's Hall each night	NO&GN
Mr. G. C. Hennessey & Rev. J. W. Handly	1909	03	20	Mandeville	LA	2 Sunday sermons in church and 2 on rear car vestibule platform	Y&MV
Mr. G. C. Hennessey & Rev. J. W. Handly	1909	03	26	Covington	LA	Heavy use of question box, 2 hour evening lectures	Y&MV
Mr. G. C. Hennessey & Rev. J. W. Handly	1909	04	05	Baton Rouge	LA	Exhibit	Y&MV
Mr. G. C. Hennessey & Rev. J. W. Handly	1909	04	06	Natchez	MS	Exhibit	NO&NW
Mr. G. C. Hennessey & Rev. J. W. Handly	1909	04	10	Red Lick	MS	Exhibit, no services, 1 week	Y&MV
Mr. G. C. Hennessey & Rev. J. W. Handly	1909	04	17	Durant	MS	Chaplains felt town deserved a church building	Y&MV
Mr. G. C. Hennessey & Rev. J. W. Handly	1909	04	24	Winona	MS	Service spoiled by noise in double train yards	Y&MV
Mr. G. C. Hennessey & Rev. J. W. Handly	1909	05	01	Water Valley	MS	Workers from railroad shop, much good to Catholics	IC
Mr. G. C. Hennessey & Rev. J. W. Handly	1909	05	08	Holly Springs	MS	Highly intelligent and cordial audiences	IC
Mr. G. C. Hennessey & Rev. J. W. Handly	1909	05	15	Jackson	TN	Starts exhibition tour to Chicago, IL	IC
Mr. G. C. Hennessey & Rev. A. W. Doran (12)	1909	05	16	Evansville	IN	Exhibit (12) From Philadelphia, PA	IC
Mr. G. C. Hennessey & Rev. A. W. Doran	1909	05	17	Decatur	IL	Exhibit	IC
Mr. G. C. Hennessey & Rev. A. W. Doran	1909	05	18	Peoria	IL	Exhibit	IC
Mr. G. C. Hennessey & Rev. A. W. Doran	1909	05	19	Springfield	IL	Exhibit	IC
Mr. G. C. Hennessey & Rev. A. W. Doran	1909	05	20	Bloomington	IL	Exhibit	IC
Mr. G. C. Hennessey & Rev. A. W. Doran	1909	05	21	Freeport	IL	Exhibit	IC
Mr. G. C. Hennessey & Rev. A. W. Doran	1909	05	22	Rockford	IL	Exhibit	IC
Mr. G. C. Hennessey & Rev. A. W. Doran	1909	05	23	Chicago	IL	Ends exhibition tour	IC
Mr. G. C. Hennessey & Rev. A. W. Doran	1909	05	24	Pullman	IL	Car in shop for repairs and waiting next mission	IC
Mr. G. C. Hennessey & Rev. A. W. Doran	1909	07	02	Clinton	IA	Starts western summer exhibition tour	NWL
Mr. G. C. Hennessey & Rev. A. W. Doran	1909	07	03	Des Moines	IA	Exhibit	NWL
Mr. G. C. Hennessey & Rev. A. W. Doran	1909	07	06	Council Bluffs	IA	Exhibit	NWL
Mr. G. C. Hennessey & Rev. A. W. Doran	1909	07	08	Lincoln	NE	Exhibit	UP
Mr. G. C. Hennessey & Rev. A. W. Doran	1909	07	14	Denver	CO	Exhibit near Union Station, 4 days	UP
Mr. G. C. Hennessey & Rev. A. W. Doran	1909	07	15	Cheyenne	WY	Exhibit	UP
Mr. G. C. Hennessey & Rev. A. W. Doran	1909	07	16	Salt Lake City	UT	Exhibit	OSL
Mr. G. C. Hennessey & Rev. A. W. Doran	1909	07	17	Ogden	UT	Ends western summer exhibition tour	OSL
Mr. G. C. Hennessey & Rev. A. W. Doran	1909	07	19	Oxford	ID	Town 3 miles from tracks, services in church	OSL
Mr. G. C. Hennessey & Rev. A. W. Doran	1909	07	21	Downey	ID	People who could not get in car used a long telegraph pole along track for seats	OSL
Rev. A. P. Doyle (13)	1909	07	22	Virginia	ID	(13) From Washington, DC	OSL
Mr. G. C. Hennessey & Rev. A. W. Doran	1909	07	24	McCammon	ID	Small circus has 2 cars on same track with chapel car	OSL
Mr. G. C. Hennessey & Rev. A. W. Doran	1909	07	25	Pocatello	ID	Car to Yellowstone Park, WY, Rev. A. P. Doyle finished services	OSL
Mr. G. C. Hennessey & Rev. A. W. Doran	1909	07	31	St. Anthony	ID	Large quantity of literature was distributed	OSL
Mr. G. C. Hennessey & Rev. A. W. Doran	1909	08	08	Idaho Falls	ID	Car most of the time on rail track in front of church	OSL
Mr. G. C. Hennessey & Rev. A. W. Doran	1909	08	14	Black Foot	ID	A Methodist conference in town with 70 preachers	OSL
Mr. G. C. Hennessey & Rev. A. W. Doran	1909	08	21	American Falls	ID	A company auditorium was used for services	OSL
Mr. G. C. Hennessey & Rev. A. W. Doran	1909	08	23	Shoshone	ID	Exhibit	OSL
Mr. G. C. Hennessey & Rev. A. W. Doran	1909	08	28	Gooding	ID	Switch engine moved car during service, free ride	OSL
Mr. G. C. Hennessey & Rev. A. W. Doran	1909	08	31	Mountain Home	ID	Terrific heat in car and bad alkali water	OSL
Mr. G. C. Hennessey & Rev. A. W. Doran	1909			Portland	OR	Car on exhibit, 3 days	NP
Mr. G. C. Hennessey & Rev. W. L. Polk (14)	1909			Seattle	WA	Exhibit, Alaska-Pacific-Yukon-Seattle Exposition, 4 weeks	NP
Mr. G. C. Hennessey & Rev. W. L. Polk	1909	10	01	Portland	OR	(14) From Portland, OR	NP
Mr. G. C. Hennessey & Rev. E. K. Cantwell (15)	1909	10	02	Rainier	OR	(15) From Portland, OR	A&CR
Mr. G. C. Hennessey & Rev. H. J. McDevitt (16)	1909	10	16	Newberg	OR	Dedication of new building, morning services in car	SP
Mr. G. C. Hennessey & Rev. D. McDonald (17)	1909	10	23	Sheridan	OR	Has started building, car was a surprise to the town	SP
Mr. G. C. Hennessey & Rev. D. McDonald	1909	10	30	Dallas	OR	Building soon to be completed, lectures in public hall	SP
Mr. G. C. Hennessey & Rev. W. L. Polk	1909			Falls City	OR	(16) From Seattle, OR	SFC&W

PERSONNEL SERVING ON CARS	Y	M	D	TOWN	ST	COMMENTS FROM ACCOUNTS, LETTERS	R R
Mr. G. C. Hennessey & Rev. W. L. Polk	1909	11	06	Blackrock	OR	A logging camp, a slight accident happen to chapel car	SFC&W
Mr. G. C. Hennessey & Rev. H. J. McDevitt	1909	11	10	Dallas	OR	Car repaired in shop, paid by logging company	SFC&W
Mr. G. C. Hennessey & Rev. H. J. McDevitt	1909	11	12	McMinnville	OR	(17) From Seattle, WA	SP
Mr. G. C. Hennessey & Rev. H. J. McDevitt	1909	11	13	Independence	OR	(18) From Corvallis, OR	SP
Mr. G. C. Hennessey & Rev. H. A. Gabriel (18)	1909	11	20	Mill City	OR	Railroad bridge washed out, could not leave when chaplains wanted to, 2 days	C&E
Mr. G. C. Hennessey & Rev. H. A. Gabriel	1909	11	22	Lyons	OR	Rev. Gabriel walked 8 miles to town to start mission	C&E
Mr. G. C. Hennessey & Rev. H. A. Gabriel	1909	11	24	Albany	OR	Stayed a little over 1 day	C&E
Mr. G. C. Hennessey & Rev. A. Lane (19)	1909	11	27	Brownsville	OR	(19) From Albany, OR.	SP
Mr. G. C. Hennessey & Rev. D. McDonald (20)	1909	11	31	Dallas	OR	(20) From Seattle, WA	SP
Mr. G. C. Hennessey & Rev. D. McDonald	1909	12	03	Halsey	OR	Methodist minister attended all evening services	SP
Mr. G. C. Hennessey & Rev. D. McDonald	1909	12	04	Harrisburg	OR	Car was full 1/2 hour before lectures started	SP
Mr. G. C. Hennessey & Rev. D. McDonald	1909	12	11	Yoncalla	OR	Car full	SP
Mr. G. C. Hennessey & Rev. D. McDonald	1909	12	18	Roseburg	OR	Car repairs, heating system and roof repairs	SP
Mr. G. C. Hennessey	1909	12	21	Portland	OR	Car too full some people had to returned home	SP
Mr. G. C. Hennessey & Rev. D. McDonald	1910	01	01	Oakland	OR	New town only 6 months, no church in town	SP
Mr. G. C. Hennessey & Rev. D. McDonald	1910	01	10	Sutherlin	OR	Challenged for open discussion about church	SP
Mr. G. C. Hennessey & Rev. D. McDonald	1910	01	15	Myrtle Creek	OR	Mayor and his family of town was in car every night	SP
Mr. G. C. Hennessey & Rev. D. McDonald	1910	01	22	Riddle	OR	Only 10 to 12 at lectures, only 2 houses and depot in town	SP
Mr. G. C. Hennessey & Rev. D. McDonald	1910	01	29	West Fork	OR	Catholics looking with eagerness for the coming of car	SP
Mr. G. C. Hennessey & Rev. D. McDonald	1910	02	10	Glendale	OR	Bad weather first night, second night car was full	SP
Mr. G. C. Hennessey & Rev. D. McDonald	1910	02	14	Leland	OR	Second night only 1 in car due to literary entertainment	SP
Mr. G. C. Hennessey & Rev. D. McDonald	1910	02	16	Merlin	OR	A divided town for or against the car	SP
Mr. G. C. Hennessey & Rev. D. McDonald	1910	02	19	Grants Pass	OR	Catholics and non-Catholics attended well each evening	SP
Mr. G. C. Hennessey & Rev. D. McDonald	1910	03	05	Drain's	OR	Catholic church was misrepresented here	SP
Mr. G. C. Hennessey & Rev. D. McDonald	1910	03	12	Cottage Grove	OR	No services	SP
Mr. G. C. Hennessey	1910	03	25	Portland	OR		SP
Mr. G. C. Hennessey & Rev. E. K. Cantwell (21)	1910	04	02	Eugene	OR	Ministers and a divinity class from the university in car	SP
Mr. G. C. Hennessey & Rev. H. A. Gabriel (22)	1910	04	16	Lebanon	OR	People in country too busy ploughing and seeding	SP
Mr. G. C. Hennessey & Rev. H. A. Gabriel	1910	04	24	Jefferson	OR	(21) From Portland, OR	SP
Mr. G. C. Hennessey & Rev. H. J. McDevitt (23)	1910	05	01	Sheridan	OR	(22) From Corvallis, OR	SFC&W
Mr. G. C. Hennessey & Rev. H. J. McDevitt	1910	05	07	Falls City	OR	(23) From Albany, OR	SP
Mr. G. C. Hennessey & Rev. H. J. McDevitt	1910	05	14	Carlton	OR	Car was the first Catholic church in town	SP
Mr. G. C. Hennessey & Rev. H. J. McDevitt	1910	05	18	McMinnville	OR		SP
Mr. G. C. Hennessey & Rev. H. J. McDevitt	1910	05	21	North Yamhill	OR	Car 1 mile from town, had to rent a hall in town	SP
Mr. G. C. Hennessey & Rev. H. J. McDevitt	1910	05	25	Trinity	OR	Building site secured	?
Mr. G. C. Hennessey & Rev. H. J. McDevitt	1910	05	28	Forest Grove	OR	Crowds increased every night to 300 to 400	SP
Mr. G. C. Hennessey & Rev. H. J. McDevitt	1910	06	04	Independence	OR	Building being remodeled and enlarged	SP
Mr. G. C. Hennessey & Rev. W. D. O'Brien (25)	1910	06	06	Portland	OR	Waiting instructions for future assignments, out of service 2 weeks	SP
Mr. G. C. Hennessey & Rev. W. D. O'Brien	1910	06	06	Portland	OR	Grain elevator fire, heat blister end of chapel car	C&E
Mr. G. C. Hennessey & Rev. E. K. Cantwell (24)	1910	06	26	Oswego	OR	(25) Bishop of Chicago, IL, and president of C.E.E.S.	C&E
Mr. G. C. Hennessey & Rev. H. J. McDevitt	1910	07	03	Dallas	OR	(24) From Portland, OR	SP
Mr. G. C. Hennessey & Rev. H. J. McDevitt	1910	07	04	Monmouth	OR	Dedicated new Catholic church, no service in car	SP
Mr. G. C. Hennessey & Rev. H. J. McDevitt	1910	07	09	Cornelius	OR	One Catholic family in town and a few others outside town	SP
Mr. G. C. Hennessey & Rev. H. J. McDevitt	1910	07	16	Portland	OR	Devout worshipers at every Mass given	SP
Mr. G. C. Hennessey & Rev. W. D. O'Brien (25)	1910	07	23	San Francisco	CA	Services in car for national convention of Hibernians	SFC&W
Mr. G. C. Hennessey & Rev. W. D. O'Brien	1910	07	24	Junction City	OR	Five Masses offered on passenger train	SP
Mr. G. C. Hennessey & Rev. W. D. O'Brien	1910	07	30	Lyons	OR	Without a Catholic church, evening crowds in car	C&E
Mr. G. C. Hennessey & Rev. W. D. O'Brien	1910	09	04	Chicago	IL	Planning for trip to Canada and east. Lv 09-02-1910	C&NW
Mr. G. C. Hennessey & Rev. W. D. O'Brien	1910	09	06	Montreal, QUE.	C	Planning for tour through Canada, 1 day	GT
Mr. G. C. Hennessey & Rev. W. D. O'Brien	1910	09	13	St. John, N.B.	C	Starts Canada northeastern tour	IR
Mr. G. C. Hennessey & Rev. W. D. O'Brien	1910	09	16	Moncton, N.B.	C	Exhibit, Cape Breton Island, 1 day	IR
Mr. G. C. Hennessey & Rev. W. D. O'Brien	1910	09	19	Sydney, N.S.	C	Exhibit, Cape Breton Island, 1 day	S&L
Mr. G. C. Hennessey & Rev. W. D. O'Brien	1910	09	22	Glace Bay, N.S.	C	Exhibit, 1 day	IR
Mr. G. C. Hennessey & Rev. W. D. O'Brien	1910	09	27	Antigonish, N.S.	C	Exhibit, 1 day	IR
Mr. G. C. Hennessey & Rev. W. D. O'Brien	1910	09	30	Ottawa, ONT.	C	Exhibit, 1 day	GT
Mr. G. C. Hennessey & Rev. W. D. O'Brien	1910	10	03	Peterborough, ONT.	C	Exhibit, 1 day	GT
Mr. G. C. Hennessey & Rev. W. D. O'Brien	1910	10	08	Toronto, ONT.	C	Exhibit, 1 day	GT
Mr. G. C. Hennessey & Rev. W. D. O'Brien	1910	10	11	London, ONT.	C	Exhibit	GT
Mr. G. C. Hennessey & Rev. W. D. O'Brien	1910	10	13	Detroit	MI	Exhibit	GT
Mr. G. C. Hennessey & Rev. W. D. O'Brien	1910	10	15	Lansing	MI	Ends northeastern tour	GT
Mr. G. C. Hennessey & Rev. W. D. O'Brien	1910	10	18	Battle Creek	MI	Car repairs, revarnished	GT
Mr. G. C. Hennessey & Rev. W. D. O'Brien	1910	10	22	South Bend	IN	Starts short western exhibition tour	GT
Mr. G. C. Hennessey & Rev. W. D. O'Brien	1910	10	25	Chicago	IL	Exhibit	GT
Mr. G. C. Hennessey & Rev. A. H. Fleming (26)	1910	11	17	Pullman	IL	Exhibit	IC
Mr. G. C. Hennessey & Rev. A. H. Fleming	1910	11	20	Chicago	IL	Exhibit	AT&SF
Mr. G. C. Hennessey & Rev. A. H. Fleming	1910	11	22	Salt Lake City	UT	Exhibit (26) From Portland, OR	SL&LA
Mr. G. C. Hennessey & Rev. A. H. Fleming	1910	11	23	Berkeley	CA	Exhibit	AT&SF
Mr. G. C. Hennessey & Rev. A. H. Fleming	1910	11	25	Oakland	CA	Exhibit	AT&SF
Mr. G. C. Hennessey & Rev. A. H. Fleming	1910	11	27	San Francisco	CA	Exhibit	AT&SF
Mr. G. C. Hennessey & Rev. A. H. Fleming	1910	11	29	San Jose	CA	Exhibit	SP
Mr. G. C. Hennessey & Rev. A. H. Fleming	1910	12	02	Sacramento	CA	Exhibit, ends short western exhibition tour	SP
Mr. G. C. Hennessey & Rev. A. H. Fleming	1910	12	10	Portland	OR	No services, ready car for missions	SP
Mr. G. C. Hennessey & Rev. A. H. Fleming	1910	12	16	Ontario	OR	The people promised faithful and prayerful reading	OSL
Mr. G. C. Hennessey & Rev. A. H. Fleming	1910	12	21	Vale	OR	Superintendent of schools invited students to listen to a lecture	OSL
Mr. G. C. Hennessey & Rev. A. H. Fleming	1910	12	24	Brogan	OR	Chapel car was the first passenger type car in town	OSL
Mr. G. C. Hennessey & Rev. A. H. Fleming	1910	12	28	Huntington	OR	Large railroad town, careless and an indifferent crowd	OSL
Mr. G. C. Hennessey & Rev. A. H. Fleming	1910	12	30	Baker City	OR	Mass in car with sisters from hospital and academy	OWR&N
Mr. G. C. Hennessey & Rev. A. H. Fleming	1911	01	01	Pleasant Valley	OR	Railroad had interest, full house to start	OWR&N

PERSONNEL SERVING ON CARS	Y	M	D	TOWN	ST	COMMENTS FROM ACCOUNTS, LETTERS	R R
Mr. G. C. Hennessey & Rev. A. H. Fleming	1911	01	04	Durkee	OR	One time a Portuguese town with a union church	OWR&N
Mr. G. C. Hennessey & Rev. A. H. Fleming	1911	01	09	Haines	OR	Property purchased, epidemic of small pox raging	OWR&N
Mr. G. C. Hennessey & Rev. A. H. Fleming	1911	01	14	North Powder	OR	Property purchased, good attendance and questions	OWR&N
Mr. G. C. Hennessey & Rev. A. H. Fleming	1911	01	22	Union	OR	Methodists were against the chapel car literature	CRO
Mr. G. C. Hennessey & Rev. A. H. Fleming	1911	01	28	Cove	OR	Steam locomotive engine broke loose from car 3 times	CRO
Mr. G. C. Hennessey & Rev. A. H. Fleming	1911	02	01	Hot Lake	OR	Rheumatism health resort, chapel car almost in a wreck	OWR&N
Mr. G. C. Hennessey & Rev. A. H. Fleming	1911	02	04	La Grande	OR	In church building for all services	OWR&N
Mr. G. C. Hennessey & Rev. A. H. Fleming	1911	02	13	Island City	OR	One Catholic family in town, people from La Grande, OR, came	OWR&N
Mr. G. C. Hennessey & Rev. A. H. Fleming	1911	02	16	Imbler	OR	No Catholic families in town, 2 day great snow storm	OWR&N
Mr. G. C. Hennessey & Rev. A. H. Fleming	1911	02	18	Elgin	OR	Six Catholic families in town, efforts to build church	OWR&N
Mr. G. C. Hennessey & Rev. A. H. Fleming	1911	02	25	Wallowa	OR	Christian minister attended, question box was stuffed	OWR&N
Mr. G. C. Hennessey & Rev. A. H. Fleming	1911	03	06	Lostine	OR	Depot 2-1/2 miles from town, used union church hall	OWR&N
Mr. G. C. Hennessey & Rev. A. H. Fleming	1911	03	08	Enterprise	OR	Church hard to get to, used court house for services	OWR&N
Mr. G. C. Hennessey & Rev. A. H. Fleming	1911	03	18	Joseph	OR	Church out of town, Catholics live away from church	OWR&N
Mr. G. C. Hennessey & Rev. A. H. Fleming	1911	03	27	La Grande	OR	No mission left car in town, Lv 04-02-1911	OWR&N
Mr. G. C. Hennessey & Rev. A. H. Fleming	1911	03	29	Summerville	OR	Lectures in the Masonic lodge building, without car	—
Mr. G. C. Hennessey & Rev. A. H. Fleming	1911	04	04	Perry	OR	A Mormon lumber mill town, large number of questions	OWR&N
Mr. G. C. Hennessey & Rev. A. H. Fleming	1911	04	07	Hilgard	OR	Only 1 store not nailed up, a deserted village	OWR&N
Mr. G. C. Hennessey & Rev. A. H. Fleming	1911	04	11	Baker City	OR	Car out of service due to Holy Week services	OSL
Mr. G. C. Hennessey & Rev. A. H. Fleming	1911	04	15	Ontario	OR	From Baker City, OR, carried seven sisters to start hospital	OSL
Mr. G. C. Hennessey & Rev. A. H. Fleming	1911	04	19	Baker City	OR	Waiting for next mission	OWR&N
Mr. G. C. Hennessey & Rev. A. H. Fleming	1911	04	22	Athena	OR	Church in town, priest lives on Indian reservation 10 miles away	OWR&N
Mr. G. C. Hennessey & Rev. A. H. Fleming	1911	04	30	Freewater	OR	On 2 state borders, no services	WWV
Mr. G. C. Hennessey & Rev. A. H. Fleming	1911	04	30	Walla Walla	OR	Trolley car to Walla Walla, OR, without car	—
Mr. G. C. Hennessey & Rev. A. H. Fleming	1911	05	06	Pendleton	OR	Church used every evening, new stone church being built	OWR&N
Mr. G. C. Hennessey & Rev. A. H. Fleming	1911	05	14	Weston	OR	End of car painted and coupler heights adjusted, $49.45	OWR&N
Mr. G. C. Hennessey & Rev. A. H. Fleming	1911	05	20	Condon	OR	Depot a distance from town, services at the academy	OWR&N
Mr. G. C. Hennessey & Rev. A. H. Fleming	1911	05	29	Umatilla	OR	Baptist chapel car 2, Emmanuel, coupled to chapel car, St. Anthony	OWR&N
Mr. G. C. Hennessey & Rev. A. H. Fleming	1911	06	05	Hermiston	OR	Many non-Catholics attended, church out of town	OWR&N
Mr. G. C. Hennessey & Rev. A. H. Fleming	1911	06	10	Stanfield	OR	Property purchased, eastern people full of business	OWR&N
Mr. G. C. Hennessey & Rev. A. H. Fleming	1911	06	20	La Grande	OR	Car has inspection and repairs	OWR&N
Mr. G. C. Hennessey	1911	07	10	La Grande	OR	Planning for missions	OWR&N
Mr. G. C. Hennessey	1911	07	17	Redmond	OR	Religious enthusiasm and interest awakened in town	OT
Mr. G. C. Hennessey	1911	08	18	Bend	OR	Weather too hot, car out of service	OT
Mr. G. C. Hennessey	1911	08	18	Madras	OR	Planning for missions	OT
Mr. G. C. Hennessey & Rev. H. J. McDevitt (27)	1911	08	26	Astoria	OR	(27) From Portland, OR	SP&S
Mr. G. C. Hennessey & Rev. H. J. McDevitt	1911	09	04	Fort Stevens	OR	Car on government ground, well attended by soldiers	GOVAT
Mr. G. C. Hennessey & Rev. H. J. McDevitt	1911	09	09	Warrenton	OR	Soldiers and people from Hammond, OR, followed car	SP&S
Mr. G. C. Hennessey & Rev. H. J. McDevitt	1911	09	16	Cascade Locks	OR	Planning and waiting for next mission	SP&S
Mr. G. C. Hennessey & Rev. T. J. Brady (28)	1911	09	26	Ione	OR	(28) From Condon, OR	OWR&N
Mr. G. C. Hennessey & Rev. T. J. Brady	1911	09	30	Heppner	OR	No lighting system in church, all services held in car	OWR&N
Mr. G. C. Hennessey & Rev. T. J. Brady	1911	10	10	Lexington	OR	Irish town, every Catholic family was delighted with visit of chapel car	OWR&N
Mr. G. C. Hennessey & Rev. T. J. Brady	1911	10	13	Hood River	OR	Chaplains said the few Catholics in town were good practical Catholics	OWR&N
Mr. G. C. Hennessey & Rev. T. J. Brady	1911	10	24	Mosier	OR	Religion strong in town, revival in Christian church	OWR&N
Mr. G. C. Hennessey & Rev. T. J. Brady	1911	10	28	Madras	OR	Property purchased for building, few Catholics here	OWR&N
Mr. G. C. Hennessey & Rev. T. J. Brady	1911	11	05	La Grande	OR	New church located 2 miles from depot	OWR&N
Mr. G. C. Hennessey & Rev. T. J. Brady	1911	11	11	Redmond	OR	No services	OWR&N
Mr. G. C. Hennessey & Rev. T. J. Brady	1911	11	11	Bend	OR	Religious enthusiasm and interest awakened in town	OWR&N
Mr. G. C. Hennessey & Rev. T. J. Brady	1911	11	27	Madras	OR	Car in shop, air brake repairs, we almost derailed train	OWR&N
Mr. G. C. Hennessey & Rev. T. J. Brady	1911	12	01	Echo	OR	Question box was not used much, church dedicated	OWR&N
Mr. G. C. Hennessey & Rev. T. J. Brady	1911	12	12	Pilot Rock	OR	Dedicated church	OWR&N
Mr. G. C. Hennessey	1911	12	12	Portland	OR	Planning and waiting for chaplain	SP
Mr. G. C. Hennessey & Rev. H. J. McDevitt (29)	1912	01	03	Portland	OR	(29) From Portland, OR	SP
Mr. G. C. Hennessey & Rev. H. J. McDevitt	1912	01	20	Gaston	OR	On a siding called Segers, 1-1/2 miles from Gaston, OR	SP
Mr. G. C. Hennessey & Rev. H. J. McDevitt	1912	01	27	Dallas	OR	A slanderous paper scattered in city against Catholics	SP
Mr. G. C. Hennessey & Rev. H. J. McDevitt	1912	01	27	Milwaukie	OR	New building not finished, all missions in car	SP
Mr. G. C. Hennessey & Rev. E. K. Cantwell (30)	1912	02	02	Portland	OR	(30) From Portland, OR	SP
Mr. G. C. Hennessey & Rev. P. L. Barrett (31)	1912	02	03	Canby	OR	(31) From Portland, OR	SP
Mr. G. C. Hennessey & Rev. P. L. Barrett	1912	02	17	Jefferson	OR	Changed chaplains aboard car	SP
Mr. G. C. Hennessey & Rev. P. L. Barrett	1912	02	19	Medford	OR	No Catholic church in town, most Catholics returned	SP
Mr. G. C. Hennessey & Rev. P. L. Barrett	1912	02	27	Talent	OR	Poles and Bohemians of the practical kind	RRV
Mr. G. C. Hennessey & Rev. P. L. Barrett	1912	02	27	Ashland	OR	Dedication of the hospital	SP
Mr. G. C. Hennessey & Rev. P. L. Barrett	1912	03	12	Jacksonville	OR	Many non-Catholics attended evening lectures	RRV
Mr. G. C. Hennessey & Rev. P. L. Barrett	1912	04	27	Harrisburg	OR	Car in shop, air brake repairs, we almost derailed train	SP
Mr. G. C. Hennessey & Rev. P. L. Barrett	1912	05	04	Eagle Point	OR	Third visit by chapel car, now about to start building	P&ER
Mr. G. C. Hennessey & Rev. P. L. Barrett	1912	05	14	Central Point	OR	Attendance so large had to move to the church	SP
Mr. G. C. Hennessey & Rev. P. L. Barrett	1912	05	18	Gold Hill	OR	Town people very busy, bad time, low attendance	SP
Mr. G. C. Hennessey & Rev. P. L. Barrett	1912	05	26	Creswell	OR	Mining town, religious indifference, poor attendance	SP
Mr. G. C. Hennessey & Rev. H. J. McDevitt (32)	1912	06	01	Portland	OR	(32) From Portland, OR	SP
Mr. G. C. Hennessey (33) & Rev. P. L. Barrett (34)	1912	06	08	La Grande	OR	(33) Transferred to Dayton, OH, to pick up new chapel car St. Peter	OWR&N
Rev. J. Murphy (35)	1912	06	20	?	OR	Car used as a church and residence	?
Rev. J. Murphy & Rev. T. J. Brady (36)	1912	06	28	Juntura	OR	Stayed 14 days	OSL
Rev. J. Murphy	1912	10	12	La Grande	OR	St. Anthony and St. Peter chapel cars coupled together	OWR&N
Mr. G. C. Hennessey	1912	10	16	Wallowa	OR	Car used as a church and residence	OWR&N
Mr. G. C. Smith & Rev. W. Hampson (38)	1912	12	21	Wallowa	OR	Placed car in shop for repairs, Lv 12-21-1912	C&E
Rev. C. M. Smith (37) & Rev. W. Hampson	1913	01	07	Summit	OR	(34) From Wallowa, OR	C&E
Rev. C. M. Smith & Rev. W. Hampson	1913	01	14	Blodgett	OR	(35) From Wallowa, OR	?
Rev. C. M. Smith & Rev. W. Hampson	1913	01	31	Wren	OR	Very small town, attentive and interested audiences	SP
Rev. C. M. Smith & Rev. W. Hampson	1913	02	10	Corvallis	OR	(36) From Condon, OR	C&E
Rev. C. M. Smith & Rev. W. Hampson	1913	03	05	Alpine	OR	(37) From Corvallis, OR	PE&E
Rev. C. M. Smith & Rev. W. Hampson	1913	03	26	Toledo	OR	Car came every 2 weeks for Sunday services ?	C&E
Rev. C. M. Smith & Rev. W. Hampson	1913	04	12	Elk City	OR	(38) From Lebanon, OR	C&E
Rev. C. M. Smith & Rev. W. Hampson	1913	04	20	Eddyville	OR	Town has 1 store and depot, hotel 1/4 mile from town	C&E

PERSONNEL SERVING ON CARS	Y	M	D	TOWN	ST	COMMENTS FROM ACCOUNTS, LETTERS	R R
Rev. C. M. Smith & Rev. W. Hampson	1913	04	26	Nashville	OR	(39) Previous situation unknown	C&E
Rev. C. M. Smith & Rev. W. Hampson	1913	05	01	Toledo	OR	Car used for church, while building church	C&E
Rev. W. J. Kane (39)	1913	07	07	Philomath	OR	Served as a chapel	C&E
	1913	07	09	Albany	OR	Shop, platforms and timbers, vestibule diaphragm, $668.03	C&E
Rev. C. M. Smith (40)	1913	09	27	Monroe	OR	(40) From Corvallis, OR	PE&E
(41)	1913	10	12	?	OR	Car out of service for summer, weather and chaplains	?
Rev. C. M. Smith & Rev. Benards (42)	1913	10	27	Cresswell	OR	Car used as a church while church was being built	OSL
Rev. C. M. Smith & Rev. W. J. Kane (43)	1914	01	08	Divide	OR	(41) Car vacant, 1 month	SP
Rev. C. M. Smith & Rev. W. J. Kane	1914	01	15	Drain	OR	Last 2 evenings many stood outside around the church	SP
Rev. C. M. Smith & Rev. W. J. Kane	1914	01	22	Roseburg	OR	Crowds too large for car, used the church	SP
Rev. C. M. Smith & Rev. W. J. Kane	1914	02	02	Glendale	OR	Local Presbyterian choir sang each evening in car	SP
Rev. C. M. Smith & Rev. W. J. Kane	1914	02	09	Grants Pass	OR	(42) Previous situation unknown	SP
Rev. C. M. Smith & Rev. W. J. Kane	1914	02	26	Ashland	OR	Many are spiritually nearsighted	SP
Rev. C. M. Smith & Rev. W. J. Kane	1914	02	28	Mill City	OR	(43) From Portland, OR	C&E
Rev. C. M. Smith & Rev. W. J. Kane	1914	03	03	Lyons	OR	As many people outside car as there are inside car	C&E
Rev. C. M. Smith & Rev. W. J. Kane	1914	03	10	Shelburn	OR	Populace displayed little enthusiasm over car	C&E
Rev. C. M. Smith & Rev. W. J. Kane	1914	03	17	Scio	OR	Bohemians and a number of non-Catholics attended	?
Rev. C. M. Smith & Rev. W. J. Kane	1914	03	24	Springfield	OR	Stayed 1 week	SP
Rev. C. M. Smith & Rev. W. J. Kane	1914	03	31	Coburg	OR	Many came to car seeking instructions	SP
Rev. C. M. Smith & Rev. W. J. Kane	1914	04	07	Independence	OR	Forty young women from state normal school came	SP
Rev. C. M. Smith & Rev. W. J. Kane	1914	04	14	Dallas	OR	Displayed much interest	SP
Rev. C. M. Smith & Rev. W. J. Kane	1914	04	21	Falls City	OR	Low attendance, not very encouraging	SFC&W
Rev. C. M. Smith & Rev. W. J. Kane	1914	04	28	Silverton	OR	Attendance discouraging, paper had bad write up	SP
Rev. C. M. Smith & Rev. W. J. Kane	1914	05	15	Albany	OR	Car repairs $.95	C&E
Rev. H. J. McDevitt (44)	1914	06	04	Silverton	OR	(44) From Portland, OR	SP
Rev. W. J. Kane	1914	06	21	Portland	OR	(45) Car vacant for summer, 2 months	PRL&P
Rev. C. M. Smith & Rev. W. J. Kane	1914	07	23	Arleta	ID		PRL&P
(45)	1914	08	01		OR	(46) From Condon, OR	?
Rev. T. J. Brady (46)	1914	10	05	Juntura	OR	Second funeral service on car	OSL
Rev. T. J. Brady	1914	11	20	Nampa	ID	(47) Car vacant for repairs 5 months	OSL
(47)	1914	12	15	Pocatello	ID	Car repairs, replaced stove and light fixtures repairs	OSL
Rev. T. J. Brady	1915	04	28	Juntura	OR	Used as church	OSL
Rev. T. J. Brady	1915	05	06	Juntura	ID	Car in shop for vestibule platform work	OSL
Rev. T. J. Brady	1915	05	13	Riverton	OR	Finishing building a chapel	SI
Rev. T. J. Brady	1915	10	09	Riverside	OR	Car near a town fire, exterior end of car fire damaged	SP
Rev. T. J. Brady	1915	11	15	Juntura	OR	Car in shop for fire damage repairs	SP
Rev. T. J. Brady	1915	11	22	Hot Springs	OR		P&IN
Mr. G. C. Hennessey	1916	04	19	Pocatello	ID	(48) Car vacant 1-1/2 months	UP
(48)	1916	08	06	Dietrich	ID	(49) From Shoshone, ID	UP
Rev. Wirtzberger (49)	1916	12	22	Dietrich	ID	Near station almost a year, 6 months used as church	UP
Rev. Wirtzberger	1917	08	25	Portland	OR	Car used as funeral car from Portland, OR, to ID	UP
Rev. Wirtzberger	1917	12	28		ID	Government returned ownership to railroads	?
Rev. A. H. Fleming (50)	1918	03	15	Fairfield	ID	Car moved with car trucks to lot in center of town	UP
Mr. G. C. Hennessey	1918	07	07	Pocatello	OR	Car repairs, exterior painted $192.42, ready 09-07-1918	UP
Rev. T. J. Brady	1918	09	16	Pleasant Valley	OR	Car used for resident priests	UP
(51)	1919	01	10	Union	OR	Last Mass in car	CO
Mr. G. C. Hennessey	1919	05	29	La Grande	OR	Car dismantled; altar, organ, pews placed in new church	UP
(52)	1919	06	16	Wishram (Fallbridge)	WA	(52) Car vacant 1-1/2 months	SP&S
	1919	06	01	Wishram	WA	Car retired, used as church and residence	SP&S
	1919	08	02	Wishram	WA	Car on railroad tracks and used as a church	SP&S
	1920	03	01	Wishram	WA	Government takes over operation of railroads due to WWI	—
	1921	12	20	Wishram	WA	Car moved with car trucks to lot in center of town	—
	1928			Wishram	WA	Car used for resident priests	—
	1929	12	29	Wishram	WA	Car dismantled; altar, organ, pews placed in new church	—
	1940	06		Yakima	WA	Altar on 3rd floor at St. Paul school	—

C.C.E.S. SECOND CAR, ST. PETER
NICKNAME: THE STEEL APOSTLE

Rev. E. G. Ledvina, C.C.E.S. vice president and general secretary designed this second Catholic car and supervised operation of chapel cars in the professional absence of Father Kelley

						THE CATHOLIC CHURCH EXTENSION SOCIETY OF THE UNITED STATES OF AMERICA	
	1908	10		Asked for car donor		Car donor Mr. Peter A. Kuntz Sr.	—
	1911	11				$25,000 total cost	—
	1911	12				Peter A. Kuntz Sr. supervised building car in shop	—
Mr. G. C. Hennessey (1) & Rev. E. B. Ledvina (2)(3)	1912	01	15	Dayton	OH	Peter A. Kuntz Sr. supervised building car in shop	—
Mr. G. C. Hennessey & Rev. E. B. Ledvina	1912	06	27	Dayton	OH	Car given to The Catholic Church Extension Society	—
Mr. G. C. Hennessey & Rev. E. B. Ledvina	1912	06	30	Dayton	OH	Car shipped from builder Barney & Smith Car Company	CH&D
Mr. G. C. Hennessey & Rev. E. B. Ledvina	1912	07	02	Hamilton	OH	Car dedication at union station, south of main tracks	CH&D
Mr. G. C. Hennessey & Rev. E. B. Ledvina	1912	07	03	Cincinnati	OH	Car starts Midwest exhibition tour	CH&D
Mr. G. C. Hennessey & Rev. E. B. Ledvina	1912	07	04	Lawrenceburg	IN	(1) Superintendent of Catholic chapel cars	CH&D
Mr. G. C. Hennessey & Rev. E. B. Ledvina	1912	07	05	North Vernon	IN	(2) Vice-president general secretary of C.C.E.S., chaplain on car	B&OSW
Mr. G. C. Hennessey & Rev. E. B. Ledvina	1912	07	06	Seymour	IN	(3) From Chicago, IL	B&OSW
Mr. G. C. Hennessey & Rev. E. B. Ledvina	1912	07	07	Loogootee	IN		B&OSW
Mr. G. C. Hennessey & Rev. E. B. Ledvina	1912	07	08	Washington	IN		B&OSW
Mr. G. C. Hennessey & Rev. E. B. Ledvina	1912	07	09	Princeton	IN		C&EI
Mr. G. C. Hennessey & Rev. E. B. Ledvina	1912	07	10	Vincennes	IN		C&EI
Mr. G. C. Hennessey & Rev. E. B. Ledvina	1912	07	11	Evansville	IN		C&EI
Mr. G. C. Hennessey & Rev. E. B. Ledvina	1912	07	12	Mt. Carmel	IL		CCC&SL
Mr. G. C. Hennessey & Rev. E. B. Ledvina	1912	07	13	Terre Haute	IN	St. Mary's-of-the-Woods school, ends Midwest exhibition tour	CCC&SL
Mr. G. C. Hennessey & Rev. E. B. Ledvina	1912	07	14	Saint Mary-of-the-Wood	IN	Exhibition tour in different sections of city, 1 month	CCC&SL
Mr. G. C. Hennessey & Rev. W. D. O'Brien (4)(5)	1912	07	16	Chicago	IL	Car starts Midwest exhibition tour, 1 day	CM&SP
Mr. G. C. Hennessey & Rev. W. D. O'Brien	1912	09	04	Elgin	IL	Exhibit 1 day, (4) Director of Child Apostle, chaplain	CM&SP
Mr. G. C. Hennessey & Rev. W. D. O'Brien	1912	09	06	Rock Island	IL	Exhibit 1 day, (5) From Chicago, IL	CM&SP
Mr. G. C. Hennessey & Rev. W. D. O'Brien	1912	09	07	Davenport	IA		CM&SP

PERSONNEL SERVING ON CARS	Y	M	D	TOWN	ST	COMMENTS FROM ACCOUNTS, LETTERS	R R
Mr. G. C. Hennessey & Rev. W. D. O'Brien	1912	09	11	La Crosse	WI	Exhibit 1 day	CM&SP
Mr. G. C. Hennessey & Rev. W. D. O'Brien	1912	09	12	Winona	MN	Exhibit 1 day	CM&SP
Mr. G. C. Hennessey & Rev. W. D. O'Brien	1912	09	13	Hastings	MN	Exhibit 1 day	CM&SP
Mr. G. C. Hennessey & Rev. W. D. O'Brien	1912	09	14	St. Paul	MN	Exhibit 1 day	CM&SP
Mr. G. C. Hennessey & Rev. W. D. O'Brien	1912	09	16	Minneapolis	MN	Exhibit 1 day	CM&SP
Mr. G. C. Hennessey & Rev. W. D. O'Brien	1912	09	17	Aberdeen	SD	Exhibit 1 day	CM&PS
Mr. G. C. Hennessey & Rev. W. D. O'Brien	1912	09	19	Miles City	MT	Exhibit 1 day	CM&PS
Mr. G. C. Hennessey & Rev. W. D. O'Brien	1912	09	21	Butte	MT	Exhibit 1 day	CM&PS
Mr. G. C. Hennessey & Rev. W. D. O'Brien	1912	09	25	Tacoma	WA	Car ends Midwest exhibition tour, 1 day	CM&PS
Mr. G. C. Hennessey & Rev. W. D. O'Brien	1912	09	28	Portland	OR	(6) From Wallowa, OR	OWR&N
Mr. G. C. Hennessey & Rev. J. F. Murphy (6)	1912	10	12	La Grande	OR	St. Peter and St. Anthony chapel cars coupled together	OWR&N
Mr. G. C. Hennessey & Rev. J. F. Murphy	1912	10	19	Haines	OR	First mission given in car	OWR&N
Mr. G. C. Hennessey & Rev. P. L. Barrett (7)	1912	10	24	Baker City	OR	Pupils from academy made a visit to car	OSL
Mr. G. C. Hennessey & Rev. P. L. Barrett	1912	10	26	Weiser	ID	(7) From Portland, OR	P&IN
Mr. G. C. Hennessey & Rev. P. L. Barrett	1912	11	02	New Meadow	ID	Infant town of 18 months	P&IN
Mr. G. C. Hennessey & Rev. P. L. Barrett	1912	11	09	Council	ID	Bad weather, small crowds, then good weather large crowds	P&IN
Mr. G. C. Hennessey & Rev. P. L. Barrett	1912	11	16	Cambridge	ID	Building almost completed, car was over crowded	P&IN
Mr. G. C. Hennessey & Rev. P. L. Barrett	1912	11	23	Midvale	ID	Question box used very extensively	OSL
Mr. G. C. Hennessey & Rev. P. L. Barrett	1912	11	30	Payette	ID	Much interest aroused, morning in car and evening in church	OSL
Mr. G. C. Hennessey & Rev. P. L. Barrett	1912	12	07	New Plymouth	ID	Children's mission well attended and nice congregation	PVR
Mr. G. C. Hennessey & Rev. P. L. Barrett	1912	12	15	Ontario	OR	Mass in car and evening in church	OSL
Mr. G. C. Hennessey	1912	12	21	Ontario	OR	Car waiting transportation passes and chaplain, 2 weeks	OSL
Mr. G. C. Hennessey & Rev. A. W. Doran (8)	1913	01	05	Montpelier	ID	Weather cold, minus 28 degrees, steam and water system frozen up	OSL
Mr. G. C. Hennessey & Rev. A. W. Doran	1913	01	13	Pocatello	ID	Car in shop for steam and water systems freeze up repairs	OSL
Mr. G. C. Hennessey & Rev. A. W. Doran	1913	01	18	Black Foot	ID	(8) From Philadelphia, PA	AR
Mr. G. C. Hennessey & Rev. A. W. Doran	1913	01	25	Idaho Falls	ID	Car in front of church, spirit of crowd good, 2 weeks	OSL
Mr. G. C. Hennessey & Rev. A. W. Doran	1913	02	14	Pocatello	ID	RR shop and yard workers in morning Mass	OSL
Mr. G. C. Hennessey & Rev. A. W. Doran	1913	03	01	Parma	ID	Car full so young men stood on the vestibule platform	OSL
Mr. G. C. Hennessey & Rev. A. W. Doran	1913	03	08	Caldwell	ID	(9) From Portland, OR	OSL
Mr. G. C. Hennessey & Rev. T. L. Cooney (9)	1913	03	16	Boise	ID	No mission car on exhibit, Holy Week and Easter holidays	OSL
Mr. G. C. Hennessey & Rev. T. L. Cooney	1913	04	05	Arrow Rock	ID	People now building a large dam, 5 years to complete	AR
Mr. G. C. Hennessey & Rev. R. E. Hampson (12)	1913	04	19	Meridian	ID	Due to hot weather car out of service, 2 weeks	OSL
Mr. G. C. Hennessey & Rev. T. L. Cooney	1913	04	26	Emmett	ID	(12) Previous situation unknown	OSL
Mr. G. C. Hennessey	1913	05	03	La Grande	OR	The chapel car was the wonder of the week	SP
Mr. G. C. Hennessey & Rev. J. F. Murphy (10)	1913	05	11	Pendleton	OR	Due to hot weather car out of service, 1 week	OWR&N
Mr. G. C. Hennessey & Rev. J. F. Murphy	1913	05	12	Umatilla	OR	Car waiting for chaplain, 1 week	OWR&N
Mr. G. C. Hennessey & Rev. J. F. Murphy	1913	05	25	Condon	OR	No mission (10) From Wallowa, OR	—
Mr. G. C. Hennessey & Rev. A. W. Doran	1913	05	26	Adams	OR	Umatilla Indian Reservation, without car	OWR&N
Mr. G. C. Hennessey & Rev. A. W. Doran	1913	06	01	Spokane	WA	Bishop O'Reilly blessed new hospital	OWR&N
Mr. G. C. Hennessey & Rev. W. D. Driscoll (11)	1913	06	05	Walla Walla	WA	All services held in car, building to start soon	OWR&N
Mr. G. C. Hennessey	1913	06	07	Miham	OR	Exhibit, 2 days	OWR&N
Mr. G. C. Hennessey	1913	06	10	Elgin	OR	Exhibit	OSL
Mr. G. C. Hennessey	1913	06	12			A few Catholics with a beautiful little church	OSL
Mr. G. C. Hennessey	1913	06	13			First few days only, only the faithful few came to the car	OSL
Mr. G. C. Hennessey	1913	06	14			(14) From Chicago, IL, president of C.C.E.S.	?
Mr. G. C. Hennessey	1913	06	15	Chicago	IL	No services	CCC&SL
Mr. G. C. Hennessey & Rev. W. D. O'Brien (14)	1913	06	17	Boston	MA	2nd Missionary Congress then on eastern exhibition trip	NYNH&H
Mr. G. C. Hennessey	1913	09	27	Rochester	NY	Exhibit, due to disrespect railroad employee dismissed	NYNH&H
Mr. G. C. Hennessey	1913	10	20	Dayton	OH	Barney & Smith Car Company, car general repairs and painting.	PCC&SL
Mr. G. C. Hennessey	1913	12	10	Richmond	IN	Exhibit	
Mr. G. C. Hennessey & Rev. R. Serrano (15)	1914	01	11	Hutchinson	KS	Mexican mission 5 days	AT&SF
Mr. G. C. Hennessey & Rev. J. P. MacCorry(16)	1914	01	29	Nickerson	KS	Stayed 1 night (15) From Texas	AT&SF
Mr. G. C. Hennessey & Rev. J. P. MacCorry	1914	01	30	Sterling	KS	Stayed 1 night	AT&SF
Mr. G. C. Hennessey & Rev. R. Serrano	1914	01	31	Florence	KS	Mexican mission, 4 days	AT&SF
Mr. G. C. Hennessey & Rev. J. P. MacCorry	1914	02	04	Eldorado	KS	Stayed 1 night (16) Previous situation unknown	AT&SF
Mr. G. C. Hennessey & Rev. R. Serrano	1914	02	04	Augusta	KS	Mexican mission, 2 days	AT&SF
Mr. G. C. Hennessey & Rev. R. Serrano	1914	02	06	Winfield	KS	Stayed 5 days	AT&SF
Mr. G. C. Hennessey & Rev. R. Serrano	1914	02	10	Wichita	KS	Car received new Coleman gas lighting system	AT&SF
Mr. G. C. Hennessey & Rev. R. Serrano	1914	02	12	Arkansas City	KS	Mexican mission, 2 days	AT&SF
Mr. G. C. Hennessey & Rev. R. Serrano	1914	02	13	Woodward	OK	No missions, all Mexicans had moved to Texas	MK&T
Mr. G. C. Hennessey & Rev. R. Serrano	1914	02	14	Harper	KS	Mexican mission, 2 days	AT&SF
Mr. G. C. Hennessey & Rev. R. Serrano	1914	02	16	Pratt	KS	Mexican mission, 5 days	AT&SF
Mr. G. C. Hennessey & Rev. R. Serrano	1914	02	18	Parsons	KS	Car in shop for Baker heater repairs, $33.40	AT&SF
Mr. G. C. Hennessey & Rev. R. Serrano	1914	02	20	Wichita	KS	Mexican mission, 2 days	AT&SF
Mr. G. C. Hennessey & Rev. R. Serrano	1914	02	21	Hutchinson	KS	RR trackmen and Mexican mission	AT&SF
Mr. G. C. Hennessey & Rev. R. Serrano	1914	02	27	Florence	KS	Stayed 5 days	AT&SF
Mr. G. C. Hennessey & Rev. R. Serrano	1914	03	03	Augusta	KS	Stayed 2 days	AT&SF
Mr. G. C. Hennessey & Rev. R. Serrano	1914	03	08	Winfield	KS	Stayed 5 days	AT&SF
Mr. G. C. Hennessey & Rev. R. Serrano	1914	03	14	Arkansas City	KS	Stayed 2 days	AT&SF
Mr. G. C. Hennessey & Rev. R. Serrano	1914	03	17	Woodward	KS	Stayed 1 day	AT&SF
Mr. G. C. Hennessey & Rev. R. Serrano	1914	03	19	Harper	KS	Mexican mission, 2 days	AT&SF
Mr. G. C. Hennessey & Rev. J. P. MacCorry (17)	1914	03	22	Pratt	KS	Car spotted 1-1/2 miles from the houses of the people	AT&SF
Mr. G. C. Hennessey & Dr. Pomperey (17)	1914	03	28	Dodge City	KS	A visit to St. Mary's of the Plains for a great meal	AT&SF
Mr. G. C. Hennessey & Rev. J. P. MacCorry	1914	04	05	Stafford	KS	Stayed 3 days	AT&SF
Mr. G. C. Hennessey & Rev. T. A. McKernan (18)	1914	04	15	Elkhart	KS	Rode to town on the rear of a long freight train	AT&SF
Mr. G. C. Hennessey & Rev. T. A. McKernan	1914	04	15	Newton	KS	Car in shop for marker light bracket repairs $.55	AT&SF
Mr. G. C. Hennessey & Rev. T. A. McKernan	1914	04	21	Hugoton	KS	Used car during the day and town hall at night	AT&SF

PERSONNEL SERVING ON CARS	Y	M	D	TOWN	ST	COMMENTS FROM ACCOUNTS, LETTERS	RR
Mr. G. C. Hennessey & Rev. T. A. McKernan	1914	04	28	Copeland	KS	Chapel car came in on a hog train, people are Catholic Russian-Germans	AT&SF
Mr. G. C. Hennessey & Rev. T. A. McKernan	1914	05	02	Hanson (Olney)	KS	(17) Previous situation unknown	AT&SF
Mr. G. C. Hennessey & Rev. T. A. McKernan	1914	06	10	Bazine	KS	Hurricane like dust storms, 3 days	AT&SF
Mr. G. C. Hennessey & Rev. T. A. McKernan	1914	05	16	Ness City	KS	Town suffered from many harvest failures	AT&SF
Mr. G. C. Hennessey & Rev. T. A. McKernan	1914	05	23	Dighton	KS	Car too small, lectures given in Baptist church	AT&SF
Mr. G. C. Hennessey & Rev. T. A. McKernan	1914	05	30	Scott City	KS	Greatest disappointment	AT&SF
Mr. G. C. Hennessey & Rev. T. A. McKernan	1914	06	01	Kansas City	KS	(18) From KS	CRI&P
Mr. G. C. Hennessey	1914	06	03	Liberal	KS		CRI&P
Mr. G. C. Hennessey	1914	06	05	Topeka	KS		CRI&P
Mr. G. C. Hennessey	1914	06	06	Wichita	KS		FL
Mr. G. C. Hennessey	1914	06	08	Mulberry	KS		AT&SF
Mr. G. C. Hennessey & Rev. C. M. Smith (19)	1914	06	16	Denver	CO	Car exhibit a failure due to a hard rain, 2 days	OWR&N
Mr. G. C. Hennessey & Rev. C. M. Smith	1914	06	19	Portland	OR	(19) From Dodge City, KS.	OWR&N
Mr. G. C. Hennessey & Rev. A. W. Doran (20)	1914	06	22	La Grande	OR	Car waiting for transportation and chaplain, 1 week	OSL
Mr. G. C. Hennessey & Rev. A. W. Doran	1914	06	30	Nampa	ID	(20) From Philadelphia, PA	OSL
Mr. G. C. Hennessey & Rev. A. W. Doran	1914	07	04	Rupert	ID	Arrived in town during the 4th of July excitement	OSL
Mr. G. C. Hennessey & Rev. A. W. Doran	1914	07	12	Burley	ID	All services in car	OSL
Mr. G. C. Hennessey & Rev. A. W. Doran	1914	07	16	Filer	ID	A traveling lecturer had been in town and was against chapel car work	OSL
Mr. G. C. Hennessey & Rev. A. W. Doran	1914	07	18	Buhl	ID	Church 2-1/2 years old, town is the end of the line	OSL
Mr. G. C. Hennessey & Rev. A. W. Doran	1914	07	26	Twin Falls	ID	Car full, placed chairs in aisle, people standing outside	OSL
Mr. G. C. Hennessey & Rev. A. W. Doran	1914	08	03	Hollister	ID	Late transportation from Twin Falls, ID, no church in town	OSL
Mr. G. C. Hennessey & Rev. A. W. Doran	1914	08	06	Pocatello	ID	Car in shop for small repairs	OSL
Mr. G. C. Hennessey & Rev. A. W. Doran	1914	08	08	St. Anthony	ID	People just started the foundation for building	OSL
Mr. G. C. Hennessey & Rev. A. W. Doran	1914	08	15	Victor	ID	Rail line open just last year	OSL
Mr. G. C. Hennessey & Rev. A. W. Doran	1914	08	17	Driggs	ID	Largest town on this line	OSL
Mr. G. C. Hennessey & Rev. A. W. Doran	1914	08	18	Tetonia	ID	A Mormon town	OSL
Mr. G. C. Hennessey & Rev. A. W. Doran	1914	08	19	Ashton	ID	Mostly Catholics are from here and some from other towns	OSL
Mr. G. C. Hennessey & Rev. A. W. Doran	1914	08	22	Roberts	ID	Mission excellent and earnest spirit	OSL
Mr. G. C. Hennessey & Rev. A. W. Doran	1914	08	29	Idaho Falls	ID	Knights of Columbus special retreat	OSL
Mr. G. C. Hennessey & Rev. A. W. Doran	1914	09	02	Arco	ID	Less than a dozen Catholics and some in name only	OSL
Mr. G. C. Hennessey & Rev. A. W. Doran	1914	09	05	Mackey	ID	All services in car, no organ in church	OSL
Mr. G. C. Hennessey & Rev. A. W. Doran	1914	09	09	Black Foot	ID	Chapel car came to town during a blinding, early snow storm	OSL
Mr. G. C. Hennessey & Rev. A. W. Doran	1914	09	12	Aberdeen	ID	Expecting to break ground soon for building	OSL
Mr. G. C. Hennessey & Rev. A. W. Doran	1914	09	20	Pocatello	ID	Italian parish, chapel car came in on freight and passenger trains	OSL
Mr. G. C. Hennessey & Rev. A. W. Doran	1914	09	27	American Falls	ID	(21) Previous situation unknown	OSL
Mr. G. C. Hennessey & Rev. R. J. Malloy (22)	1914	10	03	Glenns Ferry	ID	Urged to start building	OSL
Mr. G. C. Hennessey & Rev. R. J. Malloy	1914	10	10	Nampa	ID	Attendance increased steadily	OSL
Mr. G. C. Hennessey & Rev. R. J. Malloy	1914	10	18	Boise	ID	Catholic men's retreat in cathedral	GOVT
Mr. G. C. Hennessey & Rev. Arrequi (21)	1914	10	23	Boise	ID	Basque and Spanish people used Basque language in car	SP
Mr. G. C. Hennessey & Rev. R. J. Malloy (22)	1914	10	25	Boise	ID	Non-Catholics meetings, question box used, in cathedral	OSL
Mr. G. C. Hennessey & Rev. R. J. Malloy	1914	11	02	Donnelly	ID	(22) Previous situation unknown	SP
Mr. G. C. Hennessey & Rev. R. J. Malloy	1914	11	05	Lakeport	ID		OWR&N
Mr. G. C. Hennessey & Rev. R. J. Malloy	1914	11	07	Horseshoe Bend	ID	The saloon closed up during time of services	OSL
Mr. G. C. Hennessey & Rev. R. J. Malloy	1914	11	15	Arrow Rock	ID	Basque and Spanish was the language of the people	OSL
Mr. G. C. Hennessey	1914	11	28	Portland	OR	No mission	OWR&N
Mr. G. C. Hennessey & Rev. T. J. Brady (23)	1914	11	29	Nyssa	OR	(23) From Condon, OR	OSL
Mr. G. C. Hennessey	1914	12	08	Pocatello	ID	Minor repairs and heating plant overhauled, $192.42	OSL
Mr. G. C. Hennessey	1914	12	16	Portland	OR	Waiting transportation passes for 1915, car repairs $8.09	SP
Mr. G. C. Hennessey (25) (24)	1915	01	04	Pilot Rock	OR	Used as church & house (24) Priests from Hermiston, OR	OWR&N
Mr. G. C. Hennessey (26) (27)	1915	04	15	Pilot Rock	OR	Mission (25) To Dayton, OH, to pick up new chapel car St. Paul	—
Mr. G. C. Hennessey	1915	04	25	Pocatello	ID	Repairs, painting, and varnishing $250.	OSL
Mr. G. C. Hennessey & Rev. W. D. O'Brien (28)	1915	05	25	McCammon	ID	Bad time, local school having commencement	OSL
Mr. G. C. Hennessey & Rev. W. D. O'Brien	1915	05	29	Lava Hot Springs	ID	(26) From Alexandria, LA, car was first church	OWR&N
Mr. G. C. Hennessey & Rev. W. D. O'Brien	1915	06	06	Culver	OR	New town just made county seat, car was first church	OWR&N
Mr. G. C. Hennessey & Rev. W. D. O'Brien	1915	06	13	Redmond	OR	At one morning only 2 for Mass in car	OWR&N
Mr. G. C. Hennessey & Rev. W. D. O'Brien	1915	06	19	Bend	OR	Not gas lighting on car, services held in church	OWR&N
Mr. G. C. Hennessey & Rev. M. P. Seter (29)	1915	06	26	The Dalles	OR	Car shop working on gas lights	OWR&N
Mr. G. C. Hennessey & Rev. M. P. Seter	1915	06	25	Bend	OR	Car takes Bishop G. J. O'Reilly to Bend, OR	OSL
Mr. G. C. Hennessey & Rev. M. P. Seter	1915	06	26	Bend	OR	No mission	SP
Mr. G. C. Hennessey & Rev. M. P. Seter	1915	06	27	The Dalles	OR	No mission, waiting for chaplain, 2 weeks	OWR&N
Mr. G. C. Hennessey & Rev. M. P. Seter	1915	07	08	Nampa	ID	No mission, waiting for chaplain, 1 day	OSL
Mr. G. C. Hennessey & Rev. M. P. Seter	1915	07	15	Silver City	ID	Rode auto truck 30 miles to town, without car	OSL
Mr. G. C. Hennessey & Rev. M. P. Seter	1915	07	21	Nampa	ID	No mission	OSL
Mr. G. C. Hennessey & Rev. M. P. Seter	1915	07	24	Emmett	ID	(27) Fathers from Hermiston, OR	OSL
Mr. G. C. Hennessey & Rev. M. P. Seter	1915	07	31	Plummer	ID	Preached in local church and car on exhibit	OSL
Mr. G. C. Hennessey & Rev. M. P. Seter	1915	08	09	Murray	ID	Catholics had not been to sacraments for years	OWR&N
Mr. G. C. Hennessey & Rev. P. J. Driscoll (30)	1915	06	15	Portland	OR	(28) From Chicago, IL	SP
Mr. G. C. Hennessey & Rev. P. J. Driscoll	1915	08	22	Sacramento	CA	(29) From Haubustad, IN	SP
Mr. G. C. Hennessey & Rev. P. J. Driscoll	1915	08	25	San Jose	CA	(30) Previous situation unknown	SP
Mr. G. C. Hennessey & Rev. P. J. Driscoll	1915	09	17	San Francisco	CA	Car repairs and supplies at depot $7.92	SP
Mr. G. C. Hennessey & Rev. P. J. Driscoll	1915	09	22	Los Angeles	CA	For funeral of Los Angeles bishop and chapel car exhibition	SP
Mr. G. C. Hennessey & Rev. P. J. Driscoll	1915	09	25	San Francisco	CA	Car repairs and supplies at depot $3.78 + $11.70	SP
Mr. G. C. Hennessey & Rev. P. J. Driscoll	1915	09	29	San Francisco	CA	San Francisco Panama Exposition, 6 weeks	GOVT
Mr. G. C. Hennessey & Rev. P. J. Driscoll	1915	11	06	Portland	OR	Waiting transportation for chapel car	SP
Mr. G. C. Hennessey & Rev. W. J. Cartwright (31)	1915	11	08	Linnton	OR	No mission, car in train yard out of service, 1 month	SP
Mr. G. C. Hennessey & Rev. G. F. Quinan (32)	1915	12	06	Clatskanie	OR	1/3 Italian, 1/3 French, 1/3 German or Greek in town	SP&S
Mr. G. C. Hennessey & Rev. J. B. Donegan (33)	1915	12	13	Clatskanie	OR	Clatskanie Junction, Each night the crowds increased	SP&S
Mr. G. C. Hennessey	1915	12	20	Westport	OR	Poor weather (31) From Portland, OR	UP
Mr. G. C. Hennessey	1915	12	25	Pocatello	ID	Car in shop, old style brakes changed out, 4 weeks	SP&S
Mr. G. C. Hennessey	1916	02	11	Portland	OR	(32) Previous situation unknown	

PERSONNEL SERVING ON CARS	Y	M	D	TOWN	ST	COMMENTS FROM ACCOUNTS, LETTERS	RR
Mr. G. C. Hennessey & Rev. C. M. Smith (34)	1916	02	12	East St. John	OR	Many outside car tried to listen	SP&S
Mr. G. C. Hennessey	1916	02	23	Portland	OR	No mission	SP&S
Mr. G. C. Hennessey & Rev. W. J. Cartwright	1916	02	26	Hammond	OR	Fort Stevens, OR, about 1 mile from car	SP&S
Mr. G. C. Hennessey & Rev. J. B. Donegan	1916	03	06	Svensen	OR	Rained continually, a few Catholics in town	SP&S
Mr. G. C. Hennessey & Rev. J. B. Donegan	1916	03	09	Clifton	OR	Austrians, Italians, and Orthodox Greeks	SP&S
Mr. G. C. Hennessey & Rev. C. M. Smith (34)	1916	03	11	Linnton	OR	Along side of station, local paper reported many at car	SP
Mr. G. C. Hennessey	1916	03	19	Portland	OR	No mission	SP
Mr. G. C. Hennessey & Rev. C. M. Smith	1916	03	23	Clackamas	OR	Very small town but car sometimes crowded to limit	SP
Mr. G. C. Hennessey & Rev. C. M. Smith	1916	03	31	Portland	OR	(33) From St. John, OR	UP
Mr. G. C. Hennessey & Rev. C. M. Smith	1916	04	03	Latourelle	OR	Side track being worked on, mission started 04-06-1916	UP
Mr. G. C. Hennessey	1916	04	08	Ione	OR	interest awaked by the car's presence	UP
Mr. G. C. Hennessey & Rev. T. J. Brady (35)	1916	04	16	Heppner	OR	Car filled with mostly Catholics for 1 evening lecture	UP
Mr. G. C. Hennessey & Rev. T. J. Brady	1916	04	18	Pendleton	OR	(34) From Juntura, OR	UP
Mr. G. C. Hennessey & Rev. T. J. Brady	1916	04	29	Wasco	OR	Lectures created a profound impression on the people	UP
Mr. G. C. Hennessey & Rev. T. J. Brady	1916	05	07	Moro	OR	Last night the people went to see a high school play	UP
Mr. G. C. Hennessey & Rev. T. J. Brady	1916	05	14	Grass Valley	OR	Methodist minister asked for Catholic doctrine on baptism	UP
Mr. G. C. Hennessey & Rev. T. J. Brady	1916	05	17	Kent	OR	Not one Catholic in town, town not building after 2 fires	UP
Mr. G. C. Hennessey & Rev. T. J. Brady	1916	05	20	Shaniko	OR	Town at end of the railroad track	UP
Mr. G. C. Hennessey & Rev. T. J. Brady	1916	06	25	Pendleton	OR	No mission	UP
Mr. G. C. Hennessey & Rev. T. J. Brady	1916	06	02	Juntura	OR	No mission left car for exhibit, Lv 06-10-1916	UP
Mr. G. C. Hennessey & Rev. T. J. Brady	1916	06	04	Drewsey	OR	Poor attendance, due to baseball and movies, without car	—
Mr. G. C. Hennessey & Rev. T. J. Brady	1916	06	10	Riverside	OR	Mission in car at depot, a little distance from town	UP
Mr. G. C. Hennessey & Rev. T. J. Brady	1916	06	17	Brogan	OR	More than half of population of town in car	UP
Mr. G. C. Hennessey	1916	06	28	Vale	OR	No mission	UP
Mr. G. C. Hennessey & Rev. W. D. Cronin (36)	1916	07	08	Pocatello	ID	Car Repairs, painting and varnishing, $340	SP&S
Mr. G. C. Hennessey & Rev. W. D. Cronin	1916	10	07	Mountain Home	ID	(35) From Condon, OR	SP&S
Mr. G. C. Hennessey & Rev. W. D. Cronin	1916	10	14	Wendell	ID	Car organ repaired, mission held in church	SP&S
Mr. G. C. Hennessey & Rev. W. D. Cronin	1916	10	21	Jerome	ID	Car 1 mile from town, mission held in church	SP&S
Mr. G. C. Hennessey & Rev. W. D. Cronin	1916	10	31	Fairfield	ID	One family of 7 came 12 miles to attend Mass	SP&S
Mr. G. C. Hennessey & Rev. W. D. Cronin	1916	11	06	Hill City	ID	At 6000 ft. up, very cold	SP&S
Mr. G. C. Hennessey & Rev. W. D. Cronin	1916	11	10	Shoshone	ID	Mr. Hennessey held up a freight train for coal to heat the car and received some	SP&S
Mr. G. C. Hennessey & Rev. W. D. Cronin	1916	11	18	Hailey	ID	Freight train damaged draw bar of chapel car	SP&S
Mr. G. C. Hennessey & Rev. W. D. Cronin	1916	11	25	Richfield	ID	First wedding on car	SP&S
Mr. G. C. Hennessey & Rev. W. D. Cronin	1916	12	06	Pocatello	ID	Car in shop for draw bar repairs, coal famine	SP&S
Mr. G. C. Hennessey	1916	12	20	Portland	OR	(36) From Condon, OR	UP
Mr. G. C. Hennessey & Rev. W. J. Cartwright (37)	1917	01	20	St. Helens	OR	(37) From Portland, OR	SP&S
Mr. G. C. Hennessey & Rev. W. J. Cartwright	1917	01	29	Deer Island	OR	Lumber camp town, blizzard 6-18 inches of deep snow	SP&S
Mr. G. C. Hennessey & Rev. W. J. Cartwright	1917	02	03	Clatskanie	OR	Clatskanie Junction, plans to build church soon	SP&S
Mr. G. C. Hennessey & Rev. J. B. Donegan	1917	02	24	Rainier	OR	Repairs on car air brake system and waiting on chaplain	SP&S
Mr. G. C. Hennessey & Rev. W. D. Cronin	1917	03	05	Westport	OR	Very little religious strife here	SP&S
Mr. G. C. Hennessey & Rev. W. D. Cronin	1917	03	10	Warrenton	OR	Wife asked us to visit her dying husband at home	SP&S
Mr. G. C. Hennessey & Rev. W. D. Cronin	1917	03	18	Seaside	OR	Some have very bitter feelings against the church	SP&S
Mr. G. C. Hennessey & Rev. W. D. Cronin	1917	03	26	Scappoose	OR	Unfavorable weather but very successful mission	SP&S
Mr. G. C. Hennessey & Rev. W. D. Cronin	1917	04	03	Portland	OR	Sermons preached and instruction in Bohemian language	SP&S
Mr. G. C. Hennessey & Rev. W. J. Cartwright (41)	1917	04	03	Portland	OR	Car out of service during Easter, 1 week	UP
Mr. G. C. Hennessey & Rev. T. J. Brady (38)	1917	04	14	Oak Grove	OR	Sent a special engine 20 miles for car and built special track	SP
Mr. G. C. Hennessey & Rev. J. B. Donegan (39)	1917	04	26	Klamath Falls	OR	Opposing outside features kept people away from car	PRL&P
Mr. G. C. Hennessey & Rev. C. M. Smith	1917	05	16	Eugene	OR	Car steam line end hose charged out $3.93	SP
Mr. G. C. Hennessey & Rev. C. M. Smith	1917	05	19	Coquille	OR	(38) From Condon, OR	SP
Mr. G. C. Hennessey & Rev. C. M. Smith	1917	05	28	Myrtle Point	OR	Car waiting for transportation passes and chaplain, 1 month	SP
Mr. G. C. Hennessey & Rev. C. M. Smith	1917	06	02	Powers	OR	(39) Previous situation unknown	SP
Mr. G. C. Hennessey & Rev. C. M. Smith	1917	06	11	Marshfield	OR	Started as a lumber camp and now a nice little town	SP
Mr. G. C. Hennessey & Rev. C. M. Smith	1917	07	01	North Bend	OR	(40) From Portland, OR	SP
Mr. G. C. Hennessey & Rev. C. M. Smith	1917	07	01	Clackamas	OR	Wooden ship building plant, Catholic chapel attractive	SP
Mr. G. C. Hennessey & Rev. W. D. Cronin	1917	08	19	Portland	OR	For soldiers in camp and local town people	SP
Mr. G. C. Hennessey & Rev. W. D. Cronin (40)	1917	08	26	Berkley	CA	Car repairs, flat wheel change out	SP
Mr. G. C. Hennessey & Rev. W. J. Cartwright (41)	1917	08	28	Twin Falls	ID	Returned Bishop Glorieux of Boise, ID, for funeral	UP
Mr. G. C. Hennessey	1917	08	28	Boise	ID	(41) From Portland, OR	SP
Mr. G. C. Hennessey	1917	09	09	Portland	OR	(42) From Portland, OR	PRL&P
Mr. G. C. Hennessey & Rev. C. M. Smith (42)	1917	09	07	Kern Park-Arleta	OR	Maximum results are most encouraging, 2 weeks	PRL&P
Mr. G. C. Hennessey & Rev. C. M. Smith	1917	09	26	Oswego	OR	Conduct and enthusiastic most edifying, 10 days	SP
Mr. G. C. Hennessey & Rev. C. M. Smith	1917	10	08	Kern Park-Arleta	OR	Lv 01-10-1918	PRL&P
Mr. G. C. Hennessey & Rev. C. M. Smith	1917	11	10	Woodstock	OR	Used as church, Lv 01-10-1918	?
Mr. G. C. Hennessey & Rev. C. M. Smith	1917	12	26	Berkley	CA	(43) From San Francisco, CA	
Mr. G. C. Hennessey	1918	01	12	Pocatello	ID	Government takes over operation of railroads due to WWI	UP
Mr. G. C. Hennessey & Rev. A. H. Fleming (43)	1918	03	10	Shoshone	ID	Car in shop, overhaul and exterior painting. Lv 03-31-1918	—
Mr. G. C. Hennessey & Rev. A. H. Fleming	1918	03	15	Fairfield	ID	Many receive Extension Magazine, without car	—
Mr. G. C. Hennessey & Rev. A. H. Fleming	1918	03	20	Hailey	ID	In chapel car St. Anthony, without car	—
Mr. G. C. Hennessey & Rev. A. H. Fleming	1918	03	24	Pocatello	ID	Town closed down to hear Americanism speech, without car	—
Mr. G. C. Hennessey & Rev. A. H. Fleming	1918	04	05	Salt Lake City	UT	New mission for Italian people, without car	D&RG
Mr. G. C. Hennessey & Rev. A. H. Fleming	1918	04	21	Salt Lake City	UT	Car at depot, car on exhibit waiting for transportation	D&RG
Mr. G. C. Hennessey & Rev. A. H. Fleming	1918	04	29	Murray	UT	City mission work, without car	D&RG
Mr. G. C. Hennessey & Rev. A. H. Fleming	1918	05	05	Midvale	UT	Austrians not much interested in religion	D&RG
Mr. G. C. Hennessey & Rev. A. H. Fleming	1918	05	11	Eureka	UT	Mining town over 7000 ft, church full and with extra seats	D&RG
Mr. G. C. Hennessey & Rev. A. H. Fleming	1918	05	23	Provo	UT	Earnest appeal to provide a more decent building	D&RG
Mr. G. C. Hennessey & Rev. A. H. Fleming	1918	06	03	Thistle	UT	RR round house town, town will be moved	D&RG
Mr. G. C. Hennessey & Rev. A. H. Fleming	1918	06	15	Helper	UT	Locomotives added to trains to help push over the mountain	D&RG
Mr. G. C. Hennessey & Rev. A. H. Fleming	1918	06	15	Price	UT	Largely Italian and Greek about ready to build church	D&RG
Mr. G. C. Hennessey & Rev. A. H. Fleming	1918	06	22	Green River	UT	Very hot in car during the day	D&RG
Mr. G. C. Hennessey & Rev. A. H. Fleming	1918	06	26	Salt Lake City	UT	Car in shop again for flat wheel change out	D&RG

PERSONNEL SERVING ON CARS	Y	M	D	TOWN	ST	COMMENTS FROM ACCOUNTS, LETTERS	R R
Mr. G. C. Hennessey & Rev. A. H. Fleming	1918	06	29	Park City	UT	Town 8000 ft. high, local pastor died 1 week before car arrived	D&RG
Mr. G. C. Hennessey	1918	07	10	Albina	OR	Car in shop for cook stove and car lighting system repairs	UP
Mr. G. C. Hennessey & Rev. J. B. Donegan (44)	1918	09	14	Wheeler	OR	(44) From St. John, OR	SP
Mr. G. C. Hennessey & Rev. J. B. Donegan	1918	09	22	Tillamook	OR		SP
Mr. G. C. Hennessey & Rev. J. B. Donegan	1918	10	01	Bay City	OR	Cars out of service and stored due to Spanish Influenza	SP
Mr. G. C. Hennessey & Rev. G. A. Pramass (45)	1918	10	05	Buxton	OR	(45) Past situation unknown	SP
Mr. G. C. Hennessey & Rev. G. A. Pramass	1918	10	14	Banks	OR	Town old and set in ways, many have lived here a long time	SP
Mr. G. C. Hennessey & Rev. G. A. Pramass	1918	10	21	Portland	OR	Churches and theatres closed due to Spanish Influenza	PRL&P
Mr. G. C. Hennessey	1918	11	01	Portland	OR	All public gatherings canceled due flu, car out of service 1 month	PRL&P
Mr. G. C. Hennessey & Rev. G. F. Gusanae (46)	1918	11	30	Sherwood	OR	How little religious truth and prayers the children knew	OE
Mr. G. C. Hennessey & Rev. G. F. Gusanae	1918	12	06	Tualatin	OR	Finally curiosity got the best of people and they came to car	OE
Mr. G. C. Hennessey & Rev. G. F. Gusanae	1918	12	14	Tigard	OR	Arrived in middle of night by local freight train	OE
Mr. G. C. Hennessey	1918	12	23	Portland	OR		PRL&P
Mr. G. C. Hennessey	1919	01	21	Portland	OR	Car stored due to new tariff rates	PRL&P
Mr. G. C. Hennessey & Rev. J. B. Donegan	1919	04	26	Goldendale	WA	Spanish Influenza scare	SP&S
Mr. G. C. Hennessey & Rev. G. F. Gusanae	1919	05	03	Centerville	WA	(46) Previous situation unknown	SP&S
Mr. G. C. Hennessey & Rev. J. B. Donegan	1919	05	17	Fallbridge	WA	Railroad division point, floating population	SP&S
Mr. G. C. Hennessey & Rev. J. B. Donegan	1919	06	24	White Salmon	WA	Church on a hill 2 miles from town and train depot	SP&S
Mr. G. C. Hennessey & Rev. J. B. Donegan	1919	05	29	Stevenson	WA		SP&S
Mr. G. C. Hennessey	1919	06	05	Portland	OR	Car waiting instructions to take to shop or retire car	SP&S
Mr. G. C. Hennessey	1919	06	06	Parkrose	OR	Mission for local people, no local church building	PRL&P
Mr. G. C. Hennessey	1919	06	14	Parkrose	OR	Car stored on sliding at Ward, Sunday Mass only for 4 months	PRL&P
Mr. G. C. Hennessey	1919	09	26	Albina	OR	Car in shop for repairs and painting exterior $1426.18	PRL&P
Mr. G. C. Hennessey	1920	02	04	Portland	OR	Stored in train yard waiting for next mission, 1 month	UP
Mr. G. C. Hennessey	1920	03	01			Government returned ownership to railroads	—
Mr. G. C. Hennessey & Rev. A. W. Doran (47)	1920	06	08	Portland	OR	Working with St. Phillips Catholic Church	PRL&P
Mr. G. C. Hennessey & Rev. A. W. Doran	1920	05	17	North Portland	OR	In new section of town working with All Saints Catholic Church	PRL&P
Mr. G. C. Hennessey & Rev. A. W. Doran	1920	05	23	Portland	OR	Received telegram that car could start moving again	UP
Mr. G. C. Hennessey & Rev. A. W. Doran	1920	05	25	Woodland	WA	Mission started before chapel car on local freight got to town	UP
Mr. G. C. Hennessey & Rev. A. W. Doran	1920	06	05	Kalama	WA	(47) From Philadelphia, PA	UP
Mr. G. C. Hennessey & Rev. A. W. Doran	1920	06	05	Kelso	WA	Car 2 blocks from post office, a man over 100 years old came to car	UP
Mr. G. C. Hennessey & Rev. A. W. Doran	1920	06	13	Portland	OR	Worked in schools and men's retreat, without car	UP
Mr. G. C. Hennessey & Rev. A. W. Doran	1920	06	19	Vader	WA	Chapel car aroused more non-Catholics than Catholics	UP
Mr. G. C. Hennessey & Rev. A. W. Doran	1920	06	26	Winlock	WA	All services in car and often very crowded	UP
Mr. G. C. Hennessey & Rev. A. W. Doran	1920	07	09	Napavine	WA	People wanted church service	UP
Mr. G. C. Hennessey & Rev. A. W. Doran	1920	07	11	St. Urban	WA	Bad roads, people give many gifts for car, without car	UP
Mr. G. C. Hennessey & Rev. A. W. Doran	1920	07	17	Castle Rock	WA	Many not holding up their religion, Lv 07-23-1920	UP
Mr. G. C. Hennessey & Rev. A. W. Doran	1920	08	08	St. Anthony	ID	Fourteen Catholics from 6 nationalities, 1 day	UP
Mr. G. C. Hennessey & Rev. A. W. Doran	1920	08	16	Victor	ID	Not one Catholic in the full car, 1 night	UP
Mr. G. C. Hennessey & Rev. A. W. Doran	1920	08	17	Driggs	ID	Low numbers at lecture, 1 day	UP
Mr. G. C. Hennessey & Rev. A. W. Doran	1920	08	18	Tetonia	ID	One Catholic and 2 dozen Mormons, 1 day	UP
Mr. G. C. Hennessey & Rev. A. W. Doran	1920	08	19	Ashton	ID	Eight at lecture, 2 days	UP
Mr. G. C. Hennessey & Rev. A. W. Doran	1920	08	21	Roberts	WA		UP
Mr. G. C. Hennessey	1920	10	20	Woodland	WA		SP
Mr. G. C. Hennessey	1920	11	10	Portland	OR	Car not in service, waiting for chaplain	SP&S
Mr. G. C. Hennessey & Rev. C. M. Smith (48)	1920	11	13	Linnton	OR	(48) From Portland, OR	UP
Mr. G. C. Hennessey & Rev. C. M. Smith	1920	11	21	Bend	OR	Took Archbishop to Bend, OR, for church dedication	SP
Mr. G. C. Hennessey & Rev. C. M. Smith	1920	11	25	North Portland	OR	Hard to get chaplains on car, car out of service, 6 weeks	SP
Mr. G. C. Hennessey & Rev. E. J. McGuinness (49)	1921	01	11	Junction City	OR	(49) From Chicago, IL to Pocatello, ID and St. Anthony	SP
Mr. G. C. Hennessey & Rev. E. J. McGuinness	1921	01	11	Irving	OR	Other revival meetings in town, 1 store and 3 churches in town, 2 nights	SP
Mr. G. C. Hennessey & Rev. E. J. McGuinness	1921	01	14	Coburg	OR	Not one Catholic in the full car, 1 night	SP
Mr. G. C. Hennessey & Rev. E. J. McGuinness	1921	01	17	Springfield	OR	Many good people came one hour before services, 2 nights	SP
Mr. G. C. Hennessey & Rev. E. J. McGuinness	1921	01	20	Wendling	OR	Lumber camp, could not buy alcohol in town for car lights	SP
Mr. G. C. Hennessey & Rev. E. J. McGuinness	1921	01	26	Oakridge	OR	People got mad because car arrived too late for meeting	SP
Mr. G. C. Hennessey & Rev. E. J. McGuinness	1921	01	27	Eugene	OR		SP
Mr. G. C. Hennessey	1921	01	29	Portland	OR	Chapel car returned to storage due to no side tracks at 7 towns	SP
Mr. G. C. Hennessey	1921	02	28	North Portland	OR	Between Portland, OR, and Clifton, OR, on side track	SP&S
Mr. G. C. Hennessey	1921	03	02	North Portland	OR	(50) From Astoria, OR	SP
Mr. G. C. Hennessey & Rev. J. Waters (50)	1921	04	01	Parkrose	OR	Out of service for summer, 1-1/2 months	SP
Mr. G. C. Hennessey & Rev. J. Waters	1921	05	15	Clifton	OR	Fishing Port, Croations and Slavonians town	PRL&P
Mr. G. C. Hennessey & Rev. J. Waters	1921	05	24	Parkrose	OR	C.C.E.S. low on money for chapel cars, car stored	PRL&P
Mr. G. C. Hennessey & Rev. P. H. Griffin (51)	1921	11	19	Clackamas	OR	Widely scattered Catholics	SP
Mr. G. C. Hennessey & Rev. P. H. Griffin	1921	11	26	Warrenton	WA	(51) From Indianapolis, IN	SP
Mr. G. C. Hennessey & Rev. P. H. Griffin	1921	12	04	Clifton	OR		SP&S
Mr. G. C. Hennessey	1921	12	12	Westport	OR	Saw mill town, many non-Catholics	SP&S
Mr. G. C. Hennessey	1921	12	18	Linnton	OR	Car in shop and stored, waiting on car transportation	SP
Mr. G. C. Hennessey & Rev. H. J. McDevitt (52)	1922	05	13	Prescott	WA	Many rich Catholic moved, few Catholics left in town	UP
Mr. G. C. Hennessey & Rev. H. J. McDevitt	1922	05	13	Dayton	WA	(52) From Marshfield, OR	UP
Mr. G. C. Hennessey & Rev. H. J. McDevitt	1922	05	20	Waitsburg	WA	Car air train line repairs $3.96	UP
Mr. G. C. Hennessey & Rev. H. J. McDevitt	1922	05	27	Starbuck	WA	Nearly all Catholic RR men work on railroad or shops	UP
Mr. G. C. Hennessey & Rev. H. J. McDevitt	1922	06	03	Moscow	ID	A prosperous agricultural section of state, 1 week	UP
Mr. G. C. Hennessey & Rev. H. J. McDevitt	1922	06	16	La Crosse	WA	Morning Mass in car, services in church, 1 week	UP
Mr. G. C. Hennessey & Rev. H. J. McDevitt	1922	06	24	Pomeroy	WA	New church and building a new rectory, 1 week	UP
Mr. G. C. Hennessey & Rev. H. J. McDevitt (53)	1922	06	30	Spokane	WA	Waiting to leave for Chicago, IL	SP&S
Mr. G. C. Hennessey & Rev. H. J. McDevitt	1922	07	05	Chicago	IL	(53) Rode chapel car to Chicago, IL	BR
Mr. G. C. Hennessey & Rev. W. D. O'Brien (54)	1922	07	06	Pullman	IL	Car in shop for exterior painting and electric system, $2700	IC
Mr. G. C. Hennessey & Rev. W. D. O'Brien	1922	09	09	Chicago	IL	(54) From Chicago, IL	BR
Mr. G. C. Hennessey & Rev. W. D. O'Brien	1922	09	09	St. Cloud	MN	Start of exhibition tour, 1 day	NP
Mr. G. C. Hennessey & Rev. W. D. O'Brien	1922	09	11	Fargo	ND	Exhibit, 1 day	NP
Mr. G. C. Hennessey & Rev. W. D. O'Brien	1922	09	12	Bismarck	ND	Exhibit, 1 day	NP
Mr. G. C. Hennessey & Rev. W. D. O'Brien	1922	09	14	Miles City	MT	Exhibit, 1 day	NP

PERSONNEL SERVING ON CARS	Y	M	D	TOWN	ST	COMMENTS FROM ACCOUNTS, LETTERS	R R
Mr. G. C. Hennessey & Rev. W. D. O'Brien	1922	09	15	Billings	MT	Exhibit, 1 day	NP
Mr. G. C. Hennessey & Rev. W. D. O'Brien	1922	09	16	Helena	MT	Exhibit, 1 day	NP
Mr. G. C. Hennessey & Rev. W. D. O'Brien	1922	09	19	Missoula	MT	End of exhibition tour, 1 day	NP
Mr. G. C. Hennessey & Rev. W. D. O'Brien (55)	1922	09	20	Spokane	WA	Arrangements for next missions	UP
Mr. G. C. Hennessey & Rev. H. J. McDevitt	1922	10	21	Mica	WA	Grateful community, some "mustard seed" sowed	UP
Mr. G. C. Hennessey & Rev. H. J. McDevitt	1922	10	25	Farmington	WA	Proper publicity not given ahead of time, 3 days	UP
Mr. G. C. Hennessey & Rev. H. J. McDevitt	1922	10	29	Plummer	ID	Chapel car leaves on passenger train	CM&SP
Mr. G. C. Hennessey & Rev. H. J. McDevitt	1922	11	04	Worley	ID	A great deal of this land belongs to the Indians	CM&SP
Mr. G. C. Hennessey & Rev. H. J. McDevitt	1922	11	11	Harrison	ID	English mission, gratefully received literature	UP
Mr. G. C. Hennessey & Rev. H. J. McDevitt	1922	11	19	Harrison	ID	Italian mission, attendance at mission excellent	UP
Mr. G. C. Hennessey & Rev. H. J. McDevitt	1922	11	25	Lane	ID	Poison-laden waters destroyed the fertile valley	UP
Mr. G. C. Hennessey & Rev. H. J. McDevitt	1922	12	02	Rose Lake	ID	Cold weather, minus 18 degrees, both water and steam systems freeze up	UP
Mr. G. C. Hennessey & Rev. H. J. McDevitt	1922	12	08	Wallace	ID	Car in shop to be thawed out while on shop steam system	UP
Mr. G. C. Hennessey & Rev. H. J. McDevitt	1922	12	12	Clifton	ID	(55) From Marsifield, OR	SP&S
Mr. G. C. Hennessey & Rev. H. J. McDevitt	1923	03	01	Portland	OR		SP&S
Mr. G. C. Hennessey & Rev. H. J. McDevitt	1923	03	04	Clifton	OR	Many from Croatia and Yugoslavia	SP&S
Mr. G. C. Hennessey & Rev. H. J. McDevitt	1923	03	10	Rainier	OR	A good frame church and fine attendance at service	SP&S
Mr. G. C. Hennessey & Rev. H. J. McDevitt	1923	03	18	Burkenfield	OR	Number increasing in evening, without car	SP&S
Mr. G. C. Hennessey & Rev. H. J. McDevitt	1923	03	24	Linnton	OR	Services in church and children's services in car	SP&S
Mr. G. C. Hennessey & Rev. H. J. McDevitt	1923	04	02	Portland	OR	Car out of service, 1 week	OE
Mr. G. C. Hennessey & Rev. H. J. McDevitt	1923	04	08	Tigard	OR	Will not forget the good people and how much good done	SP&S
Mr. G. C. Hennessey & Rev. H. J. McDevitt	1923	04	16	Portland	OR	No missions	—
Mr. G. C. Hennessey & Rev. H. J. McDevitt	1923	04	21	Priest River	ID	Town favorably for lumber business	GN
Mr. G. C. Hennessey & Rev. H. J. McDevitt	1923	04	29	Priest River	ID	Italian colony 3 miles inland from car, without car	—
Mr. G. C. Hennessey & Rev. H. J. McDevitt	1923	05	06	Newport	WA	Town on the ID and WA state lines, building on choice corner lot	CM&SP
Mr. G. C. Hennessey & Rev. H. J. McDevitt	1923	05	12	Ione	WA	Evergreen mountains encircles town	GN
Mr. G. C. Hennessey & Rev. H. J. McDevitt	1923	05	21	Spokane	WA	No missions	GN
Mr. G. C. Hennessey & Rev. H. J. McDevitt	1923	05	26	Springdale	WA	Catholics proved faithful in attendance	GN
Mr. G. C. Hennessey & Rev. H. J. McDevitt	1923	06	02	Valley	WA	Many acts of kindness received	GN
Mr. G. C. Hennessey & Rev. H. J. McDevitt	1923	06	10	Jumpoff	WA	Three miles above valley, 1 week, without car	—
Mr. G. C. Hennessey & Rev. H. J. McDevitt	1923	06	16	Chewelah	WA	Short notice about car meetings, low numbers grew as meeting were held	GN
Mr. G. C. Hennessey	1923	06	25	Portland	OR	Car stored for summer, 4 months, Lv 10-18-1923	SP&S
Mr. G. C. Hennessey & Rev. H. J. McDevitt	1923	10	20	Wallace	ID	Mining town, Italian mission, side track shortage	UP
Mr. G. C. Hennessey & Rev. H. J. McDevitt	1923	10	27	Kellogg	ID	Italian mission, visited many homes	CRI&P
Mr. G. C. Hennessey & Rev. H. J. McDevitt	1923	11	03	Burke	ID	Mining town, church and much of town burned, without car	—
Mr. G. C. Hennessey (56) & Rev. H. J. McDevitt	1923	12	01	Portland	OR	(56) Resigned to enter mortuary business, Portland, OR	SP&S
(57)	1923	12	15	Portland	OR	(57) Car vacant, 3 months	SP&S
Rev. H. J. McDevitt & Rev. C. M. Smith (58)	1924	03	07	Portland	OR	(58) From Portland, OR	SP&S
Rev. H. J. McDevitt & Rev. C. M. Smith	1924	04	30	Hopemere	OR	First the car was taken to the wrong town	SP
Rev. H. J. McDevitt & Rev. C. M. Smith	1924	05	04	Springfield	OR	Fifteen hundred men now working on this new railroad line	SP
Rev. H. J. McDevitt & Rev. C. M. Smith	1924	05	11	Oakridge	OR	Car derailed twice due to weight of car, received KKK letter	SP
Rev. H. J. McDevitt & Rev. C. M. Smith	1924	06	01	Creswell	OR	Many have moved away and just 1 Catholic family left	SP
Rev. H. J. McDevitt & Rev. C. M. Smith	1924	06	25	Swisshome	OR	Town with a few dwellings and station	SP
Rev. H. J. McDevitt & Rev. C. M. Smith	1924	06	25	Mapleton	OR	A successful mission, 20 Catholics in town	SP
(59)	1924	12	02	Portland	OR	(59) Car vacant, 3 months	SP
(59)	1925	03	10	Chicago	IL	No mission	BR
(59)	1925	03	12	Pullman	IL	Car repaired and stored in shop	IC
Rev. S. Sweeney (60)(61)	1926	03	26	Chicago	IL	(60) From Chicago, IL	IC
Rev. S. Sweeney	1926	04	01	New York	NY	No mission	NYC
Rev. S. Sweeney	1926	04	02	Rocky Mount	NC	Great people, received only the kindness treatment	NYC
Rev. S. Sweeney	1926	04	06	Williamston	NC	(61) Picked up car for NC	ACL
Rev. S. Sweeney	1926	04	13	Plymouth	NC	Came to town through a forest fire 8 miles along track	ACL
Rev. S. Sweeney	1926	04	17	Farmville	NC	Colored section, great crowds, car was too long for track	ACL
Rev. S. Sweeney	1926	04	21	Belhaven	NC	Some traveled as far as 5 to 6 miles to chapel car	NS
Rev. S. Sweeney	1926	05	16	Washington	NC	Held several informal sessions	NS
Rev. S. Sweeney	1926	06	18	Aurora	NC	Two days trip to get here, then forest fire near car, 1 week	W&V
Rev. S. Sweeney (62)	1926	06	19	Oriental	NC	(62) In NC to 12-1927	NS
Rev. S. Sweeney	1927	01	02	Bayboro	NC	Crowded car every night, great future for church	NS
Rev. S. Sweeney	1927	03	24	Vanceboro	NC	Four people First night in car, 2 weeks	NS
Rev. S. Sweeney	1927	05	01	Greenville	NC	Three girls laughed all during the service	ACL
Rev. S. Sweeney	1927	05	24	Kinston	NC	First town for Father Albert	ACL
Rev. E. J. Albert (63)	1928	01	06	Maysville	NC	Second town for Father Albert	?
Rev. E. J. Albert	1928	01	30	New Bern	NC	(63) From MA, 01-01-1928	NS
Rev. E. J. Albert	1928	02	10	S	NC	From MA	NS
Rev. E. J. Albert (64)	1928	03	10	Oriental	NC	Belhaven, Bayboro, or Bell, NC	?
Rev. E. J. Albert	1928	04	10	Plymouth	NC	(64) Lv 01-17-1929 for Springfield, MA, died 02-07-1929	NS
(65)	1929	01	15	B	NC	(65) Car vacant, 4 months	NS
Rev. L. Hay (66)	1929	01	17	Center ?	NC	(66) From MA	NS
Rev. L. Hay	1929	05	10	New Bern	NC	50 missions after 2-1929 to 1-1932 ?	NS
Rev. L. Hay	1930	02	20	High Point	NC	First town outside New Bern, 1 week	NS
Rev. L. Hay	1930	03	09	Grifton	NC	Stayed 1 week	NS
(67)	1930	05	03	Randleman	NC	(67) Too hot and car out of service, vacant 4-12 months	NS
Rev. L. Hay	1930	05	10	Asheboro	NC	Much prejudice	ACL
Rev. L. Hay	1931	07	10	Atlantic City	NJ	Exhibition at Convention of the Catholic Daughters of American	HPRA&S
Rev. L. Hay	1931	08	02	Philadelphia	PA	Exhibit, 4000 passed through car, 2 days	PRR
Rev. L. Hay	1931	08	04	Baltimore	MD	Exhibit, 2 days	PRR
Rev. L. Hay	1931	08	06	Washington	DC	Exhibit, 2 days	PRR
Rev. L. Hay	1931	08	08	Richmond	VA	Exhibit, 2 days	SAL

PERSONNEL SERVING ON CARS	Y	M	D	TOWN	ST	COMMENTS FROM ACCOUNTS, LETTERS	R R
(68)				Raleigh	NC	(68) Car vacant for summer, 2 months	SAL
Rev. L. Hay	1931	08	10	Raleigh	NC	Car in overall poor condition, and may be in storage	SAL
(69)	1931	10	02	Raleigh	NC	(69) Car stored in shop, car renovated and shipped, 17 months	IC
Rev. L. Hay	1932	12	10	Pullman	IL	Car in storage and broken into, Lv 10-01-1933	SAL
	1933	04	20	Raleigh	NC	1933 to 1938 information not found, 54 months	?
(70)	1937			Other towns		Car has been reconditioned	SAL
(70)	1938	08	10	Wake Forest	NC	Car given to the Diocese of NC in 1939	SB
(70)	1939	11	11	Wake Forest	NC	(70) Chaplains not known	SB
	1940	07	20	Oxford	NC	On coal yard siding near Military and Spring Sts.	--
	1940	07	21	Oxford	NC	Used as a Church building	--
	1940	07	22	Oxford	NC	Also used by Catholics from Camp Butne	--
	1942	04	01	Oxford	NC	Also used by Catholics from Camp Butne	--
	1943			Oxford	NC	Also used by Catholics from Camp Butne	--
	1944			Oxford	NC	Special note: Car service in last 20 years not clear	--
	1945			Oxford	NC	Car may be vacant and not used for 5 years	--
	1948			Oxford	NC	Car service in last 20 years not used for 5 years	--
	1953	04	04	Oxford	NC	Car dismantled for $1669, money used for building church	--
NICKNAME - THE IRON APOSTLE							
C.C.E.S. THIRD CAR, ST. PAUL						OF THE UNITED STATES OF AMERICA	
						THE CATHOLIC CHURCH EXTENSION SOCIETY	
Rev. E. B. Ledvina, vice president and general secretary	1912	11	04	Planning for 3rd car		Car donor Mr. Peter A. Kuntz Sr., who also donated St. Peter	--
of C.C.E.S., mainly in control of chapel car operation	1913	07	17	Dayton	OH	Building car not started	--
	1914	06	10	Chicago	IL	Car plans approved, $35,000 total	--
	1914	12	17	Dayton	OH	Car given to Catholic Church Extension Society	CH&D
Mr. G. C. Hennessey (1) & Rev. A. W. Doran (2)	1915	01	10	Dayton	OH	Car shipped from builder Barney & Smith Car Company	CH&D
Mr. G. C. Hennessey & Rev. A. W. Doran	1915	01	10	Dayton	OH	Exhibition of car near train station, 2 day	L&N
Mr. G. C. Hennessey & Rev. A. W. Doran	1915	01	14	Covington	KY	Car starts south exhibition tour to New Orleans, LA	L&N
Mr. G. C. Hennessey & Rev. A. W. Doran	1915	01	20	Louisville	KY	Exhibit. (1) Superintendent of chapel cars, from car St. Peter in OR	L&N
Mr. G. C. Hennessey & Rev. A. W. Doran	1915	01	26	Owensboro	KY	Exhibit, (2) From Philadelphia, PA	L&N
Mr. G. C. Hennessey & Rev. A. W. Doran	1915	02	02	Henderson	KY	Exhibit	L&N
Mr. G. C. Hennessey & Rev. A. W. Doran	1915	02	08	Evansville	IN	Exhibit	L&N
Mr. G. C. Hennessey & Rev. A. W. Doran	1915	02	17	Nashville	TN	Exhibit, on schedule, car may not have stopped	L&N
Mr. G. C. Hennessey & Rev. A. W. Doran	1915	02	22	Atlanta	GA	Exhibit, Rev. Doran will speak at 2 city church services	L&N
Mr. G. C. Hennessey & Rev. A. W. Doran	1915	02	24	Birmingham	AL	Exhibit	L&N
Mr. G. C. Hennessey & Rev. A. W. Doran	1915	02	26	Montgomery	AL	Exhibit, car open to all for inspection, no services	L&N
Mr. G. C. Hennessey & Rev. A. W. Doran	1915	02	28	Pensacola	FL	Exhibit	L&N
Mr. G. C. Hennessey & Rev. A. W. Doran	1915	03	01	Mobile	AL	Exhibit	L&N
Mr. G. C. Hennessey & Rev. A. W. Doran	1915	03	03	Biloxi	MS	Exhibit	L&N
Mr. G. C. Hennessey & Rev. A. W. Doran	1915	03	06	Bay St. Louis	MS	Exhibit	L&N ?
Mr. G. C. Hennessey & Rev. A. W. Doran	1915	03	07	Greensburg	LA	Exhibit	L&N
Mr. G. C. Hennessey & Rev. A. W. Doran	1915	03	09	New Orleans	LA	No exhibit	L&N
Mr. G. C. Hennessey & Rev. A. W. Doran	1915	03	12	Pass Christian	MS	Car dedication speakers first to see car	L&N
Mr. G. C. Hennessey & Rev. A. W. Doran	1915	03	14	New Orleans	LA	Car dedication near L&N station and river	T&P
Mr. G. C. Hennessey & Rev. A. W. Doran	1915	03	16	Alexandria	LA	No mission, planning for missions	T&P
Mr. G. C. Hennessey & Rev. A. W. Doran	1915	03	20	Bunkie	LA	Out grew car, moved to the church, first mission of car	T&P
Mr. G. C. Hennessey (3) & Rev. A. W. Doran	1915	03	26	Alexandria	LA	(3) Returned to chapel car, St. Peter, in OR	T&P
Rev. A. W. Doran	1915	04	06	Cheneyville	LA	Town did not welcome building of Catholic church	LR&N
Rev. A. W. Doran	1915	04	11	Lecompte	LA	Most Catholics live outside town on plantations	LR&N
Rev. A. W. Doran	1915	04	17	Boyce	LA	Day in car and evenings in church, railroad division point	LR&N
Rev. A. W. Doran	1915	04	25	Colfax	LA	Very hot outside, the crowd could not get in the church	T&P
Rev. A. W. Doran	1915	05	02	Aloha	LA	Catholic in name only, people poor and in poverty	T&P
Rev. A. W. Doran	1915	05	04	Montgomery	LA	People in town know nothing of the Catholic church	T&P
Rev. A. W. Doran	1915	05	06	Robeline	LA	All services in car, no proper lights in church building	KCS
Rev. A. W. Doran	1915	05	08	Mansfield	LA	108 degrees in car, 92 degrees outside also visited sick	T&P
Rev. N. Judermannos (4)	1915	05	15	Alexandria	LA	(4) From Alexandria, LA	T&P
Rev. N. Judermannos	1915	05	16	Powhatan	LA	Very hot, 102 degrees in car, many Italians	T&P
Rev. N. Judermannos	1915	05	21	Natchitoches	LA	Car on exhibit	LR&N
Rev. N. Judermannos	1915	05	23	Clarence	LA	No mission	LR&N
Rev. N. Judermannos	1915	05	31	Grappes Bluff	LA	Oil fields	LR&N
Rev. N. Judermannos	1915	06	11	Lentzburg	LA	Without car	IC
Rev. N. Judermannos	1915	06	14	Spanish Lake	LA	Oil fields	L&A
Rev. N. Judermannos	1915	06	22	Coushatta	LA	Oil fields	L&A
(5)	1915	06	26	Crichton	LA	(5) Car vacant, stored for summer, 3 -1/2 months	L&A
Rev. O. R. McGrath (6)	1915	07	01	New Orleans	LA	(6) From New Orleans, LA	L&A
Rev. O. R. McGrath	1915	10	16	Alexandria	LA	No mission	--
Rev. O. R. McGrath	1915	10	18	Winnfield	LA	Town marshal shot 1 week before car arrived in town	T&G
Rev. O. R. McGrath	1915	10	25	Jena	LA	Sawmill town, Lv 11-07-1915	T&G
Rev. O. R. McGrath	1915	11	01	Goodpine	LA	Without car	AL&G
Rev. O. R. McGrath	1915	11	02	Trout	LA	Without car	AL&G
Rev. O. R. McGrath	1915	11	08	Tall Timber	LA	Sawmill town, wonderful timber lands owned by T&G Railway	VS&P
Rev. O. R. McGrath	1915	11	11	Rochelle	LA	Town practically belongs to T&G Railway, Lv 11-22-1915	VS&P
Rev. O. R. McGrath	1915	11	15	Eros	LA	Mission well received by all after 2nd night	VS&P
Rev. O. R. McGrath	1915	11	28	Bastrop	LA	(7) Car in shop but no car work done, vacant 1 month	VS&P
Rev. O. R. McGrath	1915	12	04	Monroe	LA	Theatrical troupe and Christmas kept people away	SP?
Rev. O. R. McGrath	1915	12	13	Rayville	LA	Weather very wet, render mission very unsatisfactory	CRI&P
Rev. O. R. McGrath	1915	12	20	Ruston	LA	(8) From Chicago, IL, vice president and general secretary of C.C.E.S.	CRI&P
(7)	1915	12	27	Arcadia	LA	Car repairs and varnished $414.57	CRI&P
Rev. E. B. Ledvina (8)	1916	01	03	Shreveport	TX	(9) Manager of chapel car St. Paul, was car cook	SP?
Mr. M. J. Cousins (9) & Rev. E. L. Mattingly (10)	1916	02	05	Eunice	LA	French Creoles and French language spoken	CRI&P
Mr. M. J. Cousins & Rev. E. L. Mattingly	1916	03	04	Mamou			CRI&P
Mr. M. J. Cousins & Rev. E. L. Mattingly	1916	03	18	Meridian	LA	Treated with great courtesy by manager of sawmill	CRI&P

PERSONNEL SERVING ON CARS	Y	M	D	TOWN	ST	COMMENTS FROM ACCOUNTS, LETTERS	R R
Mr. M. J. Cousins & Rev. E. L. Mattingly	1916	03	27	Turkey Creek	LA	(10) From New Orleans, LA	CRI&P
Mr. M. J. Cousins & Rev. E. L. Mattingly	1916	04	03	Pine Prairie	LA	Oil town in the past, now small cotton-gin in town	CRI&P
Mr. M. J. Cousins & Rev. E. L. Mattingly	1916	04	10	Elton	LA		NOT&M
Mr. M. J. Cousins & Rev. E. L. Mattingly	1916	04	16	New Orleans	LA	Car repairs, batteries and lighting repairs	IC
Mr. M. J. Cousins & Rev. E. L. Mattingly	1916	04	23	Kinder	LA	Irish, German, and French nationalities	SLIM&S
Mr. M. J. Cousins & Rev. E. L. Mattingly	1916	04	30	Oberlin	LA	Cajun, French, Catholics in name only	SLIM&S
Mr. M. J. Cousins & Rev. E. L. Mattingly	1916	06	06	Oakdale	LA	Also went to Choctaws Indians homes for a mission	SLIM&S
Mr. M. J. Cousins & Rev. E. L. Mattingly	1916	05	17	New Orleans	LA	(11) Car vacant in train yard for summer, 4-1/2 months	IC
(11)							
Mr. M. J. Cousins & Rev. E. L. Mattingly	1916	10	08	De Ridder	LA	Boys and girls did not know how to pray	LC&N
Mr. M. J. Cousins & Rev. E. L. Mattingly	1916	10	16	Fullerton	LA	Sawmill town manager had car moved to a better spot	LC&N
Mr. M. J. Cousins & Rev. E. L. Mattingly	1916	10	25	Longville	LA	People not ready to receive us due to indifference	LC&N
Mr. M. J. Cousins & Rev. E. L. Mattingly	1916	11	02	Oretta	LA	Train flag stop, no town, poor people duped by land sharks	KCS
Mr. M. J. Cousins & Rev. E. L. Mattingly	1916	11	05	De Quincy	LA	First time town celebrated Mass, people did appreciate	KCS
Mr. M. J. Cousins & Rev. E. L. Mattingly	1916	11	18	Lockport	LA	We found many Catholics had fallen away from religion	ML&T
Mr. M. J. Cousins & Rev. E. L. Mattingly	1916	11	26	Sulphur	LA	Hot water sulphur mines outside of town	LW
Mr. M. J. Cousins & Rev. E. L. Mattingly	1916	12	07	Vinton	LA	Novelty of the car brings many to the mission	LW
Mr. M. J. Cousins & Rev. J. Diederich (12)	1916	12	27	Lake Arthur	LA	Chaplain remarks during services had mayor of town to close dance hall	LW
Mr. M. J. Cousins & Rev. J. Diederich	1917	01	08	Hayes	LA	Benches taken from train depot for the people outside car	LW
Mr. M. J. Cousins & Rev. J. Diederich	1917	01	14	De Ridder	LA	(12) From New Orleans, LA	LC&N
Mr. M. J. Cousins & Rev. J. Diederich	1917	01	20	Lake Charles	LA		LW
Mr. M. J. Cousins & Rev. J. Diederich	1917	01	24	Lacassine (Rice)	LA	1 mile from town near sawmill	LW
Mr. M. J. Cousins & Rev. J. Diederich (14)	1917	02	01	Egan	LA	Prominent men of town welcome the car, large crowd	LW
Mr. M. J. Cousins & Rev. J. Diederich	1917	02	08	Paradis	LA	Town ranks second in the state in illiteracy standing	ML&T
Mr. M. J. Cousins & Rev. J. Diederich	1917	02	16	McEroy	LA	(13) From New Orleans, LA	LR&N
Mr. M. J. Cousins & Rev. W. J. Graham (13)	1917	02	24	Sorrento	LA	No church of any kind in town, mission a success	LR&N
Mr. M. J. Cousins & Rev. W. J. Graham	1917	03	03	Gonzales	LA	Knowing very little, but eager to hear the Word of God	LR&N ?
Mr. M. J. Cousins & Rev. W. J. Graham	1917	03	10	Nettie	LA	Agricultural district, bad roads for 4 months each year	LR&N
Mr. M. J. Cousins & Rev. J. A. Girven	1917	03	22	Prairieville	LA	Crowd so large we moved car 1-1/2 miles to Prairieville, LA	LR&N
Mr. M. J. Cousins & Rev. J. A. Girven	1917	03	23	Kleinpeter	LA	Mission meetings in church, without car	—
Mr. M. J. Cousins & Rev. J. A. Girven	1917	04	14	Bayou Sorrel	LA	Great interest and good questions from answer box	LR&N
Mr. M. J. Cousins & Rev. J. A. Girven	1917	04	20	Plattenville	LA	(14) From New Orleans, LA	?
Mr. M. J. Cousins & Rev. J. P. Mueller (14)	1917	04	25	Scotandville (Scotland)	LA	Town mission and mission at black university	T&P
Mr. M. J. Cousins & Rev. J. P. Mueller	1917	04	30	Wilhelm	LA		LR&N
Mr. M. J. Cousins & Rev. J. P. Mueller	1917	06	06	New Orleans	LA	In shop for new electric power plant & batteries repaired	LR&N
Mr. M. J. Cousins	1917	08	25	New Orleans	LA	Car out of service for summer, too hot, 2-1/2 months	IC
Mr. M. J. Cousins & Rev. A. B. Kalverage (15)	1917	10	06	Krotz Spring	LA	(15) From New Orleans, LA	GC
Mr. M. J. Cousins & Rev. A. B. Kalverage	1917	10	14	Lottie	LA	(16) From New Orleans, LA	GC
Mr. M. J. Cousins & Rev. A. B. Kalverage	1917	10	23	Blank	LA	Sawmill blacksmiths and carpenters worked on car	GC
Mr. M. J. Cousins & Rev. A. B. Kalverage	1917	10	31	Livonia	LA	Bad roads, started funds for church building	GC
Mr. M. J. Cousins & Rev. A. B. Girven (16)	1917	11	11	Baton Rouge	LA	Car stopped just for water and car supplies	GC
Mr. M. J. Cousins & Rev. J. A. Girven	1917	11	19	Erwinville	LA	Farm land, large crowds in and around car	GC
Mr. M. J. Cousins & Rev. J. A. Girven	1917	11	27	Oscar Crossing	LA	Italians did not speak English	T&P
Mr. M. J. Cousins & Rev. J. A. Girven	1917	12	02	Morrow (Morrows)	LA	Three saloons and much gambling, people from dry towns	T&P
Mr. M. J. Cousins & Rev. J. A. Girven	1917	12	12	Rosa	LA	Cold rain for 6 days kept attendance low	T&P
Mr. M. J. Cousins & Rev. J. H. Dreis (17)	1917	12	15	Palmetto	LA	(17) From New Orleans, LA	T&P
Mr. M. J. Cousins & Rev. J. H. Dreis	1917	12	23	Melville	LA	Circus car next to chapel car	T&P
Mr. M. J. Cousins & Rev. J. H. Dreis	1917	12	28	Fordoche	LA	Government takes over operation of railroads due to WWI	T&P
Mr. M. J. Cousins & Rev. J. H. Dreis	1918	01	05	Morley	LA		—
Mr. M. J. Cousins & Rev. J. H. Dreis	1918	01	13	Addis	LA		T&P
Mr. M. J. Cousins & Rev. J. H. Dreis	1918	01	20	Torras	LA		T&P
Mr. M. J. Cousins & Rev. J. H. Dreis	1918	01	30	Lettsworth	LA		T&P
Mr. M. J. Cousins & Rev. J. H. Dreis	1918	02	05	Batchelor	LA		T&P
Mr. M. J. Cousins & Rev. J. H. Dreis	1918	02	16	Chamberlin	LA		T&P
Mr. M. J. Cousins & Rev. J. H. Dreis	1918	03	03	Baton Rouge	LA		T&P
Mr. M. J. Cousins & Rev. B. J. Krieger (18)	1918	03	06	Hammond	LA	(18) From New Orleans, LA	Y&MV
Mr. M. J. Cousins & Rev. B. J. Krieger	1918	03	09	Stevensdale	LA	Train flag station without a town	Y&MV
Mr. M. J. Cousins (19) & Rev. B. J. Krieger	1918	03	16	Sharps	LA	(19) Has malaria	Y&MV
Mr. M. J. Cousins & Rev. B. J. Krieger	1918	03	22	Denham Springs	LA	(20) Watching car in storage, car vacant	Y&MV
Mr. M. J. Cousins & Rev. B. J. Krieger	1918	03	25	Corbin	LA	Good attendance, cold weather, but good attendance	Y&MV
Mr. M. J. Cousins & Rev. B. J. Krieger	1918	04	02	Livingston	LA	Good attendance and our friends, closed mission with tears	Y&MV
Mr. M. J. Cousins & Rev. B. J. Krieger	1918	04	16	Holden	LA	Railroad center, from first to last day car was crowded	Y&MV
Mr. M. J. Cousins & Rev. B. J. Krieger	1918	04	28	Robert	LA	Bad roads due to rain and trucks repairing levees	Y&MV
Mr. M. J. Cousins (20)(21)	1918	06	02	New Orleans	LA	Three French families are the only practical Catholics	IC
Mr. M. J. Cousins (20)	1918	07	10	Algiers	LA	Many had their ideas about Catholics changed	SP
Mr. M. J. Cousins (20)	1919	01	10	New Orleans	LA	Good crowds and appropriate donations made	IC
Mr. M. J. Cousins (20)	1919	10	03	New Orleans	LA	No mission	IC
Mr. M. J. Cousins (20)	1920	02	12	New Orleans	LA	(21) Married, away from work, 05-10-1918 to 06-31-1918	IC
Mr. M. J. Cousins (20)	1920	02	13	New Orleans	LA	(22) Pastor of new St. Leo The Great Church	IC
Rev. V. J. Prats (22)	1920	03	01	New Orleans	LA	Car stored in rail yard outside New Orleans, LA	NOT
Rev. V. J. Prats				New Orleans	LA	Car in shop, for repairs but no work started, car moved	NOT
Mr. M. J. Cousins (20)	1921	10	31	New Orleans	LA	Car in shop overhauled, painting and varnishing	NOT
				New Orleans	LA	Car stored in rail yard outside New Orleans, LA	IC
				New Orleans	LA	Items removed from car and stored in Remptorist house	IC
				New Orleans	LA	Some repairs to car made by Mr. M. J.Cousins	IC
				New Orleans	LA	On Mylam-Morgan grain & feed mill spur	IC
				New Orleans	LA	Car used for church services and living quarters	IC
				New Orleans	LA	Government retuned ownership to railroads	IC
				New Orleans	LA	No longer used as church or living quarters	IC
(23)	1921	11	03	Chicago	IL	(23) Car vacant 4 months	IC
(23)	1921	12	04	Pullman	IL		IC
Rev. E. J. McGuinness (24)	1922	09	03	Chicago	IL	Car exterior painted $396.56	IC
Rev. E. J. McGuinness	1922	10	10	Buffalo	NY	Starts on eastern exhibition tour	ER
Rev. E. J. McGuinness	1923	01	09	New York	NY	Exhibit	ER
Rev. E. J. McGuinness	1923	02	05	Babylon, LI	NY	Exhibit	PRR
						Exhibit	LI

—362—

PERSONNEL SERVING ON CARS	Y	M	D	TOWN	ST	COMMENTS FROM ACCOUNTS, LETTERS	R R
Rev. E. J. McGuinness	1923	02	21	Philadelphia	PA	Exhibit, 3 days	PRR
Rev. P. H. Griffin (25) & Rev. E. J. McGuinness	1923	03	26	Washington	DC	Exhibit, Union Station	PRR
Rev. P. H. Griffin & Rev. E. J. McGuinness	1923	03	28	Reading	PA	Exhibit	PRR
(26)	1923	04	02	Harrisburg	PA	(26) Car vacant, no chaplains	PRR
Rev. P. H. Griffin & Rev. E. J. McGuinness	1923	04	10	Harrisburg	PA	Exhibit	PRR
Rev. P. H. Griffin & Rev. E. J. McGuinness	1923	04	15	Altoona	PA	Exhibit	PRR
Rev. P. H. Griffin & Rev. E. J. McGuinness	1923	04	27	Pittsburg	PA	Exhibit in East Liberty train yard	PRR
Rev. P. H. Griffin & Rev. E. J. McGuinness	1923	05	01	Pittsburg	PA	Exhibit at PRR station, end of eastern tour	PRR
Rev. E. J. McGuinness & Rev. A. Cunneen (27)	1923	05	08	Belhaven	NC	Preached in courthouse	NS
Rev. E. J. McGuinness & Rev. A. Cunneen	1923	05	15	Aurora	NC	Children took flowers to the altar	W&V
Rev. E. J. McGuinness & Rev. A. Cunneen	1923	05	22	Greenville	NC	(27) From Union City, NJ	ACL
Rev. A. Cunneen	1923	12	03	J	NC	Near depot	?
Rev. A. Cunneen	1923	12	06	Maysville	NC	KKK letter received late, car was already to move on	ACL
Rev. A. Cunneen	1923	12	09	Morehead City	NC		NS
Rev. A. Cunneen	1923	12	11	Belhaven	NC		NS
Rev. A. Cunneen	1923	12	14	New Bern	NC		NS
Rev. A. Cunneen	1923	12	15	Beaufort	NC	Given letter by KKK to leave town	NS
Rev. A. Cunneen	1923	12	19	Oriental	NC	Local ice plant men connected car to plant steam lines	NS
(28)	1923	12	24	?	NC	(28) Car vacant	?
Rev. A. Cunneen	1924	02	16	?	NC	Kitchen damaged by gasoline stove tank explosion	?
Rev. A. Cunneen	1924	02	16	Kinston	NC	Car in shops for fire damage repairs	NS
Rev. A. Cunneen	1924	03	18	Farmville	NC		NS
Rev. A. Cunneen & Rev. P. H. Griffin (29)	1924	04	06	Plymouth	NC	(29) From Indianapolis, IN	NS
Rev. A. Cunneen & Rev. P. H. Griffin	1924	04	20	Cincinnati	OH	Exhibition trip from NC to Cincinnati, OH	C&O
Rev. P. H. Griffin	1924	05	09	Willard	OH	Car attached to the priests' special train from NY, NY	B&O
Rev. P. H. Griffin	1924	05	11	Chicago	IL	(30) Previous situation unknown	B&O
Rev. T. W. Drumm (30) & Rev. C. Lalley (31)	1924	05	16	Des Moines	IA	Lv 05-18-1924	CRI&P
Rev. T. W. Drumm & Rev. C. Lalley	1924	05	20	Groundy ?	IA	(31) Previous situation unknown	?
Rev. T. W. Drumm & Rev. C. Lalley	1924	05	27	Gravity	IA		BR
Rev. T. W. Drumm & Rev. C. Lalley	1924	06	03	Bedford	IA	KKK leaders attended lectures	BR
Rev. T. W. Drumm & Rev. C. Lalley	1924	06	10	Allerton	IA		CRI&P
Rev. T. W. Drumm & Rev. C. Lalley	1924	06	17	Humeston	IA		BR
Rev. T. W. Drumm & Rev. C. Lalley	1924	06	24	Davis City	IA	(32) From IA	BR
Rev. J. A. Troy (32)	1924	07	05	Clarinda	IA	(33) From Reno, NV	BR
Rev. W. Appleby (33)	1924	07	12	Corydon	IA		CRI&P
Rev. W. Appleby	1924	07	19	Allerton	IA	(34) Previous situation unknown	CRI&P
Rev. W. Appleby	1924	07	26	Humeston	IA		BR
Rev. W. Appleby	1924	08	02	Davis City	IA		BR
Rev. W. Appleby	1924	08	09	Kellerton	IA		BR
Rev. W. Appleby	1924	08	16	Mt. Ayr	IA		BR
Rev. W. Appleby	1924	08	23	Bedford	IA		BR
Rev. W. Appleby	1924	08	30	Gravity	IA		BR
Rev. W. Appleby	1924	09	06	New Market	IA		BR
Rev. W. Appleby	1924	09	13	Clarinda	IA		BR
Rev. W. Appleby	1924	09	20	Sydney	IA	(34) Previous situation unknown	?
Rev. Huff (34)	1924	11	10	Elk City	OK	First OK town	CRI&P
Rev. Huff	1924	11	15	Grandfield	OK	At depot	CRI&P
Rev. Huff	1924	12	12	Carnegie	OK	3 weeks, car batteries froze up and broke	CRI&P
	1925			?	OK		?
(35)	1926	03	12	Chicago	IL	(35) Car vacant and stored in shop, 7 years, car renovated	CRI&P
	1926	03	14	Pullman	IL	Chicago World's Fair, LV 10-31-1933	IC
	1933	05	27	Chicago	IL	A Century of Progress Fair, Lv 11-01-1934	IC
(36)	1934	11	02	Pullman	IL	(36) Car vacant 16 months	IC
	1936	03	10	Bearcreek	MT	Car donated to Catholic Diocese of Great Falls, MT	MW&S
	1939	04	10	Gardiner	MT	North entrance of Yellowstone Park for services	NP
(37)	1954	12	13	Gardiner	MT	Last Mass given in car at north entrance of park	NP
	1954	12	13	Gardiner	MT	(37) Car stored after church was built, 5-1/3 years	NP
	1960	03	10	Livingston	MT	NP repaired car trucks for movement at no cost	NP
	1960	04	05	Livingston	MT	Car air brake repaired for GN interchange traffic at no cost	NP
Priests (38)	1960	04	22	Helena	MT	No services, stopped on way to Summit, MT	GN
Priests	1960	05	25	Summit	MT	Used for summer season	GN
Priests	1960	09	05	Glacier Park	MT	East entrance of Glacier Park used for winter season	GN
Priests	1961	05	10	Summit	MT	(38) From Browning, MT	GN
Priests	1961	09	10	Glacier Park	MT	East entrance of Glacier Park used for winter season	GN
Priests	1962	05	10	Summit	MT	Used for summer season and abandoned, too hot, too cold	GN
(39)	1963	09	10	Glacier Park	MT	Stored on siding near East Glacier Park, vacant 3-1/2 years	GN
	1967	03	21	Glacier Park	MT	GN asked where car should be moved	GN
(40)	1967	04	18	Glacier Park	MT	(40) C.C.E.S. told GN to dispose of chapel car anyway they see fit	GN
	1967	07	01	Glacier Park	MT	GN sold car to Bovey Corporation	GN
	1967	07	03	Great Falls	MT	On way to Alder, MT	GN
	1967	07	05	Alder	MT	Car trucked to Nevada City, MT	NP
	1967	07	09	Nevada City	MT	Bovey Corporation Alder Gulch railroad museum	GN
	1996	10	01	Nevada City	MT	Car traded	—
	1996	11	10	Alder	MT	Car trucked from Nevada City, MT	MRL
	1997	01	10	Wells	MI	Restoration of car for service at museum	ELS
	1999			Duluth	MN	Lake Superior Museum of Transportation intended to be the destination after restoration	ELS

The source for this information is *The Official Guide of the Railways and Steam Navigation Lines of the United States, Porto Rico, Canada, Mexico, and Cuba*, from 1889 to 1998. These volumes were located in the holdings of the John W. Barringer III Railroad Library of the St. Louis Mercantile Library at the University of Missouri-St. Louis, Missouri; and the Transportation Collection of the Northwestern University Library, Evanston, Illinois. Railroads mentioned in the letters and journals of the chapel car missionaries and chaplains did not always coincide with the names of the railroads registered in the Official Guide. Sometimes the missionaries and chaplains used nicknames or abbreviated names of the railroads, or were inaccurate or out of date in their information.

R R	RAILROAD NAME	EP CCND	EP NM #1	EP NM #2	EP NM #2	B #1	B NM #2	B #2	B #3	B #4	B #5	B #6	B #7	CC ST. ANTHONY	CC ST. PETER	CC ST. PAUL
A&CR	Astoria & Columbia River Railroad													S		
A&NM	Arizona & New Mexico Railway		S	S												
A&P	Atlantic & Pacific Railroad															
A&SE	Arizona & South-eastern Railroad		S	S												
AA	Ann Arbor Railroad							S								
ACL	Atlantic Coast Line Railroad															S
AE	Arizona Eastern Railroad		S	S												S
AL&G	Arkansas, Louisiana & Gulf Railroad					S										
AM	Arkansas Midland Railroad															
AR	Arrow Rock Railroad		S													
AT&SF	Atchison, Topeka & Santa Fe Railway		S	S		S		S		S						S
B&A	Boston & Albany Railroad			S		S										
B&O	Baltimore & Ohio Railway or Railroad		S													S
B&OSW	Baltimore & Ohio, Southwestern Railroad					S										
BA&P	Butte, Anaconda & Pacific Railway						S									
BC&SE	Boyne City & Southeastern Railroad															
BCR&N	Burlington, Cedar Rapids & Northern Railway		S			S										
BR	Burlington Route or Railroad		S			S		S		S						S
C&A	Chicago & Alton Railroad		S			S										
C&C	Coal & Coke Railroad															
C&E	Corvallis & Eastern Railroad					S								S		
C&EI	Chicago & Eastern Illinois Railroad or Railway		S											S		
C&NW	Chicago & Northwestern Railway or System or Line	S	S			S		S		S				S		
C&O	Chesapeake & Ohio Railway					S								S		S
C&S	Colorado & Southern								S							
CB&Q	Chicago, Burlington & Quincy Railroad		S			S								S		
CCC&SL	Cleveland, Cincinnati, Chicago & St. Louis Railway		S			S		S		S		S		S		S
CGW	Chicago Great Western Railroad		S			S								S		
CH&D	Cincinnati, Hamilton & Dayton Railway or Railroad		S			S				S				S		S
CI&L	Chicago, Indianapolis & Louisville Railway					S								S		
CL&N	Cincinnati, Lebanon & Northern Railway															
CM&PS	Chicago, Milwaukee & Puget Sound Railway		S			S								S		
CM&SP	Chicago, Milwaukee & St. Paul Railroad or Railway	S	S	S		S		S		S				S		
CMStP&P	Chicago, Milwaukee, St. Paul & Pacific Railroad		S			S								S		
CO	Central of Oregon													S		
CO&G	Choctaw, Oklahoma & Gulf Railroad					S				S						
CRI&G	Chicago, Rock Island & Gulf Railway															
CRI&P	Chicago, Rock Island & Pacific Railroad or Railway	S	S			S		S		S				S		S
CRO	Central Railroad of Oregon													S		
D&H	Delaware & Hudson Railroad															
D&IM	Denver & Inter Mountain Railroad								S					S		
D&M	Detroit & Mackinac Railway													S		
D&RG	Denver & Rio Grande Railroad					S				S				S		
D&RGW	Denver & Rio Grande Western Railroad Company		S			S				S		S				
D&SL	Denver & Salt Lake Railroad or Railway					S										
DSS&A	Duluth, South Shore & Atlantic Railway	S				S										
DT&FW	Denver, Texas & Fort Worth Railroad						S									
ELS	Escanaba, Lake Superior Railroad Company															S
EP&SW	El Paso & Southwestern Railroad or Company															S
ER	Erie Railroad		S			S										
FL	Frisco Lines		S			S				S				S		
FS	Frisco System		S			S				S				S		
FS&W	Fort Smith & Western Railroad															
G&E	Greenbrier & Eastern					S										
GC	Gulf Coast Lines															S
GC&SF	Gulf, Colorado & Santa Fe Railway		S			S				S				S		
GH&SA	Galveston, Harrisburg & San Antonio Railway		S			S				S						S
GN	Great Northern Railway	S				S						S				S
GOVAT	Government Army Track															
GOVT	Government Track													S		S
GR&I	Grand Rapids & Indiana Railway					S										
GT	Grand Trunk Railway		S			S				S						
GW	Great Western Railway													S		
H&C	Hardwick & Calumet Railroad			S												
H&TC	Houston & Texas Central Railroad Company		S			S				S						
HE	Harford Eastern Railway															
HE&WT	Houston, East & West Texas Railway Company															
HIU	Holton Inter - Urban Railway															
HPRA&S	High Point, Randleman, Asheboro & Southern Railroad															
HS	Hot Springs Railroad															S
I&M	Independence & Monmouth Railway													S		

The source for this information is *The Official Guide of the Railways and Steam Navigation Lines of the United States, Porto Rico, Canada, Mexico, and Cuba*, from 1889 to 1998. These volumes were located in the holdings of the John W. Barringer III Railroad Library of the St. Louis Mercantile Library at the University of Missouri-St. Louis, Missouri; and the Transportation Collection of the Northwestern University Library, Evanston, Illinois. Railroads mentioned in the letters and journals of the chapel car missionaries and chaplains did not always coincide with the names of the railroads registered in the *Official Guide*. Sometimes the missionaries and chaplains used nicknames or abbreviated names of the railroads, or were inaccurate or out of date in their information.

R R	RAILROAD NAME	EP CCND	EP NM #1	EP NM #2	B #1	B #2	B #3	B #4	B #5	B #6	B #7	CC ST. ANTHONY	CC	ST. PETER	CC	ST. PAUL
I&SL	Iowa & St. Louis Railroad or Railway															
IC	Illinois Central Railroad	S							S			S				S
IN	Idaho Northern Railroad			S	S											
IR	Intercolonial Railway															S
IS	Idaho Southern Railroad			S	S							S				
K&M	Kanawha & Michigan Railway															
KCFS&M	Kansas City, Fort Scott & Memphis Railroad				S											
KCM&O	Kansas City, Mexico & Orient Railway				S											S
KCS	Kansas City Southern Railway				S											
KCW&G	Kansas City, Watkins & Gulf Railway				S											
L&A	Louisiana & Arkansas Railway															S
L&N	Louisville & Nashville Railroad Company															S
LA&SL	Los Angeles & Salt Lake Railroad or Railway				S											S
LC&N	Lake Charles & Northern Railway or Railroad															S
LI	Long Island Railroad															S
LR&HSW	Little Rock & Hot Springs Western Railroad															
LR&M	Little Rock & Memphis Railroad				S		S					S				S
LR&N	Louisiana Railway & Navigation Company															
LS&I	Lake Superior & Ishpeming Railroad Company or Railway			S												
LS&MS	Lake Shore & Michigan Southern Railway			S												
LW	Louisiana Western Railroad											S				S
M&N	Milner & Northside Railroad				S											
M&NR	Milwaukee & Northern Railroad			S	S											S
M&P&SRV	Maricopa & Phoenix & Salt River Valley Railroad				S							S				
M&SL	Minneapolis & St. Louis Railroad				S											
MC	Mexican Central Railroad															
MCR	Michigan Central Railroad															
MK&T	Missouri - Kansas & Texas Railway or Railroad or Lines				S		S		S			S				S
ML&T	Morgen's Louisiana & Texas Railroad															
MP	Missouri Pacific Railroad or Lines			S	S	S	S					S				S
MR	Mineral Range Railroad			S			S									
MRL	Montana Rail Link															
MSP&SSM	Minneapolis, St. Paul & Sault Ste. Marie			S	S											S
MUN	Munising Railway			S												S
MV	Midland Valley Railroad				S											S
MW&S	Montana, Wyoming & Southern Railroad											S				S
N&W	Norfolk & Western Railway															
NCB	Nevada Copper Belt Railroad															
NE	Northern Electric Railway Company - (Electric)				S		S		S			S				
NM&A	New Mexico & Arizona Railroad															
NO&GN	New Orleans & Great Northern			S	S							S				S
NO&NW	New Orleans & North West			S	S							S				S
NOT	New Orleans Terminal Company															S
NOT&M	New Orleans, Texas & Mexico Railway	S														
NP	Northern Pacific Railway Company or Railroad				S	S	S					S				S
NS	Norfolk Southern Railroad				S							S				
NWL	North Western Line															
NWP	Northwestern Pacific Railroad				S			S				S				
NYC	New York Central System											S				S
NYC&HR	New York Central & Hudson River Railroad															
NYC&SL	New York, Chicago & St. Louis Railroad				S											
NYNH&H	New York, New Haven & Hartford Railroad				S							S				
OE	Oregon Electric Railway - (Electric)				S							S				
OKC&E	Omaha, Kansas City & Eastern Railroad						S		S							
OR&N	Oregon Railroad & Navigation Company or Railway			S	S											
OSL	Oregon Short Line Railroad Company			S	S							S				S
OT	Oregon Trunk Railway				S											
OWR&N	Oregon, Western Railroad & Navigation Company				S							S				S
P&ER	Portland & Eastern Railroad				S							S				S
P&IN	Pacific Idaho & Northern Railroad or Railway			S	S							S				S
PCC&SL	Pittsburgh, Cincinnati, Chicago & St. Louis Railway				S				S							
PE	Pacific Electric Railway - (Electric)															
PE&E	Portland, Eugene & Eastern Railway				S											
PEP	Portland Electric Power Company - ((Electric)				S							S				S
PM	Pere Marquette Railroad or Railway			S	S							S				
PRL&P	Portland Railway, Light & Power Company - (Electric)			S	S		S		S			S				S
PRR	Pennsylvania Railroad				S							S				S
PV	Pecos Valley Railway or Railroad															
PVR	Payette Valley Railroad				S							S				S
PVT	Private Track															
QO&KC	Quincy, Omaha & Kansas City Railroad or Railway			S	S	S	S									

OPERATING RAILROADS STATIONS WHERE CHAPEL CARS STOPPED

The source for this information is *The Official Guide of the Railways and Steam Navigation Lines of the United States, Porto Rico, Canada, Mexico, and Cuba*, from 1889 to 1998. These volumes were located in the holdings of the John W. Barringer III Railroad Library of the St. Louis Mercantile Library at the University of Missouri-St. Louis, Missouri; and the Transportation Collection of the Northwestern University Library, Evanston, Illinois. Railroads mentioned in the letters and journals of the chapel car missionaries and chaplains did not always coincide with the names of the railroads registered in the Official Guide. Sometimes the missionaries and chaplains used nicknames or abbreviated names of the railroads, or were inaccurate or out of date in their information.

R R	RAILROAD NAME	EP CCND	EP NM #1	EP NM #2	B #1	B #2	B #3	B #4	B #5	B #6	B #7	CC	CC ST. ANTHONY	CC ST. PETER	CC ST. PAUL
RRV	Rogue River Valley Railway														
S&DA	Searcy and Des Arc Railroad				S										
S&IE	Spokane & Island Empire Railroad								S				S		
S&L	Sydney & Louisburg Railway														
S&N	Seattle & Northern Railway				S								S		
S&WP	Searcy & West Point Railroad				S										
SAL	Seaboard Air Line Railway													S	S
SB	Seaboard Railway													S	S
SC	Sierra of California														
SF	Santa Fe					S	S	S							
SFC&W	Salem, Falls City and Western Railroad or Railway												S		
SI	Spokane International Railway												S		
SL&KC	St. Louis & Kansas City														
SL&LA	Salt Lake & Los Angeles								S				S		
SL&SF	St Louis & San Francisco Railroad or Railway								S		S		S		
SL&U	Salt Lake & Utah Railway - (Electric)										S				
SLIM&S	St. Louis, Iron Mountain & Southern Railroad or Railway				S	S		S	S	S	S		S		S
SLSW	St. Louis, Southwestern Railway Lines				S	S		S							
SP	Southern Pacific Railroad or Company or Lines				S	S		S	S	S	S		S		S
SP&S	Spokane, Portland & Seattle Railroad or Railway				S	S		S							
ST&H	Saginaw, Tuscola & Huron Railroad								S						
SUN	Sunset Railway										S				
T&G	Tremont & Gulf Railway Company														
T&P	Texas & Pacific Railway				S	S		S	S				S		S
TRESL	Terminal Railroad of East St. Louis														
TSL&W	Toledo, St. Louis & Western Railroad				S				S	S	S		S		
UP	Union Pacific Railroad or System				S			S	S	S	S		S		S
VA	Vandalia Railroad									S					
VS&P	Vicksburg, Shereveport & Pacific Railway Company				S										
W&BRV	White & Black River Valley Railway							S							
W&LE	Wheeling & Lake Erie Railroad									S					
W&V	Washington & Vandemere														
WAB	Wabash Railroad Company		S		S				S	S			S		
WC	Wisconsin Central Lines or Railway				S				S	S			S		
WP	Western Pacific Railroad						S	S							
WWV	Walla - Walla Valley Railway - (Electric)							S			S		S		
WY	Wyoming Railway Company									S					
Y&MV	Yazoo & Mississippi Valley Railroad Company					S									S
YR	Yreka Railroad														

—366—

Railroads

Arizona & Southeastern, 78

Atlantic & Pacific, 78

Baltimore & Ohio, 195, 201, 202, 275, 276, 278

Big Four, 193, 194, 242

Calumet & Blue Island, 50

Canadian Grand Trunk, 169

Canadian National, 127

Canadian Pacific, 228

Central Pacific, 81, 82

    construction of transcontinental railroad, 1–5

Charleston, Clendenin & Sutton (Coal & Coke), 202, 204

Chesapeake & Ohio, 169

Chicago & Eastern Illinois, 50, 194

Chicago & Kenosha, 50

Chicago & Northern Pacific, 30

Chicago & North Western, 65, 114, 200, 222, 299

Chicago & South Eastern, 50

Chicago, Burlington & Quincy, 108, 119, 122, 192, 200, 299

Chicago, Milwaukee & Puget Sound, 121, 243

Chicago, Milwaukee & St. Paul, 88, 200, 242

Chicago, Rock Island & Pacific, 54, 200

Cincinnati Northern, 189

Choctaw, 47

Colorado & Southern, 166

Corvallis & Eastern, 232

Cotton Belt, 164

Delaware & Hudson, 105

Denver & Rio Grande, 5, 121, 145, 166, 250, 283, 299

Denver & Rio Grande Western, 298

Duluth & Manitoba, 30

Duluth, South Shore, & Atlantic, 65, 67, 71, 112

Eastern Illinois, Milwaukee & St. Paul, 193

Erie, 275

Escanaba–Lake Superior, 279

Flint & Pere Marquette, 189

Frisco & Missouri Pacific, 217

Fort Worth & Denver, 134

Galveston, Harrisburg & San Antonio, 137, 139

Grand Trunk, 228

Great Northern, 5, 18, 24, 42, 45, 88, 121, 278

Idaho & Western, 243

Idaho Southern, 86

Illinois Central, 193, 194, 224, 242

Iron Mountain, 164, 271

Iron Mountain & Southern, 47

Joliet & Blue Island, 50

Kanawha & Michigan, 202–3, 205

Lake Shore, 223

Lake Superior & Ishpeming, 71

Los Angeles & Salt Lake Railroad, 250

Louisiana River & Navigation Company, 270

Louisville & Nashville, 195, 268, 269

Manitoba, 20

Milwaukee & St. Paul, 18

Milwaukee Bay View & Chicago, 50

Minneapolis & Pacific, 18

Minneapolis & St. Louis, 113

Missouri, Kansas & Texas, 30, 134, 140, 245

Missouri Pacific, 116

Nevada Copper Belt, 144

New Orleans & Great Northern, 224

New York Central, 203

Norfolk & Western, 199

Northern Pacific, 5, 18, 20, 23–26, 30, 39–42, 44, 106, 121, 174, 278

North Western, 193

Omaha, Kansas City & Quincy, 50, 166

Oregon & Washington, 147

Oregon Central, 235

Oregon Pacific, 42, 43

Oregon Short Line, 86, 144, 145, 225, 229, 234, 245, 247

Oregon Trunk, 235

Oregon Western, 253

Oregon Western Railway & Navigation Company, 229, 230, 248, 254

Pecos Valley, 77

Pennsylvania, 275

Pere Marquette, 187, 188, 191

Philadelphia & Reading, 275

Pittsburgh & Gulf, 47

Port Huron & Northwestern, 189

Portland Electric, 148–49

Portland Railroad Light & Power, 249, 250

Rock Island, 125, 219, 270, 283

Salem Falls City & Western, 227

Salt Lake, 286

Salt Lake & Utah, 298

San Pedro, Los Angeles & Salt Lake, 289

Santa Fe, 5, 53, 78, 164

Seattle & Northern, 43

Short Line, 201

Soo, 121, 216

Southern Pacific, 5, 42, 43, 76, 79–80, 135, 138, 148, 149, 150, 151, 152, 170–71, 172, 226, 227, 230, 235, 249, 251, 271, 272, 273, 285, 286, 287

Spokane, Portland & Seattle, 249

St. Paul & Minneapolis, 20

Tacoma Eastern, 243

Texas & Pacific, 134, 269, 273, 274

Texas, Sabine Valley & Northwestern, 142

Tremont & Gulf, 271

Union Pacific, 42, 57, 123, 124, 125, 226, 254, 289, 290, 291

    construction of transcontinental railroad, 1–7

Utah & Northern, 87

Vicksburg, Shreveport & Pacific, 271

Wabash, 169, 193, 198

Western Pacific, 171

Wisconsin Central, 30, 31, 33, 39, 106, 110

Yazoo & Mississippi Valley, 223, 224